WILEY'S ENGLISH-GERMAN GERMAN-ENGLISH BUSINESS DICTIONARY

Christa Britt, Ph.D.
Lilith Schutte, Ph.D.

John Wiley & Sons, Inc.
New York • Chichester • Brisbane • Toronto • Singapore

Copyright © 1995 by Christa Britt, Raymond Britt, and Lilith Schutte

Published by John Wiley & Sons, Inc.

Library of Congress Cataloging-in-Publication Data

Britt, Christa.
   Wiley's English-German, German-English business dictionary / Christa Britt, Lilith Schutte.
     p. cm.
   Published simultaneously in Canada.
   ISBN 0-471-13401-5 (cloth : alk. paper). — ISBN 0-471-12140-1 (pbk. : alk. paper)
   1. International economic relations—Dictionaries.
   2. International economic relations—Dictionaries—German.
   3. German language—Dictionaries—English. 4. English language—Dictionaries—German. 5. English language—Business English—Dictionaries. 6. German language—Business German—Dictionaries. I. Schutte, Lilith. II. Title.
   HF1359.B75   1996
   650'.03—dc20   95-37977
                                           CIP

Contents

Preface

This dictionary of English-German, German-English business terms aims to provide the user with the most up-to-date terminology used in international business. The idea behind the creation of the dictionary was to offer a practical tool of manageable length and ease of use, rather than a major "unabridged" reference work. The criterion for the inclusion of a given term was the frequency of occurrence in the actual use of that term in international business dealings. The exclusion of infrequently used terms should greatly facilitate the user's search for everyday terms and expressions.

The authors hope that the dictionary will also prove helpful to those who teach business German to English-speaking students and business English to speakers of German. It should be a useful guide to such instructors in deciding what business terms to include in their teaching materials.

The dictionary is based on an original word frequency study funded by the EXXON Educational Foundation. It was carried out by the authors, professors of business German at the American Graduate School of International Management (AGSIM), who are native speakers of German and hold doctorates in German and English, respectively. The authors have each been teaching business German for over twenty years.

The Foundation thought AGSIM to be an ideal institution of higher learning to receive the grant and conduct the frequency study, because it is generally considered the foremost school of international management in the United States, with the longest continuous program and graduating the largest number of students annually in that field. That program combines the teaching of world business, international area studies, and modern languages into a tripartite curriculum culminating in the degree of Master of International Management (MIM).

* * *

AGSIM's resources were well suited to conduct the necessary research, since the advice of many colleagues, specialists in the above three areas, and a library specializing in relevant domestic and foreign textbooks, journals, newspapers, and documents were at the researchers' disposal.

The source materials for the word count reflect both the theory and practice of "international business." They include materials and texts used in the teaching of international business courses, as well as documents supplied by AGSIM alumni currently holding management positions in international business. These sources constitute 75 percent of the data bank used for the word count. Twenty-five percent of the source materials stem from a random sampling of relevant books in the AGSIM library.

In accordance with standard practice in the field of international business and following the cataloging system of Library of Congress holdings, the source materials used for the study were divided into five major categories: international economics (35 percent); international banking and finance (35 percent); international management (15 percent);

international marketing (10 percent); international accounting together with statistics (5 percent). The percentage representation of materials from each of these fields was based on two guidelines: (1) the percentage representation of materials from each of the six disciplines in the holdings of the AGSIM library and (2) the percentage representation of each discipline in all materials used and assigned in all AGSIM courses in these fields, percentages which closely corresponded. Within these divisions, two separate data banks, one English and one German and both selected according to the same principles, were used to establish the frequency of occurrence of all words in the source materials.

The total sample of English and German words was processed by computer, using word count programs that established lists of unique words for each language and showed the frequency of occurrence of each unique word and its cumulative frequency (the sum of the frequencies of all words up to and including the listed word). The count resulted in 14,794 unique English words and 19,352 unique German words.

In developing the English and German *business* word lists, the following criteria were used to select business terms from the lists of all words up to a cumulative frequency of 80 percent:

- Words that exclusively describe a concept, practice, procedure, or activity associated with the conduct of business
- Words that are mainly used in a general context but that have a secondary meaning and a high frequency of occurrence in business contexts

Aided by a computer program that checked for duplications, the authors translated the English as well as the German business terms, combining them into one dictionary. The English-language text samples used in the frequency study were taken from American source texts, and the German business terms were translated into American rather than British English when a variance existed.

* * *

The authors are acutely aware that a project of this kind is never really "finished." Apart from the changes in usage over time and the continuous coinage of new business terms and expressions necessitating periodic updating of the work, it can undoubtedly profit from suggestions for changes and improvements as it now stands. We fervently hope these will be forthcoming from our most important critics—students, teachers, and practitioners in the field.

Although, of course, the authors collaborated closely on the entire work, the first half (letters A through K) in both the English-German and the German-English sections was under the special care of Lilith Schutte, and the second half (letters L through Z) in both sections was the special responsibility of Christa Britt. We ask, therefore, that any suggestions be directed accordingly. Both authors may be reached at the following address:

Department of Modern Languages
American Graduate School of International Management
15249 North 59th Avenue
Glendale, AZ   85306-6000
U.S.A.

How to Use the Dictionary

In keeping with the purpose of the dictionary, only those meanings that are commonly used in a business context are given.

If an English word can be used as a noun as well as an adjective, adverb, preposition, or verb, such word categories are separated by periods and preceded by one of the following abbreviations: **n** (noun), **a** (adjective), **adv** (adverb), **p** (preposition), or **v** (verb). If there is more than one possible translation within the same word category, the translations appear in descending order of frequency of occurrence.

The gender of each noun is indicated by the *italic* abbreviation *m, f,* or *nt.* If the feminine form of a noun indicating a profession, religion, nationality, political affiliation, and so on, does not differ from the masculine form except for the addition of -in (der Manager, die Managerin), it is not separately listed. Otherwise, both forms are given (der Kunde, die Kundin). Adjectival nouns denoting persons are marked as being masculine *or* feminine (Angehörige *m/f*).

In order to help the user select the proper translation for a main entry, guide words or phrases are provided in parentheses in front of the translations. These words or phrases point to the exact area of use, or provide synonyms or other helpful pointers.

Hinweise zur Benutzung des Wörterbuchs

Dem Zweck des Wörterbuchs entsprechend werden nur die Bedeutungen, die im Geschäftsleben gewöhnlich gebraucht werden, angegeben.

Wenn ein englisches Wort sowohl als Substantiv wie auch als Adjektiv, Adverb, Präposition oder Verb gebraucht werden kann, sind die Wortgruppen durch einen Punkt getrennt. Die Kennzeichnung der Wortgruppen erfolgt durch die folgenden vorangestellten Abkürzungen: **n** (Substantiv), **a** (Adjektiv), **adv** (Adverb), **p** (Präposition), **v** (Verb). Wenn es innerhalb der gleichen Wortgruppe mehrere mögliche Übersetzungen gibt, sind die Übersetzungen in absteigender Reihenfolge der Häufigkeit des Vorkommens angeordnet.

Das Geschlecht eines Substantivs wird in Kursivdruck durch die Abkürzungen *m*, *f* oder *nt* angegeben. Wenn die weibliche Form eines Substantivs, das einen Beruf, eine Staatsangehörigkeit usw. bezeichnet, von der männlichen Form nur durch das Anfügen von -in abweicht (der Manager, die Managerin), wird sie nicht gesondert angeführt. Wenn die Formen sich anders unterscheiden, werden beide Formen angegeben (der Türke, die Türkin).

Um die Auswahl der richtigen Übersetzung zu erleichtern, befinden sich erklärende Schlüsselwörter oder Wendungen in Klammern vor den Übersetzungen. Diese Wörter oder Wendungen weisen entweder auf das Benutzungsgebiet hin, oder sie sind Synonyme oder andere erklärende Hinweise.

English-German Section

abandon *(to give up)* aufgeben; preisgeben; *(to desert)* im Stich *m* lassen; *(to leave)* verlassen; *(a claim)* fallenlassen; *(controls)* aufheben.

ability Fähigkeit *f*.

ability to save Sparfähigkeit *f*.

able fähig; *(efficient)* tüchtig; *(law)* berechtigt.

abnormal regelwidrig; anormal.

abolish *(to do away with)* beseitigen; abschaffen; *(to void)* aufheben.

abolition Abschaffung *f*; Aufhebung *f*.

abridgment *(shortening)* Kürzung *f*; *(abridged work)* gekürzte Ausgabe *f*.

abroad im (ins) Ausland *nt*; auswärts.

absence Abwesenheit *f*; *(from school, work)* Fehlen *nt*.

absent abwesend; fehlend.

absentee Abwesende *m/f*.

absolute unumschränkt; absolut.

absorb absorbieren; aufnehmen; *(liquids)* aufsaugen; *(costs)* auffangen; *(expenses)* übernehmen; *(shock)* dämpfen.

absorption limit Sättigungsgrenze *f*.

abstention Enthaltung *f*.

abstract n *(summary)* Zusammenfassung *f*; Übersicht *f*; Abriß *m*. a abstrakt. v einen Auszug *m* machen.

abundance Überfluß *m*; Fülle *f*.

abundant reichlich.

abuse n *(wrong use)* Mißbrauch *m*; *(mistreatment)* Mißhandlung *f*. v *(to use wrongly)* mißbrauchen; *(to mistreat)* mißhandeln.

accelerate beschleunigen; *(car)* Gas *nt* geben.

acceleration Beschleunigung *f*.

accept annehmen; *(invitation)* zusagen; *(bill of exchange)* akzeptieren.

acceptability Annehmbarkeit *f*.

acceptable annehmbar; akzeptabel.

acceptance Annahme *f*; *(invitation)* Zusage *f*; *(bill of exchange)* Akzept *nt*.

acceptance bank Wechselbank *f*.

acceptance credit Akzeptkredit *m*.

acceptance of liability Haftungszusage *f*.

access Zugang *m*; *(computer memory)* Zugriff *m*.

accessible zugänglich; erreichbar.

accessories Zubehör *nt*.

accident Unfall *m*; *(chance)* Zufall *m*.

accident insurance Unfallversicherung *f*.

accommodate *(housing)* unterbringen; *(to oblige)* entgegenkommen.

accommodation *(lodging)* Unterbringung *f*; Unterkunft *f*; *(quarters)* Räumlichkeit *f*; *(space)* Platz *m*; *(concession)* Entgegenkommen *nt*; *(settlement)* Verständigung *f*; Anpassung *f*.

accompany begleiten.

accomplish *(to achieve)* erreichen; schaffen; zustandebringen; *(to complete)* vollenden; *(task)* bewältigen.

accomplishment *(performance)* Leistung *f*; *(achievement)* Errungenschaft *f*; *(completion)* Bewältigung *f*.

accord n Übereinstimmung *f*. v *(to grant)* gewähren; bewilligen.

accordance Übereinstimmung *f*.

according to nach; gemäß.

according to schedule termingerecht.

according to value wertmäßig.

account n *(accounting)* Konto *nt*; *(advertising agency)* Kundenetat *m*; *(bill)* Rechnung *f*; *(report)* Bericht *m*. v *(to account for)* Rechenschaft *f* ablegen; abrechnen.

accountability Rechenschaftspflicht *f*.

accountable rechenschaftspflichtig.

accountancy Rechnungswesen *nt*.

accountant *(certified public accountant)* Wirtschaftsprüfer *m*; Rechnungsführer *m*; Sachverständige *m/f* für das Rechnungswesen *nt*; Bilanzbuchhalter *m*.

account balance Kontosaldo *m*.

account holder Kontoinhaber *m*.

accounting *(bookkeeping)* Buchführung *f*; Buchhaltung *f*; *(managerial accounting)* Rechnungswesen *nt*.

accounting principles Buchführungsgrundsätze *pl*; Bilanzierungsrichtlinien *pl*.

account number Kontonummer *f*.

accounts payable Verbindlichkeiten *pl*.

accounts payable ledger Kontokorrentbuch *nt*.

accounts receivable ausstehende Forderungen *pl*.

accounts receivable ledger Kontokorrentbuch *nt*.

accrual Zuwachs *m*; *(of interest)* Auflaufen *nt*.

accrue anwachsen; *(interest)* auflaufen; *(to accumulate)* sich ansammeln.

accumulation Ansammlung *f*; *(of interest)* Auflaufen *nt*; *(of assets)* Vermögensbildung *f*; Kumulierung *f*.

accuracy *(exactness)* Genauigkeit *f*; *(correctness)* Richtigkeit *f*.

accurate *(exact)* genau; *(correct)* richtig.

achieve erreichen; erzielen.

achievement *(act of achieving)* Erreichen *nt*; Erzielen *nt*; *(performance)* Leistung *f*; *(thing achieved)* Errungenschaft *f*.

acknowledge *(to confirm)* bestätigen; *(to recognize)* anerkennen.

acknowledgment *(confirmation)* Bestätigung *f*; *(recognition)* Anerkennung *f*.

acquire erwerben; anschaffen.

acquirer Erwerber *m*.

acquisition Erwerb *m*; Anschaffung *f*; ~ **of assets** Vermögenserwerb *m*.

act n Handlung *f*; Tat *f*; *(law)* Gesetz *nt*; *(legal transaction)* Rechtsgeschäft *nt*. v handeln; *(to behave)* sich verhalten.

act as fungieren.

action *(act)* Tat *f*; *(activity)* Tätigkeit *f*; Handlung *f*; *(public or political action)* Aktion *f*; *(lawsuit)* Klage *f*.

activation Aktivierung *f*.

active aktiv; tätig; *(market)* lebhaft.

activity Aktivität *f*; Tätigkeit *f*;
(function) Aufgabenbereich *m*.
actual tatsächlich; *(costs)* effektiv;
real.
actual situation Sachverhalt *m*.
actual wage Reallohn *m*.
actual wage level Reallohnniveau
nt.
ad Anzeige *f*; Inserat *nt*; *(TV)*
Werbespot *m*.
adapt *(to adjust)* anpassen; *(to
rework)* umarbeiten; *(machine)*
umstellen; *(text, book)* bearbeiten.
adaptability Anpassungsfähigkeit
f.
adaptation *(adjustment)* Anpassung *f*; *(reworking)* Umarbeitung *f*.
add *(figures)* zusammenrechnen;
addieren; *(to append)* hinzufügen;
hinzurechnen.
addition *(figures)* Addition *f*;
Zusammenrechnung *f*; *(supplement)* Zusatz *m*; *(to building)*
Anbau *m*.
additional zusätzlich.
address n Anschrift *f*; Adresse *f*;
(form of address) Anrede *f*;
(speech) Ansprache *f*. v adressieren; richten an; anreden;
ansprechen.
adequacy Angemessenheit *f*.
adequate angemessen.
adjust anpassen; *(to balance)* ausgleichen; *(accounts)* bereinigen;
(insurance) regulieren; *(entry)*
berichtigen; richtigstellen.
adjustable einstellbar; regulierbar.
adjustable-rate *(loan, mortgage)*
mit flexibler Verzinsung *f*.
adjustment Anpassung *f*; *(balance
sheet)* Wertberichtigung *f*; *(insurance)* Regulierung *f*; *(correction)*
Richtigstellung *f*.

adjustment program Anpassungs-
programm *nt*.
administer verwalten; *(price)* regulieren.
administration Verwaltung *f*.
administrative verwaltungsmäßig;
Verwaltungs-.
administrator Verwalter *m*; Ver-
waltungsbeamte *m*; Verwaltungs-
beamtin *f*.
admissible zulässig; erlaubt;
annehmbar.
admission Zulassung *f*; *(entrance)*
Einlaß *m*; *(admittance)* Zutritt *m*;
Eintritt *m*; *(admission price)* Eintrittspreis *m*; *(acknowledgment)*
Zugeständnis *nt*; *(membership)*
Aufnahme *f*.
admit einlassen; zulassen; *(membership)* aufnehmen; *(to concede)*
zugeben.
advance n *(money)* Vorschuß *m*;
Anzahlung *f*; *(progress)* Fortschritt
m; *(in prices)* Preissteigerung *f*. v
(to prepay) vorauszahlen; *(a task)*
vorwärtsbringen; *(to progress)*
vorwärtskommen; *(to move forward)* vorverlegen; *(an opinion)*
vorbringen; *(to rise)* aufsteigen; ~
(money on securities) lombardieren.
advancement *(furtherance)* Förderung *f*; *(progress)* Fortschritt *m*;
(promotion) Beförderung *f*.
advance payment Vorauszahlung
f.
advantage Vorteil *m*; Nutzen *m*.
advantageous vorteilhaft; günstig.
adverse ungünstig; nachteilig.
advertise werben; Reklame *f*
machen; *(in newspaper)* annoncieren; inserieren.
advertisement *(advertising)*
Reklame *f*; Werbung *f*; *(in news-*

paper) Anzeige *f*; Inserat *nt*; *(for position)* Ausschreibung *f*.

advertisement heading   Anzeigenüberschrift *f*.

advertisement photograph   Werbebild *nt*.

advertisement viewer   Anzeigenbetrachter *m*.

advertiser   Werber *m*; Inserent *m*; *(sponsor)* Werbekunde *m*.

advertising   Werbung *f*; Reklame *f*.

advertising account executive   Werbebetreuer *m*.

advertising agency   Werbeagentur *f*.

advertising appeal   Werbekraft *f*.

advertising brochure   Werbeprospekt *m*.

advertising budget   Werbeetat *m*.

advertising campaign   Werbekampagne *f*.

advertising circle   Werbekreis *m*.

advertising consultant   Werbeberater *m*.

advertising copy   Werbetext *m*; Reklametext *m*.

advertising design   Werbegestaltung *f*.

advertising director   Werbechef *m*.

advertising expenditure   Werbeaufwendung *f*.

advertising expense   Werbekosten *pl*.

advertising gimmick   Werbemasche *f*.

advertising idea   Werbeeinfall *m*; Werbeidee *f*.

advertising impact   Werbeeffekt *m*.

advertising material   Werbemittel *nt*.

advertising message   Werbebotschaft *f*.

advertising section   Anzeigenteil *m*.

advertising slogan   Werbebotschaft *f*; Werbemotto *nt*; Werbeslogan *m*.

advertising strategist   Werbestratege *m*; Werbestrategin *f*.

advertising tactic   Werbemaßnahme *f*.

advertising war   Werbekrieg *m*; Werbeschlacht *f*.

advice   Rat *m*; Ratschlag *m*; *(notification)* Benachrichtigung *f*; Avis *m/nt*.

advise   raten; beraten; *(to notify)* benachrichtigen.

adviser   Berater *m*.

advisory   Beratungs-; beratend.

advisory board   Beirat *m*; Beratungsgremium *nt*.

advisory group   Beratergruppe *f*.

advocate   n Fürsprecher *m*; Befürworter *m*. v befürworten.

affair   *(business)* Geschäft *nt*; *(matter, concern)* Angelegenheit *f*; Sache *f*.

affect   beeinflussen; sich auswirken auf.

affiliate   n Konzerngesellschaft *f*. v angliedern; anschließen.

affiliated   angeschlossen.

affirm   versichern; bekräftigen.

affluence   Wohlstand *m*; Reichtum *m*.

affluent   reich; wohlhabend.

afford   *(can afford)* sich leisten; erschwingen; *(to offer)* bieten; *(to grant)* gewähren.

affordable   erschwinglich.

age   n Alter *nt*; *(length of life)* Lebensdauer *f*; *(of age)* Mündigkeit *f*; *(period)* Zeitalter *nt*. v altern; *(to mature)* reifen.

agency   Agentur *f*; Vertretung *f*; *(public authority)* Behörde *f*;

Geschäftsstelle *f*; *(administrative)*
Verwaltungsstelle *f*.

agenda   Tagesordnung *f*.

agenda item   Tagesordnungspunkt
m.

agent   *(representative)* Vertreter *m*;
Agent *m*; *(authorized person)*
Bevollmächtigte *m/f*.

aggravate   verschlimmern; erschweren.

aggregate   n *(insurance)* Aggregat
nt. a gesamt. v ansammeln;
aggregieren.

agree   *(to consent)* zustimmen; *(to
settle)* abmachen; *(to reach an
agreement)* vereinbaren; übereinkommen; *(to concur)* übereinstimmen.

agreement   *(understanding,
arrangement)* Abmachung *f*; Übereinkommen *nt*; Vereinbarung *f*;
(sharing of opinion) Einigung *f*;
(treaty) Abkommen *nt*; *(consent)*
Zustimmung *f*; Einverständnis *nt*.

agricultural   landwirtschaftlich;
Agrar-.

agricultural act   Agrarbeschluß
m.

agricultural budget   Agrarhaushalt
m.

agricultural market   Agrarmarkt *m*.

agricultural price policy   Agrar-
preispolitik *f*.

agricultural price support   Agrar-
preisstützung *f*.

agricultural product   Agrarerzeug-
nis *nt*; Agrargut *nt*; Agrarprodukt
nt.

agricultural surplus   Agrarüber-
schuß *m*.

agricultural technology   Agrar-
technik *f*.

agricultural trade   Agrarhandel *m*.

agriculture   Landwirtschaft *f*;
Agrarwirtschaft *f*.

aid   n Hilfe *f*; Beistand *m*; Unterstützung *f*; *(promotion)* Förderung
f. v helfen; unterstützen; *(to promote)* fördern.

aim   n *(goal)* Ziel *nt*; *(purpose)*
Zweck *m*; *(intention)* Absicht *f*.
v zielen auf; abzielen auf; *(to strive
for)* erstreben.

aimless   ziellos.

aircraft   Flugzeug *nt*.

air freight   Luftfracht *f*.

airline   Fluggesellschaft *f*.

airmail   Luftpost *f*.

airplane   Flugzeug *nt*.

airport   Flughafen *m*.

air transport   Luftverkehr *m*.

alien   n *(foreigner)* Ausländer *m*;
Gebietsfremde *m/f*. a *(foreign)*
ausländisch; *(different)* fremd.

alleviate   erleichtern; mildern.

alliance   Bündnis *nt*; Bund *m*;
Gemeinschaft *f*.

alliance partner   Bündnispartner *m*.

all-inclusive price   Pauschalpreis *m*.

allocate   *(to allot)* zuteilen; zuwenden; zuweisen; *(to set apart for a
specific purpose)* bereitstellen.

allocation   *(allotment)* Zuweisung
f; Zuteilung *f*; *(setting apart for a
specific purpose)* Bereitstellung *f*;
Allokation *f*.

allocation of profit   Gewinnzuschreibung *f*.

allocation of resources   Mittelverwendung *f*.

allocative function   Verteilungsfunktion *f*.

allot   zuteilen.

allotment   Zuteilung *f*.

allow   erlauben; *(to grant)* gewähren; *(to admit)* zulassen.

allowable *(admissible)* zulässig; *(deductible)* abziehbar.

allowance *(compensation)* Vergütung *f*; *(discount)* Abzug *m*; *(allotment)* Zuteilung *f*; *(extra allowance)* Zuschuß *m*; *(small amounts allotted)* Taschengeld *nt*.

ally n Verbündete *m/f*. v sich verbünden; sich alliieren.

alter ändern; verändern; umändern.

alteration Änderung *f*; Veränderung *f*; Umänderung *f*.

alternate n *(substitute)* Ersatz *m*. a abwechselnd; wechselnd; *(on alternate days)* jeden zweiten Tag *m*. v wechseln; abwechseln.

alternative n Alternative *f*; Ausweichsmöglichkeit *f*; Ersatz *m*. a alternativ.

altitude Höhe *f*.

ambassador Botschafter *m*.

ambiguity Ungewißheit *f*; Doppeldeutigkeit *f*; Zweideutigkeit *f*.

ambiguous ungewiß; zweideutig; unklar.

ambition Ehrgeiz *m*; Strebsamkeit *f*.

ambitious ehrgeizig; strebsam.

amend berichtigen; ergänzen.

amendment Zusatz *m*; Neufassung *f*; *(law)* Novelle *f*; Gesetzesänderung *f*.

amortization Schuldentilgung *f*; Amortisation *f*; Kredittilgung *f*; *(depreciation)* Abschreibung *f*.

amortization amount Tilgungsbetrag *m*.

amortization mortgage Tilgungshypothek *f*.

amortization rate Tilgungsrate *f*.

amortize tilgen; amortisieren; *(to depreciate)* abschreiben.

amount n Betrag *m*; Summe *f*; *(quantity)* Menge *f*; Höhe *f*. v betragen; ausmachen; sich belaufen auf.

amount invested Investitionssumme *f*.

amount of capital Kapitalbetrag *m*; Kapitalhöhe *f*.

amount saved Sparbetrag *m*.

ample ausreichend; reichlich; genügend.

amplitude Umfang *m*; Fülle *f*.

analysis Analyse *f*; Aufgliederung *f*.

analysis of needs Bedarfsanalyse *f*.

analyst *(finance)* Berater *m*; Analytiker *m*; Analyst *m*.

analytical analytisch.

analyze analysieren; untersuchen.

annotation Erläuterung *f*.

announce ankündigen; bekanntmachen; *(to report)* melden.

announcement Bekanntmachung *f*; Ankündigung *f*.

annual n *(book)* Jahrbuch. a jährlich.

annual account Jahresabschluß *m*.

annual amount Jahresbetrag *m*.

annual average Jahresdurchschnitt *m*.

annual balance sheet Jahresabschluß *m*; Jahresbilanz *f*.

annual budget Jahresetat *m*.

annual comparison Jahresvergleich *m*.

annual conference Jahrestagung *f*.

annual convention Jahrestagung *f*.

annual earnings Jahresgewinn *m*; Jahresverdienst *m*.

annual financial statement Jahresabschluß *m*.

annual meeting *(stockholders)* Hauptversammlung *f*.

annual output   Jahresergebnis *nt*; Jahresproduktion *f*.

annual report   Jahresbericht *m*; Jahresgutachten *nt*.

annual returns   Jahresergebnis *nt*.

annual sales   Jahresumsatz *m*.

annual statement of accounts   Jahresabschluß *m*.

annual working hours   Jahresarbeitszeit *f*.

annuity   Rente *f*.

annuity index   Rentenindex *m*.

annuity insurance   Rentenversicherung *f*.

annuity value   Rentenwert *m*.

answer   n Antwort *f*; Bescheid *m*; *(solution)* Lösung *f*. v antworten; *(a question)* beantworten; *(to be responsible)* verantwortlich sein.

answer in the affirmative   zusagen.

anticipate   *(to await)* erwarten; *(to forestall)* vorwegnehmen.

anticipation   *(expectation)* Erwartung *f*; *(forestalling)* Vorwegnahme *f*.

antitrust agency   Kartellamt *nt*.

antitrust law   Kartellrecht *nt*.

apology   Entschuldigung *f*.

apparatus   Apparat *m*; Vorrichtung *f*.

appeal   n *(against sentence)* Berufung *f*; *(against decision)* Einspruch *m*; *(to customers)* Anklang *m*; *(request)* Aufruf *m*; Appell *m*. v *(to appeal a sentence)* Berufung *f* einlegen; *(to appeal a decision)* Einspruch *m* erheben; *(to customers)* Anklang *m* finden bei; appellieren.

appear   erscheinen.

appearance   Erscheinung *f*; *(in public)* Auftreten *nt*.

appliance   *(household)* Gerät *nt*; Vorrichtung *f*.

applicable   anwendbar; zutreffend; *(usable)* verwendbar.

applicant   Bewerber *m*; Antragsteller *m*; *(for a job)* Stellenbewerber *m*.

application   *(use)* Anwendung *f*; *(request)* Antrag *m*; *(for a position)* Bewerbung *f*; *(handling)* Handhabung *f*.

apply   anwenden; *(funds)* verwenden; *(for a position)* sich bewerben; *(to make a request)* beantragen; *(results, findings)* verwerten für; *(efforts)* zuwenden.

apply oneself   sich anstrengen.

appoint   *(to a post)* ernennen; berufen; *(to designate)* bestimmen.

appointment   *(engagement)* Verabredung *f*; Termin *m*; *(nomination)* Ernennung *f*; *(office)* Anstellung *f*; Berufung *f*; Einsetzung *f*.

appointment calendar   Terminkalender *m*.

appointment schedule   Terminkalender *m*; Terminplan *m*.

apportion   zuweisen.

appraisable   bewertbar.

appraisal   Abschätzung *f*; Bewertung *f*; *(appraised value)* Taxwert *m*.

appraise   schätzen; bewerten; *(to assess)* taxieren.

appraiser   Schätzer *m*; *(insurance)* Schadensabschätzer *m*.

appreciate   *(to value)* schätzen; *(to rise in value)* im Wert *m* steigen.

appreciation   *(valuation)* Schätzung *f*; Wertschätzung *f*; *(a rise in value)* Wertsteigerung *f*.

appreciation of principal   Kapitalzuwachs *m*.

apprentice n Lehrling *m*; Auszu-
bildende *m/f*. v in die Lehre *f*
geben.
apprenticeship Lehrstelle *f*.
apprenticeship offer Lehrstellenangebot *nt*.
approach n *(method)* Vorgehen *nt*;
(access) Annäherung *f*. v sich nähern.
approachable erreichbar;
ansprechbar.
appropriate a *(adequate)* angemessen; gemäß. v *(to allocate)*
bewilligen; *(to take possession)*
aneignen.
appropriation *(allocation)* Bewilligung *f*; *(taking possession)* Aneignung *f*.
approval Zustimmung *f*; Genehmigung *f*; Billigung *f*.
approve zustimmen; genehmigen;
billigen.
approximate a annähernd.
v nahebringen; nahekommen.
approximately zirka; schätzungsweise.
approximation annähernde Berechnung *f*; Näherungswert *m*.
arbiter Schiedsrichter *m*.
arbitrage Arbitrage *f*.
arbitrager Arbitragehändler *m*.
arbitrary willkürlich.
arbitrate schlichten.
arbitration Schlichtungsverfahren
nt.
arbitration agreement Schlichtungsabkommen *nt*.
arbitration decision Schlichtungsspruch *m*.
arbitration result Schlichtungsergebnis *nt*.
arbitrator Schlichter *m*; Schiedsrichter *m*.

area Fläche *f*; *(region)* Gebiet *nt*;
Bereich *m*.
argue diskutieren; *(to dispute)*
bestreiten; sich auseinandersetzen.
argument Argument *nt*; *(dispute)*
Streit *m*; Auseinandersetzung *f*.
arrange arrangieren; ordnen; *(to
agree upon)* vereinbaren; *(to
plan)* Vorkehrungen *pl* treffen;
(to organize) veranstalten.
arrangement Anordnung *f*; *(agreement)* Abmachung *f*; Vereinbarung
f; *(plan)* Vorkehrung *f*; *(compromise)* Vergleich *m*.
arrival Ankunft *f*; Ankommen *nt*;
Eintreffen *nt*; *(of shipment)* Eingang *m*.
arrive ankommen; eintreffen;
(shipment) eingehen.
article Artikel *m*; *(item)* Posten *m*;
(goods) Ware *f*; *(object)* Gegenstand *m*; *(clause)* Klausel *f*; *(section)* Abschnitt *m*.
ascertain feststellen; festsetzen;
(costs) ermitteln.
ascertainment Feststellung *f*;
Ermittlung *f*.
ask *(a question)* fragen; *(for a
favor)* bitten; *(to demand)* fordern;
ersuchen.
asking price Preisforderung *f*.
aspect Gesichtspunkt *m*; Aspekt
m.
assemble *(group of people)* versammeln; *(to gather objects)*
ansammeln; *(industrial installation)* montieren; *(to fit together)*
zusammensetzen.
assembly *(industrial installation)*
Montage *f*; *(group of people)* Versammlung *f*.
assembly chamber Kongreßhalle
f.

assembly line Fließband *nt.*
assembly plant Montagewerk *nt.*
assert behaupten; *(rights)* geltend machen.
assertion Behauptung *f*; *(rights)* Geltendmachung *f.*
assess *(to appraise)* einschätzen; bewerten; *(to charge with a tax)* besteuern; *(a fine)* festsetzen.
assessed value Einheitswert *m.*
assessment *(appraisal)* Einschätzung *f*; Bewertung *f*; *(taxes)* Veranlagung *f*; *(duty)* Abgabe *f.*
asset *(balance sheet)* Aktivposten *m*; *(possession)* Vermögensgegenstand *m.*
asset account Bestandskonto *nt.*
asset-creating vermögenswirksam.
assets *(balance sheet)* Aktiva *pl*; Aktivseite *f*; *(property)* Vermögen *nt*; Guthaben *nt.*
asset value Fondsvermögen *nt.*
assign *(to allot)* zuweisen; zuteilen; *(to transfer)* übertragen; *(debt)* abtreten.
assignment *(allotment)* Zuweisung *f*; *(transfer)* Übertragung *f*; *(debt)* Abtretung *f*; *(task)* Aufgabe *f.*
assist helfen; unterstützen.
assistance Hilfe *f*; Unterstützung *f.*
assistant n Gehilfe *m*; Gehilfin *f*; Assistent *m.* a *(deputizing)* stellvertretend.
associate n *(business)* Geschäftspartner *m*; Teilhaber *m*; Partner *m.* a verbunden; assoziiert. v sich verbinden; sich assoziieren; *(socially)* verkehren mit.
associated establishment Partnerinstitut *nt.*
association *(organization)* Verband *m*; Verein *m*; *(with other people)* Umgang *m*; Verkehr *m.*

association representative Verbandsvertreter *m.*
assortment *(selection)* Auswahl *f*; *(set of goods)* Kollektion *f*; Sortiment *nt.*
assume *(to suppose)* annehmen; *(an office)* übernehmen.
assumption *(supposition)* Annahme *f*; *(prerequisite)* Voraussetzung *f*; *(of duty)* Übernahme *f.*
assumption of office Amtsübernahme *f.*
assurance Zusicherung *f*; Sicherheit *f.*
assure sichern; versichern; sicherstellen.
attach *(to enclose)* beifügen; *(to fasten to)* befestigen; *(to seize)* beschlagnahmen.
attachment *(to a document)* Beilage *f*; *(seizure)* Beschlagnahme *f*; *(implement)* Zusatzgerät *nt.*
attain erreichen; erlangen.
attainable erreichbar.
attainment Erlangung *f*; Errungenschaft *f.*
attempt n Versuch *m.* v versuchen.
attend besuchen; *(to take care of)* besorgen; bedienen.
attendance Anwesenheit *f*; *(number of visitors)* Teilnehmerzahl *f*; Besucherzahl *f.*
attendant n Begleiter *m*; *(guard)* Wärter *m*; *(care taker)* Pfleger. a begleitend; zugehörig.
attention Aufmerksamkeit *f*; Beachtung *f*; *(to the attention of)* zu Händen *pl* von.
attentive aufmerksam.
attest beglaubigen; bezeugen; bestätigen; bescheinigen.
attitude Haltung *f*; Einstellung *f.*
attorney Bevollmächtigte *m/f*;

(attorney-at-law) Rechtsanwalt *m*; Rechtsanwältin *f*.

attract anziehen.

attraction Attraktion *f*; *(power to attract)* Anziehungskraft *f*; *(focus of attraction)* Anziehungspunkt *m*.

attractive attraktiv; zugkräftig; reizvoll; anziehend; *(price)* günstig.

attribute n Attribut *nt*; Merkmal *nt*; Kennzeichen *nt*. v zurechnen; zurückführen auf; zuschreiben.

attribution Zurechnung *f*; Zurück-führung *f*.

auction n Versteigerung *f*; Auktion *f*. v versteigern.

audience *(reception)* Empfang *m*; *(attending public)* Publikum *nt*; Zuhörerschaft *f*.

audit n Revision *f*; Bilanzprüfung *f*. v Revision *f* durchführen.

auditor Wirtschaftsprüfer *m*; Rechnungsprüfer *m*.

audit report Revisionsbericht *m*.

augment vergrößern; vermehren.

augmentation Vergrößerung *f*; Vermehrung *f*.

austerity *(severity)* Strenge *f*; *(simplicity)* Einfachheit *f*; *(hardship)* Entbehrung *f*.

austerity program Sparprogramm *nt*.

authentic echt.

authenticity Echtheit *f*; *(legal validity)* Rechtsgültigkeit *f*.

author Urheber *m*; Autor *m*.

authoritative maßgeblich.

authority *(government agency)* Behörde *f*; *(power, expert)* Autorität *f*; *(right to act)* Befugnis *f*; *(power of attorney)* Vollmacht *f*; *(expert)* Sachverständige *m/f*; Kenner *m*.

authorization Ermächtigung *f*;

(approval) Genehmigung *f*; Befugnis *f*.

authorize *(to grant power)* bevollmächtigen; *(to approve)* genehmigen.

autodraft Eigenwechsel *m*.

automate automatisieren.

automatic automatisch.

automatic teller machine Geldausgabeautomat *m*; Geldautomat *m*.

automation Automatisierung *f*.

autonomous unabhängig; autonom.

autonomy Autonomie *f*; Selbstregierung *f*; Selbstverwaltung *f*.

auxiliary materials *(balance sheet)* Hilfsstoffe *pl*.

availability Verfügbarkeit *f*.

available verfügbar; vorhanden.

average n Durchschnitt *m*; *(mean value)* Mittelwert *m*. a durchschnittlich. v durchschnittlich betragen; den Durchschnitt *m* berechnen.

average cost Durchschnittskosten *pl*.

average figure Durchschnittszahl *f*.

average number Durchschnittszahl *f*.

average price Durchschnittspreis *m*.

average rent Durchschnittsmiete *f*.

aviation Luftfahrt *f*.

aviation industry Luftfahrtindustrie *f*.

avoid vermeiden; umgehen.

avoidable vermeidlich; vermeidbar.

award n *(reward)* Belohnung *f*; Zuerkennung *f*; *(price)* Preis *m*; *(of contract)* Vergabe *f*. v *(to reward)* belohnen; zuerkennen; *(a price)* verleihen; *(to grant)* vergeben.

B

back n Rücken *m*; *(back page)* Rückseite *f*. **a** *(overdue)* rückständig. **adv** zurück; rückwärts. **v** *(to support)* unterstützen.

background Hintergrund *m*; *(preceding events)* Vorgeschichte *f*; *(professional experience)* Berufserfahrung *f*; *(training)* Ausbildung *f*.

backing *(help)* Hilfe *f*; *(support)* Stütze *f*; Unterstützung *f*; *(bank notes)* Deckung *f*; *(currency exchange)* Stützungskäufe *pl*.

backing money Stützungsgelder *pl*.

backlog of orders unerledigte Aufträge *pl*.

bad schlecht; ungünstig; *(check)* ungedeckt.

bad buy Fehlkauf *m*.

bad debt Forderungsausfall *m*.

bad debt insurance Kreditversicherung *f*.

bail Kaution *f*.

balance n Gleichgewicht *nt*; *(balance sheet)* Bilanz *f*; *(debit or credit account surplus)* Saldo *m*; Restsumme *f*. **v** ausgleichen; *(to balance an account)* bilanzieren; saldieren; Konto *nt* ausgleichen.

balance of current accounts Leistungsbilanz *f*.

balance of payments Zahlungsbilanz *f*.

balance of prices Preisgleichgewicht *nt*.

balance of trade Handelsbilanz *f*.

balance sheet Bilanz *f*; Bilanzaufstellung *f*.

balance sheet guidelines Bilanzrichtlinien *pl*.

balance sheet item Bilanzposten *m*.

balance sheet structure Bilanzstruktur *f*.

balance sheet total Bilanzsumme *f*; Bilanzvolumen *nt*.

ballot n *(voting ticket)* Wahlzettel *m*; Stimmzettel *m*; *(act of voting)* Abstimmung *f*. **v** abstimmen.

ballot vote Urabstimmung *f*.

bank n Bank *f*. **v** Bankgeschäfte *pl* machen.

bankable bankmäßig.

bank account Bankkonto *nt*.

bank affiliate Bankentochter *f*.

bank assets Bankvermögen *nt*.

bank automation Bankautomation *f*.

bank clientele Bankenkundschaft *f*.

bank code number Bankleitzahl *f*.

bank counselor Bankberater *m*.

bank credit Bankkredit *m*.

bank customer Bankkunde *m*; Bankkundin *f*.

bank customers Bankenkundschaft *f*.

bank depositor Einleger *m*.

bank employee Bankmitarbeiter *m*.

banker Bankier *m*.

banker's acceptance Bankakzept *nt*.

bank group   Bankenkonsortium *nt.*
banking   Bankwesen *nt.*
banking activity   Bankaktivität *f;*
Banktätigkeit *f.*
banking business   Bankgewerbe
nt.
banking center   Bankplatz *m.*
banking expertise   Bankfachwissen *nt.*
banking house   Bankhaus *nt.*
banking institution   Bankinstitut *nt.*
banking rule   Bankregel *f.*
banking service   Bankdienstleistung *f;* Bankleistung *f.*
banking syndicate   Bankenkonsortium *nt.*
bank management   Bankleitung *f;*
Bankvorstand *m.*
bank manager   Bankleiter *m.*
bank note   Banknote *f.*
bank officer   Bankbeamte *m;*
Bankbeamtin *f.*
bankroll   n Banknoten *pl.* v
finanzieren; Geldmittel *pl* bereitstellen.
bankrupt   n Konkursschuldner *m.*
a bankrott; pleite.
bankrupt company   Pleitefirma *f.*
bankruptcy   Bankrott *m;* Konkurs
m.
bankruptcy case   Konkursfall *m.*
bankruptcy judge   Konkursrichter
m.
bankruptcy law   Insolvenzrecht *nt.*
bank service charge   Bankspesen *pl.*
bank statement request   Konto-
standsabfrage *f.*
bank stocks   Bankaktien *pl.*
bank subsidiary   Bankentochter *f.*
bank supervision   Bankaufsicht *f.*
bank top management   Bankvorstand *m.*
bar   n Schranke *f;* Sperre *f; (ingot)*

Barren *m; (law)* Anwaltsstand *m.*
v ausschließen.
bargain   n Geschäft *nt;* Handel *m;*
(favorable purchase) Gelegenheitskauf *m.* v feilschen; handeln; *(to
negotiate)* verhandeln.
bargaining agent   Tarifpartner
m.
bargaining agreement   Betriebs-
vereinbarung *f;* Tarifvereinbarung
f.
bargaining round   Verhandlungsrunde *f;* Tarifrunde *f.*
bargaining strength   Verhandlungsstärke *f.*
barrier   Schranke *f;* Barriere *f.*
barter   n Tauschgeschäft *nt;*
Tauschhandel *m.* v Tauschhandel
m treiben.
barter economy   Tauschwirtschaft
f.
barter trade   Kompensationshandel *m;* Tauschgeschäft *nt.*
base   n Basis *f;* Grundlage *f.*
v basieren; begründen.
base pay   Grundgehalt *nt.*
base price   *(cost price)* Einkaufspreis
m; Grundpreis *m;* Basispreis *m.*
base salary   Grundgehalt *nt.*
basic   grundlegend; grundsätzlich;
fundamental.
basic need   Grundbedürfnis *nt.*
basic prerequisite   Grundvoraussetzung *f.*
basic regulation   Rahmenregelung
f.
basic strategy   Grundstrategie *f.*
basis   Basis *f;* Grundlage *f.*
basis of calculation   Rechnungsgrundlage *f.*
basis of information   Informa-
tionsbasis *f.*
basket   Korb *m.*

basket of commodities Warenkorb *m*.

basket of currencies Währungskorb *m*.

bear n *(stock exchange)* Baissespekulant *m*. a *(describing market)* flau. v *(to carry)* tragen; *(costs)* bestreiten; *(interest)* sich verzinsen.

bearer Inhaber *m*.

bearer note Inhaberpapier *nt*.

bearer savings bond Inhabersparbrief *m*.

bearer share Inhaberaktie *f*.

bearer stock Inhaberaktie *f*.

bear market Baisse *f*.

begin anfangen; beginnen.

beginning Beginn *m*; Anfang *m*; Start *m*.

behavior Verhalten *nt*; *(attitude)* Einstellung *f*; *(manners)* Benehmen *nt*.

behavioral control Verhaltenssteuerung *f*.

behavioral norm Verhaltensnorm *f*.

behavior of markets Marktverhalten *nt*.

behavior pattern Verhaltensweise *f*.

belief Glaube *m*; *(opinion)* Meinung *f*; *(conviction)* Überzeugung *f*.

believe glauben; meinen.

belong gehören; *(to be a member of)* angehören.

belt *(geography)* Streifen *m*; Zone *f*; *(clothing)* Gürtel *m*; *(machinery)* Riemen *m*.

beneficial vorteilhaft; nützlich.

beneficial interest Nießbrauch *m*.

beneficial use Genuß *m*.

beneficiary Begünstigte *m/f*; Bezugsberechtigte *m/f*; *(law)* Nutznießer *m*.

benefit n Vorteil *m*; Vergünstigung *f*; *(insurance)* Leistung *f*; *(non-salary compensation)* Nebenleistung *f*; *(aid)* Beihilfe *f*. v *(to favor)* begünstigen; *(to profit from)* Nutzen *m* ziehen aus.

bequeath hinterlassen.

bet n Wette *f*. v wetten.

betterment Verbesserung *f*.

bid n Angebot *nt*; Offerte *f*; *(estimate)* Kostenvoranschlag *m*; *(auction)* Gebot *nt*. v *(to auction)* bieten; *(to make an offer)* Angebot *nt* machen.

bidder Bieter *m*; Bietende *m/f*.

bid invitation Ausschreibung *f*.

bilateral zweiseitig; bilateral.

bill n Rechnung *f*; Faktura *f*; *(bank note)* Banknote *f*; *(bill of exchange)* Wechsel *m*; *(government)* Gesetzentwurf *m*; Gesetzesvorlage *f*. v berechnen; in Rechnung *f* stellen.

billholdings Wechselportefeuille *nt*.

bill of lading Konnossement *nt*.

bills in hand Wechselportefeuille *nt*.

blame n Tadel *m*; Schuld *f*. v tadeln; Schuld *f* geben.

blank n *(printed form)* Vordruck *m*; *(blank space)* leere Stelle *f*; *(lottery)* Niete *f*. a blanko; leer.

blank credit Blankokredit *m*.

blue chip Spitzenwert *m*.

board n *(committee)* Ausschuß *m*; *(council)* Rat *m*; *(executive board)* Vorstand *m*; *(board of directors)* Aufsichtsrat *m*; *(billboard)* Anschlagtafel *f*; *(meals)* Verpflegung *f*; *(ship)* Deck *nt*. v *(train, airplane)* einsteigen; *(ship)* sich einschiffen.

board meeting *(directors)* Aufsichtsratssitzung *f*; *(management)* Vorstandssitzung *f*.

board of directors Aufsichtsrat *m*.

board of directors' seat Aufsichtsratsmandat *nt*.

bond n *(debenture)* Schuldverschreibung *f*; Anleihepapier *nt*; *(industrial bond)* Obligation *f*; *(mortgage bond)* Pfandbrief *m*; *(customs)* Zollverschluß *m*; *(tie)* Bindung *f*. v *(customs)* unter Zollverschluß *m* nehmen.

bonded warehouse Zollager *nt*.

bond index Rentenindex *m*.

bond market Rentenmarkt *m*.

bond ownership Rentenbesitz *m*.

bond price Anleihekurs *m*.

bonus Prämie *f*; Sondervergütung *f*; Gehaltszuschlag *m*; *(at Christmas)* Gratifikation *f*.

book n Buch *nt*; *(ledger)* Geschäftsbuch *nt*. v *(to make reservation)* buchen.

book credit Buchkredit *m*.

bookkeeping Buchführung *f*; Buchhaltung *f*.

bookkeeping entry Buchungsposten *m*.

book of commissions Auftragsbuch *nt*; Orderbuch *nt*.

book value Bilanzwert *m*; Buchwert *m*.

boom n Hausse *f*; *(strong demand)* starke Nachfrage *f*; Hochkonjunktur *f*. v florieren; *(to rise in value)* im Wert *m* steigen.

boost n Auftrieb *m*; Ankurbelung *f*. v ankurbeln; fördern.

border n Rand *m*; *(international)* Grenze *f*. v angrenzen.

borderline case Grenzfall *m*.

borrow borgen; entleihen; *(to take out a loan)* ein Darlehen *nt* aufnehmen.

borrowed money Fremdgeld *nt*; aufgenommenes Kapital *nt*.

borrower Kreditnehmer *m*; Kreditkunde *m*, Kreditkundin *f*.

borrower's bank Hausbank *f*.

borrowing Kreditaufnahme *f*.

boss Chef *m*.

bottleneck Engpaß *m*.

bottom *(of business cycle)* Tiefpunkt *m*; Tiefstand *m*.

bottom line Saldo *m*.

boundary Grenze *f*; Grenzlinie *f*.

box n Kasten *m*; Kiste *f*; *(of cardboard)* Karton *m*; *(printed square)* Kästchen *nt*; *(post office)* Schließfach *nt*. v verpacken; *(sport)* boxen.

box office Hauptkasse *f*; *(movie)* Kinokasse *f*; *(theater)* Theaterkasse *f*.

boycott n Boykott *m*. v boykottieren.

branch *(of company)* Zweigstelle *f*; Filiale *f*; Geschäftsstelle *f*.

branch bank Tochterbank *f*; Filialbank *f*; Bankzweigstelle *f*.

branch network Filialnetz *nt*.

branch office Zweigniederlassung *f*; Niederlassung *f*; *(of a bank)* Depositenkasse *f*.

brand n *(make)* Marke *f*; Sorte *f*; *(brand product)* Markenerzeugnis *nt*. v mit seinem Warenzeichen *nt* versehen.

brand name Markenname *m*; *(trademark)* Warenzeichen *nt*.

brand new fabrikneu.

breach Bruch *m*; *(violation)* Verstoß *m*; Verletzung *f*.

breach of contract Vertragsbruch *m*.

break n *(breakage)* Bruch *m*;
(pause) Arbeitspause *f*. v brechen;
(rules) nicht einhalten.
breakdown Zusammenbruch *m*.
break even ohne Gewinn *m* und
Verlust *m* abschneiden; kostendeckend arbeiten.
breakthrough Durchbruch *m*.
breakup Auflösung *f*.
break up *(a conglomerate)* entflechten; auseinanderbrechen; *(to
dissolve)* auflösen.
bribe n Bestechung *f*. v bestechen.
bridge a gap überbrücken.
bridging of a gap Überbrückung
f.
brief n *(law)* Schriftsatz *m*. a kurz.
v informieren.
briefcase Aktentasche *f*.
briefing Einweisung *f*; Unterrichtung *f*.
broad breit; weit; ausgedehnt.
broadcast advertising Werbefunk
m.
broad product line breit gestreutes
Warensortiment *nt*.
brochure Broschüre *f*; Druckschrift
f.
brochure price Prospektpreis *m*.
broke pleite.
broker Makler *m*; Broker *m*.
brokerage Maklergeschäft *nt*.
brokerage house Brokerhaus *nt*.
budget n Budget *nt*; Haushalt *m*;
Etat *m*; Finanzplan *m*. v Haushaltsplan *m* aufstellen.
budgetary policy Haushaltspolitik
f.
budget committee Haushaltsausschuß *m*.
budget deficit Haushaltsdefizit *nt*;
Etatdefizit *nt*.

budgeting Finanzplanung *f*.
budget limitation Budgetbeschränkung *f*.
budget proposal Haushaltsvoranschlag *m*; Haushaltsentwurf *m*.
budget reduction Budgetbeschränkung *f*.
budget reorganization Haushaltssanierung *f*.
budget specialist Haushaltsexperte *m*; Haushaltsexpertin *f*.
buffer Reserve *f*; Stoßpolster *nt*.
buffer stock Vorratslager *nt*; Reservelager *nt*.
build bauen; aufbauen; *(to erect)*
errichten.
builder Bauherr *m*.
building funds Baugelder *pl*.
bulk n Masse *f*; Menge *f*. a lose;
unverpackt.
bulk buyer Großabnehmer *m*.
bulk commodity Massengut *nt*.
bulk transaction Massengeschäft
nt.
bullish phase Haussephase *f*.
bull market Hausse *f*.
burden n Last *f*. v belasten.
bureau Dienststelle *f*; Amt *nt*.
bureaucracy Bürokratie *f*.
bureaucrat Bürokrat *m*.
bureaucratic bürokratisch.
business *(company, business activity)* Geschäft *nt*; *(firm)* Firma *f*;
(plant, operation) Betrieb *m*;
(trade, industry) Gewerbe *nt*;
(economy) Wirtschaft *f*.
business account Geschäftskonto
nt.
business call Kundenbesuch *m*.
business center Geschäftszentrum
nt.
business client Firmenkunde *m*;
Geschäftskunde *m*.

business community Geschäftswelt *f*; Wirtschaftskreise *pl.*
business cycle Wirtschaftsablauf
m; Konjunkturzyklus *m*; Konjunkturverlauf *m.*
business day Geschäftstag *m.*
business development Geschäfts-
entwicklung *f.*
business expenses Geschäftskosten *pl.*
business hours Verkaufszeit *f*;
Öffnungszeit *f*; Geschäftszeit *f.*
business journal Wirtschaftszeitung *f.*
business loan Betriebskredit *m*;
Geschäftskredit *m*; Gewerbedarlehen *nt.*
businessman Geschäftsmann *m*;
Kaufmann *m.*
business management Geschäftsführung *f*; Unternehmensführung
f.
business name Handelsname *m.*
business on joint account Konsortialgeschäft *nt.*
business outlook Konjunkturaussichten *pl.*
business page *(newspaper)* Wirtschaftsteil *m.*
businesspeople Geschäftsleute *pl.*
business premises Betriebsstätte *f.*

business publication Wirtschaftsmagazin *nt.*
business purpose Geschäftszweck
m.
business report Geschäftsbericht
m.
business revival Konjunkturbelebung *f.*
business tax Gewerbesteuer *f.*
business volume Geschäftsvolumen *nt*; Geschäftsumfang *m.*
businesswoman Geschäftsfrau *f.*
busy *(occupied)* beschäftigt;
(active) tätig; *(street, town)* belebt;
(industrious) fleißig; *(telephone)*
besetzt.
buy n Kauf *m*; Erwerb *m.*
v kaufen; erwerben.
buyer Käufer *m*; *(for store)* Einkäufer *m.*
buyer's market Käufermarkt *m.*
buying behavior Kaufverhalten
nt.
buying country Abnehmerland *nt.*
buying group Abnehmergruppe *f.*
buying incentive Kaufanreiz *m.*
buying resistance Kaufzurückhaltung *f.*
buy up aufkaufen.
bylaws Statuten *pl*; Satzung *f.*

calculable berechenbar.
calculate berechnen; kalkulieren; errechnen; *(to estimate)* schätzen.
calculation Berechnung *f*; Kalkulation *f*; *(estimate)* Voranschlag *m*.
calculation of earning power Ertragsschätzung *f*.
calculator Rechenmaschine *f*; Rechner *m*.
calendar Kalender *m*.
call n Ruf *m*; *(appointment)* Berufung *f*; *(for funds)* Abruf *m*; *(telephone)* Anruf *m*; Gespräch *nt*; *(visit)* Besuch *m*; *(demand)* Nachfrage *f*. v rufen; *(to telephone)* anrufen; *(to name)* nennen; *(to be called)* heißen; *(a loan)* abrufen; *(a bond)* aufrufen.
call for additional cover Nachschußpflicht *f*.
call for funds Einforderung *f*.
calling in Einforderung *f*.
calling on customers Kundenbesuch *m*.
call money Tagesgeld *nt*.
call option Bezugsoption *f*; Kaufoption *f*.
call up abrufen.
campaign n Kampagne *f*; Feldzug *m*. v eine Kampagne *f* führen; Propaganda *f* machen.
cancel rückgängig machen; annullieren; streichen; *(order)* stornieren; *(entry)* löschen; *(meeting)* absagen; *(magazine subscription)* kündigen.
cancellation Annullierung *f*; *(abolition)* Aufhebung *f*; Ungültigkeits-

erklärung *f*; *(order)* Stornierung *f*; *(entry)* Löschung *f*; Streichung *f*; *(magazine subscription)* Kündigung *f*; *(meeting)* Absage *f*.
candidate Kandidat *m*; Anwärter *m*.
canvass n *(customers)* Kundenwerbung *f*; *(votes)* Stimmenwerbung *f*. v Kunden werben; Stimmen werben.
capability Fähigkeit *f*; Leistungsfähigkeit *f*.
capable fähig.
capacity Kapazität *f*; *(content)* Fassungsvermögen *nt*; *(ability)* Leistungsfähigkeit *f*; *(official role)* Eigenschaft *f*; *(power)* Kraft *f*; Leistungsstärke *f*.
capital Kapital *nt*; Stammvermögen *nt*; *(balance sheet)* Kapitalanteil *m*; *(funds)* Geldmittel *pl*; *(capital city)* Hauptstadt *f*; *(capital letter)* Großbuchstabe *m*.
capital account Kapitalkonto *nt*.
capital accumulation Kapitalakkumulation *f*.
capital appreciation Anlagewertsteigerung *f*; Vermögenszuwachs *m*.
capital base Kapitalbasis *f*.
capital budget Investitionsplan *m*; Investitionshaushalt *m*.
capital control Kapitalkontrolle *f*.
capital expenditure Investitionsausgabe *f*.
capital expenditure program Investitionsprogramm *nt*.
capital export Kapitalexport *m*.

capital flight Kapitalflucht *f*.

capital flow Kapitalwanderung *f*; Kapitalbewegung *f*; Kapitalstrom *m*.

capital formation Kapitalbildung *f*.

capital gain Kapitalzuwachs *m*.

capital gains Kapitalgewinn *m*; *(stock exchange)* realisierter Kursgewinn *m*.

capital goods Investitionsgüter *pl*; Produktionsmittel *pl*; Anlagegüter *pl*.

capital growth Kapitalzuwachs *m*.

capital income Kapitaleinkommen *nt*.

capital investment Kapitalanlage *f*.

capitalism Kapitalismus *m*.

capitalist Kapitalist *m*.

capitalistic kapitalistisch.

capitalization Kapitalisierung *f*; Kapitalausstattung *f*; *(capital stock)* Gesellschaftskapital *nt*.

capital market Kapitalmarkt *m*.

capital movement Kapitalverkehr *m*.

capital reduction Kapitalminderung *f*.

capital requirement Kapitalbedarf *m*.

capital resources *(bank)* Eigenkapital *nt*.

capital spending Kapitalaufwand *m*.

capital stock Grundkapital *nt*; Anfangskapital *nt*.

capital structure Kapitalstruktur *f*; Kapitalzusammensetzung *f*.

captive market monopolistischer Markt *m*.

capture n *(market)* Eroberung *f*. v *(market)* erobern.

card Karte *f*; *(ticket)* Billett *nt*; *(business card)* Visitenkarte *f*.

care n *(worry)* Sorge *f*; *(attention)* Aufmerksamkeit *f*; *(diligence)* Sorgfalt *f*; *(taking care)* Betreuung *f*; Pflege *f*; *(responsibility)* Obhut *f*. p *(care of)* bei. v sorgen für; sich kümmern um; *(to like)* mögen.

career Laufbahn *f*; Karriere *f*; Werdegang *m*.

career opportunity Berufschance *f*.

cargo Fracht *f*; Ladung *f*; Frachtgut *nt*.

cargo ship Frachtschiff *nt*.

carrier Fuhrunternehmer *m*; Transportunternehmer *m*; Spediteur *m*; *(airline)* Lufttransportgesellschaft *f*; Träger *m*.

carry tragen; *(to transport)* befördern; *(on one's person)* mitführen.

carry forward *(bookkeeping)* übertragen.

carry on *(a business)* betreiben; *(a conversation)* führen.

carry out durchführen; ausführen; vollziehen.

cartel Kartell *nt*.

cartelize kartellisieren.

case n Fall *m*; *(container)* Kasten *m*; *(law)* Rechtssache *f*; Rechtsfall *m*. v in Kisten *pl* verpacken.

case of need Notfall *m*.

case presentation Fallpräsentation *f*.

case study Fallstudie *f*.

cash n Bargeld *nt*; Barmittel *pl*; Barzahlung *f*; *(balance sheet)* Kassenbestand *m*. a bar. v *(to collect money)* einkassieren; *(to cash a check)* einlösen.

cash account Kassenkonto *nt*.

cash accounting Kassenbuchführung *f*.

cash assets reserve Bestandsreserve *f*.

cash bonus Barprämie *f.*
cash contribution Bargeldbeitrag *m.*
cash discount Skonto *m/nt.*
cash distribution Barausschüttung *f.*
cash dividend ausgeschüttete Dividende *f.*
cash flow geschäftsnotwendige Barmittel *pl.*
cashier Kassierer *m*; Kassenführer *m.*
cash ledger Kassenbuch *nt.*
cash management Kassenhaltung *f*; Geldhandel *m.*
cash market *(stock exchange)* Kassamarkt *m.*
cash position Liquiditätslage *f.*
cash price Geldpreis *m.*
cash squeeze Liquiditätsdruck *m.*
cash transaction Bargeschäft *nt.*
cash value *(insurance)* Versicherungswert *m*; Geldwert *m.*
casualty *(hurt or killed person)* Opfer *nt*; *(injured person)* Verletzte *m/f.*
casualty insurance Unfallversicherung *f.*
catalog n Katalog *m*; Verzeichnis *nt*; Liste *f.* v katalogisieren.
catalog firm Versandhaus *nt.*
catch-up effect Nachholeffekt *m.*
category Klasse *f*; Gruppe *f*; Kategorie *f.*
category of goods Gütergruppe *f.*
causal ursächlich.
cause n Ursache *f*; Anlaß *m*; *(reason)* Grund *m*; *(being in the public interest)* Anliegen *nt*; *(law case)* Rechtsstreit *m.* v verursachen; veranlassen; bewirken.
cause of loss Schadensursache *f.*
caution n Vorsicht *f*; *(prudence)*

Umsicht *f*; *(warning)* Warnung *f.* v warnen.
cautious vorsichtig; behutsam.
cease aufhören; *(firm)* erlöschen; *(payment)* einstellen.
ceiling Decke *f*; *(upper limit)* Höchstgrenze *f.*
census Volkszählung *f*; Erhebung *f.*
census year Erhebungsjahr *nt.*
center n Zentrum *nt*; Zentralstelle *f*; Mittelpunkt *m.* v sich konzentrieren; in den Mittelpunkt *m* stellen.
center of learning Bildungszentrum *nt.*
central Haupt-; zentral.
central bank Notenbank *f*; Zentralbank *f.*
central bank money Zentralbankgeld *nt.*
central bank system Notenbanksystem *nt.*
central department Hauptabteilung *f.*
centralization Zentralisierung *f*; Zusammenlegung *f.*
centralize zentralisieren.
central market Großmarkt *m.*
central pay office Hauptkasse *f.*
century Jahrhundert *nt.*
certain sicher; gewiß; bestimmt.
certainty Gewißheit *f*; Bestimmtheit *f*; Sicherheit *f*; *(reliability)* Zuverlässigkeit *f.*
certificate Bescheinigung *f*; Schein *m*; *(confirmation)* Bestätigung *f*; *(verification)* Beglaubigung *f*; *(customs)* Geleitzettel *m*; *(stock)* Anteilschein *m*; Zertifikat *nt*; *(diploma)* Zeugnis *nt.*
certificate of origin Ursprungszeugnis *nt.*
certify bescheinigen.

cessation   Beendigung *f*; Einstellung *f*.

cession   Überlassung *f*.

chain   Kette *f*; Kettenunternehmen *nt*.

chain of stores   Handelskette *f*.

chain store   Kettenladen *m*; Filialgeschäft *nt*.

chairman,-person,-woman   Vorsitzende *m/f*.

challenge   n Herausforderung *f*. v herausfordern; *(to contest)* anfechten.

chamber   Kammer *f*.

chamber of commerce   Handelskammer *f*.

change   n Änderung *f*; Veränderung *f*; *(transition)* Übergang *m*; Wandel *m*; *(balance of money returned)* herausgegebenes Geld *nt*; Wechselgeld *nt*; *(small coin)* Kleingeld *nt*. v ändern; umwandeln; wandeln; *(money)* wechseln.

change purse   Portemonnaie *nt*.

channel   n Kanal *m*; *(television)* Programm *nt*; *(path)* Weg *m*. v lenken; einschleusen.

chapter   Kapitel *nt*; Abschnitt *m*.

characteristic   n Merkmal *nt*; Kennzeichen *nt*. a charakteristisch; bezeichnend.

characterization   Charakterisierung *f*.

charge   n *(fee)* Gebühr *f*; *(bookkeeping)* Belastung *f*; Abbuchung *f*; *(cost)* Kosten *pl*; *(care)* Aufsicht *f*; *(responsibility)* Verantwortung *f*; *(load)* Ladung *f*; *(person entrusted to one's care)* Schützling *m*; *(law)* Anklage *f*; **additional ~** Aufschlag *m*. v *(to debit)* belasten; abbuchen; *(for fees)* berechnen; in Rechnung *f* stellen; *(on credit)* anschreiben; *(to entrust with)* beauftragen; *(law)* zur Last legen; *(to load)* laden.

charging of costs   Kostenbelastung *f*.

chart   Karte *f*; Tabelle *f*; *(graph)* Schaubild *nt*.

charter   n Mieten *nt*; *(by-laws)* Satzung *f*; *(charter flight)* Charterflug *m*; *(bank)* Konzession *f*. v chartern; mieten.

cheap   billig; preiswert; *(of inferior value)* minderwertig.

check   n *(draft)* Scheck *m*; *(control)* Aufsicht *f*; Überprüfung *f*; *(bill)* Rechnung *f*; *(voucher)* Gutschein *m*; *(baggage)* Aufbewahrungsschein *m*. v *(to control)* nachprüfen; *(to mark)* ankreuzen.

check guarantee   Scheckbürgschaft *f*.

check guarantee card   Scheckkarte *f*.

checking account   Scheckkonto *nt*; Girokonto *nt*; Bankkonto *nt*.

check list   Prüfliste *f*.

check presentation   Scheckeinreichung *f*.

chief   n Leiter *m*; Chef *m*. a Haupt-; hauptsächlich.

chief executive   Vorstandssprecher *m*; Vorstandsvorsitzende *m/f*; Vorstandschef *m*; Firmenchef *m*.

choice   n Wahl *f*; Auswahl *f*; *(best quality)* Auslese *f*. a ausgesucht; erstklassig.

choose   wählen; auswählen.

circa   zirka.

circle   Kreis *m*.

circular   n Rundschreiben *nt*. a kreisförmig.

circulation   Umlauf *m*; Kreislauf *m*; *(newspaper)* Auflage *f*.

circulation of money Geldumlauf *m*; Geldverkehr *m*.

circumstance Umstand *m*; Fall *m*.

circumstances Sachlage *f*; Sachverhalt *m*; *(financial condition)* Vermögensverhältnisse *pl*.

claim n *(right)* Anspruch *m*; *(demand)* Forderung *f*; *(statement)* Behauptung *f*. v *(to lay claim on)* beanspruchen; *(to demand)* fordern; *(to state)* behaupten.

class n Klasse *f*; *(rank)* Stand *m*; Rangstufe *f*; *(type)* Gattung *f*; *(lecture)* Vorlesung *f*. v klassifizieren; einstufen.

class barrier Klassenschranke *f*.

classification Klassifizierung *f*; Einteilung *f*; Aufgliederung *f*; Anordnung *f*.

classified advertisement Kleinanzeige *f*.

classify einstufen; einordnen; gruppieren; klassifizieren.

class of stocks Aktiengattung *f*.

class society Klassengesellschaft *f*.

clause Klausel *f*.

clear a klar; *(pure)* rein; *(claim)* unanfechtbar; *(unencumbered)* unbelastet. v freigeben; *(check)* verrechnen; *(computer)* löschen; *(debt)* bezahlen; *(profit)* Reingewinn *m* erzielen; *(through customs)* zollamtlich abfertigen.

clearance Freigabe *f*; *(check)* Verrechnung *f*; *(customs)* Zollabfertigung *f*; *(debts)* Zahlung *f*; *(of stock)* Lagerräumung *f*; *(distance)* Abstand *m*.

clearing *(banking)* Verrechnung *f*; Giroverkehr *m*.

clearing balance Verrechnungssaldo *m*.

clearing bank Girobank *f*.

clearinghouse Girozentrale *f*.

clearinghouse association Giroverband *m*.

clearinghouse balance Verrechnungssaldo *m*.

clearing system Verrechnungsverkehr *m*.

clearing unit Verrechnungseinheit *f*.

clerical Büro-; Schreib-.

clerical worker Büroangestellte *m/f*.

clerk kaufmännische Angestellte *m/f*; Schreibkraft *f*.

client Klient *m*; *(customer)* Kunde *m*; Kundin *f*; *(party ordering)* Auftraggeber *m*; *(law office)* Mandant *m*.

clientele Kundschaft *f*; Klientel *f*.

climax Höhepunkt *m*.

climb steigen; klettern.

close n Schluß *m*; Ende *nt*; *(accounting)* Abschluß *m*; *(business day)* Geschäftsschluß *m*. a *(capital)* knapp. v schließen; *(accounting)* abschließen.

close of the year Jahresschluß *m*.

closing of account Kontoauflösung *f*.

closing session Abschlußsitzung *f*.

closure Schließung *f*; Schluß *m*; *(fastener)* Verschluß *m*.

clout Einfluß *m*; Macht *f*.

club Verein *m*.

coalition Koalition *f*; Vereinigung *f*.

code Code *m*; Chiffrierschlüssel *m*; *(law)* Gesetzbuch *nt*; Kodex *m*.

codecide mitentscheiden.

code of commerce Handelsgesetzbuch *nt*.

codetermination Mitbestimmung *f*.

codetermine mitbestimmen.
cofounder Mitgründer *m*.
coin n Münze *f*; Geldstück *nt*.
v münzen; prägen.
coin changing machine Geld-
wechselautomat *m*.
coin collection Münzensammlung *f*.
collaboration Zusammenarbeit *f*.
collapse n Zusammenbruch *m*.
v zusammenbrechen; stürzen.
collateral n *(pledge)* Pfand *nt*;
(security) Sicherheit *f*; *(cover)*
Deckung *f*. a Neben-; seitlich;
gleichzeitig.
colleague Kollege *m*; Kollegin *f*;
Mitarbeiter *m*.
collect *(to accumulate)* sammeln;
(to cash) kassieren; einziehen; *(to
demand)* einfordern.
collect call R-Gespräch *nt*.
collection *(accumulation)* Sammlung *f*; *(cashing)* Inkasso *nt*; Einziehung *f*; *(demand)* Einforderung *f*.
collection item Inkassopapier *nt*.
collective n Gemeinschaft *f*.
a gemeinsam.
collective agreement Tarifabkommen *nt*.
collective bargainer Tarifpartner
m.
collective bargaining Tarifverhandlung *f*.
collective consignment Sammel-
sendung *f*.
collective shipment Sammelsen-
dung *f*.
collective transfer Sammelüber-
weisung *f*.
collector Sammler *m*; *(debts)*
Inkassobeamte *m*, -beamtin *f*;
(taxes) Steuereinnehmer *m*.
collector's item Sammelobjekt *nt*.
collector's value Sammlerwert *m*.

column *(pillar)* Säule *f*; *(print)*
Spalte *f*; *(newspaper feature)*
Rubrik *f*; *(figures)* Zahlenreihe *f*.
combination Verbindung *f*;
Zusammenschluß *m*; Kombination
f.
combine n Trust *m*; Pool *m*; Kombinat *nt*. v zusammenschließen;
(to merge) fusionieren; vereinen.
comeback Wiederaufstieg *m*.
come to terms sich einigen.
command n *(order)* Befehl *m*;
(control) Führungsgewalt *f*; *(leadership)* Führung *f*; *(rule)* Herrschaft *f*; *(mastery)* Beherrschung *f*.
v befehlen; anordnen; *(to have
available)* verfügen über.
command economy Planwirtschaft *f*.
commence beginnen; anfangen.
commensurate entsprechend.
comment n Kommentar *m*; Bemerkung *f*. v kommentieren; Bemerkung *f* machen.
commentary Kommentar *m*.
commerce *(trade)* Handel *m*; *(flow
of merchandise)* Warenverkehr *m*.
commercial n *(advertising)* Werbesendung *f*. a geschäftlich; kaufmännisch; kommerziell.
commercial bank Geschäftsbank *f*.
commercial center Geschäftszentrum *nt*.
commercial code Handelsgesetzbuch *nt*.
commercial debt Warenschuld *f*.
commercial establishment Handelshaus *nt*; Handelsunternehmen
nt.
commercial lender Geschäftskreditgeber *m*.
commercial loan Geschäftskredit
m; Warenkredit *m*.

commercial paper Handelspapier *nt*; Warenwechsel *m*; Wertpapier *nt*.

commercial relationship Handelsbeziehung *f*.

commercial shipment Warenversand *m*.

commercial treaty Handelsabkommen *nt*.

commission n Provision *f*; *(brokerage)* Courtage *f*; *(committee)* Ausschuß *m*; Kommission *f*; *(granting of authority)* Auftrag *m*. v beauftragen; bevollmächtigen.

commission earnings Provisionseinnahme *f*; Provisionsertrag *m*.

commissioner Beauftragte *m/f*; Bevollmächtigte *m/f*.

commission on sales Umsatzprovision *f*.

commission rate Provisionsgebühr *f*.

commission receipts Provisionsertrag *m*.

commit *(to entrust)* anvertrauen; *(to commit oneself)* sich verpflichten; *(to perpetrate)* begehen.

commitment *(obligation)* Verpflichtung *f*; Obligo *nt*; Engagement *nt*; *(consignment)* Überweisung *f*.

committee Komitee *nt*; Ausschuß *m*.

commodities Güter *pl*; Waren *pl*.

commodity Ware *f*; Erzeugnis *nt*.

commodity futures Warenterminhandel *m*.

commodity futures market Warenterminmarkt *m*.

commodity price Warenpreis *m*.

commodity sale Warenverkauf *m*.

common *(usual)* üblich; gewöhnlich; *(shared by all)* gemeinsam; *(public)* öffentlich.

common law Gewohnheitsrecht *nt*.

Common Market Gemeinsamer Markt *m*.

common stock Stammaktie *f*.

communicate mitteilen; in Verbindung stehen.

communication *(message)* Mitteilung *f*; Benachrichtigung *f*; Information *f*; *(relationship)* Verbindung *f*; *(telecommunication)* Fernmeldewesen *nt*; Kommunikation *f*; *(flow of information)* Informationsfluß *m*.

communication network Informationsnetz *nt*.

communication policy Informationspolitik *f*.

communication system Informationssystem *nt*.

communication technology Informationstechnik *f*.

community Gemeinde *f*; Gemeinschaft *f*.

company Gesellschaft *f*; *(firm)* Firma *f*; *(enterprise)* Unternehmen *nt*; *(plant)* Betrieb *m*.

company car Firmenwagen *m*.

company earnings Betriebsergebnis *nt*.

company management Unternehmensleitung *f*.

company pension Betriebsrente *f*.

comparability Vergleichbarkeit *f*.

comparable vergleichbar.

comparative vergleichend; relativ; komparativ.

comparatively vergleichsweise.

compare vergleichen.

comparison Vergleich *m*.

compartment *(department)* Abteilung *f*; Fach *nt*; *(railroad)* Abteil *nt*.

compatible   verträglich; vereinbar; zusammenpassend; *(computer)* kompatibel.

compensate   *(to make up for)* entschädigen; ausgleichen; *(to pay)* entlohnen; erstatten.

compensation   *(for damage)* Schadensersatz *m*; Abfindung *f*; Ausgleich *m*; *(salary)* Vergütung *f*; Entlohnung *f*.

compensation charge   Ausgleichsabgabe *f*.

compensatory   entschädigend; ausgleichend.

compete   konkurrieren; im Wettbewerb *m* stehen.

compete for   sich bewerben.

competence   *(ability)* Befähigung *f*; *(authority)* Zuständigkeit *f*; Kompetenz *f*; Befugnis *f*.

competent   fähig; kompetent; fachkundig.

competing country   Konkurrenzland *nt*.

competition   Konkurrenz *f*; Wettbewerb *m*; *(competing)* Konkurrenzkampf *m*.

competitive   konkurrenzfähig; wettbewerbsfähig; *(personal quality)* ehrgeizig.

competitive advantage   Wettbewerbsvorteil *m*.

competitive disadvantage   Wettbewerbsnachteil *m*.

competitiveness   Wettbewerbsfähigkeit *f*; Konkurrenzfähigkeit *f*.

competitive position   Wettbewerbsposition *f*.

competitive pricing   konkurrenzfähige Preisfestsetzung *f*.

competitor   Konkurrent *m*; Wettbewerber *m*.

compilation   Zusammenstellung *f*.

complain   sich beschweren; beanstanden; *(about faulty merchandise)* reklamieren.

complaint   Beschwerde *f*; Beanstandung *f*; *(about faulty merchandise)* Reklamation *f*.

complement   n Ergänzung *f*. v ergänzen.

complementary   komplementär; ergänzend.

complete   a vollständig. v beenden; ergänzen; fertigstellen; *(a form)* ausfüllen.

completion   Vollendung *f*; Fertigstellung *f*; Beendigung *f*; Abschluß *m*; *(of a form)* Ausfüllen *nt*.

complex   kompliziert; komplex; verzweigt; verflochten.

complexity   Kompliziertheit *f*; Verflechtung *f*; Verzweigtheit *f*.

compliance   Befolgung *f*; Einhaltung *f*.

comply   befolgen; einhalten.

component   Bestandteil *m*; Komponente *f*.

component part   Einzelteil *nt*.

composite   zusammengesetzt.

compound   n Zusammensetzung *f*. a zusammengesetzt. v zusammensetzen.

compound interest   Zinseszinsen *pl*.

comprehend   verstehen; erfassen.

comprehensive   umfassend; umfangreich.

comprehensive coverage   *(car insurance)* Vollkasko *nt*.

comprise   enthalten; einschließen; erfassen.

compromise   n Kompromiß *m*; Vergleich *m*. v einen Kompromiß *m* schließen; *(to endanger)* gefährden; *(to expose)* bloßstellen.

comptroller Rechnungsprüfer *m*; Kostenprüfer *m*; *(auditor)* Revisor *m*; Controller *m*.

compulsory obligatorisch; zwingend; pflichtmäßig.

compulsory insurance Pflichtversicherung *f*.

compulsory loan Zwangsanleihe *f*.

compulsory registration Meldepflicht *f*.

computation Berechnung *f*.

computation of interest Zinsrechnung *f*.

compute berechnen; kalkulieren.

computer Computer *m*; Elektronenrechner *m*.

computer center Rechenzentrum *nt*.

computer company Computerfirma *f*.

computer-controlled computergesteuert.

computer data Computerdaten *pl*.

computer game Bildschirmspiel *nt*.

computerize auf Datenverarbeitung *f* umstellen.

computerized cash register Computerkasse *f*.

computer keyboard Computertastatur *f*.

computer operation Computerverfahren *nt*.

computer program Computerprogramm *nt*.

computer room Rechenzentrale *f*.

computer screen Computerbildschirm *m*.

computer technology Computertechnologie *f*.

conceal *(balance sheet)* verschleiern; verheimlichen.

concealment Geheimhaltung *f*.

concede zugestehen.

concentrate sich konzentrieren; konzentrieren.

concentration Konzentration *f*.

concern n *(business)* Betrieb *m*; Unternehmen *nt*; Konzern *m*; *(interest)* Interesse *nt*; *(matter)* Angelegenheit *f*; *(worry)* Besorgnis *f*. v *(to refer to)* betreffen; *(to occupy with)* sich beschäftigen mit.

concern director Konzernchef *m*.

concerning hinsichtlich.

concern leadership Konzernführung *f*.

concern management Konzernführung *f*.

concerted gemeinschaftlich.

concession Konzession *f*; *(conceding)* Zugeständnis *nt*; *(granting)* Gewährung *f*; *(trade license)* Gewerbeerlaubnis *f*.

conciliation *(arbitration)* Schlichtung *f*; *(settlement)* Ausgleich *m*.

conclude *(agreement)* abschließen; *(to finish)* enden; beenden; *(to deduce)* folgern.

conclusion *(agreement)* Abschluß *m*; Ende *nt*; *(deduction)* Schlußfolgerung *f*.

conclusion of an agreement Vertragsabschluß *m*.

conclusion of sale Auftragsabschluß *m*.

conclusive beweiskräftig.

concur zusammentreffen; *(to agree)* übereinstimmen.

concurrence Zusammentreffen *nt*; *(agreement)* Übereinstimmung *f*.

concurrent gleichzeitig; übereinstimmend.

condition n *(prerequisite)* Bedingung *f*; Kondition *f*; *(state of being)* Lage *f*; Zustand *m*; Beschaffenheit *f*. v bedingen; *(to* *make fit)* in guten Zustand bringen; konditionieren.

conditional bedingt.

conditionality Bedingtheit *f*.

condominium apartment Eigentumswohnung *f*.

conduct n Führung *f*; *(behavior)* Verhalten *nt*. v führen; betreiben; *(to behave)* sich verhalten.

confer *(to grant)* gewähren; *(a degree)* verleihen; *(to discuss)* sich beraten.

conference Konferenz *f*; Besprechung *f*; Sitzung *f*.

confidence Vertrauen *nt*; *(in future)* Zuversicht *f*.

confident zuversichtlich.

confidential vertraulich; geheim.

confine beschränken.

confirm bestätigen; *(to corroborate)* bekräftigen.

confiscation Beschlagnahme *f*.

conflict n Konflikt *m*; Widerspruch *m*. v in Widerspruch *m* stehen; sich entgegenstehen; *(to collide)* zusammenstoßen.

conflicting widersprüchlich; sich entgegenstehend.

conflict settlement Konfliktregelung *f*.

conflict situation Konfliktfall *m*.

conform a übereinstimmend; konform. v *(to adjust)* anpassen; sich anpassen; *(to agree)* übereinstimmen; in Übereinstimmung *f* handeln.

conglomerate Konzern *m*; Großkonzern *m*.

congress Tagung *f*; Kongreß *m*.

connect verbinden; *(train)* Anschluß *m* haben.

connection Anschluß *m*; Verbindung *f*.

connoisseur Kenner *m*.

consecutive aufeinanderfolgend.

consensus Übereinstimmung *f*.

consent n Zustimmung *f*; Einwilligung *f*; Einverständnis *nt*. v zustimmen; einwilligen.

consequence Folge *f*; Auswirkung *f*.

consequent konsequent; folgerichtig; folgend.

conservation Erhaltung *f*; *(protection)* Schutz *m*.

conservative konservativ; *(cautious)* vorsichtig.

conserve erhalten; schonen.

consider in Erwägung *f* ziehen; berücksichtigen.

considerable beträchtlich; erheblich.

consideration Erwägung *f*; Berücksichtigung *f*; *(for services rendered)* Entgelt *nt*; Gegenleistung *f*.

consign *(on commission)* in Kommission *f* geben; *(to assign)* übergeben; übertragen; *(goods)* versenden.

consignment *(commission)* Kommissionsauftrag *m*; *(assigning)* Übertragung *f*; *(of goods)* Versand *m*.

consolidate vereinigen; konsolidieren; zusammenlegen.

consolidated balance sheet Konzernbilanz *f*.

consolidated company Konzernfirma *f*.

consolidated sales Konzernumsatz *m*.

consolidation *(loan)* Konsolidierung *f*; *(merger)* Fusion *f*; Zusammenlegung *f*.

consortium Konsortium *nt*.

constant konstant; gleichbleibend.
constituency Wählerschaft *f*.
constitution Verfassung *f*;
(bylaws) Satzung *f*.
constitutional verfassungsmäßig.
constitutional state Rechtsstaat *m*.
constrain *(to restrain)* beschränken; *(to force)* zwingen.
constraint *(restraint)* Beschränkung *f*; *(force)* Zwang *m*.
construct bauen; errichten; konstruieren.
construction Bau *m*; Errichtung *f*; Konstruktion *f*.
construction business Baugewerbe *nt*.
construction company Baufirma *f*; Baugesellschaft *f*.
construction financing Baufinanzierung *f*.
construction industry Bauindustrie *f*; Bauwirtschaft *f*.
construction loan Baudarlehen *nt*; Baugelder *pl*.
construction trade Baugewerbe *nt*; Bauindustrie *f*.
consulate Konsulat *nt*.
consult sich beraten lassen; konsultieren.
consultant Berater *m*; Gutachter *m*.
consultation Beratung *f*; Rücksprache *f*.
consulting firm Beratungsfirma *f*.
consume verbrauchen; konsumieren.
consumer Verbraucher *m*; Konsument *m*; *(customer)* Kunde *m*.
consumer bank Kundenkreditbank *f*.
consumer demand Verbrauchernachfrage *f*; Konsumentenwunsch *m*; Endnachfrage *f*.

consumer finance company Ratenkreditbank *f*.
consumer goods Konsumgüter *pl*.
consumer income Verbrauchereinkommen *nt*.
consumer lending Kundenkreditgewährung *f*.
consumer loan Kleinkredit *m*; Kundenkredit *m*; Anschaffungsdarlehen *nt*; *(installment loan)* Abzahlungskredit *m*.
consumer market Verbrauchermarkt *m*.
consumer price Verbraucherpreis *m*.
consumer price index Verbraucherpreisindex *m*.
consumer products Konsumgüter *pl*; Verbrauchsgüter *pl*.
consumer protection Verbraucherschutz *m*.
consumers' association Verbraucherverband *m*.
consumer survey Verbraucherumfrage *f*.
consumption Verbrauch *m*; Konsum *m*; *(food)* Verzehr *m*.
consumption expenditure Konsumausgabe *f*.
consumption function Konsumfunktion *f*.
consumption of goods Güterkonsum *m*.
consumption pattern Verbrauchsstruktur *f*.
consumption ratio Konsumquote *f*.
consumption reduction Verbrauchsminderung *f*.
consumption sector Konsumsektor *m*.
contact n Verbindung *f*; Beziehung *f*; Kontakt *m*. v Beziehungen *pl*

aufnehmen; in Verbindung *f* treten.

contain enthalten; *(to comprise)* umfassen; *(to constrain within fixed limits)* eingrenzen.

container Behälter *m*.

contemporary n Zeitgenosse *m*. a zeitgenössisch.

contend *(to compete)* sich bewerben; *(to assert)* behaupten; *(to fight)* kämpfen.

contender Bewerber *m*; *(rival)* Rivale *m*; Rivalin *f*.

content n Inhalt *m*. a zufrieden.

contention Behauptung *f*.

contest n *(competition)* Wettkampf *m*; *(customers' competition for prices)* Preisausschreiben *nt*. v anfechten; bestreiten.

contingencies *(balance sheet)* Rückstellungen *pl*.

contingency Eventualfall *m*.

contingent n Anteil *m*; Kontingent *nt*. a eventuell; unvorhergesehen.

continuance Fortbestand *m*; *(adjournment)* Vertagung *f*.

continuation Fortsetzung *f*; Weiterführung *f*.

continue *(to go on with)* fortsetzen; fortführen; *(to go on)* fortfahren; fortdauern; *(to adjourn)* vertagen.

continuity Kontinuität *f*; Stetigkeit *f*.

continuous Dauer-; laufend; fortlaufend; kontinuierlich.

contract n *(legally binding contract)* Vertrag *m*; *(agreement)* Kontrakt *m*; Abkommen *nt*. v Vertrag *m* abschließen; sich vertraglich verpflichten.

contract amount Vertragssumme *f*.

contraction Zusammenziehung *f*; Schrumpfung *f*.

contract of employment Dienstvertrag *m*.

contractor Vertragschließende *m/f*; *(building)* Bauunternehmer *m*; *(supplier)* Lieferant *m*.

contractual vertraglich.

contractual obligation Schuldverhältnis *nt*.

contrast n Gegensatz *m*; Kontrast *m*. v gegenüberstellen; vergleichen.

contribute beitragen; *(capital)* einbringen; *(charity)* spenden.

contribution Beitrag *m*; *(capital)* Einlagekapital *nt*; *(donation)* Spende *f*; *(co-insurance)* Schadensbeteiligung *f*.

contribution receipt Spendenquittung *f*.

contributor Spender *m*; Beitragsleistende *m/f*; *(capital)* Kapitaleinleger *m*.

control n Kontrolle *f*; Überwachung *f*; *(supervision)* Aufsicht *f*; *(authority)* Verfügungsgewalt *f*; *(major influence)* auschlaggebender Einfluß *m*; *(guidance)* Steuerung *f*; Lenkung *f*. v kontrollieren; überwachen; *(to supervise)* beaufsichtigen; *(to guide)* lenken; *(to regulate)* regeln.

controller Aufseher *m*; Kontrolleur *m*; *(auditor)* Rechnungsprüfer *m*; Controller *m*.

controlling function Kontrollfunktion *f*.

controlling interest Mehrheitsbeteiligung *f*; Kapitalmehrheit *f*.

controlling stockholder Großaktionär *m*.

convene sich versammeln; einberufen.

convenience Komfort *m*; Bequemlichkeit *f*; Zweckmäßigkeit *f*.

convenient zweckdienlich; geeignet.

convention Übereinkommen *nt*; Abmachung *f*; Konvention *f*; *(custom)* Gewohnheit *f*; *(meeting)* Tagung *f*.

conventional herkömmlich; konventionell.

conversion Umwandlung *f*; *(foreign currency)* Umtausch *m*; Umrechnung *f*.

conversion of debts Umschuldung *f*.

convert *(to change)* verändern; umstellen; *(foreign currency)* umrechnen; umtauschen.

convertibility Umwandelbarkeit *f*; Konvertierbarkeit *f*; Konvertibilität *f*.

convertible n *(car)* Kabriolett *nt*. a umwandelbar; konvertierbar; *(into cash)* realisierbar.

convertible bond Wandelschuldverschreibung *f*.

convertible loan Wandelanleihe *f*.

convey *(to transfer)* übertragen; übermitteln; *(to transport)* transportieren.

conveyance Übermittlung *f*; Beförderung *f*; *(real estate)* Umschreibung *f*.

cooperate zusammenarbeiten; mitwirken; mitarbeiten.

cooperation Zusammenarbeit *f*; Mitarbeit *f*; Kooperation *f*.

cooperative n Genossenschaft *f*. a genossenschaftlich; kooperativ.

cooperative bank Genossenschaftsbank *f*.

cooperative store Konsumladen *m*.

coordinate a koordiniert; gleichgestellt. v einheitlich leiten; koordinieren.

coordination Koordinierung *f*; Gleichschaltung *f*; Koordination *f*.

cope with bewältigen.

copy n Abschrift *f*; Kopie *f*; *(advertisement)* Reklametext *m*; *(document)* Ausfertigung *f*; *(book)* Exemplar *nt*. v kopieren; Abschrift *f* anfertigen.

copy of invoice Fakturakopie *f*.

copyright Urheberrecht *nt*.

corporate gesellschaftlich; körperschaftlich.

corporate concept Unternehmenskonzept *nt*.

corporate customer Firmenkunde *m*.

corporate equity Firmenvermögen *nt*.

corporate management Firmenleitung *f*; Vorstand *m*.

corporate merger Gesellschaftsfusion *f*.

corporate objective Gesellschaftsziel *nt*; Geschäftszweck *m*.

corporate officer Vorstandsmitglied *nt*.

corporate planning Unternehmensplanung *f*.

corporate policy Unternehmungspolitik *f*; Geschäftspolitik *f*.

corporate relations service Firmenbetreuung *f*.

corporate strategy Unternehmensstrategie *f*.

corporate takeover Gesellschaftsübernahme *f*.

corporation Handelsgesellschaft *f*; *(joint stock company)* Kapitalgesellschaft *f*; Körperschaft *f*.

correct a korrekt; richtig; einwandfrei. v berichtigen; richtigstellen.

correction Berichtigung *f*; Korrektur *f*; Richtigstellung *f*.

correspond *(letter)* korrespondieren; im Briefwechsel *m* stehen; *(to relate to)* entsprechen.

correspondence Briefverkehr *m*; Schriftwechsel *m*; Korrespondenz *f*; Briefwechsel *m*.

correspondent n Korrespondent *m*; Briefpartner *m*; *(newspaper)* Berichterstatter *m*. a entsprechend.

correspondent bank Korrespondenzbank *f*; Partnerbank *f*; Bankverbindung *f*.

corrupt bestechlich; korrupt.

corruption Bestechlichkeit *f*; Korruption *f*.

cost n Kosten *pl*; *(expenses)* Aufwand *m*; *(price)* Preis *m*; *(purchase price)* Anschaffungspreis *m*. v kosten.

cost accounting Selbstkostenrechnung *f*.

cost advantage Kostenvorteil *m*.

cost containment Kostenbeschränkung *f*.

cost control Kostenkontrolle *f*; Kostenüberwachung *f*.

cost cutting Kosteneinsparung *f*.

cost differential Kostenunterschied *m*.

cost-efficient kostengünstig.

cost increase Kostenerhöhung *f*; Kostensteigerung *f*.

cost inflation Kosteninflation *f*.

costly kostspielig; teuer.

cost of capital Kapitalaufwand *m*; Kapitalkosten *pl*.

cost of fringe benefits Lohnnebenkosten *pl*.

cost of labor Lohnkosten *pl*.

cost of living Lebenshaltungskosten *pl*.

cost of money Geldbeschaffungskosten *pl*.

cost of production Produktionspreis *m*.

cost overrun Kostenüberschuß *m*; Kostenüberschreitung *f*.

cost price Einstandspreis *m*; Selbstkostenpreis *m*.

cost pricing kostenorientierte Preisbildung *f*.

cost savings Kostenersparnis *f*.

cost schedule Kostensatz *m*.

cost structure Kostengliederung *f*; Kostenstruktur *f*.

cost trend Kostenentwicklung *f*.

council Rat *m*.

council of economic advisors Wirtschaftsrat *m*.

counsel n Ratschlag *m*; *(adviser)* Berater *m*. v beraten.

counselor Berater *m*; Ratgeber *m*; Rechtsberater *m*.

count n Zählung *f*; *(total count)* Gesamtsumme *f*. v zählen; rechnen; berechnen.

counter n *(service window)* Schalter *m*; *(long table)* Theke *f*; *(counting device)* Zähler *m*. adv *(counter to)* gegen. v *(to respond)* entgegnen.

counterbalance n Gegengewicht *nt*; *(bookkeeping)* Gegensaldo *m*. v kompensieren.

counterentry Gegenbuchung *f*.

counterfeit n Fälschung *f*. a gefälscht; falsch. v fälschen.

counterorder n Abbestellung *f*. v abbestellen.

counterpart Gegenstück *nt*; *(counter value)* Gegenwert *m*.

counterproposal Gegenvorschlag *m*.

counterpurchase Kompensationskauf *m*.

countertrade Kompensationshandel *m*.

countertrade economy Tauschwirtschaft *f*.

countervail ausgleichen.

country Land *nt*; Staat *m*.

country of origin Herkunftsland *nt*.

county Kreis *m*.

coupon *(bond interest)* Kupon *m*; *(gift certificate)* Gutschein *m*.

coupon bond Inhaberobligation *f*.

course *(course of study)* Kursus *m*; *(lecture)* Vorlesung *f*; *(process)* Ablauf *m*; Verlauf *m*.

course of business Geschäftsverlauf *m*.

course of one year Jahresverlauf *m*.

course of the economy Wirtschaftsverlauf *m*.

court *(court of law)* Gericht *nt*; Gerichtshof *m*; *(court chamber)* Kammer *f*.

courtesy Höflichkeit *f*; Entgegenkommen *nt*.

cover n *(backing)* Deckung *f*; *(book)* Deckel *m*; *(protection)* Schutz *m*; *(protective cover)* Hülle *f*; Umhüllung *f*; *(under separate cover)* mit getrennter Post *f*. v *(to back)* decken; *(to comprise)* umfassen; erfassen; *(to report)* berichten; *(to deal with)* behandeln.

coverage *(insurance)* Versicherungsschutz *m*; *(backing)* Deckung *f*; *(spread)* Verbreitung *f*.

cover letter Begleitbrief *m*.

craft *(handicraft)* Handwerk *nt*; *(industrial trade)* Gewerbe *nt*; *(boat)* Boot *nt*; *(aircraft)* Flugzeug *nt*.

craftsman, -person, -woman, Handwerker *m*; Gewerbetreibende *m/f*.

crash Absturz *m*; *(stocks)* Sturz *m*.

crate Kiste *f*.

create schaffen; gründen.

creation Schaffung *f*; Gründung *f*; *(thing created)* Werk *nt*.

creation of money Geldschöpfung *f*.

creative schöpferisch.

creator Schöpfer *m*; Urheber *m*.

credentials *(certificate)* Zeugnis *nt*; *(reference)* Empfehlungsschreiben *nt*; *(diplomacy)* Beglaubigungsschreiben *nt*.

credibility Glaubwürdigkeit *f*.

credible glaubwürdig; glaubhaft.

credit n Kredit *m*; *(credit side of account)* Haben *nt*; *(tax)* abzugsfähiger Betrag *m*; Freibetrag *m*; *(credit reputation)* Kreditwürdigkeit *f*; Geltung *f*; *(recognition)* Anerkennung *f*. v *(to credit an account)* gutschreiben; zuschreiben.

credit agreement Kreditvertrag *m*.

credit amount Kreditsumme *f*.

credit association Kreditanstalt *f*.

credit balance Guthaben *nt*; Aktivsaldo *m*.

credit business Kreditgewerbe *nt*.

credit card Kreditkarte *f*.

credit contraction Kreditschrumpfung *f*.

credit cooperative Kreditgenossenschaft *f*.

credit entry Gutschrift *f*; Habenbuchung *f*.

credit expansion Kreditexpansion *f*; Kreditzuwachs *m*.

credit flow Finanzierungsstrom *m*.

credit institution Kreditinstitut *nt*.

credit instrument Finanzierungsmittel *nt*.

credit insurance Kreditversicherung *f*.

credit item   Gutschrift *f*.
credit line   eingeräumter Kredit *m*;
Kreditlinie *f*; Kreditrahmen *m*;
Dispositionskredit *m*.
credit multiplier   Kreditmultiplikator *m*.
creditor   Gläubiger *m*; Kreditor *m*.
creditor bank   Gläubigerbank *f*.
creditor country   Gläubigerland *nt*.
creditor of a bankrupt's estate
Konkursgläubiger *m*.
creditor protection   Gläubigerschutz *m*.
credit rating   Kreditbeurteilung *f*.
credit risk   Kreditrisiko *nt*.
credit system   Kreditwesen *nt*.
credit terms   Kreditkonditionen *pl*.
credit transaction   Kreditgeschäft
nt.
credit union   Volksbank *f*; Kreditgenossenschaft *f*.
credit volume   Kreditvolumen *nt*.
credit voucher   Gutschrift *f*.
crisis   Krise *f*.
crisis management   Krisenmanagement *nt*.
criterion   Kennzeichen *nt*; Kriterium *nt*.
crop   n Ernte *f*. v beschneiden.
cross   n Kreuz *nt*; *(crossing of varieties)* Kreuzung *f*. a kreuzweise;
(opposite) entgegengesetzt. v *(to intersect)* überschneiden; *(to go across)* überqueren; kreuzen; *(to pass each other)* sich kreuzen; *(bill of exchange)* querschreiben.
cross-elasticity   Kreuzelastizität *f*.
crossing   *(passing)* Überquerung *f*;
(intersection) Kreuzung *f*; *(crosswalk)* Fußgängerübergang *m*.
crucial   entscheidend.
crude oil   Erdöl *nt*.
culmination   Höhepunkt *m*.

cultivate   kultivieren; pflegen; *(soil)*
bearbeiten.
cultivation   Kultivierung *f*; *(soil)*
Ackerbestellung *f*.
cultural   kulturell.
culture   Kultur *f*; Bildung *f*.
cumulative   kumulativ; anhäufend.
curb   n *(edge of sidewalk)* Bordsteinkante *f*; *(restraint)* Drosselung
f. v *(to restrain)* dämpfen; drosseln.
currency   Währung *f*; Zahlungsmittel *nt*; Valuta *f*; *(foreign currency)*
Devisen *pl*; Fremdwährung *f*.
currency account   Fremdwährungskonto *nt*; Valutakonto *nt*;
Devisenkonto *nt*.
currency adjustment   Währungsausgleich *m*.
currency fund   Währungsfonds *m*.
currency future   Devisentermingeschäft *nt*.
currency market   Devisenmarkt *m*;
Devisenbörse *f*.
currency needs   Währungsbedarf
m.
currency profit   Währungsgewinn
m.
currency rate   Währungskurs *m*.
currency reserve   Währungsreserve
f.
currency stability   Währungsstabilität *f*; Geldwertstabilität *f*.
current   n Strom *m*. a umlaufend;
laufend; *(present)* gegenwärtig;
aktuell.
current account   Girokonto *nt*;
Kontokorrentkonto *nt*; *(balance of payments)* Leistungsbilanz *f*.
current account advance   Kontokorrentkredit *m*.
current account ledger   Kontokorrentbuch *nt*.
current assets   Umlaufvermögen *nt*.

current liabilities kurzfristige Verbindlichkeiten *pl.*

current transfer laufende Transferzahlungen *pl.*

curtail einschränken; verkürzen.

curtailment Verkürzung *f.*

curve n Kurve *f.* v biegen; kurven.

cushion n Kissen *nt*; Polster *nt*; Sicherheitsfaktor *m.* v *(to absorb a shock)* abdämpfen.

custodian Treuhänder *m*; Verwahrer *m.*

custodian bank Depotbank *f.*

custodianship account Kundendepot *nt.*

custody Verwahrung *f*; Depot *nt*; *(supervision)* Aufsicht *f.*

custom Gewohnheit *f*; Gebrauch *m.*

customary üblich.

customary within an industry branchenüblich.

customer Kunde *m*; Kundin *f*; *(purchaser)* Abnehmer *m.*

customer base Kundschaft *f.*

customer contract Kundenvertrag *m.*

customer demands Kundenwünsche *pl.*

customer loyalty Kundentreue *f.*

customer needs Kundenbedürfnisse *pl.*

customer proximity Kundennähe *f.*

customer service Kundendienst *m*; Kundenberatung *f*; Kundenservice *m.*

customer service representative Kundenberater *m.*

customs *(duty)* Zoll *m*; *(administration)* Zollbehörde *f.*

customs authority Zollverwaltung *f.*

customs forwarding firm Zollspedition *f.*

customs house Zollstelle *f.*

customs officials Zollverwaltung *f.*

customs territory Zollgebiet *nt.*

cut n Schnitt *m*; *(reduction)* Kürzung *f*; Verkürzung *f*; *(price)* Ermäßigung *f*; Senkung *f.* v schneiden; *(to cut off)* abschneiden; *(to trim)* beschneiden; *(to reduce)* kürzen; *(a price)* ermäßigen.

cutback Einschränkung *f*; Abbau *m.*

cut back einschränken; abbauen.

cutthroat ruinös; halsabschneiderisch.

cycle *(business cycle)* Konjunkturzyklus *m*; Zyklus *m*; Kreislauf *m*; Periode *f.*

cyclical zyklisch; konjunkturell.

cyclical demand konjunkturbedingte Nachfrage *f.*

cyclical downturn Konjunkturabschwung *m.*

cyclical pattern Konjunkturschema *nt.*

cyclical trend Konjunkturverlauf *m.*

D

daily quotations *(stock market)* Kursblatt *nt*.

daily statement of account Tagesauszug *m*.

daisy wheel printer Typenraddrucker *m*.

damage n Schaden *m*; *(loss)* Verlust *m*. v schaden; beschädigen.

damages Schadensersatz *m*.

data Daten *pl*; Werte *pl*; Angaben *pl*; Datenmaterial *nt*.

data bank Datenbank *f*; Datenbestand *m*.

data base Datenbasis *f*.

data collection Datenerfassung *f*.

data exchange Datenaustausch *m*.

data processing Datenverarbeitung *f*.

data storage Datenspeicherung *f*.

data transmission Datenübertragung *f*.

date Datum *nt*; *(appointment)* Verabredung *f*; *(business appointment)* Termin *m*.

date of bookkeeping entry Buchungstag *m*.

date of issue Ausgabezeitpunkt *m*.

date of maturity Fälligkeitstermin *m*.

deal n Geschäft *nt*; Handel *m*; Transaktion *f*; *(agreement)* Abmachung *f*. v handeln; Handel *m* treiben; Geschäfte *pl* machen.

dealer Händler *m*; Kaufmann *m*; Kauffrau *f*; *(sales agent)* Vertreter *m*.

dealer network Händlernetz *nt*.

dealership Verkaufsagentur *f*; Verkaufsvertretung *f*.

dealings geschäftlicher Umgang *m*; Verkehr *m*.

debenture Schuldschein *m*; Schuldverschreibung *f*; Obligation *f*.

debit n *(account item)* Schuldposten *m*; Soll *nt*; Kontobelastung *f*; *(account entry)* Abbuchung *f*. v *(to debit an account)* belasten; abbuchen.

debit advice Lastschriftanzeige *f*.

debit balance Verlustvortrag *m*; Schuldsaldo *m*.

debit carryover Passivüberhang *m*.

debit column Sollseite *f*.

debit entry Lastschrift *f*.

debt Verschuldung *f*; Schulden *pl*.

debt burden Schuldenlast *f*.

debt ceiling Verschuldungsgrenze *f*.

debt crisis Schuldenkrise *f*; Verschuldungskrise *f*.

debt instrument Schuldpapier *nt*.

debt level Schuldenstand *m*.

debt market Schuldenmarkt *m*.

debt obligation Schuldschein *m*.

debtor Schuldner *m*; Debitor *m*.

debtor nation Schuldnerland *nt*.

debt rescheduling Umschuldung *f*.

debt risk Schuldenrisiko *nt*.

debts Schulden *pl*.

debt security Schuldensicherheit *f*.

debt service Schuldendienst *m*.

decelerate verlangsamen.

deceleration Verlangsamung *f*.

decentralization Dezentralisierung *f*; Auflockerung *f*.

decentralize   dezentralisieren; auflockern.

deception   Täuschung *f*; Irreführung *f*.

decide   *(to determine)* entscheiden; beschließen; *(to make up one's mind)* sich entscheiden.

decision   Entscheidung *f*; Entschluß *m*; *(law)* Urteil *nt*.

decision maker   Entscheidungsträger *m*.

decision making   Entscheidungsbildung *f*.

decision process   Entscheidungsprozeß *m*.

declaration   Erklärung *f*; *(bankruptcy)* Anmeldung *f*; *(customs)* Zolldeklaration *f*; *(property)* Vermögensangabe *f*.

declaration of intention   Grundsatzerklärung *f*.

declare   erklären; aussagen; *(to register for bankruptcy)* anmelden; *(to notify)* bekanntmachen; *(customs)* deklarieren; *(to state)* feststellen; *(dividend)* ausschütten.

decline   n Abnahme *f*; Rückgang *m*; *(worsening)* Verschlechterung *f*. v abnehmen; geringer werden; sinken; *(to worsen)* sich verschlechtern; *(invitation)* absagen.

decline in earnings   Ertragsrückgang *m*.

decline in prices   *(stock)* Kursabschlag *m*; Preisrückgang *m*.

decline in sales   Umsatzrückgang *m*; Absatzrückgang *m*.

decontrol   n Freigabe *f*; Aufhebung *f*; Abbau *m*; Liberalisierung *f*. v freigeben; aufheben; abbauen; liberalisieren.

decrease   n Abnahme *f*; Verminderung *f*; Rückgang *m*; *(cutback)*

Kürzung *f*. v abnehmen; vermindern; zurückgehen; fallen.

deduct   abziehen; *(taxes)* absetzen.

deductible   abziehbar; *(taxes)* absetzbar.

deduction   Abzug *m*; *(taxes)* Absetzung *f*; *(rebate)* Abschlag *m*.

default   n *(contract)* Vertragsverletzung *f*; Nichterfüllung *f*; Nichteinhaltung *f*; *(payment)* Verzug *m*. v seinen Verpflichtungen *pl* nicht nachkommen; *(payments)* in Verzug *m* geraten.

defect   Defekt *m*; Fehler *m*; Mangel *m*; Manko *nt*.

defend   verteidigen.

defense   Verteidigung *f*.

defer   aufschieben; verzögern; *(meeting)* vertagen.

deferral   Aufschub *m*; Verschiebung *f*.

deferred item   *(balance sheet)* Ausgleichsposten *m*.

deferred payment credit   Ratenkredit *m*.

deficiency   Mangel *m*; Manko *nt*; *(deficit)* Fehlbetrag *m*.

deficient   unzureichend; unzulänglich; fehlerhaft; ungenügend.

deficit   Defizit *nt*; Fehlbetrag *m*; *(loss)* Verlust *m*; Ausfall *m*; *(balance sheet)* Passivsaldo *m*.

deficit decrease   Defizitkürzung *f*.

define   definieren; bestimmen; abgrenzen.

defining a project   Aufgabenstellung *f*.

definite   bestimmt; deutlich; genau.

deflation   Deflation *f*.

deflationary   deflationistisch.

defraud   betrügen.

delay   n *(postponement)* Aufschub *m*; Verzögerung *f*; Verzug *m*; *(loss*

of time) Zeitverlust *m.* v *(to postpone)* verzögern; hinausschieben;
(to detain) aufhalten.

delegate   n Delegierte *m/f*; Bevollmächtigte *m/f.* v delegieren;
bevollmächtigen.

delegation   *(of authority)* Bevollmächtigung *f*; *(group of delegates)*
Abordnung *f*; Delegation *f.*

delete   *(debt)* tilgen; *(text)* ausstreichen; löschen; streichen.

deletion   Löschung *f*; Streichung *f.*

deliberate   a *(intentional)* absichtlich; wohlüberlegt; bedachtsam.
v *(to ponder)* sich überlegen; nachdenken; *(to discuss)* sich beraten.

deliberation   *(discussion)* Beratung
f; *(consideration)* Überlegung *f.*

deliver   liefern; ausliefern; *(to hand
over)* abliefern; zustellen; *(to
deliver from)* befreien; *(a speech)*
halten.

deliverable   lieferfähig.

delivery   Lieferung *f*; Auslieferung
f; *(handing over)* Ablieferung *f*;
Zustellung *f.*

delivery stop   Liefersperre *f.*

demand   n Nachfrage *f*; *(need)*
Bedarf *m*; *(claim)* Anforderung *f*;
Einforderung *f*; *(aggregate)* End-
nachfrage. v fordern; verlangen.

demand analysis   Bedarfsanalyse *f.*

demand creditor   Sichtkreditor
m.

demand deposit   Sichteinlage *f.*

demand for credit   Kreditnachfrage *f.*

demand forecast   Nachfragevorhersage *f*; Nachfrageprognose *f.*

demand growth   Nachfragezuwachs *m*; Bedarfszunahme *f.*

demographic   bevölkerungsstatistisch; demographisch.

demonstrate   vorführen; demonstrieren.

demonstration   Vorführung *f*;
Demonstration *f.*

demote   degradieren; in den
nächstniederen Rang versetzen.

denomination   *(naming)* Benen-
nung *f*; *(class)* Klasse *f*; Kategorie
f; *(bank note)* Nennwert *m* einer
Banknote *f*; *(stock)* Stückelung *f*;
(church) Konfession *f.*

density   Dichte *f.*

deny   *(to refuse)* verweigern;
abschlagen; *(to declare untrue)*
leugnen; dementieren.

department   Abteilung *f*; Arbeitsgebiet *nt*; *(government)* Ministerium *nt*; Ressort *nt*; Fachgebiet *nt.*

departmentalization   Abteilungsbildung *f.*

department store   Kaufhaus *nt*;
Warenhaus *nt.*

depend   abhängig sein von; angewiesen sein auf; abhängen von.

dependence   Abhängigkeit *f.*

dependent   n Abhängige *m/f*; *(tax
form)* Unterhaltsberechtigte *m/f.*
a unselbständig; abhängig.

dependent on price   preisabhängig.

dependent on the exchange rate
wechselkursbedingt.

dependent on time   zeitabhängig.

dependent upon sales   umsatzabhängig.

deplete   *(to empty)* entleeren; *(to
exhaust)* erschöpfen; *(to use up)*
aufbrauchen; *(to reduce)* verringern.

depletion   *(exhaustion)* Erschöp-
fung *f*; *(of assets)* Substanzverringerung *f*; Abnutzung *f.*

deploy   *(to use)* einsetzen.

deployment *(use)* Einsatz *m.*
deployment of machines Maschineneinsatz *m.*
deport ausweisen; deportieren.
deposit n *(bank)* Geldeinlage *f;* Einzahlung *f; (down payment)* Anzahlung *f; (safety deposit)*Hinterlegungssumme *f; (minerals)* Vorkommen *nt.* v *(bank)* einzahlen; *(safety deposit)* hinterlegen; *(down payment)* anzahlen.
deposit account Sparkonto *nt.*
deposit account balance Guthaben *nt.*
deposit insurance Depotversicherung *f;* Einlagenversicherung *f.*
depositor *(payer)* Einzahler *m; (for safety deposit)* Hinterleger *m; (for down payment)* Anzahler *m; (account holder)* Depositeninhaber *m;* Kontoinhaber *m.*
depository Verwahrungsort *m;* Hinterlegungsstelle *f;* Depot *nt.*
deposit transaction Einlagengeschäft *nt.*
depreciate im Wert *m* sinken.
depreciation Abwertung *f;* Entwertung *f;* Wertminderung *f.*
depreciation of a currency Geldentwertung *f.*
depress drücken; niederdrücken; herabsetzen.
depression *(economy)* Depression *f;* Wirtschaftskrise *f;* Konjunkturtief *nt; (stock market)* Baisse *f.*
deregulate freigeben; deregulieren.
deregulation Freigabe *f;* Deregulation *f.*
derivative n Derivat *nt.* a abgeleitet.
derive ableiten; herleiten; *(to receive from)* erzielen.
describe beschreiben; schildern.

description Beschreibung *f;* Schilderung *f.*
design n *(shaping)* Gestaltung *f;* Design *nt; (form)* Form *f;* Gestalt *f; (plan)* Entwurf *m; (construction)* Konstruktionszeichnung *f;* Ausführung *f; (pattern)* Muster *nt.* v entwerfen; *(to plan)* planen.
designate bezeichnen; bestimmen.
desirable wünschenswert.
desire n Wunsch *m.* v wünschen.
desk Schreibtisch *m; (school)* Pult *nt.*
desktop computer Schreibtischcomputer *m.*
destabilize destabilisieren; unsicher machen; ins Schwanken *nt* bringen.
destination Bestimmungsort *m;* Ziel *nt.*
destined bestimmt; vorgesehen.
destroy zerstören; vernichten.
destruction Zerstörung *f.*
destructive zerstörerisch.
detach ablösen; abtrennen.
detail Einzelheit *f;* Detail *nt.*
detailed ausführlich; eingehend.
detain zurückhalten; aufhalten.
detection Ermittlung *f.*
deteriorate verfallen; *(to worsen)* sich verschlechtern; *(trade)* zurückgehen; *(to spoil)* verderben.
deterioration Verfall *m; (depreciation)* Wertminderung *f; (wear and tear)* Verschleiß *m; (worsening)* Verschlechterung *f; (spoilage)* Verderb *m.*
determinable bestimmbar; festsetzbar.
determination Entschlossenheit *f; (decision)* Entschluß *m; (will)* Wille *m.*
determine bestimmen; *(to stipulate)*

festsetzen; *(to arrange)* festlegen; *(to decide)* entscheiden; *(to find out)* feststellen.

determining factor   Einflußgröße *f*.

detriment   Schaden *m*; Nachteil *m*; Beeinträchtigung *f*.

detrimental   abträglich; schädlich.

devaluation   Abwertung *f*.

devalue   abwerten.

develop   entwickeln; *(to expand)* ausbauen; *(to promote)* fördern; *(land)* erschließen.

developer   *(construction)* Bauunternehmer *m*; *(land)* Grundstückserschließer *m*.

developing country   Entwicklungsland *nt*.

development   Entwicklung *f*; *(expansion)* Ausbau *m*; *(promotion)* Förderung *f*; *(of land)* Erschließung *f*; *(housing area)* Wohnsiedlung *f*.

development bank   Entwicklungsbank *f*.

development costs   Entwicklungskosten *pl*.

development impetus   Entwicklungsimpuls *m*.

development of sales   Umsatzentwicklung *f*.

development policy   Entwicklungspolitik *f*.

development process   Entwicklungsprozeß *m*.

deviate   abweichen.

deviation   Abweichung *f*.

device   Vorrichtung *f*; *(equipment)* Gerät *nt*; Apparat *m*; *(trick)* Kunstgriff *m*.

devise   erfinden; entwerfen.

diagnose   feststellen; bestimmen; diagnostizieren.

diagnosis   Diagnose *f*; Feststellung *f*.

diagram   graphische Darstellung *f*; Schaubild *nt*; Diagramm *nt*.

dictate   *(letter)* diktieren; *(to order)* bestimmen.

differ   sich unterscheiden; *(disagreement)* anderer Meinung *f* sein.

difference   Unterschied *m*; Differenz *f*; Gefälle *nt*; *(money)* Unterschiedsbetrag *m*.

difference in exchange rate   Kursdifferenz *f*.

difference in interest   Zinsunterschied *m*; Zinsgefälle *nt*.

differential   Differenz *f*; Unterschiedsmerkmal *nt*; *(difference in prices)* Gefälle *nt*.

differentiate   unterscheiden.

differentiation   Unterscheidung *f*.

differing   unterschiedlich.

difficult   schwierig.

difficulty   Schwierigkeit *f*.

dilemma   Dilemma *nt*; Verlegenheit *f*.

diligence   Sorgsamkeit *f*; Gewissenhaftigkeit *f*.

dime   Zehncentstück *nt*.

dimension   Dimension *f*; Ausmaß *nt*; Größenordnung *f*.

diminish   abnehmen; geringer werden; reduzieren; schrumpfen.

diminution   Verminderung *f*; Abnahme *f*; Reduzierung *f*.

direct   a direkt; unmittelbar. v *(to manage)* führen; leiten; *(to guide)* lenken; steuern; *(film)* Regie führen; *(to prescribe)* vorschreiben.

direct investment   Direktinvestition *f*; Direktanlage *f*.

direction   *(instruction)* Anweisung *f*; *(managing)* Führung *f*; Leitung *f*; *(film)* Regie *f*; *(geographical orientation)* Richtung *f*; *(traffic)*

Fahrtrichtung *f; (guidance)*
Lenkung *f.*

directive Direktive *f;* Weisung *f;*
Verfügung *f;* Richtlinie *f.*

direct mail Direktpost *f; (advertis-*
ing) Postwurfsendungen *pl.*

director Direktor *m; (manager)*
Geschäftsführer *m;* Leiter *m;*
(board member) Aufsichtsratsmit-
glied *nt; (film)* Regisseur *m;*
(radio, television) Sendeleiter *m.*

director of a company Firmenchef
m.

directorship Aufsichtsratsposten
m.

direct sales Direktverkauf *m;*
Direktabsatz *m.*

disadvantage Nachteil *m; (un-*
favorable situation) ungünstige
Lage *f.*

disadvantageous nachteilig;
schädlich; abträglich.

disagio Disagio *nt.*

disagree nicht übereinstimmen; in
Widerspruch *m* stehen; uneinig
sein.

disagreement Meinungsverschiedenheit *f;* Widerspruch *m;*
Nichtübereinstimmung *f.*

disallow nicht gestatten; nicht
zugeben; *(to reject)* abweisen.

disappear verschwinden; verlorengehen.

disappoint enttäuschen; nicht
befriedigen.

disappointing enttäuschend; unbefriedigend; nicht den Erwartungen
pl entsprechend.

disappointment Enttäuschung *f;*
(failure) Fehlschlag *m;* Mißerfolg
m.

disapproval Mißbilligung *f;* Mißfallen *nt.*

disaster Unglück *nt;* Unglücksfall
m; Katastrophe *f.*

disastrous verheerend; katastro-
phal.

disburse auszahlen; ausgeben.

disbursement Auszahlung *f;* Ausgabe *f;* Auslage *f.*

discharge n *(dismissal)* Entlassung
f; (release from obligation) Entlastung *f; (of debt)* Tilgung *f; (un-*
loading) Entladen *nt.* v *(to dis-*
miss) entlassen; *(to release)* entlasten; *(to unload)* entladen.

disclaim dementieren.

disclose offenbaren; aufzeigen;
bekanntgeben; offenlegen.

disclosure Enthüllung *f;* Aufdek-
kung *f;* Bekanntgabe *f;* Eröffnung *f.*

disclosure obligation Publizitätspflicht *f.*

discontinue einstellen; aufhören.

discount n *(bill of exchange)* Diskont *m;* Zinsabzug *m; (rebate)*
Rabatt *m; (trading in futures)*
Abschlag *m; (for prompt payment)*
Skonto *m/n; (bond market)* Disagio *nt.* v abziehen; *(bill of*
exchange) diskontieren; *(to rebate)*
Rabatt *m* gewähren; *(to depreci-*
ate) im Wert *m* herabsetzen.

discounted value Diskontwert *m;*
verminderter Wert *m.*

discounter Billiganbieter *m.*

discount merchant Billighändler *m.*

discount quotation Kursabschlag
m.

discount rate increase Diskont-
satzerhöhung *f.*

discount store Verbrauchermarkt
m.

discover entdecken; feststellen.

discovery Entdeckung *f;* Auffin-
dung *f.*

discreet diskret.

discrepancy Abweichung *f*; Diskrepanz *f*.

discrete getrennt; diskontinuierlich.

discretion *(being discreet)* Diskretion *f*; *(freedom to make decisions)* Gutdünken *nt*; Ermessen *nt*.

discretionary beliebig; dem Ermessen *nt* anheimgegeben.

discriminate *(to distinguish)* unterscheiden; *(to treat unequally)* unterschiedlich behandeln; diskriminieren.

discrimination *(discernment)* Unterscheidungsvermögen *nt*; Urteilsfähigkeit *f*; *(unequal treatment)* Diskriminierung *f*; ungleiche Behandlung *f*.

discuss besprechen; diskutieren.

discussion Besprechung *f*; Diskussion *f*.

disequilibrium Unausgeglichenheit *f*; Ungleichgewicht *nt*.

disinflation Inflationsabbau *m*.

disinvesting Zurückziehung *f* von Anlagekapital *nt*.

diskette Diskette *f*.

dismantle *(factory)* demontieren; abbauen; *(committee)* auflösen.

dismiss *(employee)* entlassen; fortschicken; *(complaint)* zurückweisen; *(lawsuit)* Verfahren *nt* einstellen.

dismissal *(of employee)* Entlassung *f*; Kündigung *f*; *(complaint)* Zurückweisung *f*.

disorder Unordnung *f*; Verwirrung *f*.

disorganization Auflösung *f*; Zerrüttung *f*.

disparate ungleichartig; unvereinbar; disparat.

disparity Ungleichheit *f*; Verschiedenheit *f*.

dispatch n *(sending)* Absendung *f*; Versand *m*; *(message)* Nachricht *f*; *(hurry)* Eile *f*. v abschicken; befördern.

disperse *(funds)* verteilen; *(news)* verbreiten; *(gathering)* auflösen.

displace verlagern; verdrängen.

display n Zurschaustellung *f*; *(marketing)* Auslage *f*; *(store window)* Schaufensterauslage *f*. v auslegen; ausstellen; zeigen.

disposable verfügbar; disponibel; *(throwaway)* wegwerfbar.

disposable goods Einweggüter *pl*; Wegwerfgüter *pl*.

disposable income verfügbares Einkommen *nt*.

disposal *(arrangement)* Anordnung *f*; *(control)* Verfügung *f*; *(sale)* Absatz *m*; Veräußerung *f*; *(waste)* Beseitigung *f*.

dispose *(to arrange)* anordnen; disponieren; *(to sell)* absetzen; veräußern; *(to remove)* beseitigen.

disposition of funds Mittelverwendung *f*.

dispossess enteignen.

disproportion Mißverhältnis *nt*.

disproportionate unverhältnismäßig.

disregard n Mißachtung *f*; Geringschätzung *f*. v mißachten; geringschätzen.

disrupt unterbrechen; *(market)* spalten.

dissatisfaction Unzufriedenheit *f*; Mißfallen *nt*.

dissatisfy nicht befriedigen; unzufrieden machen.

disseminate ausstreuen; verbreiten.

dissemination Verbreitung *f*; Aus-
streuung *f*.
dissent n Meinungsverschiedenheit
f. v nicht zustimmen.
dissociate trennen; loslösen.
dissolution *(firm)* Auflösung *f*; *(cartel)* Entflechtung *f*; Liquidation *f*.
dissolve *(firm)* auflösen; liquidieren; *(cartel)* entflechten.
distance Entfernung *f*; Strecke *f*.
distant fern; weit entfernt.
distinguish *(to differentiate)* unterscheiden; *(to characterize)* kennzeichnen; charakterisieren; *(merit)*
auszeichnen.
distinguishable unterscheidbar.
distinguished ausgezeichnet;
berühmt.
distribute verteilen; streuen; *(to
allocate)* zuteilen; *(to sell)* vertreiben; absetzen; *(dividend, profit)*
ausschütten.
distribution Verteilung *f*; Streuung
f; *(apportionment)* Aufteilung *f*;
(allocation) Zuteilung *f*; *(marketing)* Vertrieb *m*; Absatz *m*; *(dividend, profit)* Ausschüttung *f*.
distribution channel Vertriebsweg
m.
distribution network Verteilernetz
nt; Vertriebsnetz *nt*.
distribution of profit Gewinnausschüttung *f*.
distribution strategy Absatzstrategie *f*; Vertriebsstrategie *f*.
distribution system Verteilungssystem *nt*; Vertriebssystem *nt*.
distributor Verteiler *m*; Wiederverkäufer *m*; *(agent)* Vertreter *m*;
(film) Verleiher *m*; *(engine)* Zünd-
verteiler *m*.
distributorship Vertriebsagentur *f*.

district Bezirk *m*; Distrikt *m*; *(city)*
Viertel *nt*; Kreis *m*.
district court Amtsgericht *nt*.
disturb stören; beunruhigen.
disturbance Störung *f*; Unruhe *f*.
diverge abweichen; auseinanderge-
hen.
divergence Abweichung *f*.
divergent abweichend; auseinan-
derlaufend.
diverse *(different)* verschieden;
ungleich; *(varied)* vielfältig; mannigfaltig.
diversification Diversifizierung *f*;
Diversifikation *f*; Verschiedenartigkeit *f*; *(investment)* Streuung *f*;
(products) Auffächerung *f*.
diversified abwechslungsreich;
mannigfaltig; *(capital)* gestreut
angelegt.
diversify diversifizieren; abwechslungsreich gestalten; variieren;
(investment) gestreut anlegen.
diversity *(difference)* Verschiedenheit *f*; Ungleichheit *f*; *(variety)*
Vielfalt *f*; Mannigfaltigkeit *f*.
divert umleiten; *(attention)*
ablenken; *(funds)* abzweigen; *(to
amuse)* zerstreuen.
divide teilen; verteilen; aufteilen.
dividend Dividende *f*; Gewinnanteil *m*.
dividend coupon Dividendenschein *m*.
dividend declaration Dividendenerklärung *f*.
dividend income Dividendenein-
nahme *f*.
dividend-paying stock Dividendenpapier *nt*.
divisibility Teilbarkeit *f*.
divisible teilbar.

division Teilung f; Aufteilung f;
(department) Abteilung f.
division manager Abteilungsleiter
m.
division of labor Arbeitsteiligkeit
f; Arbeitsteilung f.
doctrine Lehre f; Doktrin f.
document n Dokument nt; *(certified document)* Urkunde f; *(file)*
Aktenstück nt; *(evidence)* Beweisstück nt; Unterlage f. v *(to certify)*
beurkunden; *(to evidence)* schriftlich belegen; dokumentieren.
documentary draft Rembourstratte f.
documentation Dokumentation f;
Glaubhaftmachung f durch Unter-
lagen pl.
documented dokumentiert; urkundlich festgelegt; durch Unterla-
gen pl bewiesen.
dodge n Umgehungsmanöver nt.
v umgehen; vermeiden; sich
drücken.
dogma Dogma nt; Lehrsatz m;
Glaubenssatz m.
domain Bezirk m; Feld nt; *(area
of responsibility)* Aufgabengebiet
nt.
domestic *(country)* inländisch; einheimisch; innerstaatlich; *(home)*
häuslich; heimisch.
domestic bank Inlandsbank f.
domestic business Inlandsgeschäft
nt.
domestic capital Inlandskapital nt.
domestic client Inlandskunde m.
domestic commerce Binnenhandel
m.
domestic consumption Inlandsverbrauch m.
domestic content einheimischer
Gehalt m.

domestic demand Binnenbedarf
m; Binnennachfrage f.
domestic division Inlandsabtei-
lung f.
domestic economy Binnenwirtschaft f.
domestic investment inländische
Anlagen pl; Inlandsanlage f.
domestic loan Inlandsanleihe f.
domestic market Binnenmarkt m.
domestic order Inlandsbestellung f.
domestic production Inlandspro-
duktion f; Eigenerzeugung f.
dominance Vorherrschen nt;
Herrschaft f.
dominion Besitzrecht nt; Herr-
schaftsgebiet nt.
donate spenden; schenken; *(to
endow)* stiften.
donation Spende f; Schenkung f;
(endowment) Stiftung f.
donor Spender m; Geber m.
double n Doppel nt; *(copy)* Kopie
f. a doppelt. v verdoppeln.
downgrade n *(road)* Gefälle nt.
v niedriger einstufen.
downturn Abwärtsbewegung f;
(economic cycle) Konjunkturab-
schwächung f.
draft *(on bank)* Zahlungsanweisung f; *(bill of exchange)* Tratte f;
Wechsel m; *(drawing of money)*
Geldabhebung f; *(rough copy)*
Entwurf m.
draft budget Orientierungsbudget
nt.
draft credit Wechselkredit m.
draft guarantee Wechselbürgschaft f.
draft treaty Vertragsentwurf m.
draw n *(attraction)* Schlager m;
(lottery) Verlosung f; *(tie)* Unent-
schieden nt. v ziehen; *(to attract)*

anziehen; *(to issue)* ausstellen; *(a salary)* beziehen.

drawing *(bill of exchange)* Ausstellen *nt*; Ziehung; *(on an account)* Abhebung *f*.

drawing right Ziehungsrecht *nt*.

drift n *(inactivity)* Treibenlassen *nt*; *(tendency)* Tendenz *f*; *(customers)* Abwanderung *f*. v treiben.

drive n *(car)* Fahrt *f*; *(advertising campaign)* Werbefeldzug *m*; *(approach)* Anfahrt *f*; *(energy)* Schwung *m*; *(money collection)* Geldsammlung *f*. v treiben; *(car)* fahren.

drive to succeed Erfolgszwang *m*.

drop n Tropfen *m*; *(prices)* Rückgang *m*; *(stock exchange)* Baisse *f*. v fallenlassen; *(prices)* fallen.

due n *(charge)* Gebühr *f*. a gebührend; *(maturing)* fällig; *(owing)* zustehend.

dues *(charges)* Gebühren *pl*; *(membership)* Beitrag *m*.

dump n Abladeplatz *m*; Halde *f*. v abladen; *(sell cheaply)* billig abstoßen; *(export trade)* zu Schleuderpreisen *pl* verkaufen.

dumping Schleuderausfuhr *f*; Dumping *nt*.

dumping duty Ausgleichszoll *m* gegen Schleuderausfuhren *pl*.

duplicate n Duplikat *nt*; zweite Ausfertigung *f*. v kopieren; vervielfältigen.

durable langlebig; dauerhaft.

durables langlebige Gebrauchsgüter *pl*.

duration Dauer *f*.

dutiable gebührenpflichtig.

duty *(obligation)* Pflicht *f*; *(task)* Aufgabe *f*; *(customs)* Zollgebühr *f*.

duty charge Zollforderung *f*.

duty claim Zollforderung *f*.

duty-free gebührenfrei.

dwindle zusammenschrumpfen; *(prices)* sinken.

E

early früh; frühzeitig.

early retirement Vorruhestand *m*.

earmark n Kennzeichen *nt*. v kennzeichnen; *(to set aside)* zurückstellen.

earmarked zurückgestellt; *(tax)* zweckgebunden; *(account)* gesperrt.

earn erwerben; *(wages)* verdienen; *(interest)* Zinsen *pl* bringen.

earner Erwerbstätige *m/f*; Verdiener *m*.

earning Verdienen *nt*; Erwerb *m*; Ertrag *m*.

earning capacity *(company)* Ertragsfähigkeit *f*; *(person)* Erwerbsfähigkeit *f*.

earnings *(income)* Einkommen *nt*; Einkünfte *pl*; *(profit)* Gewinn *m*; Ertrag *m*; *(salary)* Gehalt *nt*; *(wages)* Verdienst *m*; Lohn *m*.

earnings statement Ertragsrechnung *f*; Gewinn- und Verlustrechnung *f*.

ease n Leichtigkeit *f*. v entspannen; *(stock prices)* nachgeben; *(monetary policy)* lockern; erleichtern.

easing Erleichterung *f*; *(monetary policy)* Lockerung *f*.

easy leicht; *(money)* leicht verdient; *(on easy terms)* zu günstigen Bedingungen *pl*.

ecological Umwelt-; ökologisch.

ecology Umwelt *f*; Ökologie *f*.

ecology-minded umweltbewußt.

econometric ökonometrisch.

economic wirtschaftlich; volkswirtschaftlich; ökonomisch; *(productive)* rentabel; *(referring to business cycle)* konjunkturell.

economic advisor Wirtschaftsberater *m*.

economic agreement Wirtschaftsabkommen *nt*.

economical wirtschaftlich; *(thrifty)* sparsam.

economic basis wirtschaftliche Grundlage *f*.

economic boom Wirtschaftsaufschwung *m*.

economic condition Wirtschaftslage *f*.

economic development Wirtschaftsentwicklung *f*.

economic domain Wirtschaftsbereich *m*.

economic entity Wirtschaftseinheit *f*.

economic expert Wirtschaftsexperte *m*; Wirtschaftsexpertin *f*.

economic growth Wirtschaftswachstum *nt*.

economic indicator Konjunkturanzeichen *nt*.

economic journal Wirtschaftszeitung *f*.

economic miracle Wirtschaftswunder *nt*.

economic model Wirtschaftsmodell *nt*.

economic performance Wirtschaftsleistung *f*.

economic plan Wirtschaftsplan *m*.

economic policy Wirtschaftspolitik *f*.

economic process Wirtschaftsablauf *m*; Wirtschaftsgeschehen *nt*.

economic recession Wirtschaftsflaute *f*.

economic recovery Konjunkturbelebung *f*.

economic rent Grundrente *f*.

economic report Konjunkturbericht *m*.

economic research Wirschaftsforschung *f*; Konjunkturforschung *f*.

economic researcher Wirtschaftsforscher *m*; Konjunkturforscher *m*.

economics *(study)* Volkswirtschaftslehre *f*; Nationalökonomie *f*; Ökonomik *f*.

economic sector Wirtschaftszweig *m*.

economic specialist Wirtschaftsfachmann *m*.

economic spokesman Wirtschaftssprecher *m*.

economic stabilization policy Konjunkturpolitik *f*.

economic statistics Wirtschaftsstatistik *f*.

economic structure Wirtschaftsstruktur *f*.

economic system Wirtschaftsordnung *f*; Wirtschaftssystem *nt*.

economic theory Wirtschaftstheorie *f*.

economic trend Wirtschaftskurs *m*; Konjunkturverlauf *m*.

economies of scale Ersparnisse *pl* durch Produktionsvergrößerung *f*; Skalenertrag *m*.

economist Wirtschaftswissenschaftler *m*; Ökonom *m*.
economize sparsam wirtschaften;
haushalten.
economy Wirtschaft *f*; *(national
economy)* Volkswirtschaft *f*; *(economic trend)* Konjunktur *f*; *(thrift)*
Sparsamkeit *f*; Ersparnis *f*.
editor-in-chief Chefredakteur *m*.
educate ausbilden; erziehen.
education Ausbildung *f*; Erziehung
f; *(educational background)* Aus-
bildungsgang *m*; *(pedagogy)* Pädagogik *f*.
educational Ausbildungs-; bil-
dend; erzieherisch; *(informative)*
belehrend.
education field Bildungswesen *nt*.
effect n Auswirkung *f*; *(in force)*
Gültigkeit *f*. v bewirken.
effective wirksam; *(in force)* gültig; *(interest)* effektiv.
effectiveness Wirksamkeit *f*;
Erfolgswirksamkeit *f*.
efficiency *(capacity)* Leistungsfähigkeit *f*; *(effectiveness of person)* Tüchtigkeit *f*; *(effectiveness)*
Wirtschaftlichkeit *f*; Effizienz *f*.
efficient *(working well)* gut funktionierend; *(productive)* leistungsfähig; *(economical)* wirtschaftlich;
effizient.
effort Bemühung *f*; Anstrengung *f*;
(work-time spent) Arbeitsaufwand
m.
elect wählen.
election Wahl *f*.
eligibility *(for job)* Eignung *f*;
Qualifikation *f*; *(for benefits)*
Berechtigung *f*.
eligible *(suitable)* geeignet; *(acceptable)* annehmbar; *(qualified)* qualifiziert; *(authorized)* berechtigt.

eliminate ausschließen; *(competition)* ausschalten; eliminieren;
beseitigen.
elimination *(of competition)* Ausschaltung *f*; Eliminierung *f*; Beseitigung *f*.
embargo Ausfuhrsperre *f*;
Embargo *nt*.
emerge hervortreten; zutage
treten.
emergence Hervortreten *nt*.
emergency Notlage *f*; Notfall *m*.
emergency measure Hilfsmaßnahme *f*.
emphasis Betonung *f*; Schwerpunkt *m*.
emphasize betonen; hervorheben;
herausstellen.
employ n Dienst *m*. v anstellen;
beschäftigen; *(to use)* verwenden.
employed angestellt; berufstätig.
employed person Erwerbsperson *f*.
employee Angestellte *m/f*; Arbeitnehmer *m*.
employee layoff Belegschaftsabbau *m*.
employer Arbeitgeber *m*.
employer association Arbeitgeberverband *m*.
employer representative Arbeitgebervertreter *m*.
employment *(act of employment)*
Anstellung *f*; *(existing employment)* Arbeitsverhältnis *nt*; Beschäftigung *f*; *(use)* Verwendung *f*.
employment agency Arbeitsvermittlung *f*.
employment office Arbeitsamt *nt*.
empower bevollmächtigen;
ermächtigen.
enable befähigen.
enact verordnen.
enactment Verordnung *f*; Erlaß *m*.

enclose einschließen; *(with letter)* beilegen.

encourage ermutigen; *(to support)* fördern.

encouragement Ermutigung *f*; *(support)* Förderung *f*.

encumber belasten.

encumbrance Belastung *f*; *(land)* Hypothekenschulden *pl*; *(assessment)* Umlage *f*.

end of the year Jahresende *nt*; Jahresultimo *nt*.

endorse *(a check)* indossieren; *(to support)* unterstützen; *(to approve)* zustimmen.

endorsement *(of a check)* Indossament *nt*; *(support)* Unterstützung *f*; *(approval)* Zustimmung *f*.

endow ausstatten; stiften.

endowment Stiftung *f*; Ausstattung *f*.

energy Energie *f*; Kraft *f*.

enforce durchsetzen; durchführen; geltend machen; *(a law)* vollstrecken.

enforcement Durchsetzung *f*; Durchführung *f*; *(law)* Vollstreckung *f*.

engage *(to bind by contract)* verpflichten; *(to employ)* einstellen.

engagement *(appointment)* Verabredung *f*; *(employment)* Anstellung *f*; *(obligation)* Verpflichtung *f*.

engineer Ingenieur *m*.

engineering works Maschinenfabrik *f*.

enhance steigern; verbessern.

enhancement Steigerung *f*; Verbesserung *f*.

enjoyment Vergnügen *nt*; Genuß *m*.

enlarge ausweiten; vergrößern.

enlist anstellen; in Anspruch *m* nehmen.

enough genug.

enrichment Bereicherung *f*.

ensure sicherstellen; sichern.

enter *(into a contract)* eingehen; *(a record)* eintragen; *(a bookkeeping entry)* verbuchen; *(a country)* einreisen; *(a room)* eintreten.

enterprise Unternehmen *nt*; Unternehmung *f*; *(business)* Geschäft *nt*; *(plant)* Betrieb *m*.

entire ganz; voll; komplett.

entire income Gesamteinkommen *nt*.

entire territory Gesamtgebiet *nt*.

entirety Gesamtheit *f*.

entitle berechtigen.

entitlement Berechtigung *f*.

entity Gebilde *nt*; Wesen *nt*; *(agency)* Dienststelle *f*; *(legal entity)* juristische Person *f*.

entrance *(entryway)* Eingang *m*; *(admission)* Eintritt *m*; Zugang *m*.

entrepreneur Unternehmer *m*.

entrepreneurial unternehmerisch.

entrepreneurial behavior Unternehmerverhalten *nt*.

entrepreneurship Unternehmertum *nt*.

entrust anvertrauen.

entry *(entrance)* Eintritt *m*; *(record)* Eintragung *f*; *(entry in account)* Buchung *f*; *(item in account)* Posten *m*; *(into country)* Einreise *f*.

enumerate aufzählen.

environment Umwelt *f*; Umgebung *f*.

environmental Umwelt-; umweltbedingt.

environmental burden Umweltbelastung *f*.

environmental group Umweltgruppe *f*.

environmentally aware   umweltbewußt.
environmentally compatible
umweltverträglich.
environmental problem   Umweltproblem *nt*.
environmental protection
Umweltschutz *m*.
environmental protectionist
Umweltschützer *m*.
environmental quality   Umweltqualität *f*.
equal   n Gleichgestellte *m/f*. a
gleich; gleichmäßig; *(possessing
equal rights)* gleichberechtigt.
v gleich sein; gleichen.
equality   *(sameness)* Gleichheit *f*;
Gleichwertigkeit *f*; *(equal rights)*
Gleichberechtigung *f*; Parität *f*.
equalization   Ausgleich *m*; Gleichstellung *f*.
equalize   ausgleichen.
equal treatment   Gleichstellung *f*.
equate   gleichsetzen.
equation   Gleichung *f*.
equilibrium   Gleichgewicht *nt*.
equilibrium price   Gleichgewichtspreis *m*.
equip   ausrüsten; einrichten.
equipment   Einrichtung *f*; Ausrüstung *f*; *(tool)* Gerät *nt*; *(machine)*
Anlage *f*.
equitable   gerecht; angemessen.
equity   *(business interest)* Nettoanteil *m*; *(invested capital)* Eigenkapital *nt*; *(capital stock)* Grundkapital *nt*.
equity capital   Grundkapital *nt*.
equity holder   Kapitaleigner *m*.
equity participation   Kapitalbeteiligung *f*.
equity share   Dividendenpapier
nt.

equivalent   n Gegenwert *m*;
Gegenleistung *f*. a gleichwertig.
era   Ära *f*; Zeitalter *nt*.
err   sich irren.
erroneous   irrig; irrtümlich.
error   Irrtum *m*; Fehler *m*; Versehen
nt.
error rate   Fehlerquote *f*.
escalate   steigern.
escalation   Steigerung *f*.
escape   n Entkommen *nt*.
v entkommen.
escape clause   Rücktrittsklausel *f*.
escrow   Treuhandvertrag *m*.
establish   *(a company)* gründen; *(to
set up)* errichten; *(to ascertain)*
feststellen.
established   *(founded)* gegründet;
(well-established) alteingeführt.
establishment   Niederlassung *f*;
Firma *f*; Betrieb *m*; *(social stratum)* Führungsschicht *f*.
establishment of contact   Kontaktnahme *f*.
establish oneself   sich etablieren.
estate   *(assets)* Eigentum *nt*; *(bankruptcy)* Konkursmasse *f*; *(land)*
Grundbesitz *m*; *(left after death)*
Erbschaftsmasse *f*; *(property)* Vermögensmasse *f*.
estimate   n *(of costs)* Voranschlag
m; *(estimation)* Schätzung *f*. v *(to
evaluate)* schätzen; abschätzen; *(to
calculate)* berechnen.
estimated value   Schätzwert *m*.
estimate of profits   Gewinnschätzung *f*.
estimation   Veranschlagung *f*; *(of
cost)* Kostenkalkulation *f*; *(esteem)*
Wertschätzung *f*.
evaluate   *(to appraise)* bewerten;
(currency) aufwerten; *(data)* auswerten.

evaluation *(appraisal)* Bewertung *f*; *(of currency)* Aufwertung *f*; *(of data)* Auswertung *f*.

even gleich; *(number)* gerade; *(plane surface)* ebenmäßig.

eviction Zwangsräumung *f*.

evidence n *(proof)* Beweismittel *nt*; Nachweis *m*; *(testimony)* Zeugenaussage *f*. v beweisen.

ex *(shipping point)* ab; *(former)* ehemalig.

exact a genau; sorgfältig. v *(to collect)* eintreiben; fordern.

examination Prüfung *f*; *(accounts)* Revision *f*; Kontrolle *f*; *(investigation)* Untersuchung *f*.

examine prüfen; *(accounts)* revidieren; durchsehen; *(to investigate)* untersuchen.

examiner Prüfer *m*; *(accountant)* Revisor *m*; *(investigator)* Untersucher *m*.

example Beispiel *nt*.

exceed übersteigen; überschreiten.

exception Ausnahme *f*; *(reservation)* Vorbehalt *m*; *(objection)* Einwand *m*.

exceptional case Ausnahmefall *m*.

excess Übermaß *nt*; Überschuß *m*.

excess capacity Überkapazität *f*.

excessive übermäßig.

excessive indebtedness Überschuldung *f*.

exchange n *(of currency)* Währungsumtausch *m*; *(rate of exchange)* Wechselkurs *m*; *(foreign exchange)* Devisen *pl*; *(stock exchange)* Börse *f*; *(of merchandise)* Umtausch *m*; Austausch *m*. v umtauschen; austauschen.

exchangeable austauschbar.

exchange bank Wechselbank *f*.

exchange control Devisenkontrolle *f*.

exchange equilibrium Zahlungsausgleich *m*.

exchange of views Meinungsaustausch *m*.

exchange profit Kursgewinn *m*.

exchange rate Wechselkurs *m*; Devisenkurs *m*; Umrechnungskurs *m*; Währungskurs *m*; Tauschrate *f*.

exchange rate change Wechselkursänderung *f*.

exchange rate fluctuations Wechselkursschwankungen *pl*.

exchange rate increase Wechselkursanstieg *m*.

exchange rate profit Wechselkursgewinn *m*.

exchange relation Tauschrelation *f*.

excise tax Verbrauchssteuer *f*.

exclude ausschließen.

exclusion Ausschließung *f*; Ausschluß *m*.

exclusive ausschließlich; nicht eingerechnet; exklusiv.

ex dividend dividendenlos.

execute *(to carry out)* ausführen; erledigen; *(a contract)* Bedingungen *pl* erfüllen; *(a judgment)* vollstrecken; vollziehen.

execution *(carrying out)* Ausführung *f*; Erledigung *f*; *(judgment)* Vollstreckung *f*.

executive n *(branch of government)* Exekutive *f*; *(in a company)* leitende Angestellte *m/f*; Führungskraft *f*. a ausübend; *(managing)* leitend; verwaltend.

executive position Führungsposition *f*.

executive staff Führungstab *m*.

executive suite Chefetage *f*.

exempt befreit; frei von.

exemption Befreiung *f*; Freistellung *f*; Ausnahmeregelung *f*; *(income tax)* Steuerfreibetrag *m*.

exercise of functions Aufgabenwahrnehmung *f*.

exercise of influence Einflußnahme *f*.

exert oneself sich bemühen.

exhibit n *(article exhibited)* Ausstellungsstück *nt*; *(exhibition)* Ausstellung *f*; *(proof)* Beweisstück *nt*; *(voucher)* Beleg *m*. v *(to display)* ausstellen.

exhibition Ausstellung *f*; *(fair)* Messe *f*; Schau *f*.

exhibitor Aussteller *m*.

exist existieren; *(to be in existence)* bestehen; *(to live)* leben.

existence Existenz *f*; Vorhandensein *nt*; *(life)* Leben *nt*.

existing commitment Altengagement *nt*.

existing installation Altanlage *f*.

expand erweitern; ausdehnen; sich entwickeln; expandieren.

expansion Erweiterung *f*; Ausdehnung *f*; Expansion *f*; Ausweitung *f*.

expect erwarten.

expectation Aussicht *f*; Erwartung *f*.

expectation for the future Zukunftserwartung *f*.

expectation of profits Gewinnerwartung *f*.

expected voraussichtlich; erwartet.

expedient n Hilfsmittel *nt*. a zweckdienlich.

expeditious prompt.

expend aufwenden; ausgeben.

expenditure Ausgabe *f*; Aufwand *m*; Aufwendung *f*; *(expenses incurred)* Spesen *pl*. additional ~ Mehrausgabe *f*.

expense Ausgabe *f*; *(costs)* Kosten *pl*; *(expenses incurred)* Spesen *pl*; *(for postage)* Portokosten *pl*; **administrative** ~ Verwaltungsaufwand *m*.

expense item Ausgabenposten *m*.

expensive teuer; aufwendig.

experience n *(knowledge)* Erfahrung *f*; Kenntnisse *pl*; *(event)* Erlebnis *nt*. v erfahren; *(to encounter)* erleben.

experienced erfahren; sachkundig.

experiment n Versuch *m*; Experiment *nt*. v experimentieren.

experimental series Versuchsreihe *f*.

expert n Experte *m*; Expertin *f*; *(skilled professional)* Fachmann *m*; Fachfrau *f*; *(person well-informed in one field)* Sachverständige *m/f*; Sachkenner *m*. a fachmännisch.

expert advisory board Sachverständigenrat *m*.

expertise Sachwissen *nt*; Expertise *f*.

expert opinion Begutachtung *f*.

expert report Expertenbericht *m*.

experts Fachleute *pl*.

expiration Erlöschen *nt*; *(becoming due)* Fälligwerden *nt*; *(termination)* Ablauf *m*.

expire erlöschen; außer Kraft treten; *(to run out)* ablaufen.

explain erklären.

explanation Erklärung *f*; Erläuterung *f*.

explanatory erklärend.

explicit ausdrücklich.

exploit ausbeuten; ausnutzen.

exploitation Ausbeutung *f*; Ausnutzung *f*.

exploration Erforschung *f*.

explore   untersuchen; sondieren; erkunden.

export   n Export *m*; Ausfuhr *f*; *(article)* Exportgut *nt*. v exportieren; ausführen.

exportation   Export *m*; Ausfuhr *f*.

export credit   Exportkredit *m*; Ausfuhrkredit *m*.

export earnings   Exportertrag *m*; Ausfuhrertrag *m*.

export economy   Exportwirtschaft *f*.

exporter   Exporteur *m*.

export financing   Exportfinanzierung *f*; Ausfuhrfinanzierung *f*.

export growth   Exportwachstum *nt*; Exportzuwachs *m*; Ausfuhrzuwachs *m*.

export guarantee   Ausfuhrgarantie *f*.

export house   Exportgeschäft *nt*.

export industry   Exportindustrie *f*.

exporting country   Exportland *nt*; Ausfuhrland *nt*.

export license   Ausfuhrgenehmigung *f*; Exportlizenz *f*.

export market   Auslandsmarkt *m*.

export order   Exportauftrag *m*; Ausfuhrauftrag *m*.

export oriented   exportorientiert.

export product   Exportprodukt *nt*.

export promotion   Exportförderung *f*; Ausfuhrförderung *f*.

export prospects   Exportaussicht *f*.

export receipts   Exporteinnahmen *pl*; Ausfuhreinnahmen *pl*.

export restriction   Exportbeschränkung *f*; Ausfuhrbeschränkung *f*.

export strength   Exportkraft *f*.

export subsidy   Exportsubvention *f*; Ausfuhrsubvention *f*.

export surplus   Exportüberschuß *m*; Ausfuhrüberschuß *m*.

export value   Ausfuhrwert *m*.

express   n *(delivery)* Eilbeförderung *f*; *(letter)* Eilbrief *m*; *(train)* Eilzug *m*. a Eil-; ausdrücklich. v ausdrücken.

expression   Ausdruck *m*.

expropriate   enteignen.

expropriation   Enteignung *f*.

extend   *(to prolong)* verlängern; *(to expand)* ausdehnen; *(bill of exchange)* prolongieren.

extension   *(prolongation)* Verlängerung *f*; *(expansion)* Ausdehnung *f*; Erweiterung *f*; Ausweitung *f*; *(bill of exchange)* Prolongierung *f*.

extension of demand   Nachfrageausweitung *f*.

extent   Umfang *m*; Höhe *f*.

external   äußerlich; *(foreign)* ausländisch; *(foreign trade)* außenwirtschaftlich.

external debts   Auslandsschulden *pl*.

external value   Außenwert *m*.

extortion   Erpressung *f*.

extra   n *(in addition)* Zugabe *f*; *(charge added)* Zuschlag *m*. a zusätzlich; extra.

extra charge   Extragebühr *f*.

extra cost   Mehraufwand *m*.

extraction   *(mining)* Gewinnung *f*.

extra earnings   Mehrerlös *m*.

extraneous   *(costs)* betriebsfremd.

extraofficial   nebenamtlich.

extraordinary item   Sonderposten *m*.

extras   *(costs)* Nebenkosten *pl*.

F

fabricate anfertigen; erzeugen; fabrizieren; *(a story)* erfinden.
face n *(person)* Gesicht *nt*; *(coin, page)* Vorderseite *f*. v gegenüberstehen; *(facts)* ins Gesicht *nt* sehen.
face amount Nennbetrag *m*.
face value Nennwert *m*; Nominalwert *m*.
face value of policy Versicherungswert *m*.
facilitate erleichtern.
facilitation Erleichterung *f*.
facilities Einrichtungen *pl*; *(plant)* Betriebsanlagen *pl*.
facility *(ease)* Leichtigkeit *f*; *(aptitude)* Gewandtheit *f*.
fact Tatsache *f*; Umstand *m*.
factor Faktor *m*; Umstand *m*; *(factoring)* Absatzfinanzierungsinstitut *nt*.
factor price Faktorpreis *m*.
factory Fabrik *f*; Fertigungsanlage *f*; Industriewerk *nt*.
factory closing Werkschließung *f*.
factory workshop Werkhalle *f*.
facts of the case Sachverhalt *m*.
fail *(to go bankrupt)* Bankrott *m* machen; in Konkurs *m* geraten; *(to be unsuccessful)* mißlingen; keinen Erfolg *m* haben; scheitern; *(examination)* durchfallen.
failure *(bankruptcy)* Konkurs *m*; Bankrott *m*; *(ill success)* Mißerfolg *m*; Fehlschlag *m*; *(insolvency)* Zahlungseinstellung *f*; *(nonperformance)* Unterlassung *f*; Nichterfüllung *f*; *(machine)* Ausfall *m*.
fair n Messe *f*; Ausstellung *f*.

a *(just)* gerecht; *(equitable)* angemessen; *(sound business practice)* reell; fair; *(impartial)* unparteiisch.
fair ground Messeplatz *m*.
fair trade lauterer Wettbewerb *m*.
fair value üblicher Marktpreis *m*.
fall n Fallen *nt*; Rückgang *m*; Niedergang *m*; *(season)* Herbst *m*; *(stock exchange)* Kurseinbruch *m*. v fallen; sinken; zurückgehen.
false falsch.
false entry Falschbuchung *f*.
false prognosis Fehlprognose *f*.
family background Herkunft *f*.
fare n Fahrpreis *m*; Fahrgeld *nt*; *(airfare)* Flugpreis *m*; *(food)* Kost *f*.
farm n Bauernhof *m*. v einen Bauernhof *m* bestellen.
farmer Landwirt *m*; Bauer *m*.
farming area Agrargebiet *nt*.
farm policy Agrarmarktpolitik *f*.
farm policy regulation Agrarmarktordnung *f*.
farm product Agrargut *nt*; Agrarprodukt *nt*.
fault Mangel *m*; Fehler *m*; *(mechanics)* Defekt *m*.
faultfinding n Krittelei *f*. a krittelig.
faulty mangelhaft; fehlerhaft.
favor n *(act of doing a favor)* Gefallen *m*; Gefälligkeit *f*; *(preference)* Vorzug *m*; *(in favor of)* zu Gunsten *pl* von. v *(to prefer)* bevorzugen; *(to favor)* begünstigen.
favoritism Begünstigung *f*.
feasibility Ausführbarkeit *f*;

Durchführbarkeit *f*; Machbarkeit
f.

feasible   durchführbar; ausführbar;
machbar.

feature   n Kennzeichen *nt*; Eigenschaft *f*; *(advertising)* Aufhänger
m; *(newspaper)* Sonderartikel *m*.
v besonders herausstellen.

federal   Bundes-; bundesstaatlich;
föderalistisch.

Federal Reserve Bank   Zentralbank *f*.

fee   *(charge)* Gebühr *f*; *(honorar-
ium)* Honorar *nt*; *(remuneration)*
Bezahlung *f*; *(government fee)*
Abgabe *f*.

feedback   Rückwirkung *f*; Resonanz *f*.

feeder plant   Zulieferbetrieb *m*.

fee increase   Gebührenerhöhung *f*.

fee waiver   Gebührenverzicht *m*.

fellow manager   Vorstandskollege
m; Vorstandskollegin *f*.

fellow partner   Mitgesellschafter *m*.

fiduciary   n Treuhänder *m*. a treuhänderisch.

field   n Feld *nt*; *(range)* Gebiet *nt*;
(market) Absatzgebiet *nt*; *(field
service)* Außendienst *m*; *(business
field)* Sparte *f*; *(subject)* Fach *nt*;
(subject area) Fachgebiet *nt*. v
(questions) beantworten.

field experience   Außendienster-
fahrung *f*.

field office   Außenstelle *f*.

field of industry   Industriebranche
f.

field operation   Außendiensttätig-
keit *f*.

field sales force   Verkaufsorganisation *f*.

fight   Kampf *m*.

figure   n *(amount)* Betrag *m*; *(num-*

ber) Zahl *f*; *(digit)* Ziffer *f*; *(diagram)* Diagramm *nt*; Abbildung *f*;
(person) Figur *f*. v berechnen;
ausrechnen.

figures   Zahlenmaterial *nt*.

file   n Akte *f*; *(file folder)* Akten-
ordner *m*; *(record)* Vorgang *m*.
v ablegen; einordnen; *(to submit)*
einreichen.

filing   Aktenablage *f*; *(registration)*
Anmeldung *f*; *(submission)* Einreichen *nt*.

fill   einfüllen; *(form)* ausfüllen;
(order) ausführen; *(position)*
besetzen.

filling a contract   Auftragsabwicklung *f*.

final   Schluß-; End-; endgültig.

final account   Endabrechnung *f*.

final assembly   Endmontage *f*.

final inventory   Endbestand *m*.

final product   Endprodukt *nt*.

final report   Schlußbericht *m*.

final result   Endergebnis *nt*.

finance   n Finanzwirtschaft *f*;
Finanzwesen *nt*; *(science)* Finanz-
wissenschaft *f*; Finanz *f*; Geldwesen *nt*. v finanzieren.

finance business   Finanzgeschäft *nt*.

finance company   Finanzierungsgesellschaft *f*; Finanzgesellschaft *f*;
Geldinstitut *nt*; *(consumer loan
company)* Kundenkreditgesellschaft *f*.

finance department   Finanzabteilung *f*.

financial   finanziell; fiskalisch.

financial affairs   Finanzgeschäfte
pl.

financial aid   Kredithilfe *f*; Finanzhilfe *f*.

financial analysis   Finanzanalyse *f*.

financial assets   Geldvermögen *nt*.

financial business Kreditgewerbe *nt.*

financial center Finanzplatz *m*; Finanzzentrum *nt.*

financial crisis Finanzkrise *f.*

financial institution Kreditinstitut *nt*; Geldinstitut *nt.*

financial instrument Kreditinstrument *nt.*

financial interest Kapitalbeteiligung *f.*

financial investment Geldanlage *f.*

financial market Finanzmarkt *m*; Geldmarkt *m.*

financial requirements Finanzbedarf *m.*

financial section *(newspaper)* Finanzteil *m.*

financial statement Bilanzabschluß *m*; Geschäftsbericht *m.*

financial statement date Bilanzstichtag *m.*

financial statement information Bilanzdaten *pl.*

financial straits Geldnot *f.*

financial transaction Finanzgeschäft *nt.*

financial worth Vermögenswert *m.*

financial year Geschäftsjahr *nt*; Bilanzjahr *nt*; Wirtschaftsjahr *nt.*

financier Geldgeber *m*; Kapitalgeber *m*; Financier *m.*

financing Finanzierung *f*; Kapitalbeschaffung *f*; Kreditwesen *nt.*

financing deficit Finanzierungsdefizit *nt.*

financing flow Finanzierungsstrom *m.*

financing rule Finanzierungsregel *f.*

find n Fund *m*; Entdeckung *f.* v finden; *(to procure)* beschaffen; besorgen.

find fault with bemängeln.

find out feststellen.

fine n Geldstrafe *f*; Ordnungsstrafe *f*; Geldbuße *f.* a fein. v mit einer Geldstrafe *f* belegen.

fine tuning Feinabstimmung *f.*

finish n Schluß *m*; Ende *nt*; *(finishing coat)* Überzug *m*; *(finishing a job)* Fertigstellung *f.* v fertigstellen; beenden; *(manufacturing process)* veredeln; fertig bearbeiten.

finished goods Fertigwaren *pl.*

finished product Fertigprodukt *nt.*

finishing *(manufacture)* Weiterverarbeitung *f*; Veredelung *f*; Fertigstellung *f.*

fire n Feuer *nt.* v *(to lay off)* herauswerfen; *(gun)* schießen.

firm n Firma *f*; *(enterprise)* Unternehmen *nt*; *(plant)* Betrieb *m*; *(business)* Geschäft *nt.* a fest. v fest werden.

firmness Festigkeit *f.*

firm order Festbestellung *f.*

first purchaser Ersterwerber *m.*

first-rate securities Spitzenpapiere *pl.*

fiscal Finanz-; finanziell; fiskalisch; steuerrechtlich.

fiscal authority Finanzverwaltung *f.*

fiscal policy Finanzpolitik *f.*

fiscal system Steuersystem *nt.*

fiscal year Rechnungsjahr *nt*; Haushaltsjahr *nt*; Wirtschaftsjahr *nt.*

fit n Zusammenpassen *nt*; *(clothes)* Sitz *m*; *(machinery)* Passung *f.* a *(qualified)* befähigt; tauglich; qualifiziert; *(suitable)* geeignet; *(physically fit)* in Form; fit. v *(to be the proper size)* passen; *(to adjust so as to fit)* anpassen; *(to fit together)* einfügen; *(to equip)* ausrüsten.

fit for work   erwerbsfähig.

fix   n *(dilemma)* Klemme *f.* v festsetzen; festlegen; *(to repair)* reparieren.

fixed   fixiert.

fixed assets   Sachanlagen *pl;* Anlagevermögen *nt.*

fixed capital revenue   Sachkapitalrendite *f.*

fixed exchange rate   fester Wechselkurs *m.*

fixed interest   Festzinsen *pl.*

fixed-interest bearing   festverzinslich.

fixed rate loan   Festzinsanleihe *f.*

fixed rate of interest   Festzins *m;* Festzinssatz *m.*

flexibility   Anpassungsfähigkeit *f;* Flexibilität *f;* Elastizität *f;* Beweglichkeit *f.*

flexible   anpassungsfähig; elastisch; flexibel.

flier   Handzettel *m.*

flight   *(flying)* Flug *m; (escape)* Flucht *f.*

flight of capital   Kapitalflucht *f.*

float   n *(currency)* freigegebener Wechselkurs *m; (banking)* schwebende Überweisung *f.* v *(currency)* freigeben; *(bond issue)* auflegen; *(to circulate)* umlaufen; floaten.

floating rate   freier Wechselkurs *m.*

floor   Grund *m;* Boden *m; (story)* Stockwerk *nt;* Stock *m;* Geschoß *nt;* Etage *f; (minimum of prices)* Mindestpreishöhe *f; (stock exchange)* Börsensaal *m.*

floor price   *(stock exchange)* Mindestpreis *m.*

floor trade   *(stock exchange)* Eigenhandel *m.*

flotation   *(putting into circulation)*

Inumlaufsetzen *nt; (issue)* Auflegung *f;* Emission *f;* Begebung *f.*

flourish   blühen; florieren; gedeihen.

flow   n *(production)* Arbeitsablauf *m;* Fluß *m;* Strom *m;* Umlauf *m.* v fließen.

flow of information   Informationsfluß *m.*

flow of trade   Handelsstrom *m.*

fluctuate   schwanken; fluktuieren.

fluctuating   variabel; schwankend.

fluctuation   Schwanken *nt;* Schwankung *f;* Fluktuieren *nt.*

follow   folgen; *(to pursue)* verfolgen; *(to observe rules)* befolgen; *(to result)* resultieren.

follower   Anhänger *m.*

food   Nahrung *f;* Nahrungsmittel *pl;* Lebensmittel *pl; (prepared meal)* Essen *nt.*

forbid   verbieten; untersagen.

force   n Zwang *m; (power)* Kraft *f;* Stärke *f; (employees)* Belegschaft *f; (validity)* Gültigkeit *f.* v zwingen.

forced saving   Zwangssparen *nt.*

forecast   n Vorausberechnung *f;* Vorhersage *f;* Prognose *f.* v vorhersagen; prognostizieren.

forecast data   Prognosedaten *f.*

forecaster   Prognostiker *m.*

forecasting error   Prognosefehler *m.*

forecasting method   Prognosemethode *f.*

foreclosure   Zwangsvollstreckung *f.*

foreign   Auslands-; ausländisch; auswärtig; fremd.

foreign affiliate   ausländische Konzerngesellschaft *f.*

foreign aid   Entwicklungshilfe *f.*

foreign assets   Auslandsaktiva *pl;* Auslandsguthaben *nt.*

foreign bank   Auslandsbank *f.*

foreign branch Auslandsfiliale *f.*
foreign capital Auslandskapital *nt.*
foreign competition Auslands-
konkurrenz *f.*
foreign country Ausland *nt.*
foreign credit Auslandskredit *m.*
foreign currency Devisen *pl*;
Fremdwährung *f.*
foreign currency option Devisenoption *f.*
foreign currency reserves Devisenreserven *pl.*
foreign currency shortage Devisenknappheit *f.*
foreign demand Auslandsnach-
frage *f.*
foreigner Ausländer *m.*
foreign exchange *(foreign*
exchange rate) Devisenkurs *m*;
(foreign currency) Devisen *pl.*
foreign exchange proceeds Deviseneinnahmen *pl.*
foreign exchange trade Devisenhandel *m.*
foreign funds Devisenbestände *pl*;
Auslandsgelder *pl.*
foreign investment Auslandsan-
lage *f*; Auslandsinvestition *f.*
foreign loan Auslandsanleihe *f.*
foreign market Auslandsmarkt *m*;
Überseemarkt *m.*
foreign order Auslandsbestellung *f.*
foreign profit Auslandsgewinn *m.*
foreign securities Auslandspa-
piere *pl.*
foreign share Auslandsaktie *f.*
foreign shipment Auslandsliefe-
rung *f.*
foreign subsidiary ausländische
Tochtergesellschaft *f*; Auslands-
tochter *f.*
foreign trade Außenhandel *m*;
Außenwirtschaft *f.*

foresight Voraussicht *f.*
forfeit n *(for breach of contract)*
Vertragsstrafe *f*; *(fine)* Geldstrafe *f*;
(forfeiture) Verwirkung *f.* v verwirken; verfallen lassen.
forge *(document)* fälschen; *(metal)*
schmieden.
form n Form *f*; Gestalt *f*; *(docu-*
ment) Formular *nt*; Vordruck *m.*
v formen; bilden; *(company)* gründen.
formal formal; *(observing rules)*
formell; offiziell; förmlich.
formality Formalität *f*; Förmlichkeit *f.*
formalize formalisieren; offiziell
machen.
formation Gestaltung *f*; *(company)*
Gründung *f*; Errichtung *f*; *(mili-*
tary) Verband *m.*
forming of opinion Meinungsbildung *f.*
formulate abfassen; formulieren.
formulation Abfassung *f*; Formulierung *f.*
fortune *(luck)* Glück *nt*; *(property)*
Vermögen *nt.*
forward a *(futures market)* Ter-
min-; *(advanced)* fortgeschritten.
v *(to ship)* befördern; *(to send on)*
nachsenden.
forward contract Terminabschluß
m.
forward cover Kurssicherung *f.*
forward currency Termindevisen *pl.*
forwarder Spediteur *m*; Absender
m.
forwarding Beförderung *f*; Spedition *f.*
forward market Terminmarkt *m.*
forward transaction Termingeschäft *nt.*
found *(a company)* gründen; *(a*

foundation) stiften; errichten; *(metal)* gießen.

foundation   Gründung *f*; *(endowed institution)* Stiftung *f*; *(supporting part)* Fundierung *f*.

founder   *(company)* Gründer *m*; *(endowment)* Stifter *m*.

founding year   Gründungsjahr *nt*.

fraction   Bruchteil *m*.

fractional value   Teilwert *m*.

framework   Gerüst *nt*; Rahmen *m*.

framework requirements   Rahmenbedingung *f*.

franchise   n Alleinverkaufsrecht *nt*; Lizenzbetrieb *m*; Konzessionserteilung *f*; Franchise *f*. v konzessionieren.

franchisee   Lizenznehmer *m*; Franchisenehmer *m*.

fraud   Betrug *m*.

fraudulent   betrügerisch.

fraudulent entry   Falschbuchung *f*.

fraught with risk   risikoreich.

free   a frei; befreit; *(without cost)* kostenlos; gratis. v befreien.

freedom   Freiheit *f*.

freelance   freiberuflich.

free of charge   kostenlos; gebührenfrei.

free of cost   kostenlos.

free trade   Freihandel *m*.

freight   Fracht *f*; Ladung *f*; Frachtgut *nt*; *(tonnage)* Laderaum *m*; *(transport charges)* Frachtkosten *pl*.

freight car   Güterwagen *m*.

freighter   Frachtschiff *nt*.

freight forwarding business   Spedition *f*.

freight traffic   Güterverkehr *m*.

frequent   a häufig. v häufig aufsuchen.

fresh supply   Nachschub *m*.

fringe benefit   Nebenleistung *f*.

fulfill   erfüllen.

fulfillment   Erfüllung *f*; Vollziehung *f*.

full   voll; ganz; völlig.

full employment   Vollbeschäftigung *f*.

full service bank   Universalbank *f*.

full-time position   Ganztagsstelle *f*.

function   n Aufgabe *f*; Funktion *f*; *(social event)* gesellschaftliche Veranstaltung *f*. v funktionieren; *(to act as)* fungieren.

functional   funktionell; fachlich; zweckmäßig.

fund   n Kapital *nt*; Geldsumme *f*; *(investment company)* Fonds *m*; *(stock)* Vorrat *m*. v finanzieren; *(treasury notes)* einlösen.

fund assets   Fondsvermögen *nt*.

funds   Finanzmittel *pl*.

fungible   vertretbar; fungibel.

futile   nutzlos.

future   n Zukunft *f*. a zukünftig.

future earnings   zukünftiger Ertrag *m*.

future leaders   Führungsnachwuchs *m*.

futures   Termingeschäfte *pl*; Terminhandel *m*.

futures contract   Terminabschluß *m*.

futures market   Terminmarkt *m*.

futures rate   Terminsatz *m*.

futures trade   Terminhandel *m*.

G

gain n *(increase)* Zunahme *f*; *(profit)* Gewinn *m*; Profit *m*; *(utility)* Nutzen *m*. v *(to earn)* verdienen; *(to profit)* gewinnen; *(to improve)* sich bessern.

gainful employment Erwerbstätigkeit *f*.

gap Lücke *f*.

gasoline Benzin *nt*.

gasoline price hike Benzinpreiserhöhung *f*.

general allgemein; *(most common)* üblich; *(not specific)* ungefähr; unbestimmt.

general agent Generalvertreter *m*.

general partner unbeschränkt haftender Gesellschafter *m*.

general tariff Einheitstarif *m*.

generate erzeugen; hervorbringen; entwickeln.

generation Generation *f*.

generic generisch.

generous großzügig.

genuine echt.

gift Geschenk *nt*; Schenkung *f*.

give a good return sich rentieren.

give away verschenken; vergeben.

giving away Vergabe *f*.

global Welt-; global; weltweit.

global demand weltweite Nachfrage *f*.

global economics Weltwirtschaft *f*; *(study)* Weltwirtschaftslehre *f*.

global market share Weltmarktanteil *m*.

goal Ziel *nt*; Zweck *m*; *(sports)* Tor *nt*.

go below a limit unterschreiten.

go down zurückgehen.

gold Gold *nt*.

gold hoarding Goldhortung *f*.

gold holder Goldbesitzer *m*.

gold holding Goldbestand *m*.

gold producer Goldproduzent *m*.

gold reserve Goldbestand *m*; Goldreserve *f*.

gold standard Goldstandard *m*.

gold supply Goldvorrat *m*.

good n *(utility)* Nutzen *m*; *(public good)* Wohl *nt*. a gut; *(financially sound)* zahlungsfähig; solvent; reell; *(valid)* gültig; *(check)* in Ordnung *f*.

goods Ware *f*; Gut *nt*; Artikel *m*.

goodwill Goodwill *m*; Firmenwert *m*.

govern regieren; *(to administer)* verwalten; leiten; *(to regulate)* bestimmen; *(law)* als Präzedenzfall dienen.

governing body Verwaltungsgremium *nt*; Direktorium *nt*.

government Regierung *f*; *(state)* Staat *m*; *(agency)* Behörde *f*; *(administration)* Verwaltung *f*.

government guarantee Staatsgarantie *f*.

government housing Sozialwohnung *f*.

government incentives for savers Sparförderung *f*.

government influence Staatseinfluß *m*.

government order Behördenauftrag *m*.

government securities Staatspapiere *pl*.

government subsidy Staatszuschuß *m.*
grace *(delay)* Frist *f.*
grace period Zahlungsfrist *f.*
grade n Rangstufe *f;* Grad *m;*
(quality of merchandise) Handelsklasse *f;* Qualität *f.* v abstufen;
einteilen.
graduate n Absolvent *m; (high
school)* Abiturient *m; (university)*
Hochschulabsolvent *m.* v einteilen; staffeln; *(from school or
university)* Schule *f* oder Hoch-
schule *f* absolvieren; mit einem
Diplom *nt* abschließen.
graduation Gradeinteilung *f;*
(from educational institution)
Ausbildungsabschluß *m.*
grant n Verleihung *f; (donation)*
Schenkung *f; (sum granted)* Unterstützungssumme *f;* Zuschuß *m; (of
request)* Gewährung *f.* v *(to concede)* gewähren; *(to approve)*
bewilligen; *(to give)* verleihen.
granting of a loan Darlehensgewährung *f.*
granting of credit Kreditgewährung *f.*
grant leave beurlauben.
graph graphische Darstellung *f.*
gratuitous unentgeltlich; gratis.
grocery store Lebensmittelladen
m.
gross n Gros *nt.* a brutto; roh;
(coarse) unfein.
gross income Bruttoeinkommen
nt.
gross margin Bruttohandelsspanne
f.
gross national product Bruttosozialprodukt *nt.*
gross profit Rohgewinn *m.*
gross sales Bruttoabsatz *m.*

group n Gruppe *f;* Klasse *f; (business concern)* Konzern *m;* Kreis *m.*
v gruppieren; anordnen.
group member Gruppenangehörige *m/f.*
group of banks Bankengruppe *f.*
group of companies Firmengruppe *f.*
grow wachsen; *(to increase)* zunehmen; *(to cultivate)* ziehen;
anbauen.
growth Wachstum *nt; (expansion)*
Ausdehnung *f; (increase)* Zunahme *f;* Vergrößerung *f; (development)* Entwicklung *f.*
growth forecast Wachstumsprognose *f.*
growth in earnings Verdienstzuwachs *m;* Ertragsentwicklung *f.*
growth in sales Umsatzsteigerung
f.
growth in the money supply
Geldmengenwachstum *nt.*
growth model Wachstumsmodell
nt.
growth path Wachstumspfad *m.*
growth policy Wachstumspolitik *f.*
growth prediction Wachstumsvorhersage *f.*
growth rate Wachstumsrate *f.*
growth sector Wachstumsbranche
f.
guarantee n Bürgschaft *f;* Garantie *f; (bill of exchange)* Aval *m/nt.*
v bürgen; gewährleisten;
garantieren; haften.
guaranteed verbrieft.
guaranteed price Garantiepreis
m.
guarantor Bürge *m.*
guaranty fund Bürgschaftsfonds
m.
guest Gast *m.*

guest worker   Gastarbeiter *m*.
guidance   Führung *f*; Leitung *f*;
(counselling) Beratung *f*.
guide   n *(manual)* Leitfaden *m*;
(person) Führer *m*. v führen;
lenken; leiten.
guideline   Richtlinie *f*.
guild   Zunft *f*.

habit   Gewohnheit *f*; Gebrauch *m*;
Gepflogenheit *f*.
half   n Hälfte *f*. a halb.
halt   n Stillstand *m*. v anhalten.
hand   n Hand *f*; *(worker)* angelern-
ter Arbeiter *m*. v aushändigen.
handle   n Handhabe *f*; *(grip)* Griff
m; *(door)* Klinke *f*; *(vessel)* Henkel
m. v handhaben; *(to treat)* behandeln; *(to process)* bearbeiten; *(to
carry out)* erledigen.
handling   *(execution)* Erledigung *f*;
Handhabung *f*; *(processing)* Bearbeitung *f*; *(treatment)* Behandlung *f*.
handout   *(leaflet)* Prospekt *m*;
Informationsmaterial *nt*; *(charity)*
Almosen *nt*.
harbor   Hafen *m*; *(refuge)* Zu-
fluchtsort *m*.
hard   hart; *(difficult)* schwierig;
(strenuous) anstrengend; mühsam;
(strict) streng.
hard currency   harte Währung *f*.
hardship   Not *f*; Bedrängnis *f*;
Härte *f*.
hardware   Eisenwaren *pl*; *(computer)* Hardware *f*.
head   n Kopf *m*; *(main)* Haupt *nt*;
(chief) Chef *m*; Leiter *m*; *(top)*
Spitze *f*. v *(to lead)* leiten; anführen; *(to direct)* lenken.
heading   Überschrift *f*.
head manager   Chefmanager *m*.

head office   Hauptverwaltung *f*.
head organization   Spitzenorganisation *f*; Spitzenverband *m*.
headquarters   Hauptgeschäftssitz
m; Hauptverwaltung *f*; Zentrale *f*;
(military) Hauptquartier *nt*.
hearing   *(deliberation)* Verhandlung *f*; *(investigation)* Voruntersuchung *f*; *(trial)* Verhör *nt*; *(ability to hear)* Gehör *nt*.
heavy   schwer; *(large or great)*
stark.
hedge   n *(stock exchange)* Dek-
kungsgeschäft *nt*; Absicherung *f*;
Sicherungsgeschäft *nt*. v Sicherungsgeschäft *nt* abschließen;
absichern; *(to avoid commitment)*
ausweichen.
height   Höhe *f*; *(summit)* Gipfel *m*.
heir   Erbe *m*; Erbin *f*.
helper   Hilfsarbeiter *m*; Gehilfe *m*;
Gehilfin *f*.
helpful   hilfreich.
help wanted advertisement   Stellenangebot *nt*.
high   n Höchststand *m*. a hoch.
higher management   obere
Betriebsführung *f*.
highest level   Höchststand *m*; *(in
hierarchy)* oberste Ebene *f*.
high-grade   hochwertig.
highly paid   hochbezahlt.
high-quality   hochwertig.

high risk hohes Risiko *nt.*

high volume business Massengeschäft *nt.*

hike n *(increase)* Anstieg *m*; Steigen *nt*; *(walking)* Wanderung *f.* v *(to increase)* steigern; *(to walk)* wandern.

hire n *(act of hiring)* Einstellung *f*; *(renting)* Miete *f.* v *(to employ)* einstellen; anstellen; *(to rent)* mieten.

histogram Säulendiagramm *nt.*

history Geschichte *f*; Darstellung *f*; *(personal)* Entwicklung *f*; *(background)* Hintergrund *m.*

hit n *(success)* Treffer *m*; Schlager *m.* v treffen; *(to reach)* erreichen.

hoard n Vorrat *m*; Schatz *m.* v anhäufen; hamstern; horten.

hold n Halt *m*; *(grip)* Griff *m*; *(influence)* Einfluß *m*; *(ship)* Laderaum *m.* v halten; *(to possess)* im Besitz *m* haben; *(capacity)* fassen; enthalten.

holder *(property)* Besitzer *m*; Inhaber

holding *(possession)* Besitz *m*; *(inventory)* Bestand *m*; *(share)* Beteiligung *f*; Anteil *m.*

holding company Holdinggesellschaft *f*; Dachgesellschaft *f.*

home n *(residence)* Wohnort *m*; Heim *nt*; *(home country)* Heimat *f.* adv *(at home)* zu Hause; *(to go home)* nach Hause.

home computer Heimcomputer *m.*

home loan financing Hausfinanzierung *f.*

home market Inlandsmarkt *m*; Binnenmarkt *m.*

home office Zentrale *f*; Hauptbüro *nt.*

homeowner Hausbesitzer *m.*

home purchase savings Bausparen *nt.*

home rule Selbstverwaltung *f.*

home savings and loan association Bausparkasse *f.*

home trading Inlandsgeschäft *nt.*

host n Gastgeber *m*; Veranstalter *m.* v *(an event)* veranstalten.

hostage Geisel *f.*

host country Aufnahmestaat *m*; Gastland *nt.*

hour Stunde *f.*

hourly wages Stundenlohn *m.*

hours worked per week Wochenarbeitszeit *f.*

house n Haus *nt*; *(firm)* Handelsfirma *f.* v unterbringen; beherbergen.

household Haushalt *m.*

housing Unterbringung *f.*

housing industry Wohnungswirtschaft *f.*

hub Zentrum *nt*; *(wheel)* Nabe *f.*

human menschlich.

humane menschenfreundlich; human.

I

idea   Idee *f*; Begriff *m*; Einfall *m*.

ideal   n Ideal *nt*; *(model)* Vorbild *nt*. a ideal; optimal; *(exemplary)* vorbildlich.

identical   identisch; *(copy)* gleichlautend.

identifiable   feststellbar; identifizierbar.

identification   *(identification card)* Ausweis *m*; *(determination)* Bestimmung *f*; Feststellung *f*; Identifizierung *f*.

identify   ausweisen; identifizieren; *(to determine)* bestimmen.

identify oneself   sich ausweisen.

identity   Identität *f*; Gleichheit *f*.

idle   a *(person)* müßig; untätig; *(capacity)* unausgenutzt; *(capital)* tot; *(machinery)* stillstehend; *(facilities)* stilliegend. v *(engine)* leerlaufen.

idleness   Untätigkeit *f*.

idle shift   Feierschicht *f*.

illegal   unrechtmäßig; ungesetzlich; rechtswidrig; illegal; unerlaubt.

illustrate   illustrieren; *(to demonstrate)* veranschaulichen.

illustration   Abbildung *f*; Illustration *f*.

illustrative   erklärend; erläuternd.

image   n Bild *nt*; Image *nt*; Erscheinungsbild *nt*. v abbilden.

imbalance   Unausgeglichenheit *f*.

imitation   Nachahmung *f*; Imitation *f*.

immaterial   *(nonessential)* unwesentlich; unerheblich; *(intangible)* immateriell.

immeasurable   unermeßlich; unmeßbar.

immediate   sofortig; unverzüglich; dringend.

immediately   sofort.

impact   n *(hit)* Aufprall *m*; *(force)* Wirkungskraft *f*; Stoßkraft *f*; *(effect)* Auswirkung *f*. v *(to impinge on)* einwirken auf; *(to press together)* zusammenpressen.

impair   beeinträchtigen; verschlechtern.

impartial   unparteiisch; unvoreingenommen.

impede   behindern; vereiteln.

impediment   Behinderung *f*; Hindernis *nt*.

impetus   Antrieb *m*; Impuls *m*; Triebkraft *f*.

impetus toward expansion   Wachstumsimpuls *m*.

implement   n *(tool)* Werkzeug *nt*; Arbeitsgerät *nt*; *(instrument)* Instrument *nt*. v ausführen; durchführen; *(contract)* erfüllen.

implementation   Ausführung *f*; Durchführung *f*; *(contract)* Erfüllung *f*.

implementation date   Ausführungstag *m*.

import   n Einfuhr *f*; Import *m*. v einführen; importieren.

importation   Einfuhr *f*; Import *m*.

import barrier   Einfuhrschranke *f*; Importbarriere *f*; Importschranke *f*.

import capacity   Importfähigkeit *f*.

import company   Importfirma *f*.

import control Einfuhrkontrolle *f*.
import curb Importdrosselung *f*.
import demand Importbedarf *m*.
importer Importeur *m*; Importkaufmann *m*; Importkauffrau *f*.
import goods Importware *f*.
import license Einfuhrbewilligung
f; Einfuhrgenehmigung *f*.
import merchandise Importgut *nt*.
import of finished goods Fertig-
warenimport *m*.
import organization Importorga-
nisation *f*.
import price Importpreis *m*; Einfuhrpreis *m*.
import price increase Importverteuerung *f*.
import protection Einfuhrschutz
m.
import quota Einfuhrkontingent
nt; Einfuhrquote *f*; Importkontingent *nt*; Importquote *f*.
import restriction Einfuhrbeschränkung *f*.
imports Einfuhrware *f*; Importar-
tikel *pl*.
import substitute Einfuhrersatz *m*.
import surcharge Importabgabe *f*.
import value Einfuhrwert *m*.
impose aufbürden; *(taxes)* auferlegen; *(charges)* erheben.
imposition Belastung *f*; *(taxes)*
Auferlegung *f*; *(charges)* Erhebung
f; *(taking advantage)* Zumutung *f*.
improve sich bessern; verbessern;
(to refine) veredeln.
improvement Verbesserung *f*;
(progress) Fortschritt *m*; *(refining)*
Veredelung *f*.
imprudent unklug; unvorsichtig.
impulse Anstoß *m*; Antrieb *m*;
Impuls *m*.
imputation Zurechnung *f*.

impute zurechnen; unterstellen.
inability Unvermögen *nt*; Unfähigkeit *f*.
inaccurate ungenau; *(false)* falsch.
inadequacy Unzulänglichkeit *f*;
Unangemessenheit *f*.
inadequate unzulänglich; unangemessen.
inadmissible unzulässig.
incalculable unkalkulierbar.
incapable unfähig.
incentive Anreiz *m*; Ansporn *m*.
incidence Vorkommen *nt*; *(distribution)* Verbreitung *f*; *(frequency)*
Häufigkeit *f*.
incident Zwischenfall *m*; Ereignis
nt.
incidental gelegentlich; beiläufig.
inclined to buy kaufwillig.
include einschließen; einbeziehen;
erfassen.
inclusion Einbeziehung *f*.
inclusive einschließlich; inklusive.
income Einkommen *nt*; *(receipts)*
Einnahme *f*; *(revenue)* Einkünfte *pl*.
income bracket Einkommensgruppe *f*.
income decrease Einkommens-
minderung *f*.
income-dependent einkommensabhängig.
income distribution Einkommensverteilung *f*.
income group Einkommensgruppe
f.
income tax Einkommenssteuer *f*.
incoming order Auftragseingang
m.
incomplete unvollständig.
inconvertibility *(bank notes)*
Nichteinlösbarkeit *f*; Nichtkonvertierbarkeit *f*.
incorporate a inkorporiert. v *(to*

constitute as corporation) als Aktiengesellschaft *f* eintragen; registrieren; inkorporieren; *(to join)* vereinigen; *(to take in)* aufnehmen; *(of a town)* eingemeinden.

incorporation *(registration)* Eintragung *f*; *(forming of corporation)* Körperschaftsgründung *f*; *(corporation)* Körperschaft *f*; Korporation *f*; *(of a town)* Eingemeindung *f*.

incorrect unrichtig; falsch.

increase n *(rise)* Anstieg *m*; Steigerung *f*; Erhöhung *f*; *(of capital)* Aufstockung *f*; *(increment)* Zunahme *f*; Zuwachs *m*. v *(to raise)* erhöhen; steigern; *(to rise)* sich erhöhen; steigen; zunehmen.

increased demand Bedarfszuwachs *m*.

increase in capital stock Kapitalerhöhung *f*.

increase in cost Verteuerung *f*.

increase in currency Geldvermehrung *f*.

increase in customers Kundenzuwachs *m*.

increase in efficiency Effizienzsteigerung *f*.

increase in imports Einfuhranstieg *m*; Einfuhrsteigerung *f*.

increase in interest Zinsanhebung *f*.

increase in prices Kursanstieg *m*.

increase in sales Absatzsteigerung *f*.

increase in the money supply Geldmengenerhöhung *f*; Geldmengenvermehrung *f*.

increase in turnover Umsatzanstieg *m*.

increase of capital stock Kapitalvermehrung *f*.

increase of deposits Depositenzuwachs *m*.

increment Zunahme *f*; Zuwachs *m*.

incur *(obligation)* eingehen; *(costs)* übernehmen; auf sich nehmen.

indebted verschuldet; verpflichtet.

indebtedness Verschuldung *f*; Verpflichtung *f*; Schuldenlast *f*.

indefinite unbestimmt; unbegrenzt.

independence Unabhängigkeit *f*; Selbständigkeit *f*.

independent unabhängig; selbständig.

index n Index *m*; Verzeichnis *nt*; *(statistics)* Meßziffer *f*; Kennziffer *f*; *(index file)* Kartei *f*. v *(to list)* registrieren; *(to link to an index)* an einen Index *m* koppeln.

indicate angeben; anzeigen; *(to point out)* hinweisen.

indication Anzeichen *nt*; Angabe *f*; *(pointing out)* Hinweis *m*.

indication of results Ergebnisangabe *f*.

indicative bezeichnend; hinweisend.

indicator Indikator *m*; Meßgröße *f*; Anzeiger *m*.

indirect indirekt; mittelbar.

indispensable unentbehrlich; unerläfllich.

individual n Einzelperson *f*; Individuum *nt*. a Einzel-; einzeln; persönlich.

individual responsibility Eigenverantwortung *f*.

induce herbeiführen; *(to cause)* verursachen; veranlassen; *(to convince)* überreden.

inducement Anreiz *m*; Antrieb *m*.

inducement to buy Kaufanreiz *m*.

industrial   industriell; gewerblich.
industrialism   Industrialismus *m*.
industrialization   Industrialisierung *f*.
industrialize   industrialisieren.
industrialized world   industriali-
sierte Länder *pl*.
industrial nation   Industrieland *nt*;
Industrienation *f*; Industriestaat *m*.
industrial plant   Industrieanlage *f*;
Industriebetrieb *m*; Industriewerk
nt.
industry   Industrie *f*; Gewerbe *nt*;
(line of industry) Branche *f*; Industriezweig *m*.
industry expert   Industriefachmann *m*; Industriefachfrau *f*;
Branchenkenner *m*.
industry forecast   Industrieprognose *f*.
industry leader   Industrieführer *m*.
industry show   Industrieausstellung *f*.
industry spokesman   Branchensprecher *m*.
ineffective   unwirksam.
inefficient   leistungsunfähig;
unwirksam; unpraktisch.
inept   ungeeignet.
inequality   Ungleichheit *f*.
inequity   Ungerechtigkeit *f*.
inexpensive   billig; preiswert.
inexperienced   unerfahren.
infant industry   schutzzollbedürftige Industrie *f*.
inferior   minderwertig; zweitklassig.
inflate   *(economy)* Inflation herbeiführen; *(prices)* hochtreiben;
aufblähen; *(tire)* aufpumpen.
inflation   Inflation *f*; Teuerung *f*.
inflationary   inflationär; inflationistisch; inflatorisch.

inflationary factor   Inflationsfaktor *m*.
inflationary pressure   Inflationsdruck *m*.
inflationary tendency   Inflations-
tendenz *f*.
inflation rate   Inflationsrate *f*.
inflow   Zugang *m*; Zufluß *m*.
influence   n Einfluß *m*; Einwirkung
f; Beeinflussung *f*. v beeinflussen.
influential   einflußreich.
influx   Zustrom *m*.
influx of funds   Mittelzufluß *m*.
inform   informieren; *(to advise)*
Auskunft *f* geben; *(to notify)*
benachrichtigen; mitteilen; *(to
brief)* unterrichten.
informal   formlos; zwanglos;
informell.
informality   Formlosigkeit *f*.
information   Information *f*; *(notification)* Benachrichtigung *f*; *(communication)* Mitteilung *f*; *(briefing)* Unterrichtung *f*; *(knowledge)*
Kenntnis *f*; *(advice)* Auskunft *f*.
information management   *(data
processing)* Datenverwaltung *f*;
Informationsmanagement *nt*.
informative   informativ.
infrastructure   Infrastruktur *f*.
infrequent   selten; nicht häufig.
infringe   *(to violate)* verstoßen; *(a
contract)* brechen; *(a patent)* verletzen.
infringement   Verstoß *m*; Verletzung *f*; Übergriff *m*.
inhabitant   Einwohner *m*.
inherit   erben.
inheritance   Erbschaft *f*; Nachlaß *m*.
initial   n *(letter)* Anfangsbuchstabe
m. a Anfangs-; Erst-; anfänglich.
v mit den Anfangsbuchstaben *pl*
unterzeichnen.

initial capital Anfangskapital *nt.*
initial cost Anschaffungspreis *m.*
initial demand Ausgangsforderung *f.*
initial investment Erstinvestition *f.*
initial reserve Anfangsreserve *f.*
initial subscriber Erstzeichner *m.*
initiate *(to start)* einleiten; anbahnen; *(to introduce)* einführen; initiieren.
initiative Initiative *f.*
injunction Vorschrift *f*; *(judicial order)* einstweilige Verfügung *f.*
injury *(damage)* Schaden *m*; *(hurt)* Verletzung *f.*
injustice Ungerechtigkeit *f*; Unrecht *nt.*
innovate Neuerungen *pl* einführen.
innovation *(innovating)* Einführung *f* von Neuerungen *pl*; Neuerung *f*; Innovation *f.*
innovative neuerungsbereit; innovativ.
input *(data processing)* Eingabe *f*; Input *m*; *(materials)* Einsatzmenge *f.*
input data Eingabedaten *pl*; Inputdaten *pl.*
input path Inputpfad *m.*
inquire *(letter)* anfragen; nachfragen.
inquiry Erkundigung *f*; *(letter)* Anfrage *f*; *(investigation)* Nachforschung; Ermittlung *f.*
insecure unstabil; unsicher.
insider Eingeweihte *m/f.*
insist bestehen auf; dringen auf.
insistence Bestehen *nt*; Nachdruck *m.*
insolvency Insolvenz *f*; Zahlungsunfähigkeit *f.*

insolvency proceedings Vergleichsverfahren *nt.*
insolvent n Zahlungsunfähige *m/f.* a insolvent; zahlungsunfähig.
inspect prüfen; besichtigen; untersuchen; inspizieren.
inspection Prüfung *f*; Inspektion *f*; Untersuchung *f*; *(on site)* Besichtigung *f.*
instability Unbeständigkeit *f*; Instabilität *f.*
install installieren; *(into office)* einsetzen.
installation *(factory)* Betriebseinrichtung *f*; Anlage *f*; *(setting up)* Installierung *f*; Aufstellung *f*; Einbau *m.*
installation cost Aufstellungskosten *pl*; Einbaukosten *pl.*
installment *(payment)* Rate *f*; *(publication)* Fortsetzung *f.*
installment credit Ratenkredit *m.*
installment payment Abzahlung *f.*
institute n Institut *nt*; Anstalt *f.* v *(to establish)* einrichten; einführen; *(to set in motion)* einleiten.
institution Anstalt *f*; Institut *nt*; Organ *nt*; Institution *f*; *(established order)* Einrichtung *f.*
institutional institutionell.
instruct anweisen; *(to teach)* unterrichten; unterweisen.
instruction Anweisung *f*; *(teaching)* Unterricht *m.*
instrument *(document)* Dokument *nt*; Urkunde *f*; *(commercial)* Papier *nt*; Instrument *nt*; *(tool)* Werkzeug *nt.*
instrumental behilflich; mitwirkend.
insufficient unzureichend; ungenügend.

insurance Versicherung *f*.

insurance company Versicherungsgesellschaft *f*; Versicherungsfirma *f*.

insurance policy Versicherungspolice *f*.

insurance premium Versicherungsbeitrag *m*.

insure versichern.

insured value Versicherungswert *m*.

insurer Versicherer *m*; Versicherungsträger *m*.

intangible immateriell.

intangibles *(assets)* immaterielle Vermögenswerte *pl*.

integrate eingliedern; integrieren.

integration Eingliederung *f*; Integration *f*; Zusammenschluß *m*.

intend beabsichtigen; vorhaben; wollen.

intended use Verwendungszweck *m*.

intensive intensiv.

intent n Absicht *f*; *(goal)* Ziel *nt*; *(resolution)* Vorsatz *m*; *(meaning)* Bedeutung *f*. a bedacht auf; gespannt.

intention Absicht *f*; *(resolution)* Vorsatz *m*.

interbank transaction Interbankgeschäft *nt*.

interest n Interesse *nt*; *(on loan)* Zinsen *pl*; *(importance)* Bedeutung *f*. v interessieren.

interest advantage Zinsvorteil *m*.

interest arrears Zinsrückstände *pl*.

interest bearing verzinslich; zinstragend.

interest calculation Zinsberechnung *f*.

interest ceiling Höchstzinsen *pl*.

interest charge Zinsaufschlag *m*.

interest coupon Zinsschein *m*.

interest credit Zinsgutschrift *f*.

interest dependency Zinsabhängigkeit *f*.

interest difference Zinsdifferenz *f*.

interest differential Zinsabstand *m*; Zinsunterschied *m*; Zinsgefälle *nt*.

interest expense Zinskosten *pl*.

interest income Zinseinkommen *nt*.

interest level Zinsniveau *nt*.

interest margin Zinsdifferenz *f*; Zinsspanne *f*.

interest on debt Schuldzinsen *pl*; Sollzinsen *pl*.

interest on deposits Bankzinsen *pl*; Habenzinsen *pl*.

interest on loan capital Darlehenzinsen *pl*.

interest owed Zinsverpflichtung *f*.

interest payment Zinszahlung *f*.

interest policy Zinspolitik *f*.

interest rate Zinssatz *m*; Zinsrate *f*.

interest rate differential Zinssatzgefälle *nt*.

interest rate increase Zinssatzerhöhung *f*.

interest receipts Zinseinnahme *f*.

interest revenues Zinseinnahme *f*.

interest yield Zinsertrag *m*; Rendite *f*.

interfere sich einmischen; *(to impair)* beeinträchtigen; *(to step in)* einschreiten.

interference Einmischung *f*; *(intervention)* Eingriff *m*; *(disturbance)* Störung *f*.

interim n Zwischenzeit *f*. a einstweilig; zwischenzeitlich; vorläufig.

interim aid Überbrückungshilfe *f*.

interim payment Zwischenzahlung *f*.
interim ruling Übergangsregelung
f.
interior n Innere *nt*; *(country)* Binnenland *nt*; Inland *nt*. a innen-;
binnen-; *(country)* binnenländisch;
inländisch.
intermediary n Mittelsmann *m*;
Mittelsperson *f*; Zwischenhändler
m. a vermittelnd.
intermediate zwischen-; dazwischenliegend.
intermediate goods Zwischenprodukt *nt*; Halbfabrikat *nt*.
internal *(plant)* innerbetrieblich;
(country) einheimisch; inländisch;
inner.
internal bond Inlandsanleihe *f*.
internal economic trend Binnenkonjunktur *f*.
international international.
international market Weltmarkt
m.
international trade Welthandel *m*.
international unit international
gebräuchliche Maßeinheit *f*.
interrelation of media Medienverflechtung *f*.
interval Zeitabstand *m*.
intervene einschreiten; sich einschalten; intervenieren.
intervention Einschreiten *nt*; Einmischung *f*; Eingreifen *nt*; *(central
bank)* Intervention *f*; *(mediation)*
Vermittlung *f*.
intervention price Interventionskurs *m*.
interview n Gespräch *nt*; *(for job)*
Vorstellungsgespräch *nt*; Unterredung *f*; *(media)* Interview *nt*.
v befragen; interviewen.
interviewee Befragte *m/f*.

interviewer Interviewer *m*;
Befrager *m*.
introduce *(to bring in new)* einführen; *(to make acquainted)*
bekanntmachen; vorstellen; *(bill)*
einbringen.
introduction Einführung *f*; *(recommendation)* Empfehlung *f*;
(presentation) Vorstellung *f*;
(book) Einleitung *f*.
invalid n Invalide *m*; Invalidin *f*;
Körperbehinderte *m/f*. a *(not
valid)* ungültig; unwirksam.
invalidate ungültig machen; außer
Kraft setzen.
invalidity Ungültigkeit *f*; Unwirksamkeit *f*.
invent erfinden.
invention Erfindung *f*.
inventiveness Erfindungsgabe *f*.
inventor Erfinder *m*.
inventory *(stock on hand)* Inventar *nt*; Bestand *m*; Lagerbestand
m; *(inventory taking)* Inventur *f*;
Bestandsaufnahme *f*.
inventory control Bestandskontrolle *f*.
inventory cost Lagerkosten *pl*.
inventory management Lagerverwaltung *f*.
invest investieren; anlegen.
investigate untersuchen; ermitteln;
nachprüfen.
investigation Untersuchung *f*;
Nachprüfung *f*; Ermittlung *f*.
investigation fee Untersuchungsgebühr *f*.
investigator Prüfer *m*; Untersucher *m*.
investment Anlage *f*; Investition *f*;
Investierung *f*; Investment *nt*.
investment adviser Anlageberater
m.

investment bank   Anlagebank *f*;
Effektenbank *f*.

investment banker   Anlagebankier
m; Effektenbankier *m*.

investment capital   Anlagekapital
nt.

investment cycle   Investitionszyklus *m*.

investment decision   Investitionsentscheidung *f*; Anlageentscheidung *f*.

investment fund   Wertpapierfond
m; Investmentfonds *m*.

investment funds   Anlagemittel *pl*.

investment gap   Investitionslücke
f.

investment in securities   Wertpapieranlage *f*.

investment level   Investitionshöhe
f.

investment loan   Investitionskredit
m.

investment of assets   Vermögensanlage *f*.

investment period   Anlagedauer *f*.

investment plan   Investitionsprogramm *nt*; Anlageplan *m*.

investment portfolio   Wertpapierbestand *m*; Wertpapierdepot *nt*;
Effektenbestand *m*.

investment premium   Investitionsprämie *f*.

investment project   Investitionsvorhaben *nt*.

investment proposal   Investitionsantrag *m*.

investment quota   Investitionsquote *f*.

investment return   Kapitalertrag *m*.

investment tip   Anlagetip *m*.

investor   Kapitalanleger *m*; Geldanleger *m*; Geldgeber *m*; Investor
m; Kapitalgeber *m*; Eigenkapitalgeber *m*.

invoice   Faktura *f*; Rechnung *f*.

irrevocable   unwiderruflich.

isolate   isolieren; absondern.

isolation   Isolierung *f*; Absonderung *f*.

isolationism   Isolationspolitik *f*.

isolationist   Isolationspolitiker *m*.

issuance   *(distribution)* Ausgabe *f*;
(securities) Emission *f*; *(document)*
Ausstellung *f*.

issue   n *(check, document)* Ausstellung *f*; *(edition)* Ausgabe *f*;
(debate) Kernpunkt *m*; *(securities)*
Emission *f*.   v *(check, document)*
ausstellen; *(to distribute)* ausgeben; *(to publish)* herausgeben;
(securities) emittieren.

issue price   Ausgabekurs *m*; Ausgabepreis *m*.

issuer   Aussteller *m*; *(securities)*
Emittent *m*.

item   *(accounting)* Posten *m*;
(object) Gegenstand *m*; *(topic)*
Punkt *m*; *(newspaper)* Notiz *f*.

itemization   Detaillierung *f*.

itemized account   Postenkonto *nt*.

itemized billing   Einzelabrechnung
f.

jeopardize gefährden.
job *(work)* Arbeit *f; (occupation)*
 Beruf *m;* Beschäftigung *f;* Job *m;*
 (position) Arbeitsstelle *f.*
job applicant Stellenbewerber *m;*
 Arbeitsuchende *m/f.*
job description Arbeitsplatzbeschreibung *f;* Aufgabengebiet *nt.*
job loss Stellenverlust *m.*
job market Arbeitsmarkt *m.*
job market condition Arbeitsmarktlage *f.*
job offer Stellenangebot *nt.*
job protection Kündigungsschutz
 m.
job sharing Arbeitsplatzaufteilung *f.*
job training Einarbeitung *f.*
join sich vereinigen; sich verbinden;
 (an association) beitreten.
joint account Gemeinschaftskonto
 nt.
joint stock company Kapitalgesellschaft *f.*
joint venture Joint-venture *nt;*
 Gemeinschaftsunternehmen *nt;*
 Gelegenheitsgesellschaft *f.*
journeyman Geselle *m.*
judge n Richter *m.* v *(in court)*
 richten; *(to evaluate)* beurteilen;
 urteilen.

judgment Urteil *nt; (verdict)*
 Urteilsspruch *m; (ability to judge)*
 Urteilsvermögen *nt; (opinion)*
 Ansicht *f.*
judicial gerichtlich; richterlich.
judiciary committee Rechtsausschuß *m.*
jump n Sprung *m.* v *(price)*
 sprunghaft steigen.
junior staff member Nachwuchskraft *f.*
jurisdiction Rechtsprechung *f;*
 (local authority) Zuständigkeit *f;*
 Gerichtsbezirk *m.*
jurist Jurist *m.*
jury *(court)* Geschworenenkol-
 legium *nt.*
just gerecht; angemessen; *(barely)*
 gerade; *(only)* nur.
justice *(fairness)* Gerechtigkeit *f;*
 (law) Recht *nt; (legal system)*
 Justizwesen *nt; (judge)* Richter
 m.
justification *(vindication)* Rechtfertigung *f; (authorization)*
 Berechtigung *f; (reason)* Begründung *f.*
justify *(to vindicate)* rechtfertigen;
 (to give reasons) begründen.

keen *(competition)* scharf; hart.
keep house wirtschaften.
keeping an account Kontoführung *f*.
keep ready bereithalten.
key Schlüssel *m*; *(index)* Kennziffer *f*; *(office machines)* Taste *f*.
keyboard Tastatur *f*.
key buyer Hauptkäufer *m*.
key country Schlüsselland *nt*.
key currency Leitwährung *f*.
key issue Hauptthema *nt*; Schlüsselfrage *f*.

key personnel Schlüsselpersonal *nt*.
key position Schlüsselstellung *f*.
key series Hauptserie *f*; Schlüsselserie *f*.
kit *(tools)* Werkzeugtasche *f*; Werkzeugausstattung *f*; *(unassembled components)* Zusammenbauausrüstung *f*.
knockdown *(machinery)* zerlegbar.
know-how praktisches Wissen *nt*; Fachwissen *nt*; Knowhow *nt*.
knowledgeable kenntnisreich.

lab Laboratorium *nt*; Labor *nt*.
label n Etikett *nt*; *(brand)* Marke *f*. v etikettieren; beschildern; kennzeichnen.
labeling Etikettieren *nt*; Kennzeichnen *nt*.
labor *(work)* Arbeit *f*; *(workforce)* Arbeitskräfte *pl*.
labor conflict Arbeitskonflikt *m*.
labor costs Arbeitskosten *pl*; Lohnkosten *pl*.
labor court Arbeitsgericht *nt*.
labor dispute Arbeitskampf *m*.
laborer ungelernter Arbeiter *m*.
labor-intensive arbeitsintensiv.
labor judge Arbeitsrichter *m*.
labor law Arbeitsrecht *nt*.

labor organization Gewerkschaftsorganisation *f*; Arbeiterorganisation *f*.
labor rate Lohntarif *m*.
labor relations Arbeitgeber/Arbeitnehmer-Verhältnis *nt*.
labor union Gewerkschaft *f*.
lack n Mangel *m*; Fehlen *nt*; Knappheit *f*. v fehlen.
lacking n Mangeln *nt*; a fehlend.
lag n Verzögerung *f*; Rückstand *m*. v zurückbleiben.
land n Land *nt*; Ländereien *pl*; Grundbesitz *m*. v landen.
landholding n Grundbesitz *m*. a Grund besitzend.
landlord Wirt *m*; Mietherr *m*; Verpächter *m*; Hauswirt *m*.

landowner Grundbesitzer *m*; Grundeigentümer *m*.

landownership Grundbesitzertum *nt*.

land register Grundbuch *nt*.

language Sprache *f*; *(manner of speech)* Redeweise *f*; *(terminology)* Terminologie *f*.

language barrier Sprachenschranke *f*.

lapse n Verfall *m*; *(contract)* Erlöschen *nt*; *(manners)* Entgleisung *f*. v verfallen; erlöschen.

large city Großstadt *f*.

large company Großfirma *f*.

large credit Großkredit *m*.

large order Großauftrag *m*.

large plant Großanlage *f*.

large-sized großformatig.

large truck Laster *m*.

last n *(shoe)* Leisten *m*. a *(in a series)* letzt; *(prior)* vorig. v *(to suffice)* reichen; *(to continue in time)* dauern.

late spät; *(tardy)* verspätet; *(deceased)* verstorben.

lateral Neben-; seitlich.

lateral transfer gleichwertiger Austausch *m*; Konzernüberweisung *f*.

lathe Drehbank *f*.

latitude Ausdehnung *f*; *(geog.)* Breite *f*; *(freedom of action)* Handlungsfreiheit *f*; Spielraum *m*.

launch n *(boat)* Barkasse *f*. v *(to put boat in the water)* zu Wasser *nt* lassen; *(first launching of a ship)* vom Stapel *m* lassen; *(enterprise)* gründen; *(product)* herausbringen; *(campaign)* starten.

launching Herausbringen *nt*; Starten *nt*; *(nautical)* Stapellauf *m*; Gründen *nt*.

lawful *(legal)* legal; *(in keeping with the law)* rechtsgemäß; *(legitimate)* rechtmäßig; *(valid in law)* rechtsgültig; *(judicial)* rechtlich.

lawmaker Gesetzgeber *m*.

law office Anwaltsfirma *f*.

law of instrumentality Mitwirkungsrecht *nt*.

law student Jurastudent *m*; Jurist *m*.

lawsuit Rechtsprozeß *m*; Klage *f*; Rechtsstreit *m*.

lawyer Rechtsanwalt *m*; Rechtsanwältin *f*; Jurist *m*.

layer n Schicht *f*. v schichten.

laying claim to Inanspruchnahme *f*.

layman Laie *m*; Nichtfachmann *m*.

layoff Entlassung *f*.

lay open aufdecken.

layout *(display)* Aufriß *m*; *(rough sketch)* Rohskizze *f*; *(arrangement)* Anordnung *f*; Anlage *f*.

lead¹ *(metal)* Blei *nt*.

lead² n *(hint)* Tip *m*. v führen.

leader Leiter *m*; Führer *m*; *(foreman)* Vorarbeiter *m*.

leader in the field Branchenführer *m*.

leadership Leitung *f*; Führung *f*.

leadership behavior Führungsverhalten *nt*.

leadership characteristic Führungseigenschaft *f*.

leadership figure Führungsfigur *f*.

leadership image Führungsimage *nt*.

leadership position Führungsposition *f*.

leadership quality Führungsqualität *f*.

leadership role führende Rolle *f*.

leadership stance Führungsverhalten *nt*.

leading führend; maßgeblich.

leading bank Konsortialführer *m*.

leading technology Spitzentechnik *f*.

leading underwriter Konsortialführer *m*.

lead product Spitzenprodukt *nt*.

leads and lags Schwankungen *pl* im Handel *m*.

leaflet Werbeprospekt *m*; Wurfblatt *nt*; Handzettel *m*.

leak n *(crack, hole)* Leck *nt*; *(information)* gezielte Indiskretion *f*. v durchsickern; durchsickern lassen.

leakage Schwund *m*.

lean a *(thin)* dünn; *(meager)* mager; *(profits)* dürftig; kümmerlich. v *(to support)* lehnen; *(to incline)* schief stehen; *(fig.)* neigen; tendieren.

learning opportunity Bildungsangebot *nt*.

lease n *(leasing to someone)* Verpachtung *f*; *(lease revenue)* Miete *f*; *(lease document)* Mietvertrag *m*. v *(to lease to someone)* verpachten; *(to rent to someone)* vermieten; *(to lease from someone)* pachten; *(to rent from someone)* mieten; *(car)* leasen.

leasehold *(leased real estate)* Pachtgrundstück *nt*; *(leasing from someone)* Pachtung *f*.

leasing Leasing *nt*.

leasing business Leasinggeschäft *nt*.

leasing charge Leasingmiete *f*.

leasing company Leasinggesellschaft *f*.

leasing rate Leasingrate *f*.

leave n *(vacation)* Urlaub *m*; *(permission)* Erlaubnis *f*. v verlassen; *(job, service)* ausscheiden.

leave behind zurücklassen; hinterlassen; *(to outdistance)* abhängen.

lecture n Vorlesung *f*; Vortrag *m*. v Vorlesung *f* halten; vortragen.

ledger Hauptbuch *nt*; Register *nt*.

leeway Spielraum *m*; Bewegungsfreiheit *f*.

legal *(lawful)* gesetzlich; *(in accordance with law)* gesetzmäßig; rechtsgemäß; juristisch; *(legitimate)* rechtmäßig; *(valid in law)* rechtskräftig; *(judicial)* rechtlich.

legal conception Rechtsauffassung *f*.

legal force Rechtskraft *f*.

legal form Rechtsform *f*.

legal residence gesetzliches Domizil *nt*.

legal rule Rechtsvorschrift *f*.

legal services juristische Dienstleistungen *pl*; Anwaltsdienste *pl*.

legal situation Rechtslage *f*.

legal status Rechtsstatus *m*.

legislation Gesetzgebung *f*.

legislative gesetzgebend.

legislative proposal Gesetzesvorlage *f*.

legislative provision Rechtsvorschrift *f*.

legislator Gesetzgeber *m*.

legitimate legitim; *(lawful)* rechtlich; gesetzlich; *(according to law)* rechtmäßig; gesetzmäßig; *(genuine)* echt.

leisure Freizeit *f*; Muße *f*.

lend leihen; verleihen; ausleihen.

lender Ausleiher *m*; Verleiher *m*; *(creditor)* Kreditgeber *m*.

lending Ausleihung *f*; *(granting credit)* Kreditgewährung *f*; Darlehensgewährung *f*.

lending institution Kreditanstalt *f*.

lending law Kreditwesengesetz *nt*.
lending officer Kreditsachbearbeiter *m*.
lend on beleihen.
lessee Pächter *m*; *(renter)* Mieter *m*.
lessor Verpächter *m*; Vermieter *m*.
let *(to allow)* lassen; zulassen; *(to rent)* vermieten.
letter Brief *m*; Schreiben *nt*; *(alphabet)* Buchstabe *m*.
letter of credit Kreditbrief *m*; Akkreditiv *nt*.
letter of intent Bereitschaftserklärung *f*; Absichtserklärung *f*.
level n Niveau *nt*; *(height)* Höhe *f*. a *(flat)* flach; *(straight)* gerade.
level of capacity Kapazitätsgrad *m*; Auslastungsgrad *m*.
level of employment Beschäftigungsgrad *m*.
level of familiarity Bekanntheitsgrad *m*.
level of investment Investitionsquote *f*.
level of jurisdiction Instanz *f*.
leverage *(mech.)* Hebelkraft *f*; *(fig.)* Einfluß *m*; *(capital)* Verhältnis *nt* von Schulden *pl* zu Wert *m* des Grundkapitals *nt*.
leveraged verschuldet.
levy n *(collection)* Eintreibung *f*; *(tax)* Steuererhebung *f*; *(troops)* Aushebung *f*. v erheben; eintreiben.
liabilities *(bookkeeping)* Passiva *pl*; Schulden *pl*.
liability *(burden)* Bürde *f*; *(debt)* Verschuldung *f*; *(obligation)* Verpflichtung *f*; *(debt)* Verbindlichkeit *f*; Obligo *nt*; *(bookkeeping)* Passivposten *m*; *(guarantee)* Haftung *f*; Haftpflicht *f*.

liability case Schadensfall *m*.
liability for risk Risikohaftung *f*.
liable haftbar; haftpflichtig; verpflichtet; verantwortlich.
liaison Verbindung *f*; Zusammenarbeit *f*; Kontakt *m*.
libel Anschwärzung *f*; Verleumdung *f*.
liberal liberal; *(generous)* freigebig; großzügig.
liberalization Liberalisierung *f*; *(loosening)* Lockerung *f*.
liberate befreien; *(capital)* flüssig machen.
license n Lizenz *f*; *(land)* Benutzungsrecht *nt*; *(patent law)* Patentausnutzung *f*; *(driving)* Führerschein *m*; *(sale)* Verkaufsrecht *nt*; *(trade)* Zulassung *f*; Konzession *f*; *(license to engage in a trade)* Gewerbeschein *m*. v *(to grant, approve)* genehmigen; *(to permit)* erlauben; *(to admit)* zulassen.
license agreement Lizenzabkommen *nt*.
license contract Lizenzvertrag *m*.
licensed lizensiert; verbrieft.
licensee Lizenzinhaber *m*; Konzessionsinhaber *m*.
license fee Lizenzgebühr *f*.
license tax Gewerbesteuer *f*.
lien Zurückbehaltungsrecht *nt*; Pfandrecht *nt*.
life expectancy Lebenserwartung *f*.
lifehold Nießbrauch *m*.
life insurance Lebensversicherung *f*.
life insurer Lebensversicherer *m*; Lebensversicherungsgesellschaft *f*.
life span Lebensdauer *f*.
lifestyle Lebensführung *f*.

lifetime demand Lebensbedarf *m.*
lifetime employment lebenslängliche Anstellung *f.*
lift *(weight)* heben; *(ban)* aufheben;
beseitigen; *(to raise)* anheben.
limit n *(border, extent)* Grenze *f;*
(barrier) Schranke *f; (line)* Linie *f;*
Limit *nt; (top amount)* Höchstbetrag *m.* v *(to delimit)* begrenzen;
(to restrict) einschränken;
beschränken; limitieren.
limitation Beschränkung *f;* Einschränkung *f;* Begrenzung *f.*
limitation of credit Kreditbeschränkung *f.*
limited line retailer Fachhändler
m.
limited partnership Kommanditgesellschaft *f.*
limited partnership interest
Kommanditeinlage *f.*
limited price Limitkurs *m.*
line Linie *f; (text)* Zeile *f; (clothes)*
Leine *f; (fishing)* Schnur *f; (business)* Gewerbezweig *m; (product)*
Warengattung *f;* Sparte *f; (assortment)* Sortiment *nt.*
line of credit Kreditlinie *f.*
line of export goods Exportsortiment *nt.*
line of products Produktgruppe *f;*
Erzeugnisgruppe *f.*
line supervisor Spartenchef *m.*
line total Zeilensumme *f.*
link n *(chain)* Glied *nt; (connection)* Anknüpfungspunkt *m;* Verbindung *f; (capital)* Kapitalverflechtung *f.* v verbinden.
liquid n Flüssigkeit *f.* a *(capital)*
flüssig; sofort realisierbar; liquide.
liquidatability Realisierbarkeit *f.*
liquidatable realisierbar.
liquidate *(business)* abrechnen;

abwickeln; *(to dissolve)* auflösen;
(to balance) saldieren; *(to amortize, pay off)* tilgen.
liquidation Liquidierung *f;* Auflösung *f; (debt)* Abtragung *f;* Tilgung *f.*
liquidation value Abwicklungswert *m;* Liquidationswert *m.*
liquidity *(money)* Geldflüssigkeit *f;*
Liquidität *f.*
liquidity assistance Liquiditätshilfe *f.*
liquidity position Liquiditätslage
f.
liquidity problem Liquiditätsproblem *nt.*
liquidity squeeze Liquiditätsdruck
m.
list n Liste *f;* Register *nt; (direc-
tory)* Verzeichnis *nt.* v *(stock)*
notieren; aufstellen; auflisten.
listed on the stock exchange
börsengängig.
listing on the stock exchange
Börseneinführung *f.*
list of precedence Rangliste *f.*
list price Listenpreis *m;* Katalogpreis *m.*
literature *(product information)*
Broschüren *pl;* Prospekte *pl.*
litigation Rechtsstreit *m;* Prozeß
m.
livelihood Lebensunterhalt *m;*
Existenzgrundlage *f;* Auskommen
nt.
living n *(livelihood)* Lebensunterhalt *m;* Existenz *f.* a *(alive)*
lebend; lebendig.
living conditions Lebensbedingungen *pl;* Lebensverhältnisse *pl.*
living standard Lebensstandard *m.*
load n Fuhre *f;* Ladung *f; (freight)*
Fracht *f; (burden)* Last *f.* v bela-

den; aufladen; *(to adulterate)* verfälschen; *(to encumber)* belasten.

loan n Anleihe *f*; Darlehen *nt*.
v leihen; verleihen; ausleihen.

loan account Kreditkonto *nt*.

loan against borrower's note Schuldscheindarlehen *nt*.

loan agreement Kreditvertrag *m*; Darlehensvertrag *m*.

loan amount Kreditsumme *f*; Anleihebetrag *m*.

loan approval Kreditgewährung *f*.

loan association Darlehenskasse *f*.

loan bank Kreditanstalt *f*.

loan business Debitorengeschäft *nt*.

loan committee Kreditausschuß *m*.

loan contract Darlehensvertrag *m*.

loan debt Darlehensschuld *f*.

loan default Kreditausfall *m*.

loan demand Kreditnachfrage *f*.

loan guarantee Anleihegarantie *f*.

loan insurance Kreditversicherung *f*.

loan on overdraft Kontokorrentkredit *m*.

loan payable Darlehensschuld *f*.

loan proceeds Anleiheerlös *m*.

loan program Darlehensprogramm *nt*.

loan repayment Kreditrückzahlung *f*.

loan term Darlehenslaufzeit *f*.

loan terms Rückzahlungsbedingungen *pl*.

lobby *(vestibule)* Vorhalle *f*; *(interest group)* Interessengruppe *f*; Machtgruppe *f*; Interessenverband *m*.

lobbyist Interessenvertreter *m*; Lobbyist *m*.

local n *(trade union)* Ortsverein *m*;

(train) Nahzug *m*; Vorortszug *m*; *(inhabitant)* Ortsbewohner *m*.
a örtlich; kommunal; heimisch.

local bank Lokalbank *f*.

local custom Ortsgebrauch *m*.

local government Lokalbehörde *f*; Gemeindeverwaltung *f*.

locality Ort *m*; Lokalität *f*; *(location)* Lage *f*.

local market heimischer Markt *m*.

local politician Kommunalpolitiker *m*.

locate örtlich festlegen; sich niederlassen; *(find)* finden.

location Niederlassung *f*; Standort *m*.

lockout Aussperrung *f*.

lock out aussperren.

lombard lending rate Lombardsatz *m*.

long-run langfristig; auf lange Sicht *f*.

long-term langfristig; auf lange Sicht *f*.

long term lange Sicht *f*.

long-term use Dauernutzung *f*.

loophole Hintertürchen *nt*; Ausweg *m*; *(law)* Gesetzeslücke *f*; *(taxes)* Schlupfloch *nt*.

lopsided schief; *(argument)* einseitig.

lose verlieren; einbüßen; zusetzen.

loser Verlierer *m*; Verlustträger *m*.

losing verlustbringend.

loss Verlust *m*; *(disadvantage)* Nachteil *m*; *(damage)* Schaden *m*.

loss accounting Verlustrechnung *f*.

loss area Verlustzone *f*.

loss generating verlustbringend.

loss in sales Umsatzeinbuße *f*; Umsatzverlust *m*.

loss of efficiency Effizienzverlust *m*.

loss of job Arbeitsplatzverlust *m*.
loss of pay Lohnausfall *m*.
loss of production Produktionsausfall *m*.
loss of revenue Einnahmeausfall
m.
loss on interest Zinsverlust *m*.
lot Teil *m*; Anteil *m*; *(real estate)*
Grundstück *nt*; *(goods)* Warenposten *m*; Lieferposten *m*; *(quantity)* Menge *f*.
low n *(stock market)* Tiefstand *m*.
a niedrig.
lower senken; herabmindern.
lowest cost Niedrigstkosten *pl*.

lowest value Niedrigstwert *m*.
low-interest period Niedrigzinsphase *f*.
low price Niedrigpreis *m*; Billigpreis *m*.
low-price competitor Billigkonkurrent *m*.
low-priced billig.
low rate Billigtarif *m*.
lucrative lukrativ; *(profitable)*
ertragbringend; gewinnbringend;
einbringlich; einträglich.
luxury Luxus *m*; *(display)*
Aufwand *m*.

machine n Maschine *f*; *(apparatus)*
Apparat *m*; *(device)* Vorrichtung *f*;
(mechanism) Mechanismus *m*.
v maschinell bearbeiten.
machine life Nutzungsdauer *f*
einer Maschine *f*.
machinery Maschinenanlage *f*;
maschinelle Anlage *f*.
machine tool Werkzeugmaschine *f*.
machine works Maschinenfabrik *f*.
macroculture Gesamtkultur *f*.
macroeconomic gesamtwirt-
schaftlich; makroökonomisch.
macroeconomic policy gesamt-
wirtschaftliche Politik *f*.
macroeconomics Makroökonomie
f.
macroeconomist Gesamtwirt-
schaftler *m*.
made gemacht; *(manufactured)*
hergestellt; angefertigt.

magazine Magazin *nt*; *(periodical)*
Zeitschrift *f*.
magisterial richterlich.
magnate Magnat *m*; *(industry)*
Großindustrielle *m/f*.
mail n Post *f*; *(items)* Postsachen *pl*;
(shipment) Postsendung *f*. v mit
der Post *f* senden; *(to post)* ein-
stecken.
mailing list Postversandliste *f*;
Adressenkartei *f*.
mailing list adressee *(customer)*
Versandkunde *m*; Versandkundin
f; Werbeadressat *m*.
mailman Briefträger *m*.
mail-order firm Versandhaus *nt*.
mail-order trade Versandhandel *m*.
main Haupt-; hauptsächlich;
wichtigst-.
main cashier's window Hauptkasse *f*.

main competitor Hauptkonkurrent *m*.

main computer Zentralrechner *m*.

mainframe *(computer)* Schrank *m*;
Systemzentraleinheit *f*; Internspei-
cher *m* eines Computersystems *nt*;
großes oder mittelgroßes Comput-
ersystem *nt*.

mainframe computer Zentralrechner *m*; Superrechner *m*.

mainland Festland *nt*; Kontinent
m.

main profession Hauptberuf *m*.

mainstay Hauptstütze *f*.

maintain *(equipment)* warten;
instandhalten; *(office, facility)*
unterhalten; *(price, quality)* aufrechterhalten; *(delivery, production schedule)* erfüllen; *(argument)*
bestehen auf; *(relationship)* aufrechterhalten.

maintenance *(servicing)* Wartung
f; *(equipment)* Instandhaltung *f*;
Aufrechterhaltung *f*.

major n *(military)* Major *m*.
a Haupt-; *(significant)* bedeutend;
(of age) mündig.

major growth area Hauptwachstumsgebiet *nt*.

major industry bedeutender Industriezweig *m*.

majority Mehrheit *f*; *(legal adult-
hood)* Volljährigkeit *f*.

majority interest Mehrheitsbeteiligung *f*.

majority ownership Mehrheitsbesitz *m*.

majority stockholder Mehrheitsaktionär *m*.

major market bedeutender Markt
m; wichtiger Markt *m*.

major product Hauptprodukt *nt*;
wichtiges Produkt *nt*.

major supplier Hauptlieferant *m*;
wichtiger Lieferant *m*.

make n *(product)* Erzeugnis *nt*;
(brand) Fabrikat *nt*; Marke *f*;
Warenzeichen *nt*. v machen; *(to
manufacture)* herstellen.

make a bid ein Angebot *nt*
machen; *(to apply)* sich bewerben.

make additional payment Geld
nachschießen.

make an effort sich bemühen.

make more expensive verteuern.

make public veröffentlichen; publizieren; herausstellen.

maker Hersteller *m*; Verfertiger *m*;
Fabrikant *m*.

make up *(to catch up)* nachholen;
(to apply cosmetics) schminken.

malfunction n Nichtfunktionieren
nt; *(car, machine)* Panne *f*. v nicht
funktionieren; eine Panne *f* erleiden.

mall *(shopping)* Einkaufszentrum
nt; Ladenstraße *f*.

mammoth n Mammuth *nt*.
a Riesen-; riesig.

mammoth company Riesenunternehmen *nt*.

manage *(to administer)* verwalten; *(to lead)* führen; leiten; *(to
operate, to run)* bewirtschaf-
ten.

manageable *(object)* handlich;
(task) leicht zu bewältigen.

management Vorstand *m*;
Geschäftsleitung *f*; Geschäftsführung *f*; Management *nt*;
(administration) Verwaltung *f*;
(handling) Handhabung *f*.

management capacity Führungs-
kapazität *f*.

management career Führungslaufbahn *f*.

management committee Direktorium *nt*.

management consultant Unternehmensberater *m*; Management Consulter *m*; Betriebsberater *m*; Industrieberater *m*.

management contract Vorstandsvertrag *m*.

management control Führungskontrolle *f*; Unternehmenskontrolle *f*.

management decision Entscheidung *f* der Geschäftsleitung *f*.

management function Managementfunktion *f*.

management functions Führungstätigkeit *f*.

management personnel Führungspersonal *nt*.

management process Führungsprozeß *m*.

management seminar Führungsseminar *nt*.

management skills Führungsfähigkeiten *pl*.

management structure Führungsstruktur *f*.

management style Führungsstil *m*.

management system Verwaltungssystem *nt*.

management team Führungsgruppe *f*; Verwaltungskörper *m*.

management trainees Führungsnachwuchs *m*.

manager Manager *m*; *(administrator)* Verwalter *m*; *(leader, head)* Leiter *m*; *(supervisor)* Vorsteher *m*.

managerial führend; geschäftsleitend; direktorial.

managerial area of responsibility Direktionsbereich *m*.

managerial problem Führungsproblem *nt*.

managing leitend; geschäftsführend; verwaltend.

managing director geschäftsführendes Vorstandsmitglied *nt*; Generaldirektor *m*; Betriebsführer *m*.

managing directorship Vorstandsvorsitz *m*.

mandate n Mandat *nt*; *(authority)* Vollmacht *f*. v einem Mandat *nt* unterstellen.

mandatory obligatorisch; zwingend; zwangsläufig; verbindlich.

mandatory accounting Buchführungspflicht *f*.

maneuver n Manöver *nt*; *(move)* Schachzug *m*; *(trick)* Kunstgriff *m*; *(wile)* Finte *f*. v manövrieren.

man hour Arbeitsstunde *f*.

manifest n öffentliche Erklärung *f*; Manifest *nt*; *(customs)* Zolldeklaration *f*; *(bill of lading)* Ladeverzeichnis *nt*; Warenverzeichnis *nt*. a offenkundig; augenscheinlich. v *(a cargo)* eine Ladung *f* anmelden.

man in charge Hauptverantwortliche *m/f*; Chef *m*.

manipulable manipulierbar; *(capable of being influenced)* beeinflußbar.

manipulate manipulieren; *(to influence)* beeinflussen.

manipulation Manipulation *f*; *(mech.)* Handhabung *f*.

manipulator Manipulator *m*; *(stocks)* Kursbeeinflusser *m*.

man-made künstlich; aus Kunststoff *m* hergestellt.

manpower menschliche Arbeitskraft *f*; *(personnel)* Personalbestand *m*.

manual n Handbuch *nt*; *(rules)* Vorschriftenbuch *nt*; *(instructions)*

Instruktionsbuch *nt.* **a** *(labor)* körperlich.

manual operation *(machine)* Handbedienung *f.*

manual training Werkunterricht *m.*

manual worker Handarbeiter *m.*

manufacture n Herstellung *f*; *(processing)* Verarbeitung *f*; Fabrikation *f*; Verfertigung *f*; Anfertigung *f*; Produktion *f.* v herstellen; anfertigen; produzieren.

manufactured article Fertigprodukt *nt.*

manufacturer Fabrikant *m*; *(maker)* Hersteller *m*; *(producer)* Produzent *m*; *(industrialist)* Industrielle *m/f*; *(tradesman, craftsman)* Gewerbetreibende *m/f.*

manufacturing Fertigung *f.*

manufacturing capability Fabrikationsfähigkeit *f*; Produktionsfähigkeit *f.*

manufacturing capacity Fabrikationskapazität *f*; Produktionskapazität *f.*

manufacturing company Produktionsgesellschaft *f*; Fabrikationsbetrieb *m*; Herstellungsfirma *f.*

manufacturing cost Anfertigungskosten *pl*; Fabrikationskosten *pl*; Herstellungskosten *pl.*

manufacturing country Erzeugerland *nt.*

manufacturing facility Produktionsanlage *f*; Herstellungsanlage *f.*

manufacturing operation Produktionsvorgang *m.*

manufacturing plant Industrieanlage *f*; Industriebetrieb *m.*

manufacturing process Herstellungsprozeß *m*; Fabrikationsprozeß *m*; Produktionsvorgang *m*; Fertigungsverfahren *nt.*

manufacturing program Produktionsprogramm *nt.*

manufacturing schedule Fertigungsplan *m*; Produktionsplan *m.*

map n Landkarte *f*; *(projection)* Meßtischblatt *nt.* v kartographisch aufnehmen.

margin Marge *f*; Differenz *f*; Spielraum *m*; *(earnings)* Verdienstspanne *f*; *(profit)* Gewinnspanne *f*; *(trade)* Handelsspanne *f.*

marginal knapp; kaum; am Rande *m.*

marginal cost Kostendifferenz *f.*

marginal cost curve Grenzkostenkurve *f.*

marginal costs Grenzkosten *pl.*

marginal product Grenzprodukt *nt.*

marginal value Grenzwert *m.*

margin deposit *(securities)* Einschußzahlung *f.*

margin requirements Einschußbedarf *m* im Effektendifferenzgeschäft *nt*; Mindesteinzahlungsbetrag *m.*

mark n Kennzeichen *nt*; *(sign)* Zeichen *nt*; *(characteristic)* Merkmal *nt*; *(stamp)* Stempel *m*; *(brand)* Marke *f*; *(currency)* Mark *f.* v markieren; *(to single out)* auszeichnen.

markdown Preisherabsetzung *f.*

market n Markt *m*; *(buyer category)* Käuferkategorie *f*; *(economy)* Wirtschaftslage *f*; *(market trend)* Konjunktur *f.* v vermarkten.

marketability Absatzfähigkeit *f*; Marktgängigkeit *f*; Gangbarkeit *f*; *(stocks)* Börsenfähigkeit *f.*

marketable marktfähig; marktgängig; absatzfähig; *(salable)* verkäuflich; umsetzbar; realisierbar.

market access   Marktzugang *m*.

market action   Marktgeschehen *nt*.

market analysis   Marktanalyse *f*; Marktuntersuchung *f*; Konjunkturdiagnose *f*.

market area   Absatzgebiet *nt*; Marktgebiet *nt*.

market balance   Marktgleichgewicht *nt*.

market condition   *(situation)* Marktlage *f*; Konjunkturlage *f*; *(prerequisite)* Marktbedingung *f*; *(fact)* Marktgegebenheit *f*.

market data   Marktdaten *pl*.

market demand   Marktnachfrage *f*.

market development   Marktentwicklung *f*; Absatzentwicklung *f*.

market dominance   Marktbeherrschung *f*.

market domination   Marktbeherrschung *f*.

market economist   Marktwirtschaftler *m*.

market economy   Marktwirtschaft *f*.

marketer   Absatzfachmann *m*.

market forces   Marktkräfte *pl*; *(effects)* Markteinwirkungen *pl*.

market forecast   Konjunkturprognose *f*.

market gap   Marktlücke *f*.

marketing   Marketing *nt*; *(theory)* Lehre *f* vom Warenabsatz *m*; *(economy)* Absatzwirtschaft *f*; *(planning)* Absatzplanung *f*; *(creating a market)* Marktschaffung *f*; *(goods, services)* Vermarktung *f*; *(sales)* Absatz *m*; Vertrieb *m*.

marketing activity   Absatztätigkeit *f*.

marketing area   Absatzbereich *m*; Absatzgebiet *nt*.

marketing audit   Vertriebsanalyse *f*; marktpolitische Unternehmensanalyse *f*.

marketing base   Absatzbasis *f*; Vertriebsbasis *f*.

marketing boss   Marketingchef *m*.

marketing channel   Absatzweg *m*.

marketing department   Marketingabteilung *f*.

marketing director   Vertriebschef *m*.

marketing expense   Vertriebskosten *pl*.

marketing expert   Marketingfachmann *m*.

marketing formula   Vertriebsformel *f*; Absatzformel *f*.

marketing function   absatzwirtschaftliche Funktion *f*.

marketing gimmick   Absatzgag *m*.

marketing management   Vertriebsleitung *f*.

marketing manager   Vertriebsleiter *m*; Marketingchef *m*.

marketing mix   *(media)* diversifizierte Absatzplanung *f*; *(products)* Warenangebotsmischung *f*; Warenpalette *f*.

marketing plan   Absatzplan *m*.

marketing policy   Vertriebspolitik *f*.

marketing potential   Absatzpotential *nt*; Absatzchancen *pl*.

marketing staff   Vertriebsstab *m*.

marketing strategist   Marketingstratege *m*; Marketingstrategin *f*.

marketing strategy   Marktstrategie *f*; Absatzstrategie *f*.

marketing survey   Absatzanalyse *f*.

marketing system   Vertriebssystem *nt*.

marketing test   Marketingtest *m*.

market leader *(firm)* Marktführer *m; (product)* Spitzenreiter *m.*

market mechanism Marktmechanismus *m.*

market objective Marktziel *nt;* Absatzziel *nt.*

market opportunity Absatzmöglichkeit *f;* Absatzgelegenheit *f;* Marktchance *f.*

market-oriented marktorientiert.

market outlook Konjunkturaussichten *pl.*

market pattern Marktgestaltung *f;* Marktstruktur *f.*

market performance Marktleistung *f.*

marketplace Markt *m.*

market position Marktposition *f;* Marktlage *f; (sales)* Absatzposition *f.*

market price Marktpreis *m; (replacement)* Wiederbeschaffungswert *m;* Verkaufskurs *m;* Verkaufspreis *m.*

market principle Marktprinzip *nt.*

market profit Kursgewinn *m.*

market rate Marktpreis *m;* Diskontsatz *m;* Tageskurs *m.*

market rate of interest Marktzinssatz *m.*

market reach Marktbreite *f.*

market-ready marktreif.

market regulation Marktregulierung *f; (rule)* Marktverordnung *f.*

market report Konjunkturbericht *m;* Geschäftsbericht *m.*

market research Marktforschung *f;* Marktuntersuchung *f; (sales)* Absatzforschung *f.*

market researcher Marktforscher *m.*

market scope Marktumfang *m.*

market segment Marktsegment *nt;* Marktteil *m; (customers)* Kundensegment *nt.*

market share Marktanteil *m.*

market size Marktgröße *f.*

market spectrum Marktbreite *f.*

market strength Marktstärke *f.*

market test Markttest *m;* Markterkundung *f.*

market upturn Marktaufschwung *m.*

market value Marktwert *m;* Gemeinwert *m;* Kaufwert *m; (replacement)* Wiederbeschaffungswert *m;* Handelswert *m; (stocks)* Kurswert *m.*

market volume Marktvolumen *nt.*

marking Kennzeichnen *nt;* Markieren *nt.*

markup Aufschlag *m.*

mark up heraufsetzen.

mass n Masse *f;* Anhäufung *f; (church service)* Messe *f.* v anhäufen.

mass consumption Massenkonsum *m.*

mass dismissal Massenentlassung *f.*

massive massiv; *(bulky)* massig; *(very big)* sehr groß; *(heavy)* schwer; *(mighty)* mächtig.

mass layoff Massenentlassung *f;* Entlassungswelle *f.*

mass market Massenmarkt *m.*

mass media Massenmedien *pl.*

mass produce fabrikmäßig herstellen; in Massen *pl* produzieren.

mass product Massenprodukt *nt.*

mass production Massenproduktion *f;* Massenfertigung *f.*

mast Mast *m.*

master n Meister *m; (proprietor)* Eigentümer *m;* Besitzer *m; (head of household)* Hausherr *m;*

(degree) Magister *m.* **v** *(a skill)* meistern; *(a subject)* beherrschen; *(a problem)* bewältigen.

master wage agreement   Manteltarif *m.*

master wage agreement contract Manteltarifvertrag *m.*

mastery   Meistern *nt*; *(rule)* Herrschaft *f*; *(power)* Macht *f*; *(preeminence)* Vorrang *m*; *(ascendancy)* Oberhand *f*; *(superiority)* Überlegenheit *f*; *(control)* Beherrschung *f.*

match   n *(complementarity)* Gegenstück *nt*; *(sameness)* Gleiche *nt*; *(equality)* Ebenbürtige *nt*; *(kitchen match)* Streichholz *nt*; *(marriage)* eheliche Verbindung *f.* **v** *(to make objects match)* passend machen; *(to compare)* vergleichen; *(to be matching)* passend sein.

material   n Material *nt*; *(raw material)* Werkstoff *m*; *(substance)* Substanz *f.* **a** materiell; real.

material cost   Materialkosten *pl*; Sachkosten *pl.*

materialist   materialistisch.

materials handling   Materialtransport *m.*

mathematical   mathematisch; rechnerisch.

matrix   Matrize *f*; Mater *f.*

matrix management   Matrixführung *f.*

matter   Materie *f*; *(material)* Stoff *m*; Substanz *f*; *(thing)* Sache *f*; *(affair)* Angelegenheit *f.*

mature   a reif; *(financial instrument)* fällig; abgelaufen; zahlbar. **v** fällig werden.

mature industry   vollentwickelte Industrie *f.*

maturity   Reife *f*; *(bond)* Fälligkeit *f*; *(time of payment)* Verfallzeit *f*; *(expiration date)* Ablauftermin *m*; Termin *m.*

maximization   Maximierung *f.*

maximize   maximieren; *(to aggrandize)* möglichst groß darstellen; *(to raise to highest degree)* auf ein Höchstmaß *nt* bringen.

maximum   n Maximum *nt*; *(ceiling)* Höchstgrenze *f.* **a** Höchst-; Größt-; maximal.

maximum amount   *(money)* Höchstbetrag *m.*

maximum period of time   Höchstdauer *f.*

maximum proceeds   Höchstertrag *m.*

maximum value   Höchstwert *m.*

mean   n *(average value)* Durchschnittswert *m*; Mittelwert *m.* **a** *(average)* durchschnittlich; *(petty)* kleinlich; *(shabby)* schäbig; *(base)* gemein. **v** meinen; *(to signify)* bedeuten.

mean inflation rate   Durchschnittsinflationsrate *f.*

meaning   *(significance)* Bedeutung *f*; *(sense)* Sinn *m.*

meaningless   *(insignificant)* bedeutungslos; *(senseless)* sinnlos.

means of promotion   Werbemittel *nt.*

means of subsistence   Unterhaltsmittel *nt.*

mean value   Durchschnittswert *m*; Mittelwert *m.*

measurability   Meßbarkeit *f.*

measurable   meßbar; absehbar.

measure   n Maß *nt*; *(instrument)* Meßinstrument *nt*; *(extent)* Ausmaß *nt*; *(circumference)* Umfang *m*; *(degree)* Grad *m*; *(step, action)* Maßnahme *f*; *(expedient)*

Maßregel *f*. v messen; *(to appor-tion)* bemessen.

measurement   Messung *f*; *(size)* Maß *nt*.

mechanical   mechanisch; maschinell.

mechanical engineer   Maschinenbauer *m*.

mechanical engineering   Maschinenbau *m*.

mechanics   Mechanik *f*.

mechanism   Mechanismus *m*; Triebwerk *nt*.

mechanization   Mechanisierung *f*; Motorisierung *f*.

media   Medien *pl*.

media law   Mediengesetz *nt*.

media magazine   Medienmagazin *nt*.

median   n Halbwert *m*. a mittelwertig.

mediation attempt   Vermittlungsversuch *m*.

mediator   Vermittler *m*; Mittler *m*.

medium   Medium *nt*; *(means)* Mittel *nt*; *(advertising)* Werbeträger *m*.

medium of exchange   Valuta *f*; Tauschmittel *nt*; Zahlungsmittel *nt*.

medium-size enterprise   Mittelbetrieb *m*.

medium-term   längerfristig; mittelfristig.

meet   n Treffen *nt*. v treffen; *(by chance)* begegnen; *(by introduction)* kennenlernen; *(financial obligation)* begleichen; *(criteria)* erfüllen; *(price)* gleichkommen; *(responsibility)* erfüllen; *(demand)* decken; *(limitation)* einhalten; *(to hold a meeting)* tagen.

meeting   Zusammenkunft *f*; Zu-sammentreffen *nt*; *(interview, briefing)* Besprechung *f*; *(consultation)* Beratung *f*; *(session)* Sitzung *f*; *(convention)* Versammlung *f*; Konferenz *f*; Tagung *f*.

member   *(association)* Mitglied *nt*; *(family)* Angehörige *m/f*.

member country   Mitgliedsland *nt*.

member of a banking syndicate   Konsortialbank *f*.

membership   Mitgliedschaft *f*; Zugehörigkeit *f*.

membership promotion   Mitgliederwerbung *f*.

membership register   Mitgliedsbuch *nt*.

membership roster   Mitgliederliste *f*; Mitgliedsbuch *nt*.

memorandum   Memorandum *nt*; *(note)* Notiz *f*; *(notation)* Vermerk *m*.

memorandum bill   Schuldwechsel *m*.

mention   n Erwähnung *f*. v erwähnen.

mercantile   handeltreibend; kaufmännisch; geschäftlich.

mercantile trade   Warenhandel *m*.

mercantilism   Merkantilismus *m*.

merchandise   Ware *f*; Handelsgut *nt*.

merchandise account   Warenkonto *nt*.

merchandise appeal   Kaufanreiz *m*.

merchandise export   Warenexport *m*.

merchandise item   Wareneinheit *f*.

merchandise market   Gütermarkt *m*.

merchandisers' fair   Verkaufsmesse *f*.

merchandise trade   Güterhandel *m*.

merchandise traffic Warenverkehr *m.*

merchandise value Warenwert *m.*

merchandising Steuerung *f* von Vertrieb *m* und Verkauf *m*; Absatzvorbereitung *f* durch Vertriebsplanung *f*; Absatzförderung *f*; Warenhandel *m.*

merchandising concern Handelsunternehmen *nt.*

merchandising scheme Verkaufsplan *m.*

merchant Kaufmann *m*; Kauffrau *f*; *(dealer)* Händler *m*; *(trader)* Handelsherr *m.*

merchant bank Handelsbank *f.*

merchant banking Remboursgeschäft *nt.*

merchant fleet Kauffahrteiflotte *f*; Handelsflotte *f.*

merchants Kaufleute *pl.*

merge zusammenschließen; verschmelzen; fusionieren.

merger Fusion *f*; Firmenzusammenschluß *m*; Verschmelzung *f*; Zusammenlegung *f.*

merger case Fusionsfall *m.*

merit n Verdienst *nt*; Vorzug *m*; Wert *m.* v *(deserve)* verdienen.

meritocracy Leistungsgesellschaft *f.*

mesh n Netzwerk *nt.* v ineinandergreifen; *(to cooperate)* zusammenarbeiten.

message Nachricht *f*; Botschaft *f*; *(advertising)* Werbeaussage *f.*

messenger Bote *m*; *(runner)* Läufer *m*; *(bank)* Kassenbote *m.*

metal Metall *nt.*

metal industry Metallindustrie *f.*

meter n Meter *m*; *(measuring device)* Meßinstrument *nt*; *(counter)* Zähler *m.* v messen; abzählen; *(mail)* freimachen.

method Methode *f*; Verfahren *nt*; Verfahrensweise *f.*

method of computation Berechnungsmethode *f.*

method of payment Zahlungsweise *f.*

method of production Produktionsweise *f.*

metric metrisch.

metropolis Großstadt *f.*

metropolitan großstädtisch.

microchip Mikrochip *m.*

microcomputer Mikrocomputer *m*; Kleincomputer *m*; Mikrorechner *m.*

microculture Mikrokultur *f*; Kleinstkultur *f.*

microeconomics Mikroökonomie *f.*

microelectronics Mikroelektronik *f.*

microfunction Mikrofunktion *f.*

microprocessor Mikroprozessor *m.*

microstructure Mikrostruktur *f.*

microtechnology Mikrotechnologie *f.*

microwave Mikrowelle *f.*

middle n Mitte *f.* a Mittel-; mittlere.

middle class Mittelstand *m.*

middle-class mittelständisch.

middleman Mittelsmann *m*; *(jobber)* Zwischenhändler *m*; *(broker)* Makler *m*; *(intermediary)* Vermittler *m*; *(reseller)* Wiederverkäufer *m.*

middle of the month Monatsmitte *f.*

midsection Mittelsektion *f*; Mittelteil *m/nt.*

midsize mittelgroß.

midyear Jahresmitte *f*; Halbjahrespunkt *m.*

midyear result Halbjahresergebnis *nt.*

militant militant; kämpferisch; aggressiv.

military n Militär *nt.* a Militär-; militärisch.

millionaire Millionär *m.*

mine n *(mining)* Zeche *f;* Bergwerk *nt; (explosive)* Mine *f.* v fördern; abbauen; *(mining)* minieren; *(explosives)* verminen.

miner Bergmann *m.*

mineral n Mineral *nt.* a mineralisch.

miners Bergleute *pl.*

minicomputer Minicomputer *m;* mittelgroßer Computer *m.*

minimize minimieren; *(to represent as minimal)* möglichst klein darstellen; *(to reduce to the minimum)* auf ein Mindestmaß *nt* verringern.

minimum Minimum *nt;* Mindestmaß *nt.*

minimum balance requirement Mindestreserve *f.*

minimum collateral Mindestsicherung *f.*

minimum interest Mindestzins *m.*

minimum size Mindestgröße *f.*

minimum working hours Mindestarbeitszeit *f.*

mining Bergbau *m.*

mining company Bergbauunternehmen *nt.*

minister n *(government)* Minister *m; (clergy)* Pastor *m.* v ministrieren; betreuen.

ministerial ministeriell; verwaltungsmäßig; amtlich.

minister of economic affairs Wirtschaftsminister *m.*

ministry *(government)* Ministerium *nt;* Ministeramt *nt;* Regierungsabteilung *f; (area of competency of a government minister)* Ressort *nt; (clergy)* kirchliches Amt *nt.*

minor n *(legal age)* Minderjährige *m/f.* a minderjährig; *(size)* klein; *(quantity)* gering; *(problem, flaw)* geringfügig.

minority Minorität *f;* Minderheit *f.*

minority participation Minderheitsbeteiligung *f.*

minority partner Minderheitsgesellschafter *m.*

mint n Münzamt *nt;* Münzanstalt *f; (fig.)* Fundgrube *f.* a *(brand new)* nagelneu. v münzen.

minute n Minute *f.* a *(size)* winzig.

misallocation Fehlallokation *f.*

miscalculate falsch berechnen; sich verrechnen.

miscellaneous *(mixed)* gemischt; vermischt; *(different)* verschieden; verschiedenartig.

misdirect fehlleiten; falsch leiten; *(mail)* falsch adressieren.

misdirection Fehlleitung *f; (mail)* falsche Adressierung *f.*

misinvestment Fehlinvestition *f.*

mislead irreführen.

mismanage falsch managen; schlecht verwalten; schlecht wirtschaften.

mismanagement Mißwirtschaft *f;* schlechte Verwaltung *f.*

miss vermissen; *(omission)* versäumen; *(airplane)* verpassen; *(to miss the mark)* verfehlen; *(to fail to meet)* verfehlen.

missing amount Fehlbetrag *m.*

mistake n Fehler *m; (bad choice)* Mißgriff *m.* v *(to mix up)* verwechseln.

mitigate mildern; *(to moderate)* mäßigen; *(alleviate)* lindern.

mix n *(mixture)* Mischung *f;* *(grouping)* Zusammenstellung *f;* *(assortment)* Sortiment *nt.* v mischen; vermischen; *(beverage)* mixen.

mixer *(stocks)* Aktie *f* mit hoher Rendite *f.*

mixture Mischung *f;* *(compound)* Zusammensetzung *f.*

mobile mobil; *(free to move)* bewegungsfrei; *(movable, agile)* beweglich.

mobility Mobilität *f;* *(freedom to move)* Bewegungsfreiheit *f;* *(labor force)* Freizügigkeit *f;* *(agility)* Beweglichkeit *f.*

mobilization Mobilisierung *f;* *(appropriation)* Bereitstellung *f.*

model n Modell *nt;* *(design)* Entwurf *m;* *(template)* Schablone *f.* v modellieren.

model case Beispielsfall *m.*

model of economic cycles Konjunkturmodell *nt.*

moderate n mäßig; *(modest)* bescheiden. v moderieren; *(to mitigate)* mäßigen; *(to mediate)* vermitteln.

moderation Mäßigung *f;* *(modesty)* Bescheidenheit *f;* *(mediation)* Vermittlung *f.*

moderator Moderator *m;* *(mediator)* Vermittler *m;* *(panel discussion)* Diskussionsleiter *m.*

modernization Modernisierung *f.*

modest bescheiden; *(moderate)* maßvoll; mäßig; *(decent)* anständig.

modification Modifikation *f;* *(change)* Änderung *f;* Modifizierung *f;* *(rearrangement)* Umstellung *f.*

modify modifizieren; *(to change)* abändern.

modular modular; *(in the manner of building blocks)* bausteinartig.

module Modul *nt;* *(building block)* Baustein *m;* *(unit in a series)* Serieneinheit *f.*

monetarism Monetarismus *m;* Geldwirtschaft *f.*

monetarist Monetarist *m;* Geldwirtschaftler *m.*

monetary geldlich; finanziell; monetär.

monetary assets Geldvermögen *nt.*

monetary authority Währungsbehörde *f;* Währungsinstanz *f.*

monetary claim Geldforderung *f.*

monetary fund Währungsfonds *m.*

monetary needs Währungsbedarf *m.*

monetary order Währungsordnung *f.*

monetary policy Währungspolitik *f;* Geldmarktpolitik *f;* Geldpolitik *f.*

monetary theory Geldtheorie *f.*

monetary unit Währungseinheit *f;* Geldeinheit *f.*

monetary value Geldwert *m.*

monetary variable währungspolitische Größe *f.*

monetize *(to establish the coinage standard)* den Münzfuß *m* festsetzen; *(to establish as legal tender)* zum gesetzlichen Zahlungsmittel *nt* machen.

money Geld *nt;* *(coinage)* Münze *f;* *(legal tender)* Zahlungsmittel *nt.*

money and capital market Kreditmarkt *m.*

money capital Geldkapital *nt.*

money debt   Geldschuld *f*.
money due   Geldforderung *f*.
money lender   Kapitalgeber *m*;
Geldgeber *m*.
money manager   Geldverwalter *m*;
(assets) Vermögensverwalter *m*.
money market   Geldmarkt *m*;
Kreditmarkt *m*.
money market business   Geldmarktgeschäft *nt*.
money market certificate   Geld-
marktpapier *nt*.
money market interest   Kapital-
marktzins *m*.
money market investment   Geldmarktanlage *f*.
money market securities   Geldmarktpapiere *pl*.
money market transaction   Geldmarktgeschäft *nt*.
money receipts   Geldeingang *m*.
money reserve   Geldreserve *f*.
money supply   Geldversorgung *f*;
(money in circulation) Geldmenge
f.
money supply policy   Geldmengenpolitik *f*.
money supply target   Geldmengenziel *nt*.
money trade   Geldhandel *m*.
money transfer   Geldübermittlung
f; Geldüberweisung *f*.
money transfers   Zahlungsverkehr
m.
monitor   n Abhörgerät *nt*; *(TV,
Computer)* Bildschirm *m*; Bildschirmgerät *nt*. v *(to supervise)*
kontrollieren; *(to check)* überwachen; *(to tap)* abhören.
monitor screen   Bildschirm *m*.
monopolist   Monopolist *m*; Monopolbesitzer *m*; *(sole trader)* Allein-
händler *m*.

monopolistic   monopolistisch.
monopolization   Monopolisierung
f.
monopolize   monopolisieren;
Monopol *nt* besitzen; *(exclusive
control)* allein beherrschen.
monopoly   Monopol *nt*; *(exclusive
right to do business)* ausschließ-
liche Gewerbeberechtigung *f*;
(market-controlling company)
marktbeherrschendes Unternehmen *nt*; *(exclusive selling right)*
Alleinverkaufsrecht *nt*; *(exclusive
manufacturing right)* Alleinherstel-
lungsrecht *nt*.
monopoly price   Monopolpreis *m*.
monopoly problem   Monopolproblem *nt*.
monthly   monatlich.
monthly average   Monatsdurchschnitt *m*.
monthly balance sheet   Monatsbilanz *f*.
monthly earnings   Monatsverdienst *m*.
monthly production   Monatsproduktion *f*.
monthly rate   Monatsrate *f*.
monthly statement of account
monatlicher Kontoauszug *m*;
Monatsauszug *m*.
month's end   Monatsende *nt*.
morale   *(workplace)* Arbeitsmoral
f.
moratorium   n Moratorium *nt*;
(payment) Zahlungsaufschub *m*;
(standstill agreement) Stillhalteabkommen *nt*.
mortgage   n Hypothek *f*; *(encum-
berment)* hypothekarische Belastung *f*; *(conventional mortgage)*
Grundpfandrecht *nt*; *(mortgage
paper)* Hypothekenbrief *m*.

v verpfänden; hypothekarisch belasten.

mortgage bank Hypothekenbank *f*; Hypothekarinstitut *nt*.

mortgage bond clearing house Pfandbriefzentrale *f*.

mortgage company Pfandbriefbank *f*.

mortgagee Geldgeber *m*.

mortgage interest Hypothekenzinsen *pl*.

mortgage-lending institution Pfandbriefbank *f*.

mortgage loan Hypothekendarlehen *nt*; Hypothekarkredit *m*.

mortgagor Hypothekenschuldner *m*.

most-favored-nation clause Meistbegünstigungsklausel *f*.

motivate motivieren; *(by exerting pressure)* antreiben.

motivation Motivation *f*.

motive Beweggrund *m*; *(impulse)* Antrieb *m*.

move n *(domicile)* Umzug *m*; *(strategy)* Schritt *m*. v bewegen; *(domicile)* umziehen; *(proceedings)* in Vorschlag *m* bringen; beantragen.

move backwards zurückgehen.

movement Bewegung *f*; *(tendency)* Tendenz *f*.

movement of freight Güterverkehr *m*.

movement of goods Warenverkehr *m*.

mover *(proceedings)*Antragsteller *m*; *(transport)* Fuhrunternehmer *m*; *(household)* Möbelspediteur *m*.

multilateral multilateral; vielseitig.

multilateral agreement multilaterales Abkommen *nt*.

multilingual vielsprachig.

multimillionaire Multimillionär *m*.

multinational multinational.

multinational company multinationale Unternehmung *f*.

multiple vielfach; mehrfach; mannigfaltig.

multiplicity Vielfältigkeit *f*; Vielheit *f*.

multiplier *(quantity)* Vermehrer *m*; *(intensification)* Verstärker *m*; *(math.)* Multiplikator *m*.

multipurpose vielzweckig.

multipurpose software Multizwecksoftware *f*; Allzwecksoftware *f*.

multisided vielseitig.

municipal kommunal; gemeindlich; *(municipally owned)* gemeindeeigen.

municipal bond kommunale Schuldverschreibung *f*; *(loan)* Kommunalanleihe *f*; *(debt)* Kommunalobligation *f*.

municipality Stadtgemeinde *f*.

municipal loan Kommunaldarlehen *nt*.

mushroom n Pilz *m*. v pilzartig aufschießen.

muster n Musterung *f*. v *(to procure)* auftreiben; *(to collect)* zusammenbringen.

mutual gegenseitig; wechselseitig.

mutual fund Kapitalanlagefonds *m*; Investmentfonds *m*; *(fund management company)* Kapitalanlagegesellschaft *f*; Investmentgesellschaft *f*.

mutual stock fund Aktienfonds *m*.

N

name n Name *m*; *(designation)* Bezeichnung *f*. v nennen; *(to appoint)* ernennen; *(date, price)* festsetzen; bestimmen; *(to state)* angeben.

name paper Solawechsel *m*.

nation Nation *f*.

national national; staatlich.

national accounts budget Nationalbudget *nt*.

national bank Nationalbank *f*.

national bankruptcy Staatsbankrott *m*.

national budget Staatsbudget *nt*; Staatshaushalt *m*.

national currency Landeswährung *f*.

national debt Staatsschuld *f*.

national deficit Staatsdefizit *nt*.

national economy Nationalökonomie *f*.

national finances Staatsfinanzen *pl*.

national income Volkseinkommen *nt*.

national income accounting Gesamtrechnung *f*.

national insolvency Staatsbankrott *m*.

nationalize verstaatlichen.

national law Bundesgesetz *nt*.

national product Sozialprodukt *nt*.

national wealth Volksvermögen *nt*; Nationalvermögen *nt*.

nationwide überregional.

native n Inländer *m*; Einheimische *m/f*; *(aborigine)* Eingeborene *m/f*. a einheimisch; heimisch.

natural natürlich; normal; *(customary)* üblich.

natural gas Erdgas *nt*.

natural gas pipeline Erdgasleitung *f*.

natural gas supplier Erdgaslieferant *m*.

natural gas supply Erdgasversorgung *f*; *(delivery)* Erdgaslieferung *f*.

naturalization Einbürgerung *f*; Naturalisierung *f*.

naturalize einbürgern; naturalisieren.

natural resources Bodenschätze *pl*.

nature Natur *f*; Art *f*; Beschaffenheit *f*.

navigation Navigation *f*; Lenkung *f*.

necessarily notwendigerweise.

necessary nötig; notwendig; *(requisite)* erforderlich.

necessity Notwendigkeit *f*; *(unavoidableness)* Unumgänglichkeit *f*.

need n *(hardship)* Not *f*; Bedürftigkeit *f*; *(wish, desire)* Bedürfnis *nt*; *(requirement)* Bedarf *m*. v brauchen; bedürfen; erfordern.

needs test Bedürfnisprüfung *f*.

needy bedürftig.

neglect n *(negligence)* Vernachlässigung *f*; *(carelessness)* Nachlässigkeit *f*; *(ommission)* Versäumnis *f,nt*; Unterlassung *f*. v vernachlässigen; versäumen; unterlassen.

negligence Vernachlässigung *f*; *(endangerment)* Fahrlässigkeit *f*; *(carelessness)* Nachlässigkeit *f*.

negligent *(endangering)* fahrlässig; *(careless)* nachlässig.

negotiable verhandlungsfähig; aushandelbar; *(bankable)* bankfähig; bankmäßig; *(endorsable)* indossierfähig; *(transferable)* begebbar; *(marketable)* handelbar; umlauffähig.

negotiate verhandeln; negoziieren; aushandeln; *(contract)* zustandebringen; abschließen; *(transfer)* übertragen.

negotiating power Verhandlungsmacht *f*.

negotiating skill Verhandlungsgeschick *nt*.

negotiation Verhandlung *f*; Negoziation *f*; *(transfer)* Übertragung *f*.

negotiation goal Verhandlungsziel *nt*.

negotiator Unterhändler *m*; Verhandlungspartner *m*; *(mediator)* Vermittler *m*.

neighborhood bank branch Depositenkasse *f*.

net n *(network)* Netz *nt*.
a *(amount)* netto; *(profit)* rein.
v *(profit)* erzielen.

net allowance Nettozuschuß *m*.

net asset value Reinvermögenswert *m*.

net capital Nettokapital *nt*.

net cash flow *(addition to liquid assets)* Nettozugang *m* an liquiden Mitteln *pl*; Abschreibungen *pl* plus nicht ausgeschüttete Gewinne *pl*.

net commodity price Nettowarenpreis *m*.

net contribution Nettobeitrag *m*; Nettozuschuß *m*.

net cost Grundpreis *m*; Nettopreis *m*; *(manufacturer's cost)* Selbstkostenpreis *m*.

net earnings Reinverdienst *m*; Nettoertrag *m*.

net export capital Nettoexportkapital *nt*.

net exports Außenbeitrag *m*.

net gain from operations Betriebsreingewinn *m*.

net income Nettoeinkommen *nt*; Reineinkommen *nt*; *(yield)* Reinertrag *m*.

net increase Nettozunahme *f*.

net interest yield Effektivzins *m*.

net investment Nettoinvestition *f*.

net loss Nettoverlust *m*; Reinverlust *m*.

net national product Nettosozialprodukt *nt*.

net price of goods Nettowarenpreis *m*.

net profit Reingewinn *m*.

net reserves Nettoreserve *f*.

net sales Nettoverkaufserlös *m*; Reinumsatz *m*.

net sales price Nettoverkaufspreis *m*.

net savings Nettoersparnis *f*.

net subsidy Nettosubvention *f*; Nettozuschuß *m*.

net surplus Nettoüberschuß *m*.

network n *(shared-interest group)* Gruppe *f*; *(technical)* Netzplan *m*; Stellennetz *nt*; *(television)* Sendernetz *nt*. v *(to seek out like-minded people for mutual benefit)* Verbindung *f* mit Gleichgesinnten *pl* aufnehmen.

network of contacts Kontaktnetz *nt*.

net worth Nettowert *m*; Eigenkapital *nt*.

neutral n *(gear)* Leerlauf *m*. a neutral; *(without party allegiance)* parteilos.

neutrality Neutralität *f*; Parteilosigkeit *f*.

newcomer Neuling *m*; *(stranger)* Fremdling *m*; *(marketing)* Außenseiter *m*.

newfangled neumodisch; hypermodern.

newly industrialized country Schwellenland *nt*.

newly produced neuproduziert.

new-rich neureich.

news *(message, report)* Nachricht *f*; *(news item)* Neuigkeit *f*; *(media)* Nachrichten *pl*.

news agency Nachrichtenagentur *f*; Nachrichtenbüro *nt*; Korrespondenzbüro *nt*.

newsletter *(internal)* internes Rundschreiben *nt*; Rundschreiben *nt*; Informationsblatt *nt*.

news magazine Nachrichtenmagazin *nt*.

newspaper Zeitung *f*; Journal *nt*; Blatt *nt*.

newspaper advertisement Zeitungsannonce *f*; Inserat *nt*; Zeitungsreklame *f*.

newsprint *(not yet printed)* Rotationspapier *nt*; *(old newspapers)* Zeitungspapier *nt*.

niche Nische *f*; *(market)* Marktnische *f*.

nil n Null. a nichts.

no-interest unverzinst.

nominal nominell; *(in name only)* nur dem Namen *m* nach.

nominal amount Nennbetrag *m*.

nominal capital Grundkapital *nt*.

nominal interest Nominalzins *m*.

nominal value Nominalwert *m*.

nominate nominieren; *(election)* aufstellen.

nomination Vorschlag *m*; Einsetzung *f*.

nomination of beneficiary Begünstigung *f*.

nonappealableness *(sentence)* Rechtskraft *f*.

nonbank Nichtbank *f*.

noncompetitive *(product, service)* nicht wettbewerbskonform; *(not competition oriented)* nicht wettbewerbsorientiert; *(unable to compete)* nicht wettbewerbsfähig.

noncompliance *(rule, regulation)* Nichtbefolgung *f*.

non-free-market country Staatshandelsland *nt*.

noninflationary inflationsfrei.

non-interest-bearing *(interest free)* zinsfrei; *(incapable of bearing interest)* unverzinslich.

nonnegotiable check Verrechnungsscheck *m*.

nonobservance *(rule, law)* Nichtbefolgung *f*.

nonpayment of credit Kreditausfall *m*.

nonproductive unproduktiv; ertraglos.

nonprofit gemeinnützig; nicht auf Gewinn *m* gerichtet.

nonreturnable bottle Einwegflasche *f*.

nonstop ununterbrochen; durchgehend; nonstop.

nonvoting nicht stimmberechtigt; stimmrechtlos.

norm Norm *f*; *(rule)* Regel *f*; *(standard)* Standard *m*.

normal normal; *(customary)* üblich; *(regular)* regelrecht.

normative normativ.

notarial notariell; vor einem Notar *m*.

notary Notar *m*.

not binding unverbindlich.

not cancellable *(order)* nicht stornierbar; *(contract)* unkündbar.

not considered unberücksichtigt.

not dismissable *(person)* unkündbar.

note n *(music)* Note *f*; *(memo)* Notiz *f*. v *(to jot down)* notieren; *(to notice)* bemerken; *(make a note)* aufschreiben; vermerken.

note payable Schuldwechsel *m*.

not harmful to the environment nicht umweltschädlich.

notice n *(attention)* Aufmerksamkeit *f*; Beachtung *f*; *(cognizance)* Kenntnisnahme *f*; *(advertisement)* Anzeige *f*; *(notification)* Ankündigung *f*; *(announcement)* Bekanntmachung *f*; *(warning)* Warnung *f*; *(job termination)* Kündigung *f*. v *(to notice)* bemerken.

noticeable bemerkbar; auffallend.

notice of discontinuance *(contract)* Kündigung *f*.

notice of dismissal *(from a job)* Kündigung *f*.

notice of redemption *(loan)* Kündigung *f*.

notice of termination *(of a job)* Kündigung *f*.

notification Ankündigung *f*; Bekanntmachung *f*; Benachrichtigung *f*; Mitteilung *f*.

notify bekanntgeben; benachrichtigen; amtlich mitteilen.

notify of departure abmelden.

not knowledgeable in the field sachfremd.

nourish ernähren.

nourishment Ernährung *f*.

nouveauriche neureich.

null zero; null.

null and void null und nichtig.

nullify aufheben; für nichtig erklären.

number n Nummer *f*; *(quantity)* Anzahl *f*; *(digit)* Ziffer *f*. v numerieren; beziffern; *(to count)* zählen.

number of applicants Bewerberzahl *f*.

number of employees Mitarbeiterzahl *f*.

number of members Mitgliederzahl *f*.

number of offers Angebotszahl *f*.

number of participants Teilnehmerzahl *f*.

number of persons employed Beschäftigungszahl *f*.

number of units Stückzahl *f*.

numerator Zählvorrichtung *f*; Zählwerk *nt*.

numerical numerisch; zahlenmäßig.

numerical data Zahlenmaterial *nt*.

numerical value Zahlenwert *m*.

numerous zahlreich.

nursing expenses Pflegekosten *pl*.

nursing insurance Pflegeversicherung *f*.

object n Gegenstand *m*; Sache *f*;
Ding *nt*; *(aim)* Ziel *nt*; *(purpose)*
Zweck *m*; *(taxes)* Steuerobjekt *nt*.
v beanstanden; nicht zustimmen.

objection Einspruch *m*; Beanstandung *f*; Einwand *m*.

objective n Ziel *nt*. a objektiv;
sachlich.

obligate verpflichten; binden; nötigen.

obligation Verpflichtung *f*; *(money
payable)* Verbindlichkeit *f*; Schuldverschreibung *f*; Engagement *nt*.

obligation to accept Annahmepflicht *f*.

obligation to pay interest Zinsverpflichtung *f*.

obligatory obligatorisch; bindend;
zwingend.

oblige verpflichten; binden; *(to
force)* zwingen; nötigen.

obliterate ausstreichen; auslöschen; *(stamp)* entwerten.

observance *(laws)* Einhaltung *f*;
(directives) Befolgung *f*; *(observation)* Beobachtung *f*; *(custom)*
Brauch *m*.

observation Beobachtung *f*; *(rules)*
Einhaltung *f*.

observe beobachten; *(to observe
rules)* einhalten; befolgen.

observer Beobachter *m*.

obsolescence Überalterung *f*.

obsolete obsolet; überholt; veraltet.

obstacle Hindernis *nt*; Hemmnis *nt*.

obstruction Hemmung *f*; *(handicap)* Behinderung *f*; *(blockage)*
Verstopfung *f*.

obtain erhalten; erlangen; bekom-

men; *(to procure)* beschaffen;
auftreiben; *(yield, profit)* erzielen;
erwirtschaften; *(to buy)* beziehen.

obtainable erhältlich; beziehbar.

obtainment *(procurement)*
Beschaffung *f*; *(goal)* Erzielung *f*.

occasion Gelegenheit *f*.

occupant Bewohner *m*; *(by force)*
Besetzer *m*.

occupation *(profession)* Beruf *m*;
(employment) Beschäftigung *f*.

occupational Berufs-; beruflich.

occupational category Berufsgruppe *f*.

occupy *(to keep busy)* beschäftigen; *(position)* innehaben;
(dwelling) bewohnen; *(by force)*
besetzen.

occur *(to take place)* stattfinden;
(to come into existence) entstehen;
(phenomenon) vorkommen.

occurrence *(incident)* Vorfall *m*;
(event) Vorkommnis *nt*; *(happen-
ing)* Ereignis *nt*; *(process)* Vorgang
m.

odd lot Spitze *f*.

odd lot amount Spitzenbetrag *m*.

of age mündig.

of equal rank gleichrangig.

offend beleidigen; *(rule)* verstoßen.

offer n Angebot *nt*; Offerte *f*; Vorschlag *m*; Ware *f*. v anbieten;
offerieren; *(to suggest)* in Vorschlag *m* bringen.

office Büro *nt*; *(branch)* Zweigniederlassung *f*; Geschäftstelle *f*;
(function) Funktion *f*; *(post,
bureau)* Amt *nt*; *(administration)*
Verwaltungsstelle *f*.

office automation Büroautomation *f.*
office desk Büroschreibtisch *m.*
office electronics Büroelektronik *f.*
office equipment Büroeinrichtung *f.*
office equipment trade fair Büromesse *f.*
office industry Büroindustrie *f.*
office machine Büromaschine *f.*
Office of Economic Security Arbeitsamt *nt.*
officer Beamte *m*; Beamtin *f*; *(company)* Vorstandsmitglied *nt*; Direktor *m*; *(military)* Offizier *m*; *(police)* Polizist *m*; *(party)* Funktionär *m.*
office routine Bürobetrieb *m.*
office space Bürofläche *f*; Büroraum *m.*
office technology Bürotechnik *f.*
office typewriter Büroschreibmaschine *f.*
office work Innendienst *m.*
official n *(government)* Beamte *m*; Beamtin *f*; Sachbearbeiter *m.* v offiziell; amtlich.
official act Amtshandlung *f.*
official channels Behördenweg *m.*
official register Amtsblatt *nt.*
officiate amtieren; fungieren.
offset n *(accounting)* Verrechnung *f*; Gegenbuchung *f*; *(printing)* Offsetdruck *m.* v verrechnen; kompensieren.
offset rate Tauschrate *f.*
offshoot Seitenzweig *m*; Seitenlinie *f*; Unterorganisation *f.*
offshore vor der Küste *f* gelegen.
of long duration langfristig; langjährig.
often oft; häufig.

of the same value gleichwertig.
oil-exporting erdölausführend.
oil facility Erdölverwertungsanlage *f.*
oil field Erdölfeld *nt*; Erdölvorkommen *nt.*
oligopolistic model Oligopolmodell *nt.*
oligopolistic situation Oligopolsituation *f.*
oligopolistic theory Oligopoltheorie *f.*
oligopoly Oligopol *nt.*
oligopoly problem Oligopolproblem *nt.*
omission Wegfall *m*; *(nonperformance)* Versäumnis *f/nt*; Unterlassung *f.*
omit auslassen; *(dividend)* ausfallen lassen.
one-way einfach; Einweg-.
one-way street Einbahnstraße *f.*
one-year period Jahresfrist *f.*
on hand vorrätig; vorliegend.
on-screen text Bildschirmtext *m.*
onset Beginn *m.*
onshore im Küstenvorland *nt.*
on time pünktlich.
open a offen. v *(door)* öffnen; *(meeting)* eröffnen.
open-door policy Politik *f* des freien Zugangs *m.*
opening *(aperture)* Öffnung *f*; *(meeting, branch)* Eröffnung *f*; *(opportunity)* Gelegenheit *f.*
opening price Anfangskurs *m.*
open market freier Markt *m*; offener Markt *m.*
open-market credit Schuldscheindarlehen *nt.*
open-market policy Offenmarktpolitik *f.*
operate *(a machine)* bedienen; *(an*

enterprise) betreiben; führen; *(surgery)* operieren; *(to be operative)*; funktionieren; verkehren.

operating *(company)* Betriebs-; *(surgery)* Operations-; operierend; *(functioning)* funktionierend.

operating capital Betriebskapital *nt.*

operating cost Betriebsunkosten *pl.*

operating instructions Betriebsanleitung *f*; Betriebsvorschrift *f.*

operating loss Betriebsverlust *m.*

operating manual Bedienungsanweisung *f.*

operating rate Beschäftigungsgrad *m.*

operation *(business)* Geschäftstätigkeit *f*; *(machine)* Bedienung *f*; Handhabung *f*; Arbeitsvorgang *m*; *(enterprise)* Unternehmung *f*; Betrieb *m*; *(surgery)* Operation *f.*

operational area Einsatzfeld *nt.*

operational capability Funktionsfähigkeit *f.*

operational headquarters Führungsstab *m*; Zentrale *f*; Hauptbüro *nt.*

operational management Betriebsführung *f.*

operation instructions Bedienungsanleitung *f.*

operator *(machine)* Bedienungsperson *f*; *(enterprise)* Unternehmer *m*; *(telephone)* Telefonvermittlungsperson *f.*

opinion poll Meinungsumfrage *f.*

opinion research Meinungsforschung *f.*

opponent Gegner *m.*

opportunity Gelegenheit *f*; *(possibility)* Möglichkeit *f*; Chance *f.*

oppose ablehnen; Widerspruch *m*

erheben; Einspruch *m* erheben; opponieren.

opposite side Gegenseite *f.*

opposition Widerstand *m*; Opposition *f.*

opt optieren; sich entscheiden.

opt for *(choice)* wählen.

optimality Optimalität *f.*

optimal planning Optimalplanung *f.*

optimal solution Optimallösung *f.*

optimization Optimierung *f.*

optimize optimieren.

optimum Optimum *nt*; Bestfall *m*; Bestwert *m.*

option Wahlmöglichkeit *f*; Entscheidungsfreiheit *f*; Alternative *f*; *(real estate)* Vorkaufsrecht *nt*; *(stock)* Optionsrecht *nt*; Bezugsrecht *nt*; Option *f.*

optional beliebig; wahlweise; freigestellt; nicht pflichtgemäß; freiwillig.

optional bond Optionsanleihe *f.*

option price Optionspreis *m.*

options market Terminmarkt *m*; Prämienmarkt *m*; Optionsmarkt *m.*

option to buy Vorkaufsrecht *nt*; Ankaufsoption *f.*

option trading Optionshandel *m*; Termingeschäft *nt.*

order n Auftrag *m*; Bestellung *f*; *(directive)* Bestimmung *f*; Anweisung *f*; Befehl *m*; Order *f*; *(arrangement, tidiness)* Ordnung *f.*
v *(to place an order)* bestellen; ordern; *(to make a determination)* bestimmen; *(to direct)* anweisen; *(to put in order)* ordnen.

order backlog unerledigter Auftragsbestand *m*; Auftragsüberhang *m*; Auftragspolster *nt.*

order book Orderbuch *nt*.
ordering activity Ordertätigkeit *f*.
orderly ordnungsmäßig.
orders in hand Auftragsbestand *m*.
order to economize Sparbeschluß *m*.
order to purchase securities Wertpapierauftrag *m*.
ordinance Verfügung *f*; Verordnung *f*; Erlaß *m*.
organization Organisation *f*; *(company)* Firma *f*; *(association)* Verband *m*; *(corporate legal entity)* Unternehmensform *f*.
organizational organisatorisch.
organization chart Stellenbesetzungsplan *m*.
organization committee Verbandsausschuß *m*.
organization doctrine Organisationslehre *f*.
organization of the market Marktordnung *f*.
organize organisieren; gründen.
orient orientieren.
orientation Orientierung *f*; *(new employee)* Arbeitsplatzeinweisung *f*.
origin Ursprung *m*; Herkunft *f*.
original n *(document)* Urschrift *f*; Original *nt*; Erstanfertigung *f*. a original; ursprünglich.
original capitalization Erstausstattung *f* mit Kapital *nt*.
original condition Anfangszustand *m*.
original equipment Erstausstattung *f*.
original stock Grundkapital *nt*.
original store Stammladen *m*.
original subscriber *(shares)* Ersterwerber *m*.

originate ins Leben *nt* rufen; hervorbringen; *(to found)* begründen; *(to come into being)* entstehen; *(to have origin)* herstammen.
originating banker Konsortialführer *m*.
originator Urheber *m*.
outcome Ergebnis *nt*; Resultat *nt*.
outfit n *(equipment, gear)* Ausrüstung *f*; Ausstattung *f*; *(enterprise)* Betrieb *m*; *(mil.)* Truppenteil *m*. v *(to equip)* ausrüsten.
outflow Abgang *m*; Abfluß *m*.
outflow of capital Kapitalabfluß *m*.
outflow of deposits Einlagenabfluß *m*.
outlaw n gesetzwidrig Handelnde *m/f*. v ungesetzlich machen.
outlay Auslage *f*; Ausgabe *f*; Kostenaufwand *m*.
outlet *(market)* Absatzmarkt *m*; *(sales office, store)* Vertriebsstelle *f*; *(high-volume customer)* Großabnehmer *m*.
outline n *(sketch)* Skizze *f*; Umriß *m*; *(draft)* Entwurf *m*. v umreissen; skizzieren.
outlook Aussicht *f*; Vorschau *f*; *(viewpoint)* Ansicht *f*; Auffassung *f*.
outlook on the future Zukunftserwartung *f*.
out of fashion unmodern; veraltet.
outperform leistungsmäßig übertreffen.
output n *(production)* Produktionsleistung *f*; *(quantity)* Produktionsmenge *f*; *(overall, total output)* Gesamtleistung *f*; *(production run)* Ausstoß *m*; *(productivity)* Leistung *f*; Output *m*. v *(computer)* ausgeben.

output boost Leistungssteigerung *f*; Outputsteigerung *f*.

output data Produktionsziffern *pl*; *(data processing)* Ausgabedaten *pl*.

output increase Leistungssteigerung *f*; Outputsteigerung *f*.

output path Outputpfad *m*.

outside capital Fremdkapital *nt*; Fremdmittel *pl*.

outside country *(European Community)* Drittland *nt*.

outside funds Fremdmittel *pl*.

outsider Außenseiter *m*; Nichtfachmann *m*.

outstanding *(bill)* unbeglichen; *(sum)* ausstehend; *(issue)* offenstehend; *(excellence)* hervorragend.

outstanding debt ausstehende Forderung *f*; Geldforderung *f*.

outstrip übersteigen; überflügeln.

outweigh überwiegen.

overall total; gesamt; pauschal.

overall costs Gesamtkosten *pl*.

overall index Gesamtindex *m*.

overall loss Gesamtverlust *m*.

overall result Gesamtergebnis *nt*.

overalls Schutzanzug *m*.

over and above extra.

overcapitalization Überkapitalisierung *f*.

overcapitalize überkapitalisieren; *(corporation)* zu hohen Nennwert *m* für das Stammkapital *nt* ansetzen.

overcharge zuviel verlangen; einen zu hohen Preis *m* verlangen.

overdraft Kontoüberziehung *f*.

overdraft credit Überziehungskredit *m*; Dispositionskredit *m*.

overdraw überziehen.

overdue *(time)* überfällig; *(in arrears)* rückständig.

overestimation Überbewertung *f*.

overextension Überschuldung *f*.

overflow n *(flooding)* Überschwemmung *f*; Überflutung *f*; *(flood)* Flut *f*. v überfließen; überlaufen.

overhaul n Überprüfung *f*; Überholung *f*; gründliche Instandsetzung *f*. v überprüfen; überholen; instandsetzen.

overhead n Festkosten *pl*; Gemeinkosten *pl*. a *(transport)* Hoch-; Luft-. oben.

overheat überheizen; *(economy)* sich überhitzen.

overload überladen; *(to overburden)* überlasten; einer zu hohen Belastung *f* aussetzen.

overnight loan Tagesgeld *nt*.

overprice n Überpreis *m*. v einen zu hohen Preis *m* ansetzen.

overproduce überproduzieren; zuviel produzieren.

overproduction Überproduktion *f*.

overseas n Übersee *f*. a überseeisch; im Ausland *nt*.

overseas buyer Auslandskunde *m*; Kunde *m* aus Übersee *f*.

overseas market Überseemarkt *m*.

overseas operation überseeische Unternehmung *f*; überseeische Geschäftätigkeit *f*.

overseas trade Überseehandel *m*; Überseegeschäft *nt*.

oversell überverkaufen; in zu großer Menge *f* verkaufen; *(stock exchange)* über den Bestand *m* verkaufen.

overstate *(to exaggerate)* übertreiben; zu hoch angeben; *(to overemphasize)* zu stark betonen; *(balance sheet)* überbewerten.

oversubscribe überzeichnen.

oversupply   n Überangebot *nt*.
v überversorgen.

overtake   *(outdistance)* überholen.

overtax   überbesteuern; zu hoch
besteuern; *(capacity)* überlasten.

over-the-counter market   Freiverkehr *m*.

overtime hour   Überstunde *f*.

overvaluation   Überbewertung *f*.

overvalue   überbewerten; überschätzen; zu hoch ansetzen.

overwork   *(others)* überfordern;
(self) sich überarbeiten; sich überanstrengen; *(equipment)* überlasten.

owe   *(money)* schulden; *(gratitude)*
verdanken.

owing   geschuldet; offenstehend.

own   a eigen. v *(to possess)*
besitzen.

owned by the people   volkseigen.

owner   Besitzer *m*; Eigentümer *m*;
Inhaber *m*; Eigner *m*.

ownership   Besitz *m*; Eigentumsrecht *nt*.

own production   Eigenproduktion
f.

own resources   Eigenmittel *pl*.

P

pack   n Packen *m*; *(bale)* Ballen *m*;
(bundle) Bündel *nt*; *(package)*
Packung *f*. v verpacken.

package   n Paket *nt*; Packung *f*;
(combined, flat rate) Pauschale *f*.
v verpacken.

package price   Paketpreis *m*; *(flat
rate)* Pauschalpreis *m*.

packaging industry   Verpackungsindustrie *f*.

packing material   Packmaterial *nt*.

pad   n *(notepad)* Notizblock *m*;
Papierblock *m*; *(for a rubber
stamp)* Stempelkissen *nt*; *(uphol-
stery)* Polster *nt*. v aufpolstern;
wattieren; *(expenses)* überhöhen.

page   n Seite *f*. v *(to call for a person)* ausrufen.

paltry   geringfügig.

pamphlet   Pamphlet *nt*; *(brochure)*
Broschüre *f*; *(prospectus)* Prospekt
m.

panel   *(group)* Ausschuß *m*; Gremium *nt*; *(wood)* Paneel *nt*.

panic   Panik *f*; *(stock exchange)*
Kurssturz *m*.

paper   Papier *nt*; Dokument *nt*;
(record) Unterlage *f*; *(draft)* Wechsel *m*.

paper loss   Scheinverlust *m*.

paperwork   Büroarbeiten *pl*;
Schreibarbeit *f*; Dokumentation *f*.

par   *(equality)* Gleichwertigkeit *f*;
(face value) Nennwert *m*.

paragraph   Absatz *m*; Paragraph
m; Abschnitt *m*.

parallel   n Parallele *f*. a parallel.
v entsprechen.

paralyse   *(trade)* lahmlegen; *(initiative)* lähmen.

paramount   von höchstem Rang
m; *(decisive)* ausschlaggebend.

paraphrase   n Umschreibung *f*.
v umschreiben.

parcel   Paket *nt*; *(land)* Grundstücksparzelle *f.*
parcel out   *(to distribute)* austeilen;
(to divide up) aufteilen.
pare   *(benefits)* beschneiden;
(expenditures) kürzen.
parent company   Muttergesellschaft *f.*
parent store   Stammladen *m.*
parity   Parität *f*; Pari *m*; *(equal
value)* Gleichwertigkeit *f.*
park   n Park *m*; *(public park)*
Anlage *f.* v parken.
parochial   Gemeinde-.
part   n Teil *m/nt*; Anteil *m*; *(spare)*
Ersatzteil *nt.* v *(to part company)*
sich trennen; *(to divide)* teilen.
partial   Teil-; teilweise.
partial privatization   Teilprivatisierung *f.*
partial value   Teilwert *m.*
participant   Teilnehmer *m*; Beteiligte *m/f*; *(part owner)* Teilhaber
m.
participate   teilnehmen; sich
beteiligen; *(to have a part)* teilhaben.
participating certificate   Genußschein *m.*
participation   Teilnahme *f*; *(share)*
Beteiligung *f*; *(decision-making)*
Mitwirkung *f*; Partizipation *f.*
participation in a fair   Messebeteiligung *f.*
particular   besonders; *(exact)*
genau; *(in detail)* ausführlich; *(fas-
tidious)* eigen.
particular case   Einzelfall *m.*
partner   Partner *m*; *(shareholder)*
Teilhaber *m*; *(company, corporation)* Gesellschafter *m*; *(partnership)* Kompagnon *m.*
partnership   Partnerschaft *f*; *(regis-*

tered partnership) Personengesellschaft *f.*
partnership share   Geschäftsanteil
m.
part-time   Teilzeit-; teilzeitlich;
(outside regular occupation)
nebenberuflich.
part-time work   Teilzeitarbeit *f.*
party   Partei *f*; *(party to a contract)*
Vertragspartei *f*; *(social gathering)*
Party *f.*
par value   Paritätswert *m*; *(nominal
value)* Nominalwert *m*; Nennwert
m; *(parity)* Parität *f*; Pari *m.*
pass   n Ausweis *m*; Passierschein *m.*
v *(a law)* verabschieden; *(to
approve)* genehmigen; *(to spend
time)* verbringen; *(a resolution)*
beschließen.
passage   *(throughway)* Durchgang
m; *(transoceanic)* Überfahrt *f*;
(book) Textstelle *f*; *(law)* Verabschiedung *f*; *(time)* Verlauf *m.*
passenger   Passagier *m.*
passenger receipts   Passagiereinnahmen *pl.*
passenger revenue   Passagiereinnahmen *pl.*
passive   passiv.
passive balance   Passivsaldo *m.*
passport   Reisepaß *m.*
past   n Vergangenheit *f.* a *(former)*
ehemalig; *(prior)* früher.
past due   überfällig.
patent   n Patent *nt.* a *(obvious)*
offenkundig.
patentable   patentierbar.
patent application   Patentanmeldung *f.*
patent fee   Patentgebühr *f.*
patent infringement   Patentrechtsverletzung *f.*
patent law   Patentrecht *nt.*

patent licensing   Patentvergabe *f*.
patent registry   Patentrolle *f*.
patron   *(supporter)* Förderer *m*;
(restaurant) Stammgast *m*.
patronage   Protektion *f*; *(artistic)*
Gönnerschaft *f*; *(financial)* Unterstützung *f*.
pattern   Muster *nt*; Vorlage *f*; *(garment)* Schnittmuster *nt*; *(habit)*
Gewohnheit *f*.
pawning   Verpfänden *nt*.
pay   n *(payment)* Bezahlung *f*;
(wage) Lohn *m*.   v bezahlen; *(to
remunerate)* entgelten.
payable   zahlbar; *(due)* fällig.
payables   Verbindlichkeiten *pl*.
payback   *(debt)* Rückzahlung *f*;
(capital) Kapitalrückfluß *m*.
payday   Zahltag *m*.
payee   Zahlungsempfänger *m*.
payment   *(paying)* Bezahlung *f*;
(amount) Zahlung *f*; *(deposit)* Einzahlung *f*; *(compensation)* Entlohnung *f*.   **additional** ~ Zuzahlung *f*.
payment difficulty   Zahlungsproblem *nt*.
payment habit   Zahlungsgewohnheit *f*.
payment in advance   Vorauszahlung *f*; Vorausleistung *f*.
payment instrument   Zahlungsmedium *nt*.
payment of dividend   Dividendenzahlung *f*.
payment of interest   Zinszahlung
f; Verzinsung *f*.
payment of wages   Lohnzahlung *f*.
payment transactions   Zahlungsverkehr *m*.
payoff   *(reward)* Belohnung *f*;
(profit) Profit *m*; *(yield)* Ertrag.
pay off   abzahlen; abtragen; *(to be
worthwhile)* sich lohnen.

payor   Zahlende *m/f*.
payout   Auszahlung *f*.
pay raise   Lohnsteigerung *f*;
Gehaltserhöhung *f*.
payroll   *(accounting)* Lohn- und
Gehaltsabrechnung *f*; Löhne- und
Gehälterliste *f*.
payroll account   Lohnkonto *nt*.
pay scale   Lohntarif *m*.
peak   n *(summit)* Gipfel *m*; Höchstpunkt *m*; *(climax)* Höhepunkt *m*;
(apex, top) Spitze *f*.   v den
Höchststand *m* erreichen.
peak demand   Spitzenbedarf *m*.
peak year   Spitzenjahr *nt*.
peasant   Kleinbauer *m*; Bauer *m*;
Bäuerin *f*.
peculiar   *(exclusive)* eigentümlich;
(strange) merkwürdig; sonderbar.
pecuniary   pekuniär; *(monetary)*
geldlich; *(financial)* finanziell.
peg   n *(stock exchange)* Kurs-
stützung *f*.   v *(price)* stützen;
(exchange rate) ansetzen.
pegged price   Stützpreis *m*.
penalty   Strafe *f*; *(fine)* Geldstrafe *f*.
pen and ink   Schreibzeug *nt*.
pending   schwebend; noch nicht
erledigt.
penetrate   durchdringen; *(market)*
eindringen.
penetration   Durchdringung *f*;
(market) Eindringen *nt*.
penny   Pfennig *m*.
pension   Pension *f*; Rente *f*; Ruhegehalt *nt*.
pension adjustment   Rentenanpassung *f*.
pension cut   Pensionskürzung *f*.
pensioner   Pensionär *m*; Rentner
m.
pension fund   Pensionsfonds *m*;
Pensionskasse *f*; Rentenfonds *m*.

pension increase Rentenerhöhung *f*; Rentenaufbesserung *f*.

pension payment Pensionszahlung *f*.

pent-up demand Nachholbedarf *m*.

people's bank Volksbank *f*.

per pro; *(citation)* laut.

per capita pro Kopf *m*.

perceive wahrnehmen.

percent n Prozent *nt*. a prozentig.

percentage Prozentsatz *m*.

percentaged prozentual.

percentage of sales prozentualer Umsatzanteil *m*.

percentage of share Anteilsquote *f*.

percentage point Prozentpunkt *m*.

percental prozentual.

percent calculation Prozentrechnung *f*.

perceptible wahrnehmbar.

perception Wahrnehmung *f*; Auffassung *f*.

per diem allowance Tagesgeld *nt*.

perfect a vollkommen; vollendet. v vervollkommnen.

perfection Vollkommenheit *f*; Vollendung *f*.

perforate perforieren; lochen.

perform leisten; ausführen; erfüllen; vollziehen.

performance *(entertainment)* Vorstellung *f*; *(achievement, productivity)* Leistung *f*; *(implementation)* Durchführung *f*; *(contract)* Erfüllung *f*; *(execution of work)* Verrichtung *f*; *(presentation)* Veranstaltung *f*.

peril Gefahr *f*; Risiko *nt*.

period Periode *f*; *(time span)* Zeitraum *m*; *(period of effectiveness)* Laufzeit *f*; *(punctuation)* Punkt *m*.

periodic periodisch; regelmäßig wiederkehrend.

periodical Magazin *nt*; Zeitschrift *f*.

period of adjustment Anpassungszeitraum *m*.

period of notice Kündigungsfrist *f*.

peripheral device *(computer)* Systemeinheit *f*.

perishable verderblich; *(goods)* kurzlebig.

perjury Meineid *m*.

permanent permanent; dauernd; beständig.

permanently unemployed person Dauerarbeitslose *m/f*.

permanent use Dauernutzung *f*.

permissible zulässig.

permit n Erlaubnisschein *m*; *(permission)* Erlaubnis *f*; *(official permission)* Genehmigung *f*. v erlauben; genehmigen; zulassen.

perpetual dauernd; immerwährend; *(annuity)* unbefristet.

perpetuate *(to eternize)* verewigen; *(to continue indefinitely)* endlos fortsetzen.

persist *(to persevere)* beharren; *(to last)* fortdauern.

persistent *(persevering)* beharrlich; *(lasting)* nachhaltig.

person Person *f*; Individuum *nt*.

personal persönlich; privat; personell.

personal account Privatkonto *nt*.

personal computer Personalcomputer *m*; Kleincomputer *m*.

personal credit Privatkredit *m*.

personal draw Privatentnahme *f*.

personal effects persönliche Habe *f*; bewegliches Eigentum *nt*.

personal income Privateinkommen *nt*.

personality Persönlichkeit *f.*
personalize individualisieren; individuell anpassen.
personal loan persönliche Anleihe *f*; Kleinkredit *m.*
personal share Namensaktie *f.*
personal tax Vermögenssteuer *f.*
personnel Belegschaft *f*; Personal *nt*; Mannschaft *f*; Mitarbeiter *pl.*
personnel cutback Belegschaftsabbau *m.*
personnel development Mitarbeiterförderung *f.*
personnel exchange Personalaustausch *m.*
personnel expenses Personalaufwendung *f*; Personalkosten *pl.*
personnel growth Personalzuwachs *m.*
personnel management Menschenführung *f*; Personalleitung *f.*
personnel policy Personalpolitik *f.*
personnel turnover Personalaustausch *m.*
person with power of attorney *(action)* Handlungsbevollmächtigte *m/f*; *(representation)* Vertretungsbevollmächtigte *m/f*; *(business)* Prokurist *m.*
perspective Perspektive *f*; Aussicht *f.*
persuade überreden; *(to convince)* überzeugen.
persuade to buy zum Kauf *m* überreden; umwerben.
persuasion Überredung *f*; *(conviction)* Überzeugung *f.*
persuasive überzeugend.
persuasive power Überredungskunst *f*; *(advertising)* Werbekraft *f.*
pertain betreffen.
pertaining to global economy weltwirtschaftlich.

pertaining to growth policy wachstumspolitisch.
pertinent question relevante Frage *f*; Sachfrage *f.*
petition n Antrag *m*; *(written petition)* Bittschrift *f.* v beantragen.
petitioning creditor Konkursgläubiger *m.*
petroleum Erdöl *nt.*
petty *(character)* kleinlich; *(concern)* geringfügig.
petty cash Portokasse *f.*
phase n Phase *f*; Stadium *nt*; *(step)* Stufe *f.* v in Phasen einteilen.
phase out auslaufen lassen; abschaffen.
philosophy Philosophie *f*; *(business)* Anschauung *f.*
phone n Telefon *nt*; Fernsprecher *m.* v telefonieren; anrufen.
photocopy n Fotokopie *f*; Ablichtung *f.* v fotokopieren; ablichten.
photograph Fotografie *f*; Lichtbildaufnahme *f.*
photographer Fotograf *m.*
photographic fotografisch.
phrase n Phrase *f*; *(expression)* Ausdruck *m.* v ausdrücken.
physical physisch; materiell; *(human body)* körperlich.
physical product Sachgut *nt.*
physical property *(possession)* Sachbesitz *m*; *(characteristic)* physische Eigenschaft *f.*
physician participating in a health insurance plan Kassenarzt *m.*
pick n *(choice)* Auswahl *f*; *(the best)* Auslese *f.* v *(to choose)* auswählen; aussuchen.
picket Streikposten *m*; *(fence)* Stakete *f.*
pickup *(acceleration)* Anzugsvermögen *nt*; *(truck)* Kleinlastwagen

m; *(economy)* Konjunkturanstieg *m*.

pick up abholen; *(to increase)* zunehmen; *(to rally)* sich erholen.

picture n Bild *nt*; Vorstellung *f*. v *(to imagine)* ausmalen.

picture screen *(movies)* Leinwand *f*; *(TV)* Bildschirm *m*.

piece n Stück *nt*. v zusammen-stücken.

piecemeal stückweise.

piecework Akkordarbeit *f*.

pie chart Kuchendiagramm *nt*.

pile n *(stack)* Stapel *m*; *(heap)* Haufen *m*; *(fabric, rug)* Felbel *m*; Noppe *f*. v stapeln; anhäufen.

pilferage Dieberei *f*; Mauserei *f*; kleiner Diebstahl *m*.

pilot n Pilot *m*; *(ship)* Lotse *m*. a *(experimental)* Versuchs-; Pilot-. v *(an airplane)* fliegen; *(to guide)* führen; *(to pilot a ship into harbor)* lotsen.

pilot installation Pilotanlage *f*.

pilot plant Versuchsanlage *f*.

pinpoint genau lokalisieren.

pin point Nadelspitze *f*; genau be-stimmter Punkt *m*.

pioneer n Pionier *m*; *(innovator)* Bahnbrecher *m*. v bahnbrechen; vorangehen.

pipe n *(tobacco)* Pfeife *f*; *(oil, gas)* Rohr *nt*; *(stove)* Röhre *f*. v pumpen.

pipeline Rohrleitung *f*.

pit n Grube *f*; *(coal)* Kohlenberg-werk *nt*; *(stock exchange)* Makler-stand *m*. v *(a fruit)* entsteinen, entkernen.

pitch n *(mineral)* Pech *nt*; *(sales)* Warenangebot *nt*; Überredung *f* zum Kauf *m*. v *(to pitch goods)* Waren *pl* anbieten; feilhalten.

pivotal *(decisive)* ausschlaggebend; *(vital)* lebenswichtig.

place n Ort *m*; Stelle *f*; *(employ-ment)* Anstellung *f*. v plazieren; *(to arrange)* anordnen; *(to invest)* investieren; *(a loan)* plazieren; *(to house)* unterbringen; *(in a job)* eine Stelle *f* vermitteln.

place an advertisement inserieren.

placement Unterbringung *f*; *(employment)* Vermittlung *f*; *(securities)* Plazierung *f*; *(capital)* Anlage *f*; Investierung *f*.

place of business Betriebsstätte *f*.

plan n Plan *m*; *(design)* Entwurf *m*; *(intent)* Vorhaben *nt*. v planen; *(design)* entwerfen.

plan development Planerstellung *f*.

planned output Planziel *nt*.

planner Planer *m*.

planning Planung *f*; Ausarbeitung *f*; Einplanung *f*.

planning error Planungsfehler *m*.

planning model Planungsmodell *nt*.

planning process Planungsprozeß *m*.

planning program Planungspro-gramm *nt*.

planning project Planungsaufgabe *f*.

planning task Planungsaufgabe *f*.

planning technique Planungstech-nik *f*.

plant n *(hort.)* Pflanze *f*; *(factory)* Fabrikanlage *f*; Werk *nt*; Betrieb *m*; *(manufacturing)* Fertigungsan-lage *f*; *(machinery)* technische Anlage *f*. v pflanzen; *(rumor)* ausstreuen.

plant equipment Betriebsausstat-tung *f*.

plant management Betriebsführung *f*; Betriebsleitung *f*.

plant regulation Betriebsvorschrift *f*.

plastic n Kunststoff *m*. a Kunststoff-; Plastik-; plastisch; aus Kunststoff *m*.

plate *(china)* Teller *m*; *(company)* Namensschild *nt*; *(car license)* Nummernschild *nt*.

platform Plattform *f*; *(railway station)* Bahnsteig *m*; *(oil drilling)* Bohrinsel *f*; *(political party)* Grundsatzerklärung *f*.

plausible einleuchtend; glaubhaft.

plea Bitte *f*; *(petition)* Gesuch *nt*; *(law court)* Plädoyer *nt*.

plead bitten; *(law court)* plädieren.

plebiscite Urabstimmung *f*.

pledge n *(deposit, security)* Pfand *nt*; *(guarantee)* Bürgschaft *f*. v verpfänden; *(security)* als Sicherheit *f* stellen.

plenary Plenar-; vollständig; uneingeschränkt.

plentiful reichlich.

plenty Fülle *f*; Überfluß *m*; Reichtum *m*.

plight Notlage *f*; Zwangslage *f*.

plot n *(land)* Grundstück *nt*; *(scheme)* Komplott *nt*. v *(to chart)* einzeichnen; *(to scheme)* anzetteln.

plug n Stöpsel *m*; *(advertisement)* unbezahlte Werbebotschaft *f*. v *(to promote)* anpreisen; *(to stop up)* verstopfen; *(to close with a stopper)* verstöpseln.

plunge n *(stock exchange)* Kurssturz *m*. v *(prices)* plötzlich fallen; stürzen.

plus n Pluszeichen *nt*; *(advantage)* Vorteil *m*. a zuzüglich.

plush n *(fabric)* Plüsch *m*. a *(luxurious)* luxuriös.

poach *(sales territory)* ins Gehege *nt* kommen; *(employees)* abwerben.

pocket n Tasche *f*. v *(to keep)* behalten; *(to reap, rake in)* einheimsen.

point n Punkt *m*; Stelle *f*; *(stock exchange)* Einheit *f*; *(discussion)* Kernpunkt *m*. v hinzeigen.

point of equilibrium Gleichgewichtspunkt *m*.

point of sale Verkaufsort *m*.

point system Punktsystem *nt*.

policy Verfahren *nt*; Politik *f*; *(insurance)* Police *f*; *(company)* Geschäftsusance *f*; Geschäftspolitik *f*.

policy dealer Policenhändler *m*.

policy decision Grundsatzentscheidung *f*.

policy holder Versicherungsnehmer *m*.

policy maker maßgebliche Person *f*.

policy statement Grundsatzerklärung *f*.

policy trader Policenhändler *m*.

political politisch.

political economist Nationalökonom *m*.

political science Politikwissenschaft *f*.

politician Politiker *m*.

politico-economic wirtschaftspolitisch.

politics Politik *f*.

polluter Umweltverschmutzer *m*.

pollution Verschmutzung *f*; *(environment)* Umweltverschmutzung *f*.

pollution control Überwachung *f*

der Umweltverschmutzung *f*;
(automobile) Abgaskontrolle *f*.

pool n *(interest group)* Interessengemeinschaft *f*; *(fund)* Fonds *m*;
(arrangement between companies)
Kartell *nt*; Trust *m*; Pool *m*. v zusammenschließen; *(resources)*
zusammenwerfen.

poor arm; *(quality)* schlecht;
(weak) schwach; *(unfavorable)*
ungünstig; *(needy)* bedürftig.

popular populär; beliebt; *(merchandise)* zugkräftig.

popularity Beliebtheit *f*.

popularize popularisieren; populär
machen.

popular price Preisschlager *m*.

populate bevölkern.

population Bevölkerung *f*; *(statistics)* Gesamtzahl *f*.

population stratum Bevölkerungsschicht *f*.

port Hafen *m*.

portable tragbar; *(pension)* übertragbar.

porter Träger *m*.

portfolio *(investment)* Depot *nt*;
Portefeuille *nt*; Portfolio *nt*; *(protective case for papers)* Mappe *f*;
(government minister) Ressort *nt*;
Geschäftsbereich *m*.

portfolio management Depotverwaltung *f*.

portfolio manager Vermögensverwalter *m*; Effektenverwalter *m*;
Portefeuillechef *m*.

portion n Portion *f*; Teil *m*; *(share)*
Anteil *m*; *(block of shares)*
Tranche *f*. v *(to divide)* einteilen.

position n Position *f*; Lage *f*; *(employment)* Stellung *f*; Arbeitsstelle
f; Stelle *f*; *(condition)* Zustand *m*;

(point of view) Standpunkt *m*.
v plazieren.

position in the hierarchy Rang-
stelle *f*.

position of power Machtstellung
f.

positive positiv; *(certain)* sicher;
(express/ly) ausdrücklich; *(firm/ly)*
fest.

possess besitzen.

possessing purchasing power
kaufkräftig.

possession Besitz *m*; Besitztum *nt*.

possibility Möglichkeit *f*; Chance
f.

possible möglich; eventuell.

post n *(employment)* Posten *m*;
Stelle *f*; *(mail)* Post *f*. v *(to publish)* anschlagen; *(a letter)* aufgeben; *(accounting)* verbuchen.

postage Porto *nt*.

postal postalisch.

postal budget Postetat *m*.

postal charges Portokosten *pl*.

postal checking account Postscheckkonto *nt*.

postal consumer Postkunde *m*.

postal expert Postexperte *m*.

postal rate Porto *nt*.

postal savings bank Postspar-
kasse *f*.

post employment benefit Pensionszahlung *f*.

post office box Postfach *nt*.

postpone aufschieben; zurückstellen.

postponement Aufschub *m*;
Zurückstellung *f*.

postwar Nachkriegs-.

postwar period Nachkriegszeit *f*.

potential n Potential *nt*; Möglichkeit *f*. a möglich; potentiell.

potential market potentieller Markt *m*; möglicher Bedarf *m*.

pound n *(weight)* Pfund *nt*; *(currency)* Pfund *nt*. v hämmern.

poverty Armut *f*.

power n Macht *f*; *(authority)* Vollmacht *f*; *(entitlement)* Berechtigung *f*; *(authorization)* Ermächtigung *f*; Befugnis *f*; *(output)* Leistung *f*; *(electricity)* Strom *m*; *(strength)* Kraft *f*. v *(an engine)* antreiben.

powerful mächtig; *(strong)* stark.

powerhouse Maschinenhaus *nt*; *(power station)* Elektrizitätswerk *nt*.

power output Leistungsabgabe *f*.

power plant Kraftwerk *nt*.

power struggle Machtkampf *m*.

power supply Stromversorgung *f*.

practical praktisch; brauchbar.

practice n *(working method)* Verfahren *nt*; *(profession)* Praxis *f*; *(custom)* Gewohnheit *f*; Praktik *f*. v praktizieren; *(profession)* ausüben; *(proficiency)* üben.

practitioner Ausübende *m/f*; Praktiker *m*; *(expert by practice)* Fachmann *m*.

pragmatic pragmatisch.

preamble Präambel *f*; *(introduction)* Einleitung *f*.

precarious prekär; unsicher.

precaution Vorsichtsmaßnahme *f*.

precautionary vorsorglich.

precautionary measure Vorsorgemaßnahme *f*.

precede vorangehen.

precedence Vortritt *m*; Vorrang *m*; *(ranking)* Rangordnung *f*.

precedent Präzedenzfall *m*; Beispielsfall *m*.

precept Regel *f*; Richtschnur *f*;

(authority) Vorschrift *f*; Verordnung *f*.

precious Edel-; wertvoll; kostbar.

precious metal Edelmetall *nt*.

precise genau; präzise.

precision Präzision *f*; Genauigkeit *f*.

preclude ausschließen.

predatory räuberisch; plündernd.

predecessor Vorgänger *m*.

predetermine *(planning)* vorplanen; *(cost)* vorkalkulieren.

predict voraussagen.

predictable vorhersagbar; voraussehbar.

prediction Voraussage *f*; Vorhersage *f*.

predisposition Neigung *f*.

predominance Vorherrschaft *f*.

predominant *(preponderant)* vorwiegend; *(ruling)* vorherrschend.

preeminent hervorragend; unübertroffen.

prefabricate vorfertigen.

prefer vorziehen; bevorzugen.

preference Bevorzugung *f*; Vorzug *m*; Präferenz *f*.

preferential Vorzugs-; bevorzugt; bevorrechtet.

preferential treatment Vorzugsbehandlung *f*; Begünstigung *f*.

preferred bevorzugt.

preferred dividend Vorzugsdividende *f*.

preferred stock Vorzugsaktien *pl*.

prejudice *(bias)* Vorurteil *nt*; *(detriment)* Beeinträchtigung *f*; Nachteil *m*; *(harm)* Schaden *m*.

preliminary vorläufig; einleitend.

preliminary product Vorprodukt *nt*.

premature vorzeitig; verfrüht.

premise Voraussetzung *f*; Prämisse *f*.

premises Räumlichkeiten *pl*; *(business - indoor)* Geschäftsräume *pl*; *(business - outdoor)* Betriebsgrundstück *nt*.

premium Zuschlag *m*; Aufschlag *m*; *(stock exchange)* Kursaufschlag *m*; *(insurance)* Prämie *f*.

premium reduction Prämiensenkung *f*.

preparation Vorbereitung *f*; *(food)* Zubereitung *f*.

preparatory effort Vorleistung *f*.

prepare vorbereiten; präparieren; *(food)* zubereiten.

prepay vorausbezahlen.

prepayment Vorausbezahlung *f*.

prerequisite Voraussetzung *f*; Vorbedingung *f*.

prerogative Vorrecht *nt*.

prescribe *(to issue an order)* vorschreiben; *(medicine)* verordnen; verschreiben; *(law)* bestimmen; vorschreiben.

prescription *(order)* Vorschrift *f*; Verordnung *f*; *(medicine)* Rezept *nt*.

presence Gegenwart *f*; *(attendance)* Anwesenheit *f*; *(existence)* Vorhandensein *nt*.

present n Geschenk *nt*; *(time)* Gegenwart *f*. a gegenwärtig; *(in attendance)* anwesend. v präsentieren; *(a plan)* vorlegen; *(a problem)* darstellen; *(to introduce)* vorstellen.

presentation *(showing)* Vorführung *f*; *(sales)* Präsentation *f*; *(introduction)* Einführung *f*; *(performance)* Veranstaltung *f*.

present value Tageswert *m*.

preservation Erhaltung *f*; Bewahrung *f*; Präservierung *f*.

preserve erhalten; bewahren; präservieren.

preside vorsitzen; Vorsitz *m* haben; präsidieren.

president Präsident *m*; Vorsitzende *m/f*; *(corporation)* Vorstandsvorsitzende *m/f*.

press n *(news medium)* Presse *f*; *(printing company)* Druckerei *f*; *(printing press)* Druckerpresse *f*; *(publishing house)* Verlag *m*. v pressen; *(a button)* drücken; *(to urge, to hurry)* drängen; *(clothes)* bügeln.

press photographer Pressefotograf *m*.

press statement Presseerklärung *f*.

pressure n Druck *m*; *(fig.)* Drängen *nt*. v *(to exert pressure, fig.)* bedrängen.

pressure group Interessenverband *m*; Lobby *f*.

pressure of prices Preisdruck *m*.

prestige Prestige *nt*; Ansehen *nt*.

prestigious angesehen.

presume annehmen; *(to take for granted)* voraussetzen; *(to dare)* sich erdreisten.

presumption Annahme *f*; *(law)* Vermutung *f*; *(impertinence)* Anmaßung *f*.

pretax Vorsteuer *f*.

pretax vor Steuerabzug *m*.

pretax lump sum Vorsteuerpauschale *f*.

prevail *(argument)* sich durchsetzen; *(condition, situation)* herrschen.

prevent verhindern; *(to avert)* verhüten.

prevention Verhinderung *f*; *(prophylaxis)* Verhütung *f*.

preview n Vorschau *f*.

v vorschauen; *(to check in advance)* vorprüfen.
previous vorherig; vorausgegangen.
previous owner Vorbesitzer *m*.
previous year's value Vorjahreswert *m*.
price n Preis *m*; *(cost)* Kosten *pl*; *(stock exchange)* Kurs *m*; Nettokurs *m*. adjusted for ~ preisbereinigt. v *(to set a price)* mit einem Preis *m* versehen; Preis *m* festsetzen; *(to find out a price)* Preis *m* feststellen.
price advance Preissteigerung *f*; *(securities, currency)* Kurssteigerung *f*.
price advantage Preisvorteil *m*; Kostenvorteil *m*.
price change Preisänderung *f*.
price change rate Preisänderungsrate *f*.
price competition Preiskonkurrenz *f*; Preiswettbewerb *m*.
price component Preisbestandteil *m*; Preiskomponente *f*.
price concession Preisnachlaß *m*.
price consciousness Preisbewußtsein *nt*.
price control Preiskontrolle *f*; Preisüberwachung *f*.
price curb Preisdämpfung *f*.
price cut Preissenkung *f*.
price cutting Preisunterbietung *f*.
price deterioration Preisverfall *m*.
price development Preisentwicklung *f*.
price difference Preisunterschied *m*; *(stocks)* Kursdifferenz *f*.
price differential Preisunterschied *m*.
price earnings ratio Ertragsverhältnis *nt*.

price effect Preiseffekt *m*.
price-elastic preiselastisch.
price elasticity Preiselastizität *f*.
price-enhancing preistreibend.
price fixing Preisabsprache *f*.
price fluctuation Preisschwankung *f*; *(securities, currency)* Kursschwankung *f*.
price increase Preiserhöhung *f*; Preisanstieg *m*; Preisauftrieb *m*; *(securities, currency)* Kursaufschlag *m*.
price increase impulse Teuerungsimpuls *m*.
price index Preisindex *m*.
price inflation Preisinflation *f*; Preisüberhöhung *f*.
priceless unbezahlbar.
price level Preishöhe *f*; Preisniveau *nt*.
price list Preisliste *f*.
price margin Preisraum *m*.
price mechanism Preismechanismus *m*.
price of gasoline Benzinpreis *m*.
price of gold Goldpreis *m*.
price of goods Güterpreis *m*.
price-raising preistreibend.
price raising Preisheraufsetzung *f*.
price range Preisklasse *f*; Preisraum *m*.
price relationship Preisrelation *f*; Preisverhältnis *nt*.
price resistance Preiswiderstand *m*.
price rise Preisanstieg *m*.
price risk *(stocks)* Kursrisiko *nt*.
price-setting preisbestimmend.
price setting Preissetzung *f*.
price signal Preissignal *nt*.
price spread Preisdifferenz *f*; Kursdifferenz *f*.
price stability Preisstabilität *f*.

price structure Preisgefüge *nt.*
price support Preisstützung *f.*
price tag Preisschild *nt*; *(cost)* Kosten *pl.*
price trend Preisentwicklung *f*; *(securities, currency)* Kursverlauf *m.*
price uncertainty Preisunsicherheit *f.*
price war Preisschlacht *f.*
pricing Preiskalkulation *f.*
pricing method Berechnungsmethode *f.*
pricing policy Preispolitik *f.*
pricing system Preissystem *nt.*
pricing theory Preistheorie *f.*
primary Primär-; Haupt-; hauptsächlich; primär; grundlegend; *(original)* ursprünglich.
primary data Primärdaten *pl.*
primary distribution Primärverteilung *f.*
primary product Grundprodukt *nt*; Primärerzeugnis *nt.*
primary reserve Kassenreserve *f.*
prime n Spitzenqualität *f.* a vorzüglich.
prime minister Ministerpräsident *m.*
prime rate Leitzins *m.*
principal n *(capital)* Kapital *nt*; *(chief)* Leiter *m*; *(senior partner)* Hauptteilhaber *m*; *(proprietor)* Firmeninhaber *m*; *(client)* Auftraggeber *m.* a Haupt-; hauptsächlich.
principal occupation Hauptberuf *m.*
principal payment Zahlung *f* aus dem Kapital *nt.*
principal stockholder Großaktionär *m.*
principle Grundsatz *m*; Prinzip *nt.*

print n Druck *m*; *(edition)* Druckauflage *f.* v drucken; *(publish)* verlegen.
printer Drucker *m.*
printout *(computer)* Datenausdruck *m.*
prior früher; vorausgehend.
priority Vorrang *m*; Priorität *f*; *(urgency)* Dringlichkeit *f.*
private privat; persönlich.
private attorney Sachverwalter *m.*
private bank Privatbank *f.*
private banking establishment Privatbankhaus *nt.*
private enterprise Privatunternehmen *nt*; private Unternehmung *f.*
private industry Privatindustrie *f.*
private ledger Privatkonto *nt.*
privately owned home Eigenheim *nt.*
private ownership *(state of being owned)* Privathand *f*; *(state of owning)* Privatbesitzertum *nt.*
private placement *(securities)* Wertpapierverkauf *m* an Private *pl*; Privatplazierung *f.*
private property Privateigentum *nt*; Privatvermögen *nt.*
private sale Privatverkauf *m.*
private sector *(economy)* Privatwirtschaft *f*; privater Wirtschaftssektor *m.*
privatization Privatisierung *f.*
privatize privatisieren.
privilege Privileg *nt*; Vorrecht *nt*; Sonderrecht *nt*; *(advantage)* Vergünstigung *f*; Begünstigung *f.*
prizewinning preisgekrönt.
probability Wahrscheinlichkeit *f.*
probability sample Stichprobenauswahl *f.*
probable wahrscheinlich; mutmaßlich.

probe n *(investigation)* Untersuchung *f*; *(examination)* Prüfung *f*; *(surgical instrument)* Sonde *f*. v untersuchen; prüfen; sondieren.

problem Problem *nt*; Schwierigkeit *f*.

problematic loan Problemkredit *m*.

procedural verfahrensrechtlich; prozessual.

procedural manner Verfahrensweise *f*.

procedural method Vorgehensweise *f*; Verfahrensweg *m*.

procedural principle Verfahrensprinzip *nt*.

procedural process Verfahrensgang *m*.

procedural step Verfahrensschritt *m*.

procedure Verfahren *nt*; Ablauf *m*; Vorgang *m*.

proceed *(to continue)* weitermachen; *(to advance)* vorgehen.

proceeding Handlungsverlauf *m*; Verfahren *nt*.

proceeds Erlös *m*; Ertrag *m*.

process n Verfahren *nt*; Vorgang *m*; *(law)* Rechtsgang *m*. v *(production)* veredeln; verarbeiten; weiterverarbeiten; aufbereiten; *(paperwork)* bearbeiten.

processing Weiterverarbeitung *f*; Aufbereitung *f*; *(paperwork)* Bearbeitung *f*.

processing an order Auftragsabwicklung *f*.

processor *(computer)* Prozessor *m*.

process technician Verfahrenstechniker *m*.

proclaim öffentlich bekanntgeben.

proclamation öffentliche Bekanntmachung *f*.

procure beschaffen; verschaffen.

procurement Beschaffung *f*.

procurement of funds Mittelbeschaffung *f*.

produce n *(fruit, vegetables)* Obst *nt* und Gemüse *nt*. v produzieren; *(agricultural products)* erzeugen; *(to manufacture)* herstellen; *(profit)* erwirtschaften.

produced again neu produziert.

producer Produzent *m*; *(agricultural products)* Erzeuger *m*; *(manufacturer)* Hersteller *m*.

producible produzierbar; herstellbar.

producing country Herkunftsland *nt*.

product Produkt *nt*; Erzeugnis *nt*; *(result)* Ergebnis *nt*.

product change Produktänderung *f*.

product choice Produktauswahl *f*; Produktpalette *f*.

product combination Produktkombination *f*.

product counterfeiting Produktfälschung *f*.

product cycle Produktzyklus *m*; Entwicklungskurve *f* eines Produkts *nt*.

product design Produktgestaltung *f*.

product development Produktentwicklung *f*.

product engineering Fertigungstechnik *f*.

product feature Produkteigenschaft *f*.

product group Produktgruppe *f*.

product imitation Produktnachahmung *f*; *(counterfeit)* Produktfälschung *f*.

product innovation Produktinnovation *f*.

production Produktion *f*; *(agricultural products)* Erzeugung *f*; *(manufacture)* Herstellung *f*; Fertigung *f*; *(productivity)* Leistung *f*; *(extraction of a natural resource)* Gewinnung *f*.

production budget Produktionsbudget *nt*.

production capacity Produktionskapazität *f*.

production equipment Produktionsausstattung *f*.

production facility Produktionsanlage *f*; Fabrikationsanlage *f*.

production factor Produktionsfaktor *m*.

production flow Fertigungsablauf *m*.

production function Produktionsfunktion *f*.

production growth Produktionswachstum *nt*.

production hall Fertigungshalle *f*.

production loss Produktionseinbuße *f*.

production manager Fertigungsleiter *m*.

production method Produktionsmethode *f*.

production network Produktionsapparat *m*.

production of gold Goldproduktion *f*.

production of goods Güterproduktion *f*.

production output Produktionsleistung *f*; *(lot)* Produktionsausstoß *m*.

production process Herstellungsverfahren *nt*; Produktionsprozeß *m*; Fertigungsprozeß *m*.

production rate Produktionsrate *f*.

production run Produktionsschub *m*.

production schedule Produktionszeitplan *m*.

production sector Produktionssektor *m*.

production share Produktionsanteil *m*.

production side Produktionsseite *f*.

production structure Produktionsstruktur *f*.

production system Produktionssystem *nt*; Produktionsapparat *m*.

production technique Produktionsverfahren *nt*; Herstellungsverfahren *nt*.

production time Produktionszeit *f*.

production unit Produktionseinheit *f*.

production volume Produktionsvolumen *nt*; Produktionsstand *m*.

productive produktiv; *(utility)* leistungsfähig; *(capacity)* leistungsstark; *(yield)* ertragbringend.

productivity Produktivität *f*; *(utility)* Leistungsfähigkeit *f*; *(capacity)* Leistungsstärke *f*; *(yield)* Ertragsfähigkeit *f*.

product line Produktionszweig *m*; Erzeugnisgruppe *f*; *(assortment)* Sortiment *nt*; Artikelgruppe *f*.

product mix gemischtes Produktionsprogramm *nt*; differenziertes Warenbündel *nt*.

product mixture Produktmischung *f*.

product offering Produktangebot *nt*.

product pirating Produktpiraterie *f*; Produktfälschung *f*.

product policy Warenpolitik *f*.

product quality Warenqualität *f*; Produktqualität *f*.

product quantity Produktmenge *f*.

product range Produktpalette *f*.

product test Warentest *m*; Produkttest *m*.

profession Beruf *m*; Fach *nt*.

professional Berufs-; Fach-; beruflich; berufsmäßig.

professional association Fachvereinigung *f*; Berufsverband *m*.

professional category Berufsgruppe *f*.

professional interest Fachinteresse *nt*.

professional representation Berufsvertretung *f*.

profit n Profit *m*; *(gain)* Gewinn *m*; *(yield)* Ertrag *m*; *(advantage)* Vorteil *m*; Nutzen *m*. v Nutzen *m* ziehen.

profitability Wirtschaftlichkeit *f*; Rentabilität *f*.

profitable gewinnbringend; rentabel; wirtschaftlich; profitabel.

profit accounting Gewinnrechnung *f*.

profit and loss statement Ertragsrechnung *f*.

profit as shown in the balance Bilanzgewinn *m*.

profit balance Gewinnsaldo *m*.

profit center *(of a business)* Ertragsbereich *m*.

profit gain Gewinnzuwachs *m*.

profit growth Gewinnanstieg *m*; Gewinnzuwachs *m*.

profit index Nutzenindex *m*.

profit margin Gewinnspanne *f*.

profit maximization Gewinnmaximierung *f*.

profit orientation Gewinnorientierung *f*; Ertragsorientierung *f*.

profit oriented gewinnorientiert.

profit rate Profitrate *f*.

profit ratio Gewinnverhältnis *nt*.

profit seeking Gewinnstreben *nt*.

profit share Gewinnquote *f*.

profit sharing Gewinnbeteiligung *f*.

profit situation Ertragssituation *f*; Ertragslage *f*.

profit target Gewinnplanziel *nt*.

profit trend Gewinntrend *m*.

prognosis Prognose *f*; Vorausschätzung *f*.

prognosticate prognostizieren.

program n Programm *nt*; Plan *m*. v Programm *nt* gestalten; *(computer)* programmieren.

program financing Programmfinanzierung *f*.

programmer Programmierer *m*.

programming Programmierung *f*.

programming language Programmiersprache *f*.

progress n Fortschritt *m*; Verlauf *m*. v fortschreiten; vorankommen.

progressive fortschrittlich.

progress payment proratarische Zahlung *f*.

progress report Tätigkeitsbericht *m*.

prohibit verbieten; untersagen.

prohibited unzulässig; verboten.

prohibition Verbot *nt*; Untersagung *f*.

prohibitive untragbar.

prohibitive tariff Schutzzoll *m*; Sperrzoll *m*.

project n Projekt *nt*; Plan *m*; Vorhaben *nt*; *(research)* Forschungsaufgabe *f*. v *(to plan)* planen; *(to calculate in advance)* vorausberechnen; *(to protrude)* vorspringen; hervorragen; herausragen; *(an image)* projizieren.

project cost Projektkosten *pl.*

projected *(planned in advance)* vorgeplant; *(calculated in advance)* vorausberechnet; *(future)* zukünftig.

project execution Projektdurchführung *f.*

project financing Projektfinanzierung *f.*

project implementation Projektdurchführung *f.*

projection *(cost, time)* Vorausberechnung *f*; *(planning)* Planung *f*; Projektion *f.*

project leader Projektleiter *m.*

project work Projektarbeit *f.*

proliferate sich stark vermehren; wuchern.

proliferation starke Vermehrung *f.*

prolific fruchtbar; produktiv.

prolong verlängern; *(bill of exchange)* prolongieren.

prominence Prominenz *f*; Wichtigkeit *f*; Bedeutung *f.*

prominent prominent; bedeutend.

promise n Versprechen *nt*; *(affirmative answer)* Zusage *f*; *(potential)* Zukunftspotential *nt.* v versprechen; zusagen.

promising vielversprechend.

promissory note Schuldschein *m*; Eigenwechsel *m*; Solawechsel *m.*

promote *(to raise in rank)* befördern; *(to advertise)* anpreisen; *(to support)* fördern.

promotion *(rise in rank)* Beförderung *f*; *(advertising)* Reklame *f*; Werbung *f*; *(marketing)* Verkaufs-

förderung *f*; *(furtherance)* Förderung *f.*

promotional Werbe-; fördernd.

promotional gift Werbegeschenk *nt.*

promotional literature Werbematerial *nt.*

promotional program Förderprogramm *nt.*

promotion manager Werbeleiter *m.*

prompt a prompt; *(without delay)* unverzüglich; *(punctual)* pünktlich. v *(to cause)* veranlassen; *(to suggest, to stimulate)* anregen; *(theater)* soufflieren.

proof Beweis *m*; *(substantiation)* Nachweis *m*; *(means of proof)* Beweismittel *nt*; *(print)* Korrekturbogen *m.*

proof of liquidity Liquiditätsnachweis *m.*

propaganda Propaganda *f*; *(publicity)* Reklame *f.*

propensity to consume Konsumfreudigkeit *f*; Konsumneigung *f.*

propensity to invest Investitionsneigung *f.*

proper richtig; *(correct)* ordnungsgemäß; *(competent)* maßgebend; zuständig.

property *(assets)* Vermögen *nt*; *(ownership)* Eigentum *nt*; *(land)* Grundstück *nt*; *(quality)* Eigenschaft *f.*

property sale Grundstücksverkauf *m.*

property tax Vermögenssteuer *f*; *(real estate)* Grundsteuer *f.*

property value Vermögenswert *m.*

proportion Proportion *f*; *(ratio)* Verhältnis *nt*; *(share)* Anteil *m.*

proportional Verhältnis-; verhältnismäßig.

proportionate angemessen; entsprechend.

proposal Vorschlag *m*; *(trade)* Angebot *nt*.

propose vorschlagen; Antrag *m* stellen; *(a candidate)* aufstellen.

proposition Vorschlag *m*; Antrag *m*.

proprietary vermögensrechtlich; einem Besitzer gehörig; *(patent)* patentrechtlich geschützt.

proprietary product Markenprodukt *nt*.

proprietor Besitzer *m*; Inhaber *m*; Eigentümer *m*; Eigner *m*.

proprietor of a commercial establishment Handelsherr *m*.

proprietorship *(legal right)* Eigentumsrecht *nt*; *(ownership, possession)* Inhaberschaft *f*; *(legal entity)* Einzelfirma *f*; Einzelunternehmung *f*.

prosecution *(implementation)* Durchführung *f*; *(law)* gerichtliche Verfolgung *f*; *(counsel for the plaintiff)* Anklagevertretung *f*; Staatsanwaltschaft *f*.

prospect n Aussicht *f*; *(sales)* potentieller Kunde *m*. v *(mining)* schürfen.

prospective voraussichtlich; zukünftig.

prospectus Werbeprospekt *m*.

prosper gedeihen; *(to flourish)* florieren.

prosperity Wohlstand *m*; Prosperität *f*; Gedeihen *nt*.

prosperous *(wealthy)* wohlhabend; *(successful)* erfolgreich.

protect schützen; *(to shield)* abschirmen.

protection Schutz *m*; Protektion *f*.

protectionism Protektionismus *m*.

protectionist n Protektionist *m*. a protektionistisch.

protective Schutz-; schützend.

protector power Schutzmacht *f*.

protector state Schutzmacht *f*.

protest n Protest *m*. v protestieren.

protocol Protokoll *nt*; Sitzungsordnung *f*; Verhandlungsordnung *f*; *(minutes)* Sitzungsbericht *m*.

prototype Prototyp *m*; Ausgangsbaumuster *nt*; erstes Modell *nt*.

prove beweisen; *(to substantiate)* nachweisen; *(to test)* prüfen; erproben; *(to turn out)* sich erweisen; *(to document)* belegen.

provide *(to procure)* verschaffen; beschaffen; besorgen; *(to supply)* versorgen; *(law)* bestimmen; *(regulation)* vorsehen.

provident vorsorglich.

provider Ernährer *m*; Versorger *m*; *(supplier)* Lieferant *m*.

province Provinz *f*; *(government portfolio)* Ressort *nt*; *(competency)* Zuständigkeit *f*.

provincial Provinz-; provinziell; kleinstädtisch.

provision *(clause)* Klausel *f*; Verfügung *f*; *(measure)* Maßnahme *f*; *(planning)* Vorsorge *f*; *(balance sheet)* Rücklage *f*; Rückstellung *f*; *(~ to guard against risk)* Risikovorlage *f*.

provisional vorläufig; provisorisch.

provisions *(foodstuffs)* Lebensmittel *pl*; *(victuals)* Proviant *m*; Mundvorrat *m*.

proxy Vollmacht *f*; *(voting power)* Stimmrechtsermächtigung *f*; *(deputyship)* Stellvertretung *f*.

proxy holder Prokurist *m*.

proxy statement Vollmachtsanweisung *f*.

proxy voting power Vollmachtsstimmrecht *nt*.

prudence *(circumspection)* Umsicht *f*; *(caution)* Vorsicht *f*; *(sagacity)* Klugheit *f*.

pub Kneipe *f*; Wirtschaft *f*.

public n Öffentlichkeit *f*; *(audience)* Publikum *nt*. a Staats-; öffentlich.

public assistance expenditure Sozialhilfeausgabe *f*.

publication *(print)* Veröffentlichung *f*; *(announcement)* Bekanntmachung *f*.

public bond Staatsschuldverschreibung *f*.

public consumption Staatsverbrauch *m*.

public enterprise Staatskonzern *m*.

public expense Staatskosten *pl*.

public finances Staatsfinanzen *pl*.

public fund öffentlicher Fonds *m*; Publikumsfonds *m*.

publicity Publizität *f*; *(advertising)* Reklame *f*; Werbung *f*.

publicity director Werbeleiter *m*.

publicity ploy Werbemanöver *nt*; Werbetrick *m*.

publicity strategist Werbestratege *m*; Werbestrategin *f*.

publicize publizieren; öffentlich bekanntmachen; *(advertising)* Reklame *f* machen.

publicly owned volkseigen; staatseigen.

public opinion poll öffentliche Meinungsumfrage *f*; Demoskopie *f*.

public policy öffentlicher Grund-

satz *m*; öffentliche Verhaltensweise *f*.

public relations Meinungspflege *f*; Vertrauenswerbung *f*.

public securities Staatspapiere *pl*.

public support *(opinion)* öffentliche Zustimmung *f*; *(aid)* staatliche Unterstützung *f*.

public works öffentliche Arbeiten *pl*; *(construction)* öffentliche Bauten *pl*.

publish veröffentlichen; verlegen.

publisher Verleger *m*; Herausgeber *m*.

pull n *(influence)* Macht *f*; Einfluß *m*; *(market force)* Sog *m*. v ziehen; *(to tear)* reißen; *(to stretch, to tug)* zerren.

pullback *(retrenchment)* Rückzug *m*; *(curtailment)* Einschränkung *f*.

pullout *(departure)* Verlassen *nt*; *(abandonment)* Aufgabe *f*.

pump priming *(economy)* Ankurbelung *f*.

punctual pünktlich.

punitive Straf-; strafend.

purchase n Kauf *m*; *(acquistion)* Erwerb *m*. v kaufen; *(to acquire)* erwerben; *(to purchase land)* ankaufen.

purchase guarantee Abnahmegarantie *f*.

purchase price Kaufpreis *m*; Anschaffungspreis *m*.

purchaser Käufer *m*; Ankäufer *m*.

purchasing agent Einkäufer *m*; Einkaufssachbearbeiter *m*.

purchasing calculation Ankaufsberechnung *f*.

purchasing commission *(percentage)* Ankaufsprovision *f*.

purchasing order Bezugsschein *m*.

purchasing power Kaufkraft *f*.

pure rein; *(genuine)* echt.

purpose Zweck *m*; *(intended use)* Verwendungszweck *m*; *(intention)* Absicht *f*.

purveyor Versorger *m*; Lieferant *m*.

put Verkaufsoption *f*.

put out a *(displeased)* ärgerlich. v herausstellen.

pyramid Pyramide *f*; pyramidenförmige Anordnung *f*; *(stock exchange)* ständig zunehmender Börsengewinn *m*; *(sales scheme)* Schneeballverkaufssystem *nt*.

pyramiding Verschachteln *nt*; Verschachtelung *f*.

qualification Fähigkeit *f*; Qualifikation *f*; Befähigung *f*; *(modification)* Einschränkung *f*; *(suitability)* Eignung *f*.

qualified person Fachkraft *f*.

qualify qualifizieren; *(to entitle)* berechtigen; *(to enable)* befähigen; *(to be entitled)* berechtigt sein; *(modify)* einschränken.

qualitative qualitativ.

quality Qualität *f*; Güte *f*; Wert *m*; *(characteristic)* Eigenschaft *f*.

quality comparison Qualitätsvergleich *m*.

quality competition Qualitätskonkurrenz *f*.

quality hierarchy Qualitätshierarchie *f*.

quality of life Lebensqualität *f*.

quality product Qualitätsprodukt *nt*.

quality standard Qualitätsnorm *f*; Qualitätsstandard *m*.

quantitative quantitativ; mengenmäßig.

quantitative index Mengenindex *m*.

quantity Menge *f*; Quantität *f*.

quantity adjustment Mengenanpassung *f*.

quantity of supply Angebotsmenge *f*.

quarter n Viertel *nt*; *(quarter year)* Vierteljahr *nt*; Quartal *nt*. v vierteilen; *(to house)* einquartieren.

quarterly n *(publication)* Vierteljahreszeitschrift *f*. a Quartals-; vierteljährlich.

quarterly review Vierteljahresprüfung *f*.

quarters *(lodging)* Quartier *nt*; Unterkunft *f*.

question n Frage *f*. v fragen.

questionable fragwürdig; *(doubtful)* zweifelhaft.

questionnaire Fragebogen *m*.

queue Warteschlange *f*.

quit *(to resign)* kündigen; *(to cease)* aufhören; *(to give up)* aufgeben.

quota Quote *f*; Kontingent *nt*; Sollvorgabe *f*; *(share in business)* Geschäftsanteil *m*.

quota agreement Kontingentsvereinbarung *f*.

quota control Quotenregelung *f*.

quota limitation Kontingentierung *f*.

quota regulation Quotenregelung *f*.

quotation *(citing)* Anführung *f*; *(citation)* Belegstelle *f*; Zitat *nt*; *(price offer)* Preisangabe *f*; Offerte *f*; *(stock exchange)* Kursnotierung *f*; Börsennotierung *f*.

quote n *(price offer)* Preisangebot *nt*; *(citation)* Zitat *nt*. v zitieren; *(to state)* angeben; *(stock exchange)* notieren.

quoted price angegebener Preis *m*; angebotener Preis *m*; *(stock exchange)* notierter Kurs *m*.

R

racket Geschäftemacherei *f*; *(shady dealings)* Schiebung *f*; Betrügerei *f*; *(noise)* Krach *m*; *(tennis, golf)* Schläger *m*.

radius Radius *m*; Umkreis *m*; *(fig.)* Wirkungskreis *m*.

railroad Eisenbahn *f*; Eisenbahnlinie *f*; *(tracks)* Schienenweg *m*.

raise n *(wage)* Lohnerhöhung *f*; *(salary)* Gehaltserhöhung *f*. v erhöhen; heraufsetzen; anheben; *(to procure)* bereitstellen.

raising efficiency Rationalisierung *f*.

raising of credit Kreditaufnahme *f*.

rally n *(stock exchange)* Erholung *f*; *(price)* Preisaufschwung *m*. v sich erholen.

random stichprobenartig; *(coincidental)* zufällig; *(hit-or-miss)* aufs Geratewohl *nt*; *(indiscriminate)* wahllos.

random sample of consumption Verbrauchsstichprobe *f*.

random sample of income Einkommensstichprobe *f*.

random test Stichprobe *f*.

range n *(choice)* Auswahl *f*; *(limits)* Spielraum *m*; Grenze *f*; *(extent)* Spanne *f*; *(scale)* Größenordnung *f*. v anordnen; *(to extend)* ausdehnen; sich erstrecken.

range of application Anwendungsbereich *m*.

range of fluctuation Schwankungsbreite *f*.

rank n Rang *m*; *(standing)* Stand *m*; *(degree)* Grad *m*; *(class)* Klasse *f*; *(order)* Ordnung *f*. a stinkend; *(fig.)* kraß. v *(to order)* einordnen; *(to range)* rangieren.

rank hierarchy Ranghierarchie *f*.

ranking list Rangliste *f*.

ranking system Rangsystem *nt*.

rarity Seltenheit *f*.

rate n Rate *f*; *(discount)* Satz *m*; *(wage)* Tarif *m*; *(currency exchange)* Kurs *m*. v *(to place)* einstufen; *(to judge)* beurteilen; bemessen.

rate bargaining round Tarifrunde *f*.

rate ceiling Höchstratengrenze *f*; Höchsttarif *m*.

rate control Tarifkontrolle *f*.

rate dispute Tarifstreit *m*.

rate hike Tariferhöhung *f*.

rate making Gebührenfestsetzung *f*; *(insurance)* Prämienfestsetzung; *(wages)* Tarifberechnung *f*.

rate of change Veränderungsrate *f.*
rate of duty Zollsatz *m*; Zolltarif *m.*
rate of growth Zuwachsrate *f*; Wachstumsrate *f.*
rate of increase Steigerungsrate *f*; Steigerungssatz *m.*
rate of inflation Inflationsrate *f.*
rate of interest Zinsrate *f.*
rate of price increase Teuerungsrate *f*; Preissteigerungsrate *f.*
rate of progress Fortschrittsrate *f.*
rate of return Kapitalverzinsung *f*; Rendite *f.*
rate policy Tarifpolitik *f.*
rate regulation Tarifregelung *f.*
ratification Ratifizierung *f.*
rating Bemessung *f.*
ratio *(of one number to another)* Verhältniswert *m*; *(balance sheet)* Wertverhältnis *nt.*
ration n Ration *f.* v zuteilen.
rationalization Rationalisierung *f.*
rationalize rationalisieren.
rationing Rationierung *f.*
raw material Rohmaterial *nt*; Rohstoff *m*; Ausgangsmaterial *nt.*
raw materials conglomerate Rohstoffkonzern *m.*
raw materials production Rohstoffgewinnung *f.*
re bezüglich; betreffs; wegen.
reach n Reichweite *f.* v reichen; *(goal)* erreichen.
reach an agreement übereinkommen.
readiness Bereitschaft *f.*
readiness to assume risk Risikobereitschaft *f.*
readjust neu ordnen; *(company)* sanieren; neu anpassen.
readjustment Neuregelung *f.*
readmission Neuzulassung *f.*

readmittance Neueintrittserlaubnis *f.*
ready to negotiate verhandlungsbereit.
real wirklich; real.
real cost Realkosten *pl.*
real estate Immobilien *pl.*
real estate fund Immobilienfonds *m.*
real estate sale Grundstücksverkauf *m.*
real growth reales Wachstum *nt.*
realign neu ausrichten; neu aufstellen.
realignment Neuausrichtung *f*; Neuaufstellung *f.*
real income Realeinkommen *nt*; wirkliches Einkommen *nt.*
realizability Realisierbarkeit *f.*
realizable realisierbar; ausführbar; *(convertible into capital)* kapitalisierbar.
realization *(awareness)* Erkenntnis *f*; *(conversion into capital)* Kapitalisierung *f*; *(conversion into fact)* Realisierung *f*; *(goal)* Verwirklichung *f*; Erzielung *f.*
realization of profit Gewinnerzielung *f.*
realize *(to be aware of)* erkennen; *(a goal)* realisieren; verwirklichen; *(capital)* kapitalisieren; *(profit)* erzielen; umsetzen.
realized income Einkommenserzielung *f.*
reallocate umverteilen; neu zuteilen; neu bereitstellen.
reallocation Umverteilung *f*; Neuzuteilung *f*; Umplazierung *f.*
reallot repartieren; neu verteilen.
real wage increase Reallohnzuwachs *m.*
real wage rate Reallohnsatz *m.*

real wages   Reallohn *m*.

reap   ernten; *(profits)* realisieren.

reappoint   wiederernennen; neu bestätigen.

reappointment   Wiederernennung *f*; Neueinstellung *f*.

reappraisal   Neubewertung *f*; Neuabschätzung *f*.

reappraise   neu bewerten; überprüfen.

rearrangement   Neuordnung *f*; Neuregelung *f*.

reasonable   sinnvoll; *(fair)* billig.

reassignment   Rückübertragung *f*; Wiederabtretung *f*.

rebate   n Rabatt *m*; Rückvergütung *f*; Abzug *m*; Preisnachlaß *m*. v Rabatt *m* gewähren.

rebound   n Wiederaufschwung *m*. v zurückschnellen; *(recover)* sich erholen.

rebuild   wiederaufbauen.

recalculate   nachrechnen.

recall   n *(product)* Rückruf *m*; *(from a post)* Zurückberufung *f*; *(memory)* Erinnerungsvermögen *nt*; *(loan)* Aufkündigung *f*. v *(to call back)* zurückrufen; *(from a post)* abberufen; abrufen; *(to remember)* sich erinnern; *(to give notice)* kündigen; *(product)* zurückziehen.

recapitalization   Neufinanzierung *f*; Neukapitalisierung *f*.

recapitulation   Zusammenfassung *f*; Rekapitulation *f*.

recapture   *(market)* wiedererobern; zurückgewinnen.

receipt   *(shipment)* Empfang *m*; Erhalt *m*; *(taking delivery)* Inempfangnahme *f*; *(for payment)* Quittung *f*; *(for shipment)* Empfangsbescheinigung *f*.

receivable   n *(balance sheet)* Forderung *f*. a ausstehend; offen.

receivables   *(balance sheet)* Forderungen *pl*; Außenstände *pl*; Kundenforderungen *pl*.

receive   empfangen; erhalten; vereinnahmen.

receiver   *(recipient)* Empfänger *m*; Übernehmer *m*; *(trust officer)* Einnehmer *m*; *(telephone)* Hörer *m*; *(radio)* Empfangsgerät *nt*; *(bankruptcy)* Konkursverwalter *m*.

recession   Konjunkturrückgang *m*; Rezession *f*; Wirtschaftsrückgang *m*.

recipient   Empfänger *m*; Empfangsberechtigte *m/f*.

recipient country   Empfängerland *nt*.

reciprocal   gegenseitig; wechselseitig; beiderseits; reziprok.

reciprocal effect   Wechselwirkung *f*.

reckon   *(compute)* berechnen; kalkulieren; *(count)* zählen.

reclaim   n Rückforderung *f*; Regenerierung *f*. v zurückfordern; regenerieren; reklamieren.

reclamation   *(land)* Kultivierung *f*; Gewinnung *f*; Wiedergewinnung *f*; Rückgewinnung *f*.

reclassification   Neuklassifizierung *f*; Neueinstufung *f*; Neueinteilung *f*.

reclassify   neu klassifizieren; neu einstufen; umgruppieren.

recommend   *(to propose)* vorschlagen; *(testimonial)* empfehlen; *(to support)* befürworten.

recommendation   *(proposal)* Vorschlag *m*; *(testimonial)* Empfehlung *f*; *(support)* Befürwortung *f*.

recommit   neu verpflichten; sich neu binden; *(resources)* neu bereitstellen.

recompense   n *(service)* Entgelt *nt*; Vergütung *f*; *(damages)* Entschädigung *f*; Wiedergutmachung *f*.
v entschädigen; vergüten; wiedergutmachen.

recompute   neu errechnen; nachrechnen.

reconcile   versöhnen; *(accounts)* abstimmen; in Übereinstimmung *f* bringen.

reconciliation   Versöhnung *f*; *(dispute)* Beilegung *f*.

reconsider   neu erwägen; nachprüfen; neu bedenken; Meinung *f* ändern.

reconsideration   Neuerwägung *f*; Nachprüfung *f*; Meinungsänderung *f*.

reconsignment   Rücksendung *f*.

reconstruct   wieder aufbauen; *(enterprise)* neu gründen.

reconstruction   Wiederaufbau *m*; *(business, enterprise)* Neugründung *f*.

reconvert   umwandeln; umstellen.

record   n *(of events)* Aufzeichnung *f*; Niederlegung *f*; *(official document)* Urkunde *f*; *(sports)* Rekord *m*; Höchstleistung *f*; *(grammophone)* Schallplatte *f*. a Rekord-.
v aufzeichnen; niederlegen; *(to enter)* eintragen; registrieren.

record date   *(payment of dividend)* Dividendentermin *m*.

recorder   *(registrar)* Registrator *m*; *(proceedings)* Protokollführer *m*; *(electronics)* Aufnahmeapparat *m*.

record level   Rekordstand *m*.

record profit   Rekordgewinn *m*.

record result   Rekordergebnis *nt*.

record year   Rekordjahr *nt*.

recoup   *(loss)* wieder einbringen; ersetzen; wiedergutmachen.

recourse   *(indemnity)* Entschädigung *f*; *(resort)* Rückgriff *m*; *(appeal)* Rekurs *m*; *(compensation)* Ersatzanspruch *m*; *(legal process)* Inanspruchnahme *f*.

recover   *(to get back)* wiederbekommen; *(debt)* einziehen; *(shipwreck)* bergen; *(health)* gesund werden; *(economy)* sich erholen.

recoverable   *(debt)* eintreibbar; *(expenses)* erstattungsfähig.

recovery   *(renewed possession)* Wiedererlangung *f*; Zurückerlangung *f*; *(health)* Gesundung *f*; *(recuperation)* Erholung *f*; *(shipwreck)* Bergung *f*; *(money)* Eintreibung *f*; Einziehung *f*.

recreate   *(to create anew)* neu schaffen.

recreation[1]   *(new creation)* Neuschaffung *f*.

recreation[2]   *(entertainment)* Freizeitvergnügen *nt*.

recruit   n Rekrut *m*; *(labor)* neue Arbeitskraft *f*. v rekrutieren; *(to enlist)* anwerben.

rectification   Richtigstellung *f*.

rectify   richtigstellen.

recuperate   sich erholen.

recyclable   wiederverwendbar.

recycle   regenerieren; *(to re-use)* rückschleusen; *(to reconstitute)* wiederaufbereiten.

redeem   einlösen; *(to buy back)* zurückkaufen; *(to amortize)* amortisieren; tilgen.

redemption   Einlösung *f*; *(buying back)* Rückkauf *m*; *(amortization)* Amortisierung *f*; *(debt)* Tilgung *f*.

redemption price   Rückzahlungskurs *m*.

redemption rate   Rückzahlungsrate *f*.

redemption value Rückzahlungswert *m.*

redeploy umgruppieren; umstrukturieren; *(resources)* neu einsetzen.

redeployment Umgruppierung *f;*
Umstrukturierung *f;* Neueinsatz *m.*

rediscount n Rediskont *m;* Diskont *m.* v rediskontieren; diskontieren.

rediscount capacity Rediskontvolumen *nt.*

rediscount quota Rediskontkontingent *nt.*

rediscount volume Rediskontvolumen *nt.*

redistribute neu verteilen; umverteilen.

redistribution Neuverteilung *f;*
Umverteilung *f.*

reduce vermindern; reduzieren; *(a
price)* ermäßigen; nachlassen; verbilligen; *(to shorten)* verkürzen;
(to cut) kürzen; zurückschrauben;
(to lessen) mindern; herabmindern.

reduced consumption Minderkonsum *m.*

reduced expenditure Minderausgabe *f.*

reduced working hours Kurzarbeit *f.*

reduction Verminderung *f;* Reduzierung *f;* *(alleviation)* Ermäßigung *f;* *(restriction)* Abbau *m;*
(deduction) Abzug *m;* *(lowering)*
Herabsetzung *f;* Senkung *f;* *(working time)* Verkürzung *f;* *(diminish-
ment)* Verringerung *f;* *(shrinkage)*
Schwund *m;* *(benefits)* Kürzung *f.*

reduction of interest Zinsermäßigung *f.*

reduction of jobs Arbeitsplatzverlust *m.*

reduction of the interest rate
Zinssenkung *f.*

redundancy Überfülle *f;* Überflüssigkeit *f.*

reelection Wiederwahl *f.*

reemployment Neuanstellung *f;*
Neuengagement *nt.*

reestablish *(relations)* wiederherstellen; *(business)* neu etablieren;
(value) neu festlegen; *(reputation)*
wiedererwerben; neugründen.

reestablishment Neugründung *f.*

refer verweisen; sich beziehen; sich
berufen.

referee in bankruptcy Konkursrichter *m.*

reference Anspielung *f;* Bezugnahme *f;* Hinweis *m;* *(testimonial)*
Empfehlung *f.*

reference number Bezugszahl *f.*

reference product Kontrollprodukt *nt.*

refer to erwähnen.

refinance refinanzieren.

refinancing Refinanzierung *f;*
Umfinanzierung *f;* *(debt payment)*
Umschuldung *f.*

refine veredeln; verfeinern; *(oil)*
raffinieren.

refinement Veredelung *f;* Verfeinerung *f;* Vervollkommnung *f;* *(personal quality)* Bildung *f;* Feinheit *f.*

refinery Raffinerie *f.*

reflationary expansiv; stimulierend.

refloat *(loan)* neu auflegen; *(ship)*
wieder flottmachen; *(currency)*
neu floaten.

reform n Reform *f;* *(rearrangement)* Umgestaltung *f;* Neugestaltung *f;* *(reconstruction)* Umbau *m;*
(new ordering) Neuordnung *f.*
v reformieren; umgestalten; neu
gestalten; umbauen.

reforward nachschicken.

refreshment Erfrischung *f*; Stärkung *f*.

refuel auftanken; nachtanken; *(economy)* wieder ankurbeln.

refund n Rückvergütung *f*; Rückerstattung *f*; Zurückzahlung *f*; *(amount)* Erstattungsbetrag *m*. v rückvergüten; zurückerstatten; zurückzahlen.

refusal Weigerung *f*; *(negative response)* ablehnende Antwort *f*; abschlägiger Bescheid *m*; *(payment)* Verweigerung *f*.

regime Regierung *f*; Verwaltung *f*; *(contract)* Güterrecht *nt*.

regimentation Reglementierung *f*.

region Region *f*; Bereich *m/nt*; *(area)* Gebiet *nt*; Gegend *f*.

regional regional; örtlich.

regional economic policy regionale Wirtschaftspolitik *f*; Standortpolitik *f*.

regional theory Standorttheorie *f*.

register n Register *nt*; Verzeichnis *nt*; *(record)* Journal *nt*; *(account book)* Kontobuch *nt*. v *(to enter)* eintragen; registrieren; *(letter)* einschreiben lassen; *(to record)* verzeichnen; erfassen.

registered share of stock Namensaktie *f*.

registration Registrierung *f*; Eintragung *f*; *(military draft)* Erfassung *f*; *(hotel, school)* Anmeldung *f*.

registration instruction Meldevorschrift *f*.

registration ordinance Meldebestimmung *f*.

regression Regression *f*.

regression analysis Regressionsanalyse *f*.

regressive regressiv.

regroup umgruppieren; neu gruppieren.

regular regelmäßig; regulär; ordnungsmäßig.

regular advertiser Dauerklient *m*; Dauerkunde *m*; Dauerkundin *f*.

regular customer Stammkunde *m*; Stammkundin *f*; Dauerkunde *m*; Dauerkundin *f*.

regularity Regelmäßigkeit *f*; *(legality)* Ordnungsgemäßheit *f*.

regularize regeln; gesetzlich festlegen.

regular rate Normaltarif *m*.

regulate regulieren; lenken; ordnen.

regulation Regulierung *f*; *(rule)* Vorschrift *f*; Bestimmung *f*; Regelung *f*; Ausführungsverordnung *f*.

regulation framework Ordnungsrahmen *m*.

regulator Ordner *m*; *(supervision)* Aufsichtsbehörde *f*; *(control)* Überwachungsstelle *f*.

regulatory regulativ; regelnd; bestimmend.

regulatory agency *(control)* Aufsichtsbehörde *f*; *(competency)* zuständige Behörde *f*.

regulatory system Regulierungssystem *nt*.

rehabilitation Rehabilitation *f*; Eingliederung *f*.

rehire wieder einstellen; wieder anstellen.

reimburse zurückerstatten; zurückbezahlen; *(to compensate)* entschädigen.

reimbursement Zurückerstattung *f*; Rückvergütung *f*; *(compensation)* Entschädigung *f*.

reinforce *(physically)* verstärken; *(policy, argument)* unterstützen.

reinforcement *(physical)* Verstärkung *f*; *(policy, argument)* Unterstützung *f*.

reinstate wieder einsetzen; wieder einstellen.

reintegration Neuintegrierung *f*; Wiedervereinigung *f*.

reinvest wieder anlegen; reinvestieren; umdisponieren.

reinvestment Reinvestition *f*; Umdisposition *f*; Neuanlage *f*.

reject n *(defective goods)* Ausschußware *f*. v *(to refuse)* ablehnen; *(to repudiate)* abweisen; zurückweisen; *(to cull)* aussondern.

rejection Zurückweisung *f*; *(refusal to accept)* Annahmeverweigerung *f*; *(repudiation)* Ablehnung *f*; *(refusal)* Absage *f*.

related to a specific field fachbezogen.

relation *(connection)* Beziehung *f*; Zusammenhang *m*; *(reference)* Bezug *m*; *(ratio)* Verhältnis *nt*.

relationship Beziehung *f*; Verhältnis *nt*.

relax entspannen; sich ausruhen; *(to loosen)* lockern.

relaxation Entspannung *f*; Erleichterung *f*.

release n Freigabe *f*; *(press)* Veröffentlichung *f*; *(quitclaim)* Verzichtserklärung *f*; *(document)* Verzichtsurkunde *f*; Übertragungsurkunde *f*; *(responsibility)* Entlastung *f*; *(resources)* Freistellung *f*. v *(to give up a claim)* Verzicht *m* erklären; *(to confer right to use)* freigeben; *(to publish)* veröffentlichen; *(to transfer)* übertragen; *(to unburden)* entlasten.

reliability Zuverlässigkeit *f*; Verläßlichkeit *f*; *(information)* Glaubwürdigkeit *f*; *(credit risk)* Kreditwürdigkeit *f*.

reliable zuverlässig; verläßlich; *(trustworthy)* vertrauenswürdig; *(sure)* sicher; *(information)* glaubwürdig; *(credit risk)* kreditwürdig.

relief *(feeling)* Erleichterung *f*; *(lightening a burden)* Entlastung *f*.

relief action Hilfsaktion *f*.

relieve erleichtern; *(guard)* ablösen.

relinquish aufgeben; *(to abandon)* verlassen; *(to cede)* überlassen; abtreten; *(to renounce)* verzichten; Verzicht *m* leisten.

relocate umsiedeln; verlagern.

remain zurückbleiben; übrigbleiben.

remaining restlich; übrig.

remaining period restliche Zeit *f*; *(contract)* Restlaufzeit *f*.

remaining time to maturity Restlaufzeit *f*.

remargin nachschießen.

remark n Bemerkung *f*. v bemerken.

remind erinnern; *(obligation)* mahnen.

reminder Mahnung *f*; *(letter)* Mahnbrief *m*.

remittance *(payment)* Zahlung *f*; *(by mail)* Geldsendung *f*; *(money order)* Geldanweisung *f*; Geldüberweisung *f*; *(electronic transfer)* Geldübermittlung *f*.

remittance order Überweisungsauftrag *m*.

remnant Überbleibsel *nt*; Überrest *m*; *(cloth)* Stoffrest *m*.

remodel ummodellieren; *(building)* umbauen; *(company)* umorganisieren.

remove entfernen.

remunerate honorieren; dotieren; *(to reimburse)* vergüten; *(to reward)* belohnen.

remuneration Dotierung *f*; Besoldung *f*; *(for work)* Arbeitsentgelt *nt* Vergütung *f*.

render abgeben; *(to cede)* aufgeben; *(payment)* bezahlen; *(to give)* leisten; *(to make)* machen.

renegotiation Neuverhandlung *f*; erneute Verhandlung *f*.

renew erneuern; *(connection)* wiederherstellen; *(to extend)* verlängern.

renewable erneuerungsfähig; *(contract)* verlängerungsfähig; *(resources)* nachwachsend.

renewal Erneuerung *f*; Verlängerung *f*; Prolongation *f*.

rent n *(rental charge)* Miete *f*; Mietzins *m*. v *(to rent from someone)* mieten; *(to rent to someone)* vermieten.

rental n Mieteinnahme *f*. a Miet-.

rental income Mietertrag *m*.

rented apartment Mietwohnung *f*.

rent increase Mietsteigerung *f*.

reopen wiedereröffnen; wieder in Betrieb *m* setzen; *(negotiation)* wiederaufnehmen.

reopening Wiedereröffnung *f*.

reorder n *(new order)* Neubestellung *f*; *(additional order)* Nachbestellung *f*. v *(to order again)* neu bestellen; *(to order more)* nachbestellen.

reorganization Neugestaltung *f*; Umorganisation *f*; Neuordnung *f*; *(company)* Sanierung *f*; *(official restructuring)* Neugründung *f*.

reorganization bond Gewinnobligation *f*.

reorganization measure Sanierungsmaßnahme *f*.

reorganization offer Sanierungsangebot *nt*.

reorganization program Sanierungsprogramm *nt*.

reorganization strategy Sanierungsstrategie *f*.

reorganize umorganisieren; *(to reshape)* neu gestalten; *(company - internal reorganization)* sanieren; *(company - official restructuring)* neu gründen.

repair n Reparatur *f*; Ausbesserung *f*; Instandsetzung *f*; Wiederherstellung *f*. v reparieren; ausbessern; instandsetzen; wiederherstellen.

repairman Techniker *m*; Mechaniker *m*; *(automotive)* Autoschlosser *m*.

repatriate n Repatriierte *m/f*; Heimkehrer *m*. v repatriieren; in die Heimat *f* zurückbringen.

repatriation Wiedereinbürgerung *f*; Rückführung *f*.

repay zurückzahlen; nochmals bezahlen; *(to make amends)* vergüten; *(to retaliate)* vergelten.

repayable rückzahlbar.

repayment Rückzahlung *f*; Rückvergütung *f*; *(debt)* Tilgung *f*; *(retaliation)* Vergeltung *f*.

repayment amount Tilgungsbetrag *m*.

repayment period Rückzahlungsfrist *f*.

repeal n Widerruf *m*; *(rescission)* Aufhebung *f*. v widerrufen; *(to rescind)* aufheben.

repeat business Wiederholungsgeschäft *nt*; *(additional sales)* Nachverkäufe *pl*.

replace *(compensation)* wieder-

beschaffen; *(to refund)* wiedererstatten; *(substitution)* ersetzen.
replaceable   ersetzbar.
replacement   *(substitute)* Ersatz *m*;
(compensation) Wiederbeschaf-
fung *f*; *(person)* Ersatzperson *f*;
Stellvertreter *m*; *(accounting)*
Anlagenerneuerung *f*.
replacement investment   Ersatzinvestition *f*.
report   n Bericht *m*; *(oral report)*
Vortrag *m*; *(news)* Meldung *f*.
v berichten; vortragen; melden.
reportable   berichtspflichtig.
reporter   Berichterstatter *m*;
Reporter *m*; *(law court)* Schriftführer *m*; Protokollführer *m*.
reporting   Berichterstattung *f*.
repositioning   Neuplazierung *f*.
represent   *(substitute)* vertreten;
(description, depiction) darstellen;
(constituency) repräsentieren.
representation   Vertretung *f*; *(sub-
stituting for a person)* Stellvertretung *f*; Repräsentation *f*; *(description)* Darstellung *f*; Schilderung *f*;
(constituency) Volksvertretung *f*.
representation of interests   Interessenvertretung *f*.
representative   n *(person substitut-
ing for another)* Stellvertreter *m*;
Repräsentant *m*; *(person empow-
ered to act for another)* Bevollmächtigte *m/f*; Agent *m*; *(congress)* Abgeordnete *m/f*; *(sales)*
Vertreter *m*. a repräsentativ.
reprint   n Wiederabdruck *m*; Wiederholungsdruck *m*; *(new edition)*
Neuauflage *f*. v wieder
abdrucken; neu drucken.
reproduce   *(letter)* kopieren; *(to
make multiple copies)* vervielfältigen.

repurchase   n Rückkauf *m*; Wiederkauf *m*. v zurückkaufen;
wiederkaufen.
reputable   angesehen; respektiert;
(trustworthy) vertrauenswürdig.
reputation   Leumund *m*; Ruf *m*;
Ansehen *nt*.
request   n Bitte *f*; *(official written
request)* Gesuch *nt*; *(invitation,
challenge)* Aufforderung *f*; *(procurement)* Anforderung *f*. v bitten;
ersuchen; auffordern; anfordern.
require   *(to demand)* verlangen; *(to
need)* benötigen; brauchen.
requirement   *(demand)* Forderung
f; *(requisite quality)* erforderliche
Eigenschaft *f*; Erfordernis *nt*; *(condition)* Bedingung *f*; *(need)*
Bedürfnis *nt*.
requisite   erforderlich.
requisition   n Anforderung *f*. v *(to
make a request)* anfordern; *(to
seize)* erfassen.
requisition slip   Bezugsschein *m*.
rerouting   Umleitung *f*.
resale   Wiederverkauf *m*; *(by
default)*Selbsthilfeverkauf *m*; *(second hand)* Verkauf *m* aus zweiter
Hand *f*; a Wiederverkaufs-.
reschedule   *(production)* neu einteilen; *(loan)* umschulden; *(time)*
neu ansetzen.
rescheduling   *(production)* Neueinteilung *f* der Produktionszeit *f*;
(loan) Umschuldung *f*.
rescind   *(rule)* aufheben; *(sale)*
rückgängig machen; *(agreement)*
annullieren.
research   n Forschung *f*; Erforschung *f*; genaue Untersuchung *f*;
(survey result) Erhebung *f*.
v forschen; erforschen; nachforschen; untersuchen.

research assignment Forschungsauftrag *m*; *(project)* Forschungsaufgabe *f*.
research center Forschungszentrum *nt*.
research engineer Forschungsin-
genieur *m*.
research expenditure Forschungsaufwand *m*.
research facility Forschungsanlage
f.
research grant Forschungsbeihilfe
f.
research institute Forschungsinstitut *nt*.
research program Forschungsprogramm *nt*.
research project Forschungspro-
ject *nt*.
research study Forschungsstudie *f*;
Forschungsarbeit *f*.
research team Forschungsteam *nt*.
resell wiederverkaufen; weiterverkaufen.
reserve n Reserve *f*; *(capital)*
Rücklage *f*; Rückstellung *f*.
v reservieren; zurückstellen; *(to
book)* buchen; *(judgment)* vorbehalten; *(seat)* belegen.
reserve adequacy Reservenzulänglichkeit *f*; Angemessenheit *f*
der Reserven *pl*.
reserve assets Währungsreserven
pl; Währungsguthaben *nt*.
reserve currency Reservewährung
f.
reserved reserviert; *(behavior)*
zurückhaltend; *(seat)* belegt.
reserve fund Reservefonds *m*;
Reservemittel *pl*.
reserve liability Nachschußpflicht *f*.
reserve position Rücklagenposition *f*.

reserve ratio Deckungssatz *m*.
reserves Reservemittel *pl*.
reserve system Reservesystem *nt*.
reservoir Reservoir *nt*; *(lake)* Staubecken *nt*.
reshipment Rücksendung *f*.
resident n Gebietsansässige *m/f*;
Ansässige *m/f*; Einwohner *m*.
a wohnhaft; ansässig.
residual n Restgröße *f*. a Rest-;
restlich.
residual amount Restbetrag *m*.
resign resignieren; *(office)* aufgeben; zurücktreten; *(job)* kündigen.
resignation Resignation *f*; *(office)*
Aufgabe *f*; Rücktritt *m*; *(job)*
Kündigung *f*.
resistance Widerstand *m*; *(material)* Resistenz *f*.
resolution Resolution *f*; Beschlußfassung *f*; *(document)* Beschluß *m*;
Entschließung *f*; Vorsatz *m*.
resolve n Resolution *f*; Entschlossenheit *f*; *(resolution)* Vorsatz *m*.
v sich entschließen; entschlossen
sein; sich etwas vornehmen.
resort Urlaubsort *m*.
resort to gebrauchen; ergreifen.
resource *(means)* Mittel *nt*; *(procurement)* Bezugsquelle *f*;
(reserves) Vorrat *m*; *(expedient)*
Hilfsquelle *f*.
respect Respekt *m*; *(reference)*
Hinsicht *f*.
respectable respektabel; seriös.
respite Atempause *f*.
respond *(survey)* respondieren;
antworten; reagieren.
respondent Antragsgegner *m*;
(survey) Respondent *m*.
response *(answer)* Antwort *f*;
Reaktion *f*.
responsibility Verantwortung *f*;

Verantwortlichkeit *f*; *(competency)* Verantwortungsbereich *m*; *(liability)* Haftung *f*.

responsibility for risk Risikohaftung *f*.

rest n Rest *m*; Restbestand *m*; *(recuperation)* Rast *f*; Ruhe *f*; *(balance sheet)* Rechnungssaldo *m*. v rasten; ruhen; sich ausruhen.

restaurant Restaurant *nt*; Gaststätte *f*.

restock aufstocken; Lager *nt* ergänzen.

restore *(to give back)* zurückgeben; wiederbringen; *(to original condition)* restaurieren; instandsetzen; *(rights)* wiedereinsetzen; *(to reimburse)* wiedererstatten; *(to replace)* ersetzen.

restrain *(to hold back)* zurückhalten; *(to restrict)* beschränken; *(to hinder)* hindern; hemmen.

restraint *(reticence)* Zurückhaltung *f*; *(restriction)* Beschränkung *f*; *(inhibition)* Hemmung *f*; *(obstacle)* Hemmnis *nt*; *(handicap)* Behinderung *f*; *(control)* Zügelung *f*.

restrict einschränken; beschränken.

restricted cash Termineinlagen *pl*; Termingelder *pl*.

restriction Einschränkung *f*; Beschränkung *f*.

restructure umstrukturieren; neu gliedern.

restructuring Neugliederung *f*; Umstellung *f*.

result n Ergebnis *nt*; Resultat *nt*. v resultieren.

result testing Erfolgskontrolle *f*.

résumé Resümee *nt*; *(vita)* Lebenslauf *m*.

resume *(activity)* wiederaufnehmen; *(position)* wiedereinnehmen.

retail n Einzelhandel *m*. a en detail. v im Einzelhandel *m* verkaufen.

retail chain Einzelhandelskette *f*.

retailer Kleinverkäufer *m*; Einzelhändler *m*.

retail house Einzelhandelsgeschäft *nt*.

retailing Einzelhandel *m*.

retail market Einzelhandel *m*.

retail outlet Verkaufsstelle *f*.

retail sales Ladenverkauf *m*.

retained earnings nichtausgeschütteter Gewinn *m*.

retainer *(contract)* Anwaltsbestellung *f*; *(fee advance)* Anwaltskostenvorschuß *m*.

retaliate vergelten; heimzahlen; Gegenmaßnahmen *pl* ergreifen.

retard *(to delay)* verzögern; *(to slow down)* verlangsamen; *(to draw out)* hinausziehen; *(to protract)* verschleppen.

rethink umdenken; überdenken; neu bedenken.

retire zurückziehen; *(committee member)* abwählen; *(bookkeeping)* ausbuchen; *(from circulation)* aus dem Verkehr *m* ziehen; *(debt)* tilgen; *(to pension off)* pensionieren; *(to go into retirement)* sich pensionieren lassen; in den Ruhestand *m* treten.

retired zurückgezogen; *(pensioned)* im Ruhestand *m*; *(committee member)* abgewählt; *(bookkeeping)* ausgebucht; *(from circulation)* aus dem Verkehr *m* gezogen.

retirement Zurückziehung *f*; Pensionierung *f*; Ruhestand *m*; *(committee member)* Abwahl *f*; *(bookkeeping)* Ausbuchung *f*; *(debt)* Tilgung *f*.

retirement benefit Altersversorgung *f.*

retirement income adjustment Rentenanpassung *f.*

retirement pay Pensionszahlung *f.*

retirement pension Altersruhegeld *nt.*

retirement provision Altersvorsorge *f.*

retirement savings plan Vorsorgesparplan *m.*

retiring *(reticent)* zurückhaltend; *(unobtrusive)* unaufdringlich; *(leaving a position)* ausscheidend.

retraction Rücknahme *f.*

retrain umschulen; neu ausbilden.

retraining Umschulung *f;* Neuausbildung *f.*

retrenchment Einschränkung *f;* Verminderung *f.*

retrieval Zurückerlangung *f;* Wiedererwerb *m;* *(computer)* Wiederauffindung *f.*

retrieve zurückerlangen; wiedererwerben; wieder auffinden; *(to salvage)* bergen.

retroactive rückwirkend.

return n *(travel)* Rückkehr *f;* *(reoccurrence)* Wiederkehr *f;* *(replacement)* Rückgabe *f;* *(report)* Meldung *f;* *(tax)* Steuererklärung *f;* *(yield)* Ertrag *m;* *(profit)* Gewinn *m;* *(shipment)* Rücksendung *f.*
v *(to come back)* zurückkehren; *(to give back)* zurückgeben; *(to go back)* zurückgehen.

returned zurückgesandt; retourniert.

return on assets Anlagenrendite *f.*

return on capital Kapitalertrag *m.*

return on equity Kapitalrendite *f.*

return on net assets Nettorendite *f* auf das Anlagevermögen *nt.*

return on sales Gewinnspanne *f.*

reunification Wiedervereinigung *f.*

reusable wiederverwendbar.

revalue *(evaluation)* neu bewerten; *(to estimate)* neu schätzen.

revamp reorganisieren.

revenue Einnahme *f;* Einkünfte *pl.*

revenue sharing Finanzausgleich *m.*

reversal Umkehrung *f;* Umschwung *m;* *(counter entry)* Stornierung *f;* *(setback)* Rückschlag *m.*

reversing entry Stornobuchung *f.*

revise umarbeiten; überarbeiten; *(examine)* überprüfen; revidieren.

revision Revision *f;* Umarbeitung *f;* Überarbeitung *f;* *(examination, check)* Überprüfung *f;* Revidierung *f;* *(revised edition)* Neufassung *f;* *(revised regulation)* Neuregelung *f.*

revision of a statute Gesetzesänderung *f.*

revitalize wiederbeleben; neu beleben; auffrischen.

revival Wiederbelebung *f;* Wiederaufleben *nt;* *(market)* Erholung *f.*

revive *(to revitalize)* wiederbeleben; wiederaufleben lassen; *(to become revitalized)* wiederaufleben; *(to recuperate)* sich erholen; *(to renew)* erneuern;

revocation Widerruf *m;* Zurücknahme *f.*

revoke widerrufen; zurücknehmen.

revolution Revolution *f;* *(mechanics)* Umdrehung *f.*

revolving sich drehend; revolvierend.

rewrite umschreiben; neu fassen.

rich reich; *(food)* reichhaltig.

rig n *(oil)* Bohrausrüstung *f.* v ausrüsten; montieren; *(price)* illegal beeinflussen.

rigging *(ship)* Takelung *f*; *(market)* Preistreiberei *f*; *(stock exchange)* Kurstreiberei *f*.

right to participate Teilnahmerecht *nt*; *(decision-making)* Mitwirkungsrecht *nt*.

right to recourse Regreßrecht *nt*.

right to social benefits Sozialanspruch *m*.

right to strike Streikrecht *nt*.

right to vote Stimmrecht *nt*.

ripe reif.

rise n Aufstieg *m*; Erhöhung *f*; Anstieg *m*; Steigerung *f*; *(increase)* Zunahme *f*; *(land contour)* Bodenerhebung *f*. v sich erhöhen; *(to climb)* steigen; aufsteigen; *(to grow)* wachsen.

rise in exchange rate Kursanstieg *m*.

rise in expenses Ausgabenanstieg *m*.

rise in exports Exportanstieg *m*.

rise in prices Preisanstieg *m*; *(stocks)* Kursanstieg *m*.

rise in spending Ausgabenanstieg *m*.

rising ansteigend; wachsend; *(prices)* anziehend.

rising price tendency Preisauftrieb *m*.

rising sales Umsatzanstieg *m*.

risk n Risiko *nt*; *(endangerment)* Gefährdung *f*; *(danger of loss)* Verlustgefahr *f*. v riskieren; *(to dare)* wagen.

risk-averse risikoscheu.

risk mixture Risikomischung *f*.

risk potential Gefahrenpotential *nt*.

risk spread Risikostreuung *f*; Risikomischung *f*.

risky riskant; *(daring)* gewagt;

(dangerous) gefährlich; *(high-risk)* risikoreich.

rival n Rivale *m*; *(competitor)* Konkurrent *m*; *(coapplicant)* Mitbewerber *m*. v rivalisieren; konkurrieren; wetteifern.

road to success Erfolgskurs *m*.

rob rauben; berauben; überfallen.

robot Roboter *m*; Automat *m*.

rock n Felsen *m*; Klippe *f*. v *(system)* erschüttern.

roll over revolvieren.

rope Strick *m*; Seil *nt*; *(extent of freedom to act)* Handlungsfreiheit *f*.

rotate drehen; rotieren.

rotating sich drehend; rotierend; *(work shifts)* stetig wechselnd.

rotation Drehung *f*; *(mechanics)* Umdrehung *f*; *(regulated change)* geregelter Wechsel *m*.

round of negotiations Verhandlungsrunde *f*.

route n Route *f*; Strecke *f*; *(way, path)* Weg *m*. v Route *f* bestimmen; Strecke *f* kennzeichnen.

routine n Routine *f*; *(procedure)* Prozedur *f*; *(customary course)* üblicher Verlauf *m*. a routinemäßig; üblich; laufend.

routing Festlegung *f* der Route *f*; Wegbestimmung *f*.

royalty Honorar *nt*; Tantieme *f*; *(license fee)* Lizenzgebühr *f*; *(copyright)* Autorenanteil *m*.

rubric Rubrik *f*; *(heading)* Titelkopf *m*.

ruin n Ruine *f*; *(figurative)* Ruin *m*; *(collapse)* Zusammenbruch *m*. v ruinieren; zugrunde richten.

ruinous ruinös; *(too daring)* halsbrecherisch.

rule n Regel *f*; *(directive)* Vorschrift

f; (decree) Verfügung *f; (guideline)* Richtlinie *f.* v *(to regulate)* regeln; *(to decree)* verfügen; *(a market)* beherrschen.

ruling n *(decision)* Entscheidung *f;* Entscheid *m;* Beschluß *m.* a *(predominant)* vorherrschend; *(decisive)* bestimmend.

run n Lauf *m;* Rennen *nt;* Fortgang *m; (strong demand)* starke Nachfrage *f; (production)* Ausstoß *m.*

v rennen; laufen; *(machine)* in Betrieb *m* sein; *(to operate a machine)* bedienen.

running laufend; umlaufend; *(in operation)* in Betrieb *m.*

rush n Eile *f; (heightened activity)* Hochbetrieb *m; (charge, assault)* Ansturm *m; (crowding)* Andrang *m.* v sich beeilen; *(to urge speed)* drängen; antreiben.

S

safe n Tresor *m.* a sicher.

safeguard n Sicherung *f; (protection)* Schutz *m; (protective device)* Schutzvorrichtung *f; (contract)* Sicherheitsklausel *f.* v sichern; sicherstellen.

safeguarding Sicherstellung *f;* sichere Aufbewahrung *f.*

safekeeping Sicherstellung *f.*

sagging sinkend; nachlassend; abgeschwächt.

salable verkäuflich; absatzfähig; gängig; handelbar.

salaried festes Gehalt *nt* beziehend.

salaried employee Gehaltsempfänger *m.*

salaries and wages Personalaufwendungen *pl;* Gehälter *pl* und Löhne *pl.*

salary Gehalt *nt;* Besoldung *f;* Salär *nt.*

salary account Gehaltskonto *nt.*

salary bargaining round Gehaltsrunde *f.*

salary cut Gehaltskürzung *f.*

salary increase Gehaltssteigerung *f;* Gehaltserhöhung *f.*

salary loss Gehaltseinbuße *f.*

salary negotiation round Einkommensrunde *f.*

salary raise Gehaltssteigerung *f.*

sale Verkauf *m;* Vertrieb *m;* Absatz *m;* Veräußerung *f; (clearance sale)* Ausverkauf *m.*

sale of gold Goldverkauf *m.*

sale of goods Warenverkauf *m.*

sale of land Grundstücksverkauf *m.*

sales agent Geschäftsreisende *m/f.*

sales and services Verkaufs- und Kundendienst *m.*

sales base Verkaufsbasis *f.*

sales branch Verkaufsfiliale *f;* Verkaufsniederlassung *f.*

sales calculation Verkaufsberechnung *f.*

sales call Vertreterbesuch *m;* Kundenbesuch *m.*

sales collapse Umsatzeinbruch *m.*

sales company Vertriebsgesellschaft *f.*

sales director   Vertriebschef *m*.
sales district   Verkaufsgebiet *nt*; Absatzgebiet *nt*.
sales estimate   Absatzschätzung *f*.
sales force   Verkaufspersonal *nt*; Verkaufsmannschaft *f*.
sales forecast   Absatzprognose *f*; Absatzvorausschätzung *f*.
sales gains   Umsatzzunahme *f*.
sales group   Vertriebsgemeinschaft *f*; Verkaufsgemeinschaft *f*.
sales lead   Verkaufstip *m*; Verkaufshinweis *m*.
sales letter   Werbebrief *m*.
sales loss   Absatzverlust *m*.
salesman, -person, -woman   Verkäufer *m*; Verkäuferin *f*.
sales management   Verkaufsleitung *f*.
sales manager   Verkaufsmanager *m*; Chefverkäufer *m*.
sales office   Verkaufsbüro *nt*; Vertriebsstelle *f*.
sales organization   Verkaufsorganisation *f*; Absatzorganisation *f*.
sales plan   Verkaufsplan *m*.
sales proceeds   Verkaufserlös *m*.
sales profit   Verkaufsgewinn *m*.
sales program   Absatzprogramm *nt*; Verkaufsprogramm *nt*.
sales projection   Absatzplan *m*.
sales-promotional   verkaufsfördernd.
sales psychology   Verkaufspsychologie *f*.
sales record   Umsatzrekord *m*.
sales representative   Verkäufer *m*; Handelsvertreter *m*.
sales result   Verkaufsergebnis *nt*; Absatzerfolg *m*.
sales revenue   Umsatzertrag *m*.
sales strategy   Verkaufsstrategie *f*; strategischer Verkaufsplan *m*.

sales tax   Umsatzsteuer *f*; Verkaufssteuer *f*.
sales territory   Absatzgebiet *nt*; Vertriebsgebiet *nt*.
sales volume   Verkaufsvolumen *nt*; Absatzvolumen *nt*; Absatzmenge *f*.
salvage   verwerten.
sample   n Warenprobe *f*; Muster *nt*. v *(to test)* probieren; nach Proben *pl* beurteilen.
sampling   Beurteilung *f* nach Proben *pl*.
sanction   n Sanktion *f*; Strafmaßnahme *f*; *(approval)* Genehmigung *f*; Billigung *f*. v genehmigen; billigen.
satellite   Satellit *m*; *(communication)* Fernmeldesatellit *m*; *(surveying)* Beobachtungssatellit *m*.
satisfaction   Zufriedenheit *f*; Befriedigung *f*; *(of a customer)* Zufriedenstellung *f*.
satisfy   *(customer)* zufriedenstellen; befriedigen.
saturate   sättigen; *(market)* durchdringen.
saturated   gesättigt; *(market)* nicht mehr aufnahmefähig.
saturation   Sättigung *f*; *(market)* Marktsättigung *f*.
saturation limit   Sättigungsgrenze *f*.
save   retten; *(money)* sparen; *(for future use)* erübrigen; *(reduce requisite amount)* ersparen.
saver   Sparer *m*.
savings account   Sparkonto *nt*.
savings activity   Spartätigkeit *f*.
Savings and Loan association   Spar- und Kreditvereinigung *f*; Hypothekenbank *f*.
savings bank   Sparkasse *f*.
savings bank customer   Sparkassenkunde *m*; Sparkassenkundin *f*.

savings bank window Sparkassenschalter *m.*

savings bond Sparbrief *m.*

savings book Sparbuch *nt.*

savings certificate Sparbrief *m.*

savings customer Sparkunde *m;* Sparkundin *f.*

savings deposit Spareinlage *f.*

savings deposits administration Spargelderverwaltung *f.*

savings funds Spareinlagenbestand *m.*

savings performance Sparleistung *f.*

savings plan Sparplan *m.*

savings premium Sparprämie *f.*

savings premium law Sparprämiengesetz *nt.*

savings promotion Sparförderung *f.*

savings rate Sparzinssatz *m.*

scab Streikbrecher *m.*

scale n Waagschale *f; (graduation)* Skala *f;* Gradeinteilung *f; (measure)* Maßstab *m;* Größenverhältnis *nt; (range)* Umfang *m;* Größenordnung *f.* v wiegen; messen; Maßstab *m* festlegen; *(mountain)* erklettern.

scale earnings Skalenertrag *m.*

scan n Überprüfung *f; (radar)* Abtastung *f; (television)*Bildauflösung *f.* v überprüfen; abtasten; *(read)* überfliegen.

scanner Radarantenne *f; (computer)* Abtaster *m.*

scanning n *(checking)* Überprüfen *nt; (radar)* Abtasten *nt; (reading)* Überfliegen *nt.* a überprüfend; abtastend; überfliegend.

scarce knapp; spärlich.

scarcity Knappheit *f;* Verknappung *f;* Mangel *m.*

schedule n Zeitplan *m; (table)* Tabelle *f.* v *(to set time)* ansetzen; *(to plan)* planen.

scheduled vorgesehen; planmäßig.

scheduler Planer *m;* Programmierer *m.*

scheduling Planen *nt;* Ansetzen *nt; (time)* Terminplanung *f; (procedure)* Ablaufsplanung *f; (travel)* Reiseplanung *f.*

schema Schema *nt;* Übersicht *f; (printing)* Satzvorlage *f.*

scheme n *(plan)* Plan *m;* Vorhaben *nt; (intrigue)* Machenschaft *f;* Intrige *f; (plot)* Komplott *nt.* v planen; intrigieren.

scope of business Geschäftsumfang *m.*

scrip Bezugsschein *m.*

season n Jahreszeit *f;* Saison *f.* – v würzen; schmackhaft machen.

seasonal Saison-; jahreszeitlich bedingt; saisonbedingt.

seasonal goods Saisonware *f.*

seasonally adjusted saisonbereinigt.

secondary sekundär; *(ranking)* zweitrangig; *(not important)* nebensächlich.

secondary appointment Nebenamt *nt.*

secondary clause Nebenbedingung *f.*

secondary data Sekundärdaten *pl.*

secondary market Zweitmarkt *m.*

secondary reserve Sekundärreserven *pl.*

seconds *(goods)* Waren *pl* zweiter Qualität *f.*

secrecy Geheimhaltung *f.*

secret Geheimnis *nt.*

secretarial help Schreibkraft *f.*

secretarial staff Schreibpersonal *nt.*

secretary Sekretär *m*; *(government)* Minister *m*; *(association)* Schriftführer *m*.

secretary general Generalsekretär *m*.

Secretary of Trade Handelsminister *m*.

secret of success Erfolgsgeheimnis *nt*.

section n Sektion *f*; Teil *m*; *(department)* Abteilung *f*. v aufteilen; *(to dissect)* zerlegen.

sector Sektor *m*; Bezirk *m*; *(segment)* Ausschnitt *m*; *(area)* Bereich *m/nt*.

sectoral sektoral.

secure a sicher; gesichert; *(protected)* geschützt. v sichern; sicher machen; absichern; *(to obtain)* erlangen.

secured gesichert; sichergestellt; *(protected)* geschützt.

securities *(collateral)* Sicherheiten *pl*; *(investments)* Wertpapiere *pl*; Effekten *pl*.

securities account Wertpapierkonto *nt*.

securities business Wertpapiergeschäft *nt*.

securities exchange Wertpapierbörse *f*; Effektenbörse *f*.

securities market Wertpapiermarkt *m*.

securities sector Wertpapierbereich *m*.

security *(safety)* Sicherheit *f*; *(protection)* Schutz *m*; *(loan)* Darlehenssicherheit *f*; Sicherheitsleistung *f*; *(investment)* Wertpapier *nt*.

security analyst Effektenberater *m*; Anlagefachmann *m*.

security deposit Sicherheitsleistung *f*; Kaution *f*.

security holdings Wertpapierbestand *m*; Wertpapiervermögen *nt*; Effektenbestand *m*.

security trading Wertpapierhandel *m*.

security turnover Wertpapierumsatz *m*.

segment n Segment *nt*; *(part)* Teil *m*; *(piece)* Stück *nt*; *(section)* Abschnitt *m*. v segmentieren; *(to section)* aufteilen.

seize ergreifen; zugreifen.

select a vorzüglich; exklusiv; auserlesen. v aussuchen; auswählen.

selected ausgewählt; ausgesucht.

selection *(choice)* Auswahl *f*; *(pick, elite)* Auslese *f*; *(assortment)* Kollektion *f*.

selection committee Jury *f*.

selection process Auswahlverfahren *nt*.

selective selektiv; *(targeted)* gezielt; *(as needed)* nach Bedarf *m*.

self-financing Selbstfinanzierung *f*.

self-government Selbstregierung *f*; Selbstverwaltung *f*.

self-interest Eigeninteresse *nt*.

self-service Selbstbedienung *f*.

sell verkaufen; *(to market)* absetzen; *(to place)* anbringen; *(to dispose of)* veräußern; *(to turn over)* umsetzen.

seller Verkäufer *m*; *(supplier)* Abgeber *m*.

seller's market Verkäufermarkt *m*; Absatzmarkt *m*; Absatzkonjunktur *f*.

seller's option Verkaufsoption *f*.

selling Verkaufen *nt*; Absetzen *nt*; Vertreiben *nt*.

selling organization Verkaufsorganisation *f*.

selling point Verkaufsstelle *f*.

selling power   Werbekraft *f.*

selling price   *(goods)* Verkaufspreis *m*; *(securities, currency)* Verkaufskurs *m.*

selling representation   Verkaufsprogramm *nt.*

selling time   Verkaufszeit *f.*

sellout   Ausverkauf *m*; *(fig.)* Verrat *m.*

semiannual result   Halbjahresergebnis *nt.*

semiconductor   Halbleiter *m.*

semiskilled   angelernt.

send   senden; schicken; *(forward)* übersenden; versenden; *(remit)* überweisen.

sending   Absenden *nt*; *(delivering)* Ausliefern *nt*; *(forwarding)* Versenden *nt*; *(transmitting)* Übersenden *nt.*

send on   nachschicken.

senior   *(age)* älter; *(rank)* ranghöher.

senior debenture   Vorzugsobligation *f.*

senior partner   Hauptinhaber *m*; Seniorpartner *m*; Seniorchef *m.*

senior salesman   Chefverkäufer *m*; Oberverkäufer *m.*

senior salesperson   Chefverkäufer *m*; Chefverkäuferin *f*; Oberverkäufer *m*; Oberveräuferin *f.*

senior saleswoman   Chefverkäuferin *f*; Oberverkäuferin *f.*

separable   trennbar; abtrennbar; *(divisible)* teilbar.

separate   a separat; einzeln; getrennt. v separieren; trennen; *(to divide up)* aufteilen.

separate assets   Sondervermögen *nt.*

separate estate   separates Vermögen *nt*; Sondervermögen *nt.*

separate voucher   Einzelbeleg *m.*

separation of property   Gütertrennung *f.*

sequence   Reihenfolge *f*; *(data processing)* Folge *f*; *(film)* Szenenfolge *f*; Bildfolge *f.*

serial   *(broadcasting)* Sendereihe *f*; *(publication)* Serie *f*; Veröffentlichungsreihe *f.*

series   Zahlenfolge *f*; Serie *f*; Reihe *f.*

servant   *(domestic)* Hausangestellte *m/f.*

serve   dienen; im Dienst stehen; *(shop)* bedienen; *(summons)* zustellen; *(food)* auftragen.

service   n Dienst *m*; *(benefit, favor)* Dienstleistung *f*; Service *m*; *(china)* Service *nt*; *(public service)* Amtstätigkeit *f*; *(restaurant)* Bedienung *f*; *(delivery of a writ)* Zustellung *f*; *(machine)* Wartung *f*; *(military)* Wehrdienst *m*; *(public utilities)* Versorgung *f.* v warten; instandhalten; *(debt)* Schuldendienst *m* leisten.

serviceable   verwendbar.

service area   Servicebereich *m.*

service business   Dienstleistungsgeschäft *nt.*

service capacity   Dienstleistungskapazität *f.*

service center   Reparaturwerkstätte *f.*

service charge   Unkostengebühr *f*; Dienstleistungsgebühr *f*; Verwaltungsgebühr *f.*

service company   Dienstleistungsfirma *f*; Dienstleistungsbetrieb *m.*

service industry   Dienstleistungsbranche *f.*

service manual   Wartungsanweisung *f*; *(operation)* Bedienungsanleitung *f.*

service network Dienstleistungsnetz *nt*.
service office *(customer service)*
Kundendienstbüro *nt*.
service organization Dienstlei-
stungsorganisation *f*.
service regulation Dienstanweisung *f*; Betriebsvorschrift *f*.
service sector Dienstleistungsbereich *m*; Dienstleistungssektor *m*;
Servicesektor *m*.
servicing staff Wartungspersonal
nt.
session Sitzung *f*; *(meeting)*
Tagung *f*.
set n Satz *m*; *(matched set)* Garnitur *f*. a fest; bestimmt. v *(a condition)* festlegen, bestimmen; *(a
price)* festsetzen; *(a deadline)*
befristen; *(to solidify)* fest
werden.
setback Rückschlag *m*; *(regression)*
Rückschritt *m*; *(stock market)* Ein-
bruch *m*; *(worsening)* Verschlechterung *f*.
set of problems Problemkomplex
m; Problematik *f*.
setting a date Terminfestlegung *f*.
settle *(bill)* begleichen; *(claim)*
zufriedenstellen; *(dispute)* beilegen; *(residence)* sich niederlassen.
settled *(fixed, set)* fixiert; *(agreed
upon)* abgemacht.
settlement *(bill)* Begleichung *f*;
(account) Zahlungsausgleich *m*;
(claim) Zufriedenstellung *f*; *(dispute)* Beilegung *f*; Einigung *f*.
settlement date Fälligkeitstermin
m.
settlement petition Vergleichsantrag *m*.
settlement proceedings Vergleichsverfahren *nt*.

settlement trustee Vergleichsverwalter *m*.
setup *(arrangement)* Einrichtung *f*;
(establishment) Etablierung *f*;
(organization) Organisation *f*;
(trap) Falle *f*.
sever abtrennen; absondern; *(relationship)* auflösen; *(communication)* unterbrechen; abbrechen.
severally *(liability)* einzeln.
severance Trennung *f*; Bruch *m*;
(diplomatic relations) Abbruch *m*.
shadow economy Schattenwirtschaft *f*.
shakeout Geschäftsaufgabe *f* der
Konkurrenz *f*; Ausbooten *nt* der
Konkurrenz *f*.
share n Anteil *m*; *(stock)* Aktie *f*;
Kapitalanteil *m*; Kapitalbeteiligung *f*; *(certificate)* Investmentzer-
tifikat *nt*. v *(to give a share)*
teilen; *(to have a share)* teilhaben.
share certificate Partizipationsschein *m*.
share earnings *(yield)* Aktienertrag
m; *(earnings)* Aktiengewinn *m*.
shareholder Aktieninhaber *m*;
Aktionär *m*; Anteilseigner *m*.
shareholders' equity *(balance
sheet)* Eigenkapital *nt*; Nettoanteil
m der Aktionäre *pl*.
shareholders' group Aktionärskreis *m*.
shareholding Aktienbeteiligung *f*;
Anteilsbesitz *m*.
shareholdings Beteiligungen *pl*;
Aktienbesitz *m*; Aktienbestände
pl.
share of authorized capital
Stammkapitalanteil *m*.
share of business Geschäftsanteil
m.

share of capital stock   Stammkapitalanteil *m.*

share of sales   Umsatzanteil *m.*

share of the market   Marktanteil *m.*

share price   Börsenkurs *m.*

shares of record   registrierte Aktien *pl.*

shares outstanding   ausgegebene Aktien *pl.*

sharpen   *(knife)* schärfen; *(fig.)* verschärfen; *(pencil)* anspitzen; *(tools)* schleifen.

shelf   Fach *nt.*

shelter   n Zuflucht *f; (protection)* Schutz *m; (home)* Obdach *nt; (tax)* steuerbegünstigte Anlage *f.* v schützen; *(to house)* beherbergen.

sheltered   geschützt.

shift   n *(displacement, repositioning)* Verlagerung *f;* Verschiebung *f; (work period)* Schicht *f; (automobile)* Gangschaltung *f; (lever)* Schalthebel *m.* v verschieben; verlagern; *(capital)* umschichten; *(automobile)* schalten.

shift performance   *(factory)* Schichtleistung *f.*

shift productivity   *(factory)* Schichtleistung *f.*

ship   n Schiff *nt.* v verschicken; absenden; verladen.

shipment   *(by sea)* Verschiffung *f; (of goods)* Warensendung *f; (load)* Ladung *f; (delivery)* Lieferung *f.*

shipper   *(water transport)* Verschiffer *m; (land transport)* Versender *m; (freight forwarder)* Spediteur *m; (railway)* Eisenbahnspediteur *m.*

shipping   *(dispatch)* Versand *m;* Versenden *nt;* Transport *m;* a Versand-.

shipping trade   Speditionsgewerbe *nt.*

shipping volume   Transportvolumen *nt.*

shoddy   wertlos; schlecht; von schlechter Qualität *f.*

shop   n Geschäft *nt;* Laden *m; (repair facility)*Werkstatt *f.* v einkaufen.

shop closing law   Ladenschlußgesetz *nt.*

shop closing time   Ladenschlußzeit *f.*

shopper   Käufer *m; (customer)* Kunde *m;* Kundin *f.*

shopping   Ladenbesuch *m; (purchasing)* Einkaufen *nt.*

shopping center   Einkaufszentrum *nt.*

shopping mall   Ladenreihe *f;* Ladenstraße *f;* Ladenpassage *f.*

shop rules   Betriebsanleitung *f.*

shortage   *(scarcity)* Knappheit *f;* Verknappung *f; (lack)* Mangel *m; (deficiency of goods)* Fehlbestand *m; (deficiency of money)* Fehlbetrag *m.*

shortage of money   Geldnot *f.*

shorten   verkürzen.

shortfall   Unterschuß *m; (imbalance)* Defizit *nt; (deficiency)* Fehlbetrag *m.*

short run   *(short term)* kurze Sicht *f; (production)* kurzer Schub *m.*

short-run   kurzfristig.

short-term   kurzfristig.

short-term liability   kurzfristige Verbindlichkeit *f.*

show a tendency   tendieren.

shrink   schrumpfen.

shrinkage   Schwund *m.*

shutdown   Stillegung *f;* Schließung

f; (work stoppage) Arbeitsunterbrechung *f;* Betriebsstörung *f.*

shut down *(factory)* stillegen; *(to close)* schließen.

shutting up shop Ladenschließung *f.*

shuttle *(loom)* Schiffchen *nt; (shuttle train)* Pendelzug *m; (space travel)* Raumfähre *f;* a *(transportation)* Pendel-.

sideline n Seitenlinie *f; (goods)* zusätzliche Ware *f;* Nebenprodukt *nt.* v beiseiteschieben; *(to divert)* abzweigen; *(fig.)* kaltstellen.

sidestep umgehen; *(to avoid)* vermeiden.

sign n Zeichen *nt;* Schild *nt; (indication)* Anzeichen *nt; (trace)* Spur *f; (characteristic)* Merkmal *nt.* v *(document)* unterzeichnen; unterschreiben.

signature Unterschrift *f;* Signatur *f;* Namenszug *m.*

significance Bedeutung *f;* Wichtigkeit *f; (research)* Bewertungsgrad *m;* Stichhaltigkeit *f.*

signing *(agreement)* Unterzeichnung *f;* Unterzeichnen *nt.*

silent schweigend; *(partner)* still; stumm.

similar ähnlich; gleichartig.

simple einfach.

simulate simulieren; vorgeben.

simulated simuliert; fingiert; *(not genuine)* unecht; künstlich.

sincere aufrichtig; seriös.

single einfach; *(unmarried)* ledig; *(sole)* einzig; *(individual)* einzeln.

single item Einzelposten *m.*

single stockholder Einzelaktionär *m.*

singular case Einzelfall *m.*

sink n *(kitchen)* Ausguß *m.* v sinken; *(fall)* fallen; sich senken; *(sink a ship)* versenken.

sister Schwester *f; (company)* Schwestergesellschaft *f.*

site Stätte *f; (scene)* Schauplatz *m; (plot of land)* Gelände *nt; (building site)* Bauplatz *m.*

situation Situation *f;* Lage *f.*

situation analysis Situationsanalyse *f.*

size n Größe *f; (extent)* Umfang *m.* v die Größe *f* bestimmen; die Größe *f* messen.

sized nach Größe *f* geordnet.

skeleton data Rahmendaten *pl.*

skeleton regulation Rahmenregelung *f.*

sketch n Skizze *f; (drawing)* Zeichnung *f; (design, plan)* Entwurf *m.* v skizzieren; zeichnen; entwerfen.

sketchy umrißartig; ungenau; *(superficial)* oberflächlich; lückenhaft.

skewed *(statistics)* verzerrt; verzogen.

skill Geschick *nt;* Fertigkeit *f; (ability)* Können *nt.*

skilled geschickt; *(worker)* gelernt.

skilled worker Facharbeiter *m;* Fachkraft *f.*

skillful geschickt; gewandt.

skim abschöpfen; *(reading)* überfliegen.

skinned enthäutet; *(fig.)* ausgeplündert; betrogen.

skyrocket n Signalrakete *f.* v hochschnellen; hochschießen.

skyrocketing n Emporschnellen *nt;* Hochschießen *nt.* a emporschnellend; hochschießend.

slacken *(demand)* nachlassen;

(stock market) flau werden; sich abschwächen.

slackness Abschwächung *f*; Nachlassen *nt*; Flauheit *f*; Flaute *f*.

slack period flaue Geschäftszeit *f*; Flaute *f*.

slag Schlacke *f*.

slag heap Schlackenhalde *f*.

slash *(price)* stark reduzieren; drastisch senken.

slashing *(public programs)* umfangreiches Streichen *nt*; *(wages)* scharfes Senken *nt*; *(price)* starkes Herabsetzen *nt*; *(production)* starkes Einschränken *nt*.

slate n *(mineral)* Schiefer *m*; *(writing tablet)* Schiefertafel *f*; *(nomination)* Kandidatenliste *f*; Vorschlagsliste *f*. v *(to plan)* vorsehen.

slender *(profits)* gering; dürftig; mager; *(person)* schlank.

slice n Scheibe *f*; *(market)* Anteil *m*. v in Scheiben *pl* schneiden.

slide n *(photography)* Diapositiv *nt*; *(stocks)* Talfahrt *f*; Rutsch *m*. v rutschen; gleiten; *(to insert)* einschieben.

sliding n Rutschen *nt*; Gleiten *nt*; *(decline)* Absinken *nt*. a *(door)* Schiebe-; *(taxes)* gestuft; gestaffelt; *(parity)* stufenflexibel; *(scale)* gleitend.

slight n *(offense)* Mißachtung *f*. a unerheblich; geringfügig; *(stature)* zierlich; schwächlich.

slim a *(slender)* schlank; *(profits)* dürftig; *(scarce)* knapp; *(poor)* armselig. v *(to reduce one's weight)* eine Schlankheitskur *f* machen.

slip n *(paper)* Zettel *m*; Schein *m*; *(mistake)* Flüchtigkeitsfehler *m*;

Schnitzer *m*; *(ship)* Gleitbahn *f*; *(garment)* Unterrock *m*. v *(into one's clothes)* schlüpfen; *(on ice)* ausgleiten; ausrutschen; *(sales)* schwinden; *(prices)* abgleiten.

slipping n *(prices)* Abgleiten *nt*; *(sales)* Schwinden *nt*. a abgleitend; schwindend.

slogan Schlagwort *nt*; Motto *nt*; *(advertising)* Werbespruch *m*.

slot n Spalt *m*; *(coin)* Einwurfschlitz *m*; *(market niche)* Nische *f*; Position *f*. v auskerben; *(to slit)* schlitzen.

slow langsam; *(dragging)* schleppend; *(retarded)* zurückgeblieben; *(sales)* flau.

slowdown Nachlassen *nt*; Geschwindigkeitsverringerung *f*; Verlangsamung *f*.

slow growth langsames Wachstum *nt*.

slowing n Verlangsamen *nt*; Verzögern *nt*. a langsamer werdend; sich verzögernd.

slow up verlangsamen; sich verlangsamen.

sluggish *(slow-moving)* schwerfällig; *(market)* stagnierend; flau.

sluggishness Schwerfälligkeit *f*; *(economy)* Flaute *f*; Stagnation *f*.

slump n Fall *m*; *(prices)* Preisverfall *m*; *(decline)* Baisse *f*; *(business cycle)* Konjunkturrückgang *m*. v absinken; fallen.

slump in sales Absatzrückgang *m*.

small business Kleinbetrieb *m*.

small company Kleinunternehmen *nt*.

small investor Kleinanleger *m*.

small loan Kleinanleihe *f*; Kleinkredit *m*.

small parcel Päckchen *nt*.

small stockholder Kleinaktionär *m*.
small-town kleinstädtisch.
small trade Handwerk *nt*.
snowball n Schneeball *m*. v *(fig.)* exponentiell zunehmen.
soar emporschnellen; rapide steigen.
soaring n Emporschnellen *nt*. a schnell hochsteigend; rapide zunehmend.
social sozial; *(pertaining to social life)* gesellschaftlich.
social assistance law Sozialrecht *nt*.
social benefits claim Sozialanspruch *m*.
social economy Sozialwirtschaft *f*; Gemeinwirtschaft *f*.
social framework Sozialgebilde *nt*.
social justice soziale Gerechtigkeit *f*; Sozialrecht *nt*.
social order Sozialordnung *f*.
social partnership Sozialpartnerschaft *f*.
social policy Sozialpolitik *f*; Gesellschaftspolitik *f*.
social security contribution Sozialversicherungsbeitrag *m*.
social security law *(body of laws)* Sozialrecht *nt*; *(individual law)* Sozialversicherungsgesetz *nt*.
social security payment Sozialabgabe *f*.
social security tax Sozialabgabe *f*.
social service *(concept)* Sozialfürsorge *f*; *(benefit)* Sozialleistung *f*.
social service contribution Sozialbeitrag *m*.
social state Sozialstaat *m*.
social system Sozialordnung *f*.
society Gesellschaft *f*; *(club)* Verein *m*.
socioeconomic sozialwirtschaftlich.

sociopolitical sozialpolitisch.
socket *(light bulb)* Fassung *f*; *(wall socket)* Steckdose *f*.
soft weich; *(irresolute)* nachgiebig; *(beverage)* alkoholfrei; *(market)* flau; *(goods)* kurzlebig.
soften weich machen; *(business cycle)* abschwächen.
software Programmierhilfe *f*; Programmausrüstung *f*; Software *f*.
software market Softwaremarkt *m*.
sold verkauft.
sole n *(foot, shoe)* Sohle *f*; *(fish)* Seezunge *f*. a *(only)* Allein-; alleinig; einzig.
sole agency Alleinvertretung *f*.
solicit *(customers)* werben; *(support)* erbitten; *(to plead)* plädieren.
solid *(matter)* fest; *(dense)* dicht; *(rigid)* starr; *(strong)* stark; *(durable)* haltbar; *(fig.)* gründlich; zuverlässig; *(financially)* kreditfähig.
solve lösen.
solvency Zahlungsfähigkeit *f*; Solvenz *f*; Bonität *f*.
solvent n *(chemistry)* Lösungsmittel *nt*. a *(financially)* zahlungsfähig; zahlungskräftig.
sophisticated *(highly developed)* hochentwickelt; *(on a high level)* auf hohem Niveau *nt* stehend; *(complex)* differenziert.
sophistication *(high development)* hochentwickelter Stand *m*; *(technically advanced)* technisch hohes Niveau *nt*; *(complexity)* Differenziertheit *f*.
sort n Sorte *f*; *(kind)* Art *f*; *(species)* Gattung *f*. v sortieren; sichten; *(to cull)* auslesen.

sound n Ton *m*; Klang *m*; *(narrows)* Meeresenge *f*; Sund *m*.
a *(healthy)* gesund; *(undamaged)* unversehrt; *(business)* solide; gut fundiert; zahlungskräftig.
v *(depth)* ausloten.

source Ursprung *m*; *(information)* Quelle *f*; *(supplier)* Lieferant *m*.

source of error Fehlerquelle *f*.

source of information Informationsquelle *f*.

sovereign n *(ruler)* Herrscher *m*.
a souverän; unumschränkt.

space n Raum *m*; *(interstice)* Zwischenraum *m*; *(interval)* Abstand *m*; *(gap)* Lücke *f*; *(outer space)* Weltraum *m*. v *(printing)* spationieren; sperren; in Zwischenräumen *pl* anordnen.

spacious *(roomy)* geräumig; *(extensive)* ausgedehnt.

span n Spanne *f*; *(bridge)* Stützweite *f*. v umspannen; umfassen.

spare n *(spare part)* Ersatzteil *nt*; Extrastück *nt*. a Reserve-. v *(forbearance)* schonen; *(to do without)* erübrigen; entbehren.

spate Flut *f*; Schwall *m*; Überschwemmung *f*.

special Sonder-; Spezial-; speziell; ungewöhnlich.

special arrangement Sonderregelung *f*.

special charge Sondergebühr *f*.

special fee Sondergebühr *f*.

specialist Spezialist *m*; *(expert)* Fachmann *m*; Sachverständige *m/f*.

specialists Fachleute *pl*.

specialization Spezialisierung *f*; Fachrichtung *f*.

specialize sich spezialisieren.

specialized spezialisiert; fachkundig.

special levy Sondererhebung *f*; Ergänzungsabgabe *f*.

special make Sonderanfertigung *f*.

special meeting Sondersitzung *f*.

special offer Sonderangebot *nt*.

special payment Sonderzahlung *f*.

special price Sonderpreis *m*.

special property Sondervermögen *nt*; *(characteristic)* besondere Eigenschaft *f*.

special-purpose saving Zwecksparen *nt*.

special regulation Sonderregelung *f*.

special session Sondersitzung *f*.

special subsidy Sondersubvention *f*.

special tariff Sondertarif *m*.

specialty Spezialität *f*; Besonderheit *f*; Fachgebiet *nt*.

specialty retailer Fachhändler *m*.

specific spezifisch; *(exact)* genau; *(express)* ausdrücklich; *(certain)* bestimmt.

specification Spezifikation *f*; *(exact representation)* genaue Angabe *f*; *(itemization)* Einzelaufstellung *f*.

specified spezifiziert; *(precisely stated)* genau angegeben.

specify spezifizieren; *(to state precisely)* genau angeben; *(to detail)* detaillieren.

speculate spekulieren; *(business dealings)* gewagte Geschäfte *pl* machen; *(to think)* nachdenken; *(to ruminate)* grübeln.

speculation Spekulation *f*; *(thinking)* Nachdenken *nt*.

speculative spekulativ.

speculative deadline Spekulationsfrist *f*.

speculative market Spekulationsmarkt *m*.

speculative period Spekulationsfrist *f*.

speculative profit Spekulationsgewinn *m*.

speculator Spekulant *m*.

speech Vortrag *m*.

speed Geschwindigkeit *f*; Schnelligkeit *f*.

speed of growth Wachstumstempo *nt*.

spend *(money)* ausgeben; verausgaben; aufwenden; *(time)* verbringen; zubringen.

spending Ausgaben *pl*; *(public,
state)* Ausgabenwirtschaft *f*.

spending behavior Ausgabenver-
halten *nt*.

spent *(money)* verausgabt; *(energy)*
erschöpft; *(flame)* erloschen; *(Zeit)*
zugebracht.

spinoff *(business)* Abstoßen *nt* eines
Geschäftszweigs *m*; *(subsidiary)*
Tochtergesellschaft *f*; *(product)*
anfallendes Nebenprodukt *nt*.

spiral n Spirale *f*; *(inflation)*
Schraube *f*. v spiralartig ansteigen.

split n Spaltung *f*; Aufteilung *f*;
(stocks) Aktiensplit *m*. v spalten;
aufteilen; splitten.

spokesman, -person, -woman
Sprecher *m*; Wortführer *m*; *(representative)* Vertrauensmann *m*; Ver-
trauensfrau *f*.

sponsor Förderer *m*; Förderin *f*;
Stifter *m*; *(advertising)* Auftraggeber *m*; *(guarantor)* Bürge *m*; Bürgin *f*; *(financial sponsor)* Geldgeber *m*.

spot n *(locality)* Ort *m*; *(place)*
Stelle *f*; *(stain)* Fleck *m*. a *(market)* Kassa-. v *(to notice)* wahrnehmen; bemerken.

spot check Stichprobe *f*.

spotlight n Scheinwerfer *m*; *(theater)* Rampenlicht *nt*. v anstrahlen; *(to attract notice to)* in den
Blickpunkt *m* rücken.

spot market Kassamarkt *m*; Spotmarkt *m*.

spot price Kassapreis *m*; Preis *m*
bei Sofortzahlung *f*.

spot rate Platzkurs *m*; Kassakurs
m.

spot transaction Kassageschäft *nt*.

spread n *(extent)* Ausdehnung *f*;
Verbreitung *f*; *(distribution)* Streuung *f*; *(span)* Spanne *f*. v ausbreiten; verbreiten; ausdehnen.

spread in interest rates Zinsspanne *f*.

spread sheet Verteilungsbogen *m*.

spur n Sporn *m*; *(incentive)* Ansporn *m*; *(railway)* Gleis *nt*.
v *(riding)* die Sporen *pl* geben;
(to urge on) anspornen.

spurt n plötzliches Vorwärtsschnellen *nt*; *(water)* Hervor-
schiessen *nt*; *(price)* plötzlicher
Preisanstieg *m*. v hochschnellen;
vor- wärtsschnellen; hervorschie-
ßen; plötzlich ansteigen.

squander verschwenden; vergeuden.

squandering n Verschwenden *nt*.
a verschwenderisch.

squeeze n *(pressure)* Druck *m*;
(tight spot) Klemme *f*; *(money)*
finanzieller Druck *m*; Geldver-
legenheit *f*; *(scarcity)* Knappheit *f*.
v drücken; unter Druck *m* setzen;
auspressen.

stability Stabilität *f*; Beständigkeit
f; Festigkeit *f*; *(physical property)*
dynamisches Gleichgewicht *nt*.

stability analysis Stabilitätsanalyse *f*.

stability law Stabilitätsgesetz *nt.*
stabilization Stabilisierung *f*; Festigung *f.*
stabilize stabilisieren; festigen.
stable beständig; gleichbleibend; *(sturdy)* stabil; haltbar; dauerhaft.
stable growth beständiges Wachstum *nt*; Dauerwachstum *nt.*
staff n Stab *m*; Personal *nt*; Belegschaft *f.* v besetzen; mit Personal *nt* versorgen.
staff department Personalabteilung *f.*
staff director Personaldirektor *m.*
staffed mit Personal *nt* versehen; personalmäßig versorgt.
staffing Stellenbesetzung *f*; Personalbesetzung *f*; *(policy)* Stellenbesetzungsplan *m.*
staff manager Personalleiter *m.*
stage of development Entwicklungsstadium *nt.*
stagnant stagnierend; stockend; *(market)* flau.
stagnate stagnieren; stocken; abflauen.
stagnation Stagnation *f*; Stockung *f.*
stake n Stütze *f*; *(betting)* Einsatz *m*; *(capital)* Einschuß *m.* v stützen; riskieren; *(to furnish with necessities)* ausrüsten; *(to advance money)* vorschießen.
stall n *(sales booth)* Verkaufsstand *m*; *(market)* Marktbude *f*; *(theater)* Sperrsitz *m.* v *(engine)* abdrosseln; *(for time)* zögern um Zeit *f* zu gewinnen.
stamp n Stempel *m*; *(postage)* Briefmarke *f*; *(product)* Kennzeichen *nt.* v stempeln; *(coin)* prägen; *(postage)* freimachen; frankieren.

stamped abgestempelt; *(coined)* geprägt; *(postage)* frankiert.
standard Standard *m*; Norm *f*; *(quality)* Gütegrad *m*; *(average)* Durchschnitt *m*; *(coinage)* Feingehalt *m*; *(level)* Niveau *nt.*
standard deviation Normalabweichung *f*; Standardabweichung *f.*
standard error Standardfehler *m.*
standard for calculation Berechnungsmaßstab *m.*
standard format Standardformat *nt.*
standardization Standardisierung *f*; Normierung *f*; Normung *f*; Vereinheitlichung *f.*
standardize standardisieren; normieren; normen; vereinheitlichen.
standardized genormt; normiert; standardisiert; vereinheitlicht.
standardized working hours Regelarbeitszeit *f.*
standard of living Lebensstandard *m*; Lebenshaltung *f.*
standard practice übliches Verfahren *nt.*
standard solution Einheitslösung *f.*
standard value Einheitswert *m.*
standby *(waiting)* Wartestellung *f*; *(readiness)* Bereitschaft *f*; *(in reserve)* Reserve *f.*
standby agreement Bereitstellungsvereinbarung *f.*
standby credit Reservekredit *m.*
standing n Stehen *nt*; *(rank)* Rang *m*; *(level)* Stand *m*; *(position)* Stellung *f*; *(importance)* Geltung *f.* a stehend; permanent.
standing order Dauerauftrag *m.*
start n Start *m*; *(departure)* Aufbruch *m*; Beginn *m.* v starten; aufbrechen; beginnen.

start a business   ein Unternehmen *nt* gründen; sich etablieren.
starting point   Ausgangspunkt *m*.
starting position   Ausgangsposition *f*.
starting year   Anfangsjahr *nt*.
start-up phase   Anlaufphase *f*.
start-up problem   Anlaufproblem *nt*; Anfangsproblem *nt*.
state   n Staat *m*; *(condition)* Zustand *m*; *(positon)* Lage *f*; Status *m*. a *(government)* Staats-. v *(to state)* statieren; *(data)* angeben; *(to remark)* ausführen; *(to present)* darlegen.
state combine   Staatskonzern *m*; Kombinat *nt*.
stated value   festgestellter Wert *m*.
state finances   Staatsfinanzen *pl*.
state indebtedness   Staatsverschuldung *f*.
state intervention   Staatsintervention *f*; Staatsdirigismus *m*.
statement   Erklärung *f*; Angabe *f*; *(account rendered)* Rechenschaftsbericht *m*; *(statement of account)* Kontoauszug *m*; *(invoice)* Rechnung *f*.
state of the art   Stand *m* der Technik *f*.
state of the economy   Wirtschaftslage *f*; Wirtschaftssituation *f*.
state of the market   Marktlage *f*; Marktkonstellation *f*.
state-owned enterprise   Staatsunternehmen *nt*.
state planner   staatlicher Planer *m*.
state subsidy   Staatssubvention *f*; Staatszuschuß *m*.
static   n *(radio)* Empfangsstörung *f*. a *(unchanging)* statisch.
statistic   statistische Angabe *f*; *(number)* statistische Ziffer *f*.

statistical   statistisch.
statistical data   statistische Daten *pl*.
statistician   Statistiker *m*.
statistics   Statistik *f*.
status symbol   Statussymbol *nt*.
statutory   satzungsmäßig.
steel mill   Stahlwerk *nt*.
steel worker   Stahlarbeiter *m*.
steer   n *(cattle)* Ochse *m*. v *(to direct)* steuern.
steering   Steuerung *f*; *(automobile)* Lenkung *f*.
stifle   ersticken; *(a rumor)* unterdrücken; *(competition)* abdrosseln.
stimulate   stimulieren; anregen; *(revitalize)* beleben; *(crank up)* ankurbeln.
stimulating   stimulierend; anregend; auftreibend.
stimulation   Stimulanz *f*; Anregung *f*; Auftrieb *m*; *(revitalization)* Belebung *f*; *(cranking up)* Ankurbelung *f*.
stint   n bestimmte Dienstperiode *f*; Arbeitsperiode *f*. v *(to be stingy)* knausern; *(to save up)* einsparen.
stipulate   festsetzen; ausbedingen; vereinbaren; vorsehen.
stipulated   festgesetzt; ausgemacht; *(contractual)* vertragsgemäß.
stipulated damages   Konventionalstrafe *f*.
stipulation   Bedingung *f*; Abmachung *f*; Vereinbarung *f*.
stock   n Stammkapital *nt*; Geschäftskapital *nt*; Aktienkapital *nt*; *(shares)* Aktien *pl*; Kapitalbeteiligung *f*; *(inventory)* Warenlager *nt*. v lagern.
stockable   lagerungsfähig.
stock allotment   Bezugsschein *m*.

stock analyst Aktienanalyst *m*.

stockbroker Börsenmakler *m*; Effektenhändler *m*; Aktienhändler *m*.

stockbroking Börsenkommissionsgeschäft *nt*; Effektengeschäft *nt*; Aktiengeschäft *nt*.

stock dividend Gratisaktie *f*; Berichtigungsaktie *f*.

stocked vorrätig; auf Lager *nt*; *(carried)* geführt.

stock evaluation Aktienbewertung *f*.

stock exchange crash Börsenkrach *m*.

stock exchange order Börsenauftrag *m*.

stock exchange price list Kursblatt *nt*.

stock exchange quotation Börsenkurs *m*.

stock exchange supervision Börsenaufsicht *f*.

stock exchange trading Börsenhandel *m*.

stockholder Aktionär *m*; Aktieninhaber *m*.

stockholders' equity Eigenkapital *nt*; Gesellschaftskapital *nt*.

stock index Börsenindex *m*.

stocking *(hose)* Strumpf *m*; *(inventory)* Lagerung *f*.

stock investment Aktienanlage *f*.

stockjobber Börsenjobber *m*; Börsenmann *m*; Börsenfrau *f*; Börsenhändler *m*; Börsenspekulant *m*.

stockjobbing Aktiengeschäft *nt*; Spekulationsgeschäft *nt*; Effektenhandel *m*.

stockkeeping Lagerhaltung *f*.

stock market Effektenbörse *f*; Wertpapierbörse *f*; Aktienbörse *f*; Aktienmarkt *m*.

stock market loss Kursverlust *m*.

stock market quotation Kurszettel *m*.

stock market report Börsenbericht *m*; Kursblatt *nt*.

stock market transaction Börsengeschäft *nt*.

stock market trend Aktientendenz *f*.

stock market turnover Börsenumsatz *m*.

stock on hand Lagerbestand *m*.

stock option Aktienbezugsrecht *nt*.

stock option plan Belegschaftsaktiensystem *nt*.

stockpile horten; aufstocken.

stockpiling Lagerwirtschaft *f*; Vorratswirtschaft *f*; Lageraufstockung *f*; Aufstockung *f*; Einlagerung *f*; *(hoarding)* Anhäufung *f*.

stock price Aktienpreis *m*; Aktienkurs *m*.

stock price gain Kursgewinn *m*.

stock purchase warrant Optionsschein *m*.

stock split Aktiensplit *m*; Aktienaufteilung *f*.

stock subscription Kapitalbeteiligung *f*.

stocktrading Aktienhandel *m*; Effektenhandel *m*.

stock transaction Aktientransaktion *f*.

stock transfer tax Börsenumsatzsteuer *f*.

stop n *(barrier)* Sperre *f*; *(bus)* Haltestelle *f*. v *(to finish)* beenden; *(to come/bring to a stop)* anhalten; *(to cease)* aufhören.

stopgap assistance Überbrückungshilfe *f*.

stop order Limit *nt*.

stoppage Anhalten *nt*; *(interrup-*

tion) Unterbrechung *f; (funds)*
Sperrung *f; (work)* Einstellung *f;*
(traffic) Stau *m.*
storable   lagerungsfähig.
storage   Lagerung *f;* Aufbewahrung *f;* Speicherung *f;* Einlagerung
f; (capacity) Lagerraum *m; (cost)*
Lagerkosten *pl.*
storage capacity   Speicherkapazität *f.*
storage performance   Speicherleistung *f.*
store   n Vorrat *m; (abundance)*
Fülle *f; (shop)* Geschäft *nt.* v speichern; aufbewahren; lagern.
stranglehold   Würgegriff *m;* Umklammerung *f.*
strapped   unzulänglich versehen.
strategic   strategisch.
stream   Strom *m; (influx)* Zustrom
m.
streamline   n Stromlinienform *f.*
v stromlinienförmig gestalten; *(to*
simplify) vereinfachen; *(to increase*
efficiency) rationalisieren; *(to*
modernize) modernisieren.
streamlining of services   Entbürokratisierung *f.*
strength   Kraft *f; (character)* Stärke
f; (potency) Potenz *f.*
strengthen   stärken; kräftigen.
strengthening   Stärkung *f; (rein-*
forcement) Verstärkung *f.*
strike   n Streik *m; (work stoppage)*
Arbeitseinstellung *f;* Arbeitsniederlegung *f.* v streiken; Arbeit *f* niederlegen.
strike against   bestreiken.
strike area   Streikgebiet *nt.*
strikebreaker   Streikbrecher *m.*
strike-free   streikfrei.
strike loss   Streikverlust *m.*
strike month   Streikmonat *m.*

striking   n Streiken *nt;* Niederlegen
nt der Arbeit *f.* a streikend; die
Arbeit *f* niederlegend; *(notice-*
able) auffallend; ins Auge *nt* fall-
end.
strip mining   Tagebaubetrieb *m.*
strongbox   Tresor *m.*
structural   strukturell; baulich.
structural adjustment   Strukturanpassung *f.*
structural change   Strukturwandel
m.
structural damage   Gebäudeschaden *m.*
structural effect   Struktureffekt *m.*
structural plan   Strukturplan *m.*
structural problem   Strukturproblem *nt.*
structural program   Strukturprogramm *nt.*
structural shift   strukturelle Veränderung *f.*
structural weakness   Strukturschwäche *f.*
structure   n Struktur *f;* Aufbau *m;*
Gefüge *nt; (building)* Gebäude *nt;*
Bauwerk *nt.* v strukturieren; aufbauen.
structuring   Strukturierung *f.*
struggle   Kampf *m.*
study   Studie *f; (room)* Arbeitszim-
mer *nt.*
study group   Arbeitskreis *m.*
subaccount   Unterkonto *nt.*
subassembly   Teilmontage *f.*
subcategorization   Untergliederung *f.*
subcommittee   Unterausschuß *m.*
subcontract   Nebenvertrag *m;*
Zulieferungsvertrag *m.*
subcontracting   Zulieferung *f.*
subcontracting firm   Zulieferbetrieb *m.*

subcontractor Zulieferant *m*;
Unterlieferant *m*; Subunternehmer
m; Zulieferer *m*.

subdivide aufgliedern; untergliedern; *(land)* parzellieren; unterteilen.

subdivision Untergliederung *f*;
(branch department) Unterabteilung *f*; *(ledger)* Unterspalte *f*; *(real
estate)* Parzellierung *f*; *(housing
development)* Wohnsiedlung *f*.

subduct zurückziehen.

subject Fach *nt*; Fachgebiet *nt*;
(topic) Thema *nt*.

subject to charges gebührenpflichtig.

subject to postage portopflichtig.

subject to registration meldepflichtig.

subject to report berichtspflichtig.

sublease Untermiete *f*.

submission Unterwerfung *f*; *(of
documents)* Eingabe *f*; Vorlage *f*;
(bidding) Submission *f*.

submit sich unterwerfen; *(document)* einreichen; vorlegen; unterbreiten.

subordinate n Untergebene *m/f*.
a untergeordnet; zweitrangig.
v unterordnen; zurückstellen.

subpart *(organization)* Unterabteilung *f*.

subscribe *(newspaper)* abonnieren.

subscriber Subscribent *m*; *(newspaper)* Abonnent *m*; Bezieher *m*;
(TV, radio, cable TV) Teilnehmer.

subscription *(newspaper)* Abonnement *nt*; *(before availability)*
Vorbestellung *f*; *(donation)* Beitrag
m; *(TV, radio, cable TV)* Teilnahme *f*; *(stocks)* Option *f*.

subsequent nachfolgend.

subsidiary Konzerngesellschaft *f*;
Tochtergesellschaft *f*; *(branch)*
Ableger *m*; Filiale *f*.

subsidiary company Tochterfirma
f; Tochterbetrieb *m*.

subsidiary enterprise Tochterunternehmen *nt*.

subsidiary institute Tochterinstitut *nt*.

subsidization Subventionierung *f*;
Bezuschussung *f*.

subsidize subventionieren; finanziell unterstützen.

subsidy Zuschuß *m*; staatliche
Unterstützung *f*; Subvention *f*.

subsidy funds Subventionsgeld *nt*.

subsidy payment Subventionszahlung *f*; Zuschußzahlung *f*.

subsidy reduction Subventionsabbau *m*.

subsidy requirements Zuschußbedarf *m*; Subventionsbedarf *m*.

subsistence Existenz *f*.

subsistence rate Existenzsatz *m*.

substandard unter der Norm *f*;
(below average) unterdurchschnittlich; *(not of full value)* nicht
vollwertig.

substitute n Substitut *nt/m*; Ersatz
m; *(imitation)* Nachahmung *f*;
(stand-in) Surrogat *nt*; *(for a person)* Stellvertreter *m*. v substitu-
ieren; ersetzen; vertreten.

substitution Substitution *f*; Ersatz
m.

subtraction Subtraktion *f*; *(deduction)* Abzug *m*.

successful erfolgreich.

successful year Erfolgsjahr *nt*.

successive aufeinanderfolgend.

successor Nachfolger *m*.

sue verklagen; Klage *f* anstrengen;
prozessieren; ersuchen.

suffice reichen; genügen; ausreichen.

sufficient genug; hinreichend.
suffrage Stimmrecht *nt.*
suggest vorschlagen.
suggested compromise Kompromißvorschlag *m.*
suit n *(man's apparel)* Anzug *m;* *(woman's apparel)* Kostüm *nt;* *(legal action)* Rechtsstreit *m;* Prozeß *m; (petition)* Gesuch *nt.* v *(to please)* gefallen; *(to be convenient)* passen; *(to be flattering)* gut stehen.
suitability Eignung *f.*
suitable geeignet; verwendbar.
sum Summe *f;* Betrag *m.*
summarize zusammenfassen.
summary Zusammenfassung *f;* *(excerpt)* Auszug *m; (sketch)* Abriß *m; (abstract)* Kompendium *nt.*
summary budget Gesamtetat *m.*
summit talks Gipfelkonferenz *f;* Gipfeltreffen *nt.*
sum total Gesamtbetrag *m.*
superannuate pensionieren.
superheated überheizt; überhitzt.
superintendent Vorsteher *m;* Aufsichtsbeamte *m;* Aufsichtsbeamtin *f.*
superior n Vorgesetzte *m/f.* a überlegen; *(excellent)* vorzüglich; *(above average)* überdurchschnittlich; *(rank)* ranghöher.
supermarket Supermarkt *m;* Großmarkt *m.*
superstructure Überbau *m; (railway)* Oberbau *m.*
supervise überwachen; beaufsichtigen; kontrollieren.
supervising n Überwachen *nt;* Beaufsichtigen *nt;* Kontrollieren *nt.* a aufsichtsführend; überwachend.
supervision Überwachung *f;* Aufsichtsführung *f.*

supervisor Aufseher *m;* Kontrolleur *m;* Aufsichtsbeamte *m;* Aufsichtsbeamtin *f.*
supervisory überwachend; aufsichtsführend.
supervisory agency Aufsichtsamt *nt.*
supervisory body Kontrollgremium *nt.*
supervisory committee Kontrollausschuß *m.*
supplement n Ergänzung *f; (newspaper)* Beilage *f; (addition)* Zusatz *m.* v ergänzen.
supplemental ergänzend; zusätzlich.
supplemental claim Nachforderung *f.*
supplementary nachträglich; *(complementary)* ergänzend.
supplementary appropriation Nachtragsetat *m;* Nachtragshaushalt *m.*
supplementary budget Nachtragsetat *m;* Nachtragshaushalt *m.*
supplier Anbieter *m;* Auslieferer *m;* Lieferant *m;* Lieferfirma *f;* *(subcontractor)* Zulieferer *m.*
supplier's credit Lieferantenkredit *m.*
supplier country Lieferland *nt.*
supply n Versorgung *f;* Belieferung *f;* Eindeckung *f; (economics)* Angebot *nt; (stock)* Vorrat *m;* Bestand *m.* v versorgen; beschaffen; beliefern; verschaffen.
supply contract Lieferabkommen *nt;* Liefervertrag *m.*
supplying n Versorgen *nt; (subcontract)* Zuliefern *nt;* Eindecken *nt.* a versorgend; zuliefernd; eindeckend.

supply of cash Bargeldversorgung
f; *(cash on hand)* Bargeldvorrat *m*.

supply schedule Angebotstabelle
f; *(delivery)* Lieferzeitplan *m*.

support n Unterstützung *f*; *(aid)*
Hilfe *f*; *(subsistence)* Unterhalt *m*.
v unterstützen; *(idea)* bejahen; *(to
give aid)* Hilfe *f* leisten; *(financially)* unterhalten; versorgen;
ernähren.

supported unterstützt; *(stock market)* gestützt.

supporting n Unterstützen *nt*;
Unterhalten *nt*. a Hilfs-; stützend;
helfend; fördernd.

support payment Unterhaltszahlung *f*.

support personnel Hilfspersonal
nt.

support price Stützpreis *m*.

support program Förderprogramm *nt*.

supranational übernational;
supranational.

surcharge Preisaufschlag *m*;
Zuschlagsgebühr *f*; *(freight)*
Frachtaufschlag *m*.

surety Sicherheit *f*; *(guarantee)*
Pfand *nt*; Kaution *f*; *(personal
guarantor)* Bürge *m*; Bürgin;
Bürgschaftsgeber *m*; Garant *m*.

surge in orders Auftragsflut *f*.

surplus Überfluß *m*; *(balance
sheet)* Überschuß *m*.

surplus accounting Gewinnrechnung *f*.

surplus allocation Rücklagendotierung *f*.

surplus capacity Kapazitätsüberschuß *m*; freie Kapazität *f*.

surplus condition Überschußlage *f*.

surplus product Überschußprodukt *nt*.

surrounding conditions Rah-
menbedingungen *pl*.

surtax Ergänzungsabgabe *f*.

surveillance Überwachung *f*;
(supervision) Beaufsichtigung *f*;
Kontrolle *f*.

survey n *(opinion research)*
Umfrage *f*; Befragung *f*; *(inspection)* Besichtigung *f*. v befragen;
prüfen; begutachten; überschauen.

survey year Erhebungsjahr *nt*.

susceptible beeinflußbar.

suspend *(to discontinue)* einstellen; *(to interrupt)* unterbrechen;
(rule) aufheben; *(public servant)*
beurlauben.

suspended eingestellt; *(rule)* aufge-
hoben; *(public service)* vorüberge-
hend des Dienstes *m* enthoben;
beurlaubt.

swamp n Sumpf *m*. v *(market)*
überschwemmen; *(work)* überladen; überfordern.

swap n Tausch *m*; *(deal)* Swapgeschäft *nt*. v tauschen; eintauschen.

swap arrangement Swapabkommen *nt*; Swapvereinbarung *f*.

sweep n *(radar)* Reichweite *f*; *(fig.)*
Einflußsphäre *f*. v *(floor)* fegen;
(radar) absuchen.

sweeping *(change)* weitreichend;
extensiv.

sweeten versüßen; *(fig.)* mundgerecht machen.

swell anschwellen; ansteigen.

swing n *(extent)* Spielraum *m*;
(margin) Marge *f*; *(economic shift)*
Umschwung *m*; *(trading credit)*
Überziehungskredit *m*. v schwingen; *(back & forth)* pendeln.

swinging n Schwingen *nt*; *(fluctuating)* Schwanken *nt*; *(back &
forth)* Pendeln *nt*. a schwingend;

schwankend; *(back & forth)* pendelnd.

switch n *(electrical)* Schalter *m*.
v schalten; *(train)* umlenken; *(loyalty)* wechseln; *(to exchange)* auswechseln.

switchboard *(factory)* Schalttafel *f*; *(communication)* Telefonzentrale *f*.

switching *(electricity)* Schalten *nt*; *(train)* Umlenken *nt*; *(loyalty)* Wechseln *nt*; *(exchange)* Auswechseln *nt*.

syndicate Syndikat *nt*; Kartell *nt*; Konsortium *nt*.

syndicate transaction Konsortialgeschäft *nt*.

syndication *(formation of syndicate)* Syndikatsbildung *f*; Konsortialbildung *f*;*(electronic media)* überregionale Ausstrahlung *f*; *(press)* überregionale Verbreitung *f*.

synthetic n Kunststoff *m*; *(fiber)* Kunstfaser *f*. a synthetisch; *(artificial)* künstlich.

systematic systematisch; *(thorough)* gründlich.

system formation Systembildung *f*.

system of taxation Steuersystem *nt*.

T

table n Tisch *m*; *(list)* Liste *f*; Verzeichnis *nt*; *(catalogue)* Tabelle *f*; *(tablet)* Tafel *f*; *(summary)* Übersicht *f*; Schema *nt*. v *(to postpone)* vertagen.

tabulate tabellarisieren; tabellarisch ordnen.

tabulating Tabellarisieren *nt*; tabellarisches Ordnen *nt*.

tabulation Tabellarisierung *f*; tabellarische Darstellung *f*.

tack n *(course)* Richtung *f*; Weg *m*; Kurs *m*. v *(to fasten)* befestigen; heften; *(nautical)* kreuzen; lavieren.

tactic taktische Maßnahme *f*; taktischer Zug *m*.

tactical taktisch; klug; planvoll.

tactics Taktik *f*.

tag n Anhänger *m*; Anhängezettel *m*; Schild *nt*; *(label)* Etikett *nt*. v bezeichnen; etikettieren; mit einem Anhänger *m* versehen.

tailspin *(airplane)* Trudeln *nt*; Spiralsturz *m*; spiralartiges Fallen *nt*.

take back zurücknehmen; *(to withdraw, retract)* zurückziehen.

take effect in Kraft *f* treten.

take in *(profit, receipts)* vereinnahmen.

take into account einkalkulieren.

takeoff *(airplane)* Abflug *m*; Start *m*.

take off *(airplane)* abfliegen; starten; *(body weight)* abnehmen; *(to deduct)* abziehen; *(apparel)* ausziehen; *(hat)* abnehmen.

take office Amt *nt* antreten.

takeover Übernahme *f*.

take over übernehmen.

take part in decision-making   mitbestimmen.

tally   n Rechnung *f*; Abrechnung *f*; *(list)* Liste *f*; *(coupon)* Kupon *m*. v zusammenzählen; nachzählen; *(to agree)* übereinstimmen.

tamper   *(to interfere)* sich einmischen; *(to meddle)* hineinpfuschen; *(to falsify)* verfälschen.

tampering   *(interference)* Einmischung *f*; *(falsification)* Verfälschung *f*.

tangible assets   Sacheigentum *nt*.

tangible expenses   Sachausgaben *f*.

tangible goods   materielle Güter *pl*.

tangible means   Sachmittel *pl*.

tap   n *(water)* Hahn *m*; *(telephone)* Mithöreinrichtung *f*. v anzapfen; *(telephone)* mithören; *(natural resources)* erschließen.

tape   n Band *nt*; *(recording)* Tonband *nt*; *(measuring)* Bandmaß *nt*; *(paper)* Papierstreifen *m*. v *(to seal)* mit Klebestreifen *m* verschließen; *(to record)* aufnehmen; *(spoken recording)* auf Band *nt* sprechen.

taped   *(sealed)* mit Klebestreifen *m* verschlossen; *(recorded)* aufgenommen; *(spoken recording)* auf Band *nt* gesprochen.

tapped   angezapft; *(telephone)* abgehört; *(natural resources)* erschlossen.

tapping   Anzapfen *nt*; *(telephone)* Mithören *nt*; *(natural resources)* Erschließen *nt*.

target   n Ziel *nt*; Zielsetzung *f*; *(goal)* Planziel *nt*. v Ziel *nt* setzen; planen; vorherbestimmen.

target audience   Zielpublikum *nt*.

target complex   Zielkomplex *m*.

target country   Zielland *nt*.

target group   Zielgruppe *f*.

target market   Kundenzielgruppe *f*.

tariff   Tarif *m*; *(customs duty)* Zolltarif *m*; Taxe *f*.

tariff agreement   Zollabkommen *nt*.

tariff autonomy   Tarifautonomie *f*.

tariff barrier   Zollschranke *f*.

tariff commission   Tarifkommission *f*.

tariff committee   Tarifausschuß *m*.

tariff control   Tarifkontrolle *f*.

tariff decision   Tarifentscheidung *nt*; *(result of wage tariff negotiation)* Tarifergebnis *nt*.

tariff duty   Tarifzoll *m*.

tariff expert   Tarifexperte *m*; Tarifexpertin *f*.

tariff increase   Tariferhöhung *f*.

tariff movement   Tarifbewegung *f*.

tariff negotiation results   Tarifergebnis *f*.

tariff policy   Tarifpolitik *f*.

tariff preference   Tarifvorzug *m*; Zollpräferenz *f*; Zollbegünstigung *f*.

tariff rate   Gebührensatz *m*; Zollsatz *m*; Tarifsatz *m*.

tariff reduction   *(general reduction)* Tarifsenkung *f*; Zollsenkung *f*; Zollabbau *m*; *(individual reduction)* Tarifermäßigung *f*.

tariff revenue   fiskalische Gebühr *f*; Finanzzoll *m*.

tariff sovereignty   Tarifhoheit *f*.

tariff value   Zollwert *m*.

task   Aufgabe *f*; *(administrative)* Verwaltungsaufgabe *f*.

task force   Aufgabengruppe *f*; Arbeitsstab *m*; *(committee)* Arbeitsausschuß *m*.

task of reconstruction   Wiederaufbauaufgabe *f.*

tax   n Steuer *f*; *(social service tax)* Abgabe *f*; Taxe *f.*   v besteuern; *(to impose exertion)* anstrengen; anspannen.

taxable   *(subject to taxation)* steuerpflichtig; abgabenpflichtig; *(capable of being taxed)* besteuerungsfähig.

tax account   Steuerkonto *nt.*

tax advantage   Steuervorteil *m.*

tax aid   Steuerhilfe *f.*

tax assessment   Steuerschätzung *f*; *(tax burden)* Steuerbelastung *f.*

taxation   *(imposition)* Besteuerung *f*; *(the field)* Steuerwesen *nt.*

taxation guideline   Steuerrichtlinie *f.*

taxation law   *(body of laws)* Steuerrecht *nt*; *(individual law)* Steuergesetz *nt.*

taxation laws   Steuergesetzgebung *f.*

tax avoidance   Steuervermeidung *f.*

tax bonus   Steuerbonus *m.*

tax burden   Steuerbelastung *f.*

tax computation   Steuerberechnung *f.*

tax consultant   Steuerberater *m.*

tax credit   Steuerguthaben *nt.*

tax deduction   Steuerabzug *m.*

tax deficit   Steuerdefizit *nt*; Steuerausfall *m.*

tax dodging   Steuerumgehung *f.*

tax estimate   Steuerschätzung *f.*

tax evasion   Steuerhinterziehung *f*; Steuerumgehung *f.*

tax-exempt   steuerfrei.

tax expert   Steuerfachmann *m*; Steuerexperte *m*; Steuerexpertin *f.*

tax haven   Steuerparadies *nt*; Steueroase *f.*

taxing authority   Steuerbehörde *f.*

tax law   Steuergesetz *nt.*

tax liability   Steuerpflicht *f.*

tax loss   Steuereinbuße *f.*

tax moneys   Steuergelder *pl.*

taxpayer   Steuerzahler *m*; Steuerpflichtige *m/f*; Besteuerte *m/f.*

tax policy   Steuerpolitik *f.*

tax progression   Steuerprogression *f.*

tax rate   Steuersatz *m.*

tax receipts   Steuereinnahmen *pl.*

tax reduction   Steuerentlastung *f*; Steuersenkung *f.*

tax reform   Steuerreform *f.*

tax regulation   Steuervorschrift *f.*

tax relief   Steuerentlastung *f*; Steuererleichterung *f*; *(aid)* Steuerhilfe *f.*

tax revenue   Steuereinnahme *f.*

tax structure   Steuersystem *nt.*

team   *(sports)* Mannschaft *f*; *(work)* Arbeitsgemeinschaft *f*; Arbeitsgruppe *f*; Team *nt.*

team of analysts   Analystenteam *nt.*

team of experts   Expertenteam *nt.*

teamwork   Gruppenarbeit *f*; Teamarbeit *f*; koordinierte Zusammenarbeit *f.*

teaser   *(marketing)* Anreiz *m*; *(advertising)* anreizende Reklame *f*; Rätselreklame *f.*

technical   technisch; fachlich.

technical director   technischer Direktor *m.*

technically inexperienced   technisch unerfahren; sachfremd.

technical manager   technischer Leiter *m.*

technical newspapers   technische Fachpresse *f.*

technical question technische Frage *f*; Sachfrage *f*.

technique Technik *f*; technische Ausführung *f*; *(method)* Methode *f*.

technocrat Technokrat *m*.

technological technologisch.

technological advance technologischer Fortschritt *m*.

technological change technologische Änderung *f*.

technological innovation technologische Neuerung *f*.

technologist Technologe *m*; Technologin *f*; Gewerbekundige *m/f*.

technology Technologie *f*; Gewerbekunde *f*.

technology strategy technologische Strategie *f*.

technology transfer Technologietransfer *m*.

telecommunications Telekommunikation *f*; *(the field)* Fernmeldewesen *nt*; *(traffic)* Fernmeldeverkehr *m*; *(technology)* Fernmeldetechnik *f*; Telekommunikationstechnik *f*.

telegram Telegramm *nt*; Drahtnachricht *f*; Depesche *f*.

telephone n Fernsprecher *m*; Telefon *nt*. v telefonieren; anrufen.

telephone wire Fernsprechleitung *f*.

television advertising Werbefernsehen *nt*.

telex Fernschreiber *m*.

teller Kassierer *m*; Kassenbeamte *m*; Kassenbeamtin *f*; Schalterbeamte *m*; Schalterbeamtin *f*.

temporary arrangement Übergangsregelung *f*.

tend tendieren.

tendency to save Sparneigung *f*.

tender n *(bid)* Lieferungsangebot *nt*; *(offer)* Offerte *f*; Anerbieten *nt*; *(submission)* Submission *f*. v anbieten; offerieren.

tendered shares angebotene Aktien *pl*.

tentative Versuchs-; *(preliminary)* vorläufig; *(experimentally)* versuchsweise; probeweise.

tentative agreement vorläufiges Übereinkommen *nt*; *(draft)* Vertragsentwurf *m*.

term n Terminus *m*; *(expression)* Ausdruck *m*; *(condition)* Vertragsbedingung *f*; *(time)* Frist *f*; Zeitdauer *f*; *(payment period)* Zahlungsfrist *f*; Termin *m*. v benennen.

term borrowing befristete Geldaufnahme *f*.

term debt befristete Schuld *f*.

term financing befristete Finanzierung *f*.

terminal n *(airport)* Terminal *nt*; Flughafengebäude *nt*; *(computer)* Endgerät *nt*; *(railway)* Endbahnhof *m*; *(tram, bus)* Endhaltestelle *f*. a End-; begrenzend; beendend.

terminate abschließen; *(job, contract)* kündigen; *(to complete)* zum Abschluß *m* bringen; *(to finish)* beenden.

terminated abgeschlossen; *(job, contract)* gekündigt; *(completed)* zum Abschluß gebracht; *(finished)* beendet.

termination *(completion)* Abschluß *m*; *(dismissal)* Kündigung *f*; *(end)* Ende *nt*.

terminology Terminologie *f*; Fachsprache *f*.

term investment befristete Investition *f*.

term of office Amtszeit *f*.

terms of trade   Austauschrelationen *pl*; Austauschverhältnis *nt*.

territory   Gebiet *nt*; Territorium *nt*; *(sales)* Vertreterbezirk *m*; *(travel)* Reisegebiet *nt*.

tertiary reserves   Reserven *pl* dritter Ordnung *f*.

test   n Test *m*; *(experiment)* Versuch *m*; *(test piece)* Probe *f*; *(examination)* Prüfung *f*; *(investigation)* Untersuchung *f*. v testen; *(to try out)* erproben; *(to examine)* prüfen; *(to investigate)* untersuchen.

test case   Testfall *m*.

testing facility   Prüfanlage *f*.

test market   Versuchsmarkt *m*.

text   *(book, document)* Text *m*; *(wording)* Wortlaut *m*; *(contents)* Inhalt *m*.

textile   *(fabric)* Webstoff *m*; Textil-; Web-.

textile maker   Textilfabrikant *m*.

text processing   Textverarbeitung *f*.

theme   *(topic)* Gegenstand *m*; *(theme song)* Kennmelodie *f*; *(motif)* Motiv *nt*.

theory of competition   Wettbewerbstheorie *f*.

theory of demand   Nachfragetheorie *f*.

theory of economic cycles   Konjunkturtheorie *f*.

theory of market trends   Marktzyklustheorie *f*.

theory of production   Produktionstheorie *f*.

Third World   Dritte Welt *f*.

threat   *(expressed threat)* Drohung *f*; *(menace)* Bedrohung *f*.

threaten   *(to express a threat)* drohen; *(to be a threat)* bedrohen.

threat of dismissal   Kündigungsdrohung *f*.

threat to existence   Existenzbedrohung *f*.

threshold   Schwelle *f*.

thrift   *(economy)* Wirtschaftlichkeit *f*; *(thriftiness)* Sparsamkeit *f*.

thrive   gedeihen; *(to flourish)* blühen; florieren; *(to prosper)* prosperieren.

thriving   n Gedeihen *nt*. a gedeihend.

throw out of power   hinauswerfen; *(by force)* stürzen.

thrust   n Stoß *m*; *(blow, stroke)* Hieb *m*; *(fig.)* Vorstoß *m*; *(of an argument)* Hauptidee *f*; Hauptrichtung *f*. v stoßen; *(to strike a blow)* hauen; *(fig.)* vorstoßen; *(to throw)* werfen.

tide over   überbrücken.

tie   n Band *nt*; *(bond, union)* Bindung *f*; *(association, connection)* Verbindung *f*; *(voting)* Stimmengleichheit *f*; *(neckwear)* Schlips *m*. v binden; *(to connect, unite)* verbinden.

tie up   *(a ship)* vertäuen; *(to dock)* anlegen; *(to obstruct)* aufhalten; lahmlegen; *(to commit)* an einen Zweck *m* binden; *(to reserve)* einbehalten; *(a contract)* abschließen.

tight   eng; *(taut)* gespannt; *(closed)* dicht; *(moisture proof)* undurchlässig; *(money)* knapp; *(niggardly)* knauserig; knickerig.

tighten   festigen; *(to strenghen)* verstärken; *(to tie more tightly)* fester binden; *(belt)* enger schnallen; *(screw)* anziehen; *(rope)* festzurren; *(restrictions)* verschärfen.

tightened   gefestigt; *(strengthened)* verstärkt; *(screw)* angezogen; *(rope)* festgezurrt; *(restrictions)* verschärft.

tightening   n Festigen *nt*; *(strengthening)* Verstärken *nt*; *(screw)* Anziehen *nt*; *(rope)* Fest-zurren *nt*; *(restrictions)* Verschär-fen *nt*; Verschärfung *f*. v *(becoming tighter)* sich verstärkend; sich verschärfend.

time deposit rate   Termingeldsatz *m*.

time deposits   Termineinlagen *pl*; Termingelder *pl*.

time difference   Zeitunterschied *m*.

time estimate   Zeitschätzung *f*.

time lag   Zeitabstand *m*; zeitliche Verschiebung *f*.

time of payment   Zahlungsfrist *f*.

time series   Zeitreihe *f*.

timetable   Zeitplan *m*; *(train schedule)* Fahrplan *m*; Kursbuch *nt*; *(airplane schedule)* Flugplan *m*.

time worked in a lifetime   Le-bensarbeitszeit *f*.

timing   Zeitwahl *f*; Terminierung *f*.

title   Titel *m*; *(legal claim)* Rechts-anspruch *m*; *(legal title)* Rechtsti-tel *m*; *(right)* Anrecht *nt*; Verfü-gungsrecht *nt*.

title register   Grundbuch *nt*.

toehold   *(point of departure)* Ansatzpunkt *m*; *(point of support)* Stützpunkt *m*.

token   n *(sign)* Zeichen *nt*; *(proof)* Beweis *m*; *(coupon)* Gutschein *m*; Bon *m*; *(pseudocurrency)* Notgeld *nt*. a *(compliance)* symbolisch.

toll   n Abgabe *f*; *(fee)* Gebühr *f*; *(telephone)* Fernsprechgebühr *f*. v *(bell)* läuten.

toll-free   gebührenfrei.

tonnage   *(load-bearing capacity)* Tragfähigkeit *f*; *(weight capacity)* Tonnengehalt *m*; Tonnenkapazität

f; *(volume capacity)* Frachtraum *m*.

tool   n Werkzeug *nt*; Instrument *nt*; *(appliance, device)* Gerät *nt*. v *(leather)* punzen.

tooling   *(leather)* Punzarbeit *f*.

top-level functionary   Spitzen-funktionär *m*.

top-level talk   Spitzengespräch *nt*.

top management   oberste Be-triebsführung *f*; oberste Leitung *f*; Spitzenkräfte *pl*.

top manager   Spitzenmanager *m*.

top position   Spitzenstellung *f*.

top price   Höchstpreis *m*; Höchst-kurs *m*; Höchststand *m*.

top product   Spitzenprodukt *nt*.

top-ranking officeholder   Spitzen-funktionär *m*.

top-ranking official   Spitzen-beamte *m*; Spitzenbeamtin *f*.

top representative   Spitzen-vertreter *m*.

top-selling   meistverkauft.

tort   Schaden *m*.

total   n *(total amount)* Gesamt-betrag *m*; Gesamtsumme *f*. a Gesamt-; Total-. v *(to add together)* zusammenzählen; addieren; *(car)* total zerstören; einen Totalschaden *m* erleiden.

total assets   Gesamtwert *m* der Aktiva *pl*.

total bank deposits   Einlagenbe-stand *m*.

total borrowings   Kreditvolumen *nt*.

total capacity   Gesamtkapazität *f*; Gesamtleistungsvermögen *nt*.

total consumption   Gesamtver-brauch *m*.

total contract amount   Gesamt-vertragssumme *f*.

total cost Gesamtkosten *pl.*

total cost curve Gesamtkosten-kurve *f.*

total demand Gesamtnachfrage *f.*

total figure Gesamtziffer *f.*

total indebtedness Gesamtver-schuldung *f.*

total interest Gesamtverzinsung *f.*

total investment Gesamtanlage *f;* Gesamtinvestition *f.*

totality Gesamtheit *f.*

total loss Gesamtverlust *m.*

total market Gesamtmarkt *m.*

total nominal amount Gesamt-nennbetrag *m.*

total nominal value Gesamtnenn-wert *m.*

total output *(productivity)* Gesamtleistung *f; (production)* Gesamtproduktion *f.*

total production Gesamtproduk-tion *f.*

total profit Gesamtgewinn *m.*

total reserves Gesamtreserven *pl.*

total revenue Gesamteinkommen *nt.*

total sales Gesamtabsatz *m;* Gesamtumsatz *m.*

total savings Gesamtersparnisse *pl.*

total stock on hand Gesamtbe-stand *m.*

total supply *(availability)* Gesamt-angebot *nt; (provision)* Gesamt-versorgung *f.*

total value Gesamtwert *m.*

total volume Gesamtvolumen *nt.*

total weight Gesamtgewicht *nt.*

tourist Tourist *m;* Gast *m.*

tout n *(racing)* Tipgeber *m.* v *(ad-vertising)* übermäßig anpreisen; aufdringlich werben.

towage *(ship)* Schleppen *nt;* Bug-sieren *nt; (car)* Abschleppen *nt; (charge)* Schleppgebühr *f.*

trade n *(field)* Fach *nt; (commerce)* Handel *m; (vocation)* Gewerbe *nt; (business)* Gewerbebetrieb *m.* v handeln; *(exchange)* tauschen.

trade account Kundenkonto *nt.*

trade agreement Handelsabkom-men *nt.*

trade association Berufsverband *m.*

trade balance Handelsbilanz *f;* Handelssaldo *m.*

trade balance deficit Handels-bilanzdefizit *nt.*

trade barrier Handelsschranke *f.*

trade credit Lieferantenkredit *f.*

trade cycle phase Konjunktur-phase *f.*

trade deficit Handelsdefizit *nt.*

trade exhibition Fachausstellung *f;* Gewerbeausstellung *f.*

trade fair Handelsmesse *f;* Gewerbemesse *f;* Fachmesse *f;* Verkaufsmesse *f.*

trade financing Geschäftsfinan-zierung *f.*

trade for own account Eigenhan-del *m.*

trade group Handelsgruppe *f.*

trade jargon Händlerjargon *m.*

trade journal Fachjournal *nt;* Handelsblatt *nt;* Fachblatt *nt.*

trade magazine Handelszeitschrift *f;* Fachzeitschrift *f.*

trademark Schutzmarke *f;* Waren-zeichen *nt.*

trademark protection Marken-schutz *m.*

trade name Firmenname *m;* Han-delsname *m;* Handelsbezeichnung *f;* Firmenbezeichnung *f; (logo)* Fir-menzeichen *nt.*

trade newspaper Handelsblatt *nt*; Verbandszeitung *f*.

trade obstruction Handelshemmnis *nt*.

trade policy Handelspolitik *f*.

trader Händler *m*; Handeltreibende *m/f*; Kaufmann *m*; Kauffrau *f*; Kaufherr *m*; Handelsmann *m*; Handelsfrau *f*.

trade relations Handelsbeziehungen *pl*.

trade representation Berufsvertretung *f*.

trade restraint Handelseinschränkung *f*.

trade restriction Handelsbeschränkung *f*; Handelshemmnis *nt*.

trade rivalry Konkurrenzkampf *m*.

trade secret Geschäftsgeheimnis *nt*.

trade service Wirtschaftsdienst *m*.

trade show Gewerbeschau *f*; Fachausstellung *f*.

tradesman Handwerker *m*; Gewerbetreibende *m/f*.

trade tax Gewerbesteuer *f*.

trade union law Gewerkschaftsgesetz *nt*.

trade war Handelskrieg *m*.

trading center Geschäftszentrum *nt*.

trading company kaufmännische Unternehmung *f* Handelsgesellschaft *f*; Erwerbsgesellschaft *f*.

trading firm Handelshaus *nt*.

trading partner Handelspartner *m*.

traffic Verkehr *m*; *(the field)* Verkehrswesen *nt*; *(commerce)* Handel *m*; *(movement)* Bewegung *f*.

trailer truck Laster *m* mit Anhänger *m*.

train n Eisenbahnzug *m*. v *(sports)* trainieren; *(job)* ausbilden.

trained *(sports)* trainiert; *(job)* ausgebildet; vorgebildet; geschult.

trainee Volontär *m*; *(intern)* Praktikant *m*; *(beginner, learner)* Anlernling *m*; Azubi *m/f*; *(junior staff member)* Nachwuchskraft *f*.

training *(sports)* Trainieren *nt*; *(job)* Ausbilden *nt*; Vorbilden *nt*; Schulen *nt*.

training center Ausbildungszentrum *nt*.

training school Berufsschule *f*; Ausbildungsstätte *f*.

tranche Tranche *f*; Abschnitt *m*.

transaction Transaktion *f*; Geschäftsabschluß *m*; Durchführung *f*; Abwicklung *f*; Vorgang *m*; Geschäftsvorfall *m*.

transaction costs Transaktionskosten *pl*.

transaction for third account Kundengeschäft *nt*.

transaction in securities Wertpapiergeschäft *nt*.

transcription Umschreibung *f*.

transfer n *(power, duties)* Übertragung *f*; *(cross entry)* Umbuchung *f*; *(remittance)* Überweisung *f*; *(order, instruction)* Anweisung *f*; *(capital, foreign currency)* Transfer *m*; *(securities)* Umschreibung *f*. v *(power, duties)* übertragen; *(cross entry)* umbuchen; *(to remit)* überweisen; *(to order, instruct)* anweisen; *(capital, foreign currency)* transferieren.

transferable share Inhaberaktie *f*.

transfer charge Übertragungsgebühr *f*; Überweisungsgebühr *f*.

transferee *(assignee)* Zessionar *m*; *(recipient of a remittance)* Überweisungsempfänger *m*; *(successor)* Übernehmer *m*; *(purchaser)* Erwerber *m*.

transfer income Transfereinkommen *nt*.

transfer in the books Umbuchung *f*; Vortrag *m*.

transfer of funds Überweisungsverkehr *m*.

transfer order Überweisungsauftrag *m*.

transfer payment Transferzahlung *f*.

transfer price Transferpreis *m*.

transit Transit *m*; *(passageway)* Durchfahrt *f*; *(crossing a body of water)* Überfahrt *f*; *(throughway)* Durchfuhr *f*; *(foot passage)* Durchgang *m*.

transition Übergang *m*.

transitional period Übergangsperiode *f*; Übergangszeit *f*.

transparency of financial statement Bilanzklarheit *f*.

transport n Transport *m*;*(commercial transport)* Spedition *f*. v transportieren.

transportable *(size, weight)* transportfähig; *(compliance with rules)* versandfähig.

transportation Transport *m*; *(means of transportation)* Verkehrsmittel *nt*.

transport ship Frachtschiff *nt*.

travel n *(trip)* Reise *f*; *(passenger traffic)* Reiseverkehr *m*; *(mech.)* Laufspanne *f*. v reisen.

travel abroad Auslandsreisen *nt*; Reisen *nt* ins Ausland *nt*.

travelling salesman, -person, -woman Geschäftsreisende *m/f*.

treasurer Finanzdirektor *m*; Leiter *m* der Finanzabteilung *f*; *(club)* Schatzmeister *m*.

treasury Finanzministerium *nt*; Schatzamt *nt*.

treasury bill Schatzanweisung *f*; kurzfristiger Schatzwechsel *m*.

treasury department Finanzministerium *nt*.

treasury note Schatzwechsel *m*.

treat behandeln; *(topic)* abhandeln.

treatment Behandlung *f*.

trend Trend *m*; *(tendency)* Tendenz *f*; *(inclination)* Neigung *f*.

trend towards intervention Interventionskurs *m*.

trial market Versuchsmarkt *m*.

tribunal Tribunal *nt*; *(legal)* Gerichtshof *m*; *(mediation)* Schiedsgericht *nt*.

trim n *(plane, ship)* Gleichgewichtslage *f*; *(car)* Innenausstattung *f*; *(store window decoration)* Schaufensterschmuck *m*. v *(to decorate)* schmücken; dekorieren; *(to load freight)* verstauen; *(to reduce cost, services)* beschneiden.

trim back zurückschrauben.

trough Trog *m*; *(basin)* Mulde *f*; *(channel)* Rinne *f*; *(depression)* Vertiefung *f*; *(weather)* Tief *nt*; *(fig.)* Tiefpunkt *m*.

truck Transporter *m*; Lastwagen *m*.

trust n Vertrauen *nt*; *(cartel)* Konzern *m*; Großunternehmen *nt*; Trust *m*; *(endowment)* Stiftung *f*; *(custody)* Treuhandverhältnis *nt*; *(estate)* Treuhandvermögen *nt*; *(investment trust company)* Kapitalanlagegesellschaft *f*; Investmentgesellschaft *f*. v vertrauen.

trust agreement Treuhandvertrag *m*; Sicherungsübereignungsvertrag *m*.

trustee Treuhänder *m*; Bevollmächtigte *m/f*; Beauftragte *m/f*; Sachverwalter *m*.

trust transaction Treuhandgeschäft *nt*.

tumble n Fall *m*; *(crash)* Sturz *m*. v fallen; stürzen.

tune n Melodie *f*. v *(instrument)* stimmen; *(engine)* abstimmen; *(radio)* einstellen.

turn n Drehung *f*; Wendung *f*; *(pol., econ. change)* Wende *f*; *(revolution)* Umdrehung *f*. v drehen; *(to turn around)* umdrehen; wenden; *(to revolve)* sich umdrehen.

turnaround Tendenzwende *f*.

turnkey *(building, installation)*

Fertig-; komplett; *(ready for startup)* anlaufbereit.

turnkey system startbereites System *nt*.

turnover Umsatz *m*.

turn over *(to turn upside down)* umdrehen; *(to sell)* umsetzen.

turnover-dependent umsatzabhängig.

turnover gain Umsatzzuwachs *m*.

turnover increase Umsatzsteigerung *f*.

two-sided zweiseitig; bilateral.

type n Typ *m*; Grundform *f*; *(kind)* Art *f*; Modell *nt*. v *(typewriter)* tippen.

type of cost Kostenart *f*.

type of investment Anlageform *f*.

typewriter Schreibmaschine *f*.

typify typisieren; repräsentieren.

ultimate goal Endziel *nt*.

umbrella organization Dachorganisation *f*; Spitzenverband *m*.

unabbreviated ungekürzt; nicht abgekürzt.

unabridged ungekürzt.

unacceptable unannehmbar.

unaccommodating unverbindlich.

unadjusted *(statistics)* nicht bereinigt.

unaffiliated ungebunden; *(independent)* unabhängig; selbständig.

unanimous einstimmig.

unauthorized unerlaubt.

unavailable *(funds)* nicht verfügbar; *(goods)* nicht erhältlich.

unbusinesslike nicht geschäftsmäßig; ungeschäftlich.

uncertainty Unsicherheit *f*.

uncertainty factor Unsicherheitsfaktor *m*.

unchanged unverändert.

uncollectable nicht beitreibbar; nicht einziehbar; uneinbringlich.

uncounted ungezählt; *(not taken into account)* ungerechnet.

uncovered *(not secured)* ungedeckt; ohne Deckung *f*; *(insurance)* unversichert.

underbid n Unterangebot *nt*; Minderangebot *nt*. v unterbieten.

undercut untergraben; *(to work*

for substandard wages) für niedrigeren Lohn *m* arbeiten; geringere Lohnanforderungen *pl* stellen; *(to underbid)* unterbieten.

undercutting *(price)* Unterbietung *f.*

underdeveloped unterentwickelt; *(backward)* rückständig; *(capable of further development)* entwicklungsfähig.

underdevelopment Unterentwicklung *f*; *(backwardness)* Rückständigkeit *f.*

underemployment Unterbeschäftigung *f*; mangelnde Beschäftigung *f.*

underestimate n Unterschätzung *f*; *(cost)* zu niedriger Kostenanschlag *m*. v unterschätzen.

underground economy Schattenwirtschaft *f.*

underissue Minderausgabe *f.*

underlying data Basisdaten *pl*; Rahmendaten *pl.*

underlying shares zugrundeliegende Anteile *pl*; *(preferred shares)* Vorranganteile *pl.*

underlying stock zugrundeliegende Aktien *pl*; *(preferred stock)* Vorrangaktien *pl.*

undermine unterminieren; untergraben.

underpaid unterbezahlt.

underpin unterbauen; untermauern; *(fig.)* unterstützen.

underprice n Schleuderpreis *m*; *(below value)* unter dem Wert *m* angesetzter Preis *m*. v Preis *m* unter dem Wert *m* ansetzen.

undersell *(by quantity)* zuwenig verkaufen; *(by price)* unter dem Marktpreis *m* verkaufen; verschleudern.

underselling Preisunterbietung *f*; Dumping *nt.*

understaffed zu schwach besetzt; unterbesetzt.

understanding *(agreement)* Absprache *f*; Übereinkommen *nt.*

understate nicht stark genug ausdrücken; nicht genügend artikulieren; bewußt mildern.

understated *(aesthetics)* dezent; unauffällig; absichtlich einfach.

undertake unternehmen; *(to take care of)* besorgen; *(to obligate oneself)* sich verpflichten.

undertaking Unterfangen *nt*; *(enterprise)* Unternehmung *f*; *(obligation)* Verpflichtung *f*; *(document)* Verpflichtungserklärung *f.*

undervalue unterbewerten; *(underestimate)* unterschätzen.

undervalued unterbewertet; zu niedrig bewertet.

underwrite Haftung *f* übernehmen; *(insurance)* versichern; *(guarantee)* garantieren.

underwriter Versicherungsagent *m*; Prämienfestsetzer *m*; Assekurant *m*; *(insurance provider)* Versicherungsgeber *m*; *(securities)* Emissionsfirma *f.*

underwriting n Übernahme *f* der Haftung *f*; *(insurance)* Übernahme *f* von Versicherungen *pl*; Tätigung *f* von Versicherungsgeschäften *pl*; *(guarantee)* Garantieren *nt*; *(securities)* Emissionsgarantie *f*. a garantierend.

underwriting guarantee Abnahmegarantie *f.*

underwriting member bank Konsortialbank *f.*

underwriting syndicate business Konsortialgeschäft *nt.*

underwriting transaction Emissionsgeschäft *nt.*

undesirable development Fehlentwicklung *f.*

undeveloped unentwickelt.

unearned income Kapitalertrag *m.*

uneconomical unwirtschaftlich; unrentabel.

unemployed arbeitslos; erwerbslos; beschäftigungslos; *(chronically)* dauerarbeitslos.

unemployment Arbeitslosigkeit *f;* Erwerbslosigkeit *f;* Beschäftigungslosigkeit *f.*

unemployment compensation Arbeitslosengeld *nt;* Arbeitslosenhilfe *f.*

unemployment crisis Beschäftigungskrise *f.*

unemployment figure Arbeitslosenzahl *f.*

unemployment rate Arbeitslosenquote *f.*

unequal ungleich.

unethical unethisch; unrecht.

unexpected unerwartet.

unexplored *(uninvestigated)* ununtersucht; *(geographic area, natural resources)* unerschlossen.

unfair *(unreasonable)* unbillig; unfair.

unfavorable ungünstig; *(disadvantageous)* unvorteilhaft.

unfeasible undurchführbar.

unfilled *(position)* unbesetzt; *(demand)* unbefriedigt; *(order)* unerfüllt.

unfinished *(task)* unvollendet; *(product)* halbfertig; *(business)* unerledigt.

unforeseeable nicht vorhersehbar; unkalkulierbar.

unfounded grundlos; unbegründet.

uniform n Uniform *f.* a gleichmäßig; gleichförmig; einheitlich.

uniformity Gleichmäßigkeit *f;* Gleichförmigkeit *f;* Einheitlichkeit *f.*

unilateral einseitig.

uninvested nicht angelegt; brachliegend.

union Vereinigung *f; (labor)* Gewerkschaft *f.*

union district Verbandsbezirk *m.*

union hall Versammlungshalle *f* der Gewerkschaft *f.*

unionist Gewerkschaftler *m.*

union leader Gewerkschaftsführer *m.*

union personnel Gewerkschaftspersonal *nt.*

unissued unausgegeben; nicht ausgegeben.

unit Einheit *f;* Stück *nt; (block of shares)* Aktienbündel *nt; (building)* Bauelement *nt.*

unite vereinen.

unit labor cost Lohnstückkosten *pl;* Arbeitsaufwand *m* pro Produktionseinheit *f.*

unit of goods Wareneinheit *f.*

unit of quantity Mengeneinheit *f.*

unit price Stückpreis *m.*

unit profit Stückgewinn *m.*

unity Einigkeit *f.*

universal bank Universalbank *f.*

unjust ungerecht.

unjustifiable unvertretbar.

unjustified unberechtigt; ungerechtfertigt.

unlawful ungesetzlich; *(prohibited)* unerlaubt.

unlimited uneingeschränkt.

unlimited credit Blankokredit *m.*

unload *(truck)* abladen; *(ship)* löschen; *(get rid of)* abstoßen; auf den Markt *m* werfen.

unloading *(truck)* Abladen *nt*; *(ship)* Löschen *nt*; *(getting rid of)* Abstoßen *nt*.

unlock *(door)* aufschließen; *(resources)* erschließen; *(capital)* freisetzen.

unoccupied beschäftigungslos; *(not busy)* nicht beschäftigt; *(space)* unbesetzt.

unpaid unbezahlt; *(bill)* unbeglichen; *(in arrears)* rückständig.

unpledged *(shares, collateral)* unverpfändet.

unproductive unproduktiv; unergiebig.

unprofitable unrentabel; gewinnlos; nicht einträglich; ertraglos.

unpublished unveröffentlicht.

unqualified *(not qualified)* nicht qualifiziert; *(unrestricted)* uneingeschränkt.

unrealized nicht verwirklicht; *(profit)* unrealisiert; *(not comprehended)* unbegriffen; unerkannt.

unreliable unzuverlässig; *(business)* unsolide; unreell.

unrequited transfer einseitige Übertragung *f*.

unresolvable *(problem)* unlösbar; *(dispute)* unschlichtbar.

unresolved ungelöst; ungeschlichtet.

unrestricted unbeschränkt; uneingeschränkt.

unsalable unverkäuflich; nicht verkaufbar.

unsecured credit Blankokredit *m*.

unsettled unerledigt; *(uncertain)* ungewiß; unbestimmt.

unskilled *(worker)* ungelernt.

unskilled laborer Hilfsarbeiter *m*.

unsold unverkauft; nicht verkauft.

unstable *(unsteady)* unbeständig; *(volatile)* volatil.

unsuitable ungeeignet.

untapped *(natural resources)* unerschlossen; *(human resources)* ungebraucht; unverwertet.

untrained ungelernt; unausgebildet.

untrustworthy nicht vertrauenswürdig; unseriös.

unusable unbrauchbar; unverwertbar; *(unfit)* untauglich.

unused ungebraucht; ungenutzt.

unwarranted *(not entitled)* unberechtigt; *(not authorized)* unbefugt; *(not justified)* ungerechtfertigt.

unwillingness to compromise Kompromißlosigkeit *f*.

unwilling to take risks risikoscheu.

unwilling to work arbeitsscheu.

unworkable *(not realizable)* nicht ausführbar; *(unusable)* unverwendbar; nicht verwendungsfähig.

up- and downturns of the market Kursschwankungen *pl*.

update *(to inform anew)* neu informieren; *(equipment)* modernisieren; *(inventory)* neu zusammenstellen.

upgrade *(to improve)* verbessern; *(in rank)* höher einstufen; *(personnel)* befördern.

upgraded *(improved)* verbessert; *(rank)* höher eingestuft; *(personnel)* befördert.

upholster polstern; beziehen.

upkeep Aufrechterhaltung *f*; *(equipment)* Instandhaltung *f*; *(cost of maintenance)* Unterhaltungskosten *pl*; *(machine)* Wartungskosten *pl*.

upstart Emporkömmling *m*.

upsurge steiler Anstieg *m*; Auftriebstendenz *f*.

upsurge in sales Umsatzanstieg *m*.

upswing Aufschwung *m*; Aufstieg *m*.

upturn Besserung *f*; Aufwärtsbewegung *f*.

upward business trend Konjunkturaufschwung *m*.

upward mobility Aufwärtsmobilität *f*; Aufstiegsmöglichkeit *f*.

upward movement Kursanstieg *m*; Aufwärtsentwicklung *f*.

upward trend steigende Tendenz *f*; Aufwärtstendenz *f*; Aufwärtstrend *m*.

urban center Ballungsgebiet *nt*; Ballungsraum *m*.

urban household städtischer Haushalt *m*.

urbanization Verstädterung *f*.

urbanize verstädtern.

urgency Dringlichkeit *f*.

usable brauchbar; verwendbar; nutzbar.

usage *(custom)* Brauch *m*;

Herkommen *nt*; *(practice)* Praxis *f*; Usance *f*.

use *(utilization)* Gebrauch *m*; Benutzung *f*; *(usefulness)* Nützlichkeit *f*; *(utility)* Nutzen *m*; *(purpose)* Zweck *m*.

useful life Nutzungsdauer *f*.

usefulness Nützlichkeit *f*.

useless nutzlos; zwecklos.

use of income Einkommensverwendung *f*.

use-oriented anwendungsbezogen.

user Benutzer *m*; Anwender *m*; Gebraucher *m*.

user industry Anwenderindustrie *f*; Gebraucherindustrie *f*.

user tax Benutzungssteuer *f*.

use to capacity n Auslastung *f*. v auslasten.

usufruct Nießbrauch *m*.

usury Wucherei *f*; Wucher *m*.

utility Brauchbarkeit *f*.

utilization Verwertung *f*; Nutzanwendung *f*; *(of a service)* Inanspruchnahme *f*; *(of data)* Auswertung *f*.

utilization theory Nutzentheorie *f*.

utilize verwerten; nutzen; auswerten.

vacation Urlaub m. *(additional ~ time)* Zusatzurlaub *m.*
vacationer Urlauber *m.*
valid *(in effect)* gültig; *(legal)* rechtlich.
validity Geltung *f*; *(force of law)* Rechtskraft *f.*
valuation Einschätzung *f*; Abschätzung *f*; *(commercial value)* Taxierung *f.*
value n Wert *m.* v wertschätzen; schätzen.
value added Werterhöhung *f*; *(taxation)* Mehrwert *m*; *(productivity)* Wertschöpfung *f.*
value added tax Mehrwertsteuer *f.*
value measure Wertmaßstab *m.*
value of goods ordered Auftragswert *m.*
value of labor Arbeitswert *m.*
value of money Geldwert *m.*
value performance Wertleistung *f.*
value setting Wertstellung *f.*
value theory Werttheorie *f.*
van Lieferwagen *m*; Transportwagen *m.*
variable variabel.
varied unterschiedlich.
various verschiedenartig.
vault Tresor *m.*
vendor *(seller)* Verkäufer *m*; *(supplier)* Lieferer *m*; Lieferant *m.*
venture n Wagnis *nt*; *(business)* Unternehmung *f.* v wagen; riskieren.
venture capital Wagniskapital *nt.*
verbal mündlich; verbal.
verdict Gerichtsurteil *nt*; *(fig.)* Urteil *nt.*

verification Beglaubigung *f*; *(confirmation)* Bestätigung *f*; *(scrutiny)* Überprüfung *f.*
verify beglaubigen; *(to confirm)* bestätigen; *(to scrutinize)* überprüfen.
version Version *f*; *(book, document)* Fassung *f.*
vertical senkrecht; vertikal.
vertical integration vertikale Integration *f*; vertikale Eingliederung *f.*
vested festbegründet; wohlerworben; *(pension plan)* unentziehbar.
veto Veto *nt*; *(objection)* Einspruch *m.*
viability Lebensfähigkeit *f.*
viable lebensfähig.
vice chairman stellvertretende Vorsitzende *m/f.*
vice president Vizepräsident *m.*
view n *(scene, landscape)* Aussicht, *f*; *(sketch)* Skizze *f*; *(perspective)* Perspektive *f*; *(opinion)* Ansicht *f.* v *(to inspect, scrutinize)* inspizieren; *(to contemplate)* betrachten.
violate *(agreement)* verletzen; *(contract)* brechen.
violation *(agreement)* Verletzung *f*; *(contract)* Bruch *m*; *(law, rule)* Verstoß *m*; Übertretung *f.*
visibility *(weather)* Sichtweite *f*; *(firm, product)* Sichtbarkeit *f.*
vogue Mode *f*; *(popularity)* Popularität *f.*
voice Stimme *f*; *(decision-making)* Mitsprache *f.*
void n leerer Raum *m*; *(gap)* Lücke *f.* a leer; *(uninhabited)* unbewohnt;

(not valid) nichtig. v *(to void a document)* ungültig machen.

volume *(book)* Band *m*; Buch *nt*; *(bulk)* Maß *nt*; Umfang *m*; *(quantity)* Menge *f*; *(content)* Volumen *nt*.

volume business Mengengeschäft *nt*.

volume discount Mengenrabatt *m*.

volume of business Geschäftsumfang *m*.

volume of money Geldmenge *f*.

volume of sales Gesamtabsatz *m*.

volume of stocks traded Börsenumsatz *m*.

volume of work Arbeitsanfall *m*; Arbeitsvolumen *nt*.

volume transaction Mengengeschäft *nt*.

voluminous umfangreich.

voluntary freiwillig.

vote n Stimme *f*. v abstimmen; *(election)* wählen.

vouch haften; garantieren.

voucher check Verrechnungsscheck *m*.

wage n Lohn *m*; Werklohn *m*; *(remuneration)* Arbeitsentgelt *nt*. v *(to undertake)* unternehmen; *(a war)* führen.

wage adjustment Lohnausgleich *m*.

wage agreement Lohnabkommen *nt*; Tarifvertrag *m*; Tarifabkommen *nt*.

wage autonomy Tarifautonomie *f*.

wage bracket Lohngruppe *f*.

wage demand Lohnforderung *f*.

wage differential Lohngefälle *nt*.

wage discussion Tarifgespräch *nt*.

wage income tax Lohnsteuer *f*.

wage level Lohnniveau *nt*.

wage negotiation Lohnverhandlung *f*.

wage negotiation talks Lohnrunde *f*.

wage paid in cash Barlohn *m*.

wage policy Lohnpolitik *f*.

wage rate Grundlohntarif *m*; Tarifsatz *m*; Lohnsatz *m*.

wage ratio Lohnquote *f*.

wage settlement Tarifabschluß *m*.

wage structure Lohnstruktur *f*.

waiting line Warteschlange *f*.

waive verzichten; *(to exempt)* erlassen.

waiver Verzicht *m*; *(declaration)* Verzichtleistung *f*; *(document)* Verzichtleistungserklärung *f*.

wallet Brieftasche *f*.

warehouse Lager *nt*; Warenlager *nt*; Speicher *m*; *(distribution warehouse)* Auslieferungslager *nt*; Magazin *nt*.

warehousing Lagerhaltung *f*; Einlagerung *f*.

warning strike Warnstreik *m*.

warrant n Ermächtigung *f*; Befugnis *f*; *(execution)* Vollziehungsbefehl *m*; Zertifikat *nt*. v *(to vouch)* sich verbürgen; garantieren; gewährleisten.

warranted garantiert; *(vouched for)* verbürgt.

warranty Garantie *f*; Gewährleistung *f*; *(against product defects)* Mängelgarantie *f*.

waste n Verschwendung *f*; *(squandering)* Vergeudung *f*; *(cargo)* Abgang *m*; Verlust *m*; *(manufacturing)* Abfall *m*; *(scrap)* Schrott *m*; *(coal)* Schlacke *f*; *(cotton)* Putzwerg *nt*; *(rubbish)* Müll *m*. v verschwenden; vergeuden; *(to sell at a loss)* verschleudern; *(to lay waste)* verwüsten.

wasted verschwendet; *(squandered)* vergeudet; *(sold at a loss)* verschleudert; *(devastated)* verwüstet.

wasteful verschwenderisch.

wasting Verschwenden *nt*; *(squandering)* Vergeuden *nt*; *(selling below cost)* Verschleudern *nt*; *(laying waste)* Verwüsten *nt*.

waterfront Kai *m*.

waterway Wasserweg *m*; Wasserstraße *f*; *(shipping lane)* Schiffahrtsweg *m*.

wave of bankruptcies Pleitewelle *f*.

wave of dismissals Entlassungswelle *f*.

wave of price increases Teuerungswelle *f*.

weak schwach; *(economy)* flau.

weaken *(to make weak)* schwächen; abschwächen; *(to become weak)* schwach werden; *(to abate)* nachlassen.

weakening n *(making weaker)* Schwächung *f*; Abschwächung *f*;

(becoming weaker) Schwächerwerden *nt*; *(abatement)* Nachlassen *nt*. a schwächend; abschwächend.

weakness Schwäche *f*; Schwachheit *f*; *(economy, market)* Flaute *f*.

wealth Reichtum *m*; Wohlhabenheit *f*; *(assets)* Vermögen *nt*; Besitz *m*.

wealthy vermögend; wohlhabend; *(in a good position)* gut situiert; *(having sufficient capital)* kapitalkräftig.

weekly average Wochendurchschnitt *m*.

weekly report Wochenbericht *m*.

weigh wiegen; *(consider)* erwägen.

weighted average Bewertungsdurchschnitt *m*.

welfare Wohlergehen *nt*; *(social service)* Wohlfahrt *f*; Sozialhilfe *f*; Fürsorge *f*.

welfare committee Sozialausschuß *m*.

welfare eligibility Sozialanspruch *m*.

welfare policy Sozialpolitik *f*.

well grounded fundiert.

well versed sachkundig.

whole n Gesamtheit *f*. a ganz; *(complete)* vollständig.

wholesale n Großhandel *m*; Großverkauf *m*; Engroshandel *m*; *(high volume sales)* Massenabsatz *m*. a en gros.

wholesale chain Großhandelskette *f*.

wholesale market Großhandelsmarkt *m*.

wholesaler Engroshändler *m*; Großhändler *m*; Großkaufmann *m*.

wholesaling Großhandelsgewerbe *nt.*

wholly owned im Alleineigentum *nt.*

willing to take risks risikofreudig.

willing to work arbeitswillig.

win gewinnen; *(acquire)* erwerben; *(earn)* verdienen; erringen.

windfall *(forestry)* Windbruch *m*; *(lucky break)* unverhoffter Glücksfall *m.*

windfall profit unerwarteter Gewinn *m.*

window Fenster *nt*; *(customer service)* Schalter *m.*

winner Gewinner *m*; *(competition)* Sieger *m*; *(product)* Schlager *m.*

winning n Gewinnen *nt.* a *(captivating)* einnehmend; gewinnend; *(victorious)* siegreich.

wire n Draht *m*; *(telegram)* Telegramm *nt*; Depesche *f*; Drahtnachricht *f.* v telegrafieren; drahten.

withdraw sich zurückziehen; zurücktreten; *(money)* abheben; entnehmen; *(support)* entziehen; *(statement)* zurücknehmen.

withdrawal Rückzug *m*; Zurückziehung *f*; *(money)* Abhebung *f*; Entnahme *f*; *(support)* Entziehung *f*; *(statement)* Rücknahme *f.*

withdrawal period *(contract)* Kündigungsfrist *f.*

withhold *(to deny)* vorenthalten; *(to keep back)* einbehalten.

withholding Zurückbehaltung *f*; Vorbehaltung *f*; *(taxes)* Abzugsverfahren *nt*; Einbehaltung *f.*

withholding wage tax Lohnsteuerabzug *m.*

within in; inside; *(time)* binnen; innerhalb.

without amortization tilgungsfrei.

without leadership führungslos.

without obligation unverbindlich.

without purpose zwecklos; *(aimless)* ziellos.

without ready money bargeldlos.

with regard to hinsichtlich.

woo umwerben.

wording of a contract Vertragstext *m.*

word processor Textprozessor *m*; Textverarbeiter *m.*

work n Arbeit *f*; Beschäftigung *f.* v arbeiten; *(mechanism)* funktionieren.

workable bearbeitungsfähig; *(capable of being carried out)* ausführbar; durchführbar.

work analysis Arbeitsanalyse *f.*

workday Arbeitstag *m.*

work enthusiasm Arbeitseifer *m.*

work environment Arbeitsumfeld *nt*; Arbeitsumgebung *f.*

worker *(blue collar)* Arbeiter *m*; *(employee)* Arbeitnehmer *m*; Arbeitskraft *f.*

worker interest Arbeiterinteresse *nt.*

workers' council Betriebsrat *m.*

worker vote Arbeiterstimme *f.*

work force Belegschaft *f*; Arbeitskräfte *pl.*

working area *(factory)* Werkbereich *m.*

working atmosphere Betriebsklima *nt.*

working balance Betriebsmittelguthaben *nt.*

working capital Betriebskapital *nt*; Umlaufkapital *nt*; Betriebsmittel *pl.*

working condition Arbeitsbedingung *f.*

working hours Arbeitszeit *f.*

working hours policy Arbeitszeit-
politik *f*.

working hours regulation
Arbeitszeitordnung *f*.

working knowledge ausreichende
Kenntnisse *pl*.

working life Lebensarbeitszeit *f*.

working woman berufstätige Frau
f; *(blue collar)* Arbeiterin *f*;
(employee) Arbeitnehmerin *f*; *(fellow employee)* Mitarbeiterin *f*.

workload *(burden)* Arbeitsbelastung *f*; *(prescribed share)* Arbeitspensum *nt*; Deputat *nt*.

workplace Arbeitsplatz *m*;
Arbeitsstätte *f*.

workplace computer Arbeits-
platzcomputer *m*.

workplace convenience Arbeits-
platzkomfort *m*.

workplace risk Arbeitsplatzrisiko
nt.

work process Arbeitsgang *m*;
Arbeitsvorgang *m*.

work rule Arbeitsregel *f*; Arbeitsrichtlinie *f*.

workshop *(enterprise)* Gewerbebetrieb *m*; *(work room)* Werkstatt *f*;
(working meeting) Arbeitstagung
f; Seminar *nt*.

work unit Arbeitseinheit *f*.

world agricultural market Weltagrarmarkt *m*.

World Bank Weltbank *f*.

World Bank subsidiary Weltbanktochter *f*.

world class Weltklasse *f*.

world economy Weltwirtschaft *f*.

world export Weltexport *m*.

world finance Weltfinanz *f*.

world market Weltmarkt *m*.

world market leader Weltmarktführer *m*.

world market price Weltmarktpreis *m*.

world market share Weltmarktanteil *m*.

world ranking Weltrangliste *f*.

world trade Welthandel *m*.

worldwide economic condition
Weltkonjunktur *f*.

worldwide economic crisis Weltwirtschaftskrise *f*.

worldwide operations weltweite
Geschäftstätigkeit *f*.

worldwide recession weltweite
Rezession *f*.

worsen sich verschlechtern.

write-off *(taxation)* Abschreibung
f; *(bookkeeping)* Ausbuchung *f*;
Abbuchung *f*.

write off *(taxation)* abschreiben;
(bookkeeping) ausbuchen;
abbuchen.

write to anschreiben.

writing utensil Schreibgerät *nt*.

written schriftlich.

written communication Schreiben
nt.

wrong falsch; *(unjust, dishonest)*
unrecht; *(mistaken)* irrig.

wrong decision Fehlentscheidung
f.

yearbook   Jahrbuch *nt*.
year-end   Jahresultimo *m*.
year of training   Ausbildungsjahr *nt*.
year under report   Berichtsjahr *nt*.
yield   n *(crop)* Ernte *f*; Ertrag *m*; *(result)* Ergebnis *nt*; *(interest)* Zinsertrag *m*; Effektivverzinsung *f*; *(stocks)* Rendite *f*. **v** erbringen;

(to give in) nachgeben; *(to bear interest)* Zinsen *pl* tragen; *(result)* ergeben.
yield index   Nutzenindex *m*.
yield on assets   Vermögensertrag *m*.
yield on interest   Zinsertrag *m*.
yield on investment   Anlagerendite *f*; Anlagekapitalrendite *f*.

Z

zero coupon   Nullkupon *m*.
zero interest   Nullzins *m*.
zero quota   Nullquote *f*.
zip code   Postleitzahl *f*.
zip code area   Postleitzahlbereich *m*.

zone   n Zone *f*; *(area)* Gebiet *nt*; *(part of area)* Teilgebiet *nt*; *(geog.)* Landstrich *m*. **v** in Zonen einteilen.

German-English Section

abändern to alter; to modify; *(Text umarbeiten)* to revise.

Abbau *m* reduction; *(Arbeitskräfte)* dismissal; cutback; *(Bergbau)* mining.

abbauen to reduce; *(Arbeitskräfte)* to dismiss; to cut back; *(Bergbau)* to mine.

Abbildung *f* illustration; figure.

abbrechen *(Arbeit)* to stop; *(Verbindungen)* to discontinue; to sever; *(Verhandlungen)* to break off.

Abbruch *m* *(Arbeit)* stoppage; *(Verbindungen)* discontinuance; severance; *(Verhandlungen)* breaking off.

abbuchen *(abschreiben)* to write off; *(Konto belasten)* to charge; to debit.

Abbuchung *f* *(Abschreibung)* write-off; *(Belastung)* charge; debit.

abdrosseln to stall; to stifle.

Abfall *m* waste.

abfassen to prepare; to formulate.

Abfassung *f* formulation.

abfinden to pay off; *(sich abfinden mit)* to accept.

Abfindung *f* compensation; *(Angestellter)* severance pay.

Abfindungszahlung *f* payoff; lump sum payment.

Abfluß *m* outflow.

Abgabe *f* *(Übergabe)* delivery; *(Abschöpfung)* levy; *(Zoll)* duty; *(Gebühr)* fee.

Abgaskontrolle *f* emission control.

Abgeordnete *m/f* *(Parlament)* representative; deputy.

abgleiten to slip.

abgrenzen to demarcate; *(definieren)* to define.

abhandeln *(Thema behandeln)* to treat; *(vom Preis)* to bargain.

abhängen *(hinter sich lassen)* to leave behind.

abhängen von to depend on.

abhängig dependent.

Abhängigkeit *f* dependence.

abheben *(Konto)* to withdraw.

Abhebung *f* *(Konto)* withdrawal.

abhören to listen in; to monitor; *(Schulaufgabe)* to quiz.

Abhörgerät *nt* monitor; bugging device.

Abiturient *m* high-school graduate.

Abkommen *nt* agreement.

abladen *(Waren)* to unload; *(Abfall)* to dump.

Ablauf *m* *(Arbeitsablauf)* procedure; *(Erlöschen)* expiration; *(Vorgang)* course.

ablaufen *(fällig werden)* to expire; *(Zeit)* to elapse; to run out.

Ablauftermin *m* date of expiration.

ablegen *(Akten)* to file; *(hinlegen)* to lay down.

Ableger *m* *(Filiale)* subsidiary.

ablehnen to reject; to oppose.

ablehnende Antwort *f* refusal.

Ablehnung *f* rejection.

ableiten to derive.

ablichten to photocopy.

Ablichtung *f* photocopy.

abliefern to deliver.

ablösen   to detach; *(Kredit)* to redeem; *(von der Arbeit)* to relieve.

abmachen   *(vereinbaren)* to agree; *(ein Geschäft)* to settle; *(regeln)* to arrange.

Abmachung *f*   *(Vereinbarung)* agreement; *(Klausel)* stipulation; *(Geschäft)* deal; *(Regelung)* arrangement.

abmelden, sich   to notify of departure.

Abnahme *f*   *(Absatz)* sale; *(Kauf)* purchase; *(Minderung)* decline; decrease; diminution.

Abnehmer *m*   *(Käufer)* purchaser; *(Benutzer)* user; *(Kunde)* customer.

Abnehmergruppe *f*   buying group.

Abnehmerland *nt*   buying country.

Abonnement *nt*   subscription.

Abonnent *m*   subscriber.

abonnieren   to subscribe.

Abordnung *f*   delegation.

abrechnen   *(Rechnung, Konto)* to settle; *(abziehen)* to deduct.

Abrechnung *f*   *(Rechnung, Konto)* settlement; statement; bill.

Abriß *m*   summary; abstract.

abrufen   to recall; to call up.

Absage *f*   *(Weigerung)* rejection; *(Auftrag, Veranstaltung)* cancellation; *(Einladung)* regret.

absagen   *(Auftrag, Veranstaltung)* to cancel; *(Einladung)* to decline; to regret.

Absatz *m*   *(Verkauf)* sale; marketing; *(Vertrieb)* distribution; *(Paragraph)* paragraph.

Absatzbasis *f*   marketing base.

Absatzbereich *m*   marketing area.

Absatzchance *f*   marketing potential.

Absatzentwicklung *f*   market development.

Absatzerfolg *m*   sales result.

Absatzfachmann *m*   marketer.

absatzfähig   salable; marketable.

Absatzfähigkeit *f*   marketability.

Absatzfinanzierungsinstitut *nt*   factor; factoring company.

Absatzförderung *f*   merchandising; sales promotion.

Absatzformel *f*   marketing formula.

Absatzforschung *f*   marketing research.

Absatzgebiet *nt*   sales district; sales territory; market area; marketing area.

Absatzgelegenheit *f*   market opportunity.

Absatzmarkt *m*   market area; market; *(Vertriebsstelle)* outlet.

Absatzmenge *f*   sales volume.

Absatzmöglichkeit *f*   market opportunity.

Absatzorganisation *f*   sales organization.

Absatzplan *m*   sales forecast; marketing plan.

Absatzposition *f*   market position.

Absatzprognose *f*   sales forecast.

Absatzrückgang *m*   decline in sales.

Absatzstrategie *f*   marketing strategy; distribution strategy.

Absatztätigkeit *f*   marketing function.

Absatzverlust *m*   sales loss.

Absatzvolumen *nt*   sales volume.

Absatzvorausschätzung *f*   sales forecast.

Absatzweg *m*   marketing channel.

Absatzwirtschaft *f*   marketing.

Absatzziel *nt*   market objective.

abschätzen   to estimate.

Abschätzung *f*   valuation; appraisal.

abschicken   to dispatch; to send

off; *(mit der Post)* to mail; *(Geld)* to remit.

abschirmen   to protect.

Abschlag *m* *(Abzug)* deduction; *(Preisminderung)* discount.

abschlagen   *(Bitte)* to deny; to refuse.

abschlägiger Bescheid *m*   refusal.

abschließen   *(enden)* to terminate; to end; *(Vertrag, Verhandlung)* to conclude; *(Konto)* to close.

Abschluß *m*   *(Beendung)* termination; completion; *(Vertrag, Verhandlung)* conclusion; *(Konto)* closing.

Abschlußsitzung *f*   closing session.

Abschnitt *m*   section; segment; paragraph; *(Zinsschein)* coupon.

abschöpfen   to skim; *(Abgaben)* to levy.

Abschöpfung *f*   skimming; *(Abgabe)* levy.

abschreiben   *(Bilanz)* to write off; *(tilgen)* to amortize; *(kopieren)* to copy; *(absagen)* to decline in writing.

Abschreibung *f*   *(Bilanz)* write-off; *(Tilgung)* amortization.

Abschrift *f*   copy.

Abschrift *f* **anfertigen**   to copy.

abschwächen   to weaken; to soften.

abschwächen, sich   to slacken.

Abschwächung *f*   weakening; slackness.

absenden   to send off; to dispatch; *(mit der Post)* to mail; *(Geld)* to remit.

Absender *m*   sender; *(Post)* return address.

Absendung *f*   dispatch; *(mit der Post)* mailing.

absetzbar   *(Steuern)* deductible;

(Abschreibung) depreciable; *(Verkauf)* salable.

absetzen   *(verkaufen)* to sell; to dispose; *(vertreiben)* to distribute; *(abziehen)* to deduct; *(vom Amt)* to dismiss; to remove.

Absetzung *f*   *(Abzug)* deduction; *(vom Amt)* removal; dismissal.

absichern   to secure; *(Börse)* to hedge.

Absicherung *f*   *(gegen Risiko)* providing security; *(Börse)* hedge.

Absicht *f*   intent; intention; *(Zweck)* purpose; *(Ziel)* aim.

Absichtserklärung *f*   letter of intent.

Absinken *nt*   sliding.

absolut   absolute.

Absolvent *m*   graduate.

absondern   *(trennen)* to separate; to set apart; *(isolieren)* to isolate.

Absonderung *f*   *(Trennung)* separation; setting apart; *(Isolierung)* isolation.

Absprache *f*   understanding.

Abstand *m*   distance; *(Zeilen)* space; *(Druckrand)* margin; *(zwischen Objekten)* clearance.

abstimmen   to vote; *(angleichen)* to adjust; *(koordinieren)* to coordinate; *(Konten)* to reconcile.

abstoßen   *(Firmenteile)* to divest; *(Effekten)* to unload; *(Lagerbestände)* to clear.

abstrakt   abstract.

abstufen   to grade.

Absturz *m*   crash.

abtasten   to scan.

Abtaster *m*   scanner.

Abteilung *f*   section; division; department.

Abteilungsbildung *f*   departmentalization.

Abteilungsleiter *m* division manager.

Abteilungstandort *m* division headquarters.

abtragen *(Schulden)* to pay off; *(Hypothek)* to amortize.

abträglich detrimental; disadvantageous.

abtrennen to sever.

abtreten *(aufgeben)* to relinquish; *(Besitz)* to assign; *(Rechtstitel)* to cede; *(übergeben)* to transfer; *(zurücktreten)* to resign.

Abtretung *f* *(Besitz)* assignment; *(Rechtstitel)* cession; *(Übergabe)* transfer.

Abtritt *m* *(Rücktritt)* resignation.

abwälzen *(Kosten)* to pass on.

abwärts downward.

Abwärtsbewegung *f* downturn.

abwechseln to alternate.

abwechselnd alternate.

abweichen to diverge; to deviate.

abweichend divergent.

Abweichung *f* divergence; deviation; discrepancy.

abweisen to reject; to disallow.

abwerten to devaluate; to devalue.

Abwertung *f* depreciation; devaluation.

abwesend absent.

Abwesende *m/f* absentee.

Abwesenheit *f* absence.

abwickeln *(erledigen)* to carry out; to handle; to operate; *(Konkurs)* to liquidate.

Abwicklung *f* *(Erledigung)* handling; operation; *(Konkurs)* liquidation.

Abwicklungswert *m* liquidation value.

abzahlen to pay off.

Abzahlung *f* installment payment.

Abzahlungsbank *f* consumer credit bank.

Abzahlungskredit *m* consumer loan.

abziehbar deductible; allowable.

abziehen to deduct; *(nachlassen)* to discount; *(subtrahieren)* to subtract.

Abzug *m* deduction; *(Rabatt)* rebate; *(Nachlaß)* reduction; allowance; *(Subtraktion)* subtraction.

abzugsfähiger Betrag *m* *(Steuern)* deduction.

addieren to total; to add.

Adresse *f* address.

Adressenkartei *f* mailing list.

Agent *m* representative; agent.

Agentur *f* agency.

aggressiv militant; aggressive.

Agrar- agrarian; agricultural.

Agrarwirtschaft *f* agriculture.

Akademiker *m* college graduate.

Akkordarbeit *f* piece work.

Akkreditiv *nt* letter of credit.

Akte *f* file.

Aktenablage *f* filing.

Aktenstück *nt* document.

Aktentasche *f* briefcase.

Aktie *f* share.

Aktien *pl* stock.

Aktienanalyst *m* stock analyst.

Aktienanlage *f* stock investment.

Aktienaufteilung *f* stock split.

Aktienbesitz *m* shareholding.

Aktienbewertung *f* stock evaluation.

Aktienbezugsrecht *nt* stock option.

Aktienbörse *f* stock market.

Aktienertrag *m* share earnings.

Aktienfonds *m* mutual stock fund.

Aktiengattung *f* class of stocks.

Aktiengesellschaft *f* public corporation.

Aktiengesetz *nt*   corporation law.
Aktiengewinn *m*   share earnings.
Aktienhandel *m*   stock trading.
Aktienhändler *m*   stockbroker.
Aktieninhaber *m*   stockholder;
shareholder.
Aktienkapital *nt*   capital stock.
Aktienkurs *m*   stock price.
Aktienmarkt *m*   stock market.
Aktienrendite *f*   earnings per
share; yield on stock.
Aktiensplit *m*   stock split.
Aktientausch *m*   stock split; spin-
off; exchange of stock.
Aktientendenz *f*   stock market
trend.
Aktion *f*   action.
Aktionär *m*   stockholder; share-
holder.
Aktionärskreis *m*   shareholders'
group.
aktiv   active.
Aktiva *pl*   assets.
Aktivität *f*   activity.
Aktivposten *m*   asset.
Aktivsaldo *m*   credit balance.
Aktivseite *f*   *(Bilanz)* assets.
aktuell   current.
Akzept *nt*   acceptance.
akzeptabel   acceptable.
akzeptieren   to accept.
allein   alone; sole.
alleinig   sole; exclusive.
Alleinverkauf *m*   exclusive sale;
sales monopoly.
Alleinvertretung *f*   sole agency.
allgemein   general.
Allokation *f*   allocation.
Allzwecksoftware *f*   multipurpose
software.
Almosen *nt*   alms; charity.
Altanlage *f*   existing installation.
alteingeführt   established.

Altengagement *nt*   existing com-
mitment.
Altersruhegeld *nt*   retirement pen-
sion.
Altersversorgung *f*   retirement
benefit.
Altersvorsorge *f*   retirement provi-
sion.
Amortisation *f*   redemption; amortization.
amortisieren   to redeem; to amortize.
Amt *nt*   office.
amtlich   official.
Amtsantritt *m*   taking office.
Amtsblatt *nt*   official register.
Amtsgericht *nt*   district court.
Amtshandlung *f*   official act.
Amtsübernahme *f*   assumption of
office.
Amtszeit *f*   term of office.
Analyse *f*   analysis.
analysieren   to analyze.
Analytiker *m*   analyst.
analytisch   analytical.
anbahnen   to initiate.
anbieten   to offer; *(als Zahlungsmittel)* to tender; *(Preis)* to quote.
Anbieter *m*   supplier.
ändern   to change; to alter; *(revidieren)* to amend.
Änderung *f*   change; *(Revision)*
amendment.
Andrang *m*   rush.
aneignen, sich   to appropriate; to
acquire.
Aneignung *f*   appropriation;
acquisition.
anerkennen   to acknowledge; to
recognize; *(zugeben)* to admit.
Anerkennung *f*   acknowledgment;
recognition; *(Zugeständnis)*
admission.

Anfahrt *f*   drive.
Anfang *m*   beginning.
anfangen   to begin; to commence.
anfänglich   initial.
Anfangs-   initial.
Anfangsbuchstabe *m*   initial.
Anfangskapital *nt*   initial capital; *(AG)* capital stock.
Anfangskurs *m*   *(Börse)* opening price.
Anfangsproblem *nt*   start-up problem.
Anfangszustand *m*   original condition.
anfechten   to contest; to challenge.
anfertigen   to manufacture; to produce.
Anfertigung *f*   manufacture; production.
Anfertigungskosten *pl*   manufacturing cost.
anfordern   to request.
Anforderung *f*   demand; request; *(Anforderungsschein)* requisition.
Anfrage *f*   inquiry.
anführen   to head; to lead; *(zitieren)* to quote.
Angabe *f*   statement; indication; *(Einzelheiten)* data; *(Auskunft)* information.
angeben   to state; to name; to indicate; *(Quelle)* to cite.
Angebot *nt*   supply; *(Vorschlag)* proposal; *(Offerte)* offer; *(Kostenvoranschlag)* bid.
angebotene Aktien *pl*   tendered shares.
Angebotstabelle *f*   supply schedule.
angefertigt   made.
angehören   to belong to.
Angehörige *m/f*   member; *(Familie)* family member.

Angelegenheit *f*   matter; concern; affair.
angelernt   semiskilled.
angemessen   just; fair; appropriate; adequate.
Angemessenheit *f*   adequacy; *(Eignung)* suitability.
angeschlossen   affiliated.
angesehen   reputable; prestigious.
angespannt   tight.
angestellt   employed.
Angestellte *m/f*   employee.
angewiesen sein auf   to depend on.
angliedern   to incorporate; to affiliate.
angrenzen   to border.
anhalten   to halt; to stop; *(andauern)* to last.
Anhalten *nt*   stoppage.
anheben   *(Preis, Qualität)* to raise; to lift.
Ankauf *m*   acquisition.
ankaufen   to purchase; to acquire.
Ankäufer *m*   purchaser; acquirer.
Anklang *m*   appeal.
Anklang *m* **finden**   to appeal.
ankommen   to arrive.
Ankommen *nt*   arrival.
ankreuzen   to check off.
ankündigen   to announce.
Ankündigung *f*   announcement.
Ankunft *f*   arrival.
ankurbeln   to stimulate; to boost.
Anlage *f*   *(Investition)* investment; *(Einrichtung)* installation; *(Ausrüstung)* equipment; *(Betrieb)* plant; *(graphische Anordnung)* layout.
Anlagebank *f*   investment bank.
Anlagebankier *m*   investment banker.
Anlageberater *m*   investment adviser.

Anlagebetrag *m*   investment capital.

Anlagedauer *f*   investment period.

Anlageentscheidung *f*   investment decision.

Anlageform *f*   type of investment.

Anlagegüter *pl*   capital goods.

Anlagemittel *pl*   investment funds.

Anlagenrendite *f*   return on assets; yield on investment.

Anlagetip *m*   investment tip.

Anlagevermögen *nt*   fixed assets.

Anlagewertsteigerung *f*   capital appreciation.

Anlaß *m*   cause.

Anlaufphase *f*   start-up phase.

anlegen   to invest.

Anleihe *f*   *(Darlehen)* loan; *(Obligation)* bond.

Anleihekurs *m*   bond price.

Anliegen *nt*   request; concern.

anmelden   to declare; to register.

Anmeldung *f*   registration; filing; declaration.

annähernd   approximate.

Annahme *f*   *(Lieferung)* acceptance; receipt; receiving; *(Gesetz)* passing; adoption; *(Vermutung)* assumption; presumption.

Annahmepflicht *f*   obligation to accept.

Annahmeverweigerung *f*   refusal of acceptance; rejection; *(Wechsel)* nonacceptance.

annehmbar   acceptable; admissible.

Annehmbarkeit *f*   acceptability.

annehmen   *(Lieferung)* to accept; to receive; *(Gesetz)* to pass; to adopt; *(vermuten)* to assume; to presume.

annoncieren   to advertise.

Annuität *f*   annuity.

annullieren   to rescind; to cancel.

Annullierung *f*   cancellation.

anordnen   *(anweisen)* to order; to direct; *(plazieren)* to arrange; to place.

Anordnung *f*   *(Anweisung)* order; directive; decree; *(Plazierung)* arrangement; placement; *(Graphik)* layout.

anpassen   to adapt; to adjust; *(angleichen)* to match; *(Kleidung)* to fit.

anpassen, sich   to conform; to adapt.

Anpassung *f*   adjustment; adaptation; accommodation.

anpassungsfähig   flexible.

Anpassungsfähigkeit *f*   flexibility; adaptability.

Anpassungszeitraum *m*   period of adjustment.

anpreisen   to promote; to plug.

Anrecht *nt*   claim; title.

Anrede *f*   address.

anreden   to address.

anregen   to stimulate.

anregend   stimulating.

Anregung *f*   stimulation.

Anreiz *m*   incentive; inducement.

Anruf *m*   call.

anrufen   to telephone; to phone; to call.

ansammeln   *(sammeln)* to collect; *(Vorräte)* to stockpile; to assemble; *(Kapital)* to accumulate.

ansammeln, sich   *(Zinsen)* to accrue; to pile up.

Ansammlung *f*   accumulation; *(Zinsen)* accrual.

Ansässige *m/f*   resident.

Ansatzpunkt *m*   starting point.

anschaffen   to acquire.

Anschaffung *f*   acquisition.

Anschaffungsdarlehen *nt* consumer loan.

Anschaffungspreis *m* initial cost; purchase price.

anschlagen to post.

Anschlagtafel *f* bulletin board; board.

anschließen to affiliate.

Anschluß *m* connection.

anschreiben *(Kredit)* to charge; to write to.

Anschrift *f* address.

Ansehen *nt* reputation; prestige.

ansetzen *(Termin)* to schedule; *(abschätzen)* to assess; *(Preis)* to quote.

Ansicht *f* point of view; outlook; *(Urteil)* judgment.

Anspielung *f* hint; allusion.

Ansporn *m* stimulus; incentive.

anspornen to stimulate; to spur.

Ansprache *f* speech; address.

Anspruch *m* claim.

Anstalt *f* institute; institution.

ansteigen to rise; to increase.

anstellen to hire; to employ; *(ernennen)* to appoint; *(zur Arbeit heranziehen)* to enlist.

Anstellung *f* *(Stellung)* position; employment; *(Ernennung)* appointment; *(Einstellung)* engagement; hiring.

Anstieg *m* rise; hike; increase.

Anstoß *m* impulse; impetus.

anstrahlen to spotlight.

anstrengen, sich to apply oneself; to strain.

Ansturm *m* rush.

Anteil *m* share; portion; *(Prozentsatz)* percentage; *(Beteiligung)* participation; holding; *(Verhältnis)* proportion.

anteilig proportionate.

Anteilschein *m* certificate.

Anteilseigner *m* shareholder.

Anteilsquote *f* percentage share.

Antrag *m* *(Gesuch)* application; *(Angebot)* tender; *(Parlament)* motion.

Antrag *m* **stellen** *(Gesuch)* to apply; *(Parlament)* to file a motion.

Antrieb *m* *(Motivierung)* motivation; impetus; impulse; *(technisch)* propulsion.

Antwort *f* response; answer; reply.

antworten to respond; to answer; to reply.

anvertrauen to entrust.

anwachsen to grow; *(Zinsen)* to accrue.

Anwalt *m* attorney at law; lawyer.

Anwaltsfirma *f* law office.

Anwärter *m* candidate.

anweisen *(überweisen)* to transfer; to remit; *(Gebrauchsanweisung)* to instruct; *(anordnen)* to direct.

Anweisung *f* *(Geld)* transfer; *(Geldanweisung)* money order; *(Befehl)* order; *(Gebrauchsanweisung)* instruction.

anwendbar applicable.

anwenden to apply.

Anwendung *f* application.

Anwendungsbereich *m* range of application.

anwendungsbezogen use-oriented.

anwerben to recruit.

anwesend present.

Anwesenheit *f* presence.

Anzahl *f* number.

anzahlen to pay a deposit.

Anzahlung *f* deposit; down payment.

Anzeichen *nt* sign; indication.

Anzeige *f* *(Ankündigung)* notice;

(Inserat) ad; advertisement; *(bei Behörde)* report; *(Zahlungsankündigung)* advice.

Anzeige *f* **aufgeben**   to advertise.

anzeigen   *(ankündigen)* to announce; to give notice; *(inserieren)* to advertise; *(bei Behörde)* to report; *(eine Zahlung ankündigen)* to advise.

Anzeigenteil *m*   advertising section.

Anzeigenüberschrift *f*   advertising heading.

Apparat *m*   machine; device; apparatus.

Appell *m*   appeal.

appellieren   to appeal.

Ära *f*   era.

Arbeit *f*   work; job; *(Ausführung)* workmanship; *(Stellung)* employment; occupation; *(Aufgabe)* task; *(das Arbeiten)* labor.

arbeiten   to work.

Arbeiter *m*   worker.

Arbeitgeber *m*   employer.

Arbeitgeber/Arbeitnehmer-Verhältnis *nt*   labor relations.

Arbeitgeberverband *m*   employer association.

Arbeitgebervertreter *m*   employer representative.

Arbeitnehmer *m*   employee.

Arbeit *f* **niederlegen**   to strike.

Arbeitsablauf *m*   work flow.

Arbeitsamt *nt*   employment office; Office of Economic Security.

Arbeitsanalyse *f*   work analysis.

Arbeitsanfall *m*   volume of work.

Arbeitsaufwand *m*   effort.

Arbeitsausschuß *m*   task force.

Arbeitsbedingung *f*   working condition.

Arbeitsbelastung *f*   workload.

Arbeitseifer *m*   work enthusiasm.

Arbeitsentgelt *nt*   compensation; remuneration.

Arbeitsgang *m*   work process.

Arbeitsgebiet *nt*   area of work.

Arbeitsgemeinschaft *f*   team; working group; *(Schule)* study group.

Arbeitsgericht *nt*   labor court.

arbeitsintensiv   labor intensive.

Arbeitskampf *m*   labor dispute.

Arbeitskomfort *m*   workplace convenience.

Arbeitskonflikt *m*   labor conflict.

Arbeitskosten *pl*   labor costs.

Arbeitskraft *f*   worker.

Arbeitskräfte *pl*   workforce; labor.

Arbeitslohn *m*   pay; wage.

arbeitslos   unemployed.

Arbeitslose *m/f*   unemployed person.

Arbeitslosengeld *nt*   unemployment compensation.

Arbeitslosenhilfe *f*   unemployment aid.

Arbeitslosenquote *f*   unemployment rate.

Arbeitslosenunterstützung *f*   unemployment aid.

Arbeitslosenzahl *f*   unemployment figure.

Arbeitslosigkeit *f*   unemployment.

Arbeitsmarkt *m*   job market.

Arbeitsmarktlage *f*   job market condition.

Arbeitsniederlegung *f*   work stoppage; walkout.

Arbeitspause *f*   break.

Arbeitspensum *nt*   workload.

Arbeitsplatz *m*   workplace.

Arbeitsplatzaufteilung *f*   job sharing.

Arbeitsplatzbeschreibung *f*   job description.

Arbeitsplatzverlust *m*   loss of job.
Arbeitsrecht *nt*   labor law.
Arbeitsrichter *m*   labor judge.
Arbeitsrichtlinie *f*   work rule.
arbeitsscheu   unwilling to work.
Arbeitsstab *m*   task force.
Arbeitsstätte *f*   workplace.
Arbeitsstelle *f*   position; job.
Arbeitstag *m*   workday.
Arbeitstagung *f*   workshop.
Arbeitsteilung *f*   division of labor.
Arbeitsuchende *m/f*   job applicant.
Arbeitsumfeld *nt*   work environment.
Arbeitsverhältnis *nt*   employment.
Arbeitsvermittlung *f*   employment agency.
Arbeitsvorgang *m*   operation; work process.
Arbeitswert *m*   value of labor.
arbeitswillig   willing to work.
Arbeitszeit *f*   working hours.
Arbitrage *f*   arbitrage.
Arbitragehändler *m*   arbitrager.
Argument *nt*   argument.
arm   poor.
Armut *f*   poverty.
arrangieren   to arrange.
Artikel *m*   goods; article.
Artikelgruppe *f*   product line.
Aspekt *m*   aspect.
Assekurant *m*   underwriter.
Assistent *m*   assistant.
assoziieren   to associate.
aufbereiten   to process.
Aufbereitung *f*   processing.
aufbewahren   to store.
Aufbewahrung *f*   storage.
Aufbewahrungsschein *m*   storage check.
aufeinanderfolgend   consecutive.
auferlegen   to impose.
Auferlegung *f*   imposition.

Auffächerung *f*   diversification.
auffallend   striking; noticeable.
auffangen   *(abmildern)* to cushion; *(Kosten)* to absorb.
Auffassung *f*   outlook; opinion; perception.
auffordern   to request.
Aufforderung *f*   request.
auffrischen   to revitalize.
Aufgabe *f*   *(Pflicht)* duty; task; *(Arbeit)* job; function; *(Arbeitszuweisung)* assignment; *(Schulaufgabe)* lesson; *(Verantwortung)* responsibility; *(Amt)* office; *(Freigabe)* release; *(Preisgabe)* abandonment; pullout; *(Absendung)* dispatch.
Aufgabengebiet *nt*   area of responsibility; job description.
Aufgabengruppe *f*   task force.
Aufgabenstellung *f*   defining a task.
Aufgabenverteilung *f*   assignment of tasks.
Aufgabenwahrnehmung *f*   exercise of functions.
aufgeben   to assign; *(absenden)* to dispatch; *(bei der Post)* to mail; *(Brief)* to post; *(preisgeben)* to relinquish; to abandon; *(aufhören)* to quit; *(Amt aufgeben)* to resign.
Aufgeld *nt*   premium.
aufgliedern   to subdivide; *(Konten)* to classify; *(Kosten)* to break down.
Aufgliederung *f*   subdivision; *(Konten)* classification; *(Kosten)* *breakdown.*
aufhalten   *(zurückhalten)* to detain.
aufhalten, sich   to stay; to remain.
aufheben   *(Gesetz)* to repeal; *(annullieren)* to cancel; to rescind;

to annul; *(Kontrollen)* to lift; to deregulate; to decontrol; to remove; to abolish; *(Vollmacht)* to revoke; *(aufbewahren)* to keep; *(Sitzung)* to adjourn; to close.

Aufhebung *f   (Gesetz)* repeal; *(Anullierung)* cancellation; invalidation; annulment; rescission; *(Kontrollen)* lifting; deregulation; removal; abolishment; *(Vollmacht)* revocation; *(Sitzung)* adjournment; closing.

aufhören   to stop; to quit; to discontinue; to cease.

aufkaufen   to buy up.

aufkommen   to arise; *(bezahlen)* to pay for; to compensate for.

aufladen   to load.

Auflage *f   (Buch)* edition; *(Zeitung)* circulation; *(Anweisung)* direction; *(Belastung)* charge.

auflaufen   to accumulate; *(Zinsen)* to accrue.

Auflaufen *nt*   accumulation; *(Zinsen)* accrual.

auflegen   *(Buch)* to publish; *(Anleihe)* to float.

Auflegung *f   (Anleihe)* flotation.

auflisten   to list.

auflösen   to dissolve; *(Firma)* to liquidate; *(Vertrag)* to cancel.

Auflösung *f*   dissolution; *(Firma)* liquidation; *(Vertrag)* cancellation.

aufmerksam   attentive.

Aufmerksamkeit *f*   attention.

Aufnahme *f*   reception; *(Zulassung)* admission; acceptance; *(Beherbergung)* accommodation; *(Eintragung)* entry; inclusion; *(Kapital)* raising; borrowing; *(einer Tätigkeit)* assumption; *(Photo)* snapshot; *(Ton, Bild)* recording.

Aufnahmeapparat *m*   recorder.

Aufnahmestaat *m*   host country.

aufnehmen   to receive; *(zulassen)* to admit; to accept; *(beherbergen)* to accommodate; *(eintragen)* to enter; to include; *(Kapital)* to raise; to borrow; *(eine Tätigkeit)* to assume; *(Ton, Bild)* to record.

Aufprall *m*   impact.

aufrechnen   to balance; to settle.

aufrechterhalten   to maintain.

Aufrechterhaltung *f*   upkeep; maintenance.

Aufriß *m*   layout.

Aufruhr *m*   disturbance.

aufschieben   to postpone; to defer.

Aufschlag *m   (Preis)* additional charge; markup; *(Prämie)* premium.

aufschreiben   to note; to write down.

Aufschub *m*   postponement; deferral.

Aufschwung *m*   upswing.

Aufseher *m*   supervisor; controller.

Aufsicht *f*   control; check.

Aufsichtsamt *nt*   regulatory agency.

aufsichtsführend   supervising; supervisory.

Aufsichtsführung *f*   supervision.

Aufsichtsrat *m*   board of directors; supervisory board.

Aufsichtsratssitzung *f*   board of directors' meeting; supervisory board meeting.

aufsteigen   to rise; to advance.

aufstellen   *(Bilanz)* to prepare; *(Maschine)* to assemble; to install; *(Bauten)* to erect.

Aufstellung *f   (Bilanz)* preparation; *(Maschine)* installation; assembly; *(Liste)* list; statement.

Aufstieg *m*   rise; advancement.

Aufstiegsmöglichkeit *f* opportunity for advancement; career opportunity; upward mobility.

aufstocken to stockpile; *(Kapital)* to increase.

Aufstockung *f* stockpiling; *(Kapital)* increase.

aufteilen to split; to section; to segment; to parcel out; to divide.

Aufteilung *f* split; distribution; division.

Auftrag *m* *(Anweisung, Bestellung)* order; *(Ernennung)* appointment; *(Pflicht)* charge; commission.

auftragen to charge with; *(Essen)* to serve.

Auftraggeber *m* *(Besteller)* customer; principal; client; *(Werbung)* sponsor.

Auftragsabwicklung *f* filling a contract; processing an order.

Auftragsbestand *m* orders on hand.

Auftragseingang *m* incoming order; receipt of order.

Auftragsflut *f* surge in orders.

Auftragspolster *nt* order backlog.

Auftragsüberhang *m* order backlog.

Auftragswert *m* value of goods ordered.

Aufwand *m* *(Luxus)* luxury; *(Ausgabe)* expenditure.

Aufwärtsbewegung *f* upturn.

Aufwärtsentwicklung *f* upward movement.

aufwenden to spend; to expend.

aufwendig expensive.

Aufwendung *f* expenditure.

aufwerten *(Währung)* to revalue.

Aufwertung *f* *(Währung)* revaluation.

aufzählen to enumerate; to list.

aufzeichnen to record.

Aufzeichnung *f* record.

Auktion *f* auction.

Ausbau *m* *(Entwicklung)* development; *(Ausdehnung)* expansion.

ausbedingen to stipulate.

ausbessern to repair.

ausbeuten to exploit.

Ausbeutung *f* exploitation.

ausbilden to train; to educate.

Ausbildung *f* education; training.

Ausbildungsabschluß *m* graduation.

ausdehnen *(ausbreiten)* to spread; *(erweitern)* to expand; *(verlängern)* to extend.

Ausdehnung *f* *(Ausbreitung)* spread; *(Wachstum)* growth; *(Erweiterung)* expansion; *(Verlängerung)* extension.

Ausdruck *m* *(Worte)* phrase; expression; *(Druck)* printout.

ausdrücken to phrase; to express.

ausdrücklich specific; explicit; express.

Auseinandersetzung *f* dispute; argument.

Ausfall *m* *(Fehlbetrag)* deficit; *(Maschine)* breakdown.

ausfallen *(Tagung, Vorlesung)* to be cancelled; *(Maschine)* to break down; *(werden)* to turn out.

Ausfuhr *f* export; exportation.

Ausfuhrauftrag *m* export order.

ausführbar workable; realizable; feasible.

Ausführbarkeit *f* feasibility.

Ausfuhrbeschränkung *f* export restriction.

Ausfuhreinnahmen *pl* export receipts.

ausführen *(exportieren)* to export; *(Bestellung)* to fill; to complete;

(durchführen) to carry out; to
implement; to execute; *(erklären)*
to state.
Ausfuhrertrag *m*   export earnings.
Ausfuhrfinanzierung *f*   export
financing.
Ausfuhrförderung *f*   export pro-
motion.
Ausfuhrgarantie *f*   export guaran-
tee.
Ausfuhrgenehmigung *f*   export
license.
Ausfuhrkredit *m*   export credit.
Ausfuhrland *nt*   exporting country.
ausführlich   detailed.
Ausfuhrsperre *f*   embargo.
Ausfuhrsubvention *f*   export subsidy.
Ausfuhrüberschuß *m*   export surplus.
Ausführung *f*   *(Durchführung)*
implementation; execution; *(Er-
klärung)* statement.
Ausführungstag *m*   implementa-
tion date.
Ausfuhrvolumen *nt*   export volume.
Ausfuhrwert *m*   export value.
Ausfuhrzuwachs *m*   export
growth.
ausfüllen   *(Formular)* to fill in; to
complete.
Ausfüllung *f*   *(Formular)* completion.
Ausgabe *f*   *(Kosten)* expense;
expenditure; *(Emission)* issue;
issuance; *(Buch)* edition; *(Zeitung)*
issue.
Ausgabekurs *m*   issue price.
Ausgabenposten *m*   expense item.
Ausgabepreis *m*   issue price.
Ausgabeverhalten *nt*   spending
behavior.

Ausgabezeitpunkt *m*   date of
issue.
Ausgangsforderung *f*   initial
demand.
Ausgangsposition *f*   starting position.
Ausgangspunkt *m*   starting point.
ausgeben   *(Geld)* to spend; to
expend; *(Geld in Umlauf setzen)*
to issue; to circulate.
ausgebildet   trained.
ausgedehnt   broad.
ausgegebene Aktien *pl*   shares
outstanding.
ausgemacht   stipulated.
ausgeprägt   distinctive.
ausgesucht   selected; choice.
ausgewählt   selected.
Ausgleich *m*   balance; balancing;
(Bezahlung) payment; *(Entschädigung)* compensation; *(Gleichstellung)* equalization; *(Abrechnung)*
settlement; *(Berichtigung)* adjustment.
ausgleichen   to balance; to equalize; *(entschädigen)* to compensate;
(berichtigen) to adjust; *(Zoll)* to
countervail.
ausgleichend   compensatory;
(Zoll) countervailing.
Ausgleichsposten *m*   *(Buchhaltung)* deferred item.
aushandeln   to negotiate.
Auskommen *nt*   livelihood.
Auskunft *f*   information.
Auslage *f*   *(Kosten)* expense; outlay; disbursement; *(Schaufenster)*
display.
Ausland *nt*   foreign country.
Ausländer *m*   foreigner.
ausländisch   foreign; external.
Auslands-   foreign.
auslassen   to omit.

auslasten   to use to capacity.

Auslastungsgrad *m*   level of capacity.

auslaufen lassen   to phase out.

ausleihen   to lend; to loan.

Ausleiher *m*   lender.

Auslieferer *m*   supplier.

ausliefern   to deliver; to supply.

Auslieferung *f*   delivery.

Auslieferungslager *nt*   warehouse.

auslöschen   to obliterate.

Ausmaß *nt*   measure; dimension.

Ausnahme *f*   exception.

Ausnahmefall *m*   exceptional case.

Ausnahmeregelung *f*   exemption.

ausnutzen   to utilize fully; *(ausbeuten)* to exploit.

Ausnutzung *f*   utilization; *(Ausbeutung)* exploitation.

ausreichen   to suffice.

ausreichend   adequate; ample; sufficient.

ausrufen   *(Namen über Lautsprecher)* to page; to call out.

ausruhen, sich   to rest; to relax.

ausrüsten   to outfit; to equip.

Ausrüstung *f*   outfit; equipment.

Ausrüstungsgut *nt*   equipment goods.

ausschalten   *(beseitigen)* to eliminate; *(Licht)* to turn off.

Ausschaltung *f*   elimination.

ausscheiden   *(Amt)* to leave.

ausschlaggebend   pivotal.

ausschließen   to exclude; to bar.

ausschließlich   exclusive.

Ausschließung *f*   exclusion.

Ausschreibung *f*   bid invitation; *(Stelle)* advertisement; *(Bekanntmachung)* announcement.

Ausschuß *m*   *(Komitee)* panel; board; commission; committee; *(Produktionsausschuß)* rejects.

Ausschußware *f*   rejects; damaged goods.

ausschütten   *(Gewinn)* to distribute; *(Dividende)* to declare.

Ausschüttung *f*   distribution.

Außendienst *m*   field service.

Außenhandel *m*   foreign trade.

Außenpolitik *f*   foreign policy.

Außenseiter *m*   newcomer; outsider.

Außenstelle *f*   field office.

Außenwert *m*   external value.

Außenwirtschaft *f*   foreign trade.

äußerlich   external.

aussperren   to lock out.

Aussperrung *f*   lockout.

ausstatten   to equip; to outfit; *(mit Kapital)* to endow.

Ausstattung *f*   equipment; outfit; *(mit Kapital)* endowment.

ausstehend   receivable; outstanding.

ausstellen   *(check, document)* to issue; *(Wechsel)* to draw; *(Waren)* to display; *(zur Schau stellen)* to exhibit.

Aussteller *m*   *(Emittent)* issuer; *(von Waren)* exhibitor.

Ausstellung *f*   *(Emission)* issuance; issue; *(Zurschaustellung)* exhibit; exhibition; *(Messe)* fair.

Ausstellungsstück *nt*   exhibit.

Ausstoß *m*   run; output.

aussuchen   to select; to pick.

Austausch *m*   exchange.

austauschbar   exchangeable.

austauschen   to exchange.

Austauschrelationen *pl*   terms of trade.

Austauschverhältnis *nt*   terms of trade.

ausüben   to practice.

Ausübende *m/f*   practitioner.

Ausverkauf *m*   sale; sellout.

Auswahl *f*   selection; choice; *(Sortiment)* assortment; range.
auswählen   to select; to pick; to choose.
Auswahlverfahren *nt*   selection process.
auswärtig   foreign.
Ausweis *m*   pass; identification card; identification badge.
ausweisen   *(deportieren)* to deport; *(in Bilanz)* to report.
ausweisen, sich   to identify oneself.
ausweiten   to enlarge; to expand.
Ausweitung *f*   expansion; extension.
auswerten   to utilize; *(Daten)* to evaluate.

Auswertung *f*   utilization; *(Daten)* evaluation.
auswirken, sich   to have an effect; to result in.
Auswirkung *f*   impact; effect; consequence.
auszahlen   to pay out; to disburse.
Auszahlung *f*   payout; disbursement.
auszeichnen   *(markieren)* to mark; to distinguish.
Auszug *m*   *(Konto)* statement; extract; excerpt.
Automat *m*   *(Verkaufsautomat)* vending machine.
Automatisierung *f*   automation.
Aval *m/nt*   guarantee.
Azubi *m/f*   trainee; apprentice.

B

bahnbrechen   to pioneer.
Bahnbrecher *m*   pioneer.
Bahnsteig *m*   platform.
Baisse *f*   slump; drop; bear market.
Ballungsgebiet *nt*   urban center; overcrowded area.
Ballungsraum *m*   urban center; overcrowded area.
Band *m*   *(Buch)* volume.
Band *nt*   *(Schreibmaschine)* ribbon; *(Bandgerät)* tape; *(Verbindung)* tie; bond.
Bank *f*   bank.
Bankaktien *pl*   bank stocks.
Bankaktivität *f*   banking activity.
Bankakzept *nt*   banker's acceptance.
Bankanlage *f*   banking investment.
Bankaufsicht *f*   bank supervision.

Bankautomation *f*   bank automation.
Bankbeamte *m*   bank officer.
Bankbeamtin *f*   bank officer.
Bankberater *m*   bank advisor.
Bankdienstleistung *f*   banking service.
Bankenausschuß *m*   banking committee.
Bankenkonsortium *nt*   banking syndicate; bank group.
Bankenkundschaft *f*   bank customers; bank clientele.
Bankensystem *nt*   banking system.
Bankentochter *f*   bank affiliate; bank subsidiary.
Bankfachwissen *nt*   banking expertise.

bankfähig negotiable.
Bankführungskraft *f* bank executive; bank manager.
Bankgeschäfte *pl* **machen** to bank.
Bankgesellschaft *f* banking corporation.
Bankgewerbe *nt* banking business.
Bankhaus *nt* banking house.
Bankier *m* banker.
Bankkonto *nt* bank account; checking account.
Bankkredit *m* bank credit.
Bankkunde *m* bank customer.
Bankleistung *f* banking service; banking performance.
Bankleiter *m* bank manager.
Bankleitung *f* bank management.
Bankleitzahl *f* bank code number.
bankmäßig bankable; negotiable.
Bankmitarbeiter *m* bank employee.
Banknote *f* bank note; bill.
Bankplatz *m* banking center.
Bankpolitik *f* banking policy.
Bankregel *f* banking rule.
Bankrott *m* bankruptcy; failure.
Bankrott *m* **gehen** to go bankrupt; to fail.
Bankschalter *m* teller's window.
Bankspesen *pl* bank service charges.
Banktätigkeit *f* banking activity.
Bankverbindung *f* correspondent bank.
Bankvermögen *nt* bank assets.
Bankwesen *nt* banking.
Bankzinsen *pl* interest on deposits; interest on bank loans.
Bankzweigstelle *f* bank branch.
bar cash.
Barausschüttung *f* cash distribution; cash dividend.

Bargeld *nt* cash.
Bargeldautomat *m* automatic teller machine.
Bargeldbeitrag *m* cash contribution; cash dues.
bargeldlos paid by check; without ready money; noncash.
Bargeldversorgung *f* supply of cash.
Bargeschäft *nt* cash transaction.
Barlohn *m* wage paid in cash.
Barmittel *pl* cash.
Barprämie *f* cash bonus.
Barren *m* bar; *(Gold)* bullion.
Barreserve *f* money reserve; *(Bank)* minimum cash reserve.
Barriere *f* barrier.
Bartergeschäft *nt* barter transaction.
Barzahlung *f* cash.
Basis *f* base; basis.
Basispreis *m* base price.
Bau *m* construction.
Bauelement *nt* unit; component.
bauen to construct; to build.
Bauer *m* farmer.
Baufinanzierung *f* construction financing; construction loan.
Baufirma *f* construction company.
Baugelder *pl* building funds; construction loan.
Baugeldkonditionen *pl* terms for construction loan.
Baugesellschaft *f* construction company.
Baugewerbe *nt* construction business; construction trade.
Bauherr *m* builder.
Bauindustrie *f* construction industry; construction trade.
Bauplatz *m* building site.
Bausparen *nt* home purchase savings.

Bausparkasse *f* home savings and loan association.
Bauunternehmer *m* developer.
Bauwirtschaft *f* construction industry.
beabsichtigen to intend.
Beachtung *f* notice; attention.
Beamte *m*, **Beamtin** *f* officer; official.
Beamtenbesoldung *f* civil service pay.
beanspruchen to claim; *(fordern)* to demand; *(belasten)* to stress.
beanstanden to find fault with; *(beklagen)* to complain about; *(Widerspruch erheben)* to object.
Beanstandung *f* *(Widerspruch)* objection; *(Beklagen)* complaint.
beantragen to apply for; *(erbitten)* to request.
beantworten to respond; to answer.
bearbeiten to process; to handle; *(Land)* to cultivate.
Bearbeitung *f* handling; processing; *(Vorbereitung)* preparation; *(Land)* cultivation.
beaufsichtigen to supervise.
Beaufsichtigung *f* supervision; surveillance.
beauftragen *(bevollmächtigen)* to authorize; to commission; *(anweisen)* to instruct; to order.
Beauftragte *m/f* trustee; *(Bevollmächtigter)* attorney; authorized person; commissioner; *(Vertreter)* agent.
Bedarf *m* need; demand.
Bedarfsanalyse *f* demand analysis; analysis of needs.
Bedarfszunahme *f* demand growth.
Bedarfszuwachs *m* increased demand.

bedeuten to mean.
bedeutend *(wichtig)* important; *(hervorragend)* prominent; major.
Bedeutung *f* importance; significance; *(Sinn)* meaning; *(einer Person)* prominence.
bedeutungslos meaningless.
bedienen *(Maschinen)* to run; to operate; *(dienen)* to attend to; to serve.
Bedienung *f* *(Maschinen)* operation; *(Dienstleistung)* service.
Bedienungsanleitung *f* operating instructions; instruction sheet; service manual.
Bedienungsperson *f* operator.
bedingt conditional.
Bedingtheit *f* conditionality.
Bedingung *f* stipulation; *(Voraussetzung)* requirement; condition.
bedrängen to pressure.
Bedrängnis *f* hardship.
bedürfen to need.
Bedürfnis *nt* requirement; need.
Bedürfnisprüfung *f* needs test.
bedürftig needy; poor.
beeilen, sich to hurry; to rush.
beeinflußbar susceptible; manipulable; capable of being influenced.
beeinflussen to influence; to affect.
Beeinflussung *f* influence.
beeinträchtigen to impair; *(schaden)* to damage.
Beeinträchtigung *f* impairment; *(Schaden)* damage.
beenden to end; to terminate; to stop; to close; *(vollenden)* to finish; to complete.
Beendigung *f* ending; termination; *(Vollendung)* completion.
befähigen to qualify; to enable.
befähigt fit; qualified.

Befähigung *f* qualification; competence.

Befehl *m* order; command.

befehlen to command; to order.

befolgen to observe; to follow; to comply with.

Befolgung *f* observance; compliance.

befördern *(Karriereaufstieg)* to promote; *(transportieren)* to ship; to transport; to forward; to dispatch; to carry.

Beförderung *f* *(Karriereaufstieg)* promotion; advancement; *(Transport)* forwarding; shipment; transport.

befragen to interview.

Befrager *m* interviewer.

Befragte *m/f* respondent; interviewee.

Befragung *f* survey.

befreien to liberate; to free; to exempt.

befreit free; exempt.

Befreiung *f* exemption; release.

befriedigen to satisfy; to settle.

Befriedigung *f* satisfaction; settlement.

befristen to set a time limit; to set a deadline.

befristete Kündigung *f* dismissal with notice.

befugen to authorize.

Befugnis *f* *(Vollmacht)* power; authority; authorization; *(Zuständigkeit)* competence.

befürworten to recommend; to advocate.

Befürworter *m* advocate; supporter.

Befürwortung *f* recommendation; endorsement.

begebbar negotiable.

Begebung *f* *(Wertpapiere)* flotation; issue.

begegnen to meet; to encounter.

Beginn *m* start; onset; beginning.

beginnen to start; to begin; to commence.

beglaubigen *(bestätigen)* to verify; *(bescheinigen)* to certify; *(bezeugen)* to attest.

Beglaubigung *f* *(Bestätigung)* verification; *(Bescheinigung)* certificate.

Beglaubigungsschreiben *nt* credentials.

begleiten to accompany.

begrenzen to limit; to restrict.

Begrenzung *f* limitation; restriction.

Begriff *m* idea; concept.

begründen *(Geschäft)* to found; to set up; *(Behauptung)* to substantiate.

Begründung *f* foundation; basis; *(Beweisführung)* argumentation.

begünstigen to benefit; to favor; *(fördern)* to promote.

Begünstigte *m/f* beneficiary.

Begünstigung *f* favoritism; *(Gläubiger)* preferential treatment; *(Steuer)* privilege.

begutachten *(Versicherung)* to survey; to appraise.

Begutachtung *f* expert opinion; appraisal.

Behälter *m* container.

behandeln to treat; to deal with; *(handhaben)* to handle.

Behandlung *f* treatment; *(Handhabung)* handling.

beharren to persist.

beharrlich persistent.

behaupten to claim; to contend; to assert.

behaupten, sich   to hold one's own; to assert oneself.

Behauptung *f*   claim; contention; assertion.

beherbergen   to shelter; to accommodate.

beherrschen   to rule; to control; *(Markt)* to dominate; *(Fähigkeit)* to master.

beherrschend   dominant.

Beherschung *f*   control; *(Markt)* domination; *(Fähigkeit)* mastery.

behilflich   helpful; instrumental.

behindern   to obstruct; to impede.

Behinderung *f*   obstruction; obstacle; *(Beschränkung)* restraint; *(körperlich)* disability.

Behörde *f*   authority; agency.

Behördenauftrag *m*   government order.

Behördenweg *m*   official channel.

behutsam   cautious.

beifügen   *(Brief)* to enclose; to attach.

Beihilfe *f*   benefit; assistance.

Beilage *f*   *(Zeitung)* supplement; insert; *(letter)* attachment; enclosure.

beiläufig   incidental.

beilegen   *(Brief)* to enclose; *(Zeitung)* to insert; *(Streit)* to settle.

Beilegung *f*   settlement; reconciliation.

Beirat *m*   advisory board.

Beispiel *nt*   example.

Beispielsfall *m*   precedent; model case.

Beistand *m*   assistance; aid.

Beitrag *m*   contribution; *(Mitgliedsbeitrag)* dues; *(Versicherungsbeitrag)* premium.

beitragen   to contribute.

Beitragsleistende *m/f*   contributor.

beitreten   to join.

bejahen   to support.

Bekanntgabe *f*   *(Benachrichtigung)* notice; *(Ankündigung)* announcement; *(Aufdeckung)* disclosure.

bekanntgeben   *(benachrichtigen)* to notify; *(ankündigen)* to announce; *(aufdecken)* to disclose.

Bekanntheitsgrad *m*   level of familiarity.

bekanntmachen   to introduce; *(ankündigen)* to announce.

bekommen   to receive; to get; to obtain.

bekräftigen   to affirm; to confirm.

beladen   to load.

Belange *pl*   interests; issues; concerns.

belasten   *(beladen)* to load; *(auferlegen)* to encumber; to burden; *(Konto belasten)* to charge; to debit.

Belastung *f*   handicap; *(Auferlegung)* encumbrance; burden; *(Konto)* charge; debit.

belaufen, sich   to amount to.

beleben   to stimulate; to encourage.

Belebung *f*   *(Konjunktur)* stimulation; recovery.

Beleg *m*   *(Beweisstück)* proof; evidence; *(Buchhaltung)* voucher; *(Akte)* record; *(Urkunde)* certificate.

belegen   *(beweisen)* to prove; to vouch; *(Vorlesung)* to register for; *(Sitzplatz)* to reserve.

belegen mit   *(Steuern)* to impose.

Belegschaft *f*   workforce; staff; personnel.

Belegschaftsabbau *m*   personnel cutback; employee layoff.

belehrend   educational.

beleihbar   eligible to serve as collateral.

beleihen   to lend on.

beliebig   optional; discretionary.

beliebt   popular.

Beliebtheit *f*   popularity.

beliefern   to supply.

belohnen   to reward; *(bezahlen)* to remunerate.

Belohnung *f*   reward; *(Bezahlung)* remuneration.

bemängeln   to find fault with.

bemerkbar   noticeable.

bemerken   *(erkennen)* to notice; to spot; *(sagen)* to remark; to note.

Bemerkung *f*   remark; comment.

Bemerkung *f* **machen**   to comment.

bemessen   to rate; to assess; to measure.

Bemessung *f*   rating; assessment.

bemühen, sich   to exert oneself; to make an effort.

Bemühung *f*   effort.

benachrichtigen   to notify; to inform; to advise.

Benachrichtigung *f*   notification; information; communication; *(Bankanzeige)* advice.

Benehmen *nt*   behavior.

benennen   to name; to entitle.

benötigen   to require.

Benutzer *m*   user.

Benutzungsrecht *nt*   license.

Benutzungssteuer *f*   user tax.

Benzin *nt*   gasoline.

beobachten   to observe.

Beobachter *m*   observer.

Beobachtung *f*   observance; observation.

Bequemlichkeit *f*   convenience; comfort.

beraten   *(Rat geben)* to counsel; to advise.

beraten, sich   to deliberate.

beratend   advisory.

Berater *m*   adviser; *(für das Geschäft)* consultant; *(Recht)* counsel; counselor.

Beratergruppe *f*   advisory group.

Beratung *f*   consultation; *(Besprechung)* meeting; deliberation.

Beratungs-   advisory.

Beratungsfirma *f*   consulting firm.

Beratungsgremium *nt*   advisory board.

berauben   to rob; to deprive.

Beraubung *f*   deprivation.

berechenbar   calculable.

berechnen   *(anrechnen)* to charge; to bill; *(ausrechnen)* to figure; to compute; to calculate; *(abschätzen)* to estimate.

Berechnung *f*   *(Belastung)* charge; *(Ausrechnung)* computation; calculation; *(Preisfeststellung)* pricing.

Berechnungsmethode *f*   method of computation; *(Preise)* pricing method.

berechtigen   to qualify; to entitle.

berechtigt   eligible; able.

Berechtigung *f*   *(Vollmacht)* power; authority; *(Rechtfertigung)* justification; *(Befähigung)* eligibility; qualification; *(Rechtsanspruch)* claim.

Bereich *m*   area; sector; region.

Bereicherung *f*   enrichment.

bereinigen   *(Statistik)* to adjust; *(Rechnung)* to settle; *(Bilanz)* to verify.

bereithalten   to keep ready.

Bereitschaft *f*   readiness; preparedness; *(in Bereitschaft)* on call.

Bereitschaftserklärung *f*   letter of intent.

bereitstellen to make available.
Bergbau *m* mining.
Bergbauunternehmen *nt* mining company.
bergen to retrieve; to recover.
Bergleute *pl* miners.
Bergwerk *nt* mine.
Bericht *m* report.
berichten to report; to cover.
Berichterstatter *m* reporter; correspondent.
Berichterstattung *f* reporting.
berichtigen *(verbessern)* to correct; *(Buchung)* to adjust.
Berichtigung *f* correction.
Berichtigungsaktie *f* stock dividend.
Berichtsjahr *nt* year under report.
berichtspflichtig reportable; subject to report.
berücksichtigen to consider; to allow for.
Berücksichtigung *f* consideration.
Beruf *m* profession; occupation; job.
beruflich professional; occupational; *(Handwerk)* vocational.
Berufschance *f* career opportunity.
Berufserfahrung *f* work experience.
Berufsschule *f* vocational school; trade school.
berufstätig employed; working.
Berufsverband *m* professional association; trade association.
Berufsvertretung *f* professional representation; trade representation.
Berufung *f* *(Ernennung)* appointment; *(Rechtsmittel)* appeal.
Berufung *f* **einlegen** to appeal.
beschaffen to procure; to provide; to supply; *(Geld)* to raise.

Beschaffenheit *f* nature; condition.
Beschaffung *f* procurement; *(Kauf)* buying; acquisition.
beschäftigen *(Angestellte)* to employ.
beschäftigen, sich to occupy oneself with; to concern oneself with.
beschäftigt occupied; busy.
Beschäftigtenzahl *f* number of persons employed.
Beschäftigung *f* *(Arbeit)* work; *(Beruf)* occupation; job; *(Anstellung)* employment.
Beschäftigungsgrad *m* level of employment; *(Industrie)* operating rate.
Beschäftigungskrise *f* unemployment crisis.
Beschäftigungslage *f* employment situation.
bescheinigen to attest; to certify.
Bescheinigung *f* certificate.
beschildern to label.
Beschlagnahme *f* confiscation; attachment.
beschlagnahmen to confiscate; to attach.
beschleunigen to accelerate.
Beschleunigung *f* acceleration.
beschließen to decide; *(Gericht)* to decree; *(Parlament)* to pass a resolution.
Beschluß *m* resolution; ruling.
Beschlußfassung *f* resolution.
beschneiden to trim; to pare; to crop.
beschränken to restrain; *(einengen auf)* to restrict; to confine; to limit.
Beschränkung *f* restraint; *(Einengung)* restriction; limitation.
beschreiben to describe.
Beschreibung *f* description.

Beschwerde *f* complaint.
beschweren, sich to complain.
beseitigen to remove; to lift; to eliminate; to abolish.
Beseitigung *f* removal; elimination.
besetzen to occupy; *(Stelle)* to staff; to fill.
besichtigen to view; *(inspizieren)* to inspect.
Besichtigung *f* inspection; *(Grundstück)* survey; *(Tourist)* sightseeing.
Besitz *m* possession; *(Eigentum)* property; *(Wertpapiere)* holding; *(Reichtum)* wealth.
besitzen to possess; *(als Eigentum)* to own; *(Wertpapiere)* to hold.
Besitzer *m* possessor; *(Eigentümer)* owner; proprietor; *(Wohnung)* occupant; *(Wertpapiere)* holder.
Besitzrecht *nt* claim.
Besoldung *f* remuneration; salary.
Besonderheit *f* specialty.
besorgen to provide; to supply; *(Haushalt)* to manage; *(kaufen)* to buy.
Besorgnis *f* concern.
besprechen to discuss.
Besprechung *f* meeting; conference; discussion.
bessern, sich to improve.
Besserung *f* *(Konjunktur)* upturn; improvement.
Bestand *m* *(Vorrat)* supply; holding; *(Inventar)* inventory.
beständig stable; permanent.
Beständigkeit *f* stability.
Bestandsaufnahme *f* taking an inventory.
Bestandskonto *nt* asset account.
Bestandskontrolle *f* inventory control.

Bestandteil *m* section; component.
bestätigen to verify; to confirm; to attest; *(einen Brief)* to acknowledge.
Bestätigung *f* verification; *(Urkunde)* certificate; *(eines Briefes)* acknowledgement.
bestechen to bribe.
bestechlich corrupt.
Bestechlichkeit *f* corruption.
Bestechung *f* payoff; bribery.
bestellen to order; *(buchen)* to reserve; *(Nachricht)* to give a message.
Bestellung *f* order; *(Buchung)* reservation; *(Nachricht)* message.
besteuern to tax; to assess.
Besteuerung *f* taxation; assessment.
besteuerungsfähig taxable; assessable.
bestimmbar determinable.
bestimmen *(entscheiden)* to determine; *(anordnen)* to direct; *(ernennen)* to appoint; *(vorsehen)* to designate; to earmark; *(zuweisen)* to assign; *(identifizieren)* to identify.
bestimmt specific; definite; *(vorgesehen)* destined; *(sicher)* certain.
Bestimmung *f* *(Entscheidung)* determination; *(Vertrag)* stipulation; clause; provision; *(Vorschrift)* directive; *(Verordnung)* regulation; *(Ziel)* destination.
Bestimmungsort *m* destination.
bestreiken to strike against.
bestreiten to dispute; to contest; to argue; *(die Kosten)* to pay for.
Bestwert *m* optimum.
Besuch *m* attendance; visit.
besuchen to attend; to visit.
Besucher *m* attendant; visitor.
Besucherzahl *f* attendance.

beteiligen, sich   to participate; to share in.

Beteiligte *m/f*   participant.

Beteiligtsein *nt*   involvement.

Beteiligung *f*   participation; holding.

betonen   to emphasize.

Betonung *f*   emphasis.

beträchtlich   considerable.

Betrag *m*   sum; figure; amount.

betragen   to amount.

betragen, sich   to behave.

betreffen   to pertain to; to concern.

betreffs   regarding.

betreiben   *(Geschäft)* to operate; to conduct.

Betreuung *f*   care.

Betrieb *m*   *(Werk)* plant; *(Fabrik)* factory; *(Unternehmen)* business; firm; company; *(Arbeitsvorgang)* operation; *(Betriebsamkeit)* activity.

betriebsam   busy.

Betriebsanlage *f*   *(Fabrik)* factory; *(Werk)* plant; industrial installation.

Betriebsanleitung *f*   operating instructions; shop rules.

Betriebsausrüstung *f*   plant equipment.

Betriebsausstattung *f*   plant equipment.

Betriebsberater *m*   management consultant.

Betriebsergebnis *nt*   company earnings.

Betriebsführer *m*   managing director.

Betriebsführung *f*   operational management; plant management.

Betriebskapital *nt*   working capital; operating capital.

Betriebskosten *pl*   operating cost.

Betriebsleitung *f*   plant management.

Betriebsmittel *pl*   working capital.

Betriebsrat *m*   workers' council.

Betriebsreingewinn *m*   net gain from operations.

Betriebsrente *f*   company pension.

Betriebsstätte *f*   business premises; place of business.

Betriebsverlust *m*   operating loss.

Betriebsvorschrift *f*   plant regulations; operating instructions; *(Eisenbahn)* service regulations.

Betrug *m*   fraud.

betrügen   to defraud; to cheat.

betrügerisch   fraudulent.

beunruhigen   to disturb.

Beunruhigung *f*   disturbance.

beurkunden   to document; to certify.

beurlauben   to grant leave; *(Beamter)* to suspend; *(Soldat)* to grant furlough.

beurteilen   to rate; to judge.

bevölkern   to populate.

Bevölkerung *f*   population.

Bevölkerungsschicht *f*   population stratum.

bevölkerungsstatistisch   demographic.

bevollmächtigen   to authorize; *(ermächtigen)* to empower.

Bevollmächtigte *m/f*   authorized person; attorney; *(Treuhänder)* trustee; *(Vertreter)* representative; agent.

Bevollmächtigung *f*   delegation of authority; authorization; *(Ermächtigung)* empowerment.

bevorrechtigt   preferential; preferred.

bevorzugen   to prefer; *(begünstigen)* to privilege; to favor.

bevorzugt   preferential; preferred.
Bevorzugung *f*   preference.
bewahren   to preserve.
Bewahrung *f*   preservation.
bewältigen   *(eine Aufgabe)* to accomplish; *(eine Schwierigkeit)* to master; to cope with.
Bewältigung *f*   *(Erledigung)* handling; *(einer Schwierigkeit)* coping with.
bewandert   skilled.
Beweggrund   *m* motive.
beweglich   mobile.
Beweglichkeit *f*   mobility; flexibility.
Bewegungsfreiheit *f*   leeway; mobility.
Beweis *m*   evidence; proof; *(Zeichen)* token; *(Beweisführung)* demonstration.
beweisen   to prove.
beweiskräftig   conclusive.
Beweismittel *nt*   proof; evidence.
Beweisstück *nt*   document; exhibit.
bewerben, sich   to apply for; *(um Lieferungen)* to make a bid; *(um einen Preis)* to compete for; *(um Stimmen)* to solicit.
Bewerber *m*   applicant; *(Lieferungen)* bidder; *(Preis)* competitor.
Bewerberzahl *f*   number of applicants.
Bewerbung *f*   application.
bewertbar   assessable.
bewerten   to evaluate; to appraise; to assess.
Bewertung *f*   evaluation; assessment; *(Schätzung)* appraisal; estimate.
Bewertungsdurchschnitt *m*   weighted average.
bewilligen   to grant; *(erlauben)* to allow; *(genehmigen)* to approve;

(Geldmittel im Parlament) to appropriate.
Bewilligung *f*   granting; *(Erlaubnis)* permission; *(Genehmigung)* approval; consent; *(Geldmittel im Parlament)* appropriation.
bewirken   to effect; to cause.
bewohnen   to occupy.
Bewohner *m*   *(Land)* inhabitant; *(Haus)* occupant.
bezahlen   to pay.
Bezahlung *f*   pay; payment.
bezeugen   to attest.
beziehen   *(Aktien)* to subscribe; *(Geld)* to draw; *(Waren)* to obtain; to buy.
beziehen auf, sich   to refer to.
Bezieher *m*   purchaser; buyer; *(Zeitung)* subscriber.
Beziehung *f*   relation; relationship; contact.
beziffern   to number.
Bezirk *m*   sector; district.
Bezug *m*   *(im Brief)* reference; *(Einkauf)* purchase; *(Gehalt)* drawing of.
Bezüge *pl*   earnings; income; *(Gehalt)* salary; pay.
Bezugnahme *f*   reference.
Bezugsberechtigte *m/f*   beneficiary.
Bezugsoption *f*   call option.
Bezugsquelle *f*   source of supply; resource.
Bezugsrecht *nt*   buying option.
Bezugsschein *m*   *(Aktien)* stock allotment; *(Auftrag)* delivery order; *(Berechtigungsschein)* scrip; *(Materialien)* requisition slip; *(Waren)* purchasing order; *(Warenbewirtschaftung)* coupon.
Bezugszahl *f*   reference number.
Bezuschussung *f*   subsidization.

bieten to bid; to offer.
Bieter *m* bidder.
Bilanz *f* balance sheet; financial statement.
Bilanzabschluß *m* financial statement.
Bilanzaufstellung *f* balance sheet.
Bilanzbuchhalter *m* accountant.
Bilanzdaten *pl* financial statement data.
Bilanzierung *f* balancing of accounts.
Bilanzjahr *nt* financial year.
Bilanzklarheit *f* transparency of financial statement.
bilanzmäßig as shown by the balance sheet.
Bilanzposten *m* balance sheet item.
Bilanzprüfung *f* audit.
Bilanzrichtlinien *pl* accounting rules.
Bilanzstichtag *m* financial statement date.
Bilanzsumme *f* balance sheet total.
Bilanzwert *m* book value.
Bild *nt* picture; image.
bilden to form.
Bildfolge *f* sequence.
Bildschirm *m* *(Computer)* monitor screen.
Bildschirmgerät *nt* monitor.
Bildschirmspiel *nt* computer game.
Bildschirmtext *m* on-screen text.
Bildung *f* education.
Bildungsangebot *nt* learning opportunity.
Bildungsbereich *m* area of education.
Bildungsinstitution *f* institution of learning.
Bildungswesen *nt* field of education.

Bildungszentrum *nt* center of learning.
Billett *nt* ticket.
billig cheap; low-priced; inexpensive; *(angemessen)* reasonable.
billig abstoßen to dump.
Billiganbieter *m* discounter.
billigen to approve; to sanction.
Billighändler *m* discount merchant.
Billigkonkurrent *m* low-price competitor.
Billigpreis *m* low price.
Billigtarif *m* low rate.
Billigung *f* sanction; approval.
binnen- domestic.
binnen *(Frist)* within.
Binnenbedarf *m* domestic demand.
Binnenhandel *m* domestic commerce.
Binnenkonjunktur *f* internal economic trend.
Binnenland *nt* interior.
binnenländisch interior.
Binnenmarkt *m* home market; domestic market; *(Europäische Union)* unified market; single market.
Binnennachfrage *f* domestic demand.
Binnenschiffahrt *f* inland navigation.
Binnenwirtschaft *f* domestic economy.
Bitte *f* request; demand.
bitten to request; to ask.
Bittschrift *f* petition.
blanko blank.
Blankokredit *m* blank credit; unsecured credit; *(unbegrenzter Kredit)* unlimited credit.
bloßstellen to expose; to compromise.

blühen to thrive; to flourish.
Bon *m* voucher; cash register receipt.
Bonität *f* solvency.
borgen to borrow.
Börse *f* exchange; *(Wertpapiere)* stock exchange; *(Waren)* commodity exchange; *(Portemonnaie)* purse.
Börsenaufsicht *f* stock exchange supervision.
Börsenauftrag *m* stock exchange order.
Börseneinführung *f* public offering; listing on the stock exchange.
Börsenfähigkeit *f* negotiability.
börsengängig listed on the stock exchange.
Börsengeschäft *nt* stock market transaction.
Börsenhandel *m* stock exchange trading.
Börsenhändler *m* stocktrader.
Börsenindex *m* stock index.
Börsenkrach *m* stock market crash.
Börsenkurs *m* stock exchange quotation; share price.
Börsenmakler *m* stockbroker; floorbroker.
Börsennotierung *f* stock quotation.
Börsenumsatz *m* stock market turnover; volume of stocks traded.
Börsenumsatzsteuer *f* stock transfer tax.
Bote *m* messenger.
Botschaft *f* message.
Botschafter *m* ambassador.
Boykott *m* boycott.
Branche *f* line of industry.
Branchenanalyse *f* industry analysis.

Branchenkenner *m* industry expert.
Branchenschlüssel *m* classification of industry.
Branchensprecher *m* industry spokesman, -person, -woman.
branchenüblich customary within an industry.
Brauch *m* usage; observance.
brauchbar practical.
Brauchbarkeit *f* usefulness; utility.
brauchen to require; to need.
brechen *(Regeln)* to violate; to break.
breit broad.
Brief *m* letter.
Briefmarke *f* stamp.
Briefpartner *m* correspondent.
Brieftasche *f* wallet.
Briefträger *m* mailman.
Briefverkehr *m* correspondence.
Briefwechsel *m* correspondence; exchange of letters.
Broker *m* broker.
Brokerhaus *nt* brokerage house.
Broschüre *f* pamphlet; brochure.
Bruch *m* breach; violation; *(Trennung)* severance; *(Waren)* breakage.
Bruchteil *m* fraction.
brutto gross.
Bruttoabsatz *m* gross sales.
Bruttoeinkommen *nt* gross income.
Bruttohandelsspanne *f* gross margin.
Bruttosozialprodukt *nt* gross national product.
Buch *nt* book; *(Hauptbuch)* ledger.
buchen *(reservieren)* to reserve; *(Konto)* to post; *(Eintragung)* to record.
Buchführung *f* bookkeeping; accounting.

Buchführungsgrundsatz *m*
accounting principle.
Buchführungspflicht *f* mandatory
accounting.
Buchhaltung *f* bookkeeping;
accounting.
Buchkredit *m* book credit.
Buchstabe *m* letter.
Buchung *f* entry; *(Reservierung)*
reservation.
Buchungsposten *m* bookkeeping
entry.
Buchungstag *m* date of bookkeep-
ing entry.
Buchwert *m* book value.
Budget *nt* budget.
Budgetbeschränkung *f* budget
limitation; budget reduction.
Bund *m* alliance.
Bundes- federal.
bundesstaatlich federal.
Bündnis *nt* alliance.
Bürde *f* burden; liability.
Bürge *m* guarantor.
bürgen to guarantee.

Bürgschaft *f* pledge; guarantee.
Büro- clerical.
Büro *nt* office.
Büroarbeiten *pl* paperwork.
Büroautomation *f* office automa-
tion.
Bürobeschäftigte *m/f* clerical
worker.
Bürobetrieb *m* office routine.
Büroeinrichtung *f* office equip-
ment.
Büroelektronik *f* office electronics.
Büroindustrie *f* office industry.
Bürokrat *m* bureaucrat.
Bürokratie *f* bureaucracy.
bürokratisch bureaucratic.
Büromaschine *f* office machine.
Büromesse *f* office equipment
trade fair.
Büroraum *m* office space.
Büroschreibmaschine *f* office
typewriter.
Büroschreibtisch *m* office desk.
Bürotechnik *f* office technology.

Chance *f* opportunity; chance.
Charakter *m* character; personality.
charakterisieren to characterize;
to distinguish.
Charakterisierung *f* characterization.
charakteristisch distinctive; characteristic.
Charterflug *m* charter flight.
chartern to charter.
Chef *m* chief executive; head; boss;
chief.

Chefetage *f* executive suite.
Chefredakteur *m* editor-in-
chief.
Chefverkäufer *m* sales manager;
senior salesman.
Chiffrierschlüssel *m* code.
Code *m* code.
Computer *m* computer.
Computerausdruck *m* computer
printout.
Computerbildschirm *m* computer
screen.

Computerdaten *pl* computer data.
Computerfirma *f* computer company.
computergesteuert computer-controlled.
Computerprogramm *nt* computer program.

Computertastatur *f* computer keyboard.
Computertechnologie *f* computer technology.
Computerverfahren *nt* computer operation.
Courtage *f* commission.

Dachgesellschaft *f* holding company.
dämpfen to curb.
darlegen to state; to explain.
Darlehen *nt* loan.
Darlehen *nt* **geben** to lend.
Darlehensgewährung *f* granting of a loan; lending.
Darlehenskasse *f* loan association.
Darlehenslaufzeit *f* loan term.
Darlehensprogramm *nt* loan program.
Darlehensschuld *f* loan payable; loan debt.
Darlehensvertrag *m* loan agreement; loan contract.
Darlehenszinsen *pl* interest on loan.
darstellen to present; to describe.
Darstellung *f* presentation; description.
Daten *pl* data.
Datenaustausch *m* data exchange.
Datenbank *f* data bank.
Datenbasis *f* data base.
Datenbestand *m* data bank.
Datenerfassung *f* data collection.
Datenmaterial *nt* data.
Datenspeicherung *f* data storage.

Datenübertragung *f* data transmission.
Datenverarbeitung *f* data processing.
Datenverwaltung *f* information management.
Datum *nt* date.
Dauer *f* duration.
Dauerarbeitslose *m/f* chronically unemployed person; permanently unemployed person.
Dauerauftrag *m* standing order.
Dauereinkommen *nt* continuous income.
dauerhaft stable; durable.
Dauerkunde *m* regular customer; *(Kreditnehmer)* continuous borrower; *(Werbung)* regular advertiser.
dauernd permanent; perpetual.
Dauernutzung *f* permanent use; long-term use.
Dauerwachstum *nt* stable growth.
dazwischenliegend intermediate.
dazwischentreten to intervene.
Debitor *m* debtor.
Debitorengeschäft *nt* loan business.
Decke *f* *(obere Grenze)* ceiling.

decken *(Bedarf)* to meet; to cover.

Deckung *f* cover; coverage; backing.

Deckungsgeschäft *nt* hedge.

Defekt *m* fault; defect.

definieren to define.

Defizit *nt* shortfall; deficit.

Defizitkürzung *f* deficit decrease.

Deflation *f* deflation.

deflationistisch deflationary.

deklarieren to declare.

Delegation *f* delegation.

delegieren to delegate.

Delegierte *m/f* delegate; deputy.

dementieren to deny; to disclaim.

demographisch demographic.

Demonstration *f* demonstration.

demonstrieren to demonstrate.

demontieren to dismantle.

Demoskopie *f* public opinion poll.

Depesche *f* wire; telegram.

Deponent *m* depositor.

Depositeninhaber *m* depositor.

Depositenkasse *f* branch office of a bank; neighborhood bank branch.

Depositenzuwachs *m* increase in deposits.

Depot *nt* *(Wertpapiere)* portfolio; custodian account; *(Aufbewahrung)* custody.

Depotbank *f* custodian bank.

Depotstimmrecht *nt* proxy.

Depotverwaltung *f* portfolio management.

Depression *f* depression.

Design *nt* design.

destabilisieren to destabilize.

Detail *nt* detail.

detaillieren to specify.

Detaillierung *f* itemization.

deutlich distinct; definite.

Devisen *pl* foreign currency; foreign exchange; international exchange.

Devisenbestände *pl* foreign exchange funds; foreign exchange holdings.

Devisenbörse *f* currency market.

Deviseneigenhandel *m* foreign exchange trading for own account.

Deviseneinnahmen *pl* foreign exchange proceeds.

Devisenhandel *m* foreign exchange trade.

Devisenknappheit *f* foreign currency shortage.

Devisenkontrolle *f* exchange control.

Devisenkurs *m* exchange rate; foreign exchange.

Devisenmarkt *m* currency market; foreign exchange market.

Devisenoption *f* foreign currency option.

Devisenreserven *pl* foreign currency reserves.

Devisentermingeschäft *nt* forward exchange transaction.

Devisenterminmarkt *m* forward exchange market.

dezent understated.

dezentralisieren to decentralize.

Dezentralisierung *f* decentralization.

Diagnose *f* diagnosis.

diagnostizieren to diagnose.

Diagramm *nt* diagram; graph.

Diapositiv *nt* film slide.

Dichte *f* density.

dienen to serve.

Diener *m* servant.

Dienst *m* *(Dienstleistung)* service; *(Anstellung)* employment.

Dienstanweisung *f* service regulation; instructions.

Dienstbote *m* servant.
Dienstleistung *f* service.
Dienstleistungsbereich *m* service sector.
Dienstleistungsbetrieb *m* service company.
Dienstleistungsbranche *f* service industry.
Dienstleistungsfirma *f* service company.
Dienstleistungsgebühr *f* service charge.
Dienstleistungsgeschäft *nt* service business.
Dienstleistungskapazität *f* service capacity.
Dienstleistungsnetz *nt* service network.
Dienstleistungssektor *m* service sector.
Dienststelle *f* government agency; bureau.
Dienstvertrag *m* employment contract.
Dienstwagen *m* company car.
Differenz *f* margin; difference.
diktieren to dictate.
direkt direct.
Direktabsatz *m* direct sales.
Direktanlage *f* direct investment.
Direktbesteuerung *f* direct taxation.
Direktinvestition *f* direct investment.
Direktive *f* directive.
Direktor *m* *(AG)* officer; director; manager.
Direktorium *nt* governing body; management committee.
Direktpost *f* direct mail.
Direktsteuer *f* direct tax.
Direktverkauf *m* direct sales.
Disagio *nt* discount; disagio.

Diskette *f* diskette.
Diskont *m* rediscount; discount.
Diskonterhöhung *f* discount rate increase.
diskontieren to rediscount; to discount.
Diskontsatz *m* market rate; discount rate.
Diskontwert *m* discounted value.
Diskrepanz *f* discrepancy.
diskret discreet.
diskriminieren to discriminate.
diskriminierend discriminatory.
Diskriminierung *f* discrimination.
Diskussion *f* discussion.
Diskussionsleiter *m* moderator.
diskutieren to discuss; to argue.
disponibel disposable; available.
disponieren *(verfügen über)* to dispose; *(Vorsorge treffen)* to arrange; to plan ahead.
Dispositionskredit *m* overdraft credit; credit line.
disqualifizieren to disqualify.
Disqualifizierung *f* disqualification.
Distrikt *m* district.
Diversifikation *f* diversification.
diversifizieren to diversify.
Diversifizierung *f* diversification.
Dividende *f* dividend.
Dividendeneinnahmen *pl* dividend income.
Dividendenerklärung *f* declaration of dividends.
dividendenlos ex dividend.
Dividendenpapier *nt* dividend-paying stock; equity share.
Dividendenrendite *f* dividend yield.
Dividendenschein *m* dividend coupon.
Dividendentermin *m* record date.

Dividendenzahlung *f*   payment of dividend.

Dokument *nt*   document; paper; *(Wertpapiere)* instrument.

Dokumentation *f*   documentation.

dokumentieren   to document.

Doppeldeutigkeit *f*   ambiguity.

doppelt   double.

dotieren   *(Gehalt)* to compensate; *(Stiftung)* to endow.

Dotierung *f*   *(Gehalt)* compensation; *(Stiftung)* endowment.

Draht *m*   wire.

drahten   to wire.

Drahtnachricht *f*   wire; telegram.

drängen   to rush; to push.

Drängen *nt*   pressure.

drastisch senken   to slash.

dringen auf   to insist.

dringend   immediate; urgent.

Dringlichkeit *f*   urgency; priority.

Drittland *nt*   third party country.

Drittlandzollsatz *m*   customs tariff for third party countries.

drohen   to threaten.

Drohung *f*   threat.

drosseln   to curb.

Drosselung *f*   curb.

Druck *m*   squeeze; pressure; *(Buchherstellung)* print.

drücken   *(niederdrücken)* to depress; *(zusammendrücken)* to squeeze.

drucken   to print.

Drucker *m*   printer.

Druckerei *f*   printing press.

Druckschrift *f*   print; printed matter.

Duplikat *nt*   duplicate.

Durchbruch *m*   breakthrough.

durchdringen   to saturate; to penetrate.

Durchdringung *f*   penetration.

Durchfahrt *f*   *(an Grenze)* transit; passage; crossing; driving through.

Durchfuhr *f*   transit.

durchführbar   workable; feasible.

Durchführbarkeit *f*   feasibility.

durchführen   to carry out; to execute; to implement; *(Regeln)* to enforce.

Durchführung *f*   execution; implementation; *(Regeln)* enforcement.

durchgehend   nonstop.

Durchschnitt *m*   standard; average.

Durchschnitt *m* **berechnen**   to average.

durchschnittlich   average.

durchschnittlich betragen   to average.

Durchschnitts-   average.

Durchschnittswert *m*   average; *(Mittelwert)* mean; mean value.

durchsehen   to examine.

durchsetzen   to enforce.

Durchsetzung *f*   enforcement.

durchsickern   to leak.

dürftig   *(Einkommen)* meager; *(Verhältnisse)* poor.

E

echt genuine; *(rechtmäßig)* legitimate; *(rein)* pure; *(verbürgt)* warranted; *(Urkunde)* authentic.

Echtheit *f* authenticity.

Effekten *pl* securities.

Effektenbank *f* investment bank.

Effektenbankier *m* investment banker.

Effektenberater *m* securities advisor.

Effektenbestand *m* investment portfolio; securities holdings.

Effektenbörse *f* stock exchange; securities exchange.

Effektenhandel *m* securities trading; stock trading.

Effektenhändler *m* stockbroker; securities dealer.

Effektenverwalter *m* portfolio manager.

effektiv effective; real; actual.

Effektivzins *m* real interest rate.

effizient efficient.

Effizienz *f* efficiency.

ehemalig past; former.

Ehrgeiz *m* ambition.

ehrgeizig ambitious.

eidesstattliche Erklärung *f* affidavit.

eigen own.

Eigenerzeugung *f* *(Inland)* domestic production; own production.

Eigenhandel *m* *(Börse)* floor trade; trade for own account.

Eigenheim *nt* privately owned home.

Eigeninteresse *nt* self-interest.

Eigenkapital *nt* *(AG)* stockholders' equity; shareholders' equity; net worth; equity; *(Bank)* capital reserves.

Eigenkapitalgeber *m* investor; financier.

Eigenmittel *pl* own resources; *(Bauherr)* building capital.

Eigenschaft *f* *(Merkmal)* property; quality; feature; attribute; trait; *(berufliche Kapazität)* capacity.

Eigentum *nt* property; *(Besitz)* possession.

Eigentümer *m* proprietor; owner; *(Wertpapiere)* holder.

Eigentumsrecht *nt* proprietorship; ownership; title.

Eigentumswohnung *f* condominium apartment.

Eigenverantwortung *f* individual responsibility.

Eigenvertrieb *m* direct selling.

Eigenwechsel *m* promissory note.

Eigner *m* proprietor; owner.

Eignung *f* qualification; *(Brauchbarkeit)* suitability.

Eilbeförderung *f* special delivery.

Eile *f* hurry; rush.

Einahmeausfall *m* loss of revenue.

Einarbeitung *f* job training.

Einbau *m* installation.

Einbaukosten *pl* installation cost.

einbehalten to withhold.

Einbehaltung *f* witholding.

einberufen to convene.

einbeziehen to include.

Einbeziehung *f* inclusion.

einbringlich lucrative.

einbürgern to naturalize.

Einbürgerung *f* naturalization.

Einbuße *f* loss.

einbüßen to lose.
eindecken, sich to provide; to
stock up.
Eindeckung *f* supply; provision.
eindringen to penetrate.
Eindringen *nt* penetration.
einfach simple; single; *(Fahrkarte)*
one-way.
Einfluß *m* influence; pull; leverage;
hold; clout.
Einflußgröße *f* determining factor.
Einflußnahme *f* exercise of influence.
einflußreich influential.
Einflußsphäre *f* sphere of influence.
einfordern to call in; to demand;
to claim.
Einforderung *f* calling in; demand.
Einfuhr *f* import; importation.
Einfuhrabwehr *f* import barriers.
Einfuhrbeschränkung *f* import
restriction.
Einfuhrbewilligung *f* import
license.
einführen *(importieren)* to import;
(errichten) to institute; *(bekannt-
machen)* to introduce.
Einfuhrersatz *m* import substitute.
Einfuhrgenehmigung *f* import
license.
Einfuhrkontingent *nt* import
quota.
Einfuhrkontrolle *f* import control.
Einfuhrpreis *m* import price.
Einfuhrquote *f* import quota.
Einfuhrschranke *f* import barrier.
Einfuhrschutz *m* import protec-
tion.
Einfuhrsteigerung *f* increase in
imports.
Einführung *f* introduction.
Einfuhrware *f* imported merchan-
dise.

Einfuhrweg *m* import channel.
Einfuhrwert *m* import value.
Eingabe *f* *(Bittschrift)* petition;
(Datenverarbeitung) input.
Eingabedaten *pl* input data.
Eingang *m* entrance; *(Waren)*
arrival; receipt.
Eingeborene *m/f* native.
eingehen *(ankommen)* to arrive;
(Geld) to come in; *(Vertrag)* to
enter into; *(Erlöschen einer Firma)*
to close down.
eingehend detailed.
eingemeinden to incorporate.
Eingemeindung *f* incorporation.
eingeräumter Kredit *m* credit
line.
Eingeweihte *m/f* insider.
eingliedern to integrate.
Eingliederung *f* integration.
Eingriff *m* intervention; interference.
einhalten *(Regeln)* to observe; to
meet; *(Gesetz)* to comply with.
Einhaltung *f* *(Regeln)* observance;
observation; *(Gesetz)* compliance.
einheimisch domestic; native;
internal.
Einheimische *m/f* native.
einheimischer Gehalt *m* domestic
content.
einheimsen to pocket.
Einheit *f* *(Stück)* unit; *(Einigkeit)*
unity.
einheitlich uniform.
Einheitlichkeit *f* uniformity.
Einheitslösung *f* standard solution.
Einheitswert *m* standard value;
(Grundstück) assessed value.
einigen, sich to reach an agreement; to come to terms.
Einigkeit *f* unity.

Einigung *f* settlement; *(Überein-stimmung)* agreement.

einkalkulieren to take into account.

einkassieren to cash.

Einkauf *m* purchase; *(Einkaufen)* shopping.

einkaufen to buy; to purchase; *(einkaufen gehen)* to shop.

Einkäufer *m* purchasing agent; buyer.

Einkaufspreis *m* purchase price; cost price; base price.

Einkaufssachbearbeiter *m* purchasing agent.

Einkaufszentrum *nt* shopping center; shopping mall.

einklagen to sue for.

Einkommen *nt* income; earnings.

einkommensabhängig income-dependent.

Einkommensgruppe *f* income bracket.

Einkommensrunde *f* salary negotiation round.

Einkommensteuer *f* income tax.

Einkommensverteilung *f* income distribution.

Einkommensverwendung *f* use of income.

Einkünfte *pl* revenue; income.

Einlage *f* *(Bank)* deposit; *(Beilage)* insert; *(Kapital)* capital contribution.

Einlagekapital *nt* capital contribution.

Einlagenabfluß *m* outflow of deposits.

Einlagenbestand *m* total bank deposits.

Einlagengeschäft *nt* deposit transaction.

Einlagenversicherung *f* deposit insurance.

Einlagerung *f* storage; warehousing; stockpiling.

einlassen to admit.

Einleger *m* bank depositor; *(Kapital)* investor.

einleiten *(den Anstoß geben)* to initiate; *(eröffnen)* to open; *(einführen)* to introduce; *(ein Gerichtsverfahren)* to institute.

einleitend preliminary.

Einleitung *f* *(Anstoß)* initiation; *(Einführung)* introduction; preface; preamble.

einleuchtend plausible.

einlösen *(tilgen)* to redeem; *(eintauschen)* to exchange; *(einen Scheck)* to cash.

Einlösung *f* *(Tilgung)* redemption; *(Scheck)* cashing; *(Eintausch)* exchange.

einmischen, sich to interfere.

Einmischung *f* interference; intervention.

Einnahme *f* revenue; receipts; *(Einkommen)* income.

Einnahmerückgang *m* decrease in revenue.

einordnen *(in Reihenfolge)* to rank; *(klassifizieren)* to classify; *(Akten)* to file.

Einplanung *f* planning.

einreichen to submit; to file.

Einreise *f* entry.

einreisen to enter.

einrichten to institute; *(ausrüsten)* to equip; *(Wohnung)* to furnish.

Einrichtung *f* *(Errichten)* setup; *(Organisation)* institution; *(Ausrüstung)* equipment; *(Möbel)* furnishing.

Einsatz *m* *(Verwendung)* use; deployment; *(Anzeige)* insertion; *(Wette)* stake.

Einsatzfeld *nt*   operational area.
einschalten, sich   to intervene.
einschätzen   to assess.
Einschätzung *f*   valuation; assessment.
einschleusen   to channel.
einschließen   to include; to comprise.
einschließlich   inclusive.
einschränken *(beschränken)* to restrict; to limit; *(verkleinern)* to curtail; to cut back.
einschränken, sich   to economize; to retrench.
Einschränkung *f*   *(Beschränkung)* restriction; limitation; *(Einsparung)* economizing; retrenchment.
einschreiben   to register; *(als Mitglied, Student)* to enroll.
Einschreiben *nt*   registered mail.
einschreiten   to interfere; to intervene.
Einschreiten *nt*   intervention.
Einschuß *m*   *(Differenzgeschäft)* margin; *(Kapital)* invested capital; stake.
Einschußbedarf *m*   *(Differenzgeschäft)* margin requirements.
Einschußzahlung *f*   margin deposit.
einseitig   unilateral; *(ungleichgewichtig)* lopsided.
einseitige Übertragung *f*   unrequited transfer.
einsetzen   *(installieren)* to install; *(gebrauchen)* to deploy; to use.
einsparen   to economize.
Einspruch *m*   veto; objection.
Einspruch *m* **erheben**   to oppose; to veto.
Einstandspreis *m*   cost price.
einstellbar   adjustable.
einstellen   *(anstellen)* to hire; to

engage; *(beenden)* to discontinue; to cease; *(Radio)* to tune; *(Maschinen)* to set.
Einstellung *f*   *(Arbeitskräfte)* employment; *(Beendung)* stoppage; cessation; *(Meinung)* attitude.
einstimmig   unanimous.
einstufen   to rate; to class; to classify.
einstweilig   interim.
einstweilige Verfügung *f*   injunction.
eintauschen   to exchange; to trade in; to swap.
einteilen   to grade; to divide; *(zur Arbeit)* to assign.
Einteilung *f*   classification; division; *(zur Arbeit)* assignment.
eintragen   to record; to register; to enter.
einträglich   lucrative.
Eintragung *f*   registration; entry.
eintreffen   to arrive.
Eintreffen *nt*   arrival.
eintreibbar   recoverable; *(Schulden)* collectable.
eintreiben   to recover; *(Schulden)* to collect.
eintreten   to enter; *(Ereignis)* to occur.
Eintritt *m*   entrance; entry; *(Zulassung)* admission; *(Ereignis)* occurrence.
Eintrittspreis *m*   admission price.
Einverständnis *nt*   consent; agreement.
Einwand *m*   objection.
einwandfrei   correct; flawless.
Einwegflasche *f*   nonreturnable bottle.
Einweggüter *pl*   disposable goods.
Einweihung *f*   initiation; dedication.

Einweisung *f* *(im Betrieb)* briefing; *(Krankenhaus)* referral.
einwilligen to consent.
Einwilligung *f* consent.
einwirken auf to influence; to impact on.
Einwirkung *f* influence; impact.
Einwohner *m* inhabitant; resident.
einzahlen to deposit.
Einzahler *m* depositor.
Einzahlung *f* payment; *(eingezahlter Betrag)* deposit.
Einzelabrechnung *f* itemized billing.
Einzelaufstellung *f* specification.
Einzelbedürfnis *nt* individual need.
Einzelbeleg *m* separate voucher.
Einzelfall *m* particular case; singular case.
Einzelfirma *f* sole proprietorship.
Einzelhandel *m* retail trade; retailing.
Einzelhandelsgeschäft *nt* retail store.
Einzelhandelskette *f* retail chain.
Einzelhändler *m* retailer.
Einzelheit *f* detail.
einzeln single; sole; individual; *(getrennt)* separate; severally.
Einzelperson *f* individual.
Einzelplanung *f* individual planning.
Einzelposten *m* single item.
Einzelteil *nt* component part.
Einzelüberweisung *f* individual remittance.
Einzelunternehmung *f* proprietorship.
einziehen to recover; *(Schulden)* to collect; *(Wohnung)* to move in.
Einziehung *f* recovery; *(Schulden)* collection.
einzig only; sole.

Eisenbahn *f* railroad.
Eisenwaren *pl* hardware.
elastisch flexible; elastic.
Elastizität *f* flexibility; elasticity.
Elektrizitätswerk *nt* utility company; power station.
eliminieren to eliminate.
Eliminierung *f* elimination.
Embargo *nt* embargo.
Emission *f* *(Banknoten, Aktien)* issuance.
Emissionsfirma *f* securities underwriter; investment banking house.
Emissionsgarantie *f* underwriting guarantee.
Emissionsgeschäft *nt* investment banking business; *(Transaktion)* issuing transaction.
Emittent *m* issuer.
emittieren to issue.
Empfang *m* *(Eingang)* receipt; *(gesellschaftliches Ereignis)* reception; *(Hotel)* reception desk.
empfangen to receive.
Empfänger *m* receiver; recipient.
Empfängerland *nt* recipient country.
Empfangsberechtigte *m/f* recipient.
Empfangsgerät *nt* receiver.
empfehlen to recommend.
Empfehlung *f* recommendation; reference; *(Einführung)* introduction.
Empfehlungsschreiben *nt* letter of recommendation.
Emporkömmling *m* upstart.
Emporschnellen *nt* soaring; skyrocketing.
Endbahnhof *m* terminal station.
Endbestand *m* final inventory.
Ende *nt* end; ending; finish; conclusion.

Endergebnis *nt* final result.
Endgerät *nt* terminal.
endgültig final.
Endmontage *f* final assembly.
Endnachfrage *f* consumer demand; aggregate demand.
Endprodukt *nt* final product.
Endziel *nt* ultimate goal.
Energie *f* energy.
Engagement *nt* *(Verpflichtung)* commitment; obligation; *(Theater)* employment.
engagieren to engage; *(Theater)* to employ; *(Kapital)* to tie up.
Engpaß *m* bottleneck.
Engroshandel *m* wholesale.
Engroshändler *m* wholesaler.
Entbürokratisierung *f* streamlining of administration.
entdecken to discover.
Entdeckung *f* find; discovery.
enteignen to dispossess; to expropriate.
Enteignung *f* expropriation; *(staatliche Enteignungsberechtigung)* eminent domain.
entfallen *(nicht anwendbar sein)* not to apply.
entfallen auf to be allotted to; to fall upon.
entfernen to remove.
Entfernung *f* distance.
entflechten to dissolve; to break up.
Entflechtung *f* dissolution; divestiture.
entgegenkommen to accommodate.
Entgegenkommen *nt* accommodation; courtesy.
entgegnen to counter.
Entgelt *nt* *(Bezahlung)* payment; *(Vertragsleistung)* consideration.

enthalten to hold; to comprise; to contain.
enthalten, sich to abstain.
Enthaltung *f* *(Stimmenabgabe)* abstention.
Enthüllung *f* disclosure; discovery.
entlassen to dismiss; to discharge.
Entlassung *f* layoff; dismissal.
Entlassungswelle *f* round of dismissals; mass layoffs.
entlasten to relieve; to release; *(ratifizieren)* to discharge.
Entlastung *f* relief; release; *(Ratifizierung)* discharge.
entleihen to borrow.
Entlohnung *f* payment; compensation.
Entnahme *f* *(Konto)* withdrawal.
entnehmen to take out; *(verstehen)* to understand from; *(Konto)* to withdraw.
entschädigen to compensate; to indemnify; *(zurückerstatten)* to reimburse.
entschädigend compensatory.
Entschädigung *f* compensation; indemnification; *(Zurückerstattung)* reimbursement.
Entscheid *m* ruling.
entscheiden to decide; to determine; to rule.
entscheiden, sich to decide; to opt.
entscheidend crucial; essential.
Entscheidung *f* ruling; decision.
Entscheidungsbildung *f* decision making.
Entscheidungsfreiheit *f* freedom of choice.
Entscheidungsprozeß *m* decision process.
Entscheidungsträger *m* decision maker.

entschließen, sich to decide; to resolve.

Entschließung *f* resolution.

Entschluß *m* determination; decision.

Entschuldigung *f* excuse; apology.

Entsorgung *f* waste removal.

entspannen to relax; to ease.

entstehen to occur; to originate; to arise.

entstellen to distort.

Entstellung *f* distortion.

enttäuschen to disappoint.

enttäuschend disappointing.

Enttäuschung *f* disappointment.

entwerfen *(Plan)* to outline; to devise; *(Konstruktion)* to design; to sketch.

Entwertung *f* devaluation; depreciation.

entwickeln to develop; *(fördern)* to promote.

entwickeln, sich to grow; to expand.

Entwicklung *f* development; *(Wachstum)* growth.

Entwicklungsbank *f* development bank.

Entwicklungshilfe *f* foreign aid.

Entwicklungsimpuls *m* development impetus.

Entwicklungskosten *pl* development costs.

Entwicklungsländer *pl* developing countries.

Entwicklungslinie *f* trend.

Entwicklungsstadium *nt* stage of development.

Entwicklungstendenz *f* trend.

Entwurf *m* *(Plan)* outline; plan; *(Modell)* model; *(Konstruktion)* design; draft; sketch.

Entwurfsänderung *f* design change.

Erbe *m* heir.

Erbe *nt* inheritance.

erben to inherit.

erbitten to solicit; to request.

erbringen to yield.

Erbschaft *f* inheritance.

Erbschaftsmasse *f* estate.

Erdgas *nt* natural gas.

Erdgasleitung *f* natural gas pipeline.

Erdgaslieferant *m* natural gas supplier.

Erdöl *nt* crude oil; petroleum.

Erdölvorkommen *nt* oil field.

Ereignis *nt* occurrence; incident.

erfahren to experience.

Erfahrung *f* experience.

erfassen *(einschließen)* to include; to comprise; *(begreifen)* to comprehend; *(statistisch)* to cover; to register.

Erfassung *f* *(amtlich)* registration; *(Statistik)* coverage.

erfinden to invent; to devise.

Erfinder *m* inventor.

Erfindung *f* invention.

Erfindungsgabe *f* inventiveness; ingenuity.

Erfolg *m* success; result.

erfolgreich successful.

Erfolgskontrolle *f* *(Werbung)* result testing.

Erfolgskurs *m* road to success.

Erfolgswirksamkeit *f* effectiveness.

Erfolgszwang *m* drive to succeed.

erforderlich requisite; necessary.

erfordern *(brauchen)* to need; *(fordern)* to require.

Erfordernis *nt* requirement.

erforschen to explore; to research.

Erforschung *f* exploration; research.

erfüllen *(eine Pflicht)* to perform; to discharge; *(einen Vertrag)* to fulfill; to implement.

Erfüllung *f* *(einer Pflicht)* performance; *(eines Vertrags)* fulfillment; implementation.

ergänzen to supplement; *(vollenden)* to complete; to amend.

ergänzend supplementary; complementary.

Ergänzung *f* supplement; complement.

Ergänzungsabgabe *f* special levy; surtax.

ergeben *(abwerfen)* to produce; to yield; *(betragen)* to amount to.

Ergebnis *nt* yield; *(Produkt)* product; outcome.

Erhalt *m* receipt.

erhalten *(bestehen lassen)* to preserve; to conserve; *(empfangen)* to receive; to obtain.

erhältlich obtainable.

Erhaltung *f* preservation; conservation; *(Instandhaltung)* maintenance.

erheblich considerable; material.

Erhebung *f* *(Umfrage)* survey; census.

Erhebungsjahr *nt* census year; survey year.

erhöhen to raise; to increase.

erhöhen, sich to rise; to increase.

Erhöhung *f* rise; increase.

erholen, sich to recover; to recuperate; *(Kurse)* to rally; *(Konjunktur)* to rebound.

Erholung *f* recovery; *(Kurse)* rally; *(Wirtschaft)* revival.

erinnern to remind.

erinnern, sich to remember; to recall.

erklären to explain; to declare.

erklärend illustrative; explanatory.

Erklärung *f* statement; explanation; declaration.

erkunden to explore.

Erkundigung *f* inquiry.

erlangen to secure; to obtain; to attain.

Erlangung *f* attainment.

Erlaß *m* ordinance; enactment.

erlassen to waive; *(Schulden)* to release; *(Verordnung)* to issue.

erlauben to permit; to license; to allow.

Erlaubnis *f* permit.

erlaubt admissible.

erläuternd illustrative.

Erläuterung *f* explanation; *(Kommentar)* annotation.

erledigen to handle; to carry out; to execute.

Erledigung *f* handling; carrying out; execution.

erleichtern to ease; to facilitate; to alleviate; *(mildern)* to mitigate.

Erleichterung *f* easing; *(Notlage)* relief; *(Strafe)* mitigation.

Erlös *m* proceeds.

erlöschen to expire; to cease; to lapse.

Erlöschen *nt* expiration.

ermächtigen to authorize; to empower.

Ermächtigung *f* *(Vollmacht)* power of attorney; authorization.

ermäßigen to reduce; to cut.

Ermäßigung *f* reduction; cut.

Ermessen *nt* discretion.

ermitteln to investigate; *(feststellen)* to ascertain.

Ermittlung *f* *(Feststellung)* ascertainment; detection; *(Berechnung)* calculation; *(Schadenabschätzung)* appraisal; (Untersuchung) inquiry; investigation.

ermutigen to encourage.

Ermutigung *f* encouragement.

ernähren to nourish; to feed; *(unterhalten)* to support.

Ernährer *m* provider.

Ernährung *f* food; nourishment.

ernennen to appoint.

Ernennung *f* appointment.

erneuern to renew; to revive.

Erneuerung *f* renewal.

erneuerungsfähig renewable.

Ernte *f* yield; crop.

ernten to harvest; to reap.

erobern to capture; to conquer.

Eroberung *f* capture; conquest.

eröffnen to open.

Eröffnung *f* *(Börse, Konto)* opening; *(Einweihung)* dedication; *(Überraschung)* disclosure.

Erpressung *f* extortion; blackmail.

erproben to test; to prove.

errechnen to calculate.

erreichbar *(erzielbar)* attainable; *(zugänglich)* accessible; *(ansprechbar)* approachable.

erreichen to reach; *(erzielen)* to attain; to achieve.

errichten *(gründen)* to found; to establish; *(aufbauen)* to construct; to build.

Errichtung *f* *(Gründung)* formation; *(Aufbau)* construction.

Errungenschaft *f* attainment; accomplishment; achievement.

Ersatzanspruch *m* recourse.

Ersatzinvestition *f* replacement investments.

Ersatzperson *f* replacement.

Ersatzteil *nt* spare part.

erscheinen to appear.

Erscheinung *f* appearance.

Erscheinungsbild *nt* image.

erschließen to unlock; to tap; *(Land)* to develop.

Erschließung *f* *(Land)* development.

erschöpfen to deplete; to exhaust.

erschweren to hamper; to hinder; to impede.

erschwingen to afford.

erschwinglich affordable.

ersetzen to substitute; to replace; to restore; to recoup.

ersparen *(sparen)* to save.

Ersparnis *f* savings.

Ersparnisse *pl* **durch Produktionsvergrößerung** *f* economies of scale.

erstatten to compensate; *(zurückgeben)* to return; to refund.

Erstausstattung *f* original equipment; *(Firma)* original capitalization.

Erstinvestition *f* initial investment.

Erstzeichner *m* initial subscriber.

ersuchen to request; to petition; to ask.

Ertrag *m* *(Rendite)* yield; *(Einkünfte)* earnings; receipts; revenue; *(Gewinn)* profit; gain; proceeds; *(Ernte)* crop.

ertragbringend productive; profitable.

ertraglos nonproductive; unprofitable.

Ertragsfähigkeit *f* productivity.

Ertragskraft *f* earning capacity.

Ertragslage *f* profit situation.

Ertragsmotiv *nt* profit motive.

Ertragsorientierung *f* profit orientation.

Ertragsrechnung *f*   earnings statement; profit and loss statement.

Ertragsrückgang *m*   decline in earnings.

erübrigen   to spare.

Erwägung *f*   consideration.

erwähnen   to mention; to refer to.

Erwähnung *f*   mention.

erwarten   to expect; to anticipate.

Erwartung *f*   expectation; anticipation.

erweitern   to expand.

Erweiterung *f*   expansion.

Erwerb *m*   *(Kauf)* purchase; acquisition; *(Einkommen)* earnings.

erwerben   *(kaufen)* to purchase; to buy; to acquire; *(verdienen)* to earn; *(Fähigkeiten)* to gain.

Erwerber *m*   *(Käufer)* purchaser; *(Verdiener für den Haushalt)* provider.

erwerbsfähig   capable of gainful employment; fit for work.

erwerbslos   unemployed.

Erwerbslosigkeit *f*   unemployment.

Erwerbstätige *m/f*   earner.

Erwerbstätigkeit *f*   gainful employment.

erwirtschaften   to produce; to obtain; to achieve.

erzeugen   to produce; to manufacture; to generate.

Erzeuger *m*   producer.

Erzeugerland *nt*   manufacturing country.

Erzeugnis *nt*   product; commodity.

Erzeugnisgruppe *f*   product line; line of products.

Erzeugung *f*   production.

erziehen   to educate.

Erziehung *f*   education.

erzielen   *(Gewinn)* to realize; *(erreichen)* to obtain; to achieve.

Erzielung *f*   *(Erreichen)* achievement; obtainment; *(Gewinn)* realization.

etablieren, sich   to establish oneself; to start a business.

Etage *f*   floor.

Etat *m*   budget.

Etatdefizit *nt*   budget deficit.

Etatmanager *m*   budget manager; *(Werbung)* account manager.

Etikett *nt*   tag; label.

etikettieren   to tag; to label.

Etikettieren *nt*   labeling.

Eventualfall *m*   contingency.

eventuell   possible; contingent.

Existenz *f*   existence; subsistence; living.

Existenzgrundlage *f*   livelihood.

existieren   to exist.

expandieren   to expand.

Expansion *f*   expansion.

Expansionskurs *m*   expansion trend.

Expansionspolitik *f*   expansionary policy.

Experiment *nt*   experiment.

experimentieren   to experiment.

Experte *m*   expert.

Expertin *f*   expert.

Expertise *f*   expertise.

Export *m*   export; exportation.

Exportanstieg *m*   rise in exports.

Exportauftrag *m*   export order.

Exportaussicht *f*   export prospects.

Exportbeschränkung *f*   export restriction.

Exporteinnahmen *pl*   export receipts.

Exportertrag *m*   export earnings.

Exporteur *m*   exporter.

Exportfinanzierung *f*   export financing.

Exportgeschäft *nt*   export house;

export business; *(Handel)* export transaction.
exportieren to export.
Exportindustrie *f* export industry.
Exportkraft *f* export strength.
Exportkredit *m* export credit.
Exportland *nt* exporting country.
Exportlizenz *f* export license.
exportorientiert export oriented.
Exportsortiment *nt* line of export goods.
Exportsteigerung *f* rise in exports.

Exportsubvention *f* export subsidy.
Exportüberschuß *m* export surplus.
Exportverbot *nt* ban on exports.
Exportvolumen *nt* export volume.
Exportwachstum *nt* export growth.
Exportwirtschaft *f* export economy.
Exportzuwachs *m* export growth.
extra extra; over and above.
Extragebühr *f* extra charge.

Fabrik *f* factory.
Fabrikanlage *f* plant.
Fabrikant *m* manufacturer.
Fabrikat *nt* product; make.
Fabrikation *f* manufacture.
Fabrikationsanlage *f* production facility.
Fabrikationsbetrieb *m* manufacturing company.
Fabrikationsfähigkeit *f* production capability.
Fabrikationskosten *pl* manufacturing costs.
Fabrikationsmethode *f* manufacturing process.
fabrikmäßig herstellen to mass produce.
fabrikneu brand new.
Fach *nt* *(Arbeitsgebiet)* field; *(Geschäftszweig)* trade; profession; business; *(Unterricht)* subject; *(Schrank)* shelf; *(Kommode)* drawer.
Fachausdruck *m* term.
Fachausdrücke *pl* terminology.

Fachausstellung *f* trade exhibition; trade show.
Fachblatt *nt* trade journal.
Fachgebiet *nt* subject area; specialty.
Fachhändler *m* specialty retailer; limited-line retailer.
Fachinteresse *nt* professional interest.
Fachjournal *nt* trade journal.
Fachkraft *f* qualified person; skilled worker.
fachkundig expert; competent in one's field.
Fachleute *pl* experts; professionals; specialists.
Fachmann *m* expert; professional; specialist.
fachmännisch professional; expert.
Fachmesse *f* trade fair.
Fachsprache *f* terminology.
Fachvereinigung *f* professional association.
Fachzeitschrift *f* trade magazine.

fähig   capable; competent; able.

Fähigkeit *f*   qualification; capability; ability.

fahren   to drive.

Fahrgeld *nt*   fare.

fahrlässig   negligent.

Fahrlässigkeit *f*   negligence.

Fahrplan *m*   timetable.

Fahrpreis *m*   fare.

Fahrt *f*   *(Reise)* trip; tour; *(Fahren)* drive; *(Überfahrt)* voyage.

Faktor *m*   factor.

Faktorpreis *m*   factor price.

Faktura *f*   invoice; bill.

Fall *m*   *(Situation)* case; circumstance; *(Sinken)* tumble; slump; decline; fall.

fallen   to fall; to sink; to tumble; to decline; to drop.

Fallen *nt*   fall.

fallen lassen   to drop; to abandon.

fällig   due; *(Obligationen)* mature; *(zahlbar)* payable.

Fälligkeit *f*   due date; *(Obligationen)* maturity.

Fälligkeitstermin *m*   due date; settlement date; *(Obligationen)* date of maturity.

fällig werden   to become due; *(Obligationen)* to mature.

Fallpräsentation *f*   case presentation.

Fallstudie *f*   case study.

falsch   *(unrichtig)* wrong; incorrect; *(gefälscht)* forged; falsified; *(Geld)* counterfeit; *(unecht)* fake; *(ungenau)* inaccurate.

falsch berechnen   to miscalculate.

Falschbuchung *f*   false entry; fraudulent entry.

fälschen   to falsify; to fake; *(Urkunde)* to forge; *(Geld)* to counterfeit.

Fälschung *f*   falsification; fake; *(Urkunde)* forgery; *(Geld)* counterfeiting.

fangen   to catch; to capture.

fassen   *(anfassen)* to grasp; *(enthalten)* to hold; *(verstehen)* to comprehend.

Fassung *f*   *(Schriftsatz)* version; *(Glühlampe)* socket; *(Einfassung)* setting; *(Haltung)* composure.

Fassungsvermögen *nt*   capacity.

fegen   to sweep.

Fehlallokation *f*   misallocation.

Fehlbestand *m*   shortage.

Fehlbetrag *m*   shortage; shortfall; deficiency; deficit; missing amount.

fehlen   to lack; to be missing.

Fehlen *nt*   lack.

fehlend   absent; missing.

Fehler *m*   mistake; error; fault; *(Material)* defect.

fehlerhaft   faulty; deficient.

Fehlerquelle *f*   source of error.

Fehlinvestition *f*   false investment; investment failure.

Fehlkauf *m*   bad buy.

fehlleiten   to misdirect.

Fehlprognose *f*   false prognosis.

Fehlschlag *m*   failure; *(Enttäuschung)* disappointment.

fehlschlagen   to fail.

feilschen   to haggle; to bargain.

Feld *nt*   domain; field.

Feldzug *m*   campaign.

fern   distant.

Fernmeldeverkehr *m*   telecommunication.

Fernmeldewesen *nt*   telecommunications; communications.

Fernschreiber *m*   telex.

Fernsprecher *m*   telephone.

Fernsprechgebühr *f*   toll; long distance rate.

Fernsprechleitung *f* telephone wire.
Fertigkeit *f* skill.
Fertigprodukt *nt* finished product; manufactured article.
fertigstellen to finish; to complete.
Fertigstellung *f* completion; *(Produktionsvorgang)* finishing.
Fertigung *f* production; manufacturing.
Fertigungsablauf *m* production flow.
Fertigungsanlage *f* factory; plant.
Fertigungshalle *f* production hall.
Fertigungsleiter *m* production manager.
Fertigungsplan *m* manufacturing schedule.
Fertigungsprozeß *m* production process.
Fertigungstechnik *f* product engineering.
Fertigungsverfahren *nt* manufacturing process.
Fertigwaren *pl* finished goods.
fesseln to constrain.
fest solid; firm.
Festbestellung *f* firm order.
fester Wechselkurs *m* fixed exchange rate.
festes Angebot *nt* firm offer; positive offer.
festgesetzt stipulated; stated.
festgestellter Wert *m* stated value.
festigen to stabilize.
Festigkeit *f* stability; resistance; firmness.
Festigung *f* stabilization.
Festkosten *pl* overhead expenses.
Festland *nt* mainland.
festlegen to state; *(bestimmen)* to determine; to set; *(Kapital)* to tie up.

festlegen, sich to make a commitment.
festnehmen to arrest.
festsetzbar determinable.
festsetzen *(ausbedingen)* to stipulate; to fix; *(bestimmen)* to determine; *(Termin)* to set; to schedule; *(Normen)* to standardize.
feststellbar identifiable.
feststellen *(bestimmen)* to determine; *(erklären)* to declare; to state; *(ermitteln)* to ascertain; to find out; to diagnose; *(Fehler)* to locate.
Feststellung *f* *(Bestimmung)* determination; *(Erklärung)* statement; declaration; *(Ermittlung)* finding; ascertainment; diagnosis; *(des Wertes)* appraisal.
festverzinslich fixed-interest bearing.
Festzins *m* fixed rate of interest.
Festzinsanleihe *f* fixed rate loan.
Festzinsen *pl* fixed interest.
Festzinssatz *m* fixed rate of interest.
Filialbank *f* branch bank.
Filiale *f* subsidiary; branch.
Filialgeschäft *nt* chain store.
Filialnetz *nt* branch network.
Finanz *f* finance.
Finanzabteilung *f* finance department.
Finanzaktiva *pl* financial assets.
Finanzamt *nt* Internal Revenue Service.
Finanzanalyse *f* financial analysis.
Finanzausgleich *m* revenue sharing.
Finanzautonomie *f* financial autonomy.
Finanzbeamte *m*, **-beamtin** *f* Internal Revenue Service officer.

Finanzbedarf *m*   financial requirements.

Finanzdirektor *m*   treasurer.

Finanzgesellschaft *f*   finance company.

Finanzhilfe *f*   financial aid.

finanziell   financial; monetary.

finanziell unterstützen   to subsidize.

finanzieren   to fund; to finance; to bankroll.

Finanzierung *f*   financing.

Finanzierungsdefizit *nt*   financing deficit.

Finanzierungsgesellschaft *f*   finance company.

Finanzierungsinstitut *nt*   finance house.

Finanzierungsregel *f*   financing rule.

Finanzierungssystem *nt*   financial plan.

Finanzierungstrom *m*   financing flow; credit flow.

Finanzkrise *f*   financial crisis.

Finanzmanagement *nt*   financial management.

Finanzmarkt *m*   financial market.

Finanzminister *m*   finance minister.

Finanzministerium *nt*   treasury; treasury department.

Finanzmittel *pl*   funds.

Finanzplan *m*   budget; financial plan.

Finanzplanung *f*   financial planning; budgeting.

Finanzplatz *m*   financial center.

Finanzpolitik *f*   fiscal policy.

Finanzpresse *f*   financial press.

Finanzproblem *nt*   financial problem.

Finanzstärke *f*   financial strength.

Finanzteil *m*   *(Zeitung)* financial page.

Finanzverwaltung *f*   financial management; financial administration; *(Behörde)* fiscal authority.

Finanzwesen *nt*   finance.

Finanzzentrum *nt*   financial center.

Finanzzoll *m*   tariff revenue.

finden   to find; to locate.

Finte *f*   maneuver.

Firma *f*   firm; business; company; *(Firmenname)* business name; trade name.

Firmenbetreuung *f*   corporate relations service.

Firmenbezeichnung *f*   trade name.

Firmenchef *m*   chief executive officer; director of a company.

Firmengruppe *f*   group of companies.

Firmeninhaber *m*   owner of company.

Firmenkunde *m*   business client; corporate customer.

Firmenkundenbetreuer *m*   company service representative.

Firmenleitung *f*   corporate management.

Firmenname *m*   trade name.

Firmenvermögen *nt*   corporate assets.

Firmenwagen *m*   company car.

Firmenwert *m*   goodwill.

Firmenzeichen *nt*   trade mark; brand.

Firmenzusammenschluß *m*   merger.

fiskalisch   financial; fiscal.

Fiskalpolitik *f*   fiscal policy.

Fläche *f*   area.

flau   weak; slow; sluggish; soft; stagnant.

Flauheit *f*   slackness.

Flaute *f*   weakness; sluggishness; slack period; slackness.

flexibel flexible.
Flexibilität *f* flexibility.
Fließband *nt* assembly line.
fließen to flow.
floaten to float.
florieren to prosper; to flourish.
Flucht *f* flight.
Flug *m* flight.
Fluggesellschaft *f* airline.
Flughafen *m* airport.
Flughafengebäude *nt* airport terminal.
Flugplan *m* flight schedule.
Flugzeug *nt* aircraft; airplane.
fluktuieren to fluctuate.
Fluktuieren *nt* fluctuation.
flüssig *(Bank, Firma)* liquid; *(Geldmarkt)* easy; *(Kapital)* available; *(Stil)* fluent.
föderalistisch federal.
Folge *f* sequence; *(Wirkung)* consequence.
Fonds *m* pool; fund.
Fondsvermögen *nt* fund assets; *(Kapitalanlagegesellschaft)* asset value.
Förderer *m* sponsor; patron.
fordern to demand; to claim.
fördern to promote; to advance; *(ermutigen)* to encourage; to boost; *(entwickeln)* to develop; *(helfen)* to aid; *(Bergbau)* to mine.
Förderprogramm *nt* promotional program; support program.
Forderung *f* requirement; *(Schulden)* debt; *(Anspruch)* claim.
Förderung *f* promotion; advancement; *(Ermutigung)* encouragement; *(Entwicklung)* development; *(Hilfe)* aid; *(Bergbau)* extraction.
Forderungen *pl* *(Bilanz)* accounts receivable.
Forderungsausfall *m* bad debt.

formal formal.
Formalität *f* formality.
Formel *f* formula.
formell formal.
formen to form.
Formgebung *f* design.
förmlich formal.
Förmlichkeit *f* formality.
formlos informal.
Formlosigkeit *f* informality.
Formular *nt* form.
formulieren to formulate.
Formulierung *f* formulation.
forschen to research.
Forschung *f* research.
Forschungsanlage *f* research facility.
Forschungsarbeit *f* research study.
Forschungsaufgabe *f* research assignment; research project.
Forschungsauftrag *m* research assignment.
Forschungsaufwand *m* research expenditure.
Forschungsbeihilfe *f* research grant.
Forschungsbereich *m* area of research; field of study.
Forschungsgebiet *nt* area of research; field of study.
Forschungsinstitut *nt* research institute.
Forschungsprogramm *nt* research program.
Forschungsprojekt *nt* research project.
Forschungsstudie *f* research study.
Forschungszentrum *nt* research center.
Fortbestand *m* continuance.
fortdauern to persist; to continue.
fortfahren to proceed; to continue.
fortführen to pursue; to continue.

fortgeschritten   advanced.
fortlaufend   continuous.
fortschreiten   to progress; to advance.
Fortschritt *m*   progress; advance; *(Verbesserung)* improvement.
fortschrittlich   progressive.
Fortschrittsrate *f*   rate of progress.
fortsetzen   to continue.
Fortsetzung *f*   continuation.
Fotograf *m*   photographer.
Fotografie *f*   photograph.
fotografisch   photographic.
Fotokopie *f*   photocopy.
fotokopieren   to photocopy.
Fracht *f*   load; freight; cargo.
Frachtaufschlag *m*   freight surcharge.
Frachtgut *nt*   freight; cargo.
Frachtkosten *pl*   freight charges.
Frachtraum *m*   tonnage.
Frachtschiff *nt*   cargo ship; freighter; transport ship.
Frage *f*   question; *(Problem)* problem; *(Kernpunkt)* issue.
Fragebogen *m*   questionnaire.
fragen   to question; to ask.
fragwürdig   questionable.
Franchisenehmer *m*   franchisee.
frankieren   to stamp.
frankiert   stamped.
frei   free; *(frei von)* exempt.
freiberuflich   self-employed; professional; *(Journalist)* freelance.
freie Kapazität *f*   surplus capacity.
freier Markt *m*   open market; free market.
freier Wechselkurs *m*   floating exchange rate.
Freigabe *f*   release; decontrol; deregulation; clearance.
freigeben   to release; to float; to decontrol; to deregulate; to clear.

freigebig   generous.
freigegebener Wechselkurs *m*   floating exchange rate.
Freihandel *m*   free trade.
Freiheit *f*   freedom.
freimachen   *(Post)* to stamp; to meter.
Freiverkehr *m*   *(Börse)* over the counter market.
freiwillig   voluntary; optional.
Freizeit *f*   leisure time.
Freizeitvergnügen *nt*   recreational fun.
Freizügigkeit *f*   mobility.
fremd   *(ausländisch)* foreign; *(unbekannt)* strange; *(Kapital)* outside.
Fremdgeld *nt*   borrowed money.
Fremdkapital *nt*   outside capital.
Fremdling *m*   stranger; newcomer.
Fremdmittel *pl*   outside capital; outside funds.
Fremdwährung *f*   foreign currency.
Frist *f*   period of time; term; *(Aufschub)* extension; grace period; *(Ultimatum)* deadline; *(Kündigungsfrist)* notice.
fristlose Kündigung *f*   dismissal without notice.
fruchtbar   fruitful; prolific; *(Boden)* fertile.
Fuhre *f*   load.
führen   to lead; *(Firma)* to manage; to operate; to conduct; *(Bücher)* to keep; *(einen Artikel)* to carry; *(lenken)* to direct; *(herumführen)* to guide.
führend   leading; managerial.
führende Rolle *f*   leadership roll.
Führer *m*   leader; *(Tourismus)* guide.
Führerschein *m*   driver's license.
Führung *f*   *(Geschäft)* management;

leadership; direction; *(Lenkung)* guidance; *(Benehmen)* conduct.

Führungsfähigkeit *f* leadership ability.

Führungsgruppe *f* management team.

Führungskontrolle *f* management control.

Führungskraft *f* executive.

Führungslaufbahn *f* management career.

führungslos without leadership.

Führungsnachwuchs *m* *(Industrie)* management trainees; *(Politik)* future leaders.

Führungspersonal *nt* management personnel.

Führungsposition *f* leadership position.

Führungsproblem *nt* managerial problem.

Führungsprozeß *m* management process.

Führungsqualität *f* leadership quality; leadership characteristics.

Führungsschicht *f* establishment.

Führungsseminar *nt* management seminar.

Führungsstab *m* executive staff; *(Militär)* operational headquarters.

Führungsstil *m* management style.

Führungsstruktur *f* management structure.

Führungstätigkeit *f* management functions.

Führungsverhalten *nt* leadership stance; leadership behavior.

Fuhrunternehmer *m* carrier; trucking company.

Fülle *f* abundance.

Fund *m* find.

fundiert funded; well-grounded; *(Anleihe)* consolidated; *(Firma)* sound.

Fundierung *f* foundation; *(Anleihe)* funding.

fungieren to function; to act as; to serve as.

Funktion *f* office; function.

Funktionär *m* official; officer.

funktionieren to work; to operate; to function.

Funktionsbereich *m* area of operation.

Funktionsfähigkeit *f* operational capability.

Fürsorge *f* *(staatlich)* welfare; *(Pflege)* care.

Fürsprecher *m* advocate.

Fusion *f* merger; consolidation.

fusionieren to merge; to combine.

G

Garantie *f* guaranty; *(des Verkäufers)* warranty.
Garantiepreis *m* guaranteed price.
garantieren to guaranty; *(verkaufte Waren)* to warrant; *(Effekten)* to underwrite.
Gast *m* guest; *(Fremdenheim)* boarder.
Gastarbeiter *m* guest worker.
Gastgeber *m* host.
Gastland *nt* host country.
Gattung *f* kind; type; sort.
Gebäude *nt* building; structure.
Gebäudeschaden *m* damage to a building; structural damages.
Geber *m* donor.
Gebiet *nt* territory; zone; region; field; area.
Gebietsansässige *m/f* resident.
Gebietsfremde *m/f* alien.
Gebot *nt* *(Anweisung)* instruction; *(Versteigerung)* bid.
Gebühr *f* charge; fee; *(Zoll)* duty; *(Lizenz)* royalty; *(Telefon)* toll.
gebührenfrei free of charge; *(Telefon)* toll free; *(zollfrei)* duty-free.
gebührenpflichtig subject to charges; *(Post)* subject to postage; *(Zoll)* dutiable.
gedeihen to thrive; to prosper; to flourish.
Gedeihen *nt* prosperity.
geeignet suitable; eligible; fit.
Gefahr *f* danger; peril; *(Risiko)* risk.
gefährden to jeopardize; to compromise; to endanger.
Gefahrenpotential *nt* risk potential.

gefährlich risky.
Gefälle *nt* downgrade; *(Unterschied)* differential.
gefälscht counterfeit; fake; falsified.
Gefüge *nt* structure.
Gegenbuchung *f* counterentry; counteritem; offset.
Gegend *f* region.
Gegengewicht *nt* counterbalance.
Gegenleistung *f* *(Vertrag)* consideration; *(Gegenwert)* equivalent.
Gegenmittel *nt* corrective.
Gegensaldo *m* counterbalance.
gegenseitig reciprocal; mutual.
Gegenstand *m* object; item; matter; article.
Gegenstück *nt* counterpart.
gegenüberstehen to face.
Gegenvorschlag *m* counterproposal.
Gegenwart *f* *(Anwesenheit)* presence; *(Zeit)* present.
gegenwärtig present.
Gegenwert *m* equivalent.
Gegenwertmittel *nt* counterpart funds.
Gehalt *m* contents; *(Fassungsvermögen)* capacity.
Gehalt *nt* pay; salary.
Gehaltsempfänger *m* salaried employee.
Gehaltserhöhung *f* pay raise; salary raise.
Gehaltskonto *nt* payroll account.
Gehaltskürzung *f* cut in pay; cut in salary.
Gehaltsrunde *f* collective bargaining.
Gehaltszuschlag *m* bonus.

geheim secret; *(vertraulich)* confidential.
Geheimhaltung *f* secrecy; concealment.
Geheimnis *nt* secret; mystery.
Gehilfe *m* assistant.
gehören to belong to.
Geisel *f* hostage.
Gelände *nt* tract of land; area; terrain.
Geld *nt* money; *(Bargeld)* cash; *(Börse)* bid; *(Kleingeld)* change.
Geldabhebung *f* withdrawal of money.
Geldanlage *f* money investment; cash item.
Geldanleger *m* investor.
Geldanweisung *f* remittance.
Geldausgabeautomat *m* automatic teller machine.
Geldautomat *m* automatic teller machine; *(Münzwechselautomat)* coin changing machine.
Geldbeschaffung *f* raising money.
Geldbuße *f* fine.
Geldeingang *m* money receipts.
Geldeinheit *f* monetary unit.
Geldeinlage *f* deposit; money paid in.
Geldentwertung *f* *(Währungsabwertung)* depreciation of the currency; *(Inflation)* inflation.
Geldforderung *f* monetary claim; *(ausstehende Gelder)* money due; outstanding debt.
Geldgeber *m* financial backer; financier; investor; *(Förderer)* sponsor.
Geldinstitut *nt* financial institution; finance company.
geldlich monetary.
Geldmarkt *m* money market; financial market.

Geldmarktanlage *f* money market investment.
Geldmarktgeschäft *nt* money market business; money market transaction.
Geldmarktpapiere *pl* money market securities; money market instruments.
Geldmarktpolitik *f* monetary policy.
Geldmenge *f* money supply.
Geldmengenerhöhung *f* increase in the money supply.
Geldmengenpolitik *f* money supply policy.
Geldmengenvermehrung *f* increase in the money supply.
Geldmengenwachstum *nt* growth in the money supply.
Geldmengenziel *nt* money supply target.
Geldnot *f* shortage of money; financial straits.
Geldpolitik *f* monetary policy.
Geldschöpfung *f* creation of money.
Geldsendung *f* remittance.
Geldstrafe *f* penalty; fine.
Geldstück *nt* coin.
Geldsumme *f* sum of money; fund.
Geldtheorie *f* monetary theory.
Geldübermittlung *f* money transfer; remittance.
Geldüberweisung *f* remittance.
Geldumlauf *m* circulation of money.
Geldverkehr *m* money transfer; circulation of money.
Geldvermehrung *f* increase in currency.
Geldvermögen *nt* monetary assets.
Geldversorgung *f* money supply.

Geldverwalter *m* financial manager; money manager.

Geldvolumen *nt* volume of money.

Geldwert *m* value of money; monetary value; *(Wert in Geld)* cash value.

Geldwertstabilität *f* currency stability.

Geldwesen *nt* finance.

Gelegenheit *f* opportunity; occasion.

Gelegenheitsgesellschaft *f* joint venture.

Gelegenheitskauf *m* bargain.

gelegentlich incidental.

gelten to be in force; *(Wert sein)* to be worth; *(Text)* to prevail.

geltend machen *(Gesetz)* to enforce; *(Anspruch)* to assert.

Geltendmachung *f* *(Gesetz)* enforcement; *(Anspruch)* assertion.

Geltung *f* *(Ansehen)* authority; standing; *(Gültigkeit)* validity; *(Wert)* value; *(Wichtigkeit)* importance.

gemäß *(angemessen)* appropriate; *(entsprechend)* in accordance with; *(zufolge)* as a result of.

Gemeinde *f* community.

Gemeindeverwaltung *f* local government.

Gemeinkosten *pl* overhead costs.

gemeinnützig nonprofit.

gemeinsam collective; common.

Gemeinsamer Markt *m* Common Market.

Gemeinschaft *f* collective; community; alliance.

Gemeinschaftskonto *nt* joint account.

Gemeinschaftsunternehmen *nt* joint venture.

Gemeinwert *m* market value.

Gemeinwirtschaft *f* social economy.

genau exact; specific; precise; definite; accurate.

genau angeben to specify.

Genauigkeit *f* precision; accuracy.

genehmigen to approve; *(erlauben)* to permit; to authorize; *(Lizenz erteilen)* to license; *(Gesetz)* to pass; *(ratifizieren)* to ratify; *(sanktionieren)* to sanction.

Genehmigung *f* approval; *(Erlaubnis)* permit; authorization; *(Ratifizierung)* ratification; *(Sanktionierung)* sanction.

Generaldirektor *m* managing director.

Generalsekretär *m* secretary general.

Generation *f* generation.

generisch generic.

genesen to recover.

genormt standardized.

Genossenschaft *f* cooperative association.

genossenschaftlich cooperative.

Genossenschaftsbank *f* cooperative bank.

genug enough; sufficient.

genügen to suffice; to be adequate.

genügend adequate; ample.

Genuß *m* enjoyment; beneficial use.

Genußschein *m* participating certificate; coupon.

Gepflogenheit *f* habit.

Gerät *nt* *(Ausrüstung)* equipment; *(Hilfsmittel)* device; *(Werkzeug)* tool; *(Haushaltsgerät)* appliance.

gerecht just; equitable; fair.

Gerechtigkeit *f* justice.

Gericht *nt* court.

gerichtlich judicial.
gerichtliche Verfolgung *f* prosecution.
Gerichtsbezirk *m* jurisdiction.
Gerichtshof *m* court.
Gerichtsurteil *nt* judgement; *(Strafprozess)* verdict.
geringfügig petty; slight; *(Betrag)* paltry.
Gerüst *nt* framework; *(Bau)* scaffold.
gesamt total; entire; overall; aggregate.
Gesamtabsatz *m* total sales; volume of sales.
Gesamtangebot *nt* total supply.
Gesamtanlage *f* total investment.
Gesamtbestand *m* total stock on hand.
Gesamtbetrag *m* total; total amount; sum total.
Gesamteinkommen *nt* entire income; total revenue.
Gesamtergebnis *nt* overall result.
Gesamtersparnisse *pl* total savings.
gesamtes Sortiment *nt* full line.
Gesamtetat *m* summary budget.
Gesamtgebiet *nt* entire territory.
Gesamtgewicht *nt* total weight.
Gesamtgewinn *m* total profit.
Gesamtheit *f* entirety; totality; whole.
Gesamtindex *m* overall index.
Gesamtinvestition *f* total investment.
Gesamtkapazität *f* total capacity.
Gesamtkosten *pl* total cost; overall costs.
Gesamtleistung *f* total output.
Gesamtleistungsvermögen *nt* total capacity.
Gesamtmarkt *m* total market.
Gesamtnachfrage *f* total demand.

Gesamtproduktion *f* total production; total output.
Gesamtrechnung *f* national income accounting.
Gesamtreserven *pl* total reserves.
Gesamtsumme *f* total; total amount.
Gesamtumsatz *m* total sales.
Gesamtverbrauch *m* total consumption.
Gesamtverlust *m* overall loss; *(Versicherung)* total loss.
Gesamtverschuldung *f* total indebtedness.
Gesamtversorgung *f* total supply.
Gesamtvertragssumme *f* total contract amount.
Gesamtverzinsung *f* total interest.
Gesamtvolumen *nt* total volume.
Gesamtwert *m* total value.
Gesamtziffer *f* total figure.
gesättigt saturated.
Geschäft *nt* business; *(Laden)* store; shop; *(Unternehmen)* enterprise; *(Firma)* firm; *(Abschluß)* deal; *(günstiger Abschluß)* bargain.
Geschäftemacherei *f* racket.
geschäftlich commercial.
Geschäftsabschluß *m* completion of transaction; closing a deal.
Geschäftsanteil *m* share of business; partnership share.
Geschäftsbank *f* commercial bank.
Geschäftsbereich *m* area of operations; function.
Geschäftsbericht *m* business report; financial statement; *(Marktbericht)* market report.
Geschäftsergebnis *nt* company result.
Geschäftsfrau *f* businesswoman; tradeswoman; *(Händlerin)* dealer.
geschäftsführend managing.

geschäftsführendes Vorstandsmitglied *nt* managing director.

Geschäftsführer *m* manager; director.

Geschäftsführung *f* management; business management.

Geschäftsgeheimnis *nt* trade secret.

Geschäftsjahr *nt* fiscal year.

Geschäftskapital *nt* *(AG)* capital stock; business capital.

Geschäftskonto *nt* business account.

Geschäftskosten *pl* business expenses.

Geschäftskredit *m* business loan; commercial loan.

Geschäftskreditgeber *m* commercial lender.

Geschäftskunde *m* business client.

geschäftsleitend managing; *(vorübergehende Leitung)* acting.

Geschäftsleitung *f* management.

Geschäftsleute *pl* businessmen; tradesmen; *(Händler)* dealers.

Geschäftsmann *m* businessman; tradesman; *(Händler)* dealer.

geschäftsnotwendige Barmittel *pl* cash flow.

Geschäftspartner *m* business associate.

Geschäftsräume *pl* business premises.

Geschäftsreisende *m/f* travelling salesman, -person, -woman; sales agent.

Geschäftsstelle *f* agency; branch; office.

Geschäftstag *m* business day.

Geschäftstätigkeit *f* operation.

Geschäftsumfang *m* volume of business; *(Geschäftskreis)* scope of business.

Geschäftsusance *f* customary business practice.

Geschäftsverlauf *m* business trend; course of business.

Geschäftsvolumen *nt* business volume.

Geschäftsvorfall *m* business case; transaction.

Geschäftswelt *f* business community.

Geschäftszeit *f* business hours.

Geschäftszentrum *nt* commercial center; business center; trading center.

Geschäftszweck *m* business purpose; corporate objective.

Geschenk *nt* present; gift.

Geschick *nt* *(Geschicklichkeit)* skill; *(Schicksal)* fate.

geschickt skilled; skillful.

Geschoß *nt* *(Haus)* floor.

geschult trained.

geschützt secure; secured.

Geselle *m* journeyman.

Gesellschaft *f* *(Geschäft)* company; *(Staat)* society.

Gesellschafter *m* partner.

gesellschaftlich social.

gesellschaftliche Veranstaltung *f* social function.

Gesellschaftsfusion *f* corporate merger.

Gesellschaftskapital *nt* stockholders' equity; capitalization.

Gesellschaftspolitik *f* *(business)* company policy; *(society)* social policy.

Gesellschaftsübernahme *f* corporate takeover.

Gesellschaftsziel *nt* corporate objective.

Gesetz *nt* act; law; statute.

Gesetzbuch *nt* code.

Gesetzentwurf *m*   bill.

Gesetzesänderung *f*   amendment; revision of a statute.

Gesetzeslücke *f*   legal loophole.

Gesetzesvorlage *f*   bill; legislative proposal.

gesetzgebend   legislative.

Gesetzgeber *m*   lawmaker; legislator.

Gesetzgebung *f*   legislation.

gesetzlich   legal; legitimate.

gesetzmäßig   legal; legitimate.

gesetzwidrig   illegal.

gesichert   secure; secured.

Gesichtspunkt *m*   aspect.

Gespräch *nt*   interview.

gestaffelt   sliding.

gestrafft   tightened.

gestuft   sliding.

gestützt   supported.

Gesuch *nt*   request; petition.

gesund   well; healthy; *(solide)* sound.

Gesundung *f*   recovery.

gewagt   risky.

gewähren   to grant; to allow.

gewährleisten   to warrant; to guarantee.

Gewährleistung *f*   warranty.

Gewährsmann *m*   *(für Informationen)* source; informant; *(Bürge)* guarantor.

Gewährung *f*   granting; grant; *(Zugeständnis)* concession.

Gewaltenteilung *f*   division of powers.

Gewerbe *nt*   *(Handwerk)* trade; *(Industrie)* industry; business.

Gewerbeausstellung *f*   trade exhibition.

Gewerbebetrieb *m*   business; manufacturing firm; trade firm; workshop.

Gewerbedarlehen *nt*   business loan.

Gewerbeerlaubnis *f*   trade concession.

Gewerbemesse *f*   trade fair.

Gewerbeschau *f*   trade show.

Gewerbeschein *m*   trade license.

Gewerbesteuer *f*   business tax; industrial tax; trade tax; license tax.

Gewerbetreibende *m/f*   manufacturer; tradesman; *(Handwerk)* craftsman.

Gewerbezweig *m*   line of trade.

gewerblich   industrial.

Gewerkschaft *f*   union; labor union.

Gewerkschaftler *m*   unionist.

Gewerkschaftsführer *m*   union leader.

Gewerkschaftsgesetz *nt*   trade union law.

Gewinn *m*   profit; gain; *(Ertrag)* return; proceeds; earnings; *(Nutzen)* benefit; *(Spiel)* winnings.

Gewinnanstieg *m*   profit growth.

Gewinnanteil *m*   *(AG)* dividend; share of profit.

Gewinnausschüttung *f*   distribution of profit.

Gewinnbeteiligung *f*   profit sharing.

gewinnbringend   profitable; lucrative.

gewinnen   to win; *(an Wert)* to gain.

Gewinner *m*   winner.

Gewinnerwartung *f*   expectation of profits.

Gewinnerzielung *f*   realization of profits.

Gewinnmaximierung *f*   profit maximization.

Gewinnobligation *f* reorganization bond.

gewinnorientiert profit oriented.

Gewinnorientierung *f* profit orientation.

Gewinnplanziel *nt* profit target.

Gewinnrechnung *f* profit accounting; surplus accounting.

Gewinnsaldo *m* profit balance.

Gewinnschätzung *f* estimate of profits.

Gewinnspanne *f* profit margin.

Gewinnstreben *nt* profit motive; profit seeking.

Gewinntrend *m* profit trend.

Gewinnung *f* *(Bodenschätze)* extraction; production; *(Förderung)* output; *(Neuland)* reclamation.

Gewinnverhältnis *nt* profit ratio.

Gewinnzuschreibung *f* allocation of profit.

Gewinnzuwachs *m* profit growth.

gewiß certain.

Gewissenhaftigkeit *f* diligence.

Gewißheit *f* certainty.

Gewohnheit *f* habit; *(Sitte)* custom; *(Übung)* practice.

Gewohnheitsrecht *nt* common law.

gewöhnlich common.

gezielt selective.

Gipfel *m* summit; peak.

Giro *nt* *(Indossament)* endorsement; *(Übertragung)* assignment; transfer.

Girobank *f* deposit clearing bank.

Girokonto *nt* current account; checking account.

Giroverband *m* clearinghouse association.

Giroverkehr *m* deposit clearing system.

Girozentrale *f* clearing house.

glaubhaft credible; plausible.

Gläubiger *m* creditor.

Gläubigerbank *f* creditor bank.

Gläubigerland *nt* creditor country.

Gläubigerpositon *f* creditor position.

Gläubigerschutz *m* creditor protection.

Gläubigerstaat *m* creditor nation.

glaubwürdig reliable; credible.

Glaubwürdigkeit *f* reliability; credibility.

gleich *(identisch)* same; identical; *(gleichwertig)* equal; *(sofort)* immediately.

gleichartig similar; *(einheitlich)* uniform.

gleichberechtigt having equal rights.

Gleichberechtigung *f* equal rights; equal status.

gleichbleibend stable; constant.

gleichförmig uniform.

Gleichförmigkeit *f* uniformity.

Gleichgewicht *nt* equilibrium; balance.

Gleichgewichtspreis *m* equilibrium price.

Gleichgewichtspunkt *m* point of equilibrium.

Gleichheit *f* *(Preise)* parity; *(Identität)* identity; *(Gleichberechtigung)* equality.

gleichlautend identical.

gleichrangig of equal rank.

Gleichschaltung *f* coordination.

gleichsetzen to equate.

Gleichstellung *f* equalization; equal treatment; equal ranking.

Gleichung equation.

gleichwertig equivalent; of the same value.

gleichzeitig concurrent.

gleiten to slide.
Gleitzeit *f* flexible working hours; flextime.
global global.
Gold *nt* gold.
Goldbesitzer *m* gold holder.
Goldbestand *m* gold holding; gold reserve.
Goldhortung *f* gold hoarding.
Goldkrise *f* gold crisis.
Goldpreis *m* price of gold.
Goldproduktion *f* production of gold.
Goldproduzent *m* gold producer.
Goldreserve *f* gold reserve.
Goldstandard *m* gold standard.
Goldverkauf *m* sale of gold.
Goldvorrat *m* stock of gold; gold supply.
Goodwill *m* goodwill.
Grad *m* degree; grade; *(Rang)* rank; *(Ausmaß)* measure.
Gradeinteilung *f* scale.
graphische Darstellung *f* graph; diagram.
gratis free; gratuitous.
Gratisaktie *f* stock dividend.
Gremium *nt* panel.
Grenze *f* *(Beschränkung)* limit; *(Abgrenzung)* border; *(Begrenzung)* boundary.
Grenzfall *m* borderline case.
Grenzkosten *pl* marginal costs.
Grenzkostenkurve *f* marginal cost curve.
Grenzlinie *f* boundary.
Grenzprodukt *nt* marginal product; end product.
Grenzwert *m* marginal value.
Gros *nt* gross; *(einer Anzahl)* majority; *(Dutzend)* dozen.
Großabnehmer *m* quantity buyer; large customer.

Großaktionär *m* principal stockholder; controlling stockholder.
Großanlage *f* large plant.
Großanleger *m* big investor.
Großauftrag *m* large order; *(Börse)* big-ticket order.
Größe *f* size.
Größenordnung *f* dimension; scale; range.
Größenverhältnis *nt* scale.
großformatig large-sized.
Großhandel *m* wholesale.
Großhandelsgewerbe *nt* wholesaling.
Großhandelskette *f* wholesale chain.
Großhandelsmarkt *m* wholesale market.
Großhändler *m* wholesaler.
Großindustrie *f* big industry.
Großindustrielle *m/f* business tycoon.
Grossist *m* wholesaler.
Großkonzern *m* big concern; conglomerate.
Großkredit *m* large credit.
Großmarkt *m* supermarket; central market.
Großstadt *f* large city; *(Weltstadt)* metropolis.
großstädtisch metropolitan.
Großunternehmen *nt* big business; big enterprise.
Großversuch *m* large-scale test.
großzügig liberal; generous.
Grundbedürfnis *nt* basic need.
Grundbesitz *m* land; landholding; estate.
Grundbesitzer *m* landowner.
Grundbesitzertum *nt* landownership.
Grundbuch *nt* land register; title register.

Grundeigentümer *m*   landowner.
gründen *(Gesellschaft)* to found;
  to form; to launch; *(einrichten)* to
  establish; *(erschaffen)* to create.
Gründer *m*   founder.
Gründerfamilie *f*   founding family.
Gründergeneration *f*   founding
  generation.
Grundform *f*   type.
Grundgehalt *nt*   base pay; base
  salary.
Grundkapital *nt*   *(AG)* capital
  stock; equity capital; original
  stock; *(Bank)* fund; capital stock;
  (Kapitaleinlage) principal; *(Nomi-
  nalkapital)* nominal capital.
Grundlage *f*   base; basis.
grundlegend   primary; basic.
gründlich   solid; systematic.
Grundlohntarif *m*   wage rate.
Grundpfandrecht *nt*   mortgage lien.
Grundpreis *m*   net cost; base price.
Grundprodukt *nt*   primary product.
Grundrente *f*   economic rent.
Grundsatz *m*   principle.
Grundsatzentscheidung *f*   policy
  decision.
Grundsatzerklärung *f*   policy
  statement; *(Völkerrecht)* declara-
  tion of intention; *(Parteipro-
  gramm)* platform.
grundsätzlich   fundamental; *(im
  Prinzip)* in principle.
Grundstrategie *f*   basic strategy.
Grundstück *nt*   lot; parcel of land;
  (Grundstückseigentum) real
  estate; property.
Grundstückserschließer *m*   devel-
  oper.
Grundstücksparzelle *f*   parcel.
Grundstücksverkauf *m*   sale of
  land; property sale; real estate sale.

Gründung *f*   formation; foundation; creation.
Gründungsjahr *nt*   founding year.
Grundvoraussetzung *f*   basic prerequisite.
Gruppe *f*   network; group.
Gruppenangehörige *m/f*   group
  member.
Gruppenarbeit *f*   teamwork.
gruppieren   to group; to classify.
gültig   valid; good; *(rechtsgültig)*
  legal; *(in Kraft)* in force; effective.
Gültigkeit *f*   validity; *(Rechtsgültigkeit)* legality.
günstig   favorable; *(vorteilhaft)*
  advantageous; *(vielversprechend)*
  promising.
günstige Gelegenheit *f*   opportunity.
Gut *nt*   *(Besitz)* property; *(Ware)*
  goods; merchandise; *(Gutshof)*
  farm.
Gutachten *nt*   expert opinion; survey.
Gutachter *m*   consultant; expert;
  (Schätzer) appraiser.
Gutdünken *nt*   discretion.
Güte *f*   quality; *(Handelsklasse)*
  grade; *(Entgegenkommen)* kind-
  ness.
Gütegrad *m*   standard; quality.
Güter *pl*   merchandise; commodities; goods.
Gütergruppe *f*   category of goods.
Güterhandel *m*   merchandise trade;
  commodities trade.
Güterkonsum *m*   consumption of
  goods.
Güterpreis *m*   price of goods.
Güterproduktion *f*   production of
  goods.

Haben *nt* *(Buchhaltung)* credit; assets.

Habenbuchung *f* credit entry.

Habenseite *f* credit side.

Hafen *m* port; harbor.

haftbar liable; *(responsible)* verantwortlich.

haften to be liable; *(garantieren)* to guarantee; to vouch.

Haftpflicht *f* liability.

haftpflichtig liable.

Haftsumme *f* amount guaranteed.

Haftung *f* liability; *(Verantwortung)* responsibility.

Halbfabrikat *nt* intermediate goods; semifinished goods.

halbfertig semifinished.

Halbleiter *m* semiconductor.

Halde *f* waste heap; dump.

Hälfte *f* half.

halsabschneiderisch cutthroat.

haltbar *(dauerhaft)* durable; *(fest)* solid; *(stabil)* stable.

Haltung *f* *(Einstellung)* attitude.

hamstern to hoard.

Handarbeiter *m* manual worker.

Handbedienung *f* manual operation.

Handbuch *nt* manual.

Handel *m* trade; commerce; *(Transaktion)* bargain; *(Geschäft)* business.

handelbar salable; *(Wertpapier)* negotiable.

handeln *(Handel treiben)* to trade; to deal; *(feilschen)* to bargain; *(tun)* to act.

Handelsabkommen *nt* commercial treaty; trade agreement; economic agreement.

Handelsbank *f* merchant bank.

Handelsbeschränkung *f* trade restriction.

Handelsbezeichnung *f* trade name.

Handelsbeziehung *f* trade relations; commercial relationship.

Handelsbilanz *f* trade balance.

Handelsbilanzdefizit *nt* trade balance deficit.

Handelsblatt *nt* trade journal.

Handelsdefizit *nt* trade deficit.

Handelseinschränkung *f* trade restraint.

Handelsfirma *f* trading company.

Handelsflotte *f* merchant fleet.

Handelsgesellschaft *f* trading company.

Handelsgesetzbuch *nt* commercial code.

Handelsgruppe *f* trade group.

Handelsgut *nt* merchandise.

Handelshaus *nt* commercial establishment; business enterprise; trading firm; trading house.

Handelshemmnis *nt* trade barrier.

Handelskammer *f* chamber of commerce; board of trade.

Handelskette *f* chain of stores.

Handelsklasse *f* grade; quality.

Handelskrieg *m* trade war.

Handelsmann *m* merchant; trader; tradesman.

Handelsmesse *f* trade fair.

Handelsname *m* trade name; business name.

Handelspapier *nt* commercial paper.

Handelspartner *m* trading partner.

Handelspolitik *f* trade policy.

Handelsschranke *f* trade barrier.

Handelsspanne *f* margin.

Handelsstrom *m* flow of trade.

Handelsvertreter *m* sales representative.

Handelswert *m* market value.

Handelszeitschrift *f* trade magazine.

handeltreibend mercantile; trading.

Handeltreibende *m/f* trader.

Händler *m* trader; merchant; dealer.

Händlerjargon *m* trade jargon.

Händlernetz *nt* dealer network.

handlich handy; manageable.

Handlung *f* act; action; *(Laden)* business.

Handwerk *nt* craft; small trade; industrial art.

Handwerker *m* craftsman; tradesman.

Handzettel *m* leaflet; flier.

Hardware *f* hardware.

harte Währung *f* hard currency.

häufig frequent; often.

Häufigkeit *f* frequency; incidence.

Hauptabteilung *f* central department.

Hauptanziehungspunkt *m* main attraction.

Hauptberuf *m* principal occupation; main profession; full-time job.

Hauptbuch *nt* ledger.

Hauptbüro *nt* main office; headquarters; home office.

Hauptgeschäftssitz *m* headquarters.

Hauptinhaber *m* principal owner.

Hauptkäufer *m* key buyer.

Hauptkonkurrent *m* main competitor.

Hauptlieferant *m* major supplier.

Hauptprodukt *nt* major product.

Hauptquartier *nt* headquarters.

Hauptrichtung *f* thrust.

hauptsächlich primary; principal; main; chief.

Hauptserie *f* key series.

Hauptstütze *f* mainstay.

Hauptthema *nt* key issue.

Hauptversammlung *f* annual meeting.

Hauptverwaltung *f* head office; headquarters.

Hauptwachstumsgebiet *nt* major growth area.

Hausbank *f* company's bank.

Hausbesitzer *m* homeowner.

Haushalt *m* household; budget.

haushalten to economize.

Haushaltsausschuß *m* budget committee; Ways and Means Committee.

Haushaltsdefizit *nt* budget deficit.

Haushaltsentwurf *m* budget proposal.

Haushaltsexperte *m* budget specialist.

Haushaltsjahr *nt* fiscal year.

Haushaltsplan *m* **aufstellen** to budget.

Haushaltspolitik *f* budgetary policy.

Haushaltssanierung *f* budget reorganization.

Haushaltsvoranschlag *m* budget proposal.

Hausse *f* bull market.

Hauswirt *m* landlord.

Heimcomputer *m* home computer.

heimisch domestic; native; home; local.

Heizöl *nt* heating oil.

hemmen to obstruct; to restrain.

Hemmnis *nt* obstruction; obstacle.

herabsetzen to lower; to reduce; to decrease; *(diskreditieren)* to disparage.

Herabsetzung *f* reduction; lowering; *(Diskreditierung)* disparagement.

heraufsetzen to increase; to raise; *(Preise)* to mark up.

herausfordern to challenge.

herausgeben to issue; *(Kleingeld)* to give change.

Herausgeber *m* publisher; editor.

herkömmlich conventional.

Herkunft *f* *(merchandise)* origin; family background; descent.

Herkunftsland *nt* country of origin.

herleiten to derive.

herstellen to manufacture; to produce; to make.

Hersteller *m* manufacturer; producer; maker.

Herstellung *f* production; manufacture.

Herstellungsanlage *f* production facility.

Herstellungsfirma *f* production company.

Herstellungskosten *pl* production costs.

Herstellungsmethode *f* production process.

Herstellungsverfahren *nt* manufacturing process; production technique.

hervorheben to emphasize.

Hilfe *f* help; aid; assistance; *(Unterstützung)* support; backing.

Hilfe *f* **leisten** to give aid; *(unterstützen)* to support.

hilfreich helpful.

Hilfsaktion *f* relief action.

Hilfsarbeiter *m* unskilled worker; helper.

Hilfsmaßnahme *f* emergency measure.

Hilfsmittel *nt* resource; *(Notbehelf)* stopgap.

Hilfspersonal *nt* support personnel.

Hilfsquelle *f* resource.

Hilfsstoffe *f* auxiliary materials.

hinausschieben to delay; to postpone.

hinauszögern to delay; to postpone.

hindern to prevent; to restrain; to hinder.

Hindernis *nt* obstacle; obstruction; impediment.

hinreichend sufficient.

hinsichtlich with regard to; in respect to; concerning; as to.

Hintergrund *m* background.

hinterlassen to leave behind; *(Vermächtnis)* to bequeath.

hinterlegen to deposit.

Hinterleger *m* depositor.

Hinterlegungsstelle *f* depository.

Hinterlegungssumme *f* deposit.

Hinweis *m* reference; indication.

hinweisen to refer to; to indicate.

hinzeigen to point.

hinzufügen to add.

hinzurechnen to add.

Hochbetrieb *m* rush.

Hochkonjunktur *f* economic boom.

hochrechnen to project.

Hochrechnung *f* projection.

hochschießen to skyrocket.

hochschnellen to spurt; to skyrocket.

Höchstbetrag *m* maximum amount; *(Preisgrenze)* limit.
Höchstdauer *f* maximum period of time.
Höchstertrag *m* maximum proceeds.
Höchstgrenze *f* maximum; ceiling.
Höchstkredit *m* line of credit.
Höchstkurs *m* top price.
Höchstleistung *f* record.
Höchstpunkt *m* peak.
Höchstratengrenze *f* rate ceiling.
Höchststand *m* high; highest level; *(Kurse)* top price.
Höchstwert *m* maximum value.
Höchstzinsen *pl* interest ceiling.
hochtreiben to inflate; to boost; to force up.
hochwertig high-grade; high-quality; high-class.
Höflichkeit *f* courtesy.
Höhe *f* height; altitude; *(Ausmaß)* extent; *(Preise)* level; *(Summe)* amount.
Höhepunkt *m* culmination; climax; peak.
Holdinggesellschaft *f* holding company.

Honorar *nt* royalty; fee.
honorieren to remunerate.
Hörer *m* *(Telefon)* receiver; *(Radio)* listener.
horten to hoard; to stockpile.
hypermodern newfangled.
Hypothek *f* mortgage; *(mit flexibler Verzinsung)* adjustable-rate mortgage.
Hypothekarinstitut *nt* mortgage bank.
hypothekarisch belasten to mortgage.
hypothekarische Belastung *f* mortgage debt.
Hypothekarkredit *m* mortgage loan.
Hypothekenbank *f* mortgage bank.
Hypothekenbrief *m* mortgage deed.
Hypothekendarlehen *nt* mortgage loan.
Hypothekenschulden *pl* encumbrance; mortgage debt.
Hypothekenzinsen *pl* mortgage interest.

Idee *f* idea.
identifizierbar identifiable.
identifizieren to identify.
Identifizierung *f* identification.
identisch identical.
Identität *f* identity.
illegal illegal.
Illustration *f* illustration.

illustrieren to illustrate.
Image *nt* image.
immateriell intangible.
immaterielle Vermögenswerte *pl* intangible assets.
Immobilien *pl* real estate.
Immobilienfonds *m* real estate investment fund.

Import *m*   import; importation.
Importabgabe *f*   import surcharge.
Importbarriere *f*   import barrier.
Importbedarf *m*   import demand.
Importdrosselung *f*   import curb.
Importeinsparung *f*   import savings.
Importeur *m*   importer.
Importfähigkeit *f*   import capacity; importability.
Importfirma *f*   import company.
Importgut *nt*   import merchandise.
importieren   to import.
Importkaufmann *m*, **-frau** *f*   importer.
Importkontingent *nt*   import quota.
Importpreis *m*   import price.
Importquote *f*   import quota.
Importschranke *f*   import barrier.
Importverteuerung *f*   import price increase.
Importware *f*   import goods.
Impuls *m*   impulse.
Index *m*   index.
Indikator *m*   indicator.
indirekt   indirect.
individualisieren   to individualize; to personalize.
individuell anpassen   to personalize.
Individuum *nt*   person; individual.
Indossament *nt*   endorsement.
indossieren   to endorse.
indossierfähig   negotiable.
industrialisieren   to industrialize.
Industrialisierung *f*   industrialization.
Industrialismus *m*   industrialism.
Industrie *f*   industry.
Industrieanlage *f*   production plant; industrial plant; manufacturing plant.
Industrieausstellung *f*   industrial show; trade show.

Industriebasis *f*   industrial base.
Industrieberater *m*   management consultant.
Industriebereich *m*   industrial sector.
Industriebetrieb *m*   manufacturing company; industrial plant.
Industriebranche *f*   field of industry.
Industriefachmann *m*   industry expert.
Industrieführer *m*   industry leader.
Industriekreis *m*   industry segment.
Industrieland *nt*   industrial country; industrial nation.
industriell   industrial.
Industrielle *m/f*   manufacturer; industrialist.
Industriemaschinen *pl*   industrial machinery.
Industrienachfrage *f*   industrial demand.
Industrienation *f*   industrial nation.
Industriepark *m*   industrial park.
Industrieproduktion *f*   industrial production; industrial output.
Industrieprognose *f*   industry forecast.
Industriestaat *m*   industrial nation.
Industriestruktur *f*   industry structure.
Industrieunternehmen *nt*   industrial enterprise.
Industrieverwaltung *f*   industrial management.
Industriewerk *nt*   factory; industrial plant.
Industriezweig *m*   line of industry; branch of industry.
ineinandergreifen   to mesh.
Inempfangnahme *f*   receipt.
Inflation *f*   inflation.

inflationär inflationary.
inflationistisch inflationary.
Inflationsabbau *m* disinflation.
Inflationsdruck *m* inflationary pressure.
Inflationsfaktor *m* inflationary factor.
inflationsfrei noninflationary.
Inflationsrate *f* rate of inflation; inflation rate.
inflatorisch inflationary.
Information *f* information; *(Nachrichten)* news; *(Kommunikation)* communication.
Informationsblatt *nt* newsletter.
Informationsfluß *m* communication; flow of information.
Informationsnetz *nt* communication network; information network.
Informationsquelle *f* source of information.
Informationsstand *m* *(Auskunftstisch)* information desk; *(Niveau)* state of information.
Informationssystem *nt* communication system.
Informationswert *m* informational value.
informativ informative.
informell informal.
informieren to inform; to brief.
Infrastruktur *f* infrastructure.
Ingenieur *m* engineer.
Inhaber *m* *(Eigentümer)* proprietor; owner; *(Besitzer)* holder; *(Wechselinhaber)* bearer.
Inhaberaktie *f* bearer share; transferable stock; bearer stock.
Inhaberobligation *f* coupon bond.
Inhaberpapier *nt* bearer note.
Inhabersparbrief *m* bearer savings bond.

Inhalt *m* content(s).
Initiative *f* initiative.
Inkasso *nt* collection.
Inkassobeamte *m* collector.
Inkassobeamtin *f* collector.
Inkassopapier *nt* collection item.
inklusiv inclusive.
Inland *nt* inland; interior; *(im Inland)* at home.
Inländer *m* *(Einheimischer)* native; *(Bürger)* citizen.
inländisch interior; internal; domestic.
Inlandsanlage *f* domestic investment.
Inlandsanleihe *f* domestic loan; internal bond.
Inlandsbank *f* domestic bank.
Inlandsbestellung *f* domestic order.
Inlandsgeschäft *nt* domestic business; home trading.
Inlandskapital *nt* domestic capital.
Inlandsmarkt *m* domestic market.
Inlandsverbrauch *m* domestic consumption.
innehaben to occupy.
Innendienst *m* office work.
Innovation *f* innovation.
innovativ innovative.
Input *m* input.
Inputdaten *pl* input data.
Inputpfad *m* input path.
Inserat *nt* ad; advertisement.
Inserent *m* advertiser.
inserieren to place an advertisement; to advertise.
insolvent insolvent.
Insolvenz *f* insolvency.
Insolvenzrecht *nt* bankruptcy law.
Inspektion *f* inspection.
inspizieren to inspect.
Instabilität *f* instability.

installieren to install.
Installierung *f* installation.
instandhalten to maintain.
Instandhaltung *f* upkeep; mainte-
nance.
Instandsetzung *f* repair; *(gründ-
liche)* overhaul.
Instanz *f* level of jurisdiction;
authority.
Institut *nt* institute; institution.
Institution *f* institution.
institutionell institutional.
Instrument *nt* *(Urkunde)* legal
instrument; deed; *(Werkzeug)* tool.
Integration *f* integration.
integrieren to integrate.
Integrität *f* integrity.
intensiv intensive.
Interbankgeschäft *nt* interbank
transaction.
Interesse *nt* interest; concern.
Interessengemeinschaft *f* *(Kar-
tell)* trust; syndicate.
Interessengruppe *f* lobby.
Interessenverband *m* lobby; pres-
sure group.
Interessenvertreter *m* lobbyist.
Interessenvertretung *f* lobby.
interessieren to interest.
interessieren, sich to be inter-
ested.
international international.
Internationalisierung *f* interna-
tionalization.
intervenieren to intervene.
Intervention *f* intervention.
Interview *nt* interview.
interviewen to interview.
Interviewer *m* interviewer.
Inventar *nt* inventory.
Inventur *f* inventory.
investieren to invest.

Investierung *f* investment.
Investition *f* investment.
Investitionsantrag *m* investment
proposal.
Investitionsausgabe *f* capital
expenditure.
Investitionsentscheidung *f*
investment decision.
Investitionsfunktion *f* investment
function.
Investitionsgüter *pl* capital goods.
Investitionshaushalt *m* capital
budget.
Investitionshöhe *f* investment
level.
Investitionskredit *m* investment
loan.
Investitionslücke *f* investment
gap.
Investitionsneigung *f* propensity
to invest.
Investitionsprämie *f* investment
premium.
Investitionsprogramm *nt* capital
expenditure plan; investment plan.
Investitionsquote *f* level of invest-
ment; investment quota.
Investitionssumme *f* amount
invested.
Investitionsvolumen *nt* investment volume.
Investitionsvorhaben *nt* investment project.
Investitionszyklus *m* investment
cycle.
Investment *nt* investment.
Investmentfonds *m* investment
fund; mutual fund.
Investor *m* investor.
irreführen to mislead.
Irreführung *f* deception; misdirection.

irrig   erroneous; false; wrong.
Irrtum *m*   error.
irrtümlich   erroneous.
Isolationspolitik *f*   isolationism.

Isolationspolitiker *m*   isolationist.
isolieren   to isolate.
Isolierung *f*   isolation.

J

Jahrbuch *nt*   yearbook; annual book.
Jahresabschluß *m*   annual balance sheet; annual financial statement; annual statement of accounts.
Jahresarbeitszeit *f*   annual working hours.
Jahresbericht *m*   annual report.
Jahresbilanz *f*   annual balance sheet.
Jahresdurchschnitt *m*   annual average.
Jahresende *nt*   end of the year.
Jahresergebnis *nt*   annual returns; annual yield; annual output.
Jahresetat *m*   annual budget.
Jahresfrist *f*   one-year period.
Jahresgewinn *m*   annual earnings.
Jahresmitte *f*   midyear.
Jahresproduktion *f*   annual production; annual output.
Jahresschluß *m*   close of the year.
Jahresstatistik *f*   annual statistics.
Jahressumme *f*   annual sum; annual total amount.

Jahrestagung *f*   annual convention; annual conference.
Jahresüberschuß *m*   annual surplus.
Jahresultimo *m*   end of the year; year-end.
Jahresumsatz *m*   annual sales.
Jahresverdienst *m*   annual earnings.
Jahresverlauf *m*   course of one year.
Jahreszeit *f*   season.
jahreszeitlich   seasonal.
Jahrhundert *nt*   century.
jährlich   annual.
Job *m*   job.
Journal *nt*   journal; register; magazine.
Jurist *m*   jurist; holder of law degree; *(Anwalt)* lawyer.
juristisch   legal.
Jury *f*   selection committee; *(Preisrichterausschuß)* committee of judges.
Justizwesen *nt*   legal system.

Kalender *m*   calendar.
Kalkulation *f*   calculation.
kalkulieren   to compute; to calculate; *(Kosten)* to estimate.
Kammer *f*   chamber; board; *(Gericht)* court.
Kampagne *f*   campaign.
Kampf *m*   struggle; fight; battle.
Kanal *m*   channel; *(Wasserstraße)* canal.
Kandidat *m*   candidate.
Kandidatenliste *f*   slate of candidates.
Kapazität *f*   capacity; *(Fachmann)* authority.
Kapazitätsüberschuß *m*   surplus capacity.
Kapital *nt*   capital; *(Eigenkapital)* equity; net worth; *(Geldmittel)* funds; resources; *(Zinsbasis)* principal.
Kapitalabfluß *m*   outflow of capital.
Kapitalanlage *f*   capital investment.
Kapitalanlagefonds *m*   mutual fund.
Kapitalanlagegesellschaft *f* investment trust company.
Kapitalanleger *m*   investor.
Kapitalanteil *m*   share in capital; capital interest; stock share; *(Beteiligung)* interest in a firm; *(Bilanz)* capital.
Kapitalaufwand *m*   cost of capital; capital spending.
Kapitalausstattung *f*   capitalization; *(Bilanz)* capital equipment.
Kapitalbasis *f*   capital base.
Kapitalbedarf *m*   capital requirement.

Kapitalbeschaffung *f*   financing.
Kapitalbeteiligung *f*   financial interest; equity participation; *(Aktienanteil)* share; stock; *(Aktienzeichnung)* stock subscription.
Kapitalbetrag *m*   amount of capital; principal amount.
Kapitalbewegung *f*   capital flow.
Kapitalbildung *f*   capital formation.
Kapitaldienst *m*   service of capital; interest payments.
Kapitaleigner *m*   capital owner; equity owner.
Kapitaleinkommen *nt*   unearned income; investment income.
Kapitaleinleger *m*   contributor of capital; investor.
Kapitalerhöhung *f*   increase in capital stock; capital increase.
Kapitalertrag *m*   unearned income; return on capital; investment return.
Kapitalexport *m*   capital export.
Kapitalflucht *f*   flight of capital; capital flight; exodus of capital.
Kapitalgeber *m*   investor.
Kapitalgesellschaft *f*   joint stock company.
Kapitalgewinn *m*   capital gain.
Kapitalhöhe *f*   amount of capital.
Kapitalismus *m*   capitalism.
Kapitalist *m*   capitalist.
kapitalistisch   capitalistic.
Kapitalkonto *nt*   capital account; equity account.
kapitalkräftig   financially sound; financially strong.
Kapitalmarkt *m*   capital market; equity market; money market.

Kapitalmehrheit *f* controlling interest; *(AG)* majority stock holding.

Kapitalminderung *f* capital reduction.

Kapitalrendite *f* yield on investment; return on equity.

Kapitalreserve *f* reserve capital; reserve fund.

Kapitalstrom *m* capital flow.

Kapitalstruktur *f* capital structure.

Kapitalverflechtung *f* cross ownership.

Kapitalverkehr *m* capital movement.

Kapitalvermehrung *f* increase of capital stock.

Kapitalwanderung *f* capital flow; capital movement.

Kapitalzusammensetzung *f* capital structure.

Kapitalzuwachs *m* capital gain; appreciation of principal; capital growth.

Kapitel *nt* chapter.

Karriere *f* career.

Karte *f* card; *(Eintrittskarte)* ticket; *(Landkarte)* map; *(Visitenkarte)* business card; *(Speisekarte)* menu.

Kartei *f* card index.

Kartell *nt* syndicate; pool; cartel.

Kartellamt *nt* antitrust agency.

Kartellrecht *nt* antitrust law.

Karton *m* cardboard; *(Schachtel)* cardboard box.

Kassageschäft *nt* cash business; *(Börse)* cash transaction; *(Devisen)* spot exchange transaction.

Kassakurs *m* *(Aktien)* cash price; *(Devisen)* spot rate.

Kassamarkt *m* cash market; *(Devisen)* spot market.

Kassapreis *m* cash price; *(Devisen)* spot price.

Kasse *f* *(Bargeld)* cash; *(Börse)* spot cash; *(Registrierkasse)* cash register; *(Kartenverkauf)* ticket window; *(Bank)* cashier's window; *(Theaterkasse)* box office; *(Kassenschalter)* pay desk; pay office; pay window; *(Krankenkasse)* health insurance.

Kassenbestand *m* cash on hand; cash balance; *(Bank)* real reserve.

Kassenbuchführung *f* cash accounting.

Kassenführer *m* cashier; *(Bank)* teller.

Kassenhaltung *f* cash management.

Kassenkonto *nt* cash account.

kassieren to cash; to collect.

Kassierer *m* *(bank)* teller; cashier.

Kasten *m* box; case.

Katalog *m* catalog.

katalogisieren to catalog.

Katalogpreis *m* list price.

Kategorie *f* category.

Kauf *m* purchase; buy; *(Erwerb)* acquisition.

Kaufanreiz *m* inducement to buy; buying incentive; merchandise appeal.

kaufen to purchase; to buy; *(erwerben)* to acquire.

Käufer *m* purchaser; buyer; *(im Laden)* shopper.

Käuferkredit *m* consumer credit.

Käufermarkt *m* buyer's market.

Kaufhaus *nt* department store.

Kaufhauskette *f* department store chain.

Kaufkraft *f* purchasing power.

kaufkräftig possessing purchasing power.

Kaufleute *pl*   business people; merchants.

Kaufmann *m*, **-frau** *f*   businessman, -woman; merchant; *(Händler)* dealer; tradesman, -woman; *(kaufmännischer Angestellter)* clerk.

kaufmännisch   commercial.

Kaufoption *f*   buying option; call option.

Kaufpreis *m*   purchase price.

Kaufverhalten *nt*   buying behavior.

Kaufwert *m*   market value.

kaufwillig   inclined to buy.

Kaufzurückhaltung *f*   buying resistance.

Kaution *f*   surety; security deposit; bail.

Kenntnis *f*   knowledge; information.

Kenntnisnahme *f*   notice; information.

kenntnisreich   knowledgeable.

Kennzeichen *nt*   sign; mark; *(Abzeichen)* badge; *(Merkmal)* feature; criterion; attribute; characteristic.

kennzeichnen   to mark; *(Waren)* to label; *(charakterisieren)* to characterize.

Kennziffer *f*   index number.

Kernpunkt *m*   main point; main issue.

Kette *f*   chain.

Kettenladen *m*   chain store.

Kirchensteuer *f*   church tax.

Kiste *f*   box; case; crate.

Klage *f*   *(Gericht)* lawsuit; *(Beschwerde)* complaint.

Klage *f* **anstrengen**   to sue.

Klang *m*   sound.

Klasse *f*   class; category; *(Handelsklasse)* grade; *(Steuerklasse)* bracket; *(Wertpapiere)* denomination.

Klassengesellschaft *f*   class society.

Klassenschranke *f*   class barrier.

klassifizieren   to classify.

Klassifizierung *f*   classification.

Klausel *f*   clause; article.

Kleinaktionär *m*   small stockholder.

Kleinanleger *m*   small investor.

Kleinanzeige *f*   classified advertisement.

Kleinbetrieb *m*   small business.

Kleincomputer *m*   personal computer.

Kleingeld *nt*   change.

Kleinkredit *m*   small loan; consumer loan; personal loan.

Kleinlastwagen *m*   pickup truck.

kleinstädtisch   provincial; small-town.

Kleinunternehmen *nt*   small company.

klettern   to climb.

Klient *m*   client.

Klientel *f*   clientele.

knapp   scarce; tight; *(vor Zahlen)* just under.

Knappheit *f*   scarcity; shortage.

Knowhow *nt*   know-how.

Koalition *f*   coalition.

Kodex *m*   code.

Kollege *m*   colleague.

Kollegin *f*   colleague.

Kollektion *f*   selection; assortment.

Komfort *m*   convenience.

Komitee *nt*   committee.

Kommanditeinlage *f*   limited partnership interest.

Kommanditgesellschaft *f*   limited partnership.

Kommentar *m*   comment; commentary.

kommentieren   to comment.

kommerziell   commercial.

Kommission *f* commission.
kommunal municipal; local.
Kommunalanleihe *f* municipal bond.
Kommunaldarlehen *nt* municipal loan.
Kommunalobligation *f* municipal bond.
Kommunalpolitiker *m* local politician.
Kommunikation *f* communication.
Kompagnon *m* partner.
komparativ comparative.
Kompensationshandel *m* countertrade; barter trade.
Kompensationskauf *m* counterpurchase.
kompliziert complex.
Komplott *nt* scheme; plot.
Komponente *f* component.
Kompromiß *m* compromise.
Kompromißlosigkeit *f* unwillingness to compromise.
Kompromißvorschlag *m* suggested compromise.
Konditionen *pl* terms.
Konferenz *f* meeting; conference.
Konferenzteilnehmer *m* conference participant; conference delegate; conference member.
Konflikt *m* conflict.
Konfliktfall *m* conflict situation.
Konfliktregelung *f* conflict settlement.
Kongreß *m* congress.
Kongreßhalle *f* congress hall; assembly chamber.
Konjunktur *f* business cycle; economic situation.
Konjunkturabschwung *m* cyclical downturn.
Konjunkturanstieg *m* cyclical upturn; upward business trend.

Konjunkturanzeichen *nt* economic indicator.
Konjunkturaufschwung *m* cyclical upturn; upward business trend.
Konjunkturaussichten *pl* business outlook; market outlook.
konjunkturbedingte Nachfrage *f* cyclical demand.
Konjunkturbelebung *f* economic recovery; business revival.
Konjunkturbericht *m* economic report; market report.
konjunkturell cyclical; economic.
Konjunkturforscher *m* economic researcher; business researcher.
Konjunkturinstitut *nt* business research institute; economic research institute.
Konjunkturlage *f* economic condition.
Konjunkturmodell *nt* model of economic cycles.
Konjunkturpolitik *f* economic stabilization policy.
Konjunkturprognose *f* economic forecast.
Konjunkturrückgang *m* recession; slump.
Konjunkturschema *nt* cyclical pattern.
Konjunkturtheorie *f* theory of economic cycles; theory of market trends.
Konjunkturtief *nt* depression.
Konjunkturverlauf *m* economic trend; cyclical trend; business cycle.
Konkurrent *m* competitor; rival.
Konkurrenz *f* competition.
konkurrenzfähig competitive.
konkurrenzfähige Preisfestsetzung *f* competitive pricing.

Konkurrenzfähigkeit *f* competitiveness.

Konkurrenzkampf *m* competition; trade rivalry.

Konkurrenzland *nt* competing country.

konkurrieren to compete.

Konkurs *m* failure; bankruptcy.

Konkursfall *m* bankruptcy case.

Konkursforderung *f* claim provable in bankruptcy; claim against a bankrupt's estate.

Konkursgläubiger *m* petitioning creditor; creditor of a bankrupt's estate.

Konkursmasse *f* bankrupt estate.

Können *nt* skill.

Konnossement *nt* bill of lading.

konservativ conservative.

konsolidieren to consolidate.

Konsolidierung *f* consolidation.

Konsortialbank *f* member bank of a syndicate; underwriting member bank.

Konsortialbildung *f* syndication.

Konsortialführer *m* leading underwriter; originating banker; leading bank.

Konsortialgeschäft *nt* syndicate transaction; underwriting syndicate business; business on joint account.

Konsortium *nt* syndicate; consortium.

konstruieren to construct.

Konstruktion *f* construction.

Konsulat *nt* consulate.

konsultieren to consult.

Konsum *m* consumption; *(Konsumladen)* cooperative store.

Konsument *m* consumer.

Konsumentenbudget *nt* consumer budget.

Konsumenteneinkommen *nt* consumer income.

Konsumentenkredit *m* consumer credit.

Konsumentenwunsch *m* consumer demand.

Konsumgewohnheit *f* consumer buying habit.

Konsumgüter *pl* consumer products.

konsumieren to consume.

Konsumneigung *f* propensity to consume.

Kontakt *m* contact; liaison.

Kontaktnahme *f* contacting.

Kontensumme *f* account balance.

Kontingent *nt* quota; *(Zuteilung)* allotment.

Kontingentierung *f* setting of quotas; rationing.

Kontingentsvereinbarung *f* quota agreement.

Kontinuität *f* continuity.

Konto *nt* account.

Kontoauflösung *f* closing of account.

Kontoauszug *m* statement of account; account statement; *(Bank)* bank statement.

Kontoführung *f* bookkeeping; *(Abteilung)* accounting department.

Kontoinhaber *m* account holder; *(Einzahler)* depositor.

Kontokorrentbuch *nt* current account ledger; *(Kreditoren)* accounts payable ledger; *(Debitoren)* accounts receivable ledger.

Kontokorrentkonto *nt* current account.

Kontokorrentkredit *m* current account advance; loan on overdraft.

Kontokosten *pl* account costs.

Kontonummer *f*   account number.

Kontostand *m*   account balance.

Kontostandabfrage *f*   request for account statement; *(Bank)* request for bank statement.

Kontoüberziehung *f*   account overdraft; overdrawn account.

Kontrakt *m*   contract.

Kontrast *m*   contrast.

Kontrollbildschirm *m*   monitor.

Kontrolle *f*   control; *(Prüfung)* examination; *(Aufsicht)* supervision; *(Überwachung)* surveillance.

Kontrollgremium *nt*   supervisory body; supervisory committee.

kontrollieren   to control; *(prüfen)* to examine; to check; to inspect; *(beaufsichtigen)* to supervise.

Kontrollprodukt *nt*   reference product.

Konventionalstrafe *f*   stipulated damages.

konventionell   conventional.

Konvertibilität *f*   *(Währung)* convertibility.

konvertierbar   convertible.

Konvertierbarkeit *f*   convertibility.

Konzentration *f*   concentration.

konzentrieren   to concentrate.

Konzern *m*   trust; group; concern; conglomerate.

Konzernbilanz *f*   consolidated balance sheet.

Konzernfirma *f*   consolidated company.

Konzerngesellschaft *f*   subsidiary; affiliate.

Konzernüberweisung *f*   lateral transfer.

Konzernumsatz *m*   consolidated sales.

Konzession *f*   *(Verkaufsrecht)* license; franchise; *(banks)* charter.

konzessionieren   to license; to franchise.

Konzessionserteilung *f*   licensing; franchising.

Kooperation *f*   cooperation.

kooperativ   cooperative.

Koordination *f*   coordination.

koordinieren   to coordinate.

koordinierte Zusammenarbeit *f*   teamwork.

Koordinierung *f*   coordination.

Kopie *f*   double; copy.

kopieren   to duplicate; to copy.

Korb *m*   basket.

Körperbehinderte *m/f*   physically handicapped person.

Körperschaft *f*   corporation.

körperschaftlich   corporate.

Körperschaftsgründung *f*   incorporation.

korrekt   correct.

Korrektur *f*   correction.

Korrekturbogen *m*   proof sheet.

Korrespondent *m*   correspondent.

Korrespondenz *f*   correspondence.

Korrespondenzbank *f*   correspondent bank.

Korrespondenzbüro *nt*   news agency.

korrespondieren   to correspond.

korrupt   corrupt.

Korruption *f*   corruption.

kostbar   precious.

kosten   to cost; *(Essen)* to sample.

Kosten *pl*   cost(s); expense(s); *(Gebühr)* charge; *(Preis)* price.

Kostenaufwand *m*   expenditure; expense; outlay.

Kostenbeschränkung *f*   cost containment.

kostendeckend arbeiten   to break even.

243

Kosteneinsparung *f* cost cutting; cost saving.
Kostenentwicklung *f* cost trend.
Kostenerhöhung *f* cost increase.
Kostenersparnis *f* cost savings.
Kostengliederung *f* cost structure.
kostengünstig cost-efficient.
Kostenkalkulation *f* estimation of cost.
Kostenkontrolle *f* cost control.
Kostenkurve *f* cost curve.
kostenlos free; free of cost; free of charge.
Kostennachteil *m* cost disadvantage.
kostenorientierte Preisbildung *f* cost-based pricing.
Kostenprüfer *m* controller.
Kostensatz *m* cost schedule.
Kostensteigerung *f* cost increase.
Kostenüberschreitung *f* cost overrun.
Kostenüberwachung *f* cost control.
Kostenunterschied *m* cost differential.
Kostenvoranschlag *m* bid; estimated charges.
Kostenvorteil *m* price advantage; cost advantage.
kostspielig costly.
Kraft *f* power; *(Stärke)* strength; *(Krafteinwirkung)* force; *(Energie)* energy; *(Arbeitskraft)* worker.
Kraftfahrzeug *nt* motor vehicle.
Kraftwerk *nt* power plant.
Kredit *m* credit; *(Darlehen)* loan; *(Ansehen)* reputation; *(Kreditwürdigkeit)* credit rating; *(mit flexibler Verzinsung)* adjustable-rate loan.
Kreditanstalt *f* lending institution; credit association; loan bank.

Kreditaufnahme *f* borrowing.
Kreditausfall *m* loan default.
Kreditausschuß *m* loan committee.
Kreditbeschränkung *f* limitation of credit; credit contraction.
Kreditbeurteilung *f* credit rating.
Kreditbrief *m* letter of credit.
Kreditexpansion *f* credit expansion.
Kreditgeber *m* lender.
Kreditgenossenschaft *f* credit cooperative; credit union; cooperative savings organization.
Kreditgewährung *f* granting of credit; lending; loan approval.
Kreditgewerbe *nt* financial business; credit business.
Kreditgrenze *f* line of credit.
Kredithilfe *f* financial aid.
Kreditinstitut *nt* financial institution; credit institution.
Kreditinstrument *nt* financial instrument.
Kreditkarte *f* credit card; bank card.
Kreditkonditionen *pl* credit terms.
Kreditkonto *nt* loan account.
Kreditlinie *f* line of credit.
Kreditmarkt *m* financial market; money and capital markets.
Kreditmultiplikator *m* credit multiplier.
Kreditnachfrage *f* demand for credit; loan demand.
Kreditnehmer *m* borrower.
Kreditor *m* creditor.
Kreditrahmen *m* line of credit.
Kreditrisiko *nt* credit risk.
Kreditrückzahlung *f* loan repayment.
Kreditsachbearbeiter *m* lending officer.
Kreditsumme *f* credit amount; loan amount.

Kredittilgung *f*   repayment of a loan; amortization.

Kreditversicherung *f*   credit insurance; bad debt insurance; loan insurance.

Kreditvertrag *m*   credit agreement; loan agreement.

Kreditwesen *nt*   lending; financing.

Kreditwesengesetz *nt*   lending law.

kreditwürdig   financially sound; creditworthy.

Kreditwürdigkeit *f*   credit standing; credit.

Kreditzuwachs *m*   credit expansion.

Kreis *m*   circle; *(Bezirk)* district; *(Landkreis)* county; *(Gruppe)* group.

Kreislauf *m*   circulation; cycle.

Kreuz *nt*   cross.

Kreuzelastizität *f*   cross elasticity.

Krise *f*   crisis.

Krisenmanagement *nt*   crisis management.

Krisenplan *m*   crisis plan; crisis strategy.

Kriterium *nt*   criterion.

Kuchendiagramm *nt*   pie chart.

kultivieren   to cultivate.

Kultivierung *f*   cultivation.

Kultur *f*   culture.

kulturell   cultural.

kumulativ   cumulative.

Kumulierung *f*   accumulation.

Kunde *m*   customer; client; *(im Laden)* shopper; *(Verbraucher)* consumer.

Kundenbedürfnisse *pl*   customer needs.

Kundenberater *m*   customer service representative.

Kundenberatung *f*   customer service.

Kundenbesuch *m*   business call; sales call; calling on customers.

Kundendepot *nt*   custodianship account.

Kundendienst *m*   customer service.

Kundendienstbüro *nt*   customer service office.

Kundenetat *m*   *(Werbung)* account.

Kundenfang *m*   canvassing.

Kundenforderungen *pl*   *(Bilanz)* accounts receivable; receivables.

Kundengeschäft *nt*   transaction for third account.

Kundenkonto *nt*   trade account.

Kundenkredit *m*   consumer loan.

Kundenkreditbank *f*   consumer bank.

Kundenkreditgesellschaft *f*   consumer finance company.

Kundenkreditgewährung *f*   consumer lending.

Kundenservice *m*   customer service.

kündigen   to give notice; to cancel; *(Arbeitgeber)* to dismiss; *(Arbeitnehmer)* to resign; to quit; *(Vertrag)* to terminate; *(Obligationen)* to call in.

Kündigung *f*   notice; cancellation; *(Arbeitgeber)* notice of dismissal; *(Arbeitnehmer)* notice of resignation; *(Vertrag)* notice of termination; *(Anleihe)* notice of redemption; *(Obligationen)* calling in.

Kündigungsfrist *f*   period of notice; *(Bank)* withdrawal period.

Kündigungsschutz *m*   job protection.

Kundin *f*   customer; client; *(im Laden)* shopper; *(Verbraucher)* consumer.

Kundschaft *f*   customer base; clientele.
Kunstfaser *f*   synthetic fiber.
Kunstgriff *m*   maneuver; device.
künstlich   artificial; synthetic; manmade.
Kunststoff *m*   synthetic material; plastic material; plastics.
Kupon *m*   coupon; stub.
Kurs *m*   *(Aktien)* price; *(Währungskurs)* rate of exchange; *(Termingeschäft)* forward rate; *(Notierung)* quotation; *(Kursus)* course; *(Umlauf)* circulation.
Kursabschlag *m*   *(Terminhandel)* discount quotation.
Kursanstieg *m*   *(Aktien)* increase in prices; upward movement.
Kursaufschlag *m*   *(Terminhandel)* premium.
Kursblatt *nt*   daily quotations; stock-market report; stock-exchange price list.
Kursbuch *nt*   *(Eisenbahn)* schedule.
Kursdifferenz *f*   *(Devisen)* difference in exchange rate.

Kurseinbruch *m*   *(Aktien)* fall in stock prices.
Kursgewinn *m*   *(Börse)* market profit; stock price gain; *(Devisengeschäft)* exchange profit.
Kursnotierung *f*   quotation.
Kursschwankung *f*   *(Devisen)* exchange rate fluctuation; *(Börse)* price fluctuation.
Kurssicherung *f*   *(Termingeschäft)* forward guaranty.
Kurssturz *m*   *(Aktien)* stock market crash; plunging stock prices.
Kursus *m*   course.
Kurswert *m*   *(Aktien)* market value.
Kurszettel *m*   *(Börse)* stock market quotation.
Kurve *f*   curve.
kurz   short; brief.
Kurzarbeit *f*   reduced working hours.
kürzen   to cut; to reduce.
kurzfristig   short-run; short-term.
Kürzung *f*   cut; reduction; decrease; *(Buch)* abridgment; condensation.

Labor *nt*   laboratory.
Laboratorium *nt*   laboratory.
Laden *m*   shop.
Ladenbesuch *m*   shopping.
Ladenpassage *f*   shopping mall.
Ladenreihe *f*   shopping mall.
Ladenschluß *m*   shop closing time; shutting up shop.
Ladenschlußgesetz *nt*   shop closing law.

Ladenstraße *f*   shopping mall.
Ladenverkauf *m*   retail sales.
Laderaum *m*   hold; *(Kapazität)* freight capacity.
Ladeverzeichnis *nt*   manifest.
Ladung *f*   load; cargo; *(Lieferung)* shipment; *(Fracht)* freight.
Lage *f*   situation; position; *(Geog.)* locality; *(Zustand)* condition; state.

Lager *nt* *(Inventar)* stock; *(Gebäude)* warehouse.
Lageraufstockung *f* replenishing stocks.
Lagerbestand *m* stock on hand; inventory.
lagerfähig storable; stockable.
Lagerhaltung *f* stock-keeping; warehousing.
Lagerkosten *pl* storage cost.
lagern *(Aufbewahrung)* to store; *(Inventar)* to stock.
Lagerraum *m* storeroom.
Lagerräumung *f* clearance.
Lagerung *f* *(Aufbewahrung)* storage; *(Inventarhaltung)* stocking.
Lagerverwaltung *f* inventory management.
Lagerwirtschaft *f* stock management; just-in-time inventory keeping.
lahmlegen to paralyse; *(boykottieren)* to boycott; *(sperren)* to block.
Lahmlegung *f* stoppage; boycott; blocking.
Laie *m* layman.
Land *nt* land; country.
landen to land.
Ländereien *pl* acreage; real estate.
Landeswährung *f* national currency.
Landkarte *f* map.
Landstrich *m* area; zone.
Landwirt *m* farmer.
Landwirtschaft *f* agriculture.
landwirtschaftlich agricultural; agrarian.
landwirtschaftliches Erzeugnis *nt* agricultural product.
langen to be sufficient.
längerfristig medium-term.
lange Sicht *f* long term.

langfristig long-term.
langjährig for many years; of long standing.
langlebig long lived; *(Güter)* durable.
langlebige Gebrauchsgüter *pl* durable goods.
langsam slow.
langsamer werdend slowing.
langsames Wachstum *nt* slow growth.
lassen to let; to allow.
Last *f* load; burden.
lasten auf to be a burden on.
Laster *m* large truck; trailer truck.
Lastschrift *f* debit entry; debit advice.
Lastwagen *m* truck.
Lauf *m* run; *(Gewehr)* barrel.
Laufbahn *f* career.
laufen to run.
laufend current; running; *(routinemäßig)* routine; *(gültig)* valid.
laufende Transferzahlungen *pl* current transfer payments.
laufendes Konto *nt* current account; demand deposit account.
Läufer *m* messenger.
Laufspanne *f* *(Mech.)* travel.
Laufzeit *f* duration.
laut loud; *(Zitat)* per.
lavieren to maneuver; to tack.
leasen to lease.
Leasing *nt* leasing.
Leasinggeschäft *nt* leasing business.
Leasinggesellschaft *f* leasing company.
Leasingmiete *f* leasing charge.
Leasingrate *f* leasing rate.
lebend living.
lebendig *(am Leben)* alive; *(lebhaft)* lively.

Lebensalter *nt* age.
Lebensarbeitszeit *f* working life.
Lebensbedarf *m* *(Unterhalt)*
means of subsistence; *(lebens-
länglicher Bedarf)* lifetime
demand.
Lebensbedingungen *pl* living
conditions.
Lebensdauer *f* life span.
Lebenserwartung *f* life expectancy
lebensfähig viable.
Lebensfähigkeit *f* viability.
Lebensführung *f* lifestyle.
Lebenshaltung *f* standard of liv-
ing.
Lebenshaltungskosten *pl* cost of
living.
lebenslängliche Anstellung *f* life-
time employment.
Lebenslauf *m* resume; curriculum
vitae; vita.
Lebensmittel *pl* groceries; *(Nahrungsmittel)* foodstuffs; *(Vorrat)*
provisions.
Lebensmittelhändler *m* grocer.
Lebensmittelladen *m* grocery
store.
Lebensqualität *f* quality of life.
Lebensstandard *m* standard of living.
Lebensunterhalt *m* livelihood; living.
Lebensverhältnisse *pl* living conditions.
Lebensversicherer *m* life insurer.
Lebensversicherung *f* life insurance.
Lebensversicherungsgesellschaft *f*
life insurance company.
lebenswichtig vital.
lebhaft lively; active.
leer empty; *(unbewohnt)* vacant;
(unbeschrieben) blank.

Leerlauf *m* neutral gear.
leerlaufen to idle.
legal lawful.
lehnen to lean.
Lehre *f* apprenticeship; *(Theorie)*
theory.
Lehre *f* **vom Warenabsatz** *m* marketing.
Lehrling *m* apprentice.
Lehrsatz *m* doctrine; theorem.
Lehrstelle *f* apprenticeship position.
Lehrstellenangebot *nt* apprenticeship offer.
leicht easy; *(Gewicht)* light.
Leichtigkeit *f* ease; facility.
leicht zu bewältigen easily manageable.
leihen to lend.
leisten to achieve; *(Dienst)* to render; *(ausführen)* to perform.
Leistung *f* achievement; accomplishment; *(Ausführung)* performance; *(Kapazität)* power; output;
(Sozial-, Nebenleistung) benefit;
(Produktion) production.
Leistungsabgabe *f* *(Elek.)* power
output.
Leistungsaustausch *m* *(Güter)*
exchange of goods; *(Dienste)*
exchange of services.
Leistungsbilanz *f* current accounts
balance.
leistungsfähig *(produktiv)* productive; *(effizient)* efficient;
(gebrauchsfähig) serviceable.
Leistungsfähigkeit *f* *(Produktivität)* productivity; *(Effizienz)* efficiency; *(Gebrauchsfähigkeit)* ser-
viceability; *(Kapazität)* capacity.
Leistungsgesellschaft *f* meritocracy.
leistungsmäßig übertreffen to
outperform.

Leistungsstärke *f* *(Kapazität)* capacity; *(Produktivität)* productivity; *(finanziell)* solvency.
leistungsunfähig unproductive; inefficient.
leiten to manage; *(führen)* to head; to direct.
leitend managing; executive.
Leiter *m* leader; manager; *(Chef)* head; chief.
Leitfaden *m* guide.
Leitlinie *f* *(Verkehr)* demarcation line.
Leitung *f* leadership; *(Führung)* guidance; direction; *(Elek.)* circuit; *(Telefon)* line.
Leitungsstelle *f* executive position.
Leitwährung *f* lead currency; key currency.
Leitzins *m* prime rate.
lenken to direct; to channel; to control; *(regulieren)* to regulate; *(führen)* to head.
Lenkung *f* control; direction; *(Fahrzeug)* steering; *(Flugzeug)* navigation.
leugnen to deny.
Leumund *m* reputation.
liberal liberal.
liberalisieren to liberalize; *(freigeben)* to decontrol.
Liberalisierung *f* liberalization; *(Freigabe)* decontrol.
Lichtbild *nt* photograph.
Lieferabkommen *nt* delivery contract; supply agreement.
Lieferant *m* *(Händler)* vendor; provider; supplier; *(Quelle)* source; purveyor; *(Auftragnehmer)* contractor.
Lieferantenkredit *m* trade credit; supplier's credit.
Lieferer *m* supplier.

lieferfähig deliverable.
Lieferfirma *f* supplier.
Lieferland *nt* procurement country.
liefern to deliver; *(versenden)* to ship.
Lieferposten *m* shipment; lot.
Liefersperre *f* delivery stop.
Lieferung *f* *(Posten)* shipment; *(Auslieferung)* delivery.
Lieferungsangebot *nt* bid; tender.
Liefervertrag *m* supply contract; *(Auslieferung)* delivery contract.
Lieferwagen *m* delivery van.
Lieferzeitplan *m* delivery schedule.
Limit *nt* limit; stop order.
limitieren to limit.
Limitkurs *m* limited price.
lindern to mitigate.
Linie *f* line; *(Kredit)* limit; line.
Liquidationswert *m* liquidation value.
liquide liquid.
liquidieren to dissolve.
Liquidierung *f* liquidation.
Liquidität *f* liquidity.
Liquiditätsausweis *m* proof of liquidity.
Liquiditätsdruck *m* liquidity squeeze; cash squeeze.
Liquiditätsgrad *m* degree of liquidity.
Liquiditätshilfe *f* liquidity assistance.
Liquiditätslage *f* liquidity position; cash position.
Liquiditätspolitik *f* liquidity policy.
Liquiditätsproblem *nt* liquidity problem.
Liste *f* list; *(Tabelle)* table; *(Warenliste)* tally; catalog.
Listenpreis *m* list price.
Lizenz *f* license.

Lizenzabkommen *nt* license agreement.

Lizenzbetrieb *m* franchise business.

Lizenzgebühr *f* license fee; *(Urheberlizenz)* royalty payment.

Lizenzinhaber *m* licensee.

Lizenzvertrag *m* license contract.

Lobbyist *m* lobbyist.

lochen to punch; to perforate.

lockern to relax.

Lockerung *f* relaxation; liberalization.

Lohn *m* wage.

Lohnabkommen *nt* wage agreement.

Lohnausfall *m* loss of pay.

Lohnausgleich *m* wage adjustment.

lohnen to be profitable.

lohnen, sich to be worthwhile; to pay off.

Lohnerhöhung *f* pay raise.

Lohnforderung *f* wage demand.

Lohngefälle *nt* wage differential; wage fluctuation.

Lohngruppe *f* wage bracket.

Lohnkonto *nt* payroll account.

Lohnkosten *pl* labor costs.

Lohnnebenkosten *pl* cost of fringe benefits.

Lohnpolitik *f* wage policy.

Lohnquote *f* wage share; wage ratio.

Lohnrunde *f* wage negotiation talks.

Lohnsatz *m* wage rate.

Lohnsteigerung *f* pay raise.

Lohnsteuer *f* wage witholding tax; income tax.

Lohnstruktur *f* wage structure.

Lohnstückkosten *pl* unit labor cost.

Lohntarif *m* pay scale; wage rate.

Lohn- und Gehälterliste *f* payroll.

Lohn- und Gehaltsabrechnung *f* payroll accounting.

Lohnverhandlung *f* wage negotiation.

Lohnzahlung *f* payment of wages.

Lokalbank *f* local bank.

Lokalbehörde *f* local authority.

Lokalität *f* locality.

lombardieren to advance money on securities.

Lombardsatz *m* lombard lending rate.

löschen *(Waren)* to unload; *(Schuld)* to cancel; *(Computer)* to clear; *(Tonband)* to erase; *(Feuer)* to extinguish.

Löschen *nt* *(Waren)* unloading.

Löschung *f* *(Schuld)* cancellation.

lose loose.

lösen *(Problem)* to solve; *(Fahrkarte)* to buy.

loslösen *(Verbindung)* to dissociate; *(physisch)* to detach.

Lösung *f* solution.

Lotse *m* *(Schiff)* pilot.

Lücke *f* gap; *(Zwischenraum)* space; *(Leere)* void.

lückenhaft *(zeitmäßig)* intermittent; *(Information)* sketchy.

Luftfahrt *f* aviation.

Luftfahrtindustrie *f* aviation industry.

Luftfracht *f* air freight.

Luftpost *f* air mail.

Lufttransportgesellschaft *f* air carrier.

Luftverkehr *m* air traffic; *(Transport)* air transportation.

lukrativ lucrative.

luxuriös luxurious.

Luxus *m* luxury.

machen to make; to do; *(Obligation)* to incur; *(Zustand beeinflussen)* to render.

Machenschaft *f* ploy; scheme.

Macht *f* power; *(Einfluß)* pull; clout.

Machtbalance *f* balance of power.

Machtbefugnis *f* authority to act.

Machtgruppe *f* power group; *(Lobby)* lobby.

mächtig mighty; *(einflußreich)* powerful.

Machtkampf *m* power struggle.

Machtstellung *f* position of power.

Machtverteilung *f* distribution of power.

Magazin *nt* *(Speicher)* warehouse; *(Zeitschrift)* periodical; magazine.

mager meager; slender; lean.

Magnat *m* magnate.

Mahnbrief *m* reminder letter.

mahnen *(Zahlung, Leistung)* to remind.

Mahnschreiben *nt* demand note.

Mahnung *f* reminder.

Major *m* major.

Makler *m* broker; middleman.

Maklergeschäft *nt* brokerage.

Maklerstand *m* broker's pit.

Makroökonomie *f* macroeconomics.

Makroökonomik *f* macroeconomics.

makroökonomisch macroeconomic.

Mammuth *nt* mammoth.

Management *nt* management.

Managementfunktion *f* management function.

Manager *m* manager.

Mandant *m* *(Recht)* client.

Mandat *nt* mandate.

Mangel *m* *(Fehlen)* lack; *(Knappheit)* scarcity; shortage; *(Defekt)* fault; *(Unzulänglichkeit)* deficiency.

Mängelgarantie *f* warranty against defects.

mangelhaft *(unzulänglich)* insufficient; *(fehlerhaft)* faulty.

mangeln to be lacking.

mangelnde Beschäftigung *f* underemployment.

Manifest *nt* manifest.

Manipulator *nt* manipulator.

manipulieren to manipulate.

Manko *nt* *(Mangel)* deficit; *(Unzulänglichkeit)* deficiency.

mannigfaltig diverse; *(diversifiziert)* diversified; *(vielfach)* multiple.

Mannigfaltigkeit *f* diversity.

Mannschaft *f* team; *(Personal)* personnel.

Manöver *nt* maneuver.

manövrieren to maneuver.

Manteltarif *m* general wage agreement; master wage agreement.

Manteltarifvertrag *m* general wage agreement contract.

Mappe *f* *(Akten)* binder; *(Zeichnungen)* portfolio.

Marge *f* margin.

Mark *f* *(Währungseinheit)* mark.

Marke *f* brand; make.

Markenbezeichnung *f* brand description.

Markenerzeugnis *nt* brand name product.

Markenname *m* brand name.

Markenpiraterie *f* brand-name piracy.

Markenprodukt *nt* proprietary product.

Markenschutz *m* trademark protection.

Markenzeichen *nt* name brand; logo.

Marketing *nt* marketing.

Marketingabteilung *f* marketing department.

Marketingchef *m* marketing manager; marketing chief.

Marketingfachmann *m* marketing expert.

Marketingstratege *m*, **-strategin** *f* marketing strategist.

Marketingtest *m* marketing test.

markieren to mark; to designate.

Markieren *nt* marking.

Markt *m* market; marketplace.

Marktanalyse *f* market anlaysis.

Marktanteil *m* market share.

Marktaufschwung *m* market upturn.

Marktbedingung *f* market condition.

marktbeherrschendes Unternehmen *nt* monopoly enterprise.

Marktbeherrschung *f* market dominance; market domination.

Marktbreite *f* *(dimension)* market reach; market spectrum.

Marktbude *f* market stall.

Marktchance *f* market opportunity.

Marktdaten *pl* market data.

Markteinwirkungen *pl* market forces.

Markterkundung *f* market survey; market test.

marktfähig marketable.

Marktforscher *m* market researcher.

Marktforschung *f* market research.

Marktführer *m* market leader.

marktgängig marketable.

Marktgängigkeit *f* marketability.

Marktgebiet *nt* market area.

Marktgegebenheit *f* market factor.

Marktgeschehen *nt* market action.

Marktgleichgewicht *nt* market balance.

Marktgröße *f* market size.

Marktkonstellation *f* state of the market.

Marktkräfte *pl* market forces.

Marktlage *f* market position; *(Zustand)* market condition.

Marktleistung *f* market performance.

Marktlücke *f* market gap; market niche.

Marktmechanismus *m* market mechanism.

Marktnachfrage *f* market demand.

Marktnische *f* market niche.

Marktordnung *f* organization of the market.

marktorientiert market-oriented.

Marktposition *f* market position.

Marktpreis *m* market price; market rate.

Marktprinzip *nt* market principle.

Marktregulierung *f* market regulation.

marktreif market-ready.

Marktsättigung *f* market saturation.

Marktschaffung *f* creating a market.

Marktsegment *nt* market segment.

Marktstellung *f* market position.

Marktstrategie *f* marketing strategy.

Marktstruktur *f* market structure.

Marktteil *m* market sector.

Markttest *m* market test.

Marktumfang *m* market scope; market size.

Marktuntersuchung *f* market analysis; market research.

Marktverhalten *nt* market behavior.

Marktvolumen *nt* market volume.

Marktwirtschaft *f* market economy.

Marktwirtschaftler *m* market economist.

Marktziel *nt* market objective.

Marktzinssatz *m* market rate of interest; going rate of interest.

Marktzugang *m* market access.

Maschine *f* machine.

maschinell mechanical.

maschinell bearbeiten to machine.

maschinelle Anlage *f* machinery.

Maschinenanlage *f* machinery.

Maschinenbau *m* mechanical engineering.

Maschinenbauer *m* mechanical engineer.

Maschineneinsatz *m* deployment of machines.

Maschinenfabrik *f* machine works; engineering works.

Maschinenhaus *nt* powerhouse.

Maß *nt* *(Volumen)* volume; *(Hohlmaß)* measure; *(Messung)* measurement.

Masse *f* mass; matter; bulk.

Massenabsatz *m* wholesale.

Massenentlassung *f* mass layoff; mass dismissal.

Massenfertigung *f* mass production.

Massengeschäft *nt* high-volume business; bulk transaction.

Massengut *nt* bulk commodity.

massenhaft en masse; in large quantity.

Massenkonsum *m* mass consumption.

Massenmarkt *m* mass market.

Massenmedien *pl* mass media.

Massenprodukt *nt* mass product.

Massenproduktion *f* mass production.

maßgeblich authoritative; leading.

maßgebliche Person *f* policymaker.

mäßig moderate; modest.

massig bulky; massive.

mäßigen to moderate; to mitigate.

Mäßigung *f* moderation.

massiv massive.

Maßnahme *f* provision; measure.

Maßregel *f* measure.

Maßstab *m* scale.

Maßstab *m* **festlegen** to scale.

maßvoll measured; modest.

Mast *m* mast.

Mater *f* matrix.

Material *nt* material.

materialistisch materialistic.

Materialtransport *m* materials handling.

Materie *f* matter.

materiell physical; material.

materielle Güter *pl* tangible goods.

Matrixführung *f* matrix management.

Matrize *f* matrix.

Mauserei *f* pilferage.

maximieren to maximize.

Maximierung *f* maximization.

Maximum *nt* maximum.

Mechanik *f* mechanics.

Mechaniker *m* mechanic; *(Reparatur)* repairman, -person, -woman.
mechanisch mechanical.
Mechanisierung *f* mechanization.
Mechanismus *m* mechanism.
Medien *pl* media.
Mediengesetz *nt* media law.
Medienmagazin *nt* media magazine.
Medienverflechtung *f* interrelation of media.
Medium *nt* medium.
Meeresenge *f* narrows; *(Sund)* sound.
Mehraufwand *m* extra cost.
Mehrausgabe *f* additional expenditure.
mehren to increase in quantity.
Mehrerlös *m* *(Verkauf)* additional proceeds; *(Verdienst)* extra earnings.
mehrfach multiple.
Mehrheit *f* majority.
mehrheitlich by majority.
Mehrheitsaktionär *m* majority stockholder.
Mehrheitsbesitz *m* majority ownership.
Mehrheitsbeteiligung *f* majority interest; controlling interest.
Mehrwert *m* value added.
Mehrwertsteuer *f* value-added tax.
Meineid *m* ' perjury.
meinen *(Bedeutung)* to mean; *(Aussage)* to state; *(Meinung sagen)* to opine.
Meinung *f* opinion.
Meinung *f* **ändern** to change [one's] mind.
Meinungsänderung *f* change of mind.
Meinungsaustausch *m* exchange of views.

Meinungsbildung *f* opinion making; opinion formation.
Meinungsforschung *f* opinion research.
Meinungspflege *f* public relations.
Meinungsumfrage *f* opinion survey; opinion poll.
Meinungsverschiedenheit *f* *(Unterschied)* difference of opinion; *(Differenz)* disagreement.
Meister *m* master.
meistern to master.
Meistern *nt* mastery.
Meldebestimmung *f* registration ordinance.
Meldepflicht *f* compulsory registration.
meldepflichtig subject to registration.
Meldevorschrift *f* registration instruction.
Meldung *f* report; return.
Melodie *f* melody; tune.
Memorandum *nt* memorandum.
Menge *f* *(Quantität)* quantity; amount; *(Posten)* lot; *(Aufstellung)* array; *(Masse)* bulk.
Mengenanpassung *f* quantity adjustment.
Mengeneinheit *f* unit of quantity.
Mengengeschäft *nt* *(Handel, Unternehmen)* volume business; *(Transaktion)* volume transaction.
Mengenindex *m* quantitative index.
mengenmäßig quantitative.
Mengenrabatt *m* volume discount.
Menschenführung *f* human resources management; personnel management.
menschlich human; *(human)* humane.

menschliche Arbeitskraft *f* manpower.

Merkantilismus *m* mercantilism.

Merkmal *nt* *(Zeichen)* sign; *(Markierung)* mark; *(Eigenschaft)* attribute; *(quantitativ)* key variable; characteristic.

meßbar measurable.

Meßbarkeit *f* measurability.

Messe *f* exposition; *(Ausstellung)* exhibition; fair; *(Kirche)* mass.

Messebeteiligung *f* participation in a fair.

Messegesellschaft *f* exhibition corporation.

Messeleitung *f* exhibition management.

messen to measure.

Messeplatz *m* fairground.

Meßgröße *f* indicator.

Meßinstrument *nt* measure; *(Richtmaß)* gauge; *(Zähler)* meter.

Meßtischblatt *nt* map.

Messung *f* measurement.

Metall *nt* metal.

Metallindustrie *f* metal industry.

Meter *m* meter.

Methode *f* method; technique.

metrisch metric.

Miet- rental.

Miete *f* rent; lease; hire.

Mieteinnahme *f* rental receipts.

mieten to rent; *(pachten)* to lease; *(Flugzeug, Jacht)* to charter.

Mieten *nt* renting; leasing; *(Flugzeug, Jacht)* chartering.

Mieter *m* lessee.

Mietertrag *m* rental income.

Mietherr *m* landlord.

Mietsteigerung *f* rent increase.

Mietvertrag *m* rental agreement; *(Pachtung)* lease agreement.

Mietwohnung *f* rented apartment.

Mietzins *m* rent.

Mikrochip *m* microchip.

Mikrocomputer *m* microcomputer.

Mikroelektronik *f* microelectronics.

Mikrofunktion *f* microfunction.

Mikrokultur *f* microculture.

Mikroökonomie *f* microeconomics.

Mikroökonomik *f* microeconomics.

Mikroprozessor *m* microprocessor.

Mikrorechner *m* microcomputer.

Mikrostruktur *f* microstructure.

Mikrotechnik *f* microtechnology.

Mikrowelle *f* microwave.

mildern to mitigate; to alleviate.

Militär- military.

Militär *nt* military.

militärisch military.

Millionär *m* millionaire.

Minderangebot *nt* underbid.

Minderausgabe *f* *(Kosten)* reduced expenditure; *(Wertpapiere)* underissue.

Minderheit *f* minority.

Minderheitsbeteiligung *f* minority participation.

Minderheitsgesellschafter *m* minority partner.

minderjährig under age; minor.

Minderjährige *m/f* minor.

Minderkonsum *m* reduced consumption.

mindern to reduce.

minderwertig inferior; *(Warenqualität)* cheap.

Mindestarbeitszeit *f* minimum working hours.

Mindesteinzahlungsbetrag *m* margin requirement; *(Konto)* minimum deposit.

Mindestgröße *f* minimum size.

Mindestmaß *nt* *(Menge)* minimum amount; *(Größe)* minimum size.

Mindestpreis *m* minimum price; floor price.

Mindestpreishöhe *f* minimum price level; price floor.

Mindestreserve *f* minimum reserves; *(Konto)* minimum balance requirement.

Mindestsicherung *f* minimum collateral.

Mindestzins *m* minimum interest.

Mine *f* mine.

Mineral *nt* mineral.

mineralisch mineral.

Minicomputer *m* minicomputer.

minieren to mine.

minimieren to minimize.

Minimum *nt* minimum.

Minister *m* *(Regierung)* secretary; *(BE)* minister.

Ministeramt *nt* *(Regierung)* department; *(BE)* ministry; *(Position)* ministerial post.

ministeriell ministerial.

Ministerium *nt* *(Regierung)* department; *(BE)* ministry.

Ministerpräsident *m* prime minister.

Ministerrat *m* council of ministers.

ministrieren to minister.

Minorität *f* minority.

Minute *f* minute.

mischen to mix.

Mischung *f* mix; mixture.

mißachten to disregard.

Mißachtung *f* disregard.

Mißbilligung *f* disapproval.

Mißbrauch *m* abuse.

mißbrauchen to abuse.

mißbräuchlich abusive.

Mißerfolg *m* failure; disappointment.

Mißfallen *nt* dissatisfaction; disapproval.

Mißgriff *m* mistake.

mißlingen to fail.

Mißverhältnis *nt* disproportion.

Mißwirtschaft *f* mismanagement.

Mitarbeit *f* cooperation.

mitarbeiten to cooperate; to contribute one's services.

Mitarbeiter *m* *(Arbeitnehmer)* employee; *(Kollege)* co-worker; colleague.

Mitarbeiter *pl* *(Arbeitnehmer)* employees; *(Personal)* personnel.

Mitarbeiterförderung *f* personnel development.

Mitarbeiterzahl *f* number of employees.

mitbestimmen to codetermine; to take part in decision-making.

Mitbestimmung *f* codetermination.

Mitbewerber *m* *(Auftrag)* rival; *(Stellung)* coapplicant.

mitentscheiden to codecide.

Mitgesellschafter *m* fellow partner.

Mitglied *nt* member.

Mitgliederwerbung *f* membership campaign.

Mitgliederzahl *f* number of members.

Mitgliedsbuch *nt* membership roster; membership register.

Mitgliedschaft *f* membership.

Mitgliedsland *nt* member country.

Mitgründer *m* cofounder.

Mithöreinrichtung *f* wire-tapping device.

Mitinhaber *m* co-owner.

Mitsprache *f* *(Entscheidungsprozeß)* voice.

Mitte *f* middle; *(Zentrum)* center.

mitteilen to communicate; *(be-*

richten) to report; *(informieren)* to inform.

Mitteilung *f* communication; information; notification.

Mittel- middle; *(Durchschnitt)* average.

Mittel *nt* means; *(Ressource)* resource; *(Zahlung)* medium.

mittelbar indirect.

Mittelbeschaffung *f* procurement of funds.

Mittelbetrieb *m* medium-size enterprise.

Mittelbindung *f* freezing of funds.

mittelfristig medium-term.

mittelgroß mid-size.

mittelgroßer Computer *m* minicomputer.

Mittelpunkt *m* center.

Mittelsektion *f* midsection.

Mittelsmann *m* middleman; intermediary.

Mittelstand *m* middle class.

mittelständisch middle class.

Mittelteil *m/nt* midsection; center part.

Mittelverwendung *f* *(Zuwendung)* allocation of resources; *(Verwendung)* disposition of funds.

Mittelwert *m* mean value; mean.

mittelwertig median.

Mittelzufluß *m* influx of funds.

Mittler *m* mediator; agent.

mitwirken *(Teilnahme)* to participate *(Zusammenarbeit)* to cooperate.

mitwirkend participatory; *(bewirkend)* instrumental.

Mitwirkung *f* *(Teilnahme)* participation; *(Zusammenarbeit)* cooperation; *(Mittel)* instrumentality.

Mitwirkungsrecht *nt* right to participate; law of instrumentality.

mixen to mix.

Möbelspediteur *m* mover; moving company.

mobil mobile.

mobilisieren to mobilize.

Mobilisierung *f* mobilization.

Mobilität *f* mobility.

Mode *f* fashion; vogue.

Modell *nt* model; type.

modellieren to model.

Moderator *m* moderator.

moderieren to moderate.

modernisieren to modernize; to update.

Modernisierung *f* modernization.

Modifikation *f* modification.

modifizieren to modify.

Modifizierung *f* modification.

Modul *nt* module.

modular modular.

möglich possible; potential.

möglicher Bedarf *m* potential need; potential market.

Möglichkeit *f* *(Chance)* possibility; *(Gelegenheit)* opportunity; *(Potential)* potential.

möglichst groß darstellen to maximize.

möglichst klein darstellen to minimize.

monatlich monthly.

Monatsauszug *m* monthly statement of account.

Monatsbilanz *f* monthly balance; monthly balance sheet.

Monatsdurchschnitt *m* monthly average.

Monatsende *nt* month's end.

Monatsmitte *f* middle of the month.

Monatspauschale *f* flat monthly charge.

Monatsproduktion *f* monthly production.

Monatsrate *f* monthly rate.

Monatsverdienst *m* monthly earnings.

monetär monetary.

Monetarismus *m* monetarism.

Monetarist *m* monetarist.

Monopol *nt* monopoly.

Monopol *nt* **besitzen** have a monopoly.

Monopolbesitzer *m* monopolist.

monopolisieren to monopolize.

Monopolisierung *f* monopolization.

Monopolist *m* monopolist.

monopolistisch monopolistic.

monopolistischer Markt *m* captive market.

Monopolpreis *m* monopoly price.

Monopolproblem *nt* monopoly problem.

Montage *f* assembly.

Montagewerk *nt* assembly plant.

montieren to assemble; to rig.

Moratorium *nt* moratorium.

Motiv *nt* theme.

motivieren to motivate.

Motivierung *f* motivation.

Motorisierung *f* motorization; mechanization.

Motto *nt* motto; slogan.

mühsam laborious; strenuous.

Mulde *f* depression; trough.

Müll *m* waste.

multilateral multilateral.

multilaterales Abkommen *nt* multilateral agreement.

Multimillionär *m* multimillionaire.

multinational multinational.

multinationale Unternehmung *f* multinational company.

Multiplikator *m* multiplier.

mundgerecht machen to make palatable.

mündig of legal age; major.

Mündigkeit *f* majority; maturity.

mündlich verbal; oral.

Mundvorrat *m* provisions.

Münzamt *nt* mint.

Münze *f* *(Geldstück)* coin; *(Münzsystem, Prägung)* coinage.

Münzeneinziehung *f* demonetization.

Münzensammlung *f* coin collection.

Muße *f* leisure.

müßig idle.

Muster *nt* *(Probe, Exemplar)* sample; *(Vorbild, Schablone)* pattern.

Musterstück *nt* prime example; sample.

mutmaßlich presumable; *(wahrscheinlich)* probable.

Muttergesellschaft *f* parent company.

N

Nabe *f* hub.

Nachahmung *f* imitation; *(Ersatz)* substitute.

nach Bedarf *m* according to need; *(Nachfrage)* according to demand.

nachbestellen to reorder.

Nachbestellung *f* reorder.

Nachdruck *m* *(Neudruck)* reprint; *(Betonung)* emphasis; *(Beharrlichkeit)* insistence.

nachfolgend successive; *(anschließend)* subsequent.

Nachfolger *m* successor.

Nachforderung *f* *(Nachfrage)* additional demand; *(Forderung)* supplemental claim; *(Steuer)* back charge.

nachforschen *(Erkundigung)* to inquire; *(Forschung)* to research.

Nachforschung *f* inquiry.

Nachfrage *f* *(ökon.)* demand.

Nachfrageausweitung *f* expansion of demand.

Nachfragefunktion *f* demand function.

nachfragen to inquire.

Nachfrageprognose *f* demand forecast.

Nachfragetheorie *f* demand theory.

Nachfragevorhersage *f* demand forecast.

Nachfragezuwachs *m* demand growth.

nachgeben to yield; to give in.

nachgiebig yielding; soft.

nach Größe *f* **geordnet** ordered by size.

nachhaltig enduring; *(hartnäckig)* persistent.

Nachholbedarf *m* pent-up demand.

Nachholeffekt *m* catch-up effect.

nachholen *(Mangel)* to make up.

Nachkriegs- postwar.

Nachkriegszeit *f* postwar period.

Nachlaß *m* estate.

nachlassen to weaken; to slacken; *(Rabatt)* to give a rebate.

Nachlassen *nt* weakening; slowdown.

nachlassend sagging.

nachlässig negligent.

nachprüfen to check; *(untersuchen)* to investigate.

Nachprüfung *f* check; *(Untersuchung)* investigation.

nachrechnen to recompute; to recalculate; *(prüfen)* to check.

Nachricht *f* news; message.

Nachrichten *pl* news.

Nachrichtenmagazin *nt* news magazine.

nachschicken to send on; *(Post)* to forward.

nachschießen to make additional payment; *(auf Aktien)* to pay a further call; *(Effektenlombard)* to call for additional cover.

nachsenden to forward.

nachtanken to refuel.

Nachteil *m* disadvantage; *(Schaden)* detriment; loss.

nachteilig disadvantageous; adverse.

nachträglich after the fact; *(ergänzend)* supplementary.

Nachtragsetat *m* supplementary

budget; *(Zuweisung)* supplementary appropriation; *(Ergänzung)* deficiency bill.

Nachtragshaushalt *m* supplementary budget; supplementary appropriation; deficiency bill.

Nachverkäufe *pl* repeat business.

nachwachsend renewable.

Nachweis *m* proof; *(Beweis)* evidence.

nachweisen to prove.

Nachwuchskraft *f* junior staff member; trainee.

nachzählen to check; to tally.

Nadelspitze *f* pin point.

nagelneu brand new; in mint condition.

nahebringen to bring close; to approximate.

nahekommen to approach.

nähern, sich to approach.

Näherungswert *m* approximation.

Nahzug *m* local train.

Namensaktie *f* registered share of stock; personal share.

Namensschild *nt* name plate.

Namenszug *m* signature.

Nationalbank *f* national bank.

Nationalbudget *nt* national accounts budget.

Nationalökonom *m* political economist.

Nationalökonomie *f* national economy; macroeconomics.

Nationalvermögen *nt* national wealth.

naturalisieren to naturalize.

Naturalisierung *f* naturalization.

natürlich natural.

Neben- by-; auxiliary; lateral.

Nebenamt *nt* *(Posten)* secondary

appointment; *(Geschäftsstelle)* auxiliary office.

nebenamtlich extraofficial.

Nebenbedingung *f* additional condition; *(Kontrakt)* secondary clause.

nebenberuflich extraprofessional.

Nebenkosten *pl* auxiliary cost; additional expense.

Nebenleistung *f* *(Lohn, Gehalt)* fringe benefit.

Nebenprodukt *nt* *(zusätzliches Produkt)* sideline; *(Abfall, Abfallprodukt)* by-product.

nebensächlich secondary.

Nebenvertrag *m* subcontract.

negoziieren to negotiate.

Negoziierung *f* negotiation.

neigen to lean; *(Tendenz)* to tend.

Neigung *f* *(Tendenz)* tendency; *(Trend)* trend; *(Geneigtheit)* predisposition.

Nennbetrag *m* face amount; nominal amount.

nennen to call; to name.

Nennwert *m* par; par value; face value.

Nennwert *m* **einer Banknote** *f* denomination.

netto net.

Nettoanteil *m* equity.

Nettoanteil *m* **der Aktionäre** *pl* shareholders' equity.

Nettoeinkommen *nt* net income.

Nettoersparnis *f* net savings.

Nettoertrag *m* net earnings.

Nettoinvestition *f* net investment.

Nettokapital *nt* net capital.

Nettokapitalexport *m* net capital export.

Nettokurs *m* *(Währung, Wertpapier)* price.

Nettopreis *m*   net price.
Nettorendite *f* **auf das Anlagever-
mögen** *nt*   net return on assets.
Nettoreserve *f*   net reserves.
Nettosozialprodukt *nt*   net
national product.
Nettoüberschuß *m*   net surplus.
Nettoverkaufserlös *m*   net sales
earnings.
Nettoverkaufspreis *m*   net sales
price.
Nettoverlust *m*   net loss.
Nettowarenpreis *m*   net commod-
ity price; net price of goods.
Nettowert *m*   net worth.
Nettozunahme *f*   net increase.
Nettozuschuß *m*   net allowance;
(Beitrag) net contribution; *(Staat)*
net subsidy.
Netz *nt*   network; net.
Netzplan *m*   network.
Netzwerk *nt*   network; mesh.
Neuabschätzung *f*   reappraisal.
Neuabschluß *m*   new contract; new
business.
Neuanlage *f*   *(Fabrik)* new plant;
(Geld) reinvestment.
neu anpassen   to readjust.
Neuanschaffung *f*   new acquisi-
tion; *(Kauf)* new purchase; *(Bank)*
new procurement.
neu ansetzen   to reschedule.
Neuauflage *f*   reprint.
neu auflegen   *(Veröffentlichung)*
to reissue; *(Anleihe)* to refloat.
neu aufstellen   *(neu errechnen)* to
recalculate.
Neuaufstellung *f*   realignment;
(Errechnung) recalculation.
neu ausbilden   to retrain.
Neuausbildung *f*   retraining.
neu ausrichten   to realign.

Neuausrichtung *f*   *(Unterneh-
mensziel)* redirection; *(Mech.)*
realignment.
neu bedenken   to rethink; to
reconsider.
neu beleben   to revitalize.
neu bereitstellen   to reallocate; to
recommit.
neu bestätigen   to reconfirm.
neu bestellen   to reorder.
Neubestellung *f*   reorder.
neu bewerten   to reevaluate; to
revalue; *(Schätzungswert)* to reappraise.
Neubewertung *f*   reappraisal.
neu binden, sich   to recommit.
neu drucken   to reprint.
neue Arbeitskraft *f*   new
employee; new recruit.
Neueinsatz *m*   new deployment.
neu einsetzen   to redeploy.
Neueinstellung *f*   new appointment.
neu einstufen   to reclassify.
Neueinstufung *f*   *(Klassifizierung)*
new classification; *(Steuer)*
reassessment.
neu einteilen   to reapportion;
(Zeit) to reschedule.
Neueinteilung *f*   *(Anordnung)*
rearrangement; *(Klassifizierung)*
reclassification.
Neueinteilung *f* **der Produktionszeit** *f*   rescheduling.
Neueintritt *m*   reentry; new entry;
(Zulassung) readmittance.
Neuengagement *nt*   new engage-
ment.
Neuentwicklung *f*   new development.
Neuerung *f*   innovation.
Neuerungen *pl* **einführen**   to
innovate.

neuerungsbereit   innovative.
neu erwägen   to reconsider.
Neuerwägung f   reconsideration.
Neuerwerbung f   new acquisition.
neu etablieren   to reestablish.
neu fassen   to reformulate; to rewrite.
Neufassung f   *(Dokument)* revision; *(Gesetz)* amendment.
neu festlegen   to reestablish.
Neufinanzierung f   refinancing; recapitalization.
neu floaten   to refloat.
Neugeschäft nt   new business; new deal.
neu gestalten   to redesign; to reshape.
Neugestaltung f   reorganization; reform.
neu gliedern   to restructure.
Neugliederung f   restructuring.
neu gründen   to reestablish; *(Unternehmen)* to reconstruct; to reorganize.
Neugründung f   reestablishment; *(Unternehmen)* reconstruction; reorganization.
neu gruppieren   to rearrange; to regroup.
Neuigkeit f   news.
neu informieren   to update.
Neukapitalisierung f   recapitalization.
neu klassifizieren   to reclassify.
Neuklassifizierung f   reclassification.
Neukredit m   new credit; new advance.
Neuling m   newcomer; *(Lehrling)* apprentice.
neumodisch   newfangled.
Neuordnung f   rearrangement; reform; reorganization.

Neuplazierung f   repositioning.
neuproduziert   newly produced; produced again; re-produced.
Neuregelung f   readjustment; revision; rearrangement.
neureich   newly rich; nouveau-riche.
neu schätzen   to reestimate; to revalue.
neutral   neutral.
Neutralität f   neutrality.
Neuverhandlung f   renegotiation.
Neuvermögen nt   new wealth; *(Aktiva)* new assets; *(Kapital)* new funds.
neu verpflichten   to reobligate; to recommit.
Neuverschuldung f   new indebtedness.
neu verteilen   to reallot; to reallocate; to redistribute.
Neuverteilung f   redistribution.
Neuzulassung f   readmission; *(Registrierung)* new registration.
neu zusammenstellen   to regroup; to reassemble.
neu zuteilen   to reallocate.
Neuzuteilung f   reallocation.
Nichtanerkennung f **einer Schuld** f   debt repudiation.
nicht angelegt   uninvested.
nicht auf Gewinn m **gerichtet**   nonprofit.
nicht ausgegeben   *(Aktien)* unissued; *(Geld)* unspent.
nichtausgeschüttete Gewinne pl   retained earnings.
Nichtbank f   nonbank.
Nichtbefolgung f   noncompliance; nonobservance.
nicht befriedigen   to dissatisfy; *(enttäuschen)* to disappoint.
nicht beitreibbar   *(Schulden)* uncollectable.

nicht bereinigt unadjusted.

nicht eingerechnet not included; exclusive of.

nicht einhalten *(Vertrag)* to break.

Nichteinhaltung *f* default.

Nichteinlösbarkeit *f* inconvertibility.

nicht einträglich unprofitable.

nicht einziehbar uncollectable.

Nichterfüllung *f* non-fulfillment; non-performance; failure; default.

nicht erhältlich unavailable.

Nichtfachmann *m* layman; amateur.

Nichtfunktionieren *nt* malfunctioning.

nicht geschäftsmäßig unbusinesslike.

nicht gestatten to disallow.

nicht häufig infrequent.

nichtig void.

Nichtkonvertierbarkeit *f* inconvertibility.

nicht mehr aufnahmefähig saturated.

nicht originär derivative.

nichts nothing; nil.

nicht stark genug ausdrücken to understate.

nicht stimmberechtigt nonvoting.

nicht übereinstimmen to disagree.

Nichtübereinstimmung *f* disagreement.

nicht verfügbar unavailable.

nicht verkaufbar unsalable.

nicht verkauft unsold.

nicht verwendungsfähig unusable.

nicht verwirklicht unrealized.

nicht vollwertig substandard.

nicht wettbewerbsfähig not competitive.

nicht wettbewerbsorientiert non-competitive.

nicht zustimmen to dissent; *(Einspruch erheben)* to object.

niederdrücken to depress.

Niedergang *m* downgrade; fall.

niederlassen, sich to locate.

Niederlassung *f* location; establishment; *(Zweigstelle)* branch office.

Niederlegen *nt* **der Arbeit** *f* work stoppage; *(Streik)* sit-down strike.

niederschreiben to record.

niedrig low.

niedriger einstufen to downgrade.

Niedrigpreis *m* low price.

Niedrigstkosten *pl* lowest cost.

Niedrigstwert *m* lowest value.

Niedrigzinsphase *f* low interest period.

Nießbrauch *m* beneficial interest; *(Grundstück)* lifehold; usufruct.

Niete *f* *(Mech.)* rivet; *(Lotterie)* blank; *(fig.)* loser.

Nische *f* niche; slot.

Niveau *nt* level; standard; niveau.

nochmals bezahlen to repay.

noch nicht erledigt pending.

noch nicht reguliert unadjusted.

noch nicht vereinbart not yet settled.

nominal nominal.

Nominalwert *m* nominal value; face value; *(Aktien)* par value.

Nominalzins *m* nominal interest.

nominell nominal.

nominieren to nominate.

nonstop nonstop.

Norm *f* standard; norm.

normal normal; natural.

Normalabweichung *f* standard deviation.

Normaltarif *m*   general tariff; regular rate.

normativ   normative.

normen   to standardize.

normieren   to standardize.

normiert   standardized.

Normierung *f*   standardization.

Normung *f*   standardization.

Not-   emergency.

Not *f*   need; hardship.

Notar *m*   notary.

notariell   notarial.

Note *f*   note.

Notenbank *f*   central bank.

Notenbanksystem *nt*   central bank system.

Noteninstitut *nt*   central note-issuing bank.

Notfall *m*   case of need; *(unerwarteter Notfall)* emergency.

notfalls   in case of need; in an emergency.

Notgeld *nt*   *(Bon)* token; emergency funds.

notieren   *(aufschreiben)* to note; *(Börsenkurse)* to list; *(Börsenkurse, BE)* to quote.

notierter Kurs *m*   quoted price.

nötig   necessary.

nötigen   to obligate; to oblige; *(zwingen)* to coerce; to force.

Notiz *f*   note; memorandum.

Notizblock *m*   notepad.

Notlage *f*   emergency.

notwendig   necessary.

notwendigerweise   as a matter of necessity; necessarily.

Notwendigkeit *f*   necessity.

Novelle *f*   *(Gesetz)* amendment; *(lit.)* novella.

null   null; nil.

Null *f*   zero.

Nullkupon *m*   zero coupon.

Nullquote *f*   zero quota.

null und nichtig   null and void.

Nullzins *m*   zero interest.

numerieren   to number.

numerisch   numerical.

Nummer *f*   *(Bekleidung)* size; number.

Nummernschild *nt*   *(Auto)* license plate.

nur   only; just.

nur dem Namen *m* **nach**   in name only; nominal.

Nutzanwendung *f*   application; utilization.

nutzbar   usable; *(produktiv)* productive.

nutzen   to utilize; to use.

nützen   to be useful; to serve.

Nutzen *m*   usefulness; benefit; profit; gain; good; *(Vorteil)* advantage.

Nutzenindex *m*   *(Ertrag)* yield index; *(Gewinn)* profit index.

Nutzenmaximierung *f*   *(Kapital)* capital maximization.

Nutzentheorie *f*   utilization theory.

Nutzen ziehen aus   to profit from; to benefit from.

nützlich   useful; beneficial.

nutzlos   useless; futile.

Nutznießer *m*   beneficiary.

Nutzung *f*   utilization; *(Einkommen)* revenue; *(Ertrag)* yield.

Nutzungsdauer *f*   useful life; *(einer Maschine)* machine life.

Nutzwert *m*   amount of revenue.

Obdach *nt* shelter.
oben upstairs; overhead.
Oberbau *m* superstructure.
obere Betriebsführung *f* upper management.
oberflächlich superficial; *(unvollständig)* sketchy.
Oberhand *f* control; mastery.
oberste Betriebsführung *f* top management.
oberste Leitung *f* top management; top leadership.
Oberverkäufer *m* senior salesman.
objektiv objective.
Obligation *f* debenture; bond.
obligatorisch obligatory; mandatory; compulsory.
Obligo *nt* liability; engagement; commitment.
obsolet obsolete.
offen open; *(Buchführung)* receivable.
offenbaren to disclose.
offener Markt *m* open market.
offenkundig established.
offenlegen to disclose; to lay open.
Offenmarktpolitik *f* open market policy.
offenstehend *(Rechnung)* outstanding; owing.
öffentlich public.
öffentlich bekanntgeben to announce; *(publizieren)* to publicize; *(ankündigen)* to proclaim.
öffentlich bekanntmachen to publicize.
öffentliche Bekanntmachung *f* public announcement.

öffentliche Arbeiten *pl* public works.
öffentliche Erklärung *f* *(Ankündigung)* public declaration; *(Erläuterung)* public explanation.
öffentlicher Grundsatz *m* public principle.
öffentliche Zustimmung *f* public support.
Öffentlichkeit *f* public.
offerieren to tender; to offer.
Offerte *f* tender; quotation; offer; bid.
offiziell official; formal.
offiziell machen to make official; to formalize.
Offizier *m* officer.
öffnen to open.
Öffnungszeit *f* business hours; opening hours.
Offsetverfahren *nt* *(Druck)* offset printing.
Ökologie *f* ecology.
ökologisch ecological.
Ökonom *m* economist.
ökonometrisch econometric.
Ökonomie *f* economy.
ökonomisch economic.
Oligopol *nt* oligopoly.
Oligopolmodell *nt* oligopolistic model.
Oligopolproblem *nt* oligopoly problem.
Oligopolsituation *f* oligopolistic situation.
Oligopoltheorie *f* oligopolistic theory.
operieren to operate.

opponieren to oppose.
Opposition *f* opposition.
optieren to opt.
optimal optimal.
Optimalität *f* optimality.
Optimallösung *f* optimal solution.
Optimalplanung *f* optimal planning.
optimieren to optimize.
Optimierung *f* optimization.
Option *f* option; *(Bezugsrecht)* subscription.
Optionsanleihe *f* optional bond; convertible bond issue.
Optionshandel *m* option trading.
Optionsmarkt *m* options market.
Optionspreis *m* option price.
Optionsrecht *nt* option privilege.
Optionsschein *m* stock purchase warrant.
Order *f* order.
Orderbuch *nt* order book.
ordern to order.
Ordertätigkeit *f* ordering activity.
ordnen to order; *(regulieren)* to regulate; *(arrangieren)* to arrange; *(aufstellen)* to array.
Ordner *m* regulator; *(Dokumente)* file; *(Heftmappe)* binder.
Ordnung *f* order; *(Rang)* rank.
Ordnungsform *f* *(Anordnung)* arrangement form; *(Klassifizierung)* classification form.

ordnungsgemäß as required; proper.
Ordnungsgemäßheit *f* *(Legalität)* regularity.
Ordnungskriterium *nt* classification criterion.
ordnungsmäßig regular; orderly.
Ordnungsrahmen *m* regulation framework.
Ordnungsstrafe *f* fine.
Organ *nt* *(med.)* organ; institution.
Organisation *f* organization.
Organisationslehre *f* organization doctrine; corporate doctrine.
organisatorisch organizational.
organisieren to organize.
orientieren to orient.
Orientierung *f* orientation.
Orientierungsbudget *nt* draft budget.
Original *nt* original.
Ort *m* locality; place.
örtlich local.
örtlich festlegen *(lokalisieren)* to localize; *(bestimmen)* to locate.
Ortsbewohner *m* local inhabitant.
Ortsgebrauch *m* local custom.
Ortsverein *m* local association.
Output *m* output.
Outputpfad *m* output path.
Outputsteigerung *f* output increase; output boost.

P

Pachteinnahme *f* leasing receipts.
pachten to lease.
Pächter *m* lessee; *(Grundbesitz)* tenant.
Pachtgeld *nt* rent.
Pachtgrundstück *nt* leased property; leasehold.
Pachtsumme *f* lease amount.
Pachtung *f* leasehold; *(Pachten)* leasing.
Päckchen *nt* package; small parcel.
Packen *m* pack; *(Stapel)* pile; stack.
Packmaterial *nt* packing material.
Packung *f* package; pack.
Pädagogik *f* pedagogy.
pädagogisch pedagogical; educational.
Paket *nt* parcel; package.
Paketpreis *m* package price.
Panik *f* panic.
Panne *f* malfunction.
Papier *nt* paper; *(Dokument)* document; instrument.
Papierblock *m* writing pad.
Papierstreifen *m* paper tape.
Paragraph *m* paragraph; *(Gesetz)* section.
parallel parallel.
Parallele *f* parallel.
Parallelität *f* parallelism.
Pari *m* par value; parity.
Parität *f* par value; parity; equality.
Paritätswert *m* par value.
Park *m* park.
parken to park.
Parkplatz *m* parking area.
Partei *f* party.
parteilos without a party; neutral.
Parteilosigkeit *f* neutrality.

Partizipation *f* participation.
Partizipationsschein *m* share certificate.
Partner *m* partner; associate.
Partnerbank *f* correspondent bank.
Partnerinstitut *nt* associated establishment.
Partnerschaft *f* partnership.
parzellieren to subdivide.
Parzellierung *f* subdivision.
Passagier *m* passenger.
Passagiereinnahmen *f* passenger receipts; passenger revenue.
passen *(Bekleidung)* to fit; *(Arrangement)* to suit.
passend machen to fit; *(angleichen)* to match; to fit.
passend sein to match; to be appropriate.
Passierschein *m* pass.
passiv passive; *(Bilanz)* unfavorable.
Passiva *pl* liabilities.
Passivposten *m* liability item.
Passivsaldo *m* deficit.
Passivseite *f* *(Buchhaltung)* debit side.
Passivüberhang *m* *(Buchung)* debit carryover.
Passung *f* fit.
Patent *nt* patent.
Patentanmeldung *f* patent application.
Patentausnutzung *f* patent license.
Patentgebühr *f* patent fee.
patentierbar patentable.
Patentrecht *nt* patent law.
patentrechtlich geschützt proprietary; patent-protected.

Patentrechtsverletzung *f* patent infringement.
Patentrolle *f* patent registry.
Patentvergabe *f* patent licensing.
pauschal overall.
Pauschale *f* *(Preis)* package.
Pauschalpreis *m* flat rate; all-inclusive price.
Pech *nt* *(Teer)* pitch; bad luck.
pekuniär pecuniary.
Pendel- shuttle.
pendeln to swing; *(Berufsverkehr)* to commute.
Pendelzug *m* shuttle train.
Pension *f* *(Ruhegeld)* pension; *(Gasthaus)* boarding house.
Pensionär *m* pensioner.
pensionieren to retire; to pension off.
Pensionierung *f* retirement.
Pensionsfonds *m* pension fund.
Pensionskürzung *f* pension cut.
Pensionszahlung *f* *(Einkommen)* retirement pay; *(Zahlung)* pension payment; *(Leistung)* postemployment benefit.
per pro; *(nach)* according to.
perforieren to perforate.
Periode *f* period; *(Zyklus)* cycle.
periodisch periodic.
permanent permanent.
Person *f* person.
Personal *nt* personnel; *(Stab)* staff.
Personalabteilung *f* personnel department.
Personalaufwendung *f* personnel expenses; salaries and wages.
Personalaustausch *m* personnel exchange; personnel turnover.
Personalbesetzung *f* staffing.
Personalbestand *m* human resources; manpower.
Personalchef *m* personnel manager.

Personalcomputer *m* personal computer.
Personaldirektor *m* personnel director.
Personalkosten *pl* personnel expenses.
Personalleitung *f* personnel management.
personalmäßig versorgt fully staffed.
Personalpolitik *f* personnel policy.
Personalzuwachs *m* personnel growth.
Personengesellschaft *f* partnership.
persönlich personal; private; individual.
Persönlichkeit *f* personality.
Perspektive *f* perspective.
Pfand *nt* surety; pledge; collateral.
Pfandbrief *m* bond.
Pfandbriefbank *f* mortgage-lending institution; mortgage company.
Pfandbriefzentrale *f* mortgage bond clearing house.
Pfandrecht *nt* lien.
Pfennig *m* penny.
Pflege *f* care; nurture.
Pflegegeld *nt* care-giving cost; *(Vormundschaft)* guardian allowance.
Pflegekosten *pl* care-giving expenses; nursing expenses.
pflegen to nurse; *(Umgang)* to cultivate; *(Talent, Beziehung)* to nurture.
Pflegeversicherung *f* nursing insurance.
Pflicht *f* duty.
pflichtgemäß according to rule.
pflichtmäßig mandatory; compulsory.

Pflichtversicherung *f* compulsory insurance.

Pfund *nt* pound; *(Währung)* pound.

Phase *f* phase.

Philosophie *f* philosophy.

physisch physical.

physische Eigenschaft *f* physical property.

Pilot *m* pilot.

Pilotanlage *f* pilot installation.

Pilz *m* mushroom; *(Schimmel)* fungus.

pilzartig aufschießen to mushroom.

Pionier *m* pioneer.

plädieren to solicit; to plead.

Plädoyer *nt* plea.

Plan *m* plan; *(Schema, Intrige)* scheme; *(Programm)* program; *(Projekt)* project.

planen to plan; *(Zeit)* to schedule; *(Ziel)* to target.

Planen *nt* planning; *(Zeit)* scheduling.

Planer *m* planner; *(Zeit)* scheduler.

Planerstellung *f* plan development.

planmäßig according to plan; *(Zeit)* on schedule.

Planung *f* planning; *(Prognose)* projection.

Planungsaufgabe *f* planning task; planning project.

Planungsfehler *m* planning error.

Planungsmodell *nt* planning model.

Planungsprogramm *nt* planning program.

Planungsprozeß *m* planning process.

Planungstechnik *f* planning technique.

Planwirtschaft *f* planned economy.

Planziel *nt* target; *(Produktion)* planned output.

plastisch plastic.

Platzkurs *m* spot rate.

plazieren to place; to position.

Plazierung *f* placement.

pleite bankrupt; broke.

Pleitefirma *f* bankrupt company.

Pleitegeier *m* bankruptcy "vulture"; someone hoping to profit from another's bankruptcy.

Pleitewelle *f* wave of bankruptcies.

plötzlich ansteigen to rise suddenly; to spurt upwards.

plötzlich fallen to plunge suddenly.

plündernd predatory.

Pluszeichen *nt* plus sign.

Police *f* *(Versicherung)* policy.

Policenhändler *m* policy dealer; policy trader.

Politik *f* policy; politics.

Politik *f* **des freien Zugangs** *m* open-door policy.

Politiker *m* politician.

Politikwissenschaft *f* political science.

politisch political.

Polizist *m* police officer.

Polster *nt* bolster; cushion.

Pool *m* pool; *(Trust)* combine.

Popularität *f* popularity; vogue.

populär machen to popularize.

Portefeuille *nt* portfolio.

Portefeuilleberater *m* investment advisor.

Portefeuillechef *m* portfolio manager.

Portemonnaie *nt* change purse.

Portfolio *nt* portfolio.

Porto *nt* postage; postal rate.

Portokasse *f* *(Geld)* petty cash; *(Behälter)* petty cash box.

Portokosten *pl* cost of postage; postal charges.

Position *f* position.

positiv positive.

Post *f* *(Postsachen)* mail; *(Unternehmen)* post office.

postalisch postal.

Posten *m* *(Stellung)* position; *(Buchführung)* entry; item.

Postenkonto *nt* itemized account.

Postetat *m* postal budget.

Postexperte *m*, **-expertin** *f* postal expert.

Postfach *nt* post office box.

Postgiroguthaben *nt* postal account credit balance.

Postkunde *m* postal customer.

Postleitzahlbereich *m* zip code area.

Postsachen *pl* mail.

Postschalter *m* window; counter position.

Postscheckamt *nt* postal savings bank.

Postscheckguthaben *nt* postal checking account credit balance.

Postscheckkonto *nt* postal checking account.

Postversandliste *f* mailing list.

Postversandwerbung *f* direct mail advertising.

Potential *nt* potential.

potentiell potential.

potentieller Kunde *m* prospective customer.

potentieller Markt *m* potential market.

Präferenz *f* preference; *(Zoll)* most favored nation treatment.

prägen to stamp; to coin.

pragmatisch pragmatic.

Praktik *f* practice.

Praktikant *m* intern; trainee.

Praktiker *m* practitioner.

praktisch practical.

praktisches Wissen *nt* knowhow.

praktizieren to practice.

Prämie *f* *(Versicherung)* premium; *(Belohnung)* bonus.

Prämienfestsetzer *m* underwriter.

Prämienfestsetzung *f* rate making.

Prämienmarkt *m* options market.

Prämiensenkung *f* premium reduction.

Prämisse *f* premise.

präparieren to prepare.

präsentieren to present.

Präsentierung *f* presentation.

präservieren to preserve.

Präservierung *f* preservation.

Präsident *m* president; *(Vorsitzender)* chairman.

präsidieren to preside.

Praxis *f* practice; *(Brauch)* usage.

Präzedenzfall precedent.

präzise precise.

Präzision *f* precision.

Preis *m* price; *(Wettbewerb)* prize; *(Belohnung)* award.

Preis *m* **bei Sofortzahlung** *f* spot price.

Preis *m* **festsetzen** to set the price; to price.

Preis *m* **feststellen** to determine price; to price.

Preis *m* **unter dem Wert** *m* **ansetzen** to price below value; to underprice.

preisabhängig dependent on price.

Preisänderung *f* price change.

Preisänderungsrate *f* price change rate.

Preisangabe *f* price quotation.

Preisangebot *nt*   price quotation.
Preisanstieg *m*   price increase; price rise.
Preisaufschlag *m*   surcharge.
Preisaufschwung *m*   price rally.
Preisauftrieb *m*   price increase; rising price tendency.
Preisausschreiben *nt*   contest.
preisbereinigt   adjusted for price.
Preisbestandteil *m*   price component.
preisbestimmend   price-setting; *(Absprache)* price-fixing.
Preisbewußtsein *nt*   price consciousness.
Preisdämpfung *f*   price curb.
Preisdruck *m*   pressure of prices; pressure on the market because of prices.
Preiseffekt *m*   price effect.
preiselastisch   price-elastic.
Preiselastizität *f*   price elasticity.
Preisentwicklung *f*   price development; price trend.
Preiserhöhung *f*   price increase.
Preisforderung *f*   price demand; asking price.
preisgarantiert   price-guaranteed.
Preisgefüge *nt*   price structure.
preisgekrönt   prizewinning.
Preisgleichgewicht *nt*   balance of prices.
Preisherabsetzung *f*   markdown.
Preisheraufsetzung *f*   price raising.
Preishöhe *f*   price level.
Preisindex *m*   price index.
Preisinflation *f*   price inflation.
Preiskalkulation *f*   price calculation; pricing.
Preisklasse *f*   price range.
Preiskonkurrenz *f*   price competition.
preislich   with regard to price.

Preisliste *f*   price list.
Preismechanismus *m*   price mechanism.
Preisnachlaß *m*   price concession; rebate.
Preisniveau *nt*   price level.
Preispolitik *f*   pricing policy.
Preisraum *m*   price range; price margin.
Preisrelation *f*   price relationship.
Preisschild *nt*   price tag.
Preisschlacht *f*   price war.
Preisschlager *m*   best market price; popular price.
Preissenkung *f*   price cut.
Preissetzung *f*   price setting.
Preissignal *nt*   price signal.
Preisstabilität *f*   price stability.
Preissteigerung *f*   advance in prices; rise in prices.
Preissteigerungsrate *f*   rate of price increase.
Preissturz *m*   price slump.
Preisstützung *f*   price support.
Preissystem *nt*   pricing system.
Preistheorie *f*   pricing theory.
preistreibend   price-enhancing; price-raising.
Preistreiberei *f*   price rigging.
Preisüberhöhung *f*   price inflation.
Preisüberwachung *f*   price control.
Preisunsicherheit *f*   price uncertainty.
Preisunterbietung *f*   underselling; price cutting.
Preisunterschied *m*   price difference; price differential.
Preisverfall *m*   price deterioration.
Preisverhältnis *nt*   price relationship.
Preisvorteil *m*   price advantage.
preiswert   reasonably priced; inexpensive.

Preiswettbewerb *m*   price competition.

Preiswiderstand *m*   price resistance.

prekär   precarious.

Presse *f*   press.

Presseerklärung *f*   press statement.

Pressefotograf *m*   press photographer.

Pressegespräch *nt*   press conference; conversation with the press.

pressiert   rushed.

Prestige *nt*   prestige.

primär   primary.

Primärdaten *pl*   primary data.

Primärerzeugnis *nt*   primary product.

Primärverteilung *f*   primary distribution.

Prinzip *nt*   principle.

Priorität *f*   priority.

privat   private; personal.

Privatbank *f*   private bank.

Privatbankhaus *nt*   private banking establishment.

Privatbesitz *m*   private property.

Privateigentum *nt*   private property; personal effects.

Privateinkommen *nt*   personal income.

Privatentnahme *f*   personal draw.

privater Wirtschaftssektor *m*   private sector of the economy.

private Unternehmung *f*   private enterprise.

Privathand *f*   private ownership.

Privatindustrie *f*   private industry.

privatisieren   to privatize.

Privatisierung *f*   privatization.

Privatkonto *nt*   personal account; private ledger.

Privatkredit *m*   personal credit.

Privatplazierung *f*   private placement.

Privatverkauf *m*   private sale.

Privatvermögen *nt*   private property.

Privileg *nt*   privilege.

pro   per; for.

Probe *f*   test; *(Muster, Kostprobe)* sample.

probeweise   tentative; on a trial basis.

probieren   to sample; to try.

Problem *nt*   problem.

Problematik *f*   set of problems; complex of problems.

Problemkredit *m*   difficult credit; *(Anleihe)* problematic loan.

Produkt *nt*   product.

Produktänderung *f*   product change.

Produktangebot *nt*   product offering.

Produkteigenschaft *f*   product property; product feature.

Produktentwicklung *f*   product development.

Produktfälschung *f*   product counterfeiting; *(Nachahmung)* product imitation; *(Piraterie)* product piracy.

Produktgestaltung *f*   product design.

Produktgruppe *f*   product group; line of products.

Produktinnovation *f*   product innovation.

Produktion *f*   production; manufacture.

Produktionsanlage *f*   production facility; manufacturing facility.

Produktionsanteil *m*   production share.

Produktionsapparat *m*   production system; production network.

Produktionsausfall *m*   loss of production.
Produktionsausstattung *f*   production equipment.
Produktionsausstoß *m*   production output.
Produktionsbudget *nt*   production budget.
Produktionseinbuße *f*   production loss.
Produktionseinheit *f*   production unit.
Produktionsfähigkeit *f*   manufacturing capability.
Produktionsfaktor *m*   production factor.
Produktionsgesellschaft *f*   manufacturing company.
Produktionskapazität *f*   production capacity; manufacturing capacity.
Produktionsleistung *f*   production output.
Produktionsmenge *f*   production volume; production output.
Produktionsmethode *f*   production method.
Produktionsmittel *pl*   means of production; *(Investitionsgüter)* capital goods.
Produktionsplan *m*   manufacturing schedule.
Produktionspreis *m*   cost of production.
Produktionsprogramm *nt*   manufacturing program; production program.
Produktionsprozeß *m*   production process.
Produktionsrate *f*   production rate.
Produktionsschub *m*   production run.
Produktionsseite *f*   production side.

Produktionssektor *m*   production sector.
Produktionsstand *m*   production volume.
Produktionsstruktur *f*   production structure.
Produktionssystem *nt*   production system.
Produktionstheorie *f*   theory of production.
Produktionsverfahren *nt*   production process.
Produktionsvolumen *nt*   production volume.
Produktionsvorgang *m*   manufacturing operation; manufacturing process.
Produktionswachstum *nt*   production growth.
Produktionsweise *f*   method of production.
Produktionszeit *f*   production time.
Produktionszeitplan *m*   production schedule.
Produktionsziffern *pl*   production output data.
Produktionszweig *m*   product line.
produktiv   productive; *(Geistesarbeit)* prolific.
Produktivität *f*   productivity.
Produktkombination *f*   product combination.
Produktmenge *f*   product quantity.
Produktmischung *f*   product mixture.
Produktpalette *f*   product range; *(Auswahl)* product choice.
Produktqualität *f*   product quality.
Produkttest *m*   product test.
Produzent *m*   producer; manufacturer.
produzieren   to produce; to manufacture.

professionell   professional.
Profit *m*   profit; gain.
profitieren   to profit.
Profitinteresse *nt*   interest in profits.
Profitrate *f*   profit rate.
Prognose *f*   prognosis; *(Vorhersage)* forecast.
Prognosedaten *pl*   forecast data.
Prognosefehler *m*   forecasting error.
Prognosemethode *f*   forecasting method.
Prognostiker *m*   forecaster.
prognostizieren   to forecast; to prognosticate.
Programm *nt*   program.
Programm *nt* **gestalten**   to program.
Programmausrüstung *f*   *(Computer)* software.
Programmfinanzierung *f*   program financing.
programmieren   to program.
Programmierer *m*   programmer.
Programmiersprache *f*   programming language.
Programmierung *f*   programming.
Projekt *nt*   project.
Projektarbeit *f*   project; *(schriftliche Arbeit)* project paper.
Projektdurchführung *f*   project implementation; *(Ausführung)* project execution.
Projektfinanzierung *f*   project financing.
Projektion *f*   projection.
Projektkosten *pl*   project cost.
Projektleiter *m*   project leader.
projizieren   to project.
pro Kopf *m*   per capita.
Prokurist *m*   *(Stellvertreter)* proxy holder; *(Handlungsbevollmächtig-*

ter) person holding power of attorney.
prolongieren   to extend; to prolong.
Prolongierung *f*   extension; prolongation.
prominent   prominent.
Prominenz *f*   prominence.
prompt   prompt; expeditious.
Propaganda *f*   propaganda.
Propaganda *f* **machen**   to campaign.
Proportion *f*   proportion.
proratarische Zahlung *f*   prorated payment; progress payment.
Prospekt *m*   *(Broschüre)* pamphlet; *(Aktien)* prospectus.
Prospekte *pl*   literature.
prosperieren   to thrive.
Prosperität *f*   prosperity.
Protektion *f*   protection; *(Gönnerschaft)* patronage.
Protektionismus *m*   protectionism.
Protektionist *m*   protectionist.
protektionistisch   protectionist.
Protest *m*   protest.
Protokollführer *m*   recorder; recording secretary.
Prototyp *m*   prototype.
Proviant *m*   provisions.
Provision *f*   commission.
Provisionseinnahme *f*   commission earnings.
Provisionsertrag *m*   commission earnings.
Provisionsgebühr *f*   commission rate.
provisorisch   provisional.
Prozedur *f*   procedure; routine.
Prozent *nt*   percent.
prozentig   per cent.
Prozentpunkt *m*   percentage point.

Prozentrechnung *f*   percentage calculation.
Prozentsatz *m*   percentage.
prozentual   percental; percentaged.
prozentueller Umsatzanteil *m*
percentage share of sales.
Prozeß *m*   process; *(Gericht)* suit;
litigation.
prozessieren   to process; *(Gericht)*
to sue.
Prozessor *m*   processor.
Prüfanlage *f*   testing facility.
prüfen   *(testen)* to test; *(untersuchen)* to examine; *(inspizieren)*
to inspect; *(sondieren)* to probe;
(begutachten) to survey.
Prüfer *m*   examiner; inspector.
Prüfliste *f*   check list.
Prüfung *f*   test; examination;
inspection.

Publikum *nt*   *(Öffentlichkeit)* public; *(Zuschauer, Zuhörer)* audience.
Publikumsfonds *m*   public fund.
publizieren   *(bekanntmachen)* to
publicize; *(veröffentlichen)* to publish.
Publizität *f*   publicity.
Publizitätspflicht *f*   disclosure
obligation.
pumpen   to pump; *(Transport
durch Rohrleitung)* to pipe.
Punkt *m*   point; item.
pünktlich   punctual; prompt; on
time.
Punktsystem *nt*   point system.
Pyramide *f*   pyramid.
pyramidenförmige Anordnung *f*
pyramidal arrangement.

Qualifikation *f*   *(Befähigung)* qualification; *(Berechtigung)* eligibility.
qualifizieren   to qualify.
qualifiziert   *(befähigt)* qualified;
(berechtigt) eligible; fit.
Qualität *f*   quality; grade.
qualitativ   qualitative.
Qualitätskontrolle *f*   quality control.
Qualitätsnorm *f*   quality standard.
Qualitätsprodukt *nt*   quality product.
Qualitätsstandard *m*   quality standard.

Qualitätsvergleich *m*   quality com-
parison.
Quantität *f*   quantity.
quantitativ   quantitative.
Quartal *nt*   quarter.
Quartals-   quarterly.
Quartier *nt*   quarters.
Quelle *f*   source; *(Wasser)* spring.
quittieren   to acknowledge; to give
a receipt.
Quittung *f*   receipt.
Quote *f*   quota.
Quotenregelung *f*   quota control;
quota regulation.

Rabatt *m*   discount; rebate.
Rabatt gewähren   to rebate; to discount.
Radarantenne *f*   scanner.
Radius *m*   radius.
Raffinerie *f*   refinery.
raffinieren   to refine.
Rahmen *m*   framework.
Rampenlicht *nt*   spotlight.
Rand *m*   border.
Rang *m*   standing; rank; echelon.
rangieren   range; rank.
Rangordnung *f*   precedence.
Rangstufe *f*   grade; class.
rapide steigen   soar.
rapide zunehmend   soaring.
Rast *f*   rest.
rasten   to rest.
Rat *m*   council; advice; board.
Rate *f*   rate; installment.
raten   to advise.
Ratgeber *m*   counselor.
rationalisieren   streamline.
Ratschlag *m*   counsel; advice.
Rätselreklame *f*   advertising teaser.
rauben   to rob.
räuberisch   predatory.
Raum *m*   space; room.
Raumfähre *f*   space shuttle.
Räumlichkeit *f*   accommodation; space.
reagieren   to react; to respond.
Reaktion *f*   reaction; response.
real   real; actual.
Realeinkommen *nt*   real income.
Realwachstum *nt*   real growth.
realisierbar   realizable; liquidatable; convertible; *(Effekten)* marketable.

Realisierbarkeit *f*   realizability; liquidatability.
realisieren   to realize.
realisierter Kursgewinn *m*   capital gain.
Realisierung *f*   realization.
Realkosten *pl*   real costs; actual costs.
Reallohn *m*   real wages; actual wages.
Reallohnniveau *nt*   actual wage level.
Reallohnsatz *m*   real wage rate.
Reallohnzuwachs *m*   real wage increase.
Realwachstum *nt*   real growth.
Rechenmaschine *f*   calculator.
Rechenschaft *f* **ablegen**   to account.
Rechenschaftsbericht *m*   accounting; statement.
Rechenschaftspflicht *f*   accountability.
Rechenzentrale *f*   computer room; central accounting office.
Rechenzentrum *nt*   computer center; business office.
rechnen   to calculate; to reckon; to count.
Rechner *m*   calculator.
rechnerisch   arithmetical; mathematical.
Rechnung *f*   invoice; bill; account; tally.
Rechnungsführung *f*   accounting.
Rechnungsgrundlage *f*   basis of calculation.
Rechnungsjahr *nt*   fiscal year.

Rechnungsprüfer *m*   auditor; controller; *(BE)* comptroller.

Rechnungssaldo *m*   balance; rest.

Rechnungswesen *nt*   accountancy; accounting.

Recht *nt*   law; right; justice.

rechtfertigen   to justify.

Rechtfertigung *f*   justification.

rechtlich   lawful; legal; legitimate; *(gültig)* valid.

rechtmäßig   lawful; legitimate.

Rechtsanspruch *m*   legal title.

Rechtsanwalt *m*   lawyer; attorney.

Rechtsauffassung *f*   judicial conception; legal conception.

Rechtsausschuß *m*   judicial panel; judiciary committee.

Rechtsberater *m*   counselor.

Rechtschaffenheit *f*   integrity; honesty.

Rechtsfall *m*   legal case.

Rechtsform *f*   legal form.

Rechtsgang *m*   legal process.

Rechtsgeschäft *nt*   legal action; legal act.

Rechtsgültigkeit *f*   legal force.

Rechtskraft *f*   legal force; validity; *(Urteil)* nonappealableness.

rechtskräftig   legal.

Rechtslage *f*   legal status; legal situation.

Rechtsprechung *f*   jurisdiction.

Rechtsprozeß *m*   lawsuit.

Rechtssache *f*   legal case.

Rechtsstaat *m*   constitutional state; free government under the law.

Rechtsstreit *m*   lawsuit; litigation.

Rechtstitel *m*   legal title.

Rechtsvorschrift *f*   legal rule; legislative provision.

rechtswidrig   contrary to law; illegal.

rechtzeitig   timely; on time.

Redeweise *f*   idiom; language.

Rediskont *m*   rediscount.

rediskontieren   to rediscount.

Rediskontkontingent *nt*   rediscount quota.

Rediskontvolumen *nt*   rediscount volume; rediscount capacity.

reduzieren   to reduce; to diminish.

Reduzierung *f*   reduction; diminution.

reell   honest; fair.

refinanzieren   to refinance.

Refinanzierung *f*   refinancing.

Reform *f*   reform.

reformieren   to reform.

Regel *f*   rule; regulation; precept; norm.

Regelarbeitszeit *f*   standardized working hours.

regellos   *(Markt)* irregular; unsettled.

regelmäßig wiederkehrend   periodic.

regeln   to issue a ruling; to regularize; to control.

regelnd   regulatory.

regelrecht   regular.

regenerieren   to regenerate; to reclaim; to recycle.

Regenerierung *f*   regeneration; reclamation.

Regie *f*   direction.

Regie führen   to direct.

regieren   to govern.

Regierung *f*   government.

Regierungsabteilung *f*   government department; *(BE)* ministry.

Regierungsstelle *f*   department; government office.

regional   regional.

Regisseur *m*   director.

Register *nt*   register; ledger; list.
Registrator *m*   recorder.
registrieren   to record; to register; to incorporate; to index.
registrierte Aktien *pl*   shares of record.
Registrierung *f*   registration.
Reglementierung *f*   regimentation.
Regression *f*   regression.
Regressionsanalyse *f*   regression analysis.
regressiv   regressive.
Regreßrecht *nt*   right of recourse to the law.
regulativ   regulatory.
regulierbar   adjustable.
regulieren   to regulate; to adjust; to administer.
Regulierung *f*   regulation; adjustment.
Regulierungssystem *nt*   regulatory system.
reich   rich; wealthy.
reichen   *(genug sein)* to suffice; to last; to reach.
reichlich   plentiful; abundant; ample.
Reichtum *m*   wealth; riches; plenty; affluence.
Reichweite *f*   grasp; reach; sweep.
reif   ripe; mature.
reifen   to ripen; to age; to mature.
Reihe *f*   row; series.
Reihenfolge *f*   sequence.
rein   pure; *(Gewinn)* net; clear; *(Frachtbrief)* clean.
Reineinkommen *nt*   net income.
Reinertrag *m*   net yield.
Reingewinn *m*   net profit.
Reingewinn *m* **erzielen**   to clear a profit.
Reinumsatz *m*   net sales.
Reinverdienst *m*   net earnings.
Reinverlust *m*   net loss.

Reinvermögenswert *m*   net asset value.
reinvestieren   to reinvest.
Reinvestition *f*   reinvestment.
Reise *f*   journey; travel; trip.
Reisegebiet *nt*   travel area.
reisen   to travel.
Reisepaß *m*   passport.
Reiseplanung *f*   travel planning; trip scheduling.
Reiseverkehr *m*   travel.
reißen   to tear; to pull.
reizvoll   attractive.
Rekapitulation *f*   recapitulation.
Reklamation *f*   complaint.
Reklame *f*   promotion; propaganda; publicity; advertisement.
Reklame machen   to publicize; to advertise.
Reklametext *m*   advertising copy.
reklamieren   *(beanstanden)* to complain; *(zurückverlangen)* to reclaim.
Rekord *m*   record.
Rekordergebnis *nt*   record result.
Rekordgewinn *m*   record profit.
Rekordjahr *nt*   record year.
Rekordstand *m*   record level.
Rekrut *m*   recruit.
rekrutieren   to recruit.
Rekurs *m*   recourse.
relativ   relative; comparative.
Remboursgeschäft *nt*   merchant banking.
Rembourstratte *f*   documentary draft.
Rendite *f*   yield; rate of return.
rennen   to run; to race.
Rennen *nt*   race; run.
rentabel   profitable; economical.
Rentabilität *f*   profitability.
Rente *f*   pension; annuity.
Rentenanpassung *f*   pension

adjustment; retirement income adjustment.

Rentenaufbesserung *f*   pension increase.

Rentenbesitz *m*   bond ownership.

Rentenfonds *m*   pension fund.

Rentenindex *m*   annuity index; bond index.

Rentenmarkt *m*   bond market.

Rentenversicherung *f*   annuity insurance.

Rentenwert *m*   annuity value.

rentieren, sich   to give a good return; *(Betrieb)* to be profitable.

Rentner *m*   pensioner.

reorganisieren   to reorganize; to revamp.

Reparatur *f*   repair.

Reparaturwerkstätte *f*   repair workshop.

reparieren   to repair; to fix.

repartieren   to reallot.

repatriieren   to repatriate.

Reporter *m*   reporter.

Repräsentant *m*   representative.

Repräsentation *f*   representation.

repräsentativ   representative.

Repräsentativstück *nt*   sample.

repräsentieren   to represent; to typify.

Reserve-   reserve; spare.

Reserve *f*   reserve; standby; buffer.

Reservekredit *m*   standby credit.

Reservelager *nt*   buffer stock.

Reservemittel *nt*   reserve fund; reserves.

Reserven *pl* **dritter Ordnung** *f*   tertiary reserves.

Reservenzulänglichkeit *f*   reserve adequacy.

Reservesystem *nt*   reserve system.

Reservewährung *f*   reserve currency.

reservieren   to reserve.

reserviert   reserved.

Reservoir *nt*   reservoir.

Resignation *f*   resignation.

resignieren   to resign.

Resolution *f*   resolution; resolve.

Resonanz *f*   resonance; *(Reaktion)* feedback; reaction.

respektiert   reputable; respected.

Ressort *nt*   portfolio; *(Fachgebiet)* field of study; *(Regierung)* department; *(BE)* ministry; *(Zuständigkeit)* province; purview.

Rest-   residual.

Rest *m*   rest; remainder; *(Rückstand)* residue.

restaurieren   to restore.

Restbestand *m*   remainder; rest.

Restlaufzeit *f*   remaining period; *(Fälligkeit)* remaining time to maturity.

restlich   remaining; residual.

Restsumme *f*   balance; *(Konto)* account balance.

Resultat *nt*   result; outcome.

resultieren   to result.

Resümee *nt*   résumé.

retourniert   returned.

retten   to retrieve; to save.

revidieren   *(prüfen)* to check; to examine; *(ändern)* to revise.

Revidierung *f*   revision.

Revision *f*   revision; examination; audit.

Revision *f* **durchführen**   to audit.

Revisionsbericht *m*   audit report.

Revisor *m*   examiner; controller.

revolvieren   to revolve; to roll over.

revolvierend   revolving.

Rezept *nt*   *(Med.)* prescription; *(Formel)* formula; *(Kochen, Backen)* recipe.

Rezession *f*   recession.

reziprok   reciprocal.
richten   to judge.
richten an   to address to.
Richter *m*   judge; justice.
richterlich   judicial; magisterial.
richtig   correct; *(korrekt)* proper.
Richtigkeit *f*   accuracy.
richtigstellen   to correct; to rectify.
Richtigstellung *f*   correction;
  adjustment; rectification.
Richtlinie *f*   rule; guideline.
Richtschnur *f*   precept.
Richtung *f*   direction; *(fig.)* tack.
Riesenunternehmen *nt*   mammoth
  company.
riesig   giant; mammoth.
ringen   to contend.
Rinne *f*   trough.
Risiko *nt*   risk.
Risikobereitschaft *f*   readiness to
  assume a risk.
risikofreudig   willing to take a risk.
Risikohaftung *f*   liability for risk;
  responsibility for risk.
Risikomischung *f*   risk mixture;
  (Fächerung) risk spread.
risikoreich   risky; fraught with risk.
risikoscheu   risk-averse; unwilling
  to take a risk.
Risikovorsorge *f*   provision to
  guard against risk.
riskant   risky.
riskieren   to risk; *(Kapital)* to venture; *(aufs Spiel setzen)* to stake.
Rivale *m*, **Rivalin** *f*   rival; contender.
rivalisieren   to rival.
Roboter *m*   robot.
roh   *(ungekocht)* raw; *(unveredelt)*
  crude; *(gefühllos)* unfeeling.
Rohgewinn *m*   gross profit.
Rohmaterial *nt*   raw material.

Rohstoffgewinnung *f*   raw materi-
  als production.
Rohstoffkonzern *m*   raw materials
  conglomerate.
Rohstoffpreis *m*   commodity price.
Rotationspapier *nt*   newsprint.
rotieren   to rotate.
rotierend   rotating.
Route *f*   route.
Route *f* **bestimmen**   to route.
Routine *f*   routine.
Rubrik *f*   rubric.
Rück-   back.
Rücken *m*   back.
Rückerstattung *f*   refund.
Rückforderung *f*   reclaim.
Rückführung *f*   repatriation.
Rückgabe *f*   return.
Rückgang *m*   *(Wirtschaft)* decline;
  (Verminderung) decrease; *(Absin-
  ken)* drop; *(Sturz)* fall.
rückgängig machen   *(Vorschrift,
  Regel)* to rescind; *(Kontrakt)* to
  cancel.
Rückgrat *nt*   spine; *(fig.)* backbone.
Rückgriff *m*   recourse.
Rückkehr *f*   return.
Rücklage *f*   reserve; provision.
Rücklagendotierung *f*   reserve
  allocation.
Rücklagenposition *f*   reserve posi-
  tion.
rückläufig   regressive; downward.
Rücknahme *f*   retraction; *(Beru-
  fung)* withdrawal.
Rückruf *m*   recall.
Rückschlag *m*   reversal; setback.
rückschleusen   *(Geld)* to recycle.
Rückschritt *m*   setback.
Rückseite *f*   reverse; back.
Rücksendung *f*   return; reconsign-
  ment; reshipment.

Rücksprache f consultation.
Rückstand m lag; *(Zahlung)* arrears; *(Summe)* arrearage; *(Aufträge)* backlog; *(Abfall)* waste.
rückständig backward; *(Wirtschaft)* underdeveloped; *(Rechnung)* unpaid; *(überfällig)* overdue; *(zurück)* behind.
Rückständigkeit f underdevelopment.
Rückstellung f provision; reserve.
Rücktritt m resignation.
Rücktrittsklausel f escape clause.
Rückübertragung f reassignment.
rückvergüten to refund.
Rückvergütung f *(Rückzahlung)* repayment; *(Zins-, Preisnachlaß)* rebate; *(Erstattung)* refund; *(Entschädigung)* reimbursement.
rückwärts backwards.
rückwirkend retroactive.
Rückwirkung f retroactive effect.
rückzahlbar repayable.
Rückzahlung f repayment; payback.

Rückzahlungsfrist f repayment period.
Rückzahlungskurs m redemption price.
Rückzahlungsrate f redemption rate.
Rückzahlungswert m redemption value.
Rückzug m withdrawal; pullback.
Ruf m call; *(Leumund)* reputation.
rügen to criticize; to censure.
Ruhe f rest.
Ruhegehalt nt pension.
ruhen to rest; *(Geschäft)* to be at a standstill.
Ruhestand m retirement.
Ruin m *(finanziell)* ruin.
Ruine f *(Bau)* ruin.
ruinieren to ruin.
ruinös ruinous.
Rundschreiben nt *(Werbung)* circular; *(Neuigkeiten)* newsletter.
Rutsch m slide.
rutschen to slide.
Rutschen nt sliding.

S

Sachanlagen pl fixed assets.
Sachbearbeiter m official.
Sachbesitz m physical property.
Sache f object; matter.
Sachgut nt physical product.
Sachlage f circumstances.
sachlich objective.
Sachverständige m/f specialist; expert; authority.
Sachverständige m/f **für das Rechnungswesen** nt accountant.

Sachwissen nt expertise.
Saison f season.
Saison- seasonal.
saisonbedingt seasonal; seasonally.
Saisonbedingtheit f seasonality.
saisongemäß seasonally.
saisonüblich seasonally.
Salär nt salary.
saldieren liquidate.
Saldo m balance.

sammeln to collect.
Sammler *m* collector.
Sammlung *f* range; collection.
sanieren to restructure; to reorganize.
Sanierung *f* restructuring; reorganization.
Sanierungsmaßnahme *f* reorganization measure.
Sanierungsstrategie *f* reorganization strategy.
Sanktion *f* sanction.
Satellit *m* satellite.
sättigen to saturate.
Sättigung *f* saturation.
Sättigungsgrenze *f* saturation point; absorption limit.
Satz *m* (*gram.*) sentence; (*Serie, Garnitur*) set; (*Zinsen*) rate.
Satzung *f* articles; (*Unternehmen*) constitution; (*Statuten*) bylaws; (*Aktiengesellschaft*) charter.
satzunggebend charter-creating.
satzungsmäßig statutory.
Satzvorlage *f* schema.
Säulendiagramm *nt* bar chart; histogram.
schäbig shabby; (*kleinlich*) mean.
Schablone *f* stencil; (*Vorlage*) model.
Schachzug *m* move; maneuver.
Schaden *m* damage; (*Verlust*) loss; (*Nachteil*) prejudice; detriment; (*jur.*) tort; (*Verletzung*) injury.
Schadenabschätzer *m* damage appraiser.
Schadenersatz *m* compensation.
Schadensfall *m* liability case.
Schadensursache *f* cause of damage; cause of loss.
schädlich harmful; detrimental; (*nachteilig*) disadvantageous.
schaffen to create.

Schaffung *f* creation.
Schallplatte *f* record.
schalten to switch; (*Getriebe*) to shift.
Schalten *nt* switching.
Schalter *m* (*elek.*) switch; (*Bahn, Post*) counter position; counter window.
Schalterbeamte *m*, **-beamtin** *f* counter clerk; (*bank*) teller.
Schalthebel *m* shift knob.
Schalttafel *f* switchboard.
scharf sharp; keen.
scharfes Senken *nt* sharp reduction; slashing.
Schattenwirtschaft *f* shadow economy; underground economy.
Schatz *m* treasure; hoard.
Schatzamt *nt* treasury.
Schatzanweisung *f* treasury bill.
schätzen to estimate; (*taxieren*) to appraise; (*wertschätzen*) to appreciate.
Schätzer *m* appraiser.
Schatzmeister *m* treasurer.
Schätzung *f* (*Kalkulation*) estimate; (*Achtung*) estimation; esteem; (*Wertschätzung*) appreciation.
schätzungsweise approximately.
Schatzwechsel *m* treasury note.
Schätzwert *m* estimated value; estimated price.
Schau *f* show; (*Ausstellung*) exhibition.
Schaubild *n* diagram; chart.
Schaufensterauslage *f* store window display.
Schaufensterschmuck *m* store window decoration.
schaukeln to swing; (*erschüttern*) to rock.
Schauplatz *m* scene; site.
Scheck *m* check.

Scheckbürgschaft *f* check guaranty (U.S.).

Scheckeinreichung *f* check presentation.

Scheckkarte *f* check guaranty card.

Scheckkonto *nt* checking account.

Scheibe *f* slice; *(Glas)* pane.

Scheidung *f* divorce.

Schein *m* certificate; voucher.

Scheinverlust *m* paper loss.

Scheinwerfer *m* searchlight; spotlight.

scheitern to fail; *(Schiff)* run aground.

Schema *nt* schema; *(Tabelle)* table; *(Diagramm)* diagram.

schenken to give; *(gemeinnützige Gabe)* to donate.

Schenkung *f* gift; *(Zuschuß)* grant; *(gemeinnützige Gabe)* donation.

Schicht *f* layer; *(Arbeit)* shift.

schichten to layer; *(stapeln)* to stack.

Schichtenleistung *f* shift performance; shift productivity.

Schichtwechsel *m* change of shift.

schicken to send; to ship.

Schiebe- sliding.

Schiebung *f* swindle; racket.

Schiedsgericht *nt* arbitration tribunal.

Schiedsrichter *m* arbitrator; referee.

schief lopsided; crooked.

Schiefer *m* slate.

Schiefertafel *f* slate.

schief stehen to lean.

Schienenweg *m* railroad; *(Gleis)* track.

schießen to shoot; to fire.

Schiff *nt* ship; boat.

Schiffahrtsweg *m* waterway.

Schiffchen *nt* *(weben)* shuttle.

Schild *nt* sign; *(Anhänger)* tag.

Schilderung *f* description; representation.

Schirm *m* umbrella.

Schlacke *f* slag; waste.

schlagen to beat; to hit.

Schlager *m* winner; *(Treffer)* hit; *(Lied)* hit song.

Schläger *m* *(Tennis)* racket; *(Baseball)* bat; *(Golf)* club.

Schlagwort *nt* slogan.

schlank slender; slim.

Schlankheitskur *f* weight loss program.

Schlankheitskur *f* **machen.** to diet; to slim.

schlecht bad; *(minderwertig)* shoddy.

schlecht bezahlt badly paid.

schlechte Verwaltung *f* mismanagement.

schlecht verwalten to mismanage.

schlecht wirtschaften to mismanage.

Schleppen *nt* towage.

schleppend slow; dragging.

Schleppgebühr *f* towage fee.

Schleuderausfuhr *f* dumping.

Schleuderpreis *m* dumping price.

schlichten to arbitrate; to settle.

Schlichter *m* arbitrator.

Schlichtung *f* arbitration; conciliation.

Schlichtungsabkommen *nt* arbitration agreement.

Schlichtungsergebnis *nt* arbitration result.

Schlichtungsspruch *m* arbitration decision.

Schlichtungsverfahren *nt* arbitration process.

schließen to close; *(Fabrik,*

Bergwerk) to shut down; *(Ansprache)* to conclude.

Schließung *f* closure; *(Fabrik, Bergwerk)* shutdown.

Schlips *m* necktie.

schlitzen to slit; to slot.

schlüpfen to slip.

Schlupfloch *nt* loophole.

Schluß- final.

Schluß *m* finish; *(Ende)* close; *(Fabrik, Bergwerk)* closure.

Schlußbericht *m* final report.

Schlüssel *m* key.

Schlüsselfrage *f* key question; key issue.

Schlüsselland *nt* key country.

Schlüsselmarkt *m* key market.

Schlüsselpersonal *nt* key personnel.

Schlüsselserie *f* key series.

Schlüsselstellung *f* key position.

Schlüsselvariable *f* key variable.

Schlußfolgerung *f* conclusion.

Schlußtermin *m* deadline.

schmackhaft machen to make palatable.

schmieden to forge.

schmücken to decorate; to trim.

Schneeball *m* snowball.

schnell hochsteigend soaring.

Schnelligkeit *f* speed.

Schnitt *m* cut.

Schnitzer *m* *(Fehler)* blunder; *(Holzschnitzer)* carver.

schonen to conserve; to preserve.

schöpferisch creative.

Schrank *m* **für Systemzentraleinheit** *f* mainframe cabinet.

Schranke *f* limit; *(Sperre)* bar; *(Handel)* barrier.

Schraube *f* screw; *(Inflation, Preis, Steuer)* spiral.

Schreibarbeit *f* paperwork.

Schreiben *nt* (Brief) letter; *(Be-*

nachrichtigung) written communication; *(Aktivität)* writing.

Schreibgerät *nt* writing utensil.

Schreibkraft *f* secretarial help; *(Büroangestellte)* clerk.

Schreibmaschine *f* typewriter.

Schreibpersonal *nt* secretarial staff.

Schreibtisch *m* desk.

Schreibtischcomputer *m* desktop computer.

Schreibzeug *nt* writing utensils; pen and ink; desk set.

Schriftführer *m* reporter; *(Verein, Komitee)* secretary.

schriftlich written; in writing.

schriftlich belegen to document.

Schriftsatz *m* declaration; brief; *(Druck)* font.

Schriftstück *nt* document.

Schriftwechsel *m* correspondence.

Schritt *m* step; *(fig.)* move.

Schrott *m* scrap; *(Abfall)* waste.

schrumpfen to shrink; *(sich verringern)* to diminish.

Schrumpfung *f* shrinkage; contraction.

Schuld *f* fault; guilt.

Schuld *f* **geben** to blame.

Schuldbuch *nt* debt register; debt ledger.

schulden to owe.

Schulden *pl* debts; *(Verbindlichkeiten)* liabilities; *(Buchführung)* accounts payable.

Schuldendienst *m* debt service.

Schuldenkrise *f* debt crisis.

Schuldenlast *f* debt burden; *(Verschuldung)* indebtedness.

Schuldenmarkt *m* debt market.

Schuldenrisiko *nt* debt risk.

Schuldensicherheit *f* collateral; debt security.

Schuldenstand *m* debt level.

Schuldentilgung *f* discharge of debt; *(Amortisierung)* amortization.

Schuldenzahlungserleichterung *f* debt payment relief.

Schuldenzahlungsverweigerung *f* debt payment refusal; debt repudiation.

Schuldforderung *f* payment demand.

Schuldner *m* debtor.

Schuldnerland *nt* debtor nation.

Schuldpapier *nt* debt instrument.

Schuldposten *m* debit.

Schuldsaldo *m* debit balance.

Schuldschein *m* promissory note; *(Schuldverschreibung)* debenture; debt obligation.

Schuldscheindarlehen *nt* loan against borrower's note; open market credit.

Schuldverhältnis *nt* contractual obligation.

Schuldverschreibung *f* debenture; *(Obligation)* bond.

Schuldwechsel *m* memorandum bill; note payable.

Schuldzinsen *pl* interest on debt.

Schule/Universität absolvieren to graduate from school/university.

Schulen *nt* training.

schürfen to scrape; *(Erze)* to prospect.

Schutz- protective.

Schutz *m* *(Natur)* protection; conservation; *(Sicherung, Schutzvorrichtung)* safeguard; *(Sicherheit)* security; *(Steuer)* shelter.

Schutzanzug *m* overalls.

schützen to protect; to shelter.

schützend protective.

Schutzgebiet *nt* protectorate.

Schutzmacht *f* protector power; protector state.

Schutzmarke *f* trademark.

Schutzvorrichtung *f* safeguard.

Schutzzoll *m* protective tariff.

schutzzollbedürftige Industrie industry in need of tariff protection.

schwach weak; *(Gesundheit)* poor.

Schwäche *f* weakness.

schwächen to weaken.

Schwächerwerden *nt* weakening.

Schwachheit *f* weakness.

Schwächung *f* weakening.

schwach werden to weaken.

Schwall *m* wave; spate.

schwanken to fluctuate.

Schwanken *nt* fluctuating; swinging.

schwankend fluctuating; swinging.

schwankend machen to destabilize.

Schwankung *f* fluctuation.

Schwankung im Handel fluctuation in trade; leads and lags.

Schwankungsbreite *f* fluctuation range; degree of fluctuation.

schweben to hover; *(Prozeß)* to be pending; to be in limbo.

schwebend pending.

schwebende Überweisung *f* floating transfer.

schweigend silent.

Schwelle *f* threshold.

Schwellenland *nt* newly industrialized country.

schwer heavy; massive; *(schwierig)* difficult.

schwerfällig sluggish; lumbering.

Schwerfälligkeit *f* sluggishness.

Schwerpunkt *m* center of gravity; focal point; emphasis.

Schwester *f* sister.
Schwestergesellschaft *f* sister company.
schwierig difficult; hard.
Schwierigkeit *f* difficulty; (Problem) problem.
schwinden to dwindle; to slip away.
Schwinden *nt* dwindling.
schwindend dwindling; slipping.
schwingen to swing.
Schwingen *nt* swinging.
schwingend swinging.
Schwund *m* shrinkage; reduction; (Flüssigkeit) leakage.
Schwung *m* momentum; drive.
schwungvoll spirited; bold.
Seezunge *f* sole.
segmentieren to segment.
Seil *nt* rope.
seinen Verpflichtungen *pl* **nicht nachkommen** to default.
Seite *f* side; (Buch) page. side.
Seitenlinie *f* sideline; (Zweig) offshoot.
Seitenzweig *m* branch; sideline; offshoot.
seitlich lateral.
Sekretär *m* secretary.
Sektion *f* section.
Sektor *m* sector.
sektoral sectoral.
sekundär secondary.
Sekundärdaten *pl* secondary data.
Sekundärreserven *pl* secondary reserves.
selbständig autonomous; independent.
Selbständigkeit *f* independence.
Selbstbedienung *f* self service.
Selbstfinanzierung *f* internal financing; self-financing.
Selbstkostenpreis *m* net cost.

Selbstkostenrechnung *f* cost accounting.
Selbstregierung *f* self-government; (Souveränität) sovereignty; (Autonomie) autonomy.
Selbstverwaltung *f* self-government; autonomy; home rule.
selektiv selective.
selten seldom; infrequent.
Seltenheit *f* rarity.
Seminar *nt* seminar; (Arbeitstagung) workshop.
Sendeleiter *m* (Radio, TV) station director.
senden to send; (Radio) to broadcast.
Sendereihe *f* serial program; series.
Sendernetz *nt* station network.
Seniorchef *m* senior partner.
senken to lower.
senkrecht vertical.
Senkung *f* cut; reduction; (Kurs) downward movement.
Serie *f* series; serial;
Serieneinheit *f* module; series unit.
seriös respectable; sincere.
Service *m* service
Servicebereich *m* service area.
Servicesektor *m* service sector.
sicher sure; safe; (gesichert) secure; (zuverlässig) reliable; (gewiß) certain; (positiv) positive.
sichergestellt secured.
Sicherheit *f* (Sicherstellung) security; (Versicherung) assurance; (Gewißheit) certainty; (Kreditdeckung) collateral; surety.
Sicherheiten *pl* securities.
Sicherheitsfaktor *m* safety factor; cushion.
Sicherheitsklausel *f* safety clause; safeguard clause.

Sicherheitsleistung *f* security; security deposit.

sicher machen to make sure; (sichern) to secure.

sichern to ensure; *(schützen)* to safeguard; *(sicherstellen)* to secure; *(versichern)* to assure.

sicherstellen to secure; (schützen) to safeguard.

Sicherstellung *f* safekeeping; safeguarding; *(Kredit)* collateral; *(Schadloshaltung)* indemnification.

Sicherung *f* safeguard; *(elek.)* fuse.

Sicherungsgeschäft *nt* **abschließen** to hedge.

Sicherungsgeschäft *nt* hedge.

Sicherungsübereignungsvertrag *m* trust agreement.

Sichtbarkeit *f* visibility.

Sichteinlage *f* demand deposit.

sichten to catch sight of; *(sortieren)* to sort.

Sichtpapier *nt* demand note.

Sichtweite *f* visibility range.

Sieger *m* victor; *(Gewinner)* winner.

siegreich victorious; winning.

Signatur *f* signature.

simulieren to simulate.

simuliert simulated.

sinken to sink; *(schwinden)* to dwindle; *(fallen)* to fall; *(abnehmen)* to decline.

sinkend sinking; sagging.

Sinn *m* sense; *(Bedeutung)* meaning.

sinnlos senseless; *(bedeutungslos)* meaningless.

Situation *f* situation.

Situationsanalyse *f* situation analysis.

Sitz *m* seat; *(Kleidung)* fit.

Sitzung *f* meeting;

Sitzungsbericht *m* minutes.

Sitzungsordnung *f* protocol.

Skala *f* scale.

Skalenertrag *m* scale earnings.

Skizze *f* sketch; *(Umriß)* outline.

skizzieren to sketch; *(umreißen)* to outline.

Skonto *m/f* cash discount.

sofort immediately.

sofortig immediate.

sofort realisierbar *(Geld)* liquid.

Software *f* software.

Softwaremarkt *m* software market.

Sog *m* pull.

Sohle *f* sole.

Solawechsel *m* promissory note; name paper.

solide *(fundiert)* sound; respectable.

Soll *nt* debit.

Sollangabe *f* debit report; debit statement.

Sollseite *f* debit side; debit column.

Sollvorgabe *f* quota.

Sollzins *m* interest on debit balance; interest on debt.

solvent solvent; *(fundiert)* sound.

Solvenz *f* solvency.

Sonde *f* probe.

Sonder- special.

Sonderanfertigung *f* special make.

Sonderangebot *nt* special offer.

Sonderartikel *m* featured article.

Sondergebühr *f* special charge; special fee.

Sonderposten *m* *(Buchführung)* special item; *(Waren)* special lot.

Sonderpreis *m* special price.

Sonderrecht *nt* privilege.

Sonderregelung *f* special regulation; special arrangement.

Sondersitzung *f* special meeting; *(Gericht)* special session.

Sondersubvention *f* special sub-
sidy.
Sondertarif *m* *(Zoll)* special tariff;
(Versicherung) special rate.
Sondervergütung *f* bonus.
Sondervermögen *nt* separate
estate; *(Aktiva)* separate assets;
(Besitz) special property.
Sonderzahlung *f* special payment.
sondieren to probe; to sound
(untersuchen) to explore.
Sorge *f* worry; care.
sorgen to care.
sorgfältig careful; *(gewissenhaft)*
diligent.
Sorgsamkeit *f* care; diligence.
Sorte *f* sort; *(Marke)* brand.
sortieren to sort.
Sortiment *nt* assortment; *(Mischung)* mix.
soufflieren to prompt.
souverän sovereign.
sozial social.
Sozialabgaben *pl* social security
payments; *(Steuer)* social security
tax.
Sozialanspruch *m* *(Forderung)*
social benefits claim; *(Berechtigung)* right to social benefits; welfare eligibility.
Sozialausschuß *m* welfare committee.
Sozialbeitrag *m* social service contribution; social security contribution.
soziale Gerechtigkeit *f* social justice.
Sozialfinanzen *pl* social service
finances.
Sozialfürsorge *f* social service.
Sozialgebilde *nt* social framework.
Sozialhilfe *f* welfare.

Sozialhilfeausgaben *pl* public
assistance expenditures.
Sozialleistung *f* social service.
Sozialordnung *f* social system
social order.
Sozialpartnerschaft *f* social partnership.
Sozialpolitik *f* social policy; welfare policy.
sozialpolitisch socio-political.
Sozialprodukt *nt* national product.
Sozialrecht *nt* *(Gerechtigkeit)*
social justice; *(Gesetzgebung)*
social assistance law; social security law.
Sozialstaat *m* social state.
sozialwirtschaftlich socioeconomic.
Sozialwohnung *f* government
housing.
Spalt *m* slit; slot.
Spalte *f* crack; *(Zeitung)* column.
spalten to split; to disrupt.
spaltend divisive; disruptive.
Spaltung *f* split; *(Teilung)* division;
partition.
Spanne *f* span; *(Ausdehnung)*
spread; *(Reichweite)* range.
Sparbeschluß *m* order to economize; decision to retrench.
Sparbetrag *m* amount saved.
Sparbrief *m* savings bond; savings
certificate.
Sparbuch *nt* savings book.
Spareinlage *f* savings deposit.
Spareinlagenbestand *m* savings
fund.
sparen to save.
Sparer *m* saver.
Sparfähigkeit *f* ability to save.
Sparförderung *f* *(Werbung)* sav-
ings promotion; *(Anreiz)* govern-
ment incentives for savers.

Spargelder *pl* savings deposits; savings deposit funds.

Spargelderverwaltung *f* savings deposits administration.

Sparkasse *f* savings bank.

Sparkassenkunde *m* savings bank customer.

Sparkassenschalter *m* savings bank window.

Sparkassenverband *m* association of savings banks.

Sparkonto *nt* savings account; deposit account.

Sparkunde *m* savings customer.

Sparleistung *f* savings performance.

spärlich meager; *(dünn)* thin.

Sparmaßnahme *f* economy measure.

Sparneigung *f* tendency to save.

Sparplan *m* savings plan.

Sparprämie *f* savings premium; *(Lebensversicherung)* initial reserve.

Sparprämiengesetz *nt* savings premium law.

Sparprogramm *nt* austerity program; savings program.

sparsam thrifty; economical.

Sparsamkeit *f* thrift; economy.

sparsam wirtschaften to economize.

Spartätigkeit *f* savings activity.

Sparte *f* line; *(Zweig)* branch; *(Gebiet)* field.

Spartenumsatz *m* branch turnover; branch sales.

Spar- und Kreditvereinigung *f* savings and loan association.

Sparzinssatz *m* savings interest rate.

spät late.

Spediteur *m* shipper; carrier.

Spedition *f* forwarding; transport; *(Speditionsgeschäft)* freight forwarding business.

Speditionsgewerbe *nt* shipping trade.

Speicher *m* warehouse.

Speicherchip *m* memory chip.

Speicherkapazität *f* *(Lager)* storage capacity; *(Computer)* memory.

Speicherleistung *f* storage performance.

speichern to store.

Speicherung *f* storage.

Spekulant *m* speculator.

Spekulation *f* speculation.

Spekulationsfrist *f* *(Zeitspanne)* speculative period; *(Stichtag)* speculative deadline.

Spekulationsgeschäft *nt* stock-jobbing.

Spekulationsgewinn *m* speculative profit.

Spekulationsmarkt *m* speculative market.

spekulativ speculative.

spekulieren to speculate.

Spende *f* donation; *(Gabe)* gift; *(Beitrag)* contribution.

spenden to donate; *(beitragen)* to contribute; to subscribe.

Spendenquittung *f* contribution receipt.

Spender *m* donor; contributor.

Sperre *f* stop; *(Bahnhof)* turnstile; bar.

sperren to stop; to bar; *(Konto)* to freeze.

Sperrminorität *f* blocking minority.

Sperrsitz *m* orchestra seat; stall.

Sperrung *f* stoppage.

Sperrzoll *m* prohibitive tariff.

Spesen *pl* expenses.

Spesenfreiheit *f* exemption from expense charges;

Spezial- special.

Spezialisierung *f* specialization.

Spezialist *m* specialist.

Spezialität *f* specialty.

speziell special; (besonders) particular.

Spezifikation *f* specification.

spezifisch specific.

spezifizieren to specify.

spezifiziert specified.

Spiel *nt* game.

Spielraum *m* leeway; (Marge) margin; (Reichweite) range; (Swing) swing.

spiralartig ansteigen spiral upwards.

spiralartiges Ansteigen *nt* spiraling rise.

Spirale *f* spiral.

Spiralflug *m* spiraling flight.

Spiralsturz *m* tailspin.

Spitze *f* (Führung) head; (Börse) odd lot; (Höchstwert) peak; (Rückversicherung) surplus.

Spitzenbeamte *m*, **-beamtin** *f* top-ranking official.

Spitzenbedarf *m* peak demand.

Spitzenbetrag *m* residual amount; (Börse) fractional amount; odd lot amount.

Spitzenfunktionär *m* top-level functionary; top-ranking office holder.

Spitzengespräch *nt* top-level talk; summit talk.

Spitzeninstitut *nt* head institute.

Spitzenjahr *nt* peak year; (Gewinn) year of highest profits.

Spitzenkräfte *pl* top management.

Spitzenmanager *m* top manager.

Spitzenorganisation *f* head organization.

Spitzenpapiere *pl* first-rate securities.

Spitzenprodukt *nt* top product; lead product.

Spitzenqualität *f* prime quality.

Spitzenreiter *m* market leader.

Spitzenstellung *f* top position.

Spitzentechnik *f* leading technology.

Spitzenverband *m* head organization; (Dachorganisation) umbrella organization.

Spitzenvertreter *m* top representative.

Spitzenwert *m* peak value; (Aktien) blue-chip stock.

splitten to split.

Sporn *m* spur.

Spotmarkt *m* spot market.

Sprache *f* language.

Sprachenschranke *f* language barrier.

Sprecher *m* spokesman.

Sprung *m* jump.

Spur *f* trace; tracks; sign.

Staat *m* state; country.

staatlich national.

staatliche Unterstützung *f* state subsidy; public support.

staatlicher Planer *m* state planner.

Staats- state.

Staatsanwaltschaft *f* prosecution.

Staatsbankrott *m* national bankruptcy; national insolvency.

Staatsbudget *nt* national budget.

Staatsdefizit *nt* national deficit.

Staatsdirigismus *m* state intervention; government control.

Staatseinfluß *m* government influence.

Staatsfinanzen *pl*   state finances; national finances; *(öffentliche Finanzen)* public finances.

Staatsgarantie *f*   government guaranty;

Staatshandelsland *nt*   state-trading nation.

Staatshaushalt *m*   national budget.

Staatskasse *f*   federal treasury *(U.S.)*; exchequer *(U.K.)*

Staatskonzern *m*   state combine; state-owned enterprise; *(öffentliches Unternehmen)* public enterprise.

Staatskosten *pl*   public expense.

Staatspapiere *pl*   government securities; public securities.

Staatsschuld *f*   national debt.

Staatsschuldverschreibung *f*   public bond.

Staatsunternehmen *nt*   state-owned enterprise.

Staatsverbrauch *m*   public consumption.

Staatsverschuldung *f*   state indebtedness.

Staatszuschuß *m*   state subsidy; government subsidy.

Stab *m*   staff.

stabil   stable; *(stark, handfest)* sturdy.

stabilisieren   to stabilize.

Stabilisierung *f*   stabilization.

Stabilität *f*   stability.

Stabilitätsanalyse *f*   stability analysis.

Stabilitätsgesetz *nt*   stability law.

Stabsabteilung *f*   staff department.

Stabsleiter *m*   staff director.

Stadium *nt*   phase.

Stadtgemeinde *f*   municipality.

städtischer Haushalt *m*   urban household.

staffeln   to graduate; to stagger.

Staffelung *f*   gradation.

Stagnation *f*   stagnation; sluggishness.

stagnieren   to stagnate.

stagnierend   stagnant; sluggish.

Stahlarbeiter *m*   steel worker.

Stahlwerk *nt*   steel mill.

Stammaktie *f*   common stock share.

Stammgast *m*   patron.

Stammkapital *nt*   common stock.

Stammkapitalanteil *m*   *(Aktiengesellschaft)* share of capital stock. *(Grundkapital)* share of authorized capital.

Stammkunde *m*   regular customer.

Stammladen *m*   parent store; original store.

Stammvermögen *nt*   capital.

Stand *m*   stand; *(Rang)* rank; standing; *(Klasse)* class.

Stand *m* **der Technik** *f*   state of the technology.

Standard *m*   standard; norm.

Standardabweichung *f*   standard deviation.

Standardfehler *m*   standard error.

Standardformat *nt*   standard format.

standardisieren   to standardize.

standardisiert   standardized.

Standardisierung *f*   standardization.

Standort *m*   location; headquarters.

Standorttheorie *f*   industrial location theory; regional theory.

Standpunkt *m*   point of view; position.

Stapel *m*   stack; *(Haufen)* pile.

stark   strong; *(fundiert)* solid; *(mächtig)* powerful.

Stärke *f*   strength.

stärken to strengthen.
starke Nachfrage *f* strong demand.
starkes Einschränken *nt* severe restriction.
starkes Herabsetzen *nt* severe reduction.
starke Vermehrung *f* proliferation.
stark reduzieren to reduce severely; to slash.
Stärkung *f* strengthening; *(Imbiß)* refreshment.
starr rigid; inflexible.
Start *m* start; *(Flugzeug)* takeoff; *(Anfang)* beginning.
startbereites System *nt* turnkey system.
starten to start; *(Flugzeug)* to take off.
Starten *nt* starting; *(Unternehmen, Kampagne)* launching.
statisch static.
Statistik *f* statistics.
Statistiker *m* statistician.
statistisch statistical.
statistische Angabe *f* statistic.
statistische Daten *pl* statistical data.
statistische Ziffer *f* statistical number.
stattfinden to take place; to occur.
Status *m* status; *(Zustand)* state.
Statussymbol *nt* status symbol.
Statut *nt* bylaw.
Staubecken *nt* reservoir.
Stehen *nt* standing.
steif stiff.
steigen to rise; *(klettern)* to climb; *(zunehmen)* to increase.
Steigen *nt* rising; *(Klettern)* climbing.
steigende Tendenz *f* upward trend.

steigern to raise; *(vermehren)* to increase; *(erhöhen)* to enhance; *(eskalieren)* to escalate.
Steigerung *f* rise; *(Zunahme)* increase; *(Erhöhung)* enhancement.
Steigerungsrate *f* rate of increase.
Steigerungssatz *m* rate of increase.
steiler Anstieg *m* steep climb; upsurge.
Stelle *f* spot; *(Ort)* place; *(Punkt)* point; *(Posten)* post; *(Stellung)* job.
Stellenangebot *nt* job offer; *(Inserat)* help wanted advertisement.
Stellenbesetzung *f* *(Planung)* staffing plan; *(Plan)* organization chart.
Stellenbewerber *m* job applicant.
Stellenverlust *m* job loss.
Stellung *f* *(Position)* position; *(Rang)* standing; position.
stellvertretend deputy; assistant.
stellvertretende Vorsitzende *m/f* vice chairperson; deputy chairperson.
Stellvertreter *m* deputy; substitute; *(Repräsentant)* representative.
Stellvertretung *f* representation; *(Vollmacht)* proxy.
Stempel *m* stamp; *(Silber)* hallmark.
Stempelkissen *nt* stamp pad.
stempeln to stamp.
Stetigkeit *f* steadiness; continuity.
Steuer *f* tax.
Steuer *nt* *(Kraftfahrzeug)* steering wheel.
Steuerabzug *m* tax deduction.
Steuerausfall *m* tax deficit.

steuerbegünstigte Anlage *f* tax-sheltered investment.

Steuerbehörde *f* taxing authority; internal revenue office.

Steuerbelastung *f* tax burden; *(anteilsmäßige Festsetzung)* tax assessment.

Steuerberater *m* tax consultant.

Steuerberechnung *f* tax computation.

Steuerbonus *m* tax bonus.

Steuereinbuße *f* tax loss.

Steuereinnahme *f* *(Staat)* tax revenue; *(Eingänge)* tax receipts.

Steuereintreiber *m* tax collector.

Steuerentlastung *f* tax reduction; tax relief.

Steuererhebung *f* tax levy.

Steuererklärung *f* tax return.

Steuererleichterung *f* tax relief.

Steuerfachmann *m* tax expert.

steuerfrei tax-exempt.

Steuerfreibetrag *m* tax-exempt amount.

Steuergelder *f* tax moneys.

Steuergesetz *nt* tax law.

Steuergesetzgebung *f* taxation laws; internal revenue code.

Steuergutschrift *f* tax credit.

Steuerhilfe *f* tax aid; tax relief.

Steuerhinterziehung *f* tax evasion.

Steuerkonto *nt* tax account.

steuern *(leiten)* to direct; *(Vehikel)* to steer.

Steueroase *f* tax haven.

Steuerobjekt *nt* tax object.

Steuerparadies *nt* tax haven.

Steuerpflicht *f* tax liability.

steuerpflichtig taxable.

Steuerpflichtige *m/f* taxpayer.

Steuerpolitik *f* tax policy.

Steuerprogression *f* tax progression.

Steuerrecht *nt* taxation law.

Steuerreform *f* tax reform.

Steuerrichtlinie *f* taxation guideline.

Steuersatz *m* tax rate.

Steuerschätzung *f* tax assessment; tax estimate.

Steuersenkung *f* tax reduction.

Steuersystem *nt* tax structure; fiscal system; system of taxation.

Steuerumgehung *f* tax dodging; tax evasion.

Steuerung *f* steering; *(Leitung)* control.

Steuervermeidung *f* tax avoidance.

Steuervorschriften *pl* tax regulations.

Steuervorteil *m* tax advantage.

Steuerwesen *nt* taxation.

Steuerzahler *m* taxpayer.

Stichhaltigkeit *f* validity; (argument) soundness.

Stichprobe *f* random test; spot check.

stichprobenartig at random.

Stichtag *m* deadline.

stiften to endow; *(spenden)* to donate; *(schenken)* to give.

Stifter *m* *(Förderer, Gönner)* sponsor; *(Gründer)* founder.

Stiftung *f* trust; *(Rechtspersönlichkeit)* foundation; *(Schenkung)* endowment.

still silent.

stillegen *(Fabrik)* to close; *(Vorgang, Maschinen)* to shut down.

Stillegung *f* *(Fabrik)* closure; *(Vorgang, Maschinen)* shutdown.

Stillhalteabkommen *nt* moratorium.

Stillstand *m* standstill; halt.

stillstehend *(Maschinen)* idle.

Stimme *f* *(Wahl)* vote; voice.
stimmen to cast a vote; *(Musikinstrument)* to tune.
Stimmengleichheit *f* tie vote.
Stimmrecht *nt* right to vote; *(Wahlrecht)* suffrage.
Stimmrechtsermächtigung *f* proxy.
stimmrechtslos nonvoting.
Stimmzettel *m* ballot.
Stimulanz *f* stimulation.
stimulieren to stimulate.
stimulierend stimulating; reflationary.
Stock *m* stick; *(Gebäude)* storey; level.
stocken to stagnate.
stockend halting; stagnant.
Stockung *f* stagnation; stoppage.
Stockwerk *nt* level; floor; storey.
Stoff *m* matter; *(Textilie)* fabric; *(Substanz)* substance; matter.
Stoffrest *m* fabric remnant.
Stöpsel *m* plug; stopper.
stören to disturb.
stornieren to cancel.
Stornierung *f* reversal; cancellation.
Storno *m* cancellation.
Stornobuchung *f* reversing entry.
Störung *f* disturbance; interference.
Stoß *m* push; thrust; *(Ausstoß)* batch.
stoßen to push; to thrust.
Stoßkraft *f* power of thrust; *(Aufprall)* impact.
Stoßpolster *nt* buffer.
Straf- punitive.
Strafe *f* punishment; *(Geldstrafe)* penalty.
strafend punitive.
straffen to tighten.

Straffen *nt* tightening.
strategisch strategic.
strebsam striving; *(ehrgeizig)* ambitious.
Strebsamkeit *f* striving; *(Ehrgeiz)* ambition.
Strecke *f* route; *(Entfernung)* distance.
Strecke *f* **kennzeichnen** to route.
streichen to eliminate; *(Farbe)* to paint.
Streichholz *nt* match.
Streichung *f* deletion; (drucktechn.) cancellation.
Streifen *m* strip; (Gürtel) belt; *(Farbstreifen)* stripe; *(Papier-, Klebe-)* tape.
Streik *m* strike.
Streikbrecher *m* strikebreaker; scab.
streiken to strike.
Streiken *nt* striking.
streikfrei strike-free.
Streikgebiet *nt* strike area.
Streikmonat *m* strike month.
Streikposten *m* picket.
Streikrecht *nt* right to strike.
Streikverlust *m* strike loss.
Streit *m* argument.
streiten to argue; to dispute.
Streitpunkt *m* point of contention; argument.
streuen *(Risiko)* to spread; *(Dividende)* to distribute; *(Investition, Produktion)* to diversify.
Streuung *f* *(Risiko)* spread; *(Dividende)* distribution; *(Investition, Produktion)* diversification.
Strick *m* rope.
Strom *m* *(elek.)* electrical power; *(Fluß)* stream; *(Fließen)* flow.
Stromlinienform *f* streamlined shape.

stromlinienförmig gestalten to streamline.

Stromversorgung *f* electrical power supply.

Struktur *f* structure.

Strukturanpassung *f* structural adjustment.

Struktureffekt *m* structural effect.

strukturell structural.

strukturelle Veränderung *f* structural change.

strukturieren to structure.

Strukturierung *f* structuring.

Strukturplan *m* structural plan.

Strukturproblem *nt* structural problem.

Strukturprogramm *nt* structural program; structural line.

Strukturschwäche *f* structural weakness.

Strukturwandel *m* structural change.

Strumpf *m* stocking.

Stück *nt* *(Akkord)* piece; *(Einheit)* unit; *(Segment)* segment.

Stückgewinn *m* unit profit.

Stückpreis *m* unit price.

stückweise piecemeal.

Stückzahl *f* number of units.

Studie *f* study.

Stufe *f* step; *(Phase)* phase.

stufenflexibel sliding.

stumm silent.

Stunde *f* hour.

Stundenlohn *m* hourly wages.

Sturz *m* *(Börse)* crash; tumble.

stürzen *(Börse)* to crash; to tumble; to slump; *(Kurse, Preise)* to collapse; to plunge; *(Regierung)* to overthrow.

Stütze *f* *(Unterstützung)* support; backing.

stützen to support; *(Kurs, Markt)* to peg.

stützend supporting.

Stützpreis *m* support price; *(Kurs, Markt)* pegged price.

Stützpunkt *m* *(Militär)* base.

Stützung *f* *(Börse)* pegging.

Stützungsgelder *pl* backing money.

Stützungskosten *pl* cost of support; *(Subvention)* cost of subsidy.

Stützweite *f* *(Bau)* support span.

Submission *f* submission; tender.

Substanz *f* substance; *(Material)* material; *(Stoff)* matter.

Substanzverringerung *f* *(Vermögen)* depletion of assets.

substituierbar replaceable.

Substitut *nt* substitute.

Substitution *f* substitution.

Subtraktion *f* subtraction.

Subunternehmer *m* subcontractor.

Subvention *f* subsidy.

subventionieren to subsidize.

Subventionierung *f* subsidization.

Subventionsabbau *m* subsidy reduction.

Subventionsbedarf *m* subsidy requirements.

Subventionsgeld *nt* subsidy funds.

Subventionszahlung *f* subsidy payment.

Summe *f* sum; *(Betrag)* amount.

summierbar capable of being totalled.

Sumpf *m* swamp.

Sund *m* sound.

Supermarkt *m* supermarket.

Superrechner *m* mainframe computer.

supranational supranational.

Surrogat *nt* surrogate; substitute.
Swapabkommen *nt* swap agreement.
Swapgeschäft *nt* swap deal; swap business.
Swapvereinbarung *f* swap arrangement.
symbolisch symbolic; token.

Syndikat *nt* syndicate.
Syndikatsbildung *f* syndication.
synthetisch synthetic.
systematisch systematic.
Systembildung *f* system formation.
Systemeinheit *f* system unit.

tabellarische Darstellung *f* tabulation.
tabellarisches Ordnen *nt* tabulating.
tabellarisch ordnen to tabulate.
tabellarisieren to tabulate.
Tabellarisieren *nt* tabulating.
Tabelle *f* table; *(Plan, Verzeichnis)* schedule; *(Schaubild, Berechnungstafel)* chart.
Tabellierung *f* tabulation.
Tadel *m* blame; censure.
tadeln to blame; to censure.
Tafel *f* *(Schaubild)* chart; *(Tabelle)* table.
Tagebaubetrieb *m* strip mining.
Tagelohn *m* daily wage.
tagen to meet; *(beraten)* to deliberate; *(Gericht)* to sit; *(Parlament)* to be in session.
Tagesauszug *m* daily statement of account.
Tagesgeld *nt* *(Bankwesen)* call money; overnight loan; *(Sitzungsgeld)* per diem.
Tageskurs *m* market rate.
Tagesordnung *f* agenda; *(Gericht)* docket.

Tagesordnungspunkt *m* agenda item.
Tageswert *m* present value.
Tagung *f* meeting; congress; *(Versammlung)* convention.
Takelung *f* rigging.
Takelwerk *nt* rigging.
Takt *m* *(Musik)* beat; *(Motor)* stroke; *(Feingefühl)* tact.
Taktik *f* tactics.
taktisch tactical.
taktische Maßnahme *f* tactic.
taktischer Zug *m* tactical move.
Talfahrt *f* slide.
Tantieme *f* *(Ertragsanteil)* royalty.
Tarif *m* tariff; *(Rate)* rate.
Tarifabkommen *nt* collective agreement; wage agreement.
Tarifabschluß *m* tariff agreement.
Tarifautonomie *f* tariff autonomy; wage autonomy.
Tarifberechnung *f* rate making.
Tarifbewegung *f* tariff movement.
Tarifergebnis *nt* tariff decision; tariff negotiating results.
Tariferhöhung *f* rate hike; tariff increase.

Tarifermäßigung *f* tariff reduction.

Tarifexperte *m* tariff expert.

Tarifgespräch *nt* bargaining talk; wage discussion.

Tarifhoheit *f* tariff authority; tariff sovereignty.

Tarifkommission *f* *(Eisenbahn)* railroad commission; *(Gewerkschaft)* collective bargaining commission; *(Zoll)* tariff commission.

Tarifkontrolle *f* tariff control; rate control.

Tarifpartner *m* bargaining agent; collective bargainer.

Tarifpolitik *f* *(Lohn)* rate policy; *(Zoll)* tariff policy.

Tarifregelung *f* *(Lohn)* rate regulation.

Tarifrunde *f* *(Lohn)* rate bargaining round.

Tarifsatz *m* *(Lohn)* wage rate; *(Zoll)* tariff rate.

Tarifsenkung *f* tariff reduction.

Tarifstreit *m* rate dispute.

Tarifverhandlung *f* collective bargaining.

Tarifvertrag *m* wage agreement.

Tarifvorzug *m* tariff preference.

Tarifzoll *m* tariff duty.

Tasche *f* *(Handtasche)* bag; *(Kleidertasche)* pocket.

Taschengeld *nt* pocket money; allowance.

Tastatur *f* keyboard.

Taste *f* key.

Tastengerät *nt* keyboard; digital device.

tätig *(berufstätig)* employed; *(beschäftigt)* busy; *(aktiv)* active.

Tätigkeit *f* action; activity.

Tätigkeitsbericht *m* progress report.

Tätigung *f* **von Versicherungsgeschäften** *pl* insurance underwriting.

Tatsache *f* fact.

tatsächlich actual.

tauglich *(Eignung)* suitable; *(Zustand)* fit.

Tausch *m* exchange; swap; *(Tauschhandel)* barter; swap.

Tauschbeziehung *f* exchange relationship; barter relationship.

tauschen to trade; to swap.

Tauschgeschäft *nt* barter; barter trade.

Tauschhandel *m* countertrade; barter trade.

Tauschhandel *m* **betreiben** to engage in countertrade.

Tauschmittel *nt* medium of exchange.

Tauschrate *f* exchange rate; barter rate; offset rate.

Tauschrelation *f* exchange relation; barter relation.

Tauschwirtschaft *f* barter economy; countertrade economy.

Taxe *f* tariff; tax.

taxieren to appraise; *(schätzen)* to estimate.

Taxierung *f* valuation.

Taxwert *m* appraisal value.

Team *nt* team.

Teamarbeit *f* teamwork.

Technik *f* technique.

Techniker *m* technician; *(Reparatur)* repairman, -person, -woman.

technisch technical.

technisch ausgefeilt technologically perfected.

technische Anlage *f* technical installation; plant.

technische Ausführung *f* technique.

technisch hohes Niveau *nt*   technologically advanced level.

Technokrat *m*   technocrat.

Technologe *m*, **Technologin** *f*   technologist.

Technologie *f*   technology.

Technologietransfer *m*   technology transfer.

technologisch   technological.

technologische Änderung *f*   technological change.

technologische Neuerung *f*   technological innovation.

technologischer Fortschritt *m*   technological advance.

technologische Strategie *f*   technological strategy.

Teil-   partial.

Teil *m*   part; *(Sektion)* section; *(Abschnitt)* segment; *(Anteil)* portion.

Teil *nt*   *(maschinell)* part; spare part.

teilbar   divisible; *(trennbar)* separable.

Teilbarkeit *f*   divisibility.

teilen   to divide; *(teilhaben, abgeben)* to share; *(trennen)* to part; *(abtrennen)* to partition.

Teilgebiet *nt*   zone.

teilhaben   to share; to participate.

Teilhaber *m*   partner; associate; *(Teilnehmer)* participant.

Teilmontage *f*   subassembly.

Teilnahme *f*   participation; *(Subskription)* subscription.

teilnehmen   to participate.

Teilnehmer *m*   participant; *(Subskribent)* subscriber.

Teilnehmerzahl *f*   number of participants.

Teilprivatisierung *f*   partial privatization.

Teilung *f*   division.

teilweise   partial.

Teilwert *m*   fractional value; partial value.

Teilzeit-   part-time.

Teilzeitarbeit *f*   part-time work.

Telefon *nt*   telephone.

telefonieren   to telephone; to call.

Telefonvermittlungsperson *f*   telephone operator.

Telefonzentrale *f*   switchboard.

telegrafieren   to wire.

Telegramm *nt*   telegram; wire.

Tendenz *f*   tendency; *(Trend)* trend.

Tendenzwende *f*   turnaround.

tendieren   to show a tendency; to tend; *(neigen)* to lean.

Termin-   forward.

Termin *m*   term; *(Endtermin)* deadline; *(Datum)* date; *(Verfallzeit)* maturity; *(Zahlungstermin)* payment due date; *(festgesetzter Zeitpunkt)* appointment.

Terminabschluß *m*   forward contract; futures contract.

Termindevisen *pl*   forward currency.

Termineinlagen *f*   time deposits; restricted cash.

Terminfestlegung *f*   setting a date.

Termingelder *pl*   time deposits; restricted cash.

Termingeldsatz *m*   time deposit rate; fixed market rate.

termingerecht   in due time; *(zeitplanmäßig)* on schedule.

Termingeschäft *nt*   option trading; forward transaction; futures trading.

Terminierung *f*   timing.

Terminkalender *m*   appointment calendar; appointment schedule; *(Gericht)* docket.

Terminmarkt *m*   options market; forward market; futures market.

Terminologie *f* terminology; *(Sprache)* language.
Terminplanung *f* scheduling.
Terminsatz *m* futures rate.
Territorium *nt* territory.
Test *m* test.
testen to test.
Testfall *m* test case.
teuer expensive; costly.
Teuerung *f* inflation.
Teuerungsimpuls *m* price increase impulse.
Teuerungsrate *f* rate of price increase.
Teuerungswelle *f* wave of price increases.
Text *m* text.
Textil- textile.
Textilfabrikant *m* textile manufacturer.
Textilware *f* textiles.
Textprozessor *m* word processor.
Textstelle *f* passage.
Textverarbeiter *m* word processor.
Textverarbeitung *f* word processing.
Theke *f* counter.
Thema *nt* topic.
theoretisch theoretical; *(spekulativ)* speculative.
Tiefpunkt *m* low point; *(Preis, Profit)* bottom; *(Wirtschaft)* trough.
Tiefstand *m* low; bottom.
tilgen *(auslöschen)* to eradicate; *(Schulden)* to retire; to redeem; to liquidate; *(Dokument)* to delete; *(Hypothek)* to amortize.
Tilgung *f* *(Anleihekapital)* retirement; *(Zurückzahlung)* repayment; *(Amortisierung)* redemption; *(Abtragung, Auflösung)* liquidation.

Tilgungsbetrag *m* repayment amount; amortization amount.
tilgungsfrei without amortization.
Tilgungsfreistellung *f* exemption from amortization.
Tilgungshypothek *f* amortization mortgage.
Tilgungsrate *f* amortization rate; sinking fund installment.
Tip *m* tip; lead.
Tipgeber *m* *(Wette)* tout.
tippen to type.
Tisch *m* table; counter.
Tischcomputeranlage *f* desktop computer system.
Tischrechner *m* desktop calculator.
Titel *m* title.
Titelkopf *m* rubric heading.
Tochterbank *f* subsidiary bank.
Tochterbetrieb *m* subsidiary company.
Tochtergesellschaft *f* subsidiary company; subsidiary.
Tochterinstitut *nt* subsidiary institute.
Tochterunternehmen *nt* subsidiary enterprise.
Ton *m* tone; sound.
Tonband *nt* audio tape.
Tonnengehalt *m* tonnage.
Tor *nt* *(Sport)* goal; gate.
tot dead; *(fig.)* idle.
Total- total.
total total; *(gesamt)* overall; complete.
tragbar portable; *(fig.)* bearable; manageable.
tragen to carry; *(fig.)* to bear; to carry.
Träger *m* *(Bahnhof)* porter; *(Versicherung)* carrier.
Tragfähigkeit *f* tonnage capacity.
trainieren to train.

Trainieren *nt*   training.
Tranche *f*   tranche; portion.
Transaktion *f*   transaction; deal.
Transaktionskosten *pl*   transaction costs.
Transfer *m*   transfer.
Transferbegünstigte *m/f*   transferee.
Transfereinkommen *nt*   transfer income.
transferieren   to transfer.
Transferpreis *m*   transfer price.
Transferzahlung *f*   transfer payment.
Transit *m*   transit.
Transport *m*   transport; *(Versand)* shipping; transportation.
Transporter *m*   truck.
transportfähig   transportable.
transportieren   to transport; to convey; to remove.
Transportunternehmer *m*   freight carrier.
Transportvolumen *nt*   shipping volume.
Transportwagen *m*   van.
Tratte *f*   draft.
treffen   to meet; *(erzielen)* to score; *(Ziel)* to hit.
Treffen *nt*   meeting; rally.
Treffer *m*   hit.
treiben   to drift; *(Fahrzeug)* to drive.
Treibenlassen *nt*   drifting.
Trend *m*   trend.
trennen   to part; to separate; to dissociate; *(abtrennen)* to partition.

trennend   disruptive.
Trennung *f*   severance; disruption; *(Ehescheidung)* divorce; separation.
Tresor *m*   strongbox; safe; vault.
Treuhandanstalt *f*   trust institution.
Treuhänder *m*   trustee; fiduciary; custodian.
treuhänderisch   fiduciary; in trust.
Treuhandgeschäft *nt*   trust transaction.
Treuhandgesellschaft *f*   trust corporation.
Treuhandverhältnis *nt*   fiduciary relationship; trust.
Treuhandvermögen *nt*   trust assets.
Treuhandvertrag *m*   trust agreement.
Tribunal *nt*   tribunal.
Triebkraft *f*   impetus.
Triebwerk *nt*   drive mechanism; engine.
Trog *m*   trough.
Tropfen *m*   drop.
Trudeln *nt*   tailspin.
Truppenteil *m*   troop outfit; troop unit.
Trust *m*   combine; trust; pool.
tüchtig   efficient; capable.
Tüchtigkeit *f*   efficiency.
Typ *m*   type.
Typenabdrucker *m*   daisy wheel printer.

U

üben to practice.
Überalterung *f* obsolescence.
Überangebot *nt* oversupply.
überanstrengen to overwork.
überarbeiten to overwork; *(Schriftstück)* to revise.
Überarbeitung *f* revision.
Überbau *m* superstructure.
überbelasten to overburden; to overwork.
überbesteuern to overtax.
überbewerten to overvalue.
Überbewertung *f* overvaluation; overestimation.
Überbleibsel *nt* remnant.
überbrücken to bridge a gap.
Überbrückungshilfe *f* stopgap assistance; interim aid.
über den Bestand *m* **verkaufen** to oversell.
überdenken to rethink.
überdurchschnittlich above average; superior.
übereinkommen to come to an understanding; to agree.
Übereinkommen *nt* understanding; agreement.
übereinstimmen to agree; *(Nachzählung)* to tally; *(derselben Meinung sein)* to concur; *(entsprechen)* to conform to.
Übereinstimmung *f* agreement; *(Meinungsgleichheit)* concurrence; *(Konsens)* consensus; *(Einklang, Vergleich)* accord; accordance.
Überfahrt *f* crossing; transit.
überfällig overdue; past due.
überfliegen to fly over; *(Dokument)* to scan.

Überfliegen *nt* flying over; *(Dokument)* scanning.
überfließen to overflow.
überflügeln to outdistance; to outstrip.
Überfluß *m* superfluity; *(Überschuß)* surplus; *(Übermaß)* excess; *(Fülle)* abundance; plenty.
Überflüssigkeit *f* redundancy; *(Überfluß)* superfluity.
Überflutung *f* overflow; flooding.
überfordern to overburden; *(Person)* to stress.
Überfülle *f* overabundance; *(Überfluß)* superfluity.
Übergang *m* transition; change; *(Verkehr)* crossing; *(Fußgänger)* crosswalk.
Übergangsregelung *f* temporary arrangement; interim ruling.
Übergangszeit *f* transitional period.
Übergriff *m* infringement.
überheizen to overheat.
überheizt superheated.
überhitzen to overheat.
überhitzt superheated.
überhöhen *(übertreiben)* to exaggerate; *(Kosten, Spesen)* to pad.
überholen *(gründlich reparieren)* to overhaul; *(Verkehr)* to pass; *(fig.)* to overtake.
Überholen *nt* *(Verkehr)* passing.
überholt obsolete.
Überholung *f* *(gründliche Reparatur, Erneuerung)* overhaul.
Überkapazität *f* excess capacity.
überkapitalisieren to overcapitalize.

Überkapitalisierung *f* overcapitalization.

überladen ornate; excessive.

überlassen to dispose of; *(aufgeben)* to relinquish; to cede.

Überlassung *f* *(Abtretung)* cession.

überlasten to overload.

überlaufen *(Ort, Sehenswürdig-
keit)* overrun; *(überfließen)* to
overflow.

überlegen superior; *(denken)* to
deliberate.

Überlegenheit *f* superiority.

Übermaß *nt* excess.

übermäßig excessive.

übermäßig anpreisen to push; to
pitch; to tout.

Übernahme *f* *(Unternehmen)* takeover; *(Verantwortung)* assumption.

Übernahmeangebot *nt* *(Unternehmen)* takeover offer; tender
offer.

übernational supranational.

übernehmen to take over; *(Verantwortung, Schulden)* to assume;
to absorb.

Übernehmer *m* transferee; receiver.

Überpreis *m* overprice.

Überproduktion *f* overproduction.

überproduzieren to overproduce.

überprüfen to review; *(bestätigen)*
to verify; *(nachprüfen)* to check.

Überprüfen *nt* checking.

Überprüfung *f* review; *(Bestätigung)* verification; *(Nachprüfung)*
check.

überreden to persuade; *(zum
Kauf)* to make a sales pitch.

Überredung *f* persuasion; *(zum
Kauf)* sales pitch.

überregional supraregional;
nationwide.

überregionale Verbreitung *f* syndication.

überregionale Ausstrahlung *f*
(Medien) syndication.

Überrest *m* remnant.

überschätzen to overestimate; to
overvalue.

überschauen to survey.

überschreiten to exceed.

Überschrift *f* heading.

Überschuldung *f* excessive indebtedness; *(Unternehmen)* overextension.

Überschuß *m* surplus; *(Übermaß)*
excess.

Überschußlage *f* surplus condition.

Überschußprodukt *nt* surplus
product.

überschwemmen to flood; to
swamp.

Überschwemmung *f* flooding;
(Überlaufen) overflow.

Übersee *f* transoceanic area; overseas countries.

Überseegeschäft *nt* overseas
trade.

Überseehandel *m* overseas trade.

überseeisch transoceanic; overseas.

überseeische Unternehmung *f*
overseas operation.

überseeische Geschäftstätigkeit *f*
overseas business activity.

Überseemarkt *m* overseas market;
foreign market.

übersenden to transmit; to send.

Übersenden *nt* transmission;
(Spedition) consignment.

Übersicht *f* general view; summary; synopsis.

übersteigen to exceed; *(überflügeln)* to outstrip.

Überstunde *f* overtime hour.

übertragbar   transferable; portable.
übertragen   to transfer; *(freigeben)* to release; *(zuweisen)* to assign.
Übertragung *f*   transfer; *(Zuweisung)* assignment.
Übertragungsgebühr *f*   transfer charge.
Übertragungsurkunde *f*   release document.
übertreffen   to beat; to exceed.
übertreiben   to exaggerate; to overstate.
Übertretung *f*   violation; *(Bruch, Verstoß)* breach.
überverkaufen   to oversell.
überversorgen   oversupply.
überwachen   to monitor; *(beaufsichtigen)* to supervise; *(kontrollieren)* to control.
Überwachen *nt*   monitoring; *(Beaufsichtigen)* supervising.
Überwachung *f*   *(Beobachtung)* surveillance; *(Beaufsichtigung)* supervision; *(Kontrolle)* control.
Überwachung *f* **der Umweltverschmutzung** *f*   environmental pollution control.
Überwachungsstelle *f*   regulatory agency.
Überwachungstechniker *m*   control technician; monitoring technician.
überweisen   to transfer.
Überweisung *f*   transfer.
Überweisungsauftrag *m*   transfer order; *(Zahlung)* remittance order.
Überweisungsgebühr *f*   transfer charge.
Überweisungsverkehr *m*   transfer of funds.
überwiegen   to outweigh; *(dominieren)* to be dominant.
überzeichnen   to oversubscribe.

überzeugen   to convince.
überzeugend   convincing; persuasive.
überzeugendes Argument *nt*   convincing argument; selling point.
Überzeugung *f*   conviction; *(Überredung)* persuasion; *(Glaube)* belief.
überziehen   *(Konto)* to overdraw.
Überziehungskredit *f*   overdraft privilege.
üblich   customary; *(gewöhnlich)* usual.
üblicher Marktpreis *m*   fair value.
üblicher Verlauf *m*   customary process.
übliches Verfahren *nt*   standard practice; customary procedure.
übrig   remaining; left over.
übrigbleiben   to remain; to be left over.
ultimo   occuring in the preceding month.
umändern   to alter.
umarbeiten   to revise; to adapt.
Umarbeitung *f*   revision; adaptation.
Umbau *m*   reorganization; *(Umstrukturierung)* restructuring.
umbauen   to remodel; *(neu organisieren)* to reorganize.
umbuchen   to transfer.
Umbuchung *f*   transfer.
umdenken   to rethink.
umdisponieren   to redispose; to rearrange; *(Investition)* to reinvest.
Umdisposition *f*   redisposition; *(Investition)* reinvestment.
umdrehen   to turn around.
Umdrehung *f*   *(Umwendung)* turn; *(Rotation)* rotation; *(Motor)* revolution.

Umfang *m*   volume; *(Maßstab)*
scale; *(Größe)* size; *(Ausmaß)*
measure; *(Ausdehnung)* extent;
(Fülle) amplitude.
umfangreich   voluminous; *(geräumig)* spacious; *(umfassend)* comprehensive.
umfangreiche Streichungen *pl*
extensive cuts.
umfassen   to span; *(einschließen)*
to include; *(enthalten, beinhalten)*
to contain; *(decken, abdecken)* to
cover.
umfassend   comprehensive.
Umfinanzierung *f*   refinancing.
Umfrage *f*   survey.
Umgang *m*   association.
Umgebung *f*   environment.
umgehen   to dodge; *(vermeiden)* to
avoid; to sidestep.
Umgehungsmanöver *nt*   dodge.
umgestalten   to reform; to
rearrange.
Umgestaltung *f*   rearrangement.
umgruppieren   to regroup; to
rearrange; *(Klassifikation)* to
reclassify; *(Einsatz)* to redeploy.
Umgruppierung *f*   rearrangement;
(Einsatz) redeployment.
Umkehrung *f*   turnaround; reversal.
Umklammerung *f*   stranglehold.
Umkreis *m*   radius; *(Nähe)* vicinity.
Umlage *f*   contribution; *(Zuteilung)*
allocation; apportionment.
umlaufen   to circulate; *(Effekten)*
to float.
umlaufend   circulating; running;
current; *(Effekten)* floating.
umlauffähig   negotiable.
Umlaufkapital *nt*   working capital.
Umlaufvermögen *nt*   current
assets.

umleiten   to divert.
umlenken   to switch.
Umlenken *nt*   switching.
ummodellieren   to remodel.
Umorganisation *f*   reorganization.
umorganisieren   to remodel; to
reorganize.
Umplazierung *f*   relocation; *(Einsatz)* redeployment.
umrechnen   to convert.
Umrechnung *f*   conversion.
Umrechnungskurs *m*   exchange
rate.
umreißen   to outline.
Umriß *m*   outline.
Umsatz *m*   turnover.
umsatzabhängig   turnover depen-
dent; dependent on sales.
Umsatzanstieg *m*   increase in
turnover; upsurge in sales.
Umsatzanteil *m*   share of sales.
Umsatzeinbruch *m*   sales collapse.
Umsatzeinbuße *f*   loss of sales.
Umsatzentwicklung *f*   develop-
ment of sales.
Umsatzertrag *m*   sales revenue.
Umsatzprovision *f*   commission on
sales.
Umsatzrekord *m*   sales record.
Umsatzrückgang *m*   decrease in
turnover; decline in sales.
Umsatzsteigerung *f*   turnover
increase; rise in sales.
Umsatzsteuer *f*   sales tax.
Umsatzverlust *m*   loss in sales.
Umsatzwachstum *nt*   growth in
sales.
Umsatzzunahme *f*   sales increase.
Umsatzzuwachs *m*   turnover gain.
umschichten   to shift; rearrange.
Umschlag *m*   turnover; *(Brief)*
envelope.
umschreiben   to circumscribe; to

paraphrase; *(umformulieren)* to rewrite; *(kopieren)* to transcribe; *(Wechsel)* to reendorse; *(übertragen)* to transfer; *(Grundstück)* to convey.

Umschreibung *f* *(Aktien)* transfer; *(Flugkarte)* rerouting; *(Schriftstück)* transcription; *(Grundbesitz)* conveyance.

umschulden to reschedule debt payments.

Umschuldung *f* debt rescheduling; *(Umwandlung)* conversion of debts; *(Neufinanzierung)* refinancing.

umschulen to retrain.

Umschulung *f* retraining.

Umschwung *m* change; *(Umkehrung)* reversal.

umsetzbar marketable.

umsetzen to sell; *(Arbeitskräfte)* to dislocate; *(Umsatz haben)* to turn over; *(realisieren)* to realize.

Umsicht *f* circumspection; *(Vorsicht)* caution.

umsiedeln to relocate.

umspannen to span.

Umstand *m* circumstance; *(Tatsache)* fact; *(Faktor)* factor.

umstellen to convert.

Umstellung *f* *(Änderung)* change; *(Neustrukturierung)* restructuring; *(Modifizierung)* modification.

Umstellungsprozeß *m* adjustment process.

umstrukturieren to restructure.

Umstrukturierung *f* restructuring.

Umtausch *m* *(Waren)* exchange; *(Währung)* conversion.

umtauschen *(Waren)* to exchange; *(Währung)* to convert.

umverteilen to redistribute; *(neu zuteilen)* to reallocate.

Umverteilung *f* reallocation; redistribution.

Umwandelbarkeit *f* convertibility.

umwandeln to convert; to change.

Umwandlung *f* conversion.

Umwelt- environmental; ecological.

Umwelt *f* environment; *(Ökologie)* ecology.

Umweltbelastung *f* environmental burden.

umweltbewußt environmentally aware; ecology-minded.

Umweltexperte *m*, **-expertin** *f* environment expert.

umweltfreundlich environment-friendly; not harmful to the environment.

Umweltgruppe *f* environmental group.

Umweltproblem *nt* environmental problem.

Umweltqualität *f* environmental quality.

Umweltschutz *m* environmental protection.

Umweltschutzauflage *f* environmental protection amendment.

Umweltschützer *m* environmentalist; environmental activist.

Umweltthema *nt* environmental topic.

Umweltverschmutzer *m* polluter.

Umweltverschmutzung *f* environmental pollution.

umweltverträglich environmentally compatible.

umwerben to woo; *(Reklame)* to pursuade; to buy.

umziehen to move.

Umzug *m* relocation; move.

unabhängig independent; autonomous.

Unabhängigkeit *f* independence.
unabkömmlich indispensable.
unanfechtbar incontrovertible; unassailable.
unangemessen inappropriate.
Unangemessenheit *f* inappropriateness.
unannehmbar unacceptable.
unaufdringlich discreet; retiring.
unauffällig inconspicuous; understated.
unausgebildet untrained.
unausgegeben *(Aktien)* unissued; *(Geld)* unspent.
Unausgeglichenheit *f* imbalance; disequilibrium.
unausgenutzt underutilized; idle.
unbefriedigend unsatisfactory; disappointing.
unbefriedigt unsatisfied.
unbefristet *(Zeit)* unlimited.
unbeglichen outstanding; *(Rechnung)* unpaid.
unbegrenzt unlimited; indefinite.
unbegründet unfounded.
unbelastet unencumbered; clear.
unberechtigt unjustified.
unberücksichtigt not considered.
unbesetzt *(Fernsprechzelle)* unoccupied; vacant; *(Posten)* unfilled.
Unbeständigkeit *f* inconstancy; instability.
unbestimmt indefinite.
unbewohnt uninhabited; empty; void.
unbezahlbar prohibitively expensive; *(unersetzlich)* priceless; *(unschätzbar)* inestimable.
unbezahlt unpaid.
unbezahlte Werbebotschaft *f* sales plug.
unbillig unfair.
unbrauchbar unusable.

undurchführbar not feasible.
uneinbringlich uncollectable.
uneingeschränkt unlimited; unrestricted; *(Konzession)* plenary; *(Revisionsvermerk)* unqualified.
uneinig sein to disagree.
unelastisch inelastic.
Unelastizität *f* inelasticity.
unentbehrlich indispensable.
unentgeltlich gratuitous; *(gratis)* free.
unentwickelt undeveloped.
unerfahren inexperienced.
unerfüllt unfulfilled.
unergiebig unproductive.
unerheblich slight; immaterial.
unerkannt unrecognized.
unerläßlich requisite; indispensable.
unerlaubt unauthorized; *(ungesetzlich)* illegal; *(bürgerliches Recht)* unlawful.
unerledigt unfinished.
unerledigte Aufträge *pl* backlog of orders.
unerledigter Auftragsbestand *m* order backlog.
unermeßlich immeasurable.
unerschlossen undeveloped; unexplored; *(Ressourcen)* untapped.
unerwartet unexpected.
unerwarteter Gewinn *m* windfall profit.
unfähig incompetent; *(außerstande)* incapable.
Unfähigkeit *f* incompetence; *(Unvermögen)* inability; *(Untauglichkeit)* disqualification.
unfair unfair.
Unfall *m* accident.
Unfallversicherung *f* casualty insurance; accident insurance.
Unfallversorgung *f* casualty compensation.

unfein unrefined; crude; gross.
ungebraucht unused; untapped.
ungebunden uncommitted; unaffiliated.
ungedeckt uncovered; *(Schulden)* unsecured.
ungeeignet unsuitable.
ungekürzt unabbreviated; *(Buchausgabe)* unabridged.
ungelernt unskilled.
ungelernter Arbeiter *m* unskilled worker; laborer.
ungelöst unresolved.
ungenau inexact; sketchy.
ungenügend insufficient; deficient.
ungenutzt unutilized; unused.
ungerechnet uncounted.
ungerecht unjust.
ungerechtfertigt unjustified.
Ungerechtigkeit *f* injustice; inequity.
ungeschäftlich unbusinesslike.
ungeschlichtet unresolved; *(Konflikt)* not arbitrated.
ungesetzlich illegal.
ungesetzlich machen to outlaw.
ungewiß uncertain; *(vieldeutig)* ambiguous.
Ungewißheit *f* uncertainty; *(Vieldeutigkeit)* ambiguity.
ungewöhnlich unusual.
ungleich unequal.
ungleichartig disparate.
Ungleichgewicht *nt* imbalance; disequilibrium.
Ungleichheit *f* inequality; *(Ungleichartigkeit)* disparity; *(Verschiedenheit)* diversity.
Unglück *nt* misfortune; *(Desaster)* disaster.
Unglücksfall *m* accident; mishap.
ungültig invalid.
Ungültigkeit *f* invalidity.

Ungültigkeitserklärung *f* cancellation.
ungültig machen to void; to invalidate.
ungünstig unfavorable; adverse.
Uniform *f* uniform.
Universalbank *f* universal bank; full service bank.
unkalkulierbar incalculable; *(unvorhersehbar)* unforeseeable.
unklar unclear; *(vieldeutig)* ambiguous.
unklug imprudent.
Unkostengebühr *f* service charge.
unkündbar *(Arbeitspersonal)* not dismissable; *(Vertrag)* uncancellable.
unlösbar unresolvable.
unmeßbar not measurable.
unmittelbar direct.
unnormal abnormal.
Unordnung *f* disorder.
unparteiisch impartial; fair.
unpraktisch impractical.
unproduktiv unproductive; nonproductive.
unrealisiert unrealized.
unrecht *(Meinung)* wrong; *(Tat)* unethical.
Unrecht *nt* injustice.
unrechtmäßig unlawful; illegal.
unreell *(unehrlich)* dishonest; *(unzuverlässig)* unreliable.
unrentabel unprofitable; uneconomical.
unrichtig incorrect.
Unruhe *f* restlessness; *(polit.)* unrest; *(Störung)* disturbance.
unschlichtbar unresolvable.
unselbständig dependent.
unseriös not respectable; *(vertrauensunwürdig)* untrustworthy.
unsicher *(Lage)* uncertain; *(prekär)*

precarious; *(Person)* unsure; *(psych., finanziell)* insecure.

Unsicherheit *f* uncertainty; precariousness.

Unsicherheitsfaktor *m* uncertainty factor.

unsicher machen to render uncertain; to destabilize.

unsolide unsound; *(unzuverlässig)* unreliable.

unstabil unstable; *(unsicher)* insecure.

untätig idle.

Untätigkeit *f* idleness.

untauglich unusable; *(ungeeignet)* unsuitable.

unten below; *(treppab)* downstairs.

unter under; below.

Unterabteilung *f* subdivision; subpart.

Unterangebot *nt* underbid.

Unterausschuß *m* subcommittee.

unterbauen to support; to underpin.

Unterbeschäftigung *f* underemployment.

unterbesetzt understaffed.

unterbewerten to undervalue.

unterbewertet undervalued.

unterbezahlt underpaid.

unterbieten to underbid; to undercut.

unterbrechen to interrupt; *(Verhandlung)* to suspend; *(Störung)* to disrupt; *(aufhören)* to discontinue.

Unterbrechung *f* interruption; *(Stopp)* stoppage.

unterbreiten to submit; *(präsentieren)* to present.

unterbringen to house; *(plazieren)* to place; *(Übernachtung)* to accommodate.

Unterbringung *f* housing; *(Plazierung)* placement; *(Übernachtung)* accommodation.

unter dem Marktpreis *m* **verkaufen** to sell below market price.

unter dem Wert *m* **angesetzter Preis** *m* underprice.

unter der Norm *f* substandard.

unter Druck *m* **setzen** to pressure; to squeeze.

unterdrücken to suppress; *(ersticken)* to stifle.

unterdurchschnittlich below average; substandard.

unterentwickelt underdeveloped.

Unterentwicklung *f* underdevelopment.

Unterfangen *nt* undertaking.

Untergebene *m/f* subordinate.

untergeordnet subordinate.

untergliedern to subdivide.

Untergliederung *f* subdivision; *(Kategorie)* subcategorization.

untergraben to undermine.

Unterhalt *m* livelihood; maintenance; *(Unterstützung)* support.

unterhalten to support; *(Unterhalt)* to maintain; *(Unterhaltung)* to entertain.

Unterhaltskosten *pl* upkeep expense.

Unterhaltszahlung *f* support payment.

Unterhändler *m* negotiator.

Unterkonto *nt* subaccount.

Unterkunft *m* accommodation; living quarters.

Unterlage *f* document; paper.

unterlassen to refrain from.

Unterlassung *f* omission; *(Befolgung)* failure.

unterlegen inferior.

Unterlieferant *m* subcontractor.
untermauern to underpin; *(unterstützen)* to support; *(verstärken)* to strengthen.
Untermiete *f* sublease.
unterminieren to undermine.
unternehmen to undertake.
Unternehmen *nt* enterprise; *(Firma)* firm; *(Konzern)* concern; *(Gesellschaft)* company.
Unternehmensberater *m* corporate consultant; management consultant.
Unternehmensform *f* corporate organization.
Unternehmensführung *f* business management.
Unternehmenskontrolle *f* management control.
Unternehmenskonzept *nt* corporate concept.
Unternehmensleitung *f* company management.
Unternehmensplanung *f* corporate planning.
Unternehmensstrategie *f* corporate strategy.
Unternehmer *m* entrepreneur.
unternehmerisch entrepreneurial.
Unternehmerschaft *f* body of entrepreneurs; entrepreneurship.
Unternehmerverband *m* entrepreneurs' association; businessmen's association.
Unternehmerverhalten *nt* entrepreneurial behavior.
Unternehmung *f* *(Projekt)* undertaking; *(Wagnis)* venture; *(Betrieb)* operation; *(Unternehmen)* enterprise.
Unternehmungspolitik *f* corporate policy.

unterordnen to subordinate.
Unterorganisation *f* subsidiary organization; *(Tochtergesellschaft)* subsidiary.
Unterredung *f* interview.
Unterricht *m* instruction.
unterrichten to inform; *(lehren)* to teach.
Unterrichtung *f* briefing.
Unterrock *m* *(Kleidung)* slip.
untersagen to prohibit; *(verbieten)* to forbid.
Untersagung *f* prohibition.
unterschätzen to underestimate; to undervalue.
unterscheidbar capable of being differentiated; distinguishable.
unterscheiden to distinguish; *(differenzieren)* to differentiate.
unterscheiden, sich to differ.
unterscheidend discriminating.
Unterscheidung *f* differentiation; discrimination.
Unterscheidungsvermögen *nt* ability to discriminate; discrimination.
Unterschied *m* difference.
unterschiedlich differing; *(verschiedenartig)* varied.
unterschiedlich behandeln to discriminate.
Unterschiedlichkeit *f* differentiation.
Unterschiedsbetrag *m* difference.
Unterschiedsmerkmal *nt* differential.
unterschreiben *(Dokument)* to sign.
unterschreiten *(Preis, Frist, Norm)* to go below.
Unterschrift *f* signature.
Unterschuß *m* shortfall; *(Defizit)* deficit.

Unterspalte *f*   subcategory; subdivision.

unterstellen   to impute.

unterstützen   to support; to back; *(Antrag, Bewerbung)* to endorse.

Unterstützen *nt*   supporting.

unterstützt   supported.

Unterstützung *f*   support; backing; *(Gönnertum)* patronage; *(Antrag, Bewerbung)* endorsement; *(Hilfe)* assistance; aid.

Unterstützungssumme *f*   grant-in-aid.

untersuchen   to investigate; *(Arzt)* to examine; *(erforschen)* to explore; *(sondieren)* to probe; *(testen)* to test.

Untersucher *m*   investigator; *(Prüfer)* examiner.

Untersuchung *f*   investigation; *(Vergehung)* probe; *(Test)* test; *(Arzt)* examination.

Untersuchungsgebühr *f*   investigation fee.

unterteilen   to subdivide.

unterwerfen, sich   to submit.

Unterwerfung *f*   submission; *(Unterjochung)* subjugation.

unterzeichnen   to sign.

Unterzeichnung *f*   signing.

untragbar   unbearable; prohibitive.

unübertroffen   unsurpassed; preeminent.

Unumgänglichkeit *f*   inevitability; *(Notwendigkeit)* necessity.

unumschränkt   sovereign; absolute.

ununterbrochen   uninterrupted; nonstop.

ununtersucht   uninvestigated; unexplored.

unverändert   unchanged.

unverbindlich   not binding; not

obligatory; *(Umgang)* unaccommodating.

unvereinbar   irreconcilable; disparate.

unverhältnismäßig   disproportionate.

unverhoffter Glücksfall *m*   windfall.

unverkäuflich   unsalable.

unverkauft   unsold.

Unvermögen *nt*   inability; *(Untauglichkeit)* disqualification.

unveröffentlicht   unpublished.

unverpackt   not packaged; *(lose)* loose; in bulk.

unverpfändet   unpledged.

unversehrt   undamaged; sound.

Unversehrtheit *f*   soundness; integrity.

unversichert   uninsured; *(ungedeckt)* uncovered.

unvertretbar   unjustifiable; unwarranted.

unverwendbar   unusable; unworkable.

unverwertbar   unusable.

unverwertet   unutilized; *(Ressourcen)* untapped.

unverzinslich   noninterest-bearing.

unverzinst   not subject to interest; no-interest.

unverzüglich   prompt; *(sofort)* immediate.

unvollendet   unfinished.

unvollständig   incomplete.

unvoreingenommen   unprejudiced; *(unparteiisch)* impartial.

unvorhergesehen   unexpected.

unvorsichtig   careless; *(unklug)* imprudent.

unwesentlich   unessential; immaterial.

unwiderruflich   irrevocable.

unwirksam   ineffective; *(ineffizient)* inefficient; *(ungültig)* invalid.
Unwirksamkeit *f*   ineffectiveness; *(Ungültigkeit)* invalidity.
unwirtschaftlich   uneconomical.
Unzufriedenheit *f*   dissatisfaction.
unzufrieden machen   to dissatisfy.
unzulänglich   inadequate; deficient.
Unzulänglichkeit *f*   inadequacy.
unzulässig   inadmissible; *(verboten)* prohibited.
unzureichend   insufficient; *(unzulänglich)* deficient.
unzuverlässig   unreliable.
Urabstimmung *f*   plebiscite; *(Lohnkampf)* ballot vote.
Urheber *m*   originator; *(Schöpfer)* creator; *(Autor)* author.
Urheberrecht *nt*   copyright.
Urkunde *f*   record; *(Instrument)* instrument; *(Dokument)* document.

urkundlich festgelegt   documented.
Urlaub *m*   leave; *(Ferien)* vacation.
Urlauber *m*   vacationer.
Urlaubsort *m*   vacation resort.
Ursache *f*   cause.
ursächlich   causal.
Urschrift *f*   original.
Ursprung *m*   source; origin.
ursprünglich   primary; original.
Ursprungszeugnis *nt*   certificate of origin.
Urteil *nt*   judgment.
urteilen   to judge.
Urteilsfähigkeit *f*   ability to judge.
Urteilsspruch *m*   verdict; *(Urteil, Strafe)* sentence; *(gerichtliche Entscheidung)* judgment.
Urteilsvermögen *nt*   ability to judge.
Usance *f*   usage.

Valuta *pl*   medium of exchange; currency
Valutakonto *nt*   currency account.
variabel   variable; *(fluktuierend)* fluctuating.
variieren   to vary; *(diversifizieren)* to diversify.
verabreden   to agree upon.
Verabredung *f*   date; *(Termin)* appointment.
verabschieden   to dismiss; *(Gesetz)* to pass.
verabschieden, sich   to take one's leave; to say goodbye.

Verabschiedung *f*   *(Gesetz)* passage.
veraltet   superannuated; obsolete; *(Mode)* out of fashion.
veränderlich   changeable; adjustable; *(Kurs)* sliding.
verändern   to change; *(umändern)* to alter; *(anpassen, einstellen)* to adjust; *(umwandeln)* to convert.
Veränderung *f*   change; *(Umänderung)* alteration.
Veränderungsrate *f*   rate of change.
veranlassen   to cause; to bring about; *(dazu bringen)* to induce; (dazu bewegen) to prompt.

veranschaulichen   to illustrate.

Veranschlagung *f*   estimate.

veranstalten   to stage; *(präsentieren)* to present; *(der Gastgeber sein)* to host; *(arrangieren)* to arrange.

Veranstalter *m*   organizer; *(Produzent)* producer; *(Gastgeber)* host; *(Sponsor)* sponsor.

Veranstaltung *f*   performance; presentation.

verantwortlich   responsible; *(rechenschaftspflichtig)* accountable; *(haftpflichtig)* liable.

Verantwortlichkeit *f*   responsibility; *(Rechenschaftspflicht)* accountability.

Verantwortung *f*   responsibility.

Verantwortungsbereich *m*   area of responsibility; *(Kompetenz)* area of competence; *(Arbeitsgebiet, Ressort)* province.

verarbeiten   to process.

Verarbeitung *f*   processing; *(Fertigung)* manufacture.

verausgaben   *(ausgeben)* to spend; *(erschöpfen)* to exhaust.

verausgabt   spent; *(physisch)* exhausted.

veräußern   to dispose of; *(verkaufen)* to sell.

Veräußerung *f*   sale.

verbal   verbal.

Verband *m*   *(Organisation)* organization; *(Gesellschaft, Verein)* association; (med.) bandage.

Verbandsausschuß *m*   organization committee.

Verbandsbezirk *m*   association district; *(Gewerkschaft)* union district.

Verbandsorgan *nt*   trade paper.

Verbandsvertreter *m*   association representative.

Verbandszeitung *f*   trade newspaper.

verbergen   to hide.

verbessern   to improve; *(höher einstufen)* to upgrade; *(intensivieren)* to enhance.

verbessernd   corrective.

verbessert   improved; *(erhöht)* upgraded.

Verbesserung *f*   improvement; enhancement; *(Schreibfehler)* correction.

verbieten   to forbid; *(untersagen)* to prohibit.

verbilligen   *(verschlechtern)* to cheapen; *(Preis reduzieren)* to reduce in price.

Verbilligung *f*   price reduction.

verbinden   to link; *(zusammentun)* to join; *(Unternehmen)* to associate; *(Telefon)* to connect.

verbinden, sich   to associate.

verbindlich   obligatory; *(Umgang)* obliging.

Verbindlichkeit *f*   *(Schuldverpflichtung)* obligation; *(Schuld, Passivposten)* liability; *(Verpflichtung)* commitment; *(Buchführung)* account payable; *(Umgang)* obligingness; civility.

Verbindung *f*   connection; *(Gesellschaft)* association; *(Kontakt)* contact; *(Kombination)* combination; *(Informationsfluß)* communication.

Verbot *nt*   proscription; prohibition.

Verbrauch *m*   consumption.

verbrauchen   to consume; *(aufbrauchen)* to use up.

Verbraucher *m*   *(Konsument)* consumer; *(Benutzer)* user.

Verbraucherbelastung *f*   consumer burden.

Verbrauchermarkt *m*   consumer market.

Verbrauchernachfrage *f*   consumer demand.

Verbraucherpreis *m*   consumer price.

Verbraucherpreisindex *m*   consumer price index.

Verbraucherschutz *m*   consumer protection.

Verbraucherumfrage *f*   consumer survey.

Verbraucherverband *m*   consumer association.

Verbrauchsminderung *f*   consumption reduction.

Verbrauchssteuer *f*   excise tax.

Verbrauchsstichprobe *f*   random sample of consumption.

Verbrauchsstruktur *f*   consumption pattern.

verbreiten   to spread; *(streuen)* to disperse; *(Information)* to disseminate.

Verbreitung *f*   *(Ausbreitung)* spread; *(Vorkommen)* incidence; *(Information)* dissemination.

verbrieft   chartered; *(lizensiert)* licensed; *(zugesichert)* guaranteed.

verbringen   *(Zeit)* to spend; *(Geld)* to squander.

verbuchen   to post; *(eintragen)* to enter.

verbünden   to ally.

Verbündete *m/f*   ally.

verbürgen   to warrant.

verbürgt   warranted.

verdanken   to owe.

verderblich   perishable.

verdienen   *(Geld, Respekt)* to earn; *(berechtigt sein)* to merit; *(gewinnen)* to gain.

Verdiener *m*   earner.

Verdienst *m*   *(Einkommen)* earnings.

Verdienst *nt*   *(fig.)* merit; credit.

Verdienstspanne *f*   margin of earnings.

Verdienstzuwachs *m*   growth in earnings; *(Gewinn)* profit increase.

verdoppeln   to double.

verdrängen   to displace.

Veredeler *m*   *(Fabrikation)* processor.

veredeln   *(verarbeiten)* to process; *(verfeinern)* to refine; *(verbessern)* to improve; *(fertigstellen)* to finish.

Veredelung *f*   refinement; *(Verbesserung)* improvement.

Verein *m*   association; *(Gesellschaft)* society; *(Klub)* club; *(Gewerkschaft)* union.

vereinbar   compatible.

vereinbaren   to arrange; *(ausbedingen)* to stipulate; *(übereinkommen)* to agree.

Vereinbarung *f*   arrangement; *(Ausbedingung)* stipulation; *(Übereinkommen)* agreement.

vereinen   to unite; *(Ziele)* to combine.

vereinheitlichen   to standardize.

vereinheitlicht   standardized.

Vereinheitlichung *f*   standardization.

vereinigen   to unite; *(zusammenlegen)* to join; *(konsolidieren)* to consolidate.

vereinigt   united; consolidated.

Vereinigung *f*   union; coalition.

vereinnahmen   to take in; *(empfangen)* to receive.

vereiteln   *(verhindern)* to prevent; *(besiegen, zu Fall bringen)* to defeat.

verewigen to perpetuate.
Verfahren *nt* procedure; *(Gericht)* proceedings; *(Prozeß)* process; *(Usance)* practice; *(Methode)* method.
Verfahren *nt* **einstellen** to dismiss an action.
Verfahrensgang *m* procedural process.
Verfahrensprinzip *nt* procedural principle.
verfahrensrechtlich procedural.
Verfahrenstechniker *m* process technician.
Verfahrensweg *m* procedural path.
Verfahrensweise *f* procedural method.
Verfall *m* *(Wertpapier)* lapse; *(Zusammenbruch)* collapse; *(Verderben)* ruination.
verfallen *(überfällig werden)* to lapse; *(Gebäude)* to go to ruin.
verfallen lassen to forfeit; *(Gebäude)* to allow to go to ruin.
Verfallzeit *f* maturity.
verfälschen *(Waren)* to adulterate; *(Urkunde)* to falsify.
Verfälschung *f* adulteration; tampering.
Verfassung *f* *(Zustand)* condition; *(Gesetz)* constitution.
verfassungsmäßig constitutional.
verfehlen to miss.
verfeinern to refine.
Verfeinerung *f* refinement.
Verfertiger *m* manufacturer; maker.
Verfertigung *f* manufacture.
Verflechtung *f* *(gegenseitige Abhängigkeit)* interdependence; *(Verstrickung)* entanglement; *(Vernetzung)* meshing.

verflochten interwoven; *(gegenseitig abhängig)* interdependent.
verfolgen to pursue; *(Plan, Absicht)* to follow; *(drangsalieren)* to persecute.
verfrüht premature.
verfügbar available.
verfügbares Einkommen *nt* disposable income.
Verfügbarkeit *f* availability.
verfügen to dispose; to direct; *(Gericht)* to rule.
Verfügung *f* rule; *(Klausel)* provision; *(Verordnung)* ordinance; *(Anordnung)* disposition; *(Direktive)* directive.
Verfügungsgewalt *f* power of disposal; control.
Verfügungsrecht *nt* title.
Vergabe *f* giving away; *(Auftrag)* placing; *(Stipendium)* awarding.
Vergangenheit *f* past.
vergeben to give away; *(Auftrag)* to place; *(Kontrakt, Stipendium)* to award.
vergeblich in vain.
vergelten to retaliate; to repay.
Vergeltung *f* retaliation; repayment.
vergeuden to squander; *(verschwenden)* to waste; *(zerstreuen)* to dissipate.
Vergleich *m* comparison; *(Schlichtung)* compromise; arrangement.
vergleichbar comparable.
Vergleichbarkeit *f* comparability.
vergleichen to compare.
vergleichend comparative.
Vergleichsanmeldung *f* settlement declaration.
Vergleichsantrag *m* settlement petition.
Vergleichsverfahren *nt* settlement

proceedings; *(Bankrott)* insolvency proceedings.

Vergleichsverwalter *m* settlement trustee.

vergleichsweise comparatively; by way of comparison.

vergrößern to enlarge; *(vermehren)* to augment.

Vergrößerung *f* enlargement; *(Wachstum)* growth; *(Zunahme)* augmentation.

Vergünstigung *f* privilege; *(Vorteil)* benefit.

vergüten to remunerate; *(kompensieren)* to recompense.

Vergütung *f* remuneration; *(Entgelt, Ersatz)* recompense; *(Entschädigung)* compensation.

verhaften to arrest.

Verhalten *nt* conduct; behavior.

verhalten, sich to conduct oneself; to behave; to act.

Verhaltensänderung *f* behavior modification.

Verhaltensnorm *f* behavioral norm.

Verhaltenssteuerung *f* behavior control.

Verhaltensweise *f* behavioral pattern.

Verhältnis *nt* relation; *(Proportion)* proportion; *(Beziehung)* relationship.

verhältnismäßig relative; *(Proportion)* proportional; proportionate.

Verhältniswert *m* ratio.

verhandeln to negotiate; *(aushandeln)* to bargain.

Verhandlung *f* negotiation; *(Anhörung)* hearing; *(Strafrecht)* trial.

verhandlungsbereit ready to negotiate.

verhandlungsfähig negotiable.

Verhandlungsgeschick *nt* negotiating skill.

Verhandlungsmacht *f* negotiating power.

Verhandlungsordnung *f* protocol.

Verhandlungspartner *m* negotiator.

Verhandlungsrunde *f* round of negotiations; *(Löhne)* bargaining round.

Verhandlungsstärke *f* bargaining strength.

Verhandlungsziel *nt* negotiation goal.

verheerend ruinous; disastrous.

verheimlichen to keep something secret; *(verstecken)* to hide; *(verbergen)* to conceal.

verhindern to prevent.

Verhinderung *f* prevention.

Verhör *nt* interrogation.

verhüten to prevent.

Verhütung *f* prevention.

Verkauf *m* sale.

Verkauf *m* **aus zweiter Hand** *f* resale.

verkaufen to sell.

Verkaufen *nt* selling.

Verkäufer *m* *(Privatverkauf)* seller; *(Händler)* vendor; *(Handelsvertreter)* sales representative; salesman; salesperson; saleswoman.

Verkäufermarkt *m* seller's market.

verkäuflich for sale; *(verkaufsfähig)* salable; marketable.

Verkaufsagentur *f* dealership.

Verkaufsbasis *f* sales base.

Verkaufsberechnung *f* sales calculation.

Verkaufsbüro *nt* sales office.

Verkaufsergebnis *nt* sales result.

Verkaufserlös *m* *(Privatverkauf)* sale proceeds.

Verkaufsfiliale *f*   sales branch.
verkaufsfördernd   sales-promotional.
Verkaufsförderung *f*   sales promotion.
Verkaufsgebiet *nt*   sales district.
Verkaufsgemeinschaft *f*   sales association.
Verkaufsgewinn *m*   sales profit.
Verkaufshinweis *m*   sales lead.
Verkaufskurs *m*   *(Effekten)* selling price; market price.
Verkaufsleitung *f*   sales management.
Verkaufsmannschaft *f*   sales team; sales force.
Verkaufsmesse *f*   trade fair; merchandisers' fair.
Verkaufsniederlassung *f*   sales branch.
Verkaufsoption *f*   seller's option; *(Börse)* put.
Verkaufsorganisation *f*   sales organization; *(Außendienst)* field sales force.
Verkaufsort *m*   point of sale.
Verkaufspersonal *nt*   sales force.
Verkaufsplan *m*   sales plan; merchandising scheme.
Verkaufspreis *m*   selling price; market price.
Verkaufsprogramm *nt*   sales program.
Verkaufspsychologie *f*   sales psychology.
Verkaufsrecht *nt*   license to sell.
Verkaufsstand *m*   sales stall.
Verkaufsstelle *f*   retail outlet.
Verkaufssteuer *f*   sales tax.
Verkaufsstrategie *f*   sales strategy.
Verkaufstip *m*   sales lead.
Verkaufs- und Kundendienst *m*   sales and customer service.

Verkaufsvolumen *nt*   sales volume.
Verkaufszeit *f*   selling time; *(Geschäftszeit)* business hours.
verkauft   sold.
Verkehr *m*   traffic; *(Umgang)* association; *(geschäftliche Beziehung)* dealings.
verkehren   *(Handel treiben)* to trade; *(Umgang pflegen)* to associate.
Verkehrswesen *nt*   transportation; *(Beförderung)* transport.
verklagen   to sue.
Verknappung *f*   scarcity.
verkürzen   to shorten; *(Text)* to abbreviate; *(Rechte)* to curtail; *(vermindern)* to reduce.
Verkürzung *f*   shortening; *(Text)* abbreviation; *(Lohn)* reduction; *(Rechte)* curtailment.
verladen   to load; to ship.
Verladen *nt*   loading; *(Spedition)* shipping.
Verlader *m*   *(Spediteur)* shipper.
Verladung *f*   loading; *(Spedition)* shipping.
verlagern   to relocate; to shift.
Verlagerung *f*   shift; dislocation; *(neu lagern)* relocation.
verlangen   to require; *(fordern)* to demand.
verlängern   to prolong; to extend; *(Kontrakt)* to renew.
Verlängerung *f*   prolongation; extension; *(Kontrakt)* renewal.
verlängerungsfähig   renewable.
verlangsamen   to slow down; *(retardieren)* to retard; to decelerate.
Verlangsamen *nt*   slowing.
Verlangsamung *f*   slowdown; deceleration.
verlassen   to leave; to abandon.

Verlassen *nt* leaving; abandonment; pullout.
verläßlich reliable.
Verläßlichkeit *f* reliability.
Verlauf *m* progress; course; *(Zeit)*
passing.
verlaufen *(Vorgang)* to progress;
(Zeit) to pass.
verlegen *(Zustand)* embarrassed.
to misplace; *(Buch)* to publish.
Verlegenheit *f* dilemma; embar-
rassment.
Verleger *m* publisher.
verleihen to lend; to loan; *(Titel,
Orden)* to confer.
Verleiher *m* lender.
Verleihung *f* grant; *(Titel, Orden)*
conferment.
verletzen to hurt; to injure; *(Vorschrift, Regel)* to violate.
Verletzung *f* injury; *(Vorschrift,
Regel)* violation; *(Verstoß)*
infringement; *(Bruch)* breach.
Verleumdung *f* libel.
verlieren to lose; *(verwirken)* to
forfeit.
Verlierer *m* loser.
verlorengehen to become lost;
(verschwinden) to disappear.
Verlosung *f* drawing.
Verlust *m* loss; *(Schaden)* damage;
(Defizit) deficit.
verlustbringend loss-generating;
losing.
Verlustgefahr *f* risk of loss.
Verlustrechnung *f* loss account-
ing.
Verlustträger *m* loser.
Verlustvortrag *m* *(Buchführung)*
debit carryover; debit balance.
Verlustzone *f* loss area.
vermarkten to market.
Vermarktung *f* marketing.

vermehren to increase; to augment.
Vermehrer *m* multiplier.
Vermehrung *f* increase; augmentation.
vermeidbar avoidable.
vermeiden to avoid; *(umgehen)* to
sidestep; to dodge.
vermeidlich avoidable.
Vermerk *m* notation.
vermerken to note; *(bestätigen,
girieren)* to endorse.
vermieten to rent; *(verpachten)* to
lease; (Br.) to let.
Vermieter *m* lessor; *(Mietherr)*
landlord.
vermindern to decrease;
(reduzieren) to reduce.
verminderter Wert *m* reduced
value; discounted value.
Verminderung *f* decrease; reduction; diminution; *(Ausgaben)*
retrenchment.
vermischen to mix.
vermischt mixed; *(verschiedenartig)* miscellaneous.
vermissen to miss.
vermitteln to mediate.
Vermittler *m* mediator; *(Unterhändler)* negotiator; *(Moderator)*
moderator.
Vermittlung *f* *(Stellung)* placement; *(Verhandlung)* mediation;
(Gesuch) intercession.
Vermittlungsversuch *m* mediation
attempt.
Vermögen *nt* wealth; fortune;
(Aktivvermögen) assets; *(Besitz)*
property; *(Macht)* power.
vermögend wealthy.
Vermögensangabe *f* declaration
of assets.
Vermögensanlage *f* investment of
assets.

317

Vermögensbildung *f* formation of wealth.

Vermögensertrag *m* yield on assets.

Vermögenserwerb *m* acquisition of assets.

Vermögensgegenstand *m* asset.

Vermögensmasse *f* estate.

vermögensrechtlich proprietary.

Vermögenssteuer *f* property tax; personal tax.

Vermögensverhältnisse *pl* financial circumstances.

Vermögensverwalter *m* portfolio manager; money manager.

Vermögenswert *m* financial worth; property value.

vermögenswirksam asset-creating.

Vermögenszuwachs *m* capital growth; capital appreciation.

Vermutung *f* presumption; *(Annahme)* assumption.

vernachlässigen to neglect.

veröffentlichen *(Buch, Artikel)* to publish; *(Information)* to release.

Veröffentlichungsreihe *f* publication series.

verordnen *(Arzt)* to prescribe; *(Erlaß)* to decree.

Verordnung *f* ordinance; decree; *(Klausel)* provision.

verpachten to lease; *(BE)* to let.

Verpächter *m* lessor; *(Pachtherr)* landlord.

Verpachtung *f* lease.

verpacken to package; *(einpacken)* to pack; *(in Karton, Schachtel)* to box.

Verpackungsindustrie *f* packaging industry.

verpassen to miss.

verpfänden to pledge; to mortgage.

Verpfändung *f* pawning;

(Grundbesitz, Lombardierung) hypothecation.

Verpflegung *f* food; board; provisions.

verpflichten *(zu einer Leistung)* to obligate; *(vertraglich)* to bind; *(zu Dank)* to oblige; *(anstellen)* to engage.

verpflichten, sich to undertake.

verpflichtet obligated; *(haftbar)* liable; *(verschuldet)* indebted.

Verpflichtung *f* *(Versprechung)* commitment; *(zu einer Leistung)* obligation; *(gesetzlich)* liability; *(Verschuldung)* indebtedness.

Verpflichtungserklärung *f* undertaking.

Verquickung *f* involvement.

verrechnen to offset; *(BE)* to set off; *(abrechnen)* to clear; *(ausgleichen)* to balance.

verrechnen, sich to miscalculate.

Verrechnung *f* offset; *(Abrechnung)* clearance; clearing.

Verrechnungseinheit *f* clearing unit.

Verrechnungssaldo *m* clearing balance; *(Scheckverkehr)* clearinghouse balance.

Verrechnungsscheck *m* nonnegotiable check; voucher check.

Verrechnungsverkehr *m* clearing system.

Verrichtung *f* *(Aufgabe)* performance.

verringern to decrease; *(reduzieren)* to reduce; *(erschöpfen)* to deplete.

Verringerung *f* reduction; *(Münzen)* debasement.

versammeln to assemble.

versammeln, sich to congregate; *(Kongress, Konferenz)* to convene.

Versammlung *f* assembly; *(Sitzung, Treffen)* meeting.
Versammmlungshalle *f* **der Gewerkschaft** *f* union hall.
Versand- shipping.
Versand *m* shipping.
versandfähig transportable.
Versandhandel *m* mail order trade; direct mail selling.
Versandhaus *nt* catalog firm; mail order firm.
versäumen *(Pflicht)* to neglect; *(Termin)* to miss.
Versäumnis *nt* neglect; omission.
Verschachtelung *f* interlocking; *(Verkaufspyramide)* pyramiding.
verschaffen *(beschaffen)* to procure; *(versorgen)* to provide; *(liefern)* to supply.
verschärfen to tighten.
Verschärfen *nt* tightening.
verschärft tightened.
Verschärfung *f* *(Gesetz)* strengthening; *(Regel, Beschränkung)* tightening.
verschenken to give away.
verschicken to ship.
verschieben to shift; to dislocate.
Verschiebung *f* shift; dislocation; *(Termin)* change.
verschieden different; *(ungleichartig)* diverse.
verschiedenartig various; diverse; *(verschieden)* different.
Verschiedenartigkeit *f* diverseness.
Verschiedenheit *f* disparity; diversity.
Verschiffer *m* shipper.
Verschiffung *f* shipping; shipment.
verschlechtern to worsen; *(beeinträchtigen)* to impair.
Verschlechterung *f* worsening; deterioration; *(Rückschlag)* setback; *(Niedergang, Verfall)* decline.
verschleiern to obscure; *(verbergen)* to conceal.
verschleudern *(Ressourcen)* to squander; *(verschwenden)* to waste; *(verkaufen)* to undersell; to dump.
Verschleudern *nt* *(Ressourcen)* squandering; *(Verschwenden)* wasting.
verschleudert *(Ressource)* squandered; *(verschwendet)* wasted.
verschlimmern to aggravate.
verschlimmern, sich to worsen.
Verschluß *m* closure; *(sichere Aufbewahrung)* safekeeping.
Verschmelzung *f* merger.
Verschmutzung *f* pollution.
verschreiben to prescribe.
verschuldet indebted; *(Unternehmen)* leveraged.
Verschuldung *f* indebtedness; *(Verbindlichkeit)* liability; *(Schuld)* debt.
Verschuldungsgrenze *f* debt ceiling.
Verschuldungskrise *f* debt crisis.
verschwenden to waste; *(vergeuden)* to squander.
Verschwenden *nt* wasting.
verschwenderisch wasteful.
verschwendet wasted; *(vergeudet)* squandered.
Verschwendung *f* waste.
verschwinden to vanish; to disappear.
Versehen *nt* error; *(Fehler)* mistake.
versenden to send.
Versenden *nt* sending; *(Verladung)* shipping.
Versender *m* shipper.

versenken to sink.
Versicherer *m* insurer; *(Agent)* insurance underwriter; *(Lieferer)* insurance provider; *(Träger)* insurance carrier.
versichern to insure; *(assekurieren)* to underwrite; *(beteuern)* to assure.
Versicherung *f* insurance.
Versicherungsagent *m* insurance agent; underwriter.
Versicherungsbeitrag *m* insurance contribution.
Versicherungsfirma *f* insurance company.
Versicherungsnehmer *m* insured person; policyholder.
Versicherungspolice *f* insurance policy.
Versicherungsschutz *m* insurance coverage.
Versicherungsträger *m* insurance carrier; insurer.
Versicherungswert *m* *(Nominalwert)* face value of policy; *(Barwert)* cash value.
versöhnen to reconcile.
versorgen to provide for; *(liefern)* to supply.
versorgend supplying.
Versorgung *f* supply; *(Dienstleistung)* service.
verspätet late.
versprechen to promise.
Versprechen *nt* promise.
verstaatlichen to nationalize.
verstädtern to urbanize.
Verstädterung *f* urbanization.
Verständigung *f* understanding; *(Übereinkommen)* accommodation.
verstärken to reinforce; to strengthen; *(intensivieren)* to intensify.

Verstärker *m* (Radio) amplifier; *(Linse)* magnifier.
verstärkt reinforced; strengthened; *(vermehrt)* increased; *(Radio)* amplified; *(intensiviert)* intensified.
Verstärkung *f* reinforcement; strengthening; *(Nachschub)* reinforcements.
verstecken to hide.
versteigern to auction.
Versteigerung *f* auction; public sale.
versteuern to pay taxes on.
verstöpseln to plug.
verstorben deceased.
Verstoß *m* violation; *(Verletzung)* infringement; *(Bruch)* breach; *(Übertretung)* contravention.
Versuch *m* attempt; *(Test)* test; *(Experiment)* experiment.
versuchen to try; to attempt.
Versuchsanlage *f* pilot plant.
Versuchsmarkt *m* test market; trial market.
Versuchsreihe *f* experimental series.
versuchsweise *f* experimentally; tentatively.
versüßen to sweeten.
vertagen to defer; *(aufschieben)* to postpone; *(Komitee)* to table; *(Gerichtsverhandlung)* to continue.
Vertagung *f* postponement; *(Gerichtsverhandlung)* continuance; deferment.
verteidigen to defend.
Verteidigung *f* defense.
verteilen *(austeilen, ausstreuen)* to distribute.
Verteilernetz *nt* distribution network.
verteilt angelegt diversely invested.

Verteilung *f* distribution.
Verteilungsbogen *m* spread sheet.
Verteilungsfunktion *f* allocative function.
Verteilungssystem *nt* distribution system.
verteuern to make more expensive.
Verteuerung *f* increase in cost.
Vertiefung *f* *(Boden)* depression; *(Einschnitt)* indentation; *(Trog)* trough.
vertikal vertical.
vertikale Eingliederung *f* vertical integration.
vertikale Integration *f* vertical integration.
Vertrag *m* treaty; *(Kontrakt)* contract; *(Abkommen)* agreement.
Vertrag *m* **abschließen** to close a contract; to contract.
verträglich compatible; agreeable.
vertraglich contractual.
vertraglich verpflichten to bind by contract; to obligate.
vertraglich verpflichten, sich to contract; to undertake.
Vertragsabschluß *m* conclusion of an agreement.
Vertragsbedingung *f* contract clause.
Vertragsbruch *m* breach of contract.
Vertragsentwurf *m* tentative agreement; draft contract.
vertragsgemäß according to contract.
Vertragspartei *f* contract party.
Vertragssumme *f* contract amount.
Vertragstext *m* wording of a contract.
Vertragsverletzung *f* contract violation; default on contract.

vertrauen to trust.
Vertrauen *nt* trust; confidence.
Vertrauensmann *m* *(Repräsentant)* representative; *(Sprecher)* spokesman.
Vertrauenswerbung *f* public relations.
vertrauenswürdig trustworthy; *(zuverlässig)* reliable; *(angesehen)* reputable.
vertraulich confidential.
vertreiben *(Konkurrenz)* to drive away; *(vermarkten)* to market.
vertretbar defensible; *(gerechtfertigt)* justifiable; *(ersetzbar)* replaceable; *(Sache)* fungible; *(Argument)* tenable.
vertreten to represent.
Vertreter *m* *(Ersatzperson)* replacement person; *(Repräsentant)* representative; *(Agent)* agent.
Vertreterbesuch *m* sales call.
Vertreterbezirk *m* sales territory.
Vertretung *f* representation; *(Agentur)* agency.
Vertrieb *m* marketing; *(Verkauf)* sales; *(Verteilung)* distribution.
Vertriebsagentur *f* distributorship.
Vertriebsanalyse *f* marketing analysis.
Vertriebsbasis *f* marketing base.
Vertriebschef *m* sales director; marketing director.
Vertriebsformel *f* marketing formula.
Vertriebsgebiet *nt* sales territory.
Vertriebsgemeinschaft *f* sales group.
Vertriebsgesellschaft *f* sales company.
Vertriebskosten *pl* marketing costs.

Vertriebsleiter *m*   marketing manager.

Vertriebsleitung *f*   marketing management.

Vertriebsnetz *nt*   distribution network.

Vertriebspolitik *f*   marketing policy.

Vertriebsstab *m*   marketing staff.

Vertriebsstelle *f*   sales office; outlet.

Vertriebsstrategie *f*   distribution strategy.

Vertriebssystem *nt*   marketing system; distribution system.

Vertriebsweg *m*   distribution channel.

verursachen   to cause; *(hervorbringen)* to induce.

verurteilen   to censure; *(Gericht)* to sentence.

vervielfältigen   *(duplizieren)* to duplicate; (kopieren) to copy.

vervollkommnen   to perfect.

Vervollkommnung *f*   *(Perfektionierung)* perfecting; *(Veredelung)* refining.

Verwahrer *m*   custodian.

Verwahrung *f*   safekeeping; *(Obhut)* custody.

Verwahrungsort *m*   repository.

verwalten   to administer; *(managen)* to manage; *(leiten)* to govern.

verwaltend   administrative.

Verwalter *m*   administrator; *(Manager)* manager.

Verwaltung *f*   administration; management.

Verwaltungs-   administrative.

Verwaltungsaufgabe *f*   administrative task.

Verwaltungsaufwand *m*   administrative expense.

Verwaltungsgebühr *f*   administra-

tion fee; *(Unkostengebühr)* service charge.

Verwaltungskörper *m*   management.

verwaltungsmäßig   administrative.

Verwaltungsstelle *f*   administrative office; *(Behörde)* administrative agency.

Verwaltungssystem *nt*   administrative system.

verwechseln   to confuse; *(verkennen)* to mistake; *(durcheinanderbringen)* to mix up.

verweigern   *(Erlaubnis)* to deny; *(Leistung)* to refuse.

Verweigerung *f*   refusal.

Verweis *m*   censure.

verweisen   to censure.

verwendbar   usable; serviceable; *(zweckmäßig)* appropriate; *(anwendbar)* applicable; *(geeignet)* suitable.

verwenden   to utilize; to use.

Verwendung *f*   use; utilization.

Verwendungszweck *m*   intended use; purpose.

verwerten   to utilize; *(Altmaterial)* to salvage.

Verwertung *f*   *(Gebrauch)* utilization.

verwickeln   to involve; *(verstricken)* to entangle.

verwirken   to forfeit.

verwirklichen   to realize.

Verwirklichung *f*   realization.

Verwirrung *f*   confusion; *(Unordnung)* disorder.

verwüsten   to lay waste; to devastate.

Verwüsten *nt*   devastating.

verwüstet   devastated; ravaged.

Verzehr *m*   *(Essen)* consumption.

verzeichnen to register; to document; to chronicle.

Verzeichnis *nt* *(Tabelle)* table; *(Liste)* list; *(Register)* index; catalog.

verzerren to distort; *(Daten)* to skew.

verzerrt distorted; *(Daten)* skewed.

Verzicht *m* renunciation; *(legaler Verzicht)* waiver.

Verzicht *m* **erklären** to renounce; *(freigeben)* to release.

Verzicht *m* **leisten** to waive; *(aufgeben)* to relinquish.

Verzichtleistung *f* *(Dokument)* waiver.

Verzichtserklärung *f* waiver declaration; release declaration.

Verzichtsurkunde *f* release document.

verzinsen to charge interest.

verzinslich interest-bearing.

Verzinsung *f* *(Ertrag)* interest yield; *(Zinssatz)* interest rate; *(Zinszahlung)* interest payment.

verzögern to retard; *(aufschieben)* to delay.

Verzögern *nt* delaying; *(Verlangsamen)* slowing.

Verzögerung *f* delay; *(Zurückbleiben)* lag.

Verzug *m* *(Zahlung)* default; *(Verzögerung)* delay.

Verzweigtheit *f* complexity.

Veto *nt* veto.

Vetorecht *nt* veto right.

vielfach multiple.

Vielfältigkeit *f* multiplicity.

Vielheit *f* multiplicity.

vielseitig multi-sided; *(multilateral)* multilateral; *(Anwendung, Begabung)* versatile.

vielsprachig multilingual.

vielversprechend promising.

vielzweckig multipurpose.

vierteilen to quarter.

Viertel *nt* quarter; *(Bezirk)* district.

Vierteljahr *nt* quarter.

Vierteljahresprüfung *f* quarterly review.

Vierteljahreszeitschrift *f* quarterly magazine.

vierteljährlich quarterly.

Vizepräsident *m* vice president.

Volksbank *f* people's bank; credit union.

volkseigen owned by the people; publicly owned.

Volkseinkommen *nt* national income.

Volksvermögen *nt* national wealth.

Volksvertretung *f* representation of the people.

Volkswirtschaft *f* national economy.

volkswirtschaftlich economic.

Volkswirtschaftslehre *f* economics.

Volkszählung *f* population census.

voll full; *(ganz)* entire.

Vollarbeitsplatz *m* full-time position.

Vollbeschäftigung *f* full employment.

vollbringen to accomplish.

vollendet accomplished; perfect; *(fertig)* completed.

Vollendung *f* perfection; *(Abschluß)* completion.

vollentwickelte Industrie *f* mature industry.

Volljährigkeit *f* majority.

Vollkasko *nt* *(Versicherung)* comprehensive coverage.

vollkommen perfect.

Vollkommenheit *f* perfection.

Vollmacht *f* *(Stimmrechtsermächti-*

gung) proxy; *(Handlungsvoll-macht)* power of attorney; *(Mandat, Auftrag)* mandate; *(Amtsgewalt)* authority.
Vollmachtsanweisung *f* proxy statement.
Vollmachtsstimmrecht *nt* proxy voting power.
vollständig whole; complete.
vollständiges Sortiment *nt* complete assortment; full line.
vollstrecken to enforce; *(Urteil)* to execute.
Vollstreckung *f* enforcement; *(Urteil)* execution.
vollziehen to execute; *(ausführen)* to carry out; to perform.
Vollziehung *f* execution; *(Erfüllung)* fulfillment.
Vollziehungsbefehl *m* warrant.
Volontär *m* intern; trainee.
Volumen *nt* volume.
vorangehen to precede; *(Neuerung)* to pioneer.
vorankommen *(Karriere)* to get ahead; *(Fortschritt)* to progress.
Voranschlag *m* estimate; *(Berechnung)* calculation.
Vorarbeiter *m* foreman; lead worker.
vorausberechnen to precalculate; *(Voranschlag)* to project cost.
vorausberechnet precalculated; *(Voranschlag)* projected.
Vorausberechnung *f* projection.
vorausbezahlen to prepay; to pay in advance.
Vorausbezahlung *f* prepayment.
Voraussage *f* prediction; forecast.
voraussagen to predict; to forecast.
Vorausschätzung *f* advance estimate; *(Prognose)* prognosis.

voraussehbar predictable.
voraussetzen to assume; *(Qualifikation)* to require.
Voraussetzung *f* *(Prämisse)* premise; *(Vorbedingung)* prerequisite; *(Annahme)* assumption.
Voraussicht *f* foresight.
voraussichtlich *(wahrscheinlich)* probable; *(erwartet)* expected.
vorauszahlen to advance money; *(im Voraus bezahlen)* to pay in advance; to prepay.
Vorauszahlung *f* advance payment.
Vorbedingung *f* prerequisite; *(Voraussetzung)* requirement.
Vorbehalt *m* reservation; proviso.
vorbehalten to reserve.
vorbereiten to prepare.
Vorbereitung *f* preparation.
Vorbesitzer *m* previous owner.
vorbestellen to subscribe.
vorbestellt subscribed.
Vorbestellung *f* subscription.
Vorbild *nt* *(Beispiel)* example; *(Ideal)* ideal.
Vorbilden *nt* training.
vorbildlich exemplary.
Vorderseite *f* front; *(Gebäude)* face.
Vordruck *m* *(Formular)* form; blank.
vorenthalten to withhold; to deprive of.
Vorfall *m* occurrence.
vorfertigen to prefabricate.
vorführen *(zeigen)* to show; *(demonstrieren)* to demonstrate.
Vorführung *f* *(präsentieren)* presentation; *(demonstrieren)* demonstration.
Vorgang *m* occurrence; process; *(Angelegenheit)* transaction; *(Verfahren)* procedure.

Vorgänger *m*   predecessor.
vorgeben   to pretend; *(simulieren)* to simulate.
vorgebildet   skilled; trained.
vorgehen   *(vorausgehen)* to precede; *(Maßnahme ergreifen)* to proceed.
Vorgehen *nt*   approach; *(Methode)* method.
Vorgehensweise *f*   procedural method.
vorgeplant   projected; planned in advance.
Vorgeschichte *f*   *(Hintergrund)* background; *(Geschichte)* history.
vorgesehen   scheduled; destined.
Vorgesetzte *m/f*   superior.
vorhaben   to intend.
Vorhaben *nt*   scheme; project; plan.
vorhanden   extant; *(zur Verfügung)* available.
Vorhandensein *nt*   existence; *(Verfügbarkeit)* availability.
vorherbestimmen   to predetermine; *(zum Ziel setzen)* to target.
vorherig   previous.
Vorherrschaft *f*   predominance.
Vorherrschen *nt*   predominance.
vorherrschend   ruling; predominant.
vorhersagbar   predictable.
Vorhersage *f*   prediction; forecast.
vorhersagen   to predict; to forecast.
Vorjahreswert *m*   previous year's value.
Vorjahreszeitraum *m*   previous year's period.
vorkalkulieren   to calculate in advance.
Vorkaufsrecht *nt*   option; option to buy.
Vorkehrung *f*   arrangement.

Vorkehrungen *pl* **treffen**   to make arrangements.
vorkommen   to occur.
Vorkommen *nt*   incidence; occurrence; *(Bergbau)* deposit.
Vorkommnis *nt*   occurrence.
Vorlage *f*   *(Unterbreitung)* submission; *(Beispiel)* example; *(Muster)* sample; *(Schablone)* stencil.
vorläufig   tentative; preliminary; *(provisorisch)* provisional; *(einstweilig)* interim.
vorlegen   to submit; to present.
Vorleistung *f*   preparatory effort; *(Zahlung)* payment in advance.
Vorlesung *f*   lecture.
vorliegend   present; *(Dokument)* on hand.
Vorortszug *m*   suburban train; local train.
Vorprodukt *nt*   preliminary product.
vorprüfen   to pretest; to preview.
Vorrang *m*   precedence; priority,
Vorrangaktien *pl*   underlying stock.
Vorranganteile *pl*   underlying shares.
Vorrat *m*   store; supply; *(Geld)* fund; *(Anhäufung)* hoard.
vorrätig   on hand; *(Inventar)* in stock.
Vorratslager *nt*   buffer stock.
Vorratswirtschaft *f*   stockpiling.
Vorrecht *nt*   prerogative; privilege.
Vorrichtung *f*   device; apparatus; machine.
Vorruhestand *m*   early retirement.
Vorsatz *m*   resolution; *(Beschlußfassung)* resolve; *(Absicht)* intent.
Vorschau *f*   preview; *(Aussichten)* outlook.
vorschauen   to preview.
vorschießen   *(Geld)* to advance.

Vorschlag *m* suggestion; *(schriftlich)* proposal; proposition; *(Empfehlung)* recommendation; *(Angebot)* offer.

vorschlagen to suggest; *(schriftlich)* to propose; *(empfehlen)* to recommend.

Vorschlagsliste *f* *(Kandidaten)* slate.

vorschreiben *(Regel)* to direct; *(verordnen)* to prescribe.

Vorschrift *f* regulation; *(Regel)* rule; *(Erfordernis)* requirement; *(Verordnung)* precept; prescription.

Vorschriftenbuch *nt* manual of rules.

Vorschuß *m* advance.

Vorsicht *f* caution.

vorsichtig careful; cautious.

Vorsichtsmaßnahme *f* precautionary measure.

Vorsitz *m* **haben** to preside.

vorsitzen to preside.

Vorsitzende *m/f* chairperson.

Vorsorge *f* provision.

Vorsorgemaßnahme *f* precautionary measure.

Vorsorgesparplan *m* retirement savings plan.

vorsorglich provident; precautionary.

vorspringen to jump ahead; *(phys.: Dach, Fels)* to project.

Vorstand *m* management; corporate management.

Vorstandschef *m* chief executive officer.

Vorstandskollege *m* fellow manager.

Vorstandsmitglied *nt* officer; corporate officer.

Vorstandssitzung *f* board meeting.

Vorstandssprecher *m* chief spokesman.

Vorstandsvertrag *m* management contract.

Vorstandsvorsitz *m* managing directorship.

Vorstandsvorsitzende *m/f* president; chief executive; chairperson of the board.

Vorsteher *m* superintendent.

vorstellen to present; *(bekanntmachen)* to introduce.

Vorstellung *f* *(Bekanntmachung)* introduction; (Theater) performance; *(Idee)* idea.

Vorsteuer *f* pretax.

Vorsteuerpauschale *f* pretax lump sum.

Vorstoß *m* thrust; *(Vorrücken, Fortschritt)* advance.

vorstoßen to forge ahead; *(vorrücken)* to advance.

Vorteil *m* advantage; benefit; *(Gewinn)* profit.

vorteilhaft advantageous; beneficial.

Vortrag *m* *(Rede)* speech; *(Bericht)* report; *(Buchführung)* balance carried forward; *(Umbuchung)* transfer in the books; *(Vorlesung)* lecture; *(Referat)* talk.

Vortritt *m* precedence.

Voruntersuchung *f* preliminary hearing.

Vorurteil *nt* prejudice.

vorwärtsbringen to advance.

vorwärtskommen to advance.

vorwärtsschnellen to spurt forward.

Vorwegnahme *f* *(Annahme)* presumption; (Voraussehen) anticipation.

vorwegnehmen *(vorgreifen)* to anticipate.

vorwiegend predominant.

vorzeitig premature.
vorziehen to prefer.
Vorzug *m* *(Vorteil)* advantage; *(Präferenz)* preference; *(Verdienst)* merit.
vorzüglich select; *(erstklassig)* prime; *(überlegen)* superior.

Vorzugsaktien *pl* preferred stock.
Vorzugsbehandlung *f* preferential treatment.
Vorzugsdividende *f* preferred dividend.
Vorzugsobligation senior debenture.

Waagschale *f* scale.
wachsen to grow; to rise.
wachsend growing; *(steigend)* rising.
Wachstum *nt* growth.
Wachstumsbedingung *f* condition necessary for growth.
Wachstumsbranche *f* growth sector.
Wachstumsimpuls *m* growth impulse.
Wachstumskraft *f* growth strength.
Wachstumsmodell *nt* growth model.
Wachstumspfad *m* direction of growth; growth path.
Wachstumspolitik *f* growth policy.
wachstumspolitisch pertaining to growth policy.
Wachstumsproblem *nt* growth problem.
Wachstumsprognose *f* growth prognosis.
Wachstumsprozeß *m* growth process.
Wachstumsrate *f* growth rate.
Wachstumstempo *nt* speed of growth.
Wachstumstheorie *f* growth theory.

Wachstumsvorhersage *f* growth prediction.
wagen to dare; *(Kapital)* to venture; *(riskieren)* to risk.
Wagnis *nt* *(Kapital)* venture.
Wahl *f* choice; *(Stimmenabgabe)* election; *(Abstimmung)* vote.
Wählbarkeit *f* eligibility for election.
wählen to choose; *(polit. Wahl)* to elect; *(sich für etwas entscheiden)* to opt for; *(Stimme abgeben)* to vote.
Wählerschaft *f* constituency.
wahllos indiscriminate; random.
Wahlmöglichkeit *f* option.
wahlweise optional.
Wahlzettel *m* ballot.
wahrnehmbar perceptible.
wahrnehmen to notice; *(empfinden, erkennen)* to perceive; *(ausfindig machen)* to spot.
Wahrnehmung *f* perception.
wahrscheinlich probable.
Wahrscheinlichkeit *f* probability.
Währung *f* currency.
Währungsausgleich *m* currency adjustment.
Währungsbedarf *m* currency

requirement; monetary require-ment.

Währungsbehörde *f*   monetary authority.

Währungsebene *f*   currency level.

Währungseinheit *f*   monetary unit.

Währungsfonds *m*   currency fund; monetary fund.

Währungsgewinn *m*   currency profit.

Währungsguthaben *nt*   reserve monetary assets.

Währungsinstanz *f*   monetary authority.

Währungskorb *m*   basket of currencies.

Währungskurs *m*   currency rate; *(Wechselkurs)* exchange rate.

Währungsordnung *f*   monetary order.

Währungspolitik *f*   monetary policy.

währungspolitische Größe *f* , monetary variable.

Währungsreserve *f*   currency reserve.

Währungsreserven *pl*   reserve assets; monetary reserves.

Währungsstabilität *f*   currency stability.

Währungssystem *nt*   currency system.

Währungsumtausch *m*   currency exchange.

Wandel *m*   change.

Wandelanleihe *f*   convertible loan.

wandeln *(ändern)* to change; *(verändern)* to alter.

wandern   to wander; to hike.

Ware *f*   commodity; *(Börse)* offering; *(Erzeugnis)* product; *(Handelsware)* merchandise; *(Güter)* goods.

Waren *pl* **anbieten**   to offer goods.

Waren *pl* **zweiter Qualität** *f*   seconds.

Warenangebot *nt*   offering of goods; supply of goods.

Warenangebotsmischung *f*   marketing mix.

Warenbuch *nt*   catalog.

Wareneinheit *f*   unit of goods; merchandise item.

Warenexport *m*   merchandise export.

Warengattung *f*   line of goods.

Warenhandel *m*   merchandising; mercantile trade.

Warenhaus *nt*   department store.

Warenhausunternehmen *nt*   department store enterprise.

Warenkonto *nt*   goods account; merchandise account.

Warenkorb *m*   basket of available commodities.

Warenkredit *m*   commercial credit.

Warenpolitik *f*   product policy.

Warenposten *m*   lot.

Warenpreis *m*   commodity price.

Warenprobe *f*   sample.

Warenqualität *f*   product quality.

Warenschuld *f*   commercial debt.

Warensendung *f*   shipment.

Warenterminhandel *m*   commodity futures trade.

Warentest *m*   product test.

Warenverkauf *m*   sale of goods; commodity sale.

Warenverkehr *m*   movement of goods; merchandise traffic.

Warenversand *m*   consignment of goods; commercial shipment.

Warenverzeichnis *nt*   *(Ladung)* manifest.

Warenwechsel *m*   commercial paper.

Warenwert *m*   merchandise value.

Warenzeichen *nt* trademark; *(Marke)* brand; *(Symbol)* logo.

warnen to warn; *(zur Vorsicht mahnen)* to caution.

warnend cautionary.

Warngerät *nt* monitor.

Warnstreik *m* warning strike.

Warnung *f* warning; *(Bekanntgabe)* notice.

warten to wait; *(Wartung)* to service; to maintain.

Wärter *m* attendant.

Warteschlange *f* waiting line; *(BE)* queue.

Wartestellung *f* standby position.

Wartung *f* service; maintenance.

Wartungskosten *pl* cost of upkeep.

Wartungspersonal *nt* maintenance staff; servicing staff.

Wasserstraße *f* waterway.

Wasserweg *m* waterway.

Web- textile.

Webstoff *m* textile.

Wechsel *m* draft; bill; paper.

Wechselbank *f* acceptance bank; exchange bank.

Wechselbürgschaft *f* draft guarantee.

Wechselgeld *nt* change.

Wechselkredit *m* draft credit.

Wechselkurs *m* exchange rate.

Wechselkursänderung *f* exchange rate change.

Wechselkursanstieg *m* exchange rate increase.

wechselkursbedingt dependent on the exchange rate.

Wechselkursgewinn *m* exchange rate profit.

Wechselkursmodell *nt* exchange rate model.

wechseln to switch; *(umtauschen)* to exchange; *(Kleidung)* to change.

Wechselportefeuille *nt* bills in hand; bill holdings.

wechselseitig reciprocal; mutual.

Wechselwirkung *f* reciprocal effect.

Weg *m* way; *(Pfad)* path; *(Bahn)* track; *(Route)* route; *(Dienstweg)* channel.

Wegbestimmung *f* routing.

Wegfall *m* *(Aufhören)* cessation; *(Auslassung)* omission.

wegwerfbar disposable.

Wegwerfgüter *pl* disposable goods.

Wehrdienst *m* military service.

weich soft.

weich machen to soften.

Weigerung *f* refusal.

Weisung *f* directive.

weit wide; *(breit)* broad.

weit enfernt distant; *(fig.)* far removed; *(idiomatisch)* far from it.

Weiterführung *f* continuation.

weitermachen to continue; to proceed.

weiterverarbeiten to process; to finish.

Weiterverarbeitung *f* processing; finishing.

weiterverkaufen to resell.

weitreichend far-reaching; sweeping.

Welt- global.

Weltagrarmarkt *m* world agricultural market.

Weltbank *f* World Bank; International Bank of Reconstruction and Development.

Weltbanktochter *f* World Bank subsidiary; World Bank affiliate.

Weltexport *m*   world export; global export.

Weltfinanz *f*   global finance.

Welthandel *m*   world trade; international trade.

Weltklasse *f*   world class.

Weltkonjunktur *f*   global economic condition.

Weltkonzern *m*   global corporation.

Weltmarkt *m*   global market; international market.

Weltmarktanteil *m*   global market share.

Weltmarktführer *m*   global market leader.

Weltmarktpreis *m*   world market price.

Weltrangliste *f*   global ranking; worldwide ranking.

Weltraum *m*   outer space.

weltweit   global.

weltweite Geschäftstätigkeit *f*   worldwide operations.

weltweite Nachfrage *f*   global demand.

weltweite Rezession *f*   worldwide recession.

Weltwirtschaft *f*   world economy.

weltwirtschaftlich   pertaining to a global economy.

Weltwirtschaftskrise *f*   global economic crisis.

Weltwirtschaftslehre *f*   global economics.

Wende *f*   turn; *(Wirtschaft, Markt)* turnaround.

wenden   to turn around.

wenden, sich   to turn.

Wendung *f*   turn.

Werbe-   advertising; promotional.

Werbeadressat *m*   mailing list addressee.

Werbeagentur *f*   advertising agency.

Werbeaufwendung *f*   advertising expenditure.

Werbeaussage *f*   advertising message.

Werbebetreuer *m*   advertising consultant; advertising account executive.

Werbebild *nt*   advertisement picture.

Werbebotschaft *f*   advertising message; advertising slogan.

Werbebrief *m*   sales letter.

Werbechef *m*   advertising director.

Werbedrehbuch *nt*   advertising script; commercial script.

Werbeeffekt *m*   advertising effect; advertising impact.

Werbeeinfall *m*   advertising idea.

Werbeetat *m*   advertising budget.

Werbefeldzug *m*   advertising campaign.

Werbefernsehen *nt*   television advertising.

Werbefotograf *m*   commercial photographer.

Werbefunk *m*   promotional broadcasting.

Werbegeschenk *nt*   promotional gift.

Werbegestaltung *f*   advertising design.

Werbeidee *f*   advertising idea.

Werbekampagne *f*   advertising campaign.

Werbekosten *pl*   advertising expenses.

Werbekraft *f*   persuasive power; advertising appeal; selling power.

Werbekreis *m*   advertising circle.

Werbekrieg *m*   advertising war.

Werbekunde *m*   advertiser; client.

Werbeleiter *m* advertising manager; promotion manager; *(Publizität)* publicity director.

Werbemasche *f* advertising gimmick.

Werbemaßnahme *f* advertising tactic; publicity ploy.

Werbemittel *nt* *(Material)* advertising material; promotional literature; *(Träger)* advertising medium; *(für Händler)* dealer aids; *(Vertreter)* sales kit.

Werbemotto *nt* advertising slogan.

werben to advertise; *(Kundschaft)* to solicit; to advertise.

Werbeplattform *f* advertising rostrum.

Werbeprospekt *m* advertising brochure; *(Reklamezettel)* handbill; *(Faltblatt)* leaflet; *(Gesellschaftsgründung)* prospectus.

Werber *m* advertiser.

Werbeschlacht *f* advertising battle.

Werbesendung *f* commercial broadcast; *(Werbespot)* advertising spot; commercial.

Werbeslogan *m* advertising slogan.

Werbespruch *m* advertising slogan; *(Reim)* jingle.

Werbestratege *m*, **-strategin** *f* advertising strategist; publicity strategist.

Werbetext *m* advertising copy.

Werbeträger *m* advertising medium.

werbewirksam effective in advertising.

Werbung *f* promotion; *(Publizität)* publicity; *(Anzeige, Inserat)* advertisement.

Werdegang *m* career.

werfen to throw; *(vorwärtswerfen)* to thrust.

Werk *nt* *(Fabrik)* plant; *(Anlage)* facility; *(Schöpfung)* creation; *(Lebenswerk)* work.

Werkbereich *m* working area.

Werkhalle *f* factory work floor; factory work room.

Werklohn *m* wage.

Werkschließung *f* factory closing.

Werkstatt *f* factory workshop.

Werkstoff *m* material.

Werkunterricht *m* manual training.

Werkzeug *nt* tool; *(Gerät)* implement; *(Instrument)* instrument.

Werkzeugausstattung *f* tool kit.

Werkzeugmaschine *f* machine tool.

Werkzeugtasche *f* tool kit.

Wert *m* value; *(Qualität)* quality; *(Verdienst)* merit; *(des Grundkapitals)* equity.

Wertberichtigung *f* value adjustment.

Werte *f* *(Statistik)* data; *(Effekten)* securities.

Werterhöhung *f* rise in value; *(Mehrwert)* added value.

wertlos without value; worthless; *(minderwertig)* shoddy.

wertmäßig according to value.

Wertmaßstab *m* value measure.

Wertminderung *f* deterioration; *(Steuererklärung)* depreciation.

Wertpapier *nt* security; commercial paper; *(Schuldverschreibung)* bond.

Wertpapieranlage *f* investment in securities.

Wertpapierauftrag *m* order to purchase securities.

Wertpapierbereich *m* securities sector.

Wertpapierbestand *m* securities holdings; *(Bilanz)* investment portfolio.

Wertpapierbörse *f* stock market; securities exchange.

Wertpapierdepot *nt* investment portfolio.

Wertpapiere *pl* securities.

Wertpapierfonds *m* investment fund.

Wertpapiergeschäft *nt* securities business; transaction in securities.

Wertpapierhandel *m* securities trading.

Wertpapierkonto *nt* securities account.

Wertpapiermarkt *m* securities market.

Wertpapierumsatz *m* securities sales.

Wertpapierverkauf *m (an Private)* private placement.

Wertpapiervermögen *nt* security holdings.

Wertschätzung *f (persönlich)* esteem; appreciation; *(Abschätzung)* appraisal.

Wertschöpfung *f* creation of value; *(Werterhöhung)* net value added.

Wertsteigerung *f* appreciation in value.

Wertstellung *f* value setting.

Werttheorie *f* value theory.

Wertverhältnis *nt* value ratio.

wertvoll valuable; *(kostbar)* precious.

Wesen *nt* essence; *(Charakter)* character; *(Rechtspersönlichkeit)* entity.

wesentlich integral; *(essentiell)* essential.

Wettbewerb *m* competition.

Wettbewerber *m* competitor.

Wettbewerbsargument *nt* argument supporting competition.

wettbewerbsfähig competitive; capable of competing.

Wettbewerbsfähigkeit *f* competitiveness.

Wettbewerbsnachteil *m* competitive disadvantage.

Wettbewerbsposition *f* competitive position.

Wettbewerbstheorie *f* theory of competition.

Wette *f* bet; *(Einsatz)* wager.

wetteifern to compete; *(rivalisieren)* to rival.

wetten to bet.

Wettkampf *m* contest; *(Wettbewerb)* competition.

Wichtigkeit *f* importance; significance; *(Prominenz)* prominence.

Widerruf *m (Güter, Posten)* recall; *(Gesetze)* repeal; *(Rechte, Privilegien)* revocation; *(Ungültigkeitserklärung)* rescission.

widerrufen to revoke; *(Gesetz)* to repeal; *(für ungültig erklären)* to rescind.

Widerspruch *m* contradiction.

Widerspruch *m* **erheben** to contradict; *(opponieren)* to oppose.

Widerstand *m* resistance; opposition.

Wiederabdruck *m* reprint.

wieder abdrucken to reprint.

wieder ankurbeln to restart; *(Wirtschaft, Markt)* to refuel.

wieder anlegen to reinvest.

wieder anstellen to rehire.

Wiederaufbau *m* reconstruction; rehabilitation.

Wiederaufbauaufgabe *f* task of reconstruction.

wiederaufbauen to reconstruct; to rebuild.

wiederaufbereiten to recycle.

Wiederaufbereitung *f* recycling.

wieder auffinden to retrieve.

Wiederauffindung *f* retrieval.

wiederaufleben to revive.

Wiederaufleben *nt* revival; *(Neubelebung)* revitalization.

wiederaufnehmen to resume; *(Verhandlung)* to reopen.

Wiederaufschwung *m* rebound; *(Erholung, Gesundung)* recovery.

Wiederaufstieg *m* comeback.

wiederbeleben to revitalize.

Wiederbelebung *f* revitalization; *(Wiederaufleben)* revival.

wiederbeschaffen to replace.

Wiederbeschaffung *f* replacement.

Wiederbeschaffungswert *m* replacement value; *(Marktwert)* market value.

wiederbringen to restore.

wieder einbringen to recoup.

Wiedereinbürgerung *f* repatriation.

wiedereinsetzen to restore; to reinstate.

wiedereinstellen to rehire; *(wiedereinsetzen)* to reinstate.

Wiedererlangung *f* recovery.

wiederernennen to reappoint.

Wiederernennung *f* reappointment.

wiedererobern to recapture.

wiedereröffnen to reopen.

Wiedereröffnung *f* reopening.

wiedererstatten to repay; *(ersetzen)* to replace; *(zurückerstatten)* to restore.

Wiedererwerb *m* reacquisition; retrieval.

wiedererwerben to retrieve; to reacquire.

wieder flottmachen *(Schiff)* to refloat; *(fig.)* to restart.

wiedergutmachen to recompense.

Wiedergutmachung *f* compensation; *(Kriegsschuld)* reparation; compensation.

wiederherstellen *(Ordnung)* to restore; *(erneuern)* to renew; *(reparieren)* to repair; *(neu etablieren)* to reestablish.

Wiederherstellung *f* restoration; *(Reparatur)* repair.

Wiederholungsdruck *m* reprint.

Wiederholungsgeschäft *nt* repeat business.

wieder in Betrieb *m* **setzen** to reopen.

Wiederkauf *m* repurchase.

Wiedervereinigung *f* reunification; *(Neuintegration)* reintegration.

Wiederverkauf *m* resale.

wiederverkaufen to resell.

Wiederverkäufer *m* reseller; *(Zwischenhändler)* middleman; *(Verteiler)* distributor.

Wiederverkaufs- resale.

wiederverwendbar reusable; recyclable.

wieder vorlegen to resubmit.

Wiederwahl *f* reelection.

wiegen to weigh.

Wille *m* will; *(Entschlossenheit)* determination.

Willenserklärung *f* statement of purpose; statement of intention.

willkürlich arbitrary.

winzig tiny; *(minuziös)* minute.

wirkliches Einkommen *nt* *(Realeinkommen)* real income.

wirksam effective.

Wirksamkeit *f* effectiveness.

Wirkungskraft *f* effective force; impact.

Wirkungskreis *m* *(Effekt)* area of effectiveness; *(Kompetenz)* radius of operation.

Wirt *m* landlord.

Wirtschaft *f* economy; economic system; *(Gastwirtschaft)* restaurant; *(Kneipe)* pub; *(Landwirtschaft)* farm.

wirtschaften to keep house; to manage.

wirtschaftlich economic; *(sparsam)* economical; *(effizient)* efficient; *(ertragbringend)* profitable.

wirtschaftliche Grundlage *f* economic basis.

Wirtschaftlichkeit *f* profitability; *(Sparsamkeit)* thrift; *(Effizienz)* efficiency.

Wirtschaftsablauf *m* economic process; *(Zyklus)* business cycle.

Wirtschaftsberater *m* economic advisor.

Wirtschaftsbereich *m* economic domain.

Wirtschaftsbotschaft *f* economic signal.

Wirtschaftsbüro *nt* economic bureau.

Wirtschaftsdialog *m* economic dialogue.

Wirtschaftsdienst *m* economic service; trade service.

Wirtschaftseinheit *f* economic entity; *(Betrieb)* self-contained unit.

Wirtschaftsentwicklung *f* economic development.

Wirtschaftsexperte *m*, **-expertin** *f* economic expert.

Wirtschaftsfachmann *m* eco-

nomic specialist; *(Theoretiker)* economist.

Wirtschaftsflaute *f* economic stagnation.

Wirtschaftsforscher *m* economic researcher.

Wirtschaftsforschung *f* economic research.

Wirtschaftsgeschehen *nt* economic process.

Wirtschaftsjahr *nt* fiscal year.

Wirtschaftskonferenz *f* economic conference.

Wirtschaftskrise *f* economic crisis.

Wirtschaftskurs *m* economic trend; course of the economy.

Wirtschaftslage *f* economic position; economic condition.

Wirtschaftsleben *nt* economic life; business.

Wirtschaftsleistung *f* economic performance; *(Produktivität)* productivity.

Wirtschaftsmagazin *nt* business publication.

Wirtschaftsminister *m* secretary of commerce.

Wirtschaftsmodell *nt* economic model.

Wirtschaftsordnung *f* economic order.

Wirtschaftsplan *m* economic plan.

Wirtschaftspolitik *f* economic policy.

wirtschaftspolitisch pertaining to economic policy.

Wirtschaftsprophet *m* economic prophet.

Wirtschaftsprüfer *m* financial auditor; accountant.

Wirtschaftsrat *m* council of economic advisors.

Wirtschaftsrückgang *m*   economic recession.

Wirtschaftssituation *f*   state of the economy.

Wirtschaftssprecher *m*   economic spokesperson.

Wirtschaftsstatistik *f*   economic statistics.

Wirtschaftsstruktur *f*   economic structure.

Wirtschaftssystem *nt*   economic system.

Wirtschaftsteil *m*   *(Zeitung)* business section.

Wirtschaftstheorie *f*   economic theory.

Wirtschaftsverlauf *m*   course of the economy.

Wirtschaftswachstum *nt*   economic growth.

Wirtschaftswissenschaftler *m*   economist.

Wirtschaftswunder *nt*   economic miracle.

Wirtschaftszeitung *f*   economic journal; *(Fachzeitschrift)* trade paper; *(Geschäftsjournal)* business journal.

Wirtschaftszone *f*   economic zone.

Wirtschaftszweig *m*   branch of the economy; *(Sektor)* economic sector.

Wochenarbeitszeit *f*   hours worked per week.

Wochenbericht *m*   weekly report.

Wochendurchschnitt *m*   weekly average.

Wohlergehen *nt*   wellbeing; *(Prosperität)* prosperity.

wohlerworben   honestly acquired; vested.

Wohlfahrt *f*   welfare.

wohlfahrtsoptimal   welfare-optimal.

wohlhabend   wealthy; prosperous; affluent.

Wohlhabenheit *f*   wealth.

Wohlstand *m*   prosperity.

wohlüberlegt   well thought out; deliberate.

Wohnort *m*   place of residence; home.

Wohnsiedlung *f*   residential subdivision; residential development.

Wohnung *f*   apartment.

Wohnungswirtschaft *f*   housing industry.

Wortführer *m*   spokesman.

Wortlaut *m*   text.

Wortverdrehung *f*   distortion; *(falsches Zitat)* misquotation.

Wucher *m*   usury.

Wucherei *f*   usury.

wuchern   *(ungehemmtes Wachstum)* to grow unchecked; *(Überwucherung)* to proliferate luxuriantly; *(Wucherei)* to engage in usury.

Wunsch *m*   wish; desire.

wünschenswert   desirable.

Würgegriff *m*   stranglehold; chokehold.

würzen   to season.

Z

Zahl *f* *(Nummer, Anzahl)* number; *(Ziffer, Preis)* figure.

zahlbar payable; *(Wertpapier)* mature.

zählen to count; *(numerieren)* to number; *(rechnen)* to reckon.

Zahlende *m/f* payor.

Zahlenfolge *f* series of numbers.

zahlenmäßig numerical.

Zahlenmaterial *nt* numerical data; figures.

Zahlenreihe *f* column of numbers.

Zahlenwert *m* numerical value.

Zähler *m* meter; *(Arith.)* numerator.

zahlreich numerous.

Zahltag *m* *(Lohn)* payday.

Zählung *f* count; *(Volkszählung)* census.

Zahlung *f* payment; *(aus dem Kapital)* principal payment.

Zahlungsanweisung *f* money order; draft.

Zahlungsaufforderung *f* demand note.

Zahlungsaufschub *m* payment deferral; *(Verlängerung)* extension.

Zahlungsausgleich *m* clearance; settlement; *(international)* exchange equilibrium.

Zahlungsbilanz *f* balance of payments.

Zahlungsbilanzkrise *f* balance of payments crisis.

Zahlungsbilanzlage *f* balance of payments position.

Zahlungseinstellung *f* stoppage of payment; *(Versäumnis)* default; *(Nichteinhaltung)* failure.

Zahlungsempfänger *m* payee.

zahlungsfähig solvent; financially sound.

Zahlungsfrist *f* term; time of payment; *(gewährter Aufschub)* extension of time; *(Wechsel)* grace period.

Zahlungsgewohnheit *f* payment habit.

zahlungskräftig solvent; sound.

Zahlungsmedium *nt* payment instrument.

Zahlungsmittel *nt* medium of exchange; *(Geld)* money; currency.

Zahlungsort *m* place of payment.

Zahlungsproblem *nt* payment difficulty.

zahlungsunfähig insolvent; illiquid.

Zahlungsunfähige *m/f* insolvent person.

Zahlungsverkehr *m* money transfers; payment transactions.

Zahlungsweise *f* method of payment.

Zählvorrichtung *f* counter.

Zählwerk *nt* counting device.

Zeche *f* *(Bergwerk)* mine.

Zeichen *nt* sign; *(Merkmal)* mark; *(Beweis)* token; *(Anzeichen)* indication.

zeichnen to draw; *(skizzieren)* to sketch; *(unterschreiben)* to sign.

Zeichnung *f* drawing; *(Skizze)* sketch.

zeigen to show; *(zur Schau stellen)* to display.

Zeile *f* line.

Zeilensumme *f* line total.

zeitabhängig dependent on time.
Zeitabstand *m* time interval.
Zeitalter *nt* age; *(Ära)* era.
Zeitdauer *f* term; *(Abschnitt)* time period.
Zeitgenosse *m*; **-genossin** *f* contemporary.
zeitgenössisch contemporary.
zeitliche Verschiebung *f* time lag.
Zeitplan *m* timetable; schedule.
Zeitraum *m* period.
Zeitreihe *f* time series.
Zeitschätzung *f* time estimate.
Zeitschrift *f* periodical; *(Magazin)* magazine.
Zeitung *f* newspaper.
Zeitungspapier *nt* newsprint.
Zeitungsreklame *f* newspaper advertisement.
Zeitunterschied *m* time difference.
Zeitverlust *m* time loss; *(Verspätung)* delay.
Zeitwahl *f* timing.
Zensur *f* censorship; *(akad.)* grade; *(BE)* mark.
Zentral- central.
zentral central.
Zentralbank *f* central bank; *(in U.S.)* Federal Reserve Bank.
Zentralbankchef *m* chairperson of the central bank; *(in U.S.)* chairperson of the Federal Reserve Bank.
Zentralbankgeld *nt* central bank money.
Zentralbankrat *m* governing board of the central bank.
Zentrale *f* headquarters; home office.
Zentralinstitution *f* central institution.
zentralisieren to centralize.
Zentralisierung *f* centralization.

Zentralrechner *m* mainframe computer; main computer.
Zentralstelle *f* center.
Zentralverband *m* central association.
Zentrum *nt* hub; center.
zerlegbar reducible; knockdown.
zerlegen to disassemble; to section.
Zerrbild *nt* distorted picture; distortion.
zerren to wrench; to pull; to tug.
Zerrüttung *f* disorganization; *(Zerfall)* disintegration.
Zerschlagung *f* *(Monopol, Kartell)* breakup.
zerstören to destroy.
zerstörerisch destructive.
Zerstörung *f* destruction.
zerstreuen to disperse; to scatter; *(Bedenken)* to dispel; to dissipate; *(belustigen)* to divert.
Zertifikat *nt* certificate; warrant.
Zessionar *m* transferee.
Zettel *m* slip of paper.
Zeugenaussage *f* witness account; *(beglaubigt)* deposition.
Zeugnis *nt* certificate; *(Diplom)* diploma; *(Empfehlung)* reference; testimonial.
ziehen to pull; to draw.
Ziehung *f* drawing.
Ziehungsrecht *nt* drawing right.
Ziel *nt* target; aim; goal; objective; *(Zweck)* object; *(Absicht)* intent; *(Ort)* destination. **~ setzen** to set a goal; to target.
zielbewußt systematic.
zielen to aim; *(Ziel setzen)* to target.
Zielfunktion *f* end function.
Zielgruppe *f* target group.
Zielkomplex *m* target complex.

Zielland *nt*   target country.
Zielpublikum *nt*   target audience.
Zielsetzung *f*   targeting.
Ziffer *f*   digit; *(Nummer)* number; *(Zahl, Preis)* figure.
Zins *m*   interest.
Zinsabhängigkeit *f*   interest dependency.
Zinsabstand *m*   interest differential.
Zinsabzug *m*   discount.
zinsähnlich   interest-like.
Zinsanhebung *f*   increase in interest.
Zinsanteil *m*   interest share; *(prozentual)* interest percentage.
Zinsaufschlag *m*   interest increase.
Zinsberechnung *f*   interest calculation.
Zinsbestandteil *m*   interest percentage.
zinsbewußt   interest-conscious.
Zinsdifferenz *f*   interest difference; *(Marge)* interest margin.
Zinseinkommen *nt*   interest income.
Zinseinnahme *f*   interest revenues; interest receipts.
zinsempfindlich   interest-sensitive.
Zinsen *pl*   interest. ~**bringen** to earn interest. ~ **tragen** to yield interest.
Zinsendienst *m*   debt service.
Zinsentwicklung *f*   interest rate development; interest rate trend.
Zinserhöhung *f*   interest increase.
Zinsermäßigung *f*   interest rebate; interest reduction.
Zinsertrag *m*   yield; yield on interest.
Zinseszinsen *pl*   compound interest.
zinsfrei   interest free; no-interest; non-interest-bearing.
Zinsgefälle *nt*   interest rate differential; interest rate fluctuation.

Zinsgutschrift *f*   interest credit.
Zinskosten *pl*   interest expense; *(Anleihe)* cost of money; interest expense.
Zinsnachteil *m*   interest disadvantage.
Zinsniveau *nt*   interest level.
Zinspolitik *f*   interest policy.
Zinsrate *f*   interest rate.
Zinsrechnung *f*   computation of interest.
Zinsrückgang *m*   decrease in the interest rate.
Zinsrückstände *pl*   interest arrears.
Zinsrutsch *m*   downward slide of interest rates.
Zinssatz *m*   interest rate.
Zinsschein *m*   interest coupon.
Zinssenkung *f*   reduction of the interest rate.
Zinsspanne *f*   spread in interest rates; interest margin.
Zinssubvention *f*   interest subsidy.
Zinsswap *m*   interest swap.
zinstragend   interest-bearing.
Zinsüberschuß *m*   interest surplus.
Zinsunterschied *m*   difference in interest rates; interest differential.
Zinsverlust *m*   loss on interest.
Zinsverpflichtung *f*   obligation to pay interest; *(Zinssumme)* interest owed.
Zinsvorteil *m*   interest advantage.
Zinszahlung *f*   interest payment.
zirka   circa; approximately.
Zitat *nt*   quotation; quote.
zitieren   to quote.
zögern   *(um Zeit zu gewinnen)* to stall for time.
Zoll *m*   *(Außenhandel)* tariff; *(Zollgebühr)* duty; *(Zollbehörde, -abfertigung)* customs; *(Maß)* inch.
Zollabbau *m*   tariff reduction.

Zollabfertigung *f* customs clearance.

Zollabkommen *nt* tariff agreement.

Zollager *nt* bonded warehouse.

zollamtlich abfertigen to clear throughcustoms.

Zollbegünstigung *f* tariff preference.

Zollbehörde *f* customs authority.

Zolldeklaration *f* customs declaration; *(Exportlieferung)* manifest.

Zollerklärung *f* customs declaration.

Zollforderung *f* duty charge; duty claim.

Zollgebiet *nt* customs territory.

Zollgebühr *f* duty.

Zollpräferenz *f* tariff preference.

Zollsatz *m* tariff rate; rate of duty.

Zollschranke *f* tariff barrier.

Zollsenkung *f* tariff reduction.

Zollspedition *f* customs expediting firm; customs forwarding firm.

Zollstelle *f* customs office; customs house.

Zolltarif *m* customs tariff; rate of duty.

Zollverwaltung *f* *(Behörde)* customs authority; *(Personal)* customs officials.

Zollwert *m* tariff value.

Zone *f* zone.

Zubehör *nt* accessories.

zuerkennen to award; *(zusprechen)* to adjudge; *(zuteilen)* to apportion.

Zuerkennung *f* award; *(Zuteilung)* apportionment.

zufällig accidental; by chance.

Zufallsfaktor *m* coincidence factor.

Zuflucht *f* shelter.

Zufluß *m* inflow.

zufrieden content; *(zufriedengestellt)* satisfied.

Zugabe *f* extra benefit.

Zugang *m* access.

zugänglich accessible.

zugeben to admit.

Zugehörigkeit *f* belonging; *(Mitgliedschaft)* membership.

Zügelung *f* restraint.

Zugeständnis *nt* concession; admission.

zugestehen to concede.

zugkräftig popular; attractive.

zugreifen to seize; to help oneself.

Zugriff *m* *(Datenverarbeitung)* access.

zugrundeliegend *(Anteile, Aktien)* underlying.

zugrunde richten to ruin.

zugunsten in favor of.

Zuhörerschaft *f* listeners; *(Publikum)* audience.

Zukunft *f* future.

zukünftig future.

zukünftiger Ertrag *m* future earnings.

Zukunftserwartung *f* future expectation; *(Aussichten)* future outlook.

Zukunftsmarkt *m* future market.

zulassen *(erlauben)* to allow; to permit; *(aufnehmen, eintreten lassen)* to admit; *(Konzession gewähren)* to license.

zulässig *(erlaubt)* permissible; *(Beweismaterial)* admissible; *(zu erlauben)* allowable.

Zulassung *f* admittance; *(Lizenz)* license; *(Aufnahme)* admittance.

Zulieferant *m* subcontractor.

Zulieferbetrieb *m* subcontracting firm; *(Fabrik)* feeder plant;

(Tochterunternehmen) manufacturing subsidiary.
Zulieferer *m* subcontractor; supplier.
Zuliefern *nt* supplying.
Zulieferung *f* subcontracted supply.
Zulieferungsvertrag *m* subcontract.
zum Abbau *m* **der Inflation** *f* **beitragend** disinflationary.
zum Abschluß *m* **bringen** to bring to a close; *(fertig machen)* to finish; *(beendigen)* to terminate.
zum Abschluß *m* **gebracht** finalized; *(fertig)* completed.
zum gesetzlichen Zahlungsmittel *nt* **machen** to monetize.
Zunahme *f* increase; gain; *(Erhöhung)* rise; *(Wachstum)* growth.
zunehmen to increase; *(wachsen)* to grow; *(Umsatz)* to pick up.
Zunft *f* *(Handwerk)* guild.
zurechnen to add; *(fig.)* to impute; to attribute.
Zurechnung *f* addition; *(fig.)* imputation; attribution.
zur Formsache *f* **machen** to formalize.
Zurschaustellung *f* display.
Zurückbehaltung *f* withholding; *(Reserve)* reserve.
Zurückbehaltungsrecht *nt* lien.
Zurückberufung *f* recall.
zurückbleiben *(noch dableiben)* to stay behind; *(nicht Schritt halten)* to fall behind; *(nachhinken)* to lag.
zurückerlangen to recover; *(wiedergewinnen)* to regain.
Zurückerlangung *f* recovery.
zurückerstatten to refund; *(entschädigen)* to reimburse.
Zurückerstattung *f* refund; *(Entschädigung)* reimbursement.

zurückfordern to reclaim.
zurückführen *(Zitat, Idee)* to attribute; *(umsiedeln)* to resettle.
zurückgeben to give back; to restore; to return.
zurückgeblieben *(Entwicklung)* backward; slow.
zurückgehen to regress; *(abnehmen)* to decrease; *(zurückkommen)* to return; *(Aufträge)* to go down; *(Einnahmen)* to fall off; *(Konjunktur)* to move backwards; *(Kurse, Preise)* to decline; *(Qualität, Wert)* to deteriorate.
zurückgesandt returned.
zurückgestellt *(Mittel)* reserved.
zurückgewinnen to recapture.
zurückgezogen retired.
zurückhalten to hold back; *(hemmen, hindern)* to restrain; *(aufhalten)* to detain.
zurückhaltend reserved; retiring.
Zurückhaltung *f* restraint.
zurückkaufen to repurchase; *(einlösen)* to redeem.
zurückkehren to return.
Zurücknahme *f* *(Ware)* return; *(Rechte, Privilegien)* revocation.
zurücknehmen to take back; *(Behauptung)* retract; *(Rechte, Privilegien)* to revoke.
zurückrufen to recall; *(telefonieren)* to call back.
zurückschnellen to rebound.
zurückschrauben to trim back; *(reduzieren)* to reduce.
zurückstellen *(Priorität)* to subordinate; *(Mittel)* to reserve; *(Termin)* to postpone.
Zurückstellung *f* *(Priorität)* subordination; *(Mittel)* reserves; *(Termin)* postponement.

zurücktreten *(Kandidatur)* to withdraw; *(Position)* to step down; *(Amt)* to resign.

zurückweisen *(Behauptung)* to repudiate; *(Vorschlag)* to reject; *(Argument)* to dismiss.

Zurückweisung *f (Behauptung)* repudiation; *(Vorschlag)* rejection; *(Argument)* dismissal.

zurückzahlen to repay; *(Entschädigung)* to reimburse; *(Rückerstattung)* to refund.

Zurückzahlung *f* refund; *(Entschädigung)* reimbursement.

zurückziehen *(Geld)* to recall; *(Einspruch)* to subduct; *(Forderung)* to take back.

zurückziehen, sich to withdraw; *(Ruhestand)* to retire.

Zurückziehung *f* withdrawal; *(Ruhestand)* retirement; *(von Anlagekapital)* disinvesting.

Zusage *f (Zusicherung)* assurance; *(Versprechen)* promise.

zusagen *(versprechen)* to promise; *(zustimmen)* to agree; to answer in the affirmative; *(Einladung)* to accept.

Zusammenarbeit *f* cooperation; collaboration.

zusammenarbeiten to cooperate; to collaborate.

Zusammenbauausrüstung *f* assembly kit.

zusammenbrechen to collapse.

Zusammenbruch *m* collapse; ruin; *(Maschine)* breakdown.

zusammenfassen to sum up; to summarize.

Zusammenfassung *f* summary; recapitulation.

zusammengefaßt summarized.

zusammengesetzt *(Mechanik)* assembled; composite; *(vermischt)* compound.

Zusammenhang *m* context; relation.

Zusammenkunft *f* gathering; *(Treffen)* meeting.

zusammenlegen to combine; *(konsolidieren)* to consolidate.

Zusammenlegung *f* consolidation; *(Kombination)* combination; *(Unternehmung)* merger; amalgamation; *(Verwaltung)* centralization.

zusammenpassend compatible.

zusammenrechnen to add up.

Zusammenrechnung *f* addition.

zusammenschließen to pool; *(vereinigen)* to combine; *(verschmelzen)* to fuse; *(fusionieren)* to merge.

zusammenschließen, sich *(sich verschmelzen)* to fuse; to amalgamate; *(sich vereinigen)* to unite.

Zusammenschluß *m* merger; *(Integration)* integration; *(Kombination)* combination.

zusammenschrumpfen to shrink; *(dahinschwinden)* to dwindle.

zusammensetzen to put together; *(Montage)* to assemble.

Zusammensetzung *f (Mischung, Mixtur)* mixture; *(Chemie)* compound.

Zusammenstellung *f* compilation; *(Mischung)* mix.

zusammenstoßen to collide; *(Kulturen)* to clash.

zusammenstücken to piece together.

zusammentreffen to meet; *(Termine, Ziele)* to coincide.

Zusammentreffen *nt* meeting.

zusammenwerfen to pool.

zusammenzählen   to total; *(nach-zählen)* to tally.

Zusammenziehung *f* contraction.

Zusatz *m* supplement; *(Hinzufü-gung)* addition; *(parl.)* amend-ment.

Zusatzgerät *nt* auxiliary unit; *(Zubehör)* attachment; *(Zwischen-stecker)* adapter.

Zusatzleistung *f* additional contri-bution; *(Produktion)* additional output.

zusätzlich   additional; supplemen-tal; extra.

Zusatzurlaub *m* additional vaca-tion time.

Zusatzverzinsung *f* additional interest.

Zuschlag *m* premium; extra amount.

Zuschlaggebühr *f* surcharge.

zuschreiben   *(Ursache)* to attribute.

Zuschreibung *f* *(Quelle)* attribu-tion; *(Widmung)* dedication; *(Bilanz)* writing up.

Zuschuß *m* allowance; *(Subven-tion)* subsidy; *(Stipendium, Über-tragung)* grant.

Zuschußbedarf *m* subsidy require-ment.

Zuschußzahlung *f* subsidy pay-ment.

zusetzen   *(einbüßen)* to lose; *(belästigen)* to pester.

Zusicherung *f* assurance.

Zustand *m* condition; state; *(Lage)* position.

zustandebringen   to accomplish.

zuständig   competent; in charge.

zuständige Behörde *f* competent agency.

Zuständigkeit *f* jurisdiction; com-petence.

zustellen   to send; *(ausliefern)* to deliver.

Zustellung *f* *(Auslieferung)* deliv-ery.

zustimmen   to agree; *(bestätigen)* to endorse; *(einwilligen)* to con-sent; *(genehmigen, gutheißen)* to approve.

Zustimmung *f* agreement; *(Bestäti-gung)* endorsement; *(Einwilligung)* consent; *(Genehmigung)* approval.

Zustrom *m* influx.

zutage treten   to come to light; *(klar werden)* to become evident; *(auftauchen)* to emerge.

zuteilen   to apportion; to allocate; *(rationieren)* to ration; *(verteilen)* to distribute; to allot.

zutreffend   applicable; *(passend)* fitting.

zuverlässig   reliable.

Zuverlässigkeit *f* reliability.

zuversichtlich   confident.

zuviel produzieren   to overpro-duce.

Zuwachs *m* increment of growth; accrual.

Zuwachsrate *f* incremental growth rate.

zuwegebringen   to accomplish.

zuweisen   *(Aufgabe)* to assign; *(Mittel)* to apportion; to allocate.

Zuweisung *f* *(Aufgabe)* assign-ment; *(Mittel)* allocation.

zuwenden   *(Mittel)* to allocate; *(Geld)* to channel.

Zuzahlung *f* additional payment; *(Effekten)* assessment.

zuzüglich   plus; additionally.

Zwang *m* coercion; compulsion.

zwanglos   informal.

Zwangsanleihe *f* forced loan; compulsory loan.

Zwangslage *f* plight; tight spot.
zwangsläufig mandatory.
Zwangsräumung eviction.
Zwangssparen *nt* forced saving.
Zwangsvollstreckung *f* foreclosure.
Zweck *m* purpose; object; *(Ziel)*
goal; aim.
zweckdienlich expedient; convenient.
zweckgebunden *(Mittel)* commit-
ted; earmarked.
zwecklos useless; without purpose;
(ziellos) aimless.
zweckmäßig functional.
Zweckmäßigkeit *f* utility; convenience.
zwecks for the purpose of.
Zwecksetzung *f* goal setting; goal
establishment.
Zwecksparen *nt* special purpose
saving.
zweideutig ambiguous; *(Witz)*
suggestive.
Zweideutigkeit *f* ambiguity; double entendre; *(Witz)* suggestive-
ness.
zweifelhaft doubtful; *(fragwürdig)*
questionable.
Zweigniederlassung *f* branch
office.

Zweigstelle *f* branch.
zweiseitig bilateral.
Zweitausfertigung *f* duplicate
copy.
zweitklassig second-rate; *(unterlegen, minderwertig)* inferior.
Zweitmarkt *m* secondary market.
zweitrangig second-rank; subordinate.
zwingen to coerce; to force; to
compel; to oblige; to constrain.
zwingend *(obligatorisch)* obligatory; *(pflichtmäßig)* mandatory;
(zwangsmäßig) compulsory;
(Grund) compelling.
Zwischen- intermediate; middle;
(Zeit) interim.
Zwischenfall *m* unforeseen occurrence; incident.
Zwischenhändler *m* middleman;
intermediary.
Zwischenprodukt *nt* intermediate
product.
Zwischenraum *m* interval; *(Lücke)*
gap.
Zwischenzahlung *f* interim payment.
Zwischenzeit *f* interim time.
zyklisch cyclical.
Zyklus *m* cycle.